# HISTORY OF ROME

# HISTORY OF
# ROME

## Michael Grant

*faber and faber*

LONDON · BOSTON

First published in Great Britain in 1978
by Weidenfeld and Nicolson
First published in this revised edition in 1979
by Faber and Faber Limited
3 Queen Square London WC1N 3AU
Reprinted in 1986
Printed in Great Britain
by Redwood Burn Ltd, Trowbridge, Wiltshire
All rights reserved
© Michael Grant Publications Ltd, 1978, 1979

*British Library Cataloguing in Publication Data*

Grant, Michael, *b.1914*
  History of Rome.
  1. Rome – History
  I. Title
  937      DG209

ISBN 0-571-11461-X

# CONTENTS

Maps and Plans                                          ix
Genealogical Tables                                     xi

## I ETRUSCAN ROME
1 Rome and Etruria                                       7
2 The Etruscan Monarchy                                 18

## II THE UNITY OF ITALY AND ROME
3 The Unification of Italy                              37
4 The Class Struggle                                    57

## III ROME AGAINST CARTHAGE
5 First Wars Against Foreign Powers                     77
6 The Changing Roman World                              89
7 The Invasion by Hannibal                             96

## IV THE IMPERIAL REPUBLIC
8 'Our Sea'                                            113
9 The New Society                                      127

## V THE FALL OF THE REPUBLIC
10 Reform and War in Italy                             145
11 Reaction and Breakdown                              161

## VI CAESAR AND AUGUSTUS
12 Caesar                                              177
13 Augustus                                            199

## VII  THE IMPERIAL PEACE

14  The Inheritors of Empire                 225
15  Imperial Society                          241
16  The Jews, Jesus and Paul                  256

## VIII  TOWARDS A NEW WORLD

17  Collapse and Recovery                     273
18  The Climax of the Pagan Empire            289
19  Supreme State and Church                  300

## IX  THE TRANSFORMATION OF EUROPE

20  The Fall of the Western Empire            321
21  The Fatal Disunities                      332
22  The Aftermath                             352

Epilogue                                      357
Notes                                         360
Ancient Sources                               393
Bibliography                                  396
Table of Dates                                401
Index                                         409

# MAPS AND PLANS

| | | |
|---|---|---|
| 1 | Etruria | 12 |
| 2 | Latium | 27 |
| 3 | Regal and Republican Rome | 30 |
| 4 | Central and Southern Italy | 48 |
| 5 | Rome's Conquest of Italy | 53 |
| 6 | The Wars Against Carthage | 81 |
| 7 | Spain, 3rd–2nd Centuries BC | 97 |
| 8 | The Eastern Mediterranean | 114 |
| 9 | The Roman Provinces 100 BC | 155 |
| 10 | Gaul | 180 |
| 11 | The Civil Wars | 190 |
| 12 | Italy | 200 |
| 13 | The Provinces at the Death of Augustus (AD 14) | 209 |
| 14 | The Roads of the Roman Empire | 213 |
| 15 | The Roman Legions in AD 23 | 226 |
| 16 | Britain | 228 |
| 17 | The Provinces at the Death of Antoninus Pius (AD 161) | 240 |
| 18 | The Empire in the 1st and 2nd Centuries AD | 247 |
| 19 | Palestine in the Time of Christ | 258 |
| 20 | The Journeys of St Paul | 266 |
| 21 | The 'Barbarian' Invasions of the 2nd and 3rd Centuries AD | 274 |
| 22 | The Administrative Dioceses of Diocletian | 301 |
| 23 | Imperial Rome | 315 |
| 24 | The Empire in the 4th and 5th Centuries AD | 322 |
| 25 | The 'Barbarian' Invasions of the 5th Century AD | 325 |
| 26 | After the Fall of the Western Empire in AD 476 | 330 |
| 27 | The Byzantine Empire at the Death of Justinian I (AD 565) | 354 |

# GENEALOGICAL TABLES

1 The family of the Scipios 134
2 The family of Caesar 178
3 The family of Augustus 207
4 The family of Septimius Severus 278
5 The family of Constantine 309
6 The family of Valentinian I 323

# INTRODUCTION

THE ROMANS ARE DIFFICULT to assess today. They employed force; yet what they accomplished by the use of it has never been equalled. For Rome conferred, indeed imposed, upon the Mediterranean area, and upon vast hinterlands in three continents, a unity which these regions had never known before. And will they ever regain it? So far they have not.

But that is by no means all. For although Rome forms part of a larger Greek–Roman story, it possessed a potent individuality of its own. The notion, which is still sometimes aired, that Roman culture was merely an imitation of its Greek models is outworn and misguided in every field. On the contrary, in the literary and visual arts alike, as well as in law and the governmental sciences, Rome's achievement was of singular originality and distinction.

Ancient Rome is also unparalleled among the great communities of the Western world because it lasted for so long. No other occidental civilization or major political unit has so far rivalled its millennial duration. For the historian it is infinitely useful that this uninterruptedly continuing, evolving society is available for his or her investigation at every phase of its growth and vigorous existence and eventual transformation.

The Roman experience is useful for two reasons. First of all, in itself, without any consideration whatever of modern comparisons and echoes. It is wonderfully worthwhile to attempt to recreate this unique phenomenon just as it was, leaving our own modern concerns out of the matter altogether. The study of such an exciting and distinctive historical process is amply justified purely and simply on its own account. Yet at the same time this interest takes on a new dimension when it is remembered that we ourselves, whether we like it or not, are Rome's heirs. In a thousand different ways, the Romans are permanently and indestructibly woven into the fabric of our own existences. They lived through many events and developments which resembled, prefigured and caused what has happened, is happening and may happen in the future to our own communities and our own selves.

The circumstances and backgrounds, it goes without saying, are in some respects radically different. But to conclude from this that people today cannot profit from such ancient history, that Rome is unable to communicate to us any relevant lessons or warnings – to use that old-fashioned phrase – is mistaken. For the past is deeply and unavoidably engrained in our own lives. It is therefore plain common sense to turn this inescapable possession to our advantage. For it can show us the good and bad and strange things of which humanity has proved to be capable, and is therefore capable still; and besides, as the philosopher George Santayana pointed out, those who cannot remember the past are condemned to repeat it. We admit that, when faced with a decision in our personal lives, we are habitually guided by the recollection of things that we ourselves have done or experienced at an earlier stage of our own lifetimes. But why limit this to our lifetimes, why assume that we cannot also learn from the experiences and decisions and achievements and mistakes of those who have lived before?

First, then, Rome should be studied entirely on its own account, and every endeavour should be made to extract its own peculiar quintessence, regardless of any guidance it may have to offer to ourselves: in the second place, however, nothing will be lost, and perhaps much gained, by seeking analogies with our own experiences as well. For both these reasons, the effort to find out as much as we can about this unique segment of world history needs no further justification.

However, the task of pursuing this aim is far from easy. That is mainly for two reasons – which at first sight seem to contradict each other. To begin with, the ancient sources, literary and archaeological alike, are often tantalizingly inadequate and uninformative. A great many of the documents that once existed have been lost, and those that survive are often enigmatic, and biased, and neglectful of many matters that we should dearly like to know about. And yet the second reason why the task is so difficult is because the quantity of this material, however unsatisfactory, is nevertheless so colossal: which is hardly surprising since it encompasses a thousand eventful years.

There are, of course, countless modern histories of ancient Rome; and to many of them I owe a profound debt. Yet they have not prevented me from persisting with this new attempt, because, however far it will fall below the greatness of the theme, I believe there is room for another book on this subject at the present time, of approximately this size and amount of detail, and planned to take into account, in so far as this can be done, the researches and discoveries and insights contributed by scholars in recent years.

But, given all this material, what principles of selection and omission ought to be adopted? First, would it be better to write a narrative story, or divide the book according to subjects? Both approaches seem equally necessary. Narrative history may be unfashionable, but a history of Rome makes no sense without it; though if it is nothing but narrative, it will miss some of the major developments, so that there will be need to pause from time to time to discuss matters in somewhat more depth. Among these matters for discussion will be social, economic and literary and artistic topics; and an effort will be made to relate these to the multiracial Roman empire as well as to Rome itself. For those who want additional names, details and comments, I have provided supplementary material in the notes. But what is trickiest of all is to establish an appropriate balance between different epochs. In particular, it is important not to neglect non-central periods which were vital to Rome's growth or evolution or transformation, even though the quantity of trustworthy evidence available for them is sometimes relatively small.

And what about our moral judgements? Are the Romans 'good' because of all their positive achievements or 'bad' because of their unmistakable brutalities? One cannot keep moral judgements out of it altogether because, as Cicero pointed out, it remains *objectively true*, in spite of debatable marginal cases, that some sorts of behaviour are good, and others bad, and no vicissitudes of taste or special circumstances can make them otherwise. But when we pass on to intellectual judgements, for example concerning the political wisdom or unwisdom of actions taken by this or that personage, the historical task becomes more delicate still. It is easy enough to sit in one's study, and perhaps never leave it, and pronounce that Scipio or Caesar or Marcus Aurelius acted sensibly or otherwise; yet chair-borne hindsight of this kind can never be based on a knowledge of all the circumstances and facts. Nevertheless, modern historians owe it to their readers to stand up and be counted and express a certain number of personal views. True, this may turn out to reveal less about ancient times than about the historian's own environment, and the prejudices it has instilled in him. However, if some of these preconceptions are consciously held, so much the better, because then at least they will be under some control. But other unconscious preconceptions, despite all vigilance, will creep through as well.

This is another way of saying that we cannot claim to be as objective as we would like to be. Like others I have tried, and no doubt without as much success as I should have wished. But at least one result of this attempt, which I believe to be good, has been the conclusion that I cannot subscribe to any unitary, all-explaining theories of Roman history. There is too much of it, and it is too varied, for any single, dominant theme to be conceded a monopoly. Just as attempts to find any *one* cause for what is described as Rome's Decline and Fall are doomed to failure – as one might surely expect when so elaborate an institution is concerned – so, too, all overall explanations of its earlier development, including theories of inevitable cycles, are doomed to failure because there are always too many loose ends.

Perhaps if one was dealing only with political history one could write it around the single guiding theme of imperial unity, and approaches to this unity and failures to achieve it. But in the wider field of the whole civilization of the Roman world, there is no single formula that will cover Fabius Maximus and Catullus and Plotinus. For they are so totally different – manifestations of a fabulous diversity and richness. If I have succeeded in giving even a hint of this richness in the present book I shall be pleased.

I owe warm acknowledgements to the following: to Professor Fergus Millar and Messrs Duckworth and Co. Ltd, and Professor R. M. Ogilvie and Fontana Paperbacks and the Harvester Press, for allowing me to see copies of their books, *The Emperor in the Roman World* and *Early Rome and the Etruscans*, before publication, and to Mr Edward de Bono and Messrs Weidenfeld and Nicolson for permission to reproduce a passage from their volume *The Greatest Thinkers*. And I want to thank Miss Christine Sandeman and Mrs Susan Loden, of the same firm, for all the work they have done to prepare the book for the press. I also appreciate greatly the constructive encouragement I have received from Mr Charles Scribner Jr, and the helpful editing of Miss Edith Poor of Charles Scribner's Sons, and I record with very great gratitude the help my wife Anne-Sophie has given me at every stage.

MICHAEL GRANT
Gattaiola

# I

# ETRUSCAN ROME

# I

# Rome and Etruria

ITALY'S CENTRAL POSITION IN the Mediterranean is a call to self-assertion, suggesting many promising opportunities if and when its population is capable of grasping them. For instead of forming a barrier between the eastern and western reaches of the sea, the country serves as a link between them, open to maritime channels on either side. Moreover, the curiously elongated shape of the peninsula provides, next only to Greece, the longest coastline in Europe. For every fifty-nine square miles of land there is a mile of shore; whereas Spain, for example, only has one to a hundred and forty-five. Besides, Italy is significantly placed in relation to the continental lands to its north. It is far enough removed from them to escape many of their turmoils, yet near enough to gain a share of whatever cultural advances are in the making.

At least three-quarters of Italy's territory consists of hills. They rise into the harshly ribbed vertebrae of the Apennines which dominate the whole land, curving down from the north-western seaboard to the eastern, Adriatic coast, and then back again to Italy's toe. Yet there are also plains at the foot of this mountainous mass; they provide convenient inland corridors, and for the most part enjoy a relatively temperate and humid climate, which, in early times, opened up possibilities of agriculture on a scale that no other Mediterranean country had ever before been able to attempt. In comparison with other parts of the world, and particularly with the little, less bountiful plains of Greece, these regions seemed welcoming indeed.

The greatest of the plains is the Po Valley in the north between the Apennines and the Alps. However, that region, known to the Romans as Gaul this side of the Alps (Cisalpine Gaul), is part of the continental land-mass rather than of the peninsula itself; and throughout more than half the period covered by this book it was not yet regarded as part of Italy at all. Yet in the south, too, even more fertile districts are to be found, especially along the west coast which was more attractive than the east because its

mountains are not so steep, and recede farther from the sea. On this shore
lay, above all, the Campanian plain, centred round the Gulf of Cumae (Bay of
Naples) and, to its north, the 230-mile stretch of lowland Latium; and then,
north of Latium, there was Etruria, separated from it by the River Tiber,
which, although smaller than the Po, is the largest river, and possesses the
most extensive drainage area, of peninsular Italy.

Descending from the central massif, the Tiber becomes navigable in its
lower reaches, like so many other rivers of the world on which important,
durable settlements have likewise been founded. And fifteen miles from the
Mediterranean, or twenty for those travelling on its stream – far enough to
provide warning of maritime raiders, but near enough to give it ready access
to the sea – was the lowest of the river's feasible crossing points: at Rome.
This crossing, close to an island in the river, linked together the lowest
stretches of firm ground on either bank at the point where the Tiber turns
and breaks through a low range to the marshy coastal plain, before debouch-
ing at the only possible harbour for many miles in either direction.

It was a crossing of vital importance, since it coincided with the most
convenient of the few longitudinal routes of Italy, a route which provided
the main line of communications along the whole of the western and more
populous flank of the country. Moreover, like London and Paris, the site
commanded easy progress not only across the river, but along its course as
well. For both upon its waters and by the road that lay beside it there was
access to precious, rare salt-pans on the shore; and inland the continuation
of the same road up the Tiber valley led by fairly easy passes into the central regions of the land.

Once the inhabitants of Rome became strong enough, they would be able
to dominate these vital passages in all directions. However, this potentiality
was a challenge and a peril as much as an advantage. For people at an
important junction are as likely to reap suffering as profit, and the men and
women who came and lived here were open to aggression from all sides, and
needed all the protection they could get.

They got it from the cliffs on which they planted their settlements, for
the river lay in a deep trough at this point, and the settlers came to live on
the hills and hillocks above its southern bank. These heights were between
100 and 300 feet above sea level – a series of flat-topped spurs projecting,
more sharply than now, towards the Tiber, and safely raised above the
floods to which its valley was exposed. Ravines, former tributaries of the
river, divided the hills from one another, and to a lesser extent from
the main plateau of the hinterland as well.

The site of Rome enjoyed a good water-supply at all seasons, and was
within easy reach of fertile soil. It had seen human occupation, at least at
sporadic intervals, from a very early date. The skull of a single-tusked

elephant that lived some two million years ago has been found in its alluvial sands, and the soil beneath a suburb has yielded a Neanderthal man's skull more than 30,000 years old. Other discoveries include the flint and copper implements of people who lived in the place early in the second millennium before our era.

Not long afterwards, in about 1600 BC, men and women with unfamiliar customs made their first appearance in Italy. They buried (inhumed) the bodies of their dead, practised a semi-nomadic pastoral economy, and made excellent bronze work and decorated pottery. These settlers are described as representatives of the 'Apennine culture' because they lived on either side of that range, to its north in the valley of the Po, and to its south in Etruria which extended down as far as Rome's river the Tiber; contrary to the view that prevailed until recently, the Etruscan sector of the culture probably developed more rapidly than the other. Moreover, from c. 1400 BC onwards this culture gained strength on the south bank of the Tiber, too, and left traces inside Rome itself, where objects that belonged to them have been found on the low ground near the river upon the site of the Forum Boarium or cattle market – to which they may have been transported from a neighbouring hill.

It is possible, though not certain, that the men and women who lived on the site of Rome at that time were already speaking the Indo-European speech which later became Latin and Italian. And there is also quite a likelihood that from the time of these Bronze Age settlers onwards, habitation continued without a break: in other words, that the city which exists today was founded by the middle of the second millennium BC.

A new phase, archaeologically better documented, began early in the last millennium BC, when new groups of migrants gradually moved to this location. These were the descendants of men and women who had probably been settled for some generations in the area later called Latium and now the southern part of Lazio, a roughly triangular, well-watered country consisting of rolling plains furrowed into gullies and undulating folds. Some thirty miles deep and sixty miles long, Latium extended from the borders of Campania as far north as the Tiber and the site of Rome. Before 1000 BC, the populations which had established themselves in this region had apparently been joined by immigrants of mixed origins coming by sea from the Balkans in small, isolated, pioneering groups.

Whatever may have been the case with their predecessors, these settlers probably spoke a primitive dialect related to Latin. They engraved bronze skilfully, but supplemented this talent by a growing familiarity with the use of iron, a knowledge they had acquired along the sea-routes from the Aegean. In contrast to their predominantly pastoral forerunners, they ploughed the soil with light ploughs and did not bury but burnt (cremated) their dead. They form one of the main streams of Iron Age history. But another too became increasingly apparent, for Latium also contained people, coming perhaps originally from southern Italy, who like the Bronze Age people of the previous millennium did not cremate their dead but buried them. This element gradually became dominant in Latium and greatly increased its prosperity.

One of the nuclei of these Latin communities was the Alban Mount (Monte Cavo), thirteen miles south-east of Rome. Its peak was a natural fortress some 3,000 feet in height, dominating a semi-circle of cone-shaped hills. The Alban Mount was a former volcano, which had ceased to be active in about the fourth millennium BC. By that time, however, its eruptions had guaranteed the future wealth of the area, by covering the marshy clay plain for miles around with layers of new soil containing phosphates and potash. This mixture, with the addition of decaying leaves from the forests of fir, pine, chestnut and beech that still covered the territory, made the sodden clay especially fertile when drained.

By the early years of the first millennium the settlement of the Alban area and of Latium was nearing completion, and nomadism was finally giving way to intensive cultivation. It was at this juncture that some of the Iron Age settlers moved into Rome. Groups of shepherds and farmers gradually moved across from the Alban region until they came to the Tiber and built their huts upon the Roman hills which were particularly attractive because they provided communications with Etruria beyond the river. First of all (the latest archaeological discoveries indicate a date during the tenth century BC) groups of these people settled on the level summit of the isolated and well-protected Palatine Hill, and in the marshy, moat-like valley of the Forum which lay between it and the Quirinal, Esquiline and Capitoline Hills. Next, in the ninth and eighth centuries BC, further immigrants came and settled on the Quirinal, guarded by steep ravines on three sides; and then others established themselves on the Esquiline as well. The precipitous Capitoline and the Caelian, rising north-west and east of the Palatine respectively, also received inhabitants in an early period, though at what stage cannot yet be determined.

And these people not only dwelt on the hills and the Forum that lay between them, but also deposited the remains of their dead near their dwellings. The two types of interment, characteristic of the two groups of Iron Age settlers, are both found, cremation and burial (inhumation). The cremators dug small, deep, circular pits, within which they placed large globular jars, with stone slats as lids, containing urns in which the burnt ashes of the dead person were laid. Often the urn was a little model of one of the huts in which the people themselves lived – a design that seems to have originated in Latium. As for the inhumers, they buried the bodies in hollowed-out logs or rough stone sarcophagsi, which they laid in long rectangular pits or trenches, sometimes lined with stones. The two types of

interment, cremation and inhumation, are sometimes found side by side on
Roman sites, and even, on occasion, in such close proximity that graves of
the two kinds actually cut into one another. But whether the practitioners
of these two customs differed from one another in race we cannot say. All
that it is safe to conjecture from these first Iron Age cemeteries at Rome is
that the two groups, whoever they were, gradually mixed and amalgamated
both with each other and with whatever sparse populations they already
found living on the hilltops when they arrived.

Rome, according to the traditional belief, was founded in 753 BC. But the
date is wholly mythical – too late for the first regular settlements, and too
early for the time of true urbanization. It is worth while to note how this
fictitious date came to be fixed. In the first place, the city's period of
monarchic rule was widely, and probably correctly, believed to have come
to an end in the last years of the sixth century BC. Now, to fill the preceding
period, later Romans could only muster the names of seven kings of varying
authenticity. To accommodate these seven kings, and the more or less
legendary events associated with them, it seemed necessary to suppose that
their reigns had covered two or three hundred years: which, working
back from their expulsion shortly before 500 BC, fixed the foundation of
Rome in the ninth or eighth century.

And so one later historian favoured 814 BC for this foundation – on an
entirely erroneous principle, because his only aim was to synchronize the
event with the origin of Rome's later arch-enemy Carthage, which was
believed to have been founded at that date. Another writer preferred 748–7
instead – on the equally fallacious grounds that this provided a convenient
period of exactly 400 years before a recorded celebration of the Secular
Games, a religious festival which marked periods of time, often centuries,
and had been celebrated, it was believed, in 348 BC. However, an alternative
date for the foundation, favoured by another ancient historian, was 751 –
the move from 748–7 being made to permit the interpolation of certain
names which this author wished to insert in the list of annually elected
consuls. And then a writer of the first century BC, Varro, needing two more
years for the same sort of reason, fastened upon 753 instead. That, ultimately, became canonical; but it is as wholly speculative and unsound a date
as any of the others.

In seeking, that is to say, to reconstruct the early history and chronology
of Rome, its abundant patriotic and partisan myths and legends have to be
distrusted. And yet those, unfortunately, are the only literary material that
we possess for all these early centuries before any reliable historical facts
are available. The myths are immensely important, because they tell us
what later generations of Romans believed about their country, and how
their minds worked. But to find out what had actually happened in early

days we are compelled, for the most part, to have recourse not to these stories but to archaeological excavation; and the record that this provides for us is sometimes entirely different from the stories told by the mythographers.

Another example of the same difficulty is provided by Rome's Etruscan period. Rome was at one time, as archaeological evidence reveals, a largely Etruscan city. Its myths do not deny that this was so. Yet the strange love-hate attitude which later Romans exhibited towards the Etruscans (and which is apparent, for instance, in many passages of Virgil's poetry) reflects such great discomfort about this period of foreign domination, far back in the past though it was, that most of the salient facts are obscured, and can only be partially recovered by painstaking archaeological research.

In the first place this tells us, and is telling us in ever greater detail year by year, who the Etruscans were. Their city-states flourished in the seventh and sixth centuries BC, in a homeland which roughly corresponded with what is now southern Tuscany and northern Lazio, covering a highly varied territory stretching 200 miles from the Arno to the Tiber, and inland as far as the Apennines. The individual but varied Etruscan people inhabiting this region, who called themselves 'Rasenna', displayed an art with pronounced oriental characteristics. Their splendid gold jewellery, for example, and the architectural themes and techniques which they employed to spectacular effect (preserved nowadays, when their cities have otherwise scarcely survived, mainly in grandiose rock-cut tombs), were strongly reminiscent of the near east: to some extent Asia Minor, but also the coastlands of Syria and Phoenicia (Lebanon), and historic Mesopotamia and Assyria beyond them.

Now similar trends were apparent in the art of Greece, too, during its 'orientalizing' phase which was precisely at the time of the greatest Etruscan art. Orientalizing tendencies had first begun to pervade Greece late in the eighth century BC, because the country's isolation, following its so-called 'Dark Age' during the convulsions at the beginning of the millennium, was beginning to come to an end. The monopoly of the eastern Mediterranean, which had passed during the previous chaotic period from Mycenae and other places in Greece to the Semitic cities of Tyre and Sidon in Phoenicia, was at this time challenged once again by the Greeks, whose own ships, as well as those of the Phoenicians, began to bring them objects of eastern trade and workmanship, thus causing oriental motifs to flood into Greek art. The lead was taken by the maritime isthmus city of Corinth, whose artists, as well as those from its offshoots or colonies on either side of the Adriatic, extensively painted such eastern themes on their vases. In these polychrome paintings, new patterns of animals and winged monsters replace the former geometric designs. This representational, illustrative type of art had long been familiar in Syria and Egypt and Assyria. But in Greece the introduction of these tendencies proved epoch-making, releasing novel creative forces, and endowing the rising civilization with a new and distinctive personality.

And they in their turn conveyed the new orientalizing influences to Etruria, both directly from the mainland of Greece and indirectly through their colonies of Magna Graecia in south Italy. For Etruria became one of the chief export markets of the Greeks. And so their painted vases, filled with amber, tin, lead and luxury goods, flooded into the country. And the Etruscans employed immigrant craftsmen from Corinth and its colonies; Etrusco-Corinthian pottery dominated the local markets from c. 600 BC, when a Greek-speaking community made its appearance at Graviscae (Porto Clementino), one of the ports of the Etruscan city of Tarquinii (now Tarquinia).

Etruscan art absorbed this Greek influence thoroughly. Yet the result seems strangely different and individual; just as Etruscan society, too, is in many ways alien from Greece, for example in its strange mixture of intense religious feeling with brutal physical force, and in the prominence it accorded to women, almost unparalleled in western lands until the present century. At its more pedestrian levels, the art of Etruria merely resembles an off-beat provincial variation of Greek art, such as could be found in other fringe areas of Hellenic culture in Europe and Asia. At its best, on the other hand, it achieves authentic, imposing originality.

The most typical features of Etruscan temples, their lofty platforms and roomy, colonnaded porches, are clearly un-Greek. Moreover an Etruscan statue like the Apollo of Veii (*c.* 500 BC) adds to its Greek shape and manner an un-Greek gross and forceful abundance of life, and an unclassical treatment of detail. These are partly the artist's own contribution; but they are also based on an apprehension of the eastern past which was more direct among the Etruscans than among the Greeks. For the orientalizing tendency is unmistakably sharper and deeper in Etruria. And this must have been the result of links with the near east so strong that they are best explained not merely by indirect contacts with that area, for example through trade with orientalizing Corinth, but by the supposition that the Etruscans themselves, or at least their ruling class, had originally been of eastern origin: a tradition believed by themselves and accepted by the Greek historian Herodotus, who regarded them as immigrants from Lydia in Asia Minor.

Indeed, the likelihood that they originated from some region of the near east – whether Lydia or elsewhere – is demonstrated not only by the artistic echoes and parallels, but by other evidence as well. For example, their belief in revealed religion and in specific methods of divination seems to go back to that part of the world. Moreover, their mining of copper, and then iron, was highly reminiscent of Asia Minor and regions beyond. They exploited this activity on a scale which, by ancient standards, was prodigious. Indeed, it was the copper available to Populonia, on the Etruscan coast, which evidently first brought these adventurers to the country and gave them their huge prosperity – and the weapons which maintained it. Moreover, their success was further guaranteed by extremely effective agriculture, making use of sophisticated methods of drainage and soil conservation which recall the techniques of Mesopotamia. And there is epigraphic evidence of eastern connexions, too, since inscriptions from the Aegean island of Lemnos reveal that its people spoke a language resembling Etruscan.

We can read the twenty-six characters of the alphabet used by the Etruscans, which they evolved from the letters employed by Greek colonists in south-western Italy. However, our fifty bilingual inscriptions

in which Etruscan is juxtaposed with another language unfortunately fail
to disclose the nature of this tongue, or even to show whether it forms part
of the Indo-European stock to which Greek and Latin belong. But that
now seems on the whole improbable, a conclusion which, like the Lemnos
inscriptions, suggests that the language of the Etruscans is yet another of
their institutions that seems to come from the east: thus confirming the view
that they themselves, or their governing class, were likewise of eastern
origin.

If so, it may be supposed that in the years round 700–675 BC – at a time
when Asia Minor and the lands beyond it were suffering from especially
troubled conditions – a succession of small bands of immigrants from some
unidentifiable eastern territory, following perhaps in the wake of reconnaissances by earlier traders, arrived upon the shores of Etruria. And there,
running their ships aground on the flat, grey-black beaches, they seized
the hill-spurs nearby and fortified them with wooden palisades, and established upon them, in due course, the powerful city-states which we know as
Etruscan. They did so with the collaboration, willing or forced, of the
peoples whom they found already in residence there; for, despite the
sudden upsurge suggestive of a new cultural element, there is also a strong
measure of archaeological continuity on the sites.

The Etruscans owed to their eastern forebears, as well as to the Greeks
when they subsequently got to know them, a marked talent for urbanization,
and this was encouraged by the compulsion, imposed by Italy's geography,
to cluster together on the relatively few sites that were eligible and attractive. And so the Etruscans created their cities, first near the coast, and then
on inland sites towards the middle course of the Tiber. Traditionally there
were twelve such communities in Etruria, though it is hard to draw up a
complete list for any given time; and besides, archaeology has revealed a
number of townships far exceeding that total. But twelve was the approximate number of their major city-states. In spite of traditions that there had
once been a single king over the whole country, each of these cities seems
to have been independent of all the rest. Once a year they sent delegates
over their excellent roads to a joint gathering at the shrine of Voltumna,
which has not yet been identified but was probably not far from Lake
Volsiniensis (Bolsena). Yet the political initiatives which this loose cult
union attempted were apparently rare and generally ineffectual. True, its
member cities no doubt maintained shifting patterns of alliances with one
another. But they had grown up in physical isolation, kept apart by the
wooded and hilly country which surrounded them. In consequence, each
city usually tended to act on its own.

And indeed these states were not only independent but highly individual, and distinguished from each other by sharp political, social and cultural

differences – almost as great, perhaps, as those which distinguished, say, Athens and Sparta in Greece. This point, too rarely appreciated, is of major importance to early Roman history, which was influenced at most significant junctures, not by the Etruscans as a whole, but by this or that Etruscan city-state. Owing to the inadequate state of our sources, we cannot always say which of these cities exercised such effect at any given moment. But obviously, to a large extent, Rome is likely to have been most greatly influenced by the southern communities, which lay so close to the Tiber. They were Tarquinii (Tarquinia), Caere (Cerveteri) and Veii: only forty, twenty and twelve miles distant respectively from Rome. These south Etruscan cities, standing on their hilltops in close proximity to the coast, were livelier and more cosmopolitan, more open and receptive to Greek and other foreign contacts, than their middle and north Etruscan counterparts which lay beyond almost untouched forests in the interior. And so it was they, Tarquinii, Caere and Veii, that developed a particularly brilliant and prosperous culture in *c.* 670–630 BC and supplied the formative stimulus and inspiration which transformed Rome from a huddle of hut villages into a city.

For by the early seventh century BC, the communities on the several spurs of the Palatine, Esquiline and Caelian had joined together at least for religious purposes and perhaps politically as well. The unit they now formed was the Septimontium or Seven Hills (different from, and smaller than, the later Seven Hills of Rome). Then, perhaps in *c.* 625–620, the low-lying area later known as the Forum was systematically drained, and it was probably at this juncture that Rome's Great Drain, the Cloaca Maxima, was dug through it – at first in the form of an open trench. Thus the Forum was able to start its long career as a meeting place and market for the unified Roman hills. Within another quarter of a century, the momentum quickened still further; the Forum, and the Sacred Way that connected it with the other quarters of the town, received their first permanent pavements, and the Forum Boarium (cattle market) near the river, too, was regularly laid out.

And it was at about the same time that a further decisive step was taken towards the unification of the city. For now the northernmost spurs, the Quirinal and Viminal, joined the growing community. Before long, the expanded township began to make use of the rocky Capitoline as a common citadel. Whether the earlier, smaller amalgamation, the Septimontium, had only been for purposes of common worship or had been more comprehensive, this new and larger Rome of the Four Regions, as it was called, was a completely unified entity, its boundaries marked with a sacred furrow by a bronze ploughshare drawn by a white bull and white cow.

It still cannot be proved for certain that these developments were directly due to the example or counsel of Rome's Etruscan neighbours. But this seems highly probable. For the appearance of such rapid internal changes, accompanied, as excavations show, by the transformation of a purely domestic economy into a community of professional handicrafts, suggests that some such powerful external agency was at work. Moreover contacts between Iron Age Latium and southern Etruria were nothing new; they had been taking place from the mid-eighth century onwards, and Rome had participated in them almost from the start, progressively assimilating its material culture to that of the Etruscans. And it is in the last quarter of the seventh century BC, at just about the time when the Forum was drained, that the first pottery and metalwork from the nearby Etruscan cities of Caere and Veii begin to appear at Rome. The place is evidently on the way to becoming an Etruscan town.

# 2

# The Etruscan Monarchy

WHAT INTERESTED THE ETRUSCANS about Rome, in the first place, was
not its own attractions but its position on the way south to the uniquely
inviting land of Campania. For behind this same coast, starting ninety miles
beyond Rome, lay the Campanian plain, incredibly favoured by nature.
Traversed by two rivers and fanned by moist winds, this territory of spongy
volcanic earth enjoyed relatively mild and short winters. Moreover, its soil,
retaining enough of the abundant seasonal rainfall to resist three months of
summer drought, became capable of producing in some districts as many
as three grain crops every year, in addition to a catch-crop of vegetables as
well.

But the Greeks reached Campania before the Etruscans, for in the eighth
century BC Greek colonists, attracted by the fertility of the area – as well as
by the possibility of trading with Etruria – chose Cumae, on the coast just
north-west of the gulf named after it, and now known as the Bay of Naples,
for their earliest settlement on the mainland of Italy; and it became a great
centre for the sale of grain and for the diffusion of Greek influence over the
greater part of south Italy and Sicily, known to the ancients as Magna
Graecia for this reason. But before 600 BC the migrants or armies of certain
Etruscan city-states forced their way into Campania, and founded, or refounded, the leading city of the fertile lowlands, Capua (Santa Maria
Capua Vetere), seventeen miles north of Neapolis (Naples). From Capua
the Etruscans began to extend their influence over the greater part of the
Campanian plain, though they did not succeed in controlling Cumae itself.

Whether they had first come to Campania by land or by sea cannot be
determined. But in any case they rapidly found it desirable both to create
a land-route to these new southern dependencies, and to possess harbours
on the way to them as well. That brought them into Latium, which lay
between Campania and themselves; so that during the seventh century BC
many leading Latin towns became subject to Etruscan city-states, at least
to the extent that those city-states controlled their communications and

imposed ruling classes upon them. And above all, it was the Etruscans who stimulated an enormous development of Latium's agriculture, introducing, after the model of their own country, a system of irrigation based on drainage channels (*cuniculi*), about five feet deep and two or three feet wide. Cut into the volcanic soil over almost the whole Latin plain stretching northwards from Campania and southwards from Rome, the channels made it practicable for this potentially fertile region to be cultivated with unprecedented intensity and the entire territory rescued from the marsh, just as the Dutch later reclaimed their lowlands from the sea.

It was impossible for the Etruscans to hold Latium without also taking Rome which lay between Latium and themselves. The town was on their very borders, and its river crossing was essential for their access to the Latin plain. There was also the added attraction of Rome's salt-trade from the river-mouth, since salt was essential to the Etruscan cities, and they could not obtain it from any other source. So those were the reasons why Rome came under Etruscan influence. As we saw in the last chapter, when discussing the stages of its urbanization, the decisive period of that process seems to have been the last quarter of the seventh century BC. Nor was it long before influence took the form of overt political control, and Rome, as its own subsequent writers were obliged to admit, came under the rule of an Etruscan monarch.

What sort of place did he find? Above all else, it was a religious community. For the Romans had from the earliest period cherished a powerful, pervasive and peculiar religion. Centuries later, Cicero praised their continuing conviction that everything is subordinate to divine rule and direction. Roman religion was based on mutual trustfulness (*fides*) between the divine powers or gods on the one hand, and men and women on the other. The trust accorded by the gods, and their benevolence – what was called the 'peace of the gods' (*pax deorum*), a balance of nature in which divine powers and human beings worked in harmony – could be secured by meticulous ritual: and not so much, as more recent religions would maintain, by good moral behaviour, since for centuries there was no very prominent moral element in Roman religion. Nevertheless, this idea of the divine peace indirectly exercised a moral influence, since the respect which it induced for vows made to the gods was extended, in the course of time, to vows made to other human beings as well.

Yet the individual human being was not what mattered in the religion of the Romans; for they saw this as a group affair, not a matter for individuals. And indeed the same applied to the whole of Roman life, in which individuality was submerged in family, clan and state. The family or household, and the clan (*gens*) or group of households – comparable to similar institutions in most other ancient Indo-European speaking peoples – were of overriding importance. The head of the family (*paterfamilias*) was absolute; there is nothing, perhaps, in any other known culture quite as extreme as this long-lasting patriarchal assertion. Although the *pater-familias* might call in, by custom, a council of male relatives, and although he habitually left the running of his house to his wife, it was he who monopolized all rights. In the home, his word was literally law – and so long as he remained alive his sons never came of age.

Thus he controlled, among much else, domestic cult, which played a mighty part in daily life. The household deities were worshipped every day and at every meal, and no important family event could take place without securing divine approval. Whether domestic or communal worship came earliest is disputed; but in any case the latter was a magnified version of the former. Vesta, worshipped by her Vestal Virgins beside the Forum in her round straw hut which later became a temple, was the hearth-goddess of the Roman state. But she was equally prominent in family cult as well, symbolizing the solidarity of the home as well as the nation.

Roman religion possessed no sacred writings except invocations and prayers, and its priests were not a caste set apart, but men following secular careers. Yet it was none the less real for all that. 'To understand the success of the Romans,' declared the Greek historian Dionysius of Halicarnassus at the turn of our era, 'you must understand their piety.' The gods were national, invisible, potent citizens of whatever country they favoured, and the Romans, duly performing manifold observances towards them, believed that they favoured Rome.

Yet these powers that inspired their awe and reverence, which is what *religio* meant, were regarded as mysterious and unknowable, and for a long time were scarcely seen as personal beings. For in the earliest times, the Romans, like many other Italians, lacked the Greek taste for seeing their deities in personalized anthropomorphic form; so that the temple of Vesta contained no image at all. They also in those early days lacked the desire to clothe their gods and goddesses in a mythology. Instead, they were inclined to see divine force, or divinity, operating as pure function or act, both in human activities like opening doors or giving birth to children, and in natural phenomena, such as the movement of the sun and stars and the seasons of the soil.

Yet this impersonal concept was already becoming gradually modified from a very ancient date, when Greek ideas first began to come in, both directly and through the medium of Etruria. For example, Vesta, even though she lacked a statue, was the same, etymologically and by assimilation, as the Greek Hestia. And Mars, the first god to be recognized by the Romans (as by other Italians too) as chief of all the divinities, was identified with the Greek Ares. Nevertheless, their religion retained its independence, because their deities remained somewhat different from those of the Greeks: Mars, for example, was not entirely a war-god like Ares, since he was rather the protector of the whole people, in agriculture as well as war. Indeed, he shared an ancient sanctuary in the Forum, known as the Regia, with the power of fertility, Ops Consiva. The first cult building on the Regia site, replacing earlier huts and burials, was a stone-founded and stone-walled precinct dating from the later seventh century BC. It contained a monument of which the purpose is still unknown; perhaps it was dedicated to Mars. As the name 'Regia', suggests, early Rome was a monarchy: for the word comes from *rex*, king, and the Regia was therefore in all probability the building in which the king had his residence.

That Rome had originally been ruled by kings was unanimously asserted by its subsequent historians. Before Etruscan rule began, there had already been, according to this tradition, four non-Etruscan monarchs. Most or all of these four names are either of dubious historicity or downright fictitious: notably the alleged city founder Romulus, which just means 'the man of Rome'. Yet the memory that Rome had been a monarchy was authentic, and is confirmed by the survival of the royal title *rex* into later times, after the kings had gone, when it came to be borne by a priest known as the *rex sacrorum*, 'king' of religious affairs – residing, as the early monarchs had apparently resided, in the Regia. Yet about the most ancient phases of this kingship we know practically nothing, except that, as the survival of the *rex sacrorum* suggests, it included religious duties. The office, perhaps, was not necessarily hereditary or adoptive, but elective, as in the city-states of primitive Greece.

From the beginning, so later tradition maintained, the Roman state was divided into three units, known as tribes (*tribus*). Some scholars suggest that this division represented a racial distinction, corresponding to three different components in the original Roman state; but this is uncertain, and they may instead have been groups of clans without any clear ethnic differentiation. In any case, the threefold division is likely to have been made in the first place in order to facilitate military and financial censuses of the people. The names of the three tribes are Etruscan, and this could mean either that they are Etruscanized designations of units that had already existed under different names before the Etruscan monarchy, or, alternatively, that they were new institutions which the Etruscan monarchy first brought into existence. The latter is the more natural interpretation; and if we accept it, these tribes may reasonably be ascribed to the earlier times of Etruscan influence, perhaps towards the end of the seventh century BC.

The three tribes were subdivided into ten *curiae* or wards, each comprising a number of clans or groups of families (once again, not necessarily differentiated by race); a similar kind of organization seems to have existed in other Latin towns, and perhaps in Etruscan communities as well. It was upon these *curiae*, and upon the tribes into which they were grouped, that the earliest recognizable Senate was based, for it contained 300 members, that is to say, 30 from each *curia* and 100 from each tribe. These senators were selected by the kings from the *patres familias* – the heads of the clans and of their component families – and were known as *patres conscripti*; how freely they debated under the monarchy we cannot tell. The *curiae* also met together in a body to form the earliest Assembly Rome possessed, the *comitia curiata*. Probably this merely ratified decisions which had been made by the king, perhaps after he had consulted with the Senate; though when a king died, the Assembly may have played a part in electing his successor. The curial system also seems to have been the basis of Rome's most primitive military organization. This comprised an army or legion (*legio*) of 3,000 infantry and 300 cavalry, that is to say, 1,000 and 100 respectively from each of the tribes, and 100 and 10 respectively from each *curia*.

Owing to the Etruscan tribal nomenclature on which these developments are based, it is possible that they ought to be synchronized with the fifth name on Rome's traditional king list; for he was Etruscan and brings us to firmer ground, since he represents the Etruscan takeover of Rome, which is a historical fact. Roman legend tells that this first of the city's Etruscan kings succeeded peacefully to the throne – though such a tradition may be merely a patriotic device to scotch the idea that Rome had ever been forcibly subjective to foreigners. His name was said to be Tarquinius Priscus (i.e. the elder, in contrast with his son Tarquinius Superbus, who became king later): and his origin was attributed to one of the earliest Etruscan cities, Tarquinii, on a high plateau not far from the sea; forty miles north-west from Rome. But this homeland may have been invented for him by later historians because the record of a monarch named Tarquinius at Rome so obviously recalled the name of the place. There is an alternative possibility that the Tarquins came from Caere (Cerveteri). It was much closer to Rome, and more intimately connected with it: and the mausoleum of their family has been discovered there, with their name 'Tarchna' latinized as 'Tarquitius'.

The traditional dates of Priscus' reign are 616–579 BC, and here tradition harmonizes for the first time with the findings of archaeology, which ascribe the decisive stages of Rome's urbanization to the last quarter of the seventh century. The Etruscans may, then, have established political control of the city at precisely that time; though some would argue, instead, that their monarchy only started in *c.* 575. But it is not at all certain that the legends are right when they tell of *two* Etruscan kings of Rome bearing the name of Tarquin. There may have been more than two; or there may have been only one, retrospectively subdivided into two so as to attribute 'good' deeds to the first, and bad tyrannical deeds to the second (Superbus meaning 'the arrogant'), with whom the monarchy was believed to have come to an unlamented end.

It was apparently in this Etruscan period that the rulers of Rome quit their earlier royal residence in the Regia and established themselves instead, and built a citadel, on the precipitous, defensible Capitoline Hill, while their followers settled between the Capitoline and Palatine in 'Etruscan Street', the Vicus Tuscus. Moreover, excavators' reports of the destruction in c. 600 BC of small towns including Politorium (Castel di Decima) ten miles south of Rome may bear witness to a territorial drive by the Etrusco–Roman monarchy in this direction.

How Etruscan did Rome now become? Opinions differ. As inscriptions show, there was a Latin-speaking population under an Etruscan-speaking ruling class. Nevertheless, it has been argued recently that there was deep interpenetration and fusion between the two ethnic and linguistic groups, and that Rome did, at this time, turn into a more or less homogeneous Etruscanized city. Support for this view from later Roman historians cannot be expected, because it would have been unacceptable to the national pride. Yet to a certain extent at least, that is what must have happened. For the later institutions of the Romans still continued to embody highly important Etruscan features. Their religion contained much that was Etruscan, including the calendar. Their mythology, too, when they came to have one, owed much to the same source; for example the adoption of Aeneas as Rome's precursor, perpetuated by Virgil who was himself partly Etruscan, is traceable back to the city's occupation by that people, among whom Aeneas was revered.

Moreover, whereas they had taken their alphabet, with modifications, from Greece, either directly or through the medium of the Greek city of Cumae in Campania, the Romans then proceeded to borrow their own, after further changes, from their Etruscan neighbours and overlords. That is why, like the Etruscan alphabet, it is short in vowels and redundant in the C, K, and Q group: and the letter-forms of the earliest Latin inscriptions bear the same witness to Etruscan origins. And from the same source, once again, came much Roman ceremonial, and the names of families and localities, and many architectural achievements (gateways, bridges, arches, designs of houses), numerous styles and themes of pictorial art, and highly developed agricultural methods.

True, most of these borrowings, except for the last, had little effect on the illiterate, impoverished majority of the population of the region, who had to live, as always, not far from the borders of bare subsistence. But at all higher levels the influence of the Etruscans was deeply pervasive: which is scarcely surprising, since it was only due to them that Rome had become a city at all.

•    •    •    •    •    •

Midway in the Tarquinian régime, and, to be exact, between the suspect
pair of Tarquins, legend inserted the mysterious King Servius Tullius. The
dates given for his reign are 578–535 BC, but they are entirely unreliable,
and indeed this monarch is more richly encrusted with fictitious myth, if
possible, than any of the kings who supposedly come before or after him.
Servius Tullius was said to be a Latin, although a rival theory declared him to
be Etruscan. But his name is Latin, and he is best thought of as a member of
the native population that dated back to pre-Etruscan times. However,
he apparently pursued the development and expansion of Rome on the lines
of his Etruscan predecessor; and indeed, he was credited with a thorough
overhaul of the institutions of the Roman state. Many object that the reform
attributed to him, like so much else in the historians' account of the kings,
ought instead to be assigned to a date perhaps as much as two centuries
later. Yet these measures are appropriate to the stage of evolution that the
community seems to have reached in his day and may be discussed at this
point.

What happened was that the three original tribes of Rome were replaced
by twenty-one new ones, four in the city and seventeen in Rome's rural
appendages. These new tribes represented local, geographical divisions:
and the urban tribes correspond with the Four Regions of Rome which
seem to have been established slightly earlier, in about 600 BC. Even if it is
not quite certain that the three earlier tribes had been instituted for census
reasons, this was surely the purpose of Servius' twenty-one new ones:
they were basic units for raising levies and collecting taxes. As to the rural
tribes – of which the geographical delimitation remains uncertain – sixteen out of the seventeen of them were known, at least in later historical
times, by the names of families that were eminent at Rome: and it is possible
that these names go back to Servian times. Nevertheless, if this was so,
their naming in such a way was not much more than a sop to the aristocracy: for the novel insistence on a territorial residential basis meant a
diminution of family loyalties and enabled the enfranchisement of Etruscan
and other immigrants who lacked these allegiances and reserved their
allegiance not for any family but for the monarch.

Moreover, under the same king, or at least at the same period, a completely new military system was inaugurated, according to which the size of
the army was doubled to 6,000 and based no longer on the *curiae* or tribes
but on 60 'centuries' of 100 men each.

This change had highly important effects both of a political and of a
military nature. On the political side it meant that the Assembly of *curiae*,
the *comitia curiata*, was replaced for most practical purposes by a new
Assembly of Centuries, the *comitia centuriata*. This made for greater
efficiency since the curial system, having been based on wards, had proved
unadaptable to an expanding city; for example, it cannot have worked well

when citizens moved, and it was ill-adjusted to dealing with individual immigrants. After the monarchy was over, it would become the official duty of the *comitia centuriata* to elect chief magistrates, and to decide on peace or war. What powers it already possessed under the kings we cannot tell. However, although larger than those previously enjoyed by the *comitia curiata*, they were probably still not large. It seems likely that only the king or his nominee decided what measures should be brought before the centuriate Assembly, and that when this was done it could only accept or (less likely) reject them without debate. In other words, the *comitia centuriata* was a useful organ of the monarch's authority, and might have some say in state decisions, but there was nothing very democratic about it. Besides, the ruler tried to eliminate alternative loyalties by making these Assemblymen, in their capacity as soldiers, take the oath to himself.

Moreover there was no question of 'one man, one vote'. Voting was not by heads but by groups, and the procedure was so organized that the richer groups were predominant. For the new army on which the centuriate Assembly was based consisted of property owners graded according to wealth. On this basis, the infantry were divided into five classes, of which the first and richest provided no less than 80 of the 193 centuries of voting units, while those, richer still, who could pay for horses provided another 18, so that the wealthy or relatively wealthy filled more than half of the total number of centuries of which the Assembly was constituted. Here, then, was a political system in which, while birth was no longer the dominant consideration, it had given place not to democracy, but to property ownership.

This manning of the new army by property-owners, men rich enough to provide their own arms and armour, directly echoes changes in military organization that had been occurring elsewhere, first in Greece and then in Etruria. From about 750 BC the Greeks had begun to develop heavy infantry equipment, partly under Assyrian influence and partly through contact with the metal-workers of central Europe. And thereafter, more completely from about 675, Greek military history had shown a slow and piecemeal adoption of this sort of equipment – round shield, defensive metal body-armour, and thrusting spear – with the tactical corollary that these heavily armed soldiers ('hoplites', from *hopla*, arms) fought in a closely-knit line or phalanx. They were all men who possessed sufficient property of their own to equip themselves with the full array of this personal armour. Then from about 650 BC the hoplite shield began to appear in Etruria too, as archaeological finds and vase paintings reveal, and during the course of the sixth century the full set of hoplite arms came into standard use among the Etruscans.

And so this military innovation arrived at Rome as well. Its attribution to

Servius Tullius, or at least to the general period during which he appears to have ruled, finds confirmation in an Esquiline tomb of the early sixth century BC, in which a bronze shield was discovered like those adopted in the hoplite reforms of Greece and Etruria. Such were the arms of the men who provided Rome with its greatly enlarged reservoir of recruits, who were to achieve such astonishing military triumphs in the years to come. And each spring, before setting out to war, they sat and deliberated in the *comitia centuriata* and endowed it with a military *esprit de corps*; it was the Roman Army in Assembly, orderly obedience its second nature.

This was then, to a large extent, a middle-class army, containing the men whom the prosperity of Etruscan Rome had encouraged to flourish. But it was also still an aristocratic army to the extent that the land-owning noble clans, being the richest section of the population, continued to play a prominent part in the manning of the infantry. And the eighteen centuries of cavalry ('equites', knights) also, who formed the richest group, no doubt consisted chiefly of nobles. Yet the reforms of the middle-class hoplite infantry gradually deprived these horsemen of a dominant role in military operations; though it may be conjectured that they remained the personal bodyguard of the kings.

Servius encircled at least the northern part of his city of the Four Regions with a rampart. This was not what is now known as the 'Wall of Servius Tullius', which encircles the larger area of a later Rome and does not go back further than the fourth century BC. Yet surviving remains of another earthwork can be attributed to a considerably earlier date than the 'Wall', since they are partly built over sixth-century tombs and were found to contain a fragment of Athenian pottery datable, at the very latest, to c. 470 BC, and perhaps to a period two or even five decades earlier. Traditionally, King Servius Tullius died in 535 BC, but, as was suggested, there is no firm basis for that exact date, and the earthen defence-work may reasonably, if conjecturally, be ascribed to him; not only on the somewhat vague grounds that he was believed to be the builder of such a wall in ancient times, and that this tradition fits in with his general measures to extend Rome's strength, but because similar ramparts were being built at other Latin and Etruscan towns at about the same epoch. The Roman earthwork was apparently rather more than twenty-five feet high, with a ditch in front. It was erected on the vulnerable open plateau on the north side of the town, from the Quirinal along the brow of the Viminal towards the northern end of the Esquiline, so as to block the heads of the valleys leading from the interior of Latium to Rome.

For a rapidly developing city-state like Rome was certain to inspire many enmities. Moreover, Servius, as we have seen, appears to have been a Latin, an interloper in the line of Etruscan kings, and thus a provocation to a number of his neighbours. Yet he also seems to have been an expansionist in the Etruscan tradition. For although our sources are obscure and tendencious, it may well have been in his time that Rome emerged as the leading power of north-western Latium. The dominant feature of this land, the Alban Mount (Monte Cavo), had become a common religious sanctuary for the Latin communities around. It was devoted to the sky-divinity Jupiter (Diou-pater, the bright one), at first simply an impersonal power of the heavens, manifesting itself in different ways – a power worshipped in common by the Indo-European speaking peoples and some of their predecessors, and here known as Jupiter Latiaris. On the slopes of the mountain was the town of Alba Longa (Castelgandolfo), famous in Virgil's legend as the parent city of Rome, although this is unconfirmed by archaeology.

Whether Alba Longa founded other towns of Latium as further legends recount, and if so how many, must remain equally uncertain. But its headship of a loosely knit league of Latin towns from about the tenth century BC onwards, when it began to control the main inland route to the south, deserves acceptance. The towns of Latium, being grouped in inward-looking fashion round a plain, were readily inclined to form associations of this kind, of which there seem to have been several; and Alba Longa, on the slopes of the revered Alban Mount, was eminently suited to take the lead of one of them.

However, Alba Longa was only about twelve miles from Rome, and with aggressive monarchs on the Roman throne a clash was bound to come. It came, and Rome won. Legend ascribes the victory to a pre-Etruscan king of the city, and archaeology confirms that the balance of power between the Albans and Romans was already beginning to shift from the ninth or eighth century BC: but the final eclipse of Alba Longa, and of other towns of north-west Latium as well, may be regarded as forming part of a general Roman expansion at about the time of Servius Tullius, during the sixth century. There is no reason to doubt the tradition that after the decisive confrontation, some of Alba's leading families then came to Rome and were admitted to its aristocracy, settling, in some cases, upon the Caelian hill.

And while extending their rule in this north-westerly direction, the Romans of this epoch also seem to have expanded the same distance south-westwards as far as the coast, and to have established the port of Ostia at the mouth of the Tiber – beyond Politorium which had already been reduced earlier – in order to exploit the adjoining salt-beds. This event, too, was attributed by tradition to an earlier king, but once again may tentatively be ascribed to the time of Servius Tullius. It is true that archaeological evidence on the site of Ostia itself has so far totally failed to reveal any settlement whatsoever dating back as far as the time of the kings. But this may only be because the settlement in question was located outside the later Roman harbour town, on ground which has not yet been fully explored. However 'regal' Ostia probably existed.

And Rome's first wooden bridge, the Pons Sublicius replacing the island ford, may well belong to the same time as this first Ostia. For when the salt had been collected at the river-mouth it was hard work to convey it to the city by river, which meant taking it upstream. This was, it is true, sometimes done, with the aid of tow ropes. But cargoes also frequently had to be transported by land, along the left bank; so that the Romans needed the bridge to move the salt across the Tiber, to its Etruscan purchasers and others beyond.

Servius Tullius, if such innovations are to be attributed to him personally, again had the outside world in mind when he added an appendage to Rome of the Four Regions. This he did by building an important temple on the Aventine Hill which lay just beyond the city's boundaries to the south. It was a shrine of Diana, 'the bright one' like Jupiter, and at the same time a goddess of forests who helped women by giving them children. It had been believed until recently that Servius, by constructing this temple, was deliberately superseding a similar, widely frequented, cult of Diana near the Latin town of Aricia, in an old volcanic crater valley at the foot of the Alban Mount sixteen miles south-east of Rome. But now this view needs modification, since, although the Aventine shrine cannot yet be completely reconstructed, archaeologists have offered reasons for believing that its Arician counterpart was probably the later of the two. Nevertheless, the Aventine shrine may well have been intended, if not to eclipse Aricia, at least to attract dispossessed immigrants from its territory and other parts of Latium, and that could well be why it was located outside the boundaries of the city. Evidently it enjoyed considerable prestige in the area, since its regulations, we learn, were accepted by other Latin towns, for example Tibur (Tivoli).

But the inspiration for the Aventine cult may have come not from Latium but from Greek cities whose federal worships Servius Tullius was seeking to imitate. And, in particular, his model is likely to have been Massilia. This great and influential port on the southern coast of France, founded in *c.* 600 BC (under the name of Massalia) by Greek seafarers from Asia Minor, had come to dominate the Mediterranean shores from southern Spain to where the border between France and Italy exists today. Its settlers had borrowed and imported the worship of their goddess Artemis from its world-centre at the ancient Greek city of Ephesus (Selçuk) on the coast of Asia Minor – and with this Ephesian sanctuary the Roman cult of Diana, who was early identified with Artemis, possessed a manifest connexion. For the Aventine shrine of the goddess was the possessor, perhaps from the outset, of a statue of the many-breasted type that was peculiarly characteristic of Ephesus; very probably the Romans obtained it from Massilia. At all events, its introduction to Rome represented a decisive step, a more decisive step than earlier cults of Mars and other deities, towards the personal, anthropomorphic interpretation of gods and goddesses.

The importation of this statue of Artemis-Diana, whether from Ephesus or Massilian intermediaries, is significant for another reason also, because it confirms that early Rome did not obtain all its Hellenic influences through the medium of Etruria, but derived some of them direct from the Greeks who were struggling with the Etruscans for the dominance of the western Mediterranean. This is confirmed by the geographical situation of the Aventine temple, standing guard over the river-wharves of the Tiber, which formed a centre for Greek (as well as eastern) traders very early on. And, below the north-western end of the Aventine, stood a very ancient altar (the Ara Maxima) which tells the same story. For it was dedicated to Hercules, who was the same as Heracles, the Greek god of traders, and the location of his altar at that spot intended him to preside over these commercial activities.

But another, even grander, new Roman shrine was more Etruscan than Greek. This was the temple of Jupiter the Best and Greatest, and of Juno and Minerva, on the Capitoline Hill, beside the citadel where the Etruscan

kings resided. According to tradition the two Etruscan monarchs Tarquinius Priscus and his son Tarquinius Superbus, who reigned before and
after Servius Tullius respectively, each played a part in the foundation of
the temple, Priscus by dedicating it and getting the work started and
Superbus by completing its construction. But the involvement of Priscus
may only be a retrospective fiction designed to ascribe the inception of this
great project to the 'good' monarch rather than to his 'bad' disgraced son:
whereas the truth of the matter probably is that the temple was entirely
due to the initiative of Superbus. If so, then it belongs to the very end of the
Etruscan monarchy, traditionally placed in the last years of the sixth century BC. The temple was, for the most part, in the Etruscan manner, with a
terracotta statue of a fully personalized Jupiter executed by a famous
Etruscan sculptor.

Jupiter the sky-god was called Best and Greatest, said Cicero, because he makes us prosperous; but also because, under Etruscan influence, he was now the successor of Mars as the principal god of the Romans. When he first began to assume this function, at a somewhat earlier date, he had still been associated with Mars, and with another antique Italian god Quirinus, the god of the Quirinal Hill; they formed a triad or trinity. But now the triad were Jupiter, Juno, and Minerva. The names, in these forms, were Italian, but they had Etruscan (as well as Greek) counterparts, and the linkage of these three divinities is Etruscan. It was a grouping that may have been seen in other parts of Rome already. But it was here that it became famous, on the Capitol, where the trinity was worshipped in a shrine divided into three sections (*cellae*), such as are also found at other Etruscan centres.

But the most significant feature of the Capitoline temple was its extra-ordinary size and grandeur. With its deep, Etruscan, porch of three rows of six columns, and a row of free-standing columns down each side (a less universal Etruscan feature), it measured 180 feet in width and over 200 feet in length: as its sixteen-foot-high stone platform, so characteristic of Italian as opposed to Greek temples, reveals – for much of this still survives, though little more of the original structure is now to be seen. These huge dimensions made it, as far as we can tell, the largest temple of its time in the entire Etruscan sphere, while not many exceeded its size in Greek lands either. And although in the Etruscan fashion the super-structure was only made of wood, the building was of marvellous splen-dour, colourfully decorated with lavish paintwork and many monuments.

And then, perhaps almost immediately after the dedication of this glittering temple, the Etruscan monarchy of Rome, in the person of Tarquinius Superbus, fell from power and ceased to exist. Superbus had made a treaty with strategic Gabii (Castiglione), ten miles to the east, the site of abundant recent archaeological discoveries, and had also apparently planted garrisons a good deal farther afield. But in the end he was overthrown. The traditional date of his expulsion, 510 BC, must be regarded with grave suspicion, because that is also the year in which the last tyrant of Athens was expelled from his city, and Greek historians could not resist inventing the coinci-dence.* But Tarquinius Superbus probably fell not more than three or four years afterwards, and a rival theory that the Etruscan monarchy at Rome did not end until the 450s has gained little support.

For in other parts of Italy too, including Etruria, monarchies were losing their grip and collapsing in these last years of the sixth century BC. More-over, it was a period when the Etruscans in Latium and Campania were generally in retreat, hard pressed by their enemies the Greeks. In particular, Aristodemus of the Greek city of Cumae, the bitter rival of the city states of

* The Table of Dates at the end synchronizes some of the major events in Roman and Greek history.

Etruria, had repulsed Etruscan and other attackers in 529, in the marshes and woods north of his native city; and nearly twenty years later he defeated Etruscan forces once again, this time at Aricia, a victory which enabled him to become the autocratic ruler of his home-town. The first of these engagements weakened Etruscan power in general, and probably helped, in the long run, to undermine Tarquinius Superbus. The second clash seems to have taken place shortly after Superbus' expulsion, and must have made it more difficult for him (or for that matter any other Etruscan) to seize control of Rome ever again.

Incidentally, this second battle also gave the town of Aricia, which had helped in the successful fight, the temporary headship of a loose religious and perhaps also political confederation, such as Alba Longa had possessed in earlier years. The pre-eminence of Alba had been based on the worship of Jupiter Latiaris, and Aricia's was founded on its shrine of Diana overlooking Lake Nemorensis (Nemi), to which reference was made above. Alba Longa had succumbed to the Romans, but this time Rome, its monarchy fallen, was no longer in a position to oppose or suppress the Aricians; and so they exploited their cult of Diana, deliberately seeking to outbid the Roman shrine of the same goddess on the Aventine. Nor did Aricia have to worry too much about possible encroachments from other Etruscan-dominated cities in the area either, since Rome was not the only Latin town where the Etruscans had lost their authority, or were rapidly losing it. For their defeat at Aricia was part of a general collapse of their rule over wide areas of Latium. As Latins and hill-tribesmen profited from their troubles to move in across their lines of communications, other Latin cities in addition to Aricia were recorded as conducting successful rebellions; so that the Etruscan power in Latium was broken. Moreover, archaeologists have shown that the life of certain towns in Etruria itself now came to an end at about the same time.

Such, then, was the fall of Rome's Etruscan rulers. However, despite the equal misfortunes of their compatriots in other parts of Latium and Campania, they did not, during the troubled years that followed, accept their ejection by the Romans as final. In the first place, Tarquinius Superbus tried, unsuccessfully, to engineer his own return. And Lars Porsenna of the inland Etruscan city-state of Clusium (Chiusi), acting independently of the Tarquins – for he was by no means their friend – marched eighty miles southwards upon Rome, and attacked it in a sudden raid. Moreover, contrary to the patriotic legend enshrined in Macaulay's *Lay of Horatius*, defender of the Sublician Bridge, it appears that Lars Porsenna actually captured the city and held on to it for a time, until the setback at Aricia (in which his son commanded the defeated army) compelled him to leave.

Nor was Porsenna the only Etruscan adventurer who briefly forced his way into the disorganized towns – and some of these raiders were even able to settle with their troops inside its boundaries upon the Caelian Hill. So Rome had good reason to remain highly apprehensive of continued and renewed raids from Etruria, which lay so close. And such raids, from time to time, continued to occur; while inside the city, too, Etruscan influence still remained strong. Nevertheless, no really serious attempt was made by any of the Etruscan states to recover Rome or Latium, or even the greater lost prize of Campania beyond. Indeed the latter country became even more manifestly irrecoverable after Syracuse, the greatest Greek city in Sicily, had subjected the Etruscans to another defeat off Cumae in 474 BC.

Yet their lack of perseverance in the south did not by any means signify that this remarkable people was exhausted. For the reason, strangely enough, why they were willing to turn away from Campania and Latium was because certain of their city-states were, at this very moment, launching a commercial (perhaps also political) drive in the opposite direction, to the region which the Romans later called Cisalpine Gaul. The main centre of their new dominion was Felsina (Bologna), refounded on the site of an ancient town; Marzabotto, seventeen miles to its south-west, gives us a unique picture of what an ancient Etruscan city looked like; Virgil was descended from Etruscan forebears who had founded Mantua; and the Greek ports of Adria (Atria) and Spina on the mouths of the Po are shown by excavations to have possessed substantial Etruscan trading communities – the enmity between Greeks and Etruscans, which was so apparent on the west coast of Italy, apparently being absent. This new, northern enterprise of the Etruscans, though it survived long enough to bring writing and civilization to continental Europe, did not last for more than a hundred years. But, for the time being, it increasingly absorbed their energy and attention. As far, therefore, as the menace from Etruria was concerned, Rome found itself able to enjoy a respite.

# II

# THE UNITY OF
# ITALY AND ROME

# 3

# The Unification of Italy

THE WORST OF THE grim difficulties which descended upon the Romans after the fall of the Tarquins still remain to be described. For although the Etruscan menace soon declined for the time being, the city continued to suffer from an abundance of other enemies eager to take advantage of its diminished position. In consequence the greater part of the two centuries that followed witnessed constant, uphill fights against each one of them, in turn, or often simultaneously: sometimes they were fights upon which the very survival of Rome depended.

In the first place, its immediate neighbours and relatives the Latins, once the power of the Etruscan Tarquins was removed, immediately became recalcitrant. For it was at about this time that the legend-encrusted town of Lavinium, near the sea sixteen miles from Rome, threw off its allegiance to the Romans, and asserted its claims as common sanctuary of a group of Latin coastal towns. This union, or league, conflicted with Roman interests, and in *c.* 496 BC a memorable battle was fought beside the volcanic depression of Lake Regillus (Pantano, now drained). Regillus belonged to the territory of Tusculum (near Frascati), which took the military lead in resisting the Romans. However, in the engagement that followed, Rome's heavy armed infantry, supported by its mounted knights (*equites*), proved superior to the old-fashioned Latin cavalry and won a decisive victory. As a result, the Romans incorporated in their own religion two deities who had been worshipped in Tusculum since very early times – a borrowing characteristic of their religious practice, intended to transfer and attract to themselves the power and following of the divinities of defeated states. The twin gods thus acquired after Regillus were Castor and Pollux, the Greek Dioscuri – horsemen who were believed to have helped the Romans magically in the victorious battle and who from now on became the patrons of the cavalry or knights of Rome.

But the battle may not have been as decisive as the legends of the Romans subsequently reported, since soon afterwards they made a treaty with the

Latin towns on a basis not of superiority but of equality. Rome was only to provide the combined army with its general when its turn to do so arrived; on this understanding the treaty provided for reciprocal support in war against common enemies from the neighbouring hills. And it probably also stipulated mutual recognition of private rights – a foretaste of the sensible, statesmanlike measures which were destined, in later years, to take the Romans step by step to imperial power. But they had no such power yet; otherwise they would not have agreed to such an equally balanced arrangement. Nevertheless, this was not equality with each and every Latin city individually, since Rome made its treaty with these communities jointly and as a whole; which implied that the Romans, though no longer forceful enough to dominate Latium as they had under the Etruscan monarchy, were still sufficiently strong to be recognized as the equal of the principal Latin cities combined.

And before long the balance began to tilt further in favour of the Romans. The first sign of their superior pretensions came in about 415 BC when they were entrusted with the organization of the Latin Festival on the Alban Mount. And very soon afterwards, profiting by a quarrel between Aricia and another Latin city Ardea (a primitive port), Rome moved ahead farther by signing treaties with at least one and perhaps both of them *separately*, and with Lavinium as well. This did not mean that it now considered that these towns, or any one of them, had now become its equal; it meant instead that it was prepared to flout the Latin League by making private arrangements, advantageous to itself, with any one of the league's individual members with which it desired to associate itself in this way. This was a foretaste of further Roman encroachments to come. But, for the most part, the equilibrium was still not openly upset.

This relative harmony with the Latins was imperatively needed, since the menace from the Apennines, to Latins and Romans alike, was severe. Their remote valleys, deep glens and high plateaux fostered isolated shepherd communities, speaking Oscan which was an Indo-European relative of Latin. These pastoral peoples, living tough lives wholly lacking in Mediterranean amenities, greatly coveted Latium's access to the sea and superior fertility and winter pasture-land. And so, for a century and more after the downfall of the Tarquins, they attacked the Latins and Romans and engaged in many fluctuating seesaw struggles for the critical mountain passes.

The tribes which led these persistent onslaughts were the Volsci and Aequi. The main threat came from the Volsci who had come down from the heavily forested central Italian mountains during the sixth century BC, and had established themselves in the middle reaches of the Liris (Garigliano) valley in south-east Latium, which provided the main inland route down into Campania. Then, tempted by the maritime plain, they moved right up to the regions south-east of the Alban Mount, on the very doorstep of Rome's Latin allies. From 494 BC onwards these Volsci looted and raided Latin and Roman territory almost every year. They only weakened after Rome, in about 377, had captured their coastal stronghold Antium (Anzio), the only really useful port of Latium, protected by a promontory from the north-west winds. Nevertheless, Antium was then lost by the Romans again and had to be recaptured in 338, when the ships the Volsci had based on the port were captured. This was the termination of their independent existence. As time went on, they succumbed gradually to Romanization, and almost ceased to exist as a separate entity.

The highland Aequi also came down from the hills, compelled by the overpopulation of their meagre slopes north-east of Rome. In about 484 they captured and fortified Algidus, a narrow strategic pass on the east side of the Alban Mount, through which passed the inland Via Latina, for many years the only road from Rome to the south. Then, for fifty years or more, sometimes allied with the Volsci or others, they waged unceasing strife against the Latins and Romans. At last, however, in about 431 they were dislodged from Algidus, retiring gradually to their central Italian fastnesses, where they too, within the course of the following century, were eventually Romanized – by virtual extermination.

The chief interest of these petty, repetitive, and for many years inconclusive wars against the Volsci and Aequi lay in the invention by the Latin League in the 490s, or even before, of *federal Latin colonies*. These were not whole territories like Britain's 'colonies' in North America and elsewhere, but were towns, with tracts of cultivable land around them – settlements of farmer–soldiers, to whom newly acquired or recovered lands were allotted on lease or by freehold gift. These colonies, somewhat resembling in this respect the *kibbutzim* of Israel, were intended to provide potential Latin bases against external enemies, and to influence local life in favour of pacific agriculturalism. At first they were established on the eastern borders of Latium, and the next century and a half witnessed the foundation of fourteen such settlements in these and other regions. Although the strategic points at which they were established were no doubt selected by the Latin League only after consultation with Rome, these were Latin and not Roman foundations, and the Roman citizens among their settlers had to forfeit that status on arrival and become citizens of the Latin League instead. It was not until a good deal later that the Romans borrowed for themselves this fruitful idea, which was to play such an immense part in their future development of Italy.

The enemies against whom the Latins and Romans joined forces also included the Oscan-speaking Sabines, who lived in independent Apennine hilltop villages north-north-east of Rome. Once again they had long coveted the superior resources of the plain of Latium. In later Roman traditions, they were famed for their courage and strong morality and religious devotion. In due course some of them adopted a rudimentary urban life, notably at sites whose strategic location revealed their desire to secure a supply of Ostian salt; a desire that was highly distasteful to Rome, which had made a treaty with Gabii to keep them at bay. However, only a very few years after the start of the Roman Republic, one of the leaders of the Sabines, Attus Clausus, was so eager for a share of Rome's amenities that, with the agreement of its authorities and presumably of its Latin allies as well, he moved his whole clan of 4,000 or more relatives and supporters to Roman territory, where he settled them and became the founder of Rome's great Claudian clan (c. 505 BC), and similar Sabine origins were later claimed by other Roman clans and families as well. At first, however, the Roman hopes that by admitting these immigrants they had scotched the menace of the Sabines were disappointed, because their raids continued almost without intermission. In about 496 BC the raiders reached the city's ramparts, and about thirty-six years later their successors even briefly occupied the Capitoline citadel itself, before an army from Latin Tusculum helped to eject them.

Then in 449 Rome defeated the Sabines severely, following this up, as it liked to do, by assimilating a Sabine god Sancus, under the name of Dius Fidius who was given the significant function of watching over oaths and treaties and good faith (*fides*) between nations; a matter presided over by priestly officials (*fetiales*), who by proving that all Rome's wars were just, exercised from this time onwards an excellent effect upon Roman morale. Thereafter, during the next 150 years, hostilities with the Sabines diminished and vanished, and the amalgamation of the two peoples was gradually accomplished, to a large extent because of the mutual advantage of transferring sheep between summer (Sabine) and winter (Latin) pasturage.

It had been a major piece of good fortune to Latium and Rome (helped on by able diplomacy) that these hostile Volscian, Aequian and Sabine neighbours were too poorly organized ever to unite effectively against them; for that could have meant the reduction to impotence of Latins and Romans alike. And this was all the luckier, as far as Rome was concerned, because the gravest of all the threats to its existence came at the very same time from yet another and all too familiar source – Etruria, just across the Tiber.

After the termination of the Etruscan kingship in Rome, as we saw, there had been a confused period during which, in addition to all the other enemies of Rome, Etruscan adventurers made raids upon the city, sometimes successfully, and yet at the same time, despite the ejection of the monarchy, Etruscan influence in Rome itself continued to linger on. In the end, the peril proved greater than the influence: for one Etruscan city-state, Veii, was intolerably close, only twelve miles away. This extremely short distance between the two places meant that neither could ever feel safe from the other. Veii was powerful, and its geographical position extremely strong. For it was situated on a steep, sheer plateau, and surrounded on three sides by a moat of running water, including, beneath the eastern end of the citadel, the River Cremera (Valchetta) which went on to flow into the Tiber five miles north of Rome.

Originally, like Rome, a group of hut villages which amalgamated into a single Iron Age settlement, Veii had become by 600 BC not a symbiotic Etruscan–Italian community, such as Rome seems to have been, but a purely Etruscan city, and a city of which the wealth and culture, during the century that followed, contributed greatly to the rising prosperity of Etruscanized Rome, which was linked to its territory by the Sublician Bridge. The extensive possessions of Veii were guarded by a ring of bulwark-colonies and peripheral bases, fed by roads for heavy wheeled traffic leading in every direction – including the direction of Rome. Furthermore, Veii excelled in the Etruscan techniques of cultivation and irrigation, and supplied agricultural exports over a wide area.

In comparison with the various hill tribesmen who subjected Rome to harassment, it found these powerful, advanced people infinitely more formidable rivals. Given such extreme proximity, their competing demands for markets and land and coastal salt were bound to lead to serious clashes, and had probably done so as early as the seventh century BC. For the Tiber was a highway that had to be controlled either by Veii or by Rome; in the long run, no compromise was possible.

In the later 480s, the recently established Roman Republic had been mainly controlled by the clan of the Fabii. They were traditionally connected with Etruria, and owned land towards Veii; in consequence, they were recognized by their fellow-Romans as the defenders of the Etruscan frontier, which they guarded with a private army of their own. So it was now against the threat from Veii that the Fabii threw this semi-feudal force into the field. At first the hostilities amounted to little more than an exchange of cattle-raids, but by setting up a block house near the Cremera, to command the stream and adjoining roads, the Fabian clan transformed this minor skirmishing into open warfare. But in the disastrous battle of the Cremera which ensued (*c.* 476–475), 300 members and dependants of the Fabii perished, and the block house was destroyed by the enemy. The whole west side of the Tiber was now impregnably in the hands of the Veians, and they may even have occupied the Janiculum hill which rose above its bank and looked straight across at Rome.

But next, after the Etruscans' crushing defeat by the Greeks in 474, Veii felt it advisable to make a truce with its Roman neighbours across the river. Then, after the middle of the century, the balance of power again shifted in Rome's favour: and it began to prepare for a final showdown. One of the principal bones of contention was the town of Fidenae (Castel Giubileo) on the eastern bank of the Tiber, just opposite the spot where the Cremera joins its larger stream. This place was the first station on the salt road (Via Salaria), and the hill on which it stood controlled the lowest river ford above Rome. So Fidenae was a highly strategic post, which neither Veii nor Rome was willing to allow the other to possess; and it apparently changed hands more than once, first in earlier times and then in the first part of the fifth century BC.

In about 444, the Romans felt aware that a major war with Veii lay ahead. For they now made a radical change in their method of government, replacing the two annually elected consuls (instituted at the beginning of the Republic) by three (later six) army officers with consular power (*tribuni militum consulari potestate*), an arrangement which was retained for most of the next eighty years;* the character and rank of these officials show that military needs were the primary consideration. And in the following year a new magistracy, the censorship, was created. Its two joint occupants, men of very senior status, were to be elected every four years for a duration of eighteen months in order to make up and maintain the official list of citizens. Once again the primary purpose was military, for the censorship was intended to facilitate recruitment, which had become a complicated matter owing to the property-holding qualifications required for those serving in the army.

Fortified by these preparations, the Romans now felt ready to move against Veii; and they were all the more eager to do so because they themselves were suffering from famine and pestilence, and stood in urgent need of new land. So in about 435 or 425 they passed to aggressive action, and once again occupied Fidenae. An appeal directed by Veii to the Etruscan confederation met with no response. This was a significant proof of the country's lack of unity, which was to prove suicidal. Its immediate result was to prompt the Veians to strengthen their natural defences against likely Roman attacks. Wherever possible, the cliffs on which the city stood were cut back to make them more precipitous, and round other parts of the 480-acre periphery an earthen rampart with a stone breastwork was constructed.

For the occupation of Fidenae by the Romans meant full-scale war; probably the most fateful of all the wars they ever fought, since their very existence depended on the outcome. It was they who took the initiative, and they placed Veii under siege. The fighting, conducted with unprecedentedly large forces, seems to have gone on intermittently for at least six or seven years, though perhaps not for the ten described by tradition. In the end, the Romans succeeded in advancing on the northward side of the walls, and occupying the only neck of territory which offered level access to the city from this direction. Now this piece of land happened to contain one

---

* For a slightly earlier intermission in the consulship, when the consuls were temporarily replaced by *decemviri*, see below, p. 64.

of the agricultural drainage tunnels or *cuniculi* which irrigated the whole of this territory; coming in from the open country it passed under the walls, and thus entered into Veii itself. This tunnel, then, the Romans cleared, using it to move a small body of men into the middle of the enemy city, which in this way fell into their hands. The hero of the day was Camillus, who, despite the mythical nature of many of his alleged exploits, nevertheless emerges as a partially historical figure, the earliest the Republic can offer. Shortly before the siege began, he had compelled the Romans to adopt continuous military service, without intermissions for harvesting, and he had introduced regular pay: and it was he who carried the campaign to its triumphant conclusion.

The Romans severely damaged and partly destroyed the captured stronghold, razing its defences and turning out many or all of its inhabitants. This elimination of a city-state's independent existence was a sinister innovation in Rome's military history, and a sign of the critical gravity of the war. In keeping with the religious solemnity of their victory the Romans, as on other occasions, took over the defeated enemy's patron deity as their own, establishing her cult on the Aventine Hill just outside the walls of their own city. She was Juno, who was already worshipped on the Roman Capitol as an associate of Jupiter, but at Veii enjoyed an independent and magnificent cult, with the special title of Regina, the Queen. For here, as in other parts of early Italy, she stood for vitality and youthfulness and thus for political and military strength; and from now onwards she would no longer watch over Veii but over Rome.

The downfall of this first great Etruscan city to succumb to the Romans was a turning point, for not only did it remove an enormous, hampering obstacle to their progress, but it almost doubled the size of their territory as well. The newly conquered lands, linked by the excellent Etruscan roadsystem, were distributed as individual allotments to Roman citizen-farmers, without very much consideration being given to the Latin confederate cities, which were shown by this largely Roman victory to be outmatched, both singly and corporately, by the victors. Moreover, Rome's fame was spreading to new lands; for after the victory Camillus dedicated a war memorial, a golden bowl, in Apollo's oracular sanctuary at Delphi in Greece. As an intermediary in this enterprise he probably employed the Etruscan city-state of Caere (Cerveteri), which alone of nearby cities had close connexions with Delphi: it had failed to help its neighbour and compatriot Veii in the siege. And so the triumphant Romans began to appear in a wider context than Italy, among the nations of the world.

However, a formidable setback was on the way, at the hands of the Celtic Gauls. Celtic-speaking peoples had, in the eighth and seventh centuries BC, moved out of central Europe as far as Spain and Britain, and then during the fifth century they gradually crossed the Alps and expelled the Etruscan settlers from most of northern Italy – henceforward called after them, by the name of Gaul this side of the Alps, or Cisalpine Gaul. Some of the Celts who spread through Europe lived peacefully and even luxuriously; and they developed a lively, swinging, swelling art, based principally on the free use of contemporary Greek and Etruscan models, but also echoing eastern influences, notably from Scythia (south Russia). But the Gauls who swarmed into the valley of the Po were more warlike. They had developed a frightening, if somewhat barbaric, military organization, including cavalry with iron horseshoes – an innovation in ancient warfare – and infantry carrying finely tempered slashing broad-swords.

In about 387–386 BC, under their king Brennus, 30,000 of these immigrants drove southwards from the Po valley into the Italian peninsula itself, in the hope of acquiring additional land and plunder. Learning of this move, the Romans may have sent a reconnaissance force to the inland Etruscan city of Clusium (Chiusi), which the Gallic force was threatening. At all events, the Gauls decided to abandon their attack on Clusium, and moved rapidly down against Rome itself. Only eleven miles from the city, beside the Tiber's little tributary the Allia (Fossa Regina), they were confronted by an army of 10,000–15,000 Romans. Whether some Latins, too, formed part of these troops is uncertain; but in any case it was the largest force Rome itself had ever put into the field. However, in the battle that followed, the Roman phalanx of heavy-armed spear-carrying soldiers was rushed by the much faster cavalry and infantry of the Gauls and outreached by their swords. The Roman army was routed, and most of its soldiers plunged into the nearby stream and were drowned. This blackest of all days in the history of Rome left it wholly without any men to defend it.

Brennus and his men marched on, and three days later arrived at the city, which, with the possible exception of the Capitol, they proceeded to overrun, setting its buildings on fire, as a layer of burnt debris at the edge of the Forum still shows today – broken roof-tiles, and carbonized wood and clay: Rome had fallen to its first barbarian conquerors, something that was not to happen again for 800 years. The Romans never forgot this horrifying and humiliating event, and, like their successful siege of Veii a few years earlier, it brought them to the attention of the outside world: for it attracted the notice of Greek historians. Yet the Gauls were soon bought off and departed, because they had received news that their own lands in the north were threatened by external foes. And henceforward, despite the occasional raids that they still launched into the peninsula, they lacked the stability to offer a permanent threat.

In this crisis, the Romans owed a debt to their surviving Etruscan neighbour, the city-state of Caere. It was situated on the edge of bare downland a mere twenty miles from Rome, very close to the sea where it possessed three little ports. The Caeritans had gained great wealth and importance both from their metal-workings and their widespread Greek and oriental connexions. It was these links which had enabled them to confer substantial commercial and cultural benefits upon Rome during its monarchy – of which they were possibly the originators. And then, later, they had acted as intermediary with the pan-Hellenic shrine of Delphi in the celebration of Rome's victory over Veii – a victory which they themselves had helped to bring about by failing to support their own besieged compatriots, with whom they had long been on bad terms. Now, during the invasion by the Gauls, they had helped Rome once again, not only by giving refuge to the sacred objects from its temples but by exerting military pressure to hasten Brennus' departure. They were glad to help the Romans, because Greek threats and raids that menaced their own sea-coast meant that they needed Roman assistance in their turn.

Responding to this friendly attitude, Rome granted Caere a novel, privileged status (386?). This *hospitium publicum*, as it was called, entitled its people to come to Rome on terms of equality with Rome's own citizens in matters of private jurisdiction, and to enjoy freedom from local taxes, as Romans would likewise at Caere. This proved a historic formula, because Rome later extended it, with adaptations, to many other cities also. For the present, however, what had been achieved by this understanding was to safeguard the new frontier-line which the conquest of Veii had enabled the Romans to push forward into Etruria. Nevertheless, in *c*. 353 BC, Caere had the temerity to reverse its friendly policy, joining its sister-state of Tarquinii in objecting forcibly to what was by now a too painfully manifest inferiority to Rome. But the rising was soon brought to order, and the Caeritans were forgivingly accorded a hundred-year truce.

After the onslaught of the Gauls the Romans no longer considered their city sufficiently protected by the old earth rampart of Servius Tullius. So in 378 BC they erected a massive new wall, one of the great defensive works of the age, of which the large portions that can still be seen today bear the erroneous name of the 'Wall of Servius Tullius'. It was made of volcanic stone from recently captured Veii, and planned by contractors whom masons' marks show to have been Greeks. More than twelve feet thick and twenty-four feet high, the new wall enclosed a larger area than the previous rampart, including the historic Seven Hills of Rome: the Palatine and Caelian, and the adjacent and independently fortified Capitol; the whole of the Esquiline, Quirinal and Viminal to the north (portions of which had been included in the old perimeter); and the newly included Aventine to the south, together with the adjacent Circus Maximus where chariot races were held. This fourth-century wall encompassed an area of over 1,000 acres. This meant that the new Rome possessed by far the largest perimeter of any city in Italy, being more than twice the size of recently demolished Veii, and more than four times the dimensions of Caere. A prominent part in the creation of the wall was played by Camillus who had been the hero of the siege of Veii, and who later, after the grave setback of the Gallic invasion, led the Romans into a rapid and vigorous recovery.

But their major problem was now with their Latin confederates. Between these ostensibly equal partners, the pendulum had already begun to swing in the direction of the Romans before the fifth century was half over, and then, after the conquest of Veii, their monopoly of the conquered farmlands had emphasized their growing superiority rather crudely. Under the shock of the subsequent Gallic invasion, however, Rome decided to display tact to the Latins by giving them, after all, a share in the settlement and defence of the newly conquered Etruscan lands, in which, accordingly, two Latin colonies were planted.

Yet the sentiments of the cities of the Latin confederacy towards Rome were deteriorating. They had not, it is true, been disloyal for the most part during the Gallic invasion, since they had been just as alarmed as the Romans. But several of the largest Latin towns now began to prefer independence to their Roman alliance. Thus in 381 the citizens of Tusculum, although wholly surrounded by Roman territory, seemed on the verge of hostile action. But at this juncture Rome successfully wooed them with an offer of incorporation into its own state, and full Roman citizenship into the bargain. This was a fruitful new idea for the future – a Latin city had been given all Rome's privileges and transformed from a Latin into a Roman community, while nevertheless retaining its own city organization and self-government.

Significant, too, was the whole concept that Roman citizenship could be extended in such a way; Athens and Sparta and Corinth had never effectively learnt such a lesson, and a Greek monarch later noted that this sort of arrangement was a peculiar source of Rome's strength, providing invaluable numerical superiority over its successive enemies. In the previous century no city or individual would have found it attractive to change Latin for Roman status. But now that the Romans were stronger than the Latins, feelings had changed. For one thing, possession of Rome's citizenship was a safeguard against arbitrary violence on the part of its officials; and the local aristocracies of the Latin towns were not averse to such mergers, since they often possessed intimate links with their Roman counterparts already. Indeed the Tusculan nobles adapted themselves so enthusiastically to the new order that they henceforward supplied Rome with numerous consuls – a greater number, over the course of the years, than any other single city.

In 366 BC the consuls, now definitively revived after eighty years of intermittent military government, were given a junior colleague, the praetor, to relieve them of much civil jurisdiction so that they could have a freer hand for the warfare that still seemed likely to lie ahead. For hostile attitudes to Rome were now spreading among the Latin communities. One of their leading malcontents was Praeneste (Palestrina). This princely ancient town, on the Apennine spur dominating a major road to Campania, had formerly been an important outpost of the Etruscans, who gave it a lavish prosperity rivalling the cities of their own homeland. And the place was also the possessor of a great shrine and oracle of Fors Fortuna, the bringer of increase, from which Rome had derived its cult of that goddess. During the fourth century BC the Praenestines may have remained outside the Latin League; at any rate they relished the growth of Rome so little that they sided with its Volscian enemies and even employed Gaulish mercenaries to fight against its troops.

Another unsatisfactory Latin city, from the Roman point of view, was the no less antique Tibur (Tivoli), eighteen miles from the city. Like Praeneste, this town dominated an important road, from its high hill above a Tiber tributary, and it became a powerful member of the Latin League, surrounded by several dependent communities. During the fourth century, however, it appears to have engaged in frequent skirmishes against the Romans, and may even have severed relations with them altogether. But in 358 Rome succeeded in reimposing the old treaty upon this and other Latin cities, probably on less favourable terms involving a measure of military control.

The Romans also took a decisive step by extending their sphere of influence into Campania. Its leading town, Capua (Santa Maria Capua Vetere), thirteen miles inland, was the second city in all Italy, enriched by the great fertility of the region and destined to become famous for its skilful working of bronze. It had been the capital of an Etruscan sphere in Campania during the seventh and sixth centuries BC, but thereafter its Etruscan rulers were replaced by the Samnites. These tough hill-men, descended from the more advanced Sabines and speaking a form of Oscan akin to theirs, had come from fortified strongpoints high up in the centre of the peninsula. As their population increased, they began to covet the productive Campanian lowlands, and not only Etruscan Capua but Greek Cumae fell into their hands (c. 438–421 BC). Before long, these Samnite immigrants controlled a league of Campanian cities, readily absorbing the Greek and Etruscan flair for business and becoming a distinct Campanian nation, less warlike than their invading forebears. In about 343, the members of this confederation, threatened by fresh waves of invasions from Samnium, took the fateful step of appealing under Capua's leadership to the Romans. Thereupon Rome, in the hope of agricultural benefits, decided to make its entrance into this large, rich area, and responded to the Campanian appeal, an event which set up a whole series of chain-reactions affecting much larger areas.

At first, however, things did not go smoothly for the Romans, since their army mutinied at having to fight so far afield (342). Moreover, Capua soon regretted its appeal to them and sided with the Latins instead – who had now become openly hostile to Rome. For they had interpreted the Roman intervention in Campania as a menacing attempt to encircle themselves, and, when the operation seemed to be failing, they felt encouraged to ask the Roman government for a full restoration of their own previous parity and equality. These proposals were sharply rejected, and war between Rome and the Latins soon followed.

It was one of the bitterest wars the Romans ever had to fight – and the first in which they can be seen to have employed a well-planned, long-term strategy. This eventually brought catastrophe to the Latins and their Campanian allies, whose cavalry, fighting poorly, suffered a heavy defeat at Trifanum, not far from Capua. At this point, the Campanians made a

separate peace with Rome, which proceeded to assert control over the
northern part of their country. And then, over the next two years, the Latin
cities too were obliged to submit, one after another.

When the fighting had ended, the Latin League was broken up (388). It
had lost the struggle because its members were too disunited. A very long
epoch had come to an end: the day of the Latins was done for ever, except
as a component of Roman power.

But Rome now showed a gift for conciliatory organization which no important states of the ancient world, including those of the otherwise cleverer
Greeks, had ever displayed before. For the Romans dealt with the defeated
Latins not in a spirit of vindictiveness, which would have thwarted its own
purpose, but with cool common sense: and it dealt with them not by imposing any overall, bureaucratic solution, but by making piecemeal arrangements with each individual city, as the facts of every separate case seemed
to require.

In the first place, Aricia and three other places near Rome were granted
full Roman citizenship like Tusculum nearly half a century earlier; Roman
territory was thus expanded to 4,500 square miles, with a population of at
least a million. Secondly, Tibur and Praeneste, although deprived of some
land, retained formal independence, and their earlier alliances with Rome
were confirmed. Thirdly, the other ancient Latin cities, while likewise permitted to retain their former status, were allowed treaties only with Rome,
and not with each other. And Rome granted the male inhabitants of this
category of city a new sort of right, 'citizenship without franchise' (*civitas
sine suffragio*). This was, in effect, a partial, halfway Roman citizenship, by
virtue of which the men of these places, while not normally given the 'public'
right to vote in Rome's elections (which they could in any case rarely have
exercised since they lived too far away), were granted 'private' rights,
notably the right to enter into contracts with a Roman according to Roman
law (*commercium*), and the entitlement to marry a Roman without forfeiting
inheritance of paternity rights (*conubium*). This idea, apparently developed
from the guest-right privilege granted to Etruscan Caere some forty years
earlier, was tried out first on the member towns of the Campanian League
and a Volscian group: and only then, after these experiments, was it
extended to the Latin cities and later to the Sabines as well.

It was an ingenious and not unattractive arrangement. Admittedly, it was
imposed on a unilateral basis by the dominant Romans who, unlike their
partners, were free to enjoy their own civic rights in *all* the cities with which
they were associated. Furthermore, these communities had to follow Rome's
foreign policy, and were also obliged, in the event of war, to raise and pay a
quota of troops for 'mutual defence' – which meant, in effect, the service of
Rome's needs, though it was assumed that these would coincide with their

own. Yet these soldiers were allowed to serve in their own cities' contingents, under commanders of whom half were their own compatriots; and the Romans avoided the Greek error of imposing standing garrisons. For, except in times of crisis, they had little cause to make demands or interfere, secure in the knowledge that the Latin cities were ruled by landed nobilities allied to their own. Nor did these communities have to pay the tax on property (*tributum*) which fell upon Roman citizens in times of emergency.

For a long time, therefore, this halfway Roman citizenship escaped the slur of inferior status; and it worked. The outstanding political acuteness of the Romans enabled them to get the balance right. Their aim was to maintain control over the Latins and others without offending local feeling; and that, as the relative contentment of these associates amply demonstrated, is what they for the most part achieved, over a prolonged period of time. Indeed Latium, from now on, was so closely and inseparably knit together with Rome that Virgil could later write of the Latins, in addition to the Romans, as the rulers of the world.

Among the Latin 'colonies' established during the previous century and a half, seven were authorized by Rome to retain special privileges, but the rest, like other Latin cities, received the novel halfway status. Henceforward, there was an ever-growing number of such colonies, which were effective bulwarks of empire carefully located so as to guard the possessions of Rome and its associates from external enemies, and prepare the way for future forward leaps.

Typical of these new Latin colonies was Cales (Calvi, near Capua), which now became a centre of Roman authority in Campania. Plots of land at this settlement were allotted to more than 2,000 families of Latin, Roman and Campanian settlers. Far distant from the capital by the colonizing standards of the time, Cales became a pattern for future extensions of 'Latinity' – which now meant Roman power. Another somewhat later foundation of the same type, Cosa (Ansedonia) on the mid-Etruscan coast (273 BC), shows the remains of capacious cisterns, a neatly rectangular street plan modelled on Greek urbanism in south Italy and Sicily, the remains of a voting place for the annual elections of local officials, and strong polygonal walls with eighteen towers and three main gates. For it was upon these Latin colonies that the task of defence chiefly fell, and they were planned to form an iron ring round Rome's remaining enemies in central Italy.

But a further and at first secondary, though in the long run more durable, instrument of power invented in the later fourth century BC was the purely *Roman* colony, including no allies among its settlers but Roman citizens only. Colonies of this type were once again placed at skilfully selected strategic vantage points; for example, all the earliest foundations of this type were planned to serve as coastguard stations. These Roman colonies were always linked directly to Rome by a solid and continuous stretch of Roman territory, which meant that they needed fewer defenders, and could therefore operate with a much smaller quota of settlers than their Latin counterparts. For Rome did not want to send too many potential fighters so far afield; and in any case, there were not all that many families willing to go to such places, where their metropolitan citizen rights hardly seemed to count any longer. So these Roman colonies only comprised 300 families each, only a seventh as many as there were to be at their large Latin counterparts such as Cales.

One of the very first Roman colonies, perhaps sent out a decade or so before the final downfall of the Latin League, was at Ostia, beside the mouth of the Tiber. Ostia had probably first been taken control of by the Romans some two centuries earlier, but now a more determined effort to occupy the place was made. For one of these groups of 300 Roman citizen families was sent to settle there, inside a rectangular fort of five acres, designed like a camp with two geometrically planned intersecting main streets and a strong stone wall, which 300 male settlers could man if they stood six feet apart. The colony's primary function was to defend the Tiber mouth from maritime enemies and pirates, thus saving Rome from the necessity of maintaining a permanent fleet, which it still wanted to avoid. But although there was scarcely a harbour at the mouth of the delta-forming river, Ostia also regulated trade, supervised the collection of salt, exacted the payment of customs, and stored grain and other foodstuffs, which could then go on by road or river up to Rome.

Twenty-seven miles farther down the coast, Antium (Anzio) too, after its final capture from Volscians in 338 BC, was given a Roman colony, apparently augmented by native settlers; and in 317, in response to complaints, the place was granted autonomous local government like the Latin colonies, thus establishing a new and permanent precedent for these much smaller Roman citizen foundations. Thirty-eight miles lower down again, at the remotest extremity of Roman territory, a third maritime Roman colony was established in 329 at another former Volscian town, Tarracina (Terracina), each settler being allotted one and a third acres of land. By 218 BC the number of coastal Roman colonies had risen to twelve; and by this time there were more than that number again maintaining guard over river crossings, exits from mountain passes, and road centres. They were all potential sites for army bases, and were often resented by their neighbours, so that the colonists had good reason to remain loyal to Rome.

Altogether, if we include not only the two types of colony but individual allotments outside colonies as well, 60,000 holdings were established between 343 and 264 BC, so that the area thus occupied was multiplied three-fold, to a total of some 50,000 square miles: and the settlers who manned them provided a mighty contribution not only to agriculture but to defence – and future aggression.

Outstanding among the enemies whom these colonists had to confront were the Samnites, warlike peasants and herdsmen who lived in unwalled villages throughout the landlocked valleys and grey limestone uplands of the Apennines. The Samnite nation in this central Italian homeland was divided into four large tribes, which were linked together in a loose but sometimes militarily effective league, and sent delegates to a federal assembly. In the middle of the fourth century BC these Samnites were Italy's largest political unit, possessing twice the territory and population of the Romans.

It was pressure of population, with inadequate agricultural land to feed it, that had brought some of their compatriots down into Campania. But now the separate confederacy which they formed in that country had been overwhelmed by Rome: and this the Samnites who had remained in central Italy could not tolerate. The Latin colony of Cales also provoked them, and so did another established in 328–327 at Fregellae (Opri) on the River Liris (Garigliano), which was their border with the Romans. So the Samnites now took advantage of internal dissensions at one of the chief cities of Campania, the ancient Greek foundation of Neapolis (Naples), to occupy it with a garrison – which the Romans drove out, thus precipitating the long and complicated Second or Great Samnite War (327–304 BC).

Its first important campaign, in 321, inflicted upon the Romans their worst defeat for over sixty years, the entrapment and humiliating surrender of a whole army at the Caudine Forks, east of Capua. After this disaster they were obliged to evacuate Cales and Fregellae, and stopped fighting altogether for five years. Moreover, on the resumption of the fighting, the Samnites won further victories, which culminated in an alarming incursion into Latium itself. Yet in the end they could not prevent Rome from re-founding the two Latin colonies they had lost and settling five others as well – further fetters upon Samnite expansion.

Rome also created a potent new instrument of warlike policy by building the Appian Way (Via Appia) traversing the 132 miles from Rome to Capua, mostly across the coastal plain. For the more ancient Via Latina, following an upper inland route, was uncomfortably vulnerable to attacks from Samnium, to which the new Via Appia was not exposed. The forerunner of so many other Roman roads in three continents, weapons of peace as well as war, this 'Queen of Roads' was constructed, as far as possible, on a straight course, with bridges or paved fords to carry it across rivers, while viaducts spanned marshy territory. By such means, the second Samnite War was eventually won by the Romans. Their success left their enemies firmly excluded from southern Italy, and much inferior to the victors in land and population alike.

ROME'S CONQUEST OF ITALY

Mediolanum
Verona
Placentia
Mutina
Pisae
Ariminum
Arretium
Ancona
Volaterrae
Perusia
Firmum
Asculum
Vetulonia
Reate
Aesernia
Volsinii
CORSICA
Rome
Ardea
Arpi
Venusia
Capua
Tarentum
Neapolis
Nola
Metapontum
SARDINIA
Thurii
Rhegium
Locri
SICILY

■ Roman and Latin territory 298 B C
≡ Roman gains 298-263 B C
||| Roman allies 298 B C
∷ Roman allies 298-263 B C
/// annexations 241-218 B C

0        100
miles

But a Third Samnite War (298–290) was still to follow. In 296 the Samnite commander broke out northwards to join forces with a frightening combination of anti-Roman allies – Gauls, Etruscans and Umbrians. However, while the Etruscans were kept at home by a diversion, the Roman army won an important battle at Sentinum (Sassoferrato) in the Apennines. It was one of the most northerly points where they had ever so far set foot, and never before had so many troops been engaged. Yet the victory was not decisive, because hostilities still continued for another six years. Fortunes varied, but finally the territory of the Samnites was penetrated by the Roman forces and ravaged from end to end, so that they had to give in.

Rome's success in this war decided the whole future fate of peninsular Italy. It had been a ferocious, patient struggle, in which the Samnites had clung to valley after valley with dogged determination. But the Romans had learnt to exploit their interior lines in order to split the enemy into isolated blocks, and the Latin colonies which they had continued to found served the same purpose of dividing the central Italian tribes one from another. And so the enemy were gradually driven up the hills away from their winter pastures, and worn down.

In the process, the Roman army had become a good deal larger than before. It was now subdivided into two legions. Each legion was a masterpiece of organization, more mobile than the Greek phalanx which had served as the original model because a legion contained an articulated group of thirty smaller units (maniples), each of which could manoeuvre and fight separately on its own, in rough mountainous country as well as on the plains, either in serried ranks or open order, thus combining compactness with flexibility. Moreover, every maniple was formed into three lines, of which each one in turn could advance through the line ahead, replacing it and enabling it to draw back for rest and replenishment. This new manipular legion, tested to the uttermost against the Samnites, was to prove the key to Rome's future success.

Earlier in the century, the Roman state had begun to provide standard weapons and equipment, an important stage towards the creation of a professional army. And so all legionaries wore helmets, breastplates and leg guards (greaves), and carried swords; and thrusting javelins had been superseded by javelins for throwing, more than six feet long, half wood and half iron. This new weapon had probably been introduced during the Samnite Wars. Those campaigns, coming on top of the Romans' ceaseless hostilities with so many of their neighbours during the previous two centuries and more, had forged their army into a terrible weapon. It was perfectly suited to the dour perseverance which characterized the citizens of Rome, enabling them to respond so efficiently to each successive external threat – real or imagined, since as their sphere of interests continually widened, it was hard to know whether the threats were authentic or imaginary. However, the Romans were so amply fortified by their religious leaders with the belief that all their ways were just that they could never suppose that the military measures they were taking might be morally wrong. And that being so, as the great Greek historian Polybius noted, they were not generally reluctant to employ force, when they felt that force was needed.

They were also capable of atrocious cruelty. But what made the Romans so remarkable was the combination of these unpleasant traits with a talent for patient political reasonableness which was unique in the ancient world. They had displayed this gift before, and now they showed it once again: for now the defeated Samnites were offered, in spite of all Rome's raw wounds from the recently ended hostilities, the same treaty terms that had been proposed to them at the end of the previous (second) war. Rome's treaties with other states were either 'equal' or 'unequal'. But the latter formula, explicitly stating the inferiority of the other party, was increasingly becoming the choice the Romans preferred and it was this type of 'agreement' which was accorded to the Samnites.

Such treaties, intended for peoples not close or reliable enough to be accorded the half-citizenship of the Latins, were an integral and essential part of Rome's Italian system, and explain why its dependents and subjects were regularly known as 'allies' (*socii*). Yet the treaties entered into by the Romans being bilateral, their allies were not normally permitted to be allies one with another as well; in this sense, there was no confederacy in Roman Italy. Like the Latins, these other allies had to provide troops if requested, and when their treaties with Rome were 'unequal', the requests were likely to be somewhat more peremptory. Yet their aristocracies, even if somewhat less close than the Latin nobilities to their Roman counterpart, were generally known personally to its members and regarded by them with sympathy; and this sort of friendly relationship with local governing classes was Rome's blueprint for its imperial future. The Romans protected their local rulers from internal revolutions, and left them alone to rule their own peoples according to their own laws and with a minimum of conformity; and the peoples in question could be reminded that, without having to pay taxes to Rome, they were securing from it protection and peace. Besides, from about 289 BC, drawing on their extensive spoils of Italian bronze, the Romans developed from earlier experiments a coinage to meet the common commercial and industrial needs of the area. In this, as in other respects, association with the Romans proved beneficial rather than restrictive.

On the whole, Rome found it advisable, and was encouraged by its religion, to keep its bargains with its allies, displaying a self-restraint, a readiness to compromise, and a calculated generosity which the world had never seen before. And so the allies too had little temptation to feel misused. The proud Samnites, it was true, had lost a considerable amount of their land to Roman settlers, and among them disaffection still continued to linger beneath the surface. But they were only a few out of a grand total of 120 Italian communities with which Rome, in due course, formed perpetual alliances. For after the end of the Samnite wars a network of such agreements was extended across the whole of central Italy.

The whole Roman approach was empirical, working from precedent to precedent according to each individual case, the relationship with every community in turn being considered on its own merits. This complex multiplication of differing agreements seems like a classic example of the cynical principle 'divide and rule'. And so it was. But like the earlier understandings with the Latins, it was reckoned and weighed out so acutely, with that instinctive hard, practical Roman genius for common-sense statecraft, that the system, unlike any of its partial Greek models, proved successful for generation after generation. That was how the Romans accomplished their first major historical achievement, the creation of Italy. They could speak on behalf of the country and claim to represent it in a way that no other ancient city-state had ever before been able to speak for the territories it had brought under its control. And so when, as we shall soon see, a major military crisis arose later in the century, Rome was able to muster nearly 400,000 Roman and allied troops: and even under supreme pressure most of them would still remain conspicuously loyal.

# 4

# The Class Struggle

DURING THESE 170 YEARS of almost incessant fighting, the Roman community had found itself racked by the gravest internal disturbances it was to experience for many centuries to come.

When the Etruscan dynasty of the Tarquins was overthrown shortly before 500 BC, tradition maintained that the headship of the state had immediately passed from the expelled monarch to a pair of consuls elected every year. Efforts have been made in modern times to dispute this view and speak of an interim period lasting for some decades, or even for a century and a half, in which there was indeed a new Republic, but a Republic governed initially not by two such annually elected functionaries but by a single one chosen, with subordinates, for one or two years at a time; on the analogy of certain Etruscan cities which were likewise moving at this time from regal towards Republican government. But this is somewhat unlikely. Certainly there was provision in the Roman constitution for the nomination of a single autocratic dictator in an emergency – but only temporarily, for a period of six months at most, and never in any continuous succession. It seems therefore that we must instead accept the strong tradition, based on the lists (Fasti) which purport to record all these appointments, which maintained that there were pairs of top officials from the beginning of the Republic: though for 150 years or more, these pairs were probably called, not yet consuls, but praetors, from *prae-ire*, to march ahead or precede.

However let us, for the sake of convenience, describe the two colleagues as consuls from the beginning. The character of consular office was significant and contradictory, because it sharply combined supremacy and limitation. The consuls were supreme in that each of them was invested with absolute *imperium*, the administrative power conferring command of the army and the interpretation and execution of the law. In Rome, therefore, unlike modern Britain, the centre of political gravity lay not in the legislative but in the executive, and this executive was not 'responsible' to the community or Senate or Assembly from day to day, but 'representative', limited only by law. In these respects the United States of America is somewhat closer than Britain to ancient Rome – whose ideas it deliberately borrowed – in that the power of the American President, despite sharp modern disputes on the subject, is likewise limited by nothing but the law. In ancient Rome, however, the 'magistrates', as these officials were called – as well as the relatively, remarkably, few lesser magistrates, added later on – were subject to fewer limitations than the President of the United States (to take a single example, they enjoyed immunity from prosecution while in office). This state of affairs corresponded with the Romans' marked respect for lawful public authority, and their inherited, disciplined conviction that it ought to be obeyed. And this large power vested in the executive obviously gave it a greater possibility of getting things done. But on the debit side, the situation, though it admittedly left room for criticism to be directed against the consuls, inhibited the development of democracy in any modern western sense.

Yet although responsible to no one, and limited only by the law in the exercise of their duties, the consuls nevertheless were subject to two practical restrictions. In the first place, they were only elected for a single year. And secondly, being a pair, they were subject to one another's vetoes. For since the power of each was all-pervading, neither one could prevail over the other; if they disagreed, it was understood that the colleague who was against action could veto his fellow-consul who was for it. The retention of a negative veto of this kind was not altogether inadvisable, since the annually elected consuls might be stupid or incompetent, or arrogantly obstinate. Yet they also possessed the inherited training of their class, which produced, very often, a remarkable spirit of consensus, and an attitude of selfless sacrifice to the needs of the community as a whole. The consuls also possessed the opportunity, which was generally, if not always, advantageous, of being able to consult the other representatives of their own experienced clique, since these were their fellow-members of the Senate.

The members of this body, which retained its numerical strength of 300 for nearly half a millennium, had naturally gained more say in affairs after the monarchy was expelled, an act in which they surely played a substantial part; and from that time onwards they admitted officials and other notables to join the heads of the families who had formerly monopolized their ranks. The Senate possessed no executive powers. But it advised the elected officials on domestic and foreign policy, and finance and religion, and counselled them on legislative proposals as well – though it was generally willing enough to give a free hand to these officials, who were their fellow senators and belonged to the same clans and families as themselves. And the consuls on their side, despite their extensive constitutional powers, were likely enough to defer to the Senate's advice, for the same reasons – and also because the brief annuality of their own office made them vulnerable after it was over. Besides, the senators were endowed with redoubtable prestige, due to their positions and family traditions and achievements. The Latin word for this prestige, *auctoritas*, conveyed a very urgent call for respect and deference, and the individual *auctoritas* of each senator added up in combination to a corporate influence which, in a country that depended to an exceptional extent on collective endeavours, remained strong enough to survive all the growing pains of the Republic and keep on guiding its policies for centuries.

That is not, of course, to deny that there were dissensions within the ranks of the Senate itself. No doubt there were, at all periods. Yet for a very long time there was nothing resembling a divergence of party programmes. It was rather a matter of shifting networks of personal and collective associations, as clans and families, or sometimes individuals, combined temporarily with one another in rival groups. But any disagreements which thereby arose did not greatly inhibit the effectiveness of the early Republican Senate as a whole, even in the face of a whole host of foreign and internal oppositions and problems.

Since the Senate remained, in law, purely advisory, it was not the body which elected the consuls year by year. This was the Assembly of Roman citizens (*comitia centuriata*) which had received its shape, it was said, from King Servius Tullius. However, this Assembly had been weighted from the beginning so that the centuries of the well-to-do possessed far greater voting power than the poor. Moreover, candidates for the consulship were proposed to the Assembly *by the senators*, from their own ranks. The Assembly, it was true, enacted laws and declared war and peace, and perhaps already conducted trials. Yet the senators, with their superior prestige and wealth, controlled its votes on all such occasions. In many respects, therefore, the legal appearance of democracy was sharply corrected by what in fact happened.

The historian Polybius, keenly studied and followed by the makers of the American constitution, looked back from the second century BC and enormously admired the Roman state for the internal equilibrium which, despite all its problems, it had maintained over so many hundreds of years; and this he ascribed to Rome's system of mutual automatic balances and checks between its legislative, executive and judicial institutions. Yet the equilibrium to which he devoted this praise rested on a quaint cluster of unspecific, impalpable, illogical customs and conventions which were called into play empirically and pragmatically as each successive situation demanded. Indeed Polybius himself appreciated this, pointing out that the system had developed 'not according to a theory but through frequent conflicts and practical crises'. Yet there was not any authentic 'balance' at all, since the Assembly's formal power so greatly exceeded any power it possessed in reality.

This curious gulf between fact and appearance was created by one of the most important factors in Roman life, which continued to influence it profoundly for centuries. This was the institution of *clientela*. Roman society was a structure composed of powerful *patroni* and their dependent clients (*clientes*). The client was a free man who entrusted himself to the patronage of another and received protection from him in return. The client helped his patron to succeed in public life and furthered his interests by every means in his power, and in return the patron looked after his client's private affairs, and gave him financial or legal support.

Such mutual arrangements are not unparalleled in other societies, but the Roman institution was remarkable for its all-pervasiveness and binding cogency. *Clientela* was hereditary; it was also heavily charged with feeling and emotion. A man was supposed to rate his clients even before his own relations by marriage. A law of the mid-fifth century BC damns and curses any patron who behaves fraudulently towards his client. *Clientela*, it is true, was probably not enforceable by legal sanctions. But that was immaterial beside the powerful quasi-religious force it had attained by long and universally respected custom. The keynotes of this force were *Fides*, mutual good faith – worshipped as a goddess, according to tradition, from the dimmest early past – and *Pietas*, the dutiful respect owed to patrons just as it was owed to parents and fatherland and gods.

Here was another reason why the Assembly, for all its impressive democratic-sounding 'powers', could never be a truly democratic body. For not only were its richest members in possession of disproportionate voting power, but those Assemblymen who lacked wealth were, for the most part, clients of rich men and senators, in whose favour therefore, or in favour of whose friends and relations, they were in duty bound to cast their votes in the annual elections to state offices. On the credit side it might be said that a poor client's relationship to his patron, based on inescapable ties of good faith, gave his life a meaning and security which poor people in other countries have frequently lacked, and still lack today. Nevertheless, *clientela* acted as a powerful brake on democratic development: and indeed helped to prevent it from ever taking place.

For one thing, this relationship between patrons and clients reflected the basic division of Roman society, existent when the Republic started or earlier still, between patricians and plebeians. After the beginning of the Republic, as we have seen, although the Senate was apparently not increased in size, it came to include not only heads of families (*patres familias*) but other prominent personages as well. And since these were very often the sons, descendants or relatives of the *patres familias*, they became known, because of this relationship, as *patricii*.

The patricians exercised power not only through their clients but by virtue of a monopoly, hallowed by custom, of inherited religious rights, including the administration of major cults and the power to consult the gods (*auspicia*), and the control of law and the calendar which were both religious in character. During the fifth century BC some fifty-three patrician clans (*gentes*) are known – less, apparently, than there had been under the kings, though some names may be lost – comprising a closed body of not more than 1,000 families. At the outset of the Republic there was a small inner ring of especially powerful patrician clans, notably the Aemilii, Cornelii and Fabii. And to these were added, after their immigration from Sabine territory, the Claudii as well.

However, these patricians comprised less than one-tenth of the total citizen population of Rome, and possibly not more than one-fourteenth. The remaining large majority of the inhabitants (apart from a number of slaves, a normal feature of ancient societies) were the plebeians (*plebs*): and the sharp political and social distinction that separated them from the patricians was the outstanding feature of early Republican social history. To some extent *clientela* kept the plebeians happy, since their patrons were obliged by insistent moral sanctions to give them help. But although all clients were plebeians, not all plebeians were clients; for example immigrant traders were left out in the cold. Besides, the most that a patron could do, or was willing to do, was not always enough to prevent discontent. For one thing, the plebeians were completely excluded from influential positions, including the consulships and, initially, membership of the Senate. This was a point which rankled among the more powerful and prosperous of the plebeians – who alone among that order could afford the costs of holding office, so that it was they who were often seen leading movements of plebeian protest. To this extent, successive Roman attempts at social reform or revolution were merely the endeavours of a few men at the top of the unprivileged plebeian class to climb to higher status, sometimes with the support of this or that opportunistic patrician.

But there was a great deal more to the internal disturbances of the early Republic than that. While exclusion from office was only frustrating for a few prominent plebeians at the top, the remaining plebeians, who covered a very wide spectrum ranging right down to the bottom of the 'free' social scale, wanted not so much power as rescue and protection from the abuses of power which were being committed by others. Many of these men had suffered grievous impoverishment from the abrupt fall in Rome's prosperity and resources after the expulsion of the Etruscan monarchs. For, when this happened, the city had sunk right back to the status of a purely agrarian community operating at a low subsistence level: and what with the active competition offered by their Latin allies, and harassment from enemies on every side, there just was not enough tolerable soil available, on the small territory of the early Republic, to give everyone a living. Besides, much of this territory was public land (*ager publicus*), inaccessible to the plebeians; and, even if one of them did possess land of his own, he very often had to go and fight in one of the unceasing frontier wars, and when he came back his farm had gone to ruin in his absence.

In these conditions, crippling grain shortages occurred time after time. They brought famines; and to ward them off, the Romans founded a temple of the grain goddess Ceres (*c.* 496 or 493). The worship of Ceres was essentially a cult of the plebeians. It was borrowed from the Greek city of Cumae, where her Greek counterpart Demeter was one of the leading divinities. This Greek origin was significant, since the Roman temple was located beneath the Aventine Hill, in an area near the cattle market and the river wharves which was a centre for Greek traders: and it was to the Greeks that the poor of Rome, as of other places, looked for ideas of democracy – and, for ideas, sometimes, of popular, plebeian-based, one-man rule, for which would-be autocrats allegedly made three separate bids at Rome during these early years of the Republic. The economic situation in the fifth century was bad, due not only to the shortages and famines but to the shattering epidemics which came in their wake. And in the hope of removing these further terrible accompaniments of all their internal and external troubles the Romans continued their religious borrowings by taking over the great Greek healing god Apollo, in whose honour they built a temple in about 431 BC.

As a result of the disastrous agricultural situation, a large number of plebeians fell desperately into debt. All debt legislation of the ancient world, in which rates of interest were very high indeed, seem to us alarmingly stringent; and the Roman laws were no exception. Worst of all, if a man could not pay his debts, and had exhausted other means of raising money, he only had his own body left to pledge, and so he became, on default, not indeed precisely a slave but a 'man in fetters' (*nexus*), whose position amounted in practice to very much the same: a chattel and prisoner reduced to inherited serfdom to his creditor, with little hope of ever recovering his lost freedom again. In the first century of the Republic, as very often later, debt was a crucial and catastrophic problem. Indeed, it must be regarded as the chief reason for the bitter hostility which now developed between the plebeians and their patrician governing class; for it was the state authorities' unjust and arbitrary enforcement of the laws of debt which caused plebeian indignation and sense of grievance to reach boiling point.

Yet the patrician government could not do without the plebeians, since those of them who possessed the requisite property qualifications were needed as soldiers: and this consciousness that they were indispensable encouraged the plebeians to resort to collective protests. Since trade unions and general strikes had not been heard of, their protests took the form of secessions. *Secessio* signifies their 'retirement' from the rest of the Roman community, in the sense of a literal physical departure. To suggest that all the recorded secessions were threats that were never carried out is unconvincing, since the tradition to the contrary is too persistent. What we are told is that the plebeians, or a proportion of them, moved away from the city – presumably with their families – to one of the hills beyond its periphery: a remarkable example of organized collective bargaining, which virtually created a temporary state within a state, and split the nation in two. What is more, the plebeians were reported to have made withdrawals of this kind no less than five times during the first two and a quarter centuries of the Republic. It is true that since later historians made a practice of inventing duplicates and mirror-images of recent events and inserting them into their picture of the distant, little-known past, there probably were not as many as *five* of these secessions. Nevertheless, to reject all but the last of them is still unduly sceptical. For it seems reasonable to accept, tentatively, the very earliest secession as well, since the new social and economic problems at the outset of the diminished, embattled Republic must have been acute.

What seems to have happened, then, on the first of these occasions (494 BC), was that a body of plebeians marched up the Aventine Hill which was still outside the walls of Rome at this time, and belonged, as we have seen, to an area frequented by Greek traders familiar with democratic ideas. And once there, following an old Italian formula, the plebeians all swore to one another a corporate oath of mutual support. Their secession, followed by this oath, proved effective because, in order to prevent the nation and the army from disintegrating, the patrician authorities felt obliged to grant their main request. This demanded the creation of a small number of functionaries to represent plebeian interests. These tribunes of the plebeians or of the people (*tribuni plebis*), as they were called, would have the duty of interceding against the acts of any state official in order to protect plebeians from execution or arrest or molestation – including a takeover by their creditors. The tribunes, who thus became the defenders of the plebeians just as patrons were obliged to defend their clients, did not draw their power from any law – they were not state officials or 'magistrates' – but derived it from an oath sworn by the plebeians to safeguard their inviolability, any infringement of which would provoke a curse and incur pain of death. The first holders of these tribunates were plebeians of substance and ambition. Their office was a strange and unprecedented institution, with a long, varied and fateful future, during which it sometimes contrived to protect the private rights of its constituents; though not always, and it never succeeded in making Rome into a democracy.

Shortly after the establishment of the tribunate, a quarrel developed about the land owned by the state (*ager publicus*). For the patricians preferred to maintain this public ownership, which enabled them to settle on such territory and treat it as their own, while the plebeians on the other hand wanted it to be distributed among themselves. While this dispute was still under way, constitutional agitation in 471 BC obliged the state authorities to agree to the establishment of a special Council of which the members were to be exclusively plebeians (*concilium plebis*). It was the task of the *tribuni plebis* to summon this council, tribe by tribe, to meetings, at which the annual elections of their own successors took place and various kinds of measures (*plebiscita*) were moved and passed, and lawsuits and trials of certain categories were conducted. This existence of the plebeian council created what seems to modern students an almost ludicrously complicated state of affairs according to which, in addition to the principal Assembly (*comitia centuriata*), and its semi-obsolete predecessor (*comitia curiata*), there was now what amounted virtually to a third. But the *concilium plebis* was not, initially, an official organ of the Roman state, since it was not for nearly another two centuries that its enactments came to be accorded equal validity with the laws. Until then, they were merely expressions of the plebeians' will and intent, and noted as such by the government – which generally found it advisable to accept them.

All this was being done against a background of famine, pestilence, and savage frontier warfare against numerous enemies. In these desperate circumstances, the plebeians, who bore the brunt of the miseries and the fighting, felt more discontented than anyone else, out of the conviction that every privilege which they had so far attained was merely formal and that nothing substantial had been done to relieve their social and economic miseries. Nor did they really know, legally speaking, how they stood, since the laws were not written down, and were interpreted by the college of priests (*pontifices*) who at this time were all still patricians. It was this issue which played a dominant part in the plebeians' next demands: and these demands became so violent and pressing that in 451 BC the normal appointments to consulships were temporarily suspended and a commission of ten patricians, the *decemviri*, under the chairmanship of Appius Claudius, was appointed to write down a collection of laws. The product of their labours was enacted by the Assembly of the centuries as a statute and openly published, as had never been done before, for all to see, on tablets that were set up in the Forum: the Twelve Tables. The original tablets were destroyed in the invasion by the Gauls some sixty years later, but considerable and apparently typical portions of the texts have come down to us in scattered and often re-edited quotations by later authorities.

In demanding that such a step should be taken, the plebeians were inspired by the Greek ideas they had heard around the Aventine and its wharves: for the establishment of a code of laws as a means of political compromise was an expedient very familiar to the Greeks. Indeed, tradition maintained that before carrying out their work the decemvirs had made a journey to Athens – which is unlikely, though they may have visited the Greek cities of southern Italy and Sicily or at least may have studied their procedures. True, whether the Twelve Tables ought to be regarded as displaying any extensive or specific Greek influence at all is far from certain, especially as they do not constitute a Greek-type code but are a mosaic of varied, incomplete provisions. However, much that we find in them is attributable in a general way to Rome's contacts with Greek thought, directly and through Etruria, over the previous 150 years.

The surviving excerpts and adaptations of the Twelve Tables constitute by far our most precious information about Rome of the fifth century BC. Their field is the Civil Law, the law regarding the rights and duties of Roman citizens (*cives Romani*) and the relation of one citizen to another – which was the only law Rome had for many centuries. The contents of the Tables form a strange mixture of widely ranging principles and minor details, of law private and public and criminal, of rules about matters ranging from communal hygiene to personal safety. What is quite clear, however, even from the somewhat modernized Latin in which these regulations have come down to us, is that the men who originally framed and drafted their short gnomic sentences were hard, practical thinkers who were able to express themselves in terse, plain and almost painfully exact language, and already possessed in full measure that unparalleled talent for precise legal definition which is one of Rome's greatest gifts to humanity.

The impact of the Twelve Tables upon later generations was enormous. After their disappearance in the Gaulish invasion they were meticulously reconstructed and remained legally valid. Indeed, they were traditionally seen, with a measure of respectful exaggeration, as the source of much or most of the whole body of Roman law; and for century after century they retained a dominant position in the education of every Roman citizen.

This massively triumphant subsequent career of the Twelve Tables might lead us to conclude that the efforts of the decemvirs who drew them up had been successful. Paradoxically enough, however, their initial publication of the Tables was extremely badly received – by the very plebeians for whose benefit the entire exercise had been conducted. For the decemvirs had not, to any significant extent, regarded it as part of their job to introduce into their compilation any new measures to improve the plebeians' lot.

On the contrary, their duty, as they interpreted it, was merely to reduce to visible statute form the most important regulations of the already existing customary law, with only insignificant additions or adjustments. By carrying out this task, and thereby publishing abroad the more socially significant and controversial of the rules which had hitherto been known only to the patricians, they believed they had done quite enough to satisfy plebeian demands – and that they could, therefore, in the interests of the patricians, safely evade having to do anything more. But plebeian contentment was not forthcoming.

Nevertheless, to ourselves scrutinizing the Tables, it seems impressive that a people at such a relatively early stage of development were so clearly able to disentangle law from religion, deriving the sanction of their legal pronouncements not from any divine or wholly or partly legendary lawgiver, as so many of their predecessors in other places had done, but from a sense of justice and equity, still narrow yet already strong. The Twelve Tables also show a surprisingly precocious clarity of conception in dealing with contract and property. And they proposed, as we saw earlier, a death penalty for any patron who cheated his client; though that, like the rest of these provisions, was presumably nothing new.

Moreover, in the measures regarding marriage, archaism is not untempered by liberalism. In the earliest days Roman matrimony granted every husband the power of *manus*, which bestowed on him the same rights over his wife as his status as father of the family also gave him over their children. But a slight weakening of the husband's authority was already sanctioned by the Twelve Tables, according to which his wife, after she had reached the age of twenty-five, retained possession of her property. This right, it is true, was still subject to formal control by a guardian, and according to the Twelve Tables a mother had no right of succession to an intestate son. However, despite such official limitations, the *materfamilias* enjoyed, by custom, great respect and influence, being required to supervise, for example, the education of her young children. On the lips of men, it is true, there was much stress on women's place and duties in the home. But they lived and went out and about with a liberty which far exceeded the conditions of their Greek counterparts, and instead recalled the freedom enjoyed by the women of Etruria. The Twelve Tables give some idea how far this comparative emancipation had gone.*

Up to a point, too, though the details are much disputed, the Tables safeguarded a Roman citizen's capital rights. For they confirmed that the only court which might hear a capital charge and impose a death sentence was the Assembly of the centuries (*comitia centuriata*) – which at least

* By another law of the Tables, a wife could avoid her husband's legal control by passing three nights each year away from his house. In due course, there also developed free marriage, based on mutual consent, which gave the husband no authority over his wife.

meant that he could not incur this peril from any other court. But that might not be particularly comforting, especially as summary capital jurisdiction by officials was not ruled out. Nor was the ferocious severity of the law of debt sufficiently mitigated. It was all very well adding, as was done, that the execution of a court order against debtors must be delayed for thirty days, and that the creditor must feed them adequately and not overload them with chains. But it was not yet made clear that there must always be a court order before he took forcible action; and above all the bitter fact remained that he was still eventually permitted to take his debtors over as permanent *nexi* or serfs. Moreover, the very fact that the Tables defined these and other already existing social hardships, far from improving the atmosphere as had been hoped, meant that when people saw in writing all the rules and sanctions which had been imposed on them and still were in force they felt appalled.

The decemvirs therefore failed to win the approval of the plebeians; as indeed the legends surrounding their endeavours faithfully recall, though they add numerous melodramatic embroideries. The decemvirate continued into a second year of office, during which a veto on intermarriage between patricians and plebeians was apparently confirmed. But then the decemvirs fell from power, and the normal succession of consulships was restored. Their downfall was achieved by a second secession in 449 BC, once again, it would appear, to the Aventine Hill, which in an attempt at conciliation under pressure had been allocated to them as agricultural or building land some seven years earlier. The years 449 and 447 also witnessed legislative measures in favour of the plebeians, which strengthened and confirmed certain of their existing institutions but were exaggerated by later historical tradition because the fall of the decemvirs seemed, retrospectively, such an important and progressive landmark. Then, in 445, the ban on intermarriage between patricians and plebeians may have been lifted. Or more probably – since the patricians, backed by their clients, continued for years to fight every position foot by foot – this was only an attempt to remove it, which did not prove successful. This conclusion is suggested by the continuing decline in the number of patrician families, who carried their persistent distaste for intermarrying to the lengths of class suicide.

In the following year the succession of consuls was temporarily broken when groups of army officers were appointed instead. This was primarily for military purposes (page 42). But the new system which continued, not merely for a year or two, like the earlier substitution by decemvirs, but for nearly eighty years (with interruptions), also served the cause of the plebeians, who were able to gain an occasional place among these military officers that they had not yet succeeded in gaining among the consuls; though the most prominent member of the new leadership was the winner of the war against Veii, Camillus, who was a patrician.

Towards the end of Camillus' career, however, the consulate was restored; and after a prolonged struggle two tribunes of the people, Licinius and Sextius, re-elected, it was said, for as long as ten years (376–367), carried a proposal that one of the consuls could henceforward always be a plebeian. Very soon, individual plebeians were attaining positions of great and long-lasting political power; and only twenty-five years after the Licinian–Sextian measure, the inclusion of a plebeian among every pair of consuls became obligatory. The censorship, too (page 42), became accessible to plebeians by 351 at the latest, and in 339 it was decreed that one censor must always come from their ranks. The effect of these changes was to create a new ruling class, no longer an entirely patrician aristocracy but a nobility consisting of those men, patrician and plebeian alike, whose ancestry had included consuls or censors or dictators – which is what the term 'noble' came to mean. And within the next century plebeian clans such as the Marcii and Decii and Curii, in addition to those who had come from Tusculum and elsewhere, succeeded in establishing themselves among the leaders of this new oligarchy of nobles.

Plebeians of lesser rank were aided by the creation of a new office of state, the praetorship, in 366. This 'urban praetor' was to undertake legal and other civilian functions in order to leave the two consuls free for military duties. But incidentally this innovation also helped the plebeians, since the interests of the underprivileged were benefited by the successive praetors' yearly 'edicts'. Higher officials of the Roman state were accustomed to proclaim by edict, on annual appointment to their office, the major policies which they proposed to follow as its occupants. Among such edicts those of the praetor, owing to his legal responsibilities, were of special significance for the development of private law, and ultimately became even more important than the Twelve Tables, and the source of a great deal of later legislation. It was true that, like other senior functionaries, the praetors were merely supposed to apply regulations that were already in force rather than institute new ones; but in fact their edicts formulated a multitude of new rules and improvements adapted to the increasing complexity of society. They included many remedies for unfairness and abuse, and were guided, subject to a certain latent and not always conscious class bias, by tolerant flexibility and massive fairness, the 'equity' of which the Twelve Tables had already shown signs.

Nevertheless, such improvements only became apparent over the years. For the time being, even if the annexations of Veii and its territory meant that more land was now available, many people remained in the grim clutches of poverty and debt. Licinius and Sextius tried to do something about this by providing that the interest which a debtor had already paid should be deducted from the amount of debt he still owed. Although the tribunes added, in order not to distress creditors too much, that this balance must then be repaid in annual instalments within a period not exceeding three years, their proposal was, by ancient standards, distinctly radical; so that it reminded conservatives of alarming demands for a clean slate that had become a feature of Greek city states. For such reasons, these relief enactments evidently remained ineffective, for we hear of no fewer than four further endeavours to mitigate debt hardships within the course of the next fifty years, and there was even an attempt to veto borrowing on interest altogether (*c.* 342). Its aim was to prevent hardships and abuses; but it must also have made it much more difficult for impoverished people to secure the loans they wanted.

Licinius and Sextius also established limits on the amount of land that could be owned by any one person. This was intended to appease the land-hunger of the poor, and to make sure that they secured an adequate share of conquered territories; but it seems to have become a dead letter before long. Nevertheless the endeavours of these two tribunes of the people, dim figures though they are, to ease the conditions of the plebeians were unprecedented and impressive, the most important internal reforms since the foundation of the Republic. And it was fitting, though perhaps still over-optimistic, that in the crisis year of their principal measures Camillus vowed a temple to Concord, thus echoing the principle often invoked by Greek cities, under the name of Homonoia, in order to end their internal disharmonies.

The next decades witnessed further perceptible advances in social progress and unity, so that Rome went into its decisive struggle against the Latin cities (Chapter 3) with a reasonable degree, if not of Concord, at least of public acquiescence. Whatever the deficiencies of the system from a democratic viewpoint, it proved of decisive importance for the future that Rome, convulsed by these social dissensions at the same time as it was attacked by foreign foes on every side, had prevented the internal strife from reaching suicidal proportions; so that it was given a free hand to suppress each of its foreign enemies in turn, vastly expanding its territory and resources in the process.

Yet in the acute emergency of the Second and Great Samnite War (327–304 BC), fresh measures of social appeasement still seemed urgently necessary in order to ensure that Rome's plebeian soldiers would continue to fight. The most far-reaching step was taken by the consul Poetelius, probably in 326 BC, shortly after the beginning of the war. As we have seen, there had already been many measures earlier in the century, designed to relieve the position of debtors; but the reforms of Poetelius, although obscure to us today, were apparently more comprehensive and effective.

True, the supposition that he altogether abolished the ancient custom by which a debtor could be sold up and become the permanent hereditary bondman (*nexus*) of his creditor seems unlikely. Yet he improved on the Twelve Tables by insisting that in all circumstances a court judgement was necessary before this extreme step could be taken. He may also have enacted that loans could be made on the security of the property of the borrower instead of his person, and that creditors, therefore, must be prepared to accept whatever property debtors offered as a payment. Although this was not the end of the problem, since it was destined to recur, even more urgently, within not many decades, these measures were evidently far more important for most Romans than any military or political developments of the day, and almost significant enough to justify the later enthusiasm of the historian Livy, who declared that the legislation of Poetelius inaugurated a new era of liberty for the Roman plebeians.

Of outstanding importance, too, though scarcely less enigmatic, are the social reforms introduced shortly afterwards, by the first of all Romans who can be regarded as a historical personage, Appius Claudius, censor in 312 BC. Appius Claudius, known as Caecus, 'blind' – which he became in his old age – was a remarkable man. For one thing, he was the writer of a series of pungent moral sayings in verse, thus becoming the first known personage in Latin literature. Furthermore, during his censorship he inaugurated two mighty engineering and building traditions, by constructing, first, the precursor of Rome's aqueducts, the Aqua Appia, which brought water to the city from the Sabine hills in an underground tunnel (including one mile of overground conduit), and, secondly, the Via Appia or Appian Way which was to play an active part in the strategy of the Second Samnite War.

Moreover, although himself a patrician, Appius Claudius also employed his censorship to increase the part played by the plebeians in public life. A desire to secure their effective service in the armies fighting the war may have also been in his mind. But his principal aim was apparently to further the interests of a class disqualified from army service, the landless urban population – whom no reformer had ever tried to help before. Appius' intention was probably to avoid discontent and turbulence on the home front; but at any rate, whatever his motives, he helped these city poor. In the long run, his efforts on their behalf enjoyed some success, since from now onwards the plebeian council felt a special responsibility for this section of the population; though the effects of his measures were by no means conspicuous immediately, since some of them were rescinded only eight years after they had first been enacted.

As censor, Appius Claudius also admitted the sons of former slaves (freedmen) to the Senate, a step which even many centuries later would still have seemed revolutionary, and was in fact reversed by the consuls of the following year. More lasting in its beneficial effects on the plebeians was a further development, in 304 BC, which Appius appears to have instigated by a calculated indiscretion. This was the publication by his secretary Cnaeus Flavius, who had become a state official, of a manual of correct forms of legal procedure. Despite the disclosure of laws in the Twelve Tables, the knowledge of these technicalities had hitherto still remained a monopoly of the patrician college of priests (*pontifices*). But now their publication made them available to future generations of lay jurists. This event, and the powerful opposition it aroused in conservative circles, created an atmosphere of perilous tension – and Flavius the perpetrator of the courageous deed, like Camillus before him, dedicated a shrine to the spirit of Concord. It was probably no coincidence, or at least part of the same series of progressive events, that a law of 300 BC gave all citizens the right to appeal (*provocatio*) against capital sentences imposed by any official; and another measure of the same date made half the membership of the *pontifices* plebeian.

In 298 the third and last Samnite War began, and it lasted for eight years. The ferocious struggle ended in victory, but also in financial exhaustion; and the plebeians of middle rank who had been serving in the army, did so, like many before them, at the cost of the prosperity of their farms, which often fell into decay, so that despite the Poetelian law they fell heavily into debt. So restless did they become, and so grave was the consequent friction, that in accordance with the constitution a dictator, Quintus Hortensius, was appointed as a temporary expedient to meet the emergency (287 BC).

What economic measures Hortensius took, we are not sure. But it is at least known that he passed a law of a constitutional nature in favour of the plebeians, providing that the resolutions of their council (*concilium plebis*) should have the force of law and be binding upon the whole community, patricians and plebeians alike, without the need for the national Assembly (*comitia centuriata*) or Senate to concur. Thus a right that had been claimed for more than 150 years was conceded, and the decisions of the plebeians were now every bit as valid as those of the executive. At very long last, the struggle between the orders had ended. True the Roman people, acting through the Assembly, had already been sovereign at a much earlier date – in the eyes of the law; but not in reality. Now, when the plebeians' measures had gained full legal acceptance – and for the next century and a half, they provided the greater part of Rome's legislation – it might seem that the people's sovereignty had been brought to completion; and the Hortensian law which produced this result has sometimes been hailed as the triumph of democracy.

But that it was not, for three reasons. In the first place, whatever measures Hortensius may have taken to clear up the debt situation did not prove permanently effective, any more than the enactments that had gone before them: so that democracy in the economic and social fields was still out of reach and sight. Secondly, the plebeian council, though it could, on occasion, be swayed by agitators opposed to the establishment, was normally controlled by its richest members, just as thoroughly as the national Assembly was. And thirdly, the council's guiding spirits, the tribunes of the people who possessed the power of vetoing the actions of all Roman magistrates, were cleverly won over by the other side. This happened by gradual stages. First (the dates are uncertain) they were allowed to sit in the Senate and listen to debates. Next they received the right to put motions to the Senate. And finally – and this had happened before the end of the century – they were even authorized to convene the Senate, and preside over its sessions. None of this was unacceptable to the tribunes themselves, for they were often men who wanted to pursue official careers: as they were finally in a position to do, now that Rome possessed a dominant nobility composed of plebeians as well as patricians.

If things had gone the other way, and the tribunes of the people had continued to develop their formal powers of obstruction, the whole machinery of government might well have been paralysed, and that, at least, was a result which this hampering of their obstructive capacity prevented. Yet, from the standpoint of the oppressed plebeians, this transformation of the tribunes from protesters into henchmen of the government signified that the struggle between the orders, though won in a formal sense, had in other and more important respects been lost. It proved harder for the poor, henceforward, to find champions: for the new sort of pro-government tribunes placed their vetos at the disposal of the Senate instead – and the Senate was glad to use them for its own purposes, not only in order to keep their fellow plebeians down, but to prevent ambitious state officials from getting out of hand.

By ancient and modern standards alike, the Roman class struggle had been impressively peaceable. True, it had not been quite as 'reasonably' conducted as patriotic ancient historians later maintained; the threats of secession, for example, were open blackmail. Nevertheless, the struggle had at least been carried on, for all these long years, with a minimum of physical violence, and through due process of law. Its termination has been called by some the high water mark of the Republic's political achievement. Yet, instead, it has been found disappointing by revolutionary or liberal historians, who look for continuous social progress and do not find it here. However, its absence is hardly surprising giving the highly conservative character of the Roman people, patricians and plebeians alike, whose whole society depended fundamentally upon *clientela* and ancestral tradition and the habit of obedience to authority and group and community. Besides, this system, patched together by what may seem to us a peculiar and unsatisfactory series of compromises, at least passed the pragmatic test: because it worked. Indeed, it continued to work with relatively little change, for at least as long as any politico-social system has ever worked in the history of the western world. And in the process, despite all its manifest faults, this system enabled Rome to face its mortal enemies with an imposingly united front, such as few modern states could display today.

# III

# ROME AGAINST CARTHAGE

# 5

# First Wars Against Foreign Powers

THE GREEK CITIES, WHICH so abundantly filled southern Italy and Sicily that they were described as Magna Graecia, did not have much to do with the Romans before 300 BC. But the end of the Samnite War brought the territory of Rome's subject allies far down towards the south, within easy range of some of these Greek towns. The most important of them, on the mainland, was Taras, the Roman Tarentum, now Taranto on the gulf of that name. Tarentum lay astride an isthmus between a shallow protected bay and a tidal lagoon, and possessed an almost impregnable citadel. Larger than Rome in the early third century BC, the city derived great prosperity out of wool from its hinterland, dyed with the purple of the murex mussels in the city's habour. From this port, the safest and most spacious on any Italian coast, the dyed wool was profitably exported to Greece and elsewhere; and so was grain, another product of Tarentum's large and fertile inland possessions. The Tarentines were governed by a democracy which, although somewhat aggressive, displayed (by Greek standards) relative stability. They possessed the largest fleet in Italy and an army of 15,000 men, but this, since their expansionist tendencies were not matched by military talent, they often supplemented by hiring mercenaries. The duty of these was to protect Tarentum's frontiers from its Lucanian neighbours (related to the Samnites) by keeping them in a state of semi-dependence.

The Tarentines had an old agreement with Rome, according to which it undertook not to send ships into their gulf, which they regarded as their own sphere of influence. Nevertheless, an eventual confrontation looked inevitable after Rome, during the last days of the Samnite Wars, founded in 291 a Latin colony of exceptionally large dimensions at Venusia (Venosa), near the far end of defeated Samnium. Surrounded on three sides by deep ravines, and dominating from its lofty ridge the most considerable river of southern Italy, Venusia was primarily designed by the Romans to split off the Samnites from their Lucanian neighbours. But it was also less than ninety miles from Tarentum, whose ruling democratic party regarded its establishment as a strong provocation; Rome seemed to be deliberately setting itself against the freedom of the Tarentines to extend their possessions in southern Italy any further.

This growing tension came to a head in 282 when the Greek city of Thurii, across the gulf from the Tarentines, was attacked by Lucanian raiders and appealed to the Romans; and they, after hesitation, responded, and duly sent a fleet to place a garrison in Thurii. Tarentum regarded this as a clear breach of the agreement not to send ships into its gulf, but the Romans considered that this agreement had become obsolete through lapse of time. Such were the misunderstandings, often genuine enough, which continually accompanied Rome's half-conscious imperial advances from this time onwards.

The Tarentines sank the Roman fleet, killing its admiral; and they drove the offending garrison out of Thurii, jeering at the bad Greek spoken by envoys sent by Rome. They also applied for help, as was their custom, to a Greek military adventurer, in this case King Pyrrhus of Epirus just across the Adriatic. Pyrrhus, who claimed descent from Alexander the Great, was one of the foremost of the minor rulers and rent-an-army generals who had proliferated since Alexander's death half a century earlier. Accepting the invitation from Tarentum, he proclaimed that he would put an end to the Roman power threatening the freedom of the western Greeks. Then he sailed for south Italy, taking with him 25,000 mercenaries, the most highly esteemed professional soldiers of their day, many of them veterans of extensive military experience. And so the Romans had to prepare for the first battles they had ever fought against a Greek army and a Greek ruler.

The basis of Pyrrhus' force was a phalanx of 20,000 men. In battle, lined up in depth, they displayed a front which bristled with the heads of their long lances as impenetrably as a barbed wire entanglement; and their task was to hold the Roman army while their cavalry on the wings turned its rear or flank. Pyrrhus also brought with him a contingent of twenty frightening Indian war-elephants which he innovated by using, not frontally like tanks, as was the custom, but laterally, so that they could join the horsemen in attacking the enemy's flanks.

His first battle against the Romans was fought at Heraclea (Policoro), a coastal colony of Tarentum lying to its west. The legions stood up well to Pyrrhus' phalanx, which proved somewhat unwieldy. But his elephants routed the Roman horses – which could never face these animals untrained – and then charged the flank of the legionaries, putting them to flight, though at a heavy cost of Epirot as well as Roman lives. Thereupon, joined by Samnites and Lucanians, the king marched right on up into Latium; but in the disappointing absence of further defections to his cause, he soon decided to fall back. In the next year, with a larger force, he won another of his costly victories – known henceforward as 'Pyrrhic' after him – in a battle near Ausculum (Ascoli Satriano) in northern Apulia. The Romans resisted his phalanx for a whole day, but on the following day, with the help of his elephants, he forced them back; though they avoided total disaster by regaining their fortified camp. At this point, Pyrrhus made an offer of peace, demanding little more than freedom for Tarentum and its allies. But at the instigation of the aged Appius Claudius the Blind, the proposal was turned down. For he saw a great future for the Romans in southern Italy. And he also believed that they should never treat with an enemy while he was still faring reasonably well.

Next, in autumn 278, Pyrrhus moved on to Sicily; probably he had always intended to do this, seeing the island as a base for further Mediterranean conquests. Once again, he scored military successes – and once again they were without any definitive result. So, three years later, he returned once again to the Italian mainland. There he engaged a Roman army at Beneventum (Benevento) in western Apulia, formerly a Samnite town. But the result of the battle went against him, or was at best inconclusive and damaging, because the Romans had by now discovered that his elephants, if wounded by javelins, got out of control and could be made to trample their own soldiers down. By this time, Pyrrhus' force had been reduced to only one-third of its original size. In order, therefore, to avoid being caught between two Roman armies, he felt obliged to draw back to Tarentum. And from there, before long, he evacuated Italy altogether and returned to Greece, where he was killed two years later at Argos by a tile thrown down from a house-top by a woman.

Pyrrhus was a clever tactician, but lacked persistence and long-term concentration, embarking on too many mutually inconsistent projects and oscillating between excessive hopefulness and gloom. Moreover, although in south Italy and Sicily the Romans were fighting farther from their homeland than he was, his excellent Greek professional army was no match for the combined military resources of their astutely unified, and abundantly populated allies and colonies. The outcome of the war had effectively demonstrated that the Greek states of south Italy could no longer stand against Rome, and in 272 the Tarentines accepted the alliance that was proposed to them. The Romans were becoming conscious of their imperial responsibilities; it was probably in this decade that some south Italian mint, so far unidentified, produced the first silver coinage to be issued in their name, followed in about 269 by issues minted at the capital itself.

And so, within four generations after the lowest point in the Romans' fortunes, the whole of peninsular Italy down to its southernmost regions had come under their control. Moreover, this victory won by the Republic in its first war against a Greek army had been noted in the wider Greek lands of the east, where Pyrrhus' defeat was rightly seen by perceptive

observers as a portent of things to come. For the first time Rome was
recognized, among these nations, as a powerful military state; and one of
the great successor kingdoms of Alexander, Egypt of the Ptolemies, now
proceeded to establish diplomatic relations with its government.

Rome's war with Pyrrhus had also brought it into much closer contact than
ever before with the largest western Mediterranean power, Carthage in
north Africa, in the country that is now Tunisia. And from now onwards
the problems threatening the peaceful coexistence of the two powers rapidly
multiplied.

During the later eighth century BC, when most Mediterranean trading
was in the hands of the Semitic Phoenicians living on the coastland of Lebanon, one of their leading cities, Tyre (Sur) founded an offshoot on these
shores far to its west, calling it the 'New City' of Carthage (Kart-Hadasht).
Probably the proximity of purple-beds contributed to the selection of the
site. But it was also well chosen, like other foundations of the Phoenicians,
so as to safeguard vital points along their western maritime lifelines. In this
chain, Carthage was of exceptional importance, because of its position at
the narrow waist of the Mediterranean. Situated on a peninsula in the
recesses of the gulf of Tunis, it was well protected from the interior by
steep hills; and among its several beaches a long, narrow bay behind a small
headland provided a spacious and sheltered port, later amplified by two
artificial harbours, half a mile from the citadel hill.

For three-quarters of a century Carthage was simply a colony of Tyre,
but from then onwards, apart from nominal and decreasing ties, it became
independent. By the early third century BC its population was three times
that of Rome. Its inhabitants, allowed a share of the city's commercial
profits, were content to remain sluggishly non-political, while the republican government owed its stability and strength (much admired by the
Greeks) to the small, tenacious, cautious, money-making, ruling class which
– despite keen internal jealousies – exercised control like the directorate of
a big commercial company. These rulers were served by a navy and an
army largely composed of Africans and mercenaries, since it was considered
advisable to exempt the Carthaginians themselves from military service,so as
to leave them free to conduct their trading. Under this régime, by 650 BC,
Carthage had taken over and greatly enlarged the old Phoenician trading-
posts and settlements all round the western Mediterranean. And they
created many new posts too, selecting, like their predecessors, carefully
spaced out anchorages on offshore islands or promontories or river estuaries,
with suitable sheltered beaches.

Above all, like their fellow Phoenicians before them, these Carthaginian
seafarers urgently wanted metals. Now the country best able to provide
them was Spain. But to sail due westwards in that direction without any

THE WARS AGAINST CARTHAGE

intermediate stopping-places would have incurred all the hazards of an unwelcoming north African coast and a hostile current: so they needed bases upon the islands on the way. A particularly vital link in this chain was western Sicily, where Carthage assumed leadership of the already existing Phoenician colonists, establishing its main base at Panormus (Palermo), which commanded a superb harbour and fertile hinterland. Greek attempts to dislodge the settlers were unsuccessful, and henceforward for 300 years it remained the firm policy of the Carthaginians to retain this Sicilian foothold. In Sardinia, too, they inherited and developed at least four ports, confirming their power in the region by a naval victory over their Greek rivals off Corsica (c. 535 BC). The possession of all these island bases also enabled them, for a time, to keep the Greeks away from Spain, their principal objective; where Carthage was consequently able to take over and develop important Phoenician settlements at Malaca (Malaga) on the Mediterranean, and even on the Atlantic coast at Gades (Cadiz), which had easy access to the southern Spanish mines.

Moreover, the Carthaginians' strongpoints in Sardinia gave them access to a second important source of metals also, namely Etruria. In their victorious naval battle against the Greeks off Corsica, they had been allies of the Etruscans, and they even had a share in two of the ports of Etruscan Caere: at one of them, Pyrgi, bilingual Etruscan and Phoenician inscriptions have been found, and the other was called Punicum – which meant 'Carthaginian' in Latin.

And meanwhile they were extremely active in Africa as well. Among their leadership, there was a traditional difference of opinion about the relative merits of maritime and continental ventures, and at different times both policies resulted in large extensions of their influence in Africa. By sea, the west coast of the continent was explored as far down as Sierra Leone. And the land empire established by Carthage in north Africa was larger than that of any previous Mediterranean state, Egypt only excepted. Despite the deserts adjoining its territory, Tunisia has large alluvial pockets rich in natural phosphates and highly productive of wheat, vines, olives and fruit, all of which the Carthaginians cultivated with unprecedented skills, recorded in famous agricultural handbooks. By the fifth century BC, they had taken over and developed the entire 20,000 square miles of this plain – thus enabling Carthage to push westwards into Algeria and Morocco, and opening up a land route into the interior of Africa.

It was only a matter of time before this empire came into conflict with the new Mediterranean power of the Romans. Carthage was just 130 miles across the strait from Sicily, and its settlements at the harbour of Etruscan Caere were barely thirty miles distant from Rome; moreover, at that city itself there is also likely evidence for early trading by the Carthaginians. Indeed, they were believed, perhaps correctly, to have signed an agreement with the Romans at about the time of the foundation of the Roman Republic: it seems to have confirmed Carthage's monopoly of the western Mediterranean, but to have guaranteed Italian coast-towns against its attacks. Another treaty is datable to 348 BC, and it was renewed in 279, this time because the Carthaginians shared Rome's hostility to Pyrrhus.

Once he had left Italy, however, relations between the two powers sharply deteriorated. The breaking point came when the local ruling group at Messana (Messina), situated on the straits separating Sicily from the Italian peninsula, invited the Carthaginians to occupy their city and help them suppress the internal and external opponents of their régime; and the invitation was accepted. But this upset the Greek cities of south Italy which had now become allies or dependents of Rome, since they saw Carthaginian domination of the narrows as a menace to their own safety and prosperity.

When, therefore, the men in charge of Messana changed their minds and appealed to Rome instead, and the south Italian cities added their own urgent persuasion, its government accepted the challenge (264) – the Senate had been hesitant, but was overruled by the Assembly, which wanted plunder. So war became inevitable. Its ostensible aim was to decide the future of Messana; the huge ramifications of the hostilities that this was going to involve could not be foreseen.

For this First Punic War, which side was to blame? Surely both. Rome had pushed its territories forward to a point where supposed threats directed against themselves or against their allies by this neighbouring great power could all too easily be made into a pretext for a clash; while at Carthage, too, there was a powerful element which would stop at nothing to secure more trade. Had its leaders, in 279, received an informal Roman assurance of a free hand in Sicily? Perhaps they had, and perhaps this was what had prompted them to intervene at Messana. But in any case Rome and Carthage were so divergent in culture, so mutually uncomprehending, that differences were almost impossible to bridge by diplomatic methods.

So, Rome as well as Carthage having responded to Messana's appeal, the Romans embarked successfully on the considerable task of transporting two legions across the strait to occupy the city, and the Carthaginian admiral who had failed to stop them was crucified by his own government. But the focal point of this initial phase of the First Punic War was the Greek city-state of Syracuse, on the east Sicilian coast. The most populous city in the Greek world, Syracuse stood on the side of a deep bay; the bay was partly closed by its island-citadel, which was joined to the rest of the city by a mole and dominated the entrances to active ports on either side. The Syracusans were the leaders of a flourishing mercantile society, and issued a particularly spectacular silver coinage to serve their commercial operations.

It was for the protection against the king of Syracuse, Hiero II, that Messana had initially appealed to the Carthaginians, and it was in order to thwart his expansion that they had accepted the appeal. It is therefore surprising to find that Hiero, at the outset of the First Punic War, entered into an alliance with Carthage against Rome. For, even apart from what had happened at Messana, this was a strange decision for a Sicilian Greek and a Syracusan, brought up to regard Carthage as the enemy. Yet Hiero must have believed Rome to represent, ultimately, an even greater peril than the traditional Carthaginian foe. However, driven back by a strong Roman military offensive, he almost immediately went into reverse and sought for peace with the Romans after all. They responded prudently, requiring an indemnity and perhaps tribute, but conceding him a fifteen-year alliance and the control of thirty miles of territory. He remained Rome's loyal ally until his death forty-eight years later, and a new institution had come into being: the foreign 'client' kingdom beyond the frontiers of the Roman state but its dependent – an extension of the custom according to which, within its borders, individual clients depended on their individual patrons.

In spite of further victories in the following year, the Romans rapidly came to the conclusion that the limited war which they had originally launched would settle nothing, and a satisfactory peace could only be achieved by driving the Carthaginians out of Sicily altogether. Yet this could only be done if they had a navy, which they did not possess and never had possessed on any substantial scale. So they now proceeded to construct a fleet from virtually nothing, built of the timber which Italy provided in far greater quantities than Carthage. This enterprising decision to challenge the naval supremacy of the Carthaginians, who had been sending ships as far as Sierra Leone before the unseamanlike Romans knew anything about nautical matters at all, was the most extraordinary feature of the war. It lasted for no less than twenty-three years, and for the greater part of this time the Romans kept more than 200 warships simultaneously in being.

In 260 BC they began by constructing a fleet 140 strong. The ships they built, modelled on one they had captured from the Carthaginians, were massive quinqueremes; this was the standard type of war vessel of contemporary Greek states, carrying marines and a crew of 300 sailors, divided into groups of five to an oar, of whom only one or two had to be skilled. In order to frustrate the superior naval dexterity of the enemy by making the sea fights as much like land battles as possible, the Romans equipped their craft with 'ravens' (*corvi*). These were boarding bridges or gangways tied to the mast with a rope, and hinged, or more probably slotted, so that they could be released and let drop on the enemy's decks: fixed underneath the *corvus* was a heavy iron spike or beak which crashed through the planks of the Carthaginian ship, thus holding it fast for boarding by the marines.

Equipped with these instruments the Roman fleet embarked on the second phase of the war, which witnessed the largest naval engagements that the Greco-Roman world had ever seen or would ever see again. The first of these engagements was at Mylae (Milazzo), off the north-east coast of Sicily. The 'ravens' worked well, and fifty enemy ships were destroyed (250); but the Romans did not yet possess the nautical knowledge to follow up their success. Then, four years later, off Cape Ecnomus in southern Sicily (near Licata), they won the most grimly contested naval battle ever fought in ancient times in western waters. After the warships in the Roman centre had moved forward and become perilously enveloped, those on the wings managed to extricate them by determined grappling and boarding, and the enemy was very badly mauled.

This victory inaugurated the third phase of the war, for it threw the

north African shores wide open to the Romans. Their general Regulus
made an unopposed landing, and advanced to within a single day's march
of Carthage itself. Then, seeing that the Carthaginians were harassed by a
rebellion in the interior, he seized the opportunity to offer them peace. But
his terms were so stringent that the fighting continued: and the Carthaginians made good use of a Spartan mercenary leader, Xanthippus. In
spring 255, the two armies clashed in the Bagradas (Medjerda) valley.
There Regulus' force, punctured by the enemy's elephants and encircled by
their cavalry, was annihilated, and he himself was taken prisoner. A Roman
fleet came to retrieve the situation and won a preliminary victory, but was
unable to rescue him; and on the way home it was wrecked by a storm and
lost more than 250 ships.

After these disasters the attempt to invade north Africa was abandoned,
and the war entered its fourth and last phase in which the Romans, with
one new fleet after another, renewed their attempts to gain victory in Sicily.
This new period began well for them with the capture of Panormus, which
confined the Carthaginians to the western tip of the island. Nevertheless,
hostilities dragged on for another thirteen years – to a large extent because
of the Romans' further enormous, exhausting losses from storms, due to the
inexperience of their admirals. Eventually, however, with the aid of a forced
loan from their richest citizens, they raised yet another fleet; by this time
the ships were lighter quinqueremes, without the *corvi* which had proved
perilously top-heavy. The Romans were nearly exhausted and this was the
very last fleet they could ever have afforded to raise; but it proved successful.
For, with its help, they completed the investment of the main surviving
Carthaginian strongholds in western Sicily, and then won an easy, total
naval victory near the offshore Aegates (Egadi) islands. Thereupon Carthage
was forced to accept peace (241); and soon afterwards, fittingly enough, the
unit of the Roman bronze coinage began to display a ship's prow as its
design.

The Greek historian Polybius called this prolonged war the fiercest and
bloodiest struggle that had ever been fought; both sides had lost appalling
numbers of men and ships. Although the Romans could call on the services
of sailors and shipbuilders from Greek south Italy and Etruria, in every
branch of expertise and tactics, especially engineering, the Carthaginians
were still superior. And yet they had lost. They had lost partly because of
the grave initial failure of their commanders to prevent the Romans from
crossing into Sicily. It was true that the Roman command system too was
faulty, because the consuls were very often incompetent to manage a fleet;
and besides, one of them was recalled home every year to preside at the
annual elections, and was accustomed to take his army with him – half the
total Roman force. But every Carthaginian general suffered from an even
more intractable dilemma: if he was defeated, he might be crucified by his

government, and if he won it suspected his future intentions so deeply that reinforcements often failed to reach him. Besides, that government was deeply divided within itself, with the major landowning group far less interested in the war than in developing the continental territory of Africa. For these reasons, the Carthaginian generals could never deliver the final blow, and had to settle for a war of exhaustion. But in that sort of fighting they proved to be at a disadvantage against Rome, since their mercenaries lacked any patriotic incentive to fight: whereas the legions, on the other hand, were manned by men who belonged to a political system which Rome had welded into an effective unity.

Defeated Carthage was not yet removed from the face of the earth. But it was forbidden to send ships into Italian waters ever again, and was compelled to pay a large indemnity over the next ten years. And, above all, it was obliged to evacuate Sicily altogether. For the Romans felt that they must take it over in order to forestall the possibility of the Carthaginians ever returning to it, which would have threatened Italy once more. And Rome was eager to lay hands on the abundant Sicilian grain. So with the exception of Hiero II's state of Syracuse and a few other cities, which remained officially independent as client allies, the Romans now proceeded to annex the whole of the island. In order to recoup their war losses and cover the expenses of the administration, they borrowed Hiero's efficient and famous tax system in order to levy direct taxation or tribute in the form of tithes (a tenth part of the crop). For even though most of Sicily was now part of their own territory, they decided that its people, being foreigners unfamiliar with Roman ways – and only mediocre soldiers – should commute the military service required of other subjects and allies by paying tax instead.

This annexation of Sicily was a fateful step. For it brought the Romans outside Italy, of which the island was not in ancient times a part, and gave them their first overseas province. An entirely new and lasting stage in Roman history had begun: the epoch of imperialism outside the mother country. It was appropriate enough that some forty years later a Latin poet, Naevius, who came from near Capua, chose this war among all others as the theme of his epic glorifying the power of Rome.

Yet it was, perhaps, unfortunate for the Romans that their first province had belonged to Carthage. For, in annexing this island, Rome also took over the Carthaginian mercantile idea that such possessions were intended to be a source of profit: of which the provincial governor was at liberty to take his share. In 227 it was decided that this official should be an additional praetor appointed each year for the purpose. But, as the term *provincia* (sphere of military command) indicates, the Romans evolved no specific theory of provincial administration, merely prolonging war-time conditions in amended form, and providing the governor with only a very small staff. Indeed they did not envisage the province as a unit at all, but rather as a group of city-states which enjoyed various different relations with the ruling power, but in general, although paying direct taxation to Rome, were permitted to levy indirect taxes from their own subjects. In addition the Sicilian province, like other provinces after it, included a fair amount of public land, confiscated by the Roman state, which then leased it out, very often, to the cities or their inhabitants.

The loss of Sicily, then, was the gravest of the damage imposed on the Carthaginians after their defeat. Yet such losses, though enormous, were still less serious than new disasters in which they found themselves involved in the very next year after the First Punic War had come to an end. For at this juncture, 20,000 of their mercenary troops, who had been brought back to north Africa, broke into violent mutiny because their pay was in arrears. Then this polyglot mass of warriors, from more than half a dozen different peoples, proceeded to declare themselves an independent state, issuing a wide range of separatist coins; and they marched inland upon Carthage itself. Moreover, at the very same time, the subject races of the African hinterland likewise seized the chance to take up arms against their oppressors. It was not until after more than three years of this Mercenary ('Truceless') War, comprising the most savage fighting and most inhuman atrocities ever recorded, that the mercenaries were finally annihilated.

Now during these convulsions, the Romans, who had so recently been the enemy of Carthage but were now bound to it by an agreement, came readily to its assistance; for they regarded the mercenaries in Africa as an international danger threatening to unleash general anarchy. But when, immediately afterwards, the fellow soldiers of these rebels in Sardinia as well broke into revolt against the Carthaginians and appealed to Rome (238), it became clear that the view of the Roman government had radically changed. For it now proceeded to send troops to the island's south-western coast to help the dissidents – and seize control of the Carthaginian fortresses. Carthage could do nothing, and the Romans went on to annex Sardinia and Corsica, just as they had annexed Sicily earlier, adding insult by demanding a further indemnity.

Whatever explanations were offered at the time, this forcible annexation of Sardinia and Corsica was the act of a nervous bully, and showed that the famous Roman 'good faith' (*fides*) was non-existent, or at least was regarded as inapplicable to non-Italians. Nor was the annexation justified on economic grounds, since, although use was made of Sardinia's grain, little was done to develop its important mineral resources for a long time to come. For Rome was acting out of pure opportunism, seizing the chance thus given it to guard against a possible resurgence of Carthaginian warlike feeling – a short-sighted measure, since in fact their aggressive action did everything possible to revive such emotions among its victims. The two islands were made into a second, single Roman province, paying a tithe like

the Sicilians, and a new praetorship was created, once again, to supply it
with annually appointed governors (227). The only comfort for Carthage, a
small one, was that although the people of Sardinia, who were of mixed
non-Italian stock, were greatly despised by the Romans, it took the Roman
authorities well over a century to pacify the mountainous interior of this
newly acquired territory.

# 6

# The Changing Roman World

IN A BID FOR popularity, designed to keep up morale at the outset of the First Punic War, the government of Rome had introduced an institution of horrifying brutality which retained an enormous following throughout the whole of the subsequent history of the city: the gladiatorial combat, a national sport and a psychological safety valve. It is possible that duels of this kind were an invention of the Etruscans, who had employed them, in the first instance, as religious ceremonies involving the sacrifice of war prisoners to the shades of their own fallen warriors; and then they kept these contests on for amusement, recording them on grave-urns of the third century BC.

Earlier, however, than any Etruscan artistic representations of these fights are Samnite paintings depicting them, which date from not long after 400. It may well therefore have been from Samnium rather than Etruria that Rome learnt to stage these grisly entertainments; indeed, for a long time the Romans themselves regarded 'gladiator' and 'Samnite' as synonymous terms. But if so, there were probably intermediaries in this borrowing, namely the Samnite settlements in Campania, in whose chief city Capua, long renowned for its leadership in this activity, appeared early paintings of armed, helmeted gladiators scarred by wounds and dripping with blood.

At all events, in 264 BC similar fights were first seen at Rome. For, at a funeral in the cattle-market in that year, two sons of the dead man exhibited three simultaneous gladiatorial combats – a figure which was to rise, within the next half-century, to twenty-two such contests staged on a single occasion. The sanguinary cruelty of these sports betrays the existence of a powerful streak of sadism in the ancient Roman and Italian character.

But if the First Punic War was the occasion for this sanguinary innovation, it also witnessed, paradoxically enough, many novel humanizing influences derived from the Greek world. For whereas the Romans, despite ties with that world of a more or less tenuous or transient nature going back hundreds of years, had hitherto remained more or less immune to the profounder effects of Greece, the war, providing many new contacts with south Italy and Sicily, had brought a considerable number of Greeks from those parts, so that there was an influx of Greek culture as well.

For example Livius Andronicus, a Greek or half-Greek who had come from the principal city of south Italy, Tarentum, as a prisoner of war, opened up altogether new ground – as far as we can tell – since he not only, it would seem, became the first, or one of the first, teachers of Greek literature at Rome, but virtually invented Roman poetry. For, adjusting the clanking Latin tongue to Greek verse forms, he wrote tragic dramas based on classical Athenian models; and one of them was performed, by a remarkable innovation, at the Victory Games of 240 BC. He also wrote an adaptation of Homer's *Odyssey* in Latin, which, although little has survived, and his style was by later standards somewhat craggy, evidently displayed considerable skill. With Livius, two thousand years of Latin literature had vigorously begun – and it had begun on a characteristic note, combining Greek influence and inspiration with the very different Latin language and the Roman, Italian, ethos which it reflected. That is to say, the Greek world had created the climate in which those who wrote Latin found themselves able to develop their own unquestionable originality.

The period of the First Punic War also produced two landmarks in the evolution of Roman law. The first started from what seemed an insignificant happening. In 253 BC the chief priest (*pontifex maximus*) Titus Coruncanius – the first plebeian to hold that office – commenced the practice of admitting his students to his legal consultations, and perhaps admitting members of the general public as well. This step carried farther forward the reform of fifty-one years earlier, by which the publication of the forms of judicial procedure had broken the monopoly of such knowledge previously enjoyed by the college of priests. This disclosure had created a new need to interpret the law; and now, therefore, Coruncanius began the training of the first men who would practise as Roman lay jurists (*iurisprudentes*).

These personages, whose long line was thus inaugurated, did not usually practise as advocates (which was left to professional orators), but were advisers, teachers, writers, and public figures. They exercised their legal influence at every point, counselling praetors and other officials and judges, assisting individual citizens in a wide variety of matters, and giving answers (*responsa prudentium*) on questions of law submitted for their attention. To these queries, the best of them responded with a combination of steadying legality and liberal equity – a Roman blend which appeared also in the court decisions that bore their mark. For in these secular lawcourts it became established, over the years, that legal rules could not be laid down merely by the arbitrary act of the public officials who presided over them, men not likely to be learned in the law. So the jurists sat in on their trials and judgements, and made their vital contribution. In court and out of it, they had to ask themselves what was implied in the ordinary informal acts and happenings of everyday life, and what the normal effect of these happenings would be: and on these conclusions they ruled. The gradual public recognition of their rulings as valid and efficacious was one of the lasting triumphs of Roman civilization.

Not being advocates, the detachment of these lawyers from the practical results of any lawsuit raised their pronouncements above mere partisan biases. True, working from customs, precedents and experience as they did, this famous objectivity, like that of other Roman legal personages before and after them, was sometimes limited, not always consciously, by the feelings, attitudes and aims of the oligarchy to which they belonged – which is why so much of Roman law is concerned with maintaining the rules of private property. Nevertheless, it was such jurists who directly or indirectly built a huge part of the imposing structure of Roman law. For their interpretations, revisions and enlargements of the Twelve Tables and other statutes and praetors' edicts, and their legal formulations of many customs that had never been formulated before, advanced Rome's previous legislative creations at innumerable points. And so the jurists became the central figures of Roman law for many successive generations; during which time they did much to create the way of life that the western world has followed ever since.

Other far-reaching developments originated from a further event of the First Punic War: namely the establishment in 242 BC of a second praetorship at Rome to supplement the much older city praetorship established in 366 BC. This new official was the *praetor peregrinus* (*c.* 242).* It was his task to deal with legal cases in which at least one of the contestants was a non-Roman (*peregrinus*), that is to say either a foreigner or a subject of Rome who did not possess Roman citizenship – a category which would soon display continuous increases in size, corresponding with each successive overseas annexation.

The concept behind this new peregrine praetorship had never found legal expression before, because hitherto Roman law, as formulated in the Twelve Tables and other legislative pronouncements, had all been Civil Law (*ius civile*), that is to say had dealt exclusively with the relations between one Roman citizen (*civis*) and another, foreigners being, strictly speaking, without rights. The new post of the *praetor peregrinus*, therefore, represented a major enlargement of this previously non-ecumenical Roman viewpoint, extending it, in due course, to wider issues of many kinds – the

---

* The praetors appointed to govern Sicily, and then Sardinia–Corsica, were the third and fourth.

sort of issues, inevitably, in which the constructive, equitable methods of the rising lay jurists were relevant and helpful. So the law which the peregrine praetor administered might be described as Civil Law with its more formal parts omitted, stressing its universal rather than its narrowly national implications.

, The creation of this new office also contributed largely to the evolution of one of the most potent and effective ideas that the Romans ever originated. This was the 'law of nations' (*ius gentium*) of which the history, involving various changes of meaning, has extended right up into our own times. In the period when the term first began to be formulated, during the later third and second centuries BC, it defined those portions of the Roman Law that were open to citizens and non-citizens alike: that is to say, those branches with which the new *praetor peregrinus* was concerned. Both his office, and the concept of the *ius gentium* which it helped to develop, evolved out of the growth of commercial, social, and political relations between Rome and other states.

Legal ideas of this sort were not altogether new to the world. For other ancient nations, also, although they likewise had originally thought in terms of a law applicable only to their citizens, had nevertheless evolved rough and ready codes for the benefit of their traders; and besides from early Greek times onwards, specific treaties between one city-state and another had sought to guarantee the mutual protection which these commercial interests required. And then Rome too, although not directly copying Greek influences, had proceeded along somewhat similar lines when it granted its subject allies a sort of half-citizenship, which conferred trading and matrimonial rights (*commercium, conubium*). But now, in addition, as the peregrine praetorship gradually extended its scope, many questions of marriage and status and succession, and points relating to contracts for sale and hire and work and services, gradually received legal definition in relation to non-citizens even if they possessed no such special allied rights at all.

Later jurists attributed the obligatory force of this application to 'the law of nations', *ius gentium*. In employing this concept, they were making the large assumption that it rested on some corpus of legal principles which was universally acceptable. In consequence, as more time passed, *ius gentium* came to be elevated into a philosophical ideal of 'natural law' interpreted as a set of precepts valid everywhere in the world. Later still the ramifications of the term became even more immense, since it was held to signify the rules governing relations between states – which are now grouped together under public international law.

This *ius gentium*, which was stimulated and rendered inevitable by the peregrine praetorship, demonstrated that a body of law could be established upon a foundation acceptable to the members of different peoples and races at any and every phase of social, economic and political evolution: and so it

brought the laws of the Romans nearer to universal applicability than any
others that have ever been devised, and uniquely displayed their genius for
social organization. Above all, *ius gentium* was redolent of common sense;
which is, indeed, characteristic of Roman law as a whole. Its exponents,
like English lawyers later on, were often reluctant to specify the principles
which guided them. Yet a Roman jurist was boldly prepared to offer
generalizations, not indeed for their own sake, but in order to solve each
specific set of problems that had to be confronted; thus striking the shrew-
dest balance between theory and practice, and having the best of both.
Moreover, the great majority of these generalizations have never, in all the
intervening centuries, been discredited or discarded – and in most cases not
even reformulated, since they had been set out from the first in carefully
thought out language of a clarity and sharpness that could not be improved
upon. Roman law was much superior, in precision and substance alike, to
the legal systems of the Greeks, in spite of their rich jurisprudence.

Nevertheless, law is one thing and litigation is another, and even the
Romans found that perfect fairness in regard to the latter was hard to come
by. For it would be unrealistic to see the processes of the ancient Roman
lawcourts (*iudicia publica*), despite the impressive laws and concepts they
were called upon to put into effect, in too rosy a light. For one thing these
courts, like the people who worked for them, consciously or unconsciously
served the ruling class; and besides, there was no real professional tradition
of impartial justice, and no organized police to enforce it, any more than
there was to be in later western countries until well after the 1800s. Roman
litigants also experienced many vexatious delays, though even the twentieth
century AD still has its share of these. And the limits of free speech and free
political action would have seemed to us excessively narrow. Nevertheless
a great proportion of Rome's available intellectual power and subtlety,
throughout the whole millennium of antiquity, was poured into the development of its law, and since then it has continued to have a history lasting
for two further millennia. Moreover, in the course of that prolonged period,
it has often seemed that the whole principle of order as a bulwark against
chaos, indeed the very survival of civilization itself, depended upon the
maintenance of the legal structure the Romans left behind them.

In the last chapter it was pointed out that the Roman class struggle had
ended in formal victories for the plebeians, but that these ostensible successes were, in practical fact, converted into a victory for the nobility
instead: not indeed the ancient patrician class, but the new nobility of those
men, patricians and plebeians alike, who belonged to families who could
boast at least one consulship at some time in the past. In this new order,
the plebeian council (*concilium plebis*) which had now gained full validity
for its decisions, played an effective and essential part. Yet the poor possessed

very little say in those decisions since they were guided by nobles – and besides, the council's membership, like that of the national Assembly (*comitia centuriata*), was dominated by the middle class of substantial peasants.

This middle class included many men who, like the poor, were clients of dominant noble patrons. Other members of this same intermediate category, however, were sufficiently independent to stand up, from time to time, for the under-privileged. Thus on one notable occasion in the 230s they directly challenged the wishes of the nobility, in the interests of those who were impoverished and landless. The clash originated from an event that had taken place half a century earlier, in 283 BC; Rome's annexation from the Gauls of the Ager Gallicus, the Adriatic coastal district south of the Po. Yet this territory, together with the area that lay north of the river (Cispadane and Transpadane Gaul respectively, the joint components of Cisalpine Gaul) had never been made part of Italy – and apart from the foundation of a Roman and a Latin colony, Rome had made extremely little use of its lands, initially because there had been no demand for them. Yet later the situation had changed, because the First Punic War produced ex-soldiers who had seen their farms gone to ruin while they were away on active service, and who therefore demanded to be given new land to replace what they had lost: so that during the difficult decade which followed the conclusion of the war, there was intense popular pressure for the break-up of the Ager Gallicus into small, individual allotments.

The agitation was led by a tribune of the people, Gaius Flaminius, a 'new man' outside the patricio-plebeian nobility. But the senators, who held valuable leaseholds in this region, objected to any such distribution, whereupon Flaminius, with the aid of other 'new' gentry whose public careers he agreed to assist, carried the proposal through the plebeian council over the heads of the protesting Senate. This high-handed action was believed to be without precedent in recorded Roman history: Flaminius had disclosed the secret that policy could, against all tradition, be made outside the Senate. What he had done was censured by later conservative historians, since it set the precedent, a century later, for a whole mass of other agrarian measures. Indeed, during that future period there were no less than forty such proposals, which in some cases were much more revolutionary in character than Flaminius' bill and were blamed for the downfall of the Republic. More radical writers, on the other hand, believed he had struck a valuable blow against oppression.

However at this juncture a new generation of Gauls was threatening to avenge their defeat of half a century earlier, which had led to the loss of those Adriatic lands. In consequence, Flaminius' proposed distribution of the Ager Gallicus was denounced by his Roman opponents as a gratuitous act of provocation against the Gauls: because it introduced substantial

Roman manpower into this delicate border area. In 225, therefore, a coalition of Gallic tribes sought to remedy this situation by violent means, launching an army of 70,000 men with powerful cavalry and war-chariots, in an attack which penetrated deep into the peninsula. But at Telamon (Talamone), halfway down the Etruscan coast, this force, while retreating in order to store its plunder in safety, was hemmed in between two Roman armies, and in the subsequent engagement the Gauls, fighting back to back, were almost annihilated. Never again did an army of their people cross the Apennines, though the Romans never forgot the first terrible onslaughts of these naked warriors, with their flashing gold necklaces and bracelets.

Flaminius did not hold a command at the time of the victory, but he succeeded, in spite of his non-noble background, in winning a consulship in 223. And after that, he marched north – regardless of a senatorial order to come back to Rome – and led the first army ever to cross the Po, the precursor of later expeditions which would eventually transform this area into a populous and flourishing part of the Italy from which it had so long been excluded.

# 7

# The Invasion by Hannibal

IT WAS NOT THE Gauls, however, but once again the Carthaginians, who offered the greatest menace to Italy in the 220s BC. This time the threat came from the armies they maintained in Spain. Their dominant position in that peninsula was a new phenomenon, or rather the revival of an old one. For Carthage had earlier possessed a Spanish coastal empire; but during the middle years of the third century BC, when it lost the First Punic War and was expelled from Sicily and Sardinia and Corsica, it had also, under pressure from Greek Massilia (Marseille), which competed for the western Mediterranean ports, been deprived of almost the whole of its former Spanish dominions: until finally little more than Gades (Cadiz) and the Straits of Gibraltar remained in its hands. But after putting an end to the ferocious Mercenary Revolt, the Carthaginians achieved a startling revival, and, employing their subject lands in Algeria and Morocco as stepping stones, soon proceeded to build up a Spanish empire all over again. The agents of this recovery were the most able family Carthage ever produced, the house of the Barcids. In spite of determined political opponents, they had gained an impressive position at home, and now they established themselves for several decades in Spain, establishing a hereditary line of semi-independent governors.

The first of the family to set himself up there was Hamilcar Barca, who had played a distinguished part in the First Punic War, when he earned substantial credit for the resistance which postponed his side's defeat. Then, when the war was over, and when he had again fulfilled a leading role in the suppression of the rebellious mercenaries, he was authorized by his government in 237 BC to proceed to Spanish waters: his task was to recapture territories and resources in compensation for the loss of Sicily and the other islands. His successes in Spain were impressive. Starting from Gades, he reconquered most of the southern and eastern regions of the country as far north as Cape Ifach and Cape Nao, halfway up the coast; and near the

SPAIN, 3RD - 2ND CENTURIES B C

Pyrenees Mts

CELTIBERI

R Ebro

Numantia

Tarraco

R Douro

NEARER SPAIN
(TARRACONENSIS)

Saguntum

Ebusus I

R Tagus

Sierra de
Toledo

C Nao
C Ifach

Acra Leuce

LUSITANI

Baecula

Carthago
Nova

FURTHER SPAIN
(BAETICA)

R Baetis

Ilipa

Malaca

Gades

0    50 miles

limits of this occupation, beside lands which recalled the most fertile territories of north Africa, he established a port and capital at Acra Leuce, the
White Promontory (Alicante). Already the Spanish territories he had occupied were larger and richer than the Carthaginians had ever ruled in the
country before: and the Spaniards, men of mixed Celtic and Iberian stock
famous for their physical endurance, provided him with a new army – the
best Carthage had ever possessed throughout its history. The finely tempered Celtic swords which these soldiers carried were the products of the
immensely rich mines the conquests included. And their share in the
revenues from these mines that went to Hamilcar's political enemies at
Carthage induced them not to obstruct him.

In 229, however, he was drowned. His son-in-law Hasdrubal, who succeeded him, moved his headquarters farther south, in order to be near his
home base. The site he chose, Carthago Nova or New Carthage (Cartagena), stood on a peninsula commanding one of the best harbours in the

world; and it was protected from the interior by a lagoon, while a valley nevertheless gave it access to the abundant silver mines its townsmen exploited. Yet although Hasdrubal had selected this more southerly capital, he pushed the frontier of the new Carthaginian Spain a long way to the north, advancing to the banks of the River Iberus (Ebro), halfway up to the Pyrenees. And he also expanded his conquests deep into the interior, arranging a co-ordinated series of alliances and treaties in vast areas of this hinterland, which the Greeks who had settled in the same country had never succeeded in achieving.

Then Hasdrubal was murdered (221) and the command passed to his brother-in-law Hannibal, the son of Hamilcar Barca who had originally brought him out to Spain. Hannibal pushed still farther inland as far as the upper River Douro and the Tagus; and his diplomatic methods earned him considerable popularity among the Spaniards. However, one coastal town south of the Ebro, Saguntum, decided to resist him. With the Romans, on the other hand, this place was more friendly and indeed, under the direction of an anti-Carthaginian party, it may have formed some sort of alliance with them. At all events, it was to Rome that the Saguntines now appealed – perhaps not for the first time. And Rome took the fateful step of responding favourably. Before long, its delegates were on their way to Hannibal at Carthago Nova, in order to transmit the Senate's command that he should keep his hands off Saguntum. A peace party at Carthage was in favour of complying, but Hannibal rejected the ultimatum, and pressed on with the blockade of Saguntum, which fell to him after a savage eight months' siege (219). The Romans angrily ordered the Carthaginian government to hand Hannibal over to them – a demand that was predictably turned down. Debate at Rome about what should be done next was keen and bitter; but finally its envoy told the Carthaginians that their refusal to surrender Hannibal meant war. The curtain was now going up for the most terrible of all Rome's struggles, and the most far reaching in its results – the Second Punic War (218).

The rights and wrongs of the war are hard to determine, since much hinges on an obscure treaty which Rome had made with Hasdrubal in 226. According to the Greek historian Polybius, it was agreed, at this meeting, that the Carthaginians were not to cross the River Ebro in arms. This was a point on which Rome would be eager to insist, in order to calm the apprehensions of Massilia, which was its long-standing ally. For this Greek city, as it had shown by its hostility towards the earlier Carthaginian empire in Spain, had long been anxious for the safety of its own trading stations on that country's east coast; and it still possessed Spanish outposts north of the Ebro. Moreover, there was a second and more direct reason why Rome did not want the Carthaginians to cross the river. This was because of the fear that they might march right up the Pyrenees and across them, and then traverse the south of France and move down into Cisalpine Gaul (north Italy), where they could help the Gauls against Rome. And it appears that in 226 Hasdrubal agreed to the urgent Roman stipulation that he should not march north of the Ebro. But he would never have consented to such a restriction unless the Romans, at the same time, had agreed that they themselves would not interfere south of the river – at Saguntum, for example (even if it had been previously recognized as their ally). There must, therefore, have been a second clause in the Ebro agreement to this effect.

But, if that was so, how did the Romans justify their subsequent breach of the understanding? Probably on the grounds that the treaty of 226 had been negotiated with Hasdrubal himself on a personal basis only, and had never been ratified by the Carthaginian government. And that may well have been the case. Nevertheless, the real and underlying motive of the Romans' action, as so often in their subsequent history, was a profound suspicion of the foreigner: in this case, of Hasdrubal's successor Hannibal, whom they suspected of planning a major campaign across the Ebro. As to his own attitude, he must have known that his siege of Saguntum, whether it violated a formal Carthaginian treaty with the Romans or not, involved a serious risk of war against them. The legend was that his father had once made him swear eternal hatred towards the Romans. But in any case, whatever the truth of that, he evidently felt determined to avenge his country's defeat in the First Punic War and Rome's perfidious behaviour after it had ended. And he believed that the new Spanish empire his family had won, rich in minerals and warriors, gave him a wonderful opportunity to carry out these plans of vengeance and reversal.

But the Romans too were confident in their human resources: and so now they declared war. They intended to send forces to Spain, via the land route and Massilia; and to send them to the north African homeland of Carthage as well. However, both these designs were forestalled by Hannibal's audacious decision to invade Italy. This came as a surprise to Rome, which knew he had constructed no fleet. But instead he made for Italy by the difficult land-route. He took with him, on the final stage of the march, some 40,000 men, comprising well-trained Carthaginian-officered Spanish infantry and excellent African (Numidian) cavalry, with thirty-seven elephants. And he confidently hoped to augment this army on arrival in north Italy by winning over anti-Roman Gauls and Rome's Italian subject allies; in this way he would be able to cut off the vast reservoir of Roman–Italian manpower before it could ever be drawn upon.

In April 218 BC, brushing aside native opposition, he transferred his army across the Rhône, and then in the early autumn he crossed the Alps. The mountains were treacherous going, because of premature falls of snow: but Rome's belief that they would stop an army from getting through them proved mistaken. Nevertheless, when Hannibal came down into the Po valley he had only 26,000 men left: and the Senate's generals hoped to wear him down by a series of delaying actions. But they were almost at once defeated in two successive battles, on a northern and then a southern tributary of the Po. First, on the River Ticinus, where they tried to engage Hannibal's tired army before it could recover, a skirmish between advance guards displayed his cavalry's superior speed, equipment and training so clearly that the Romans fell back across the river to the Apennine foothills, and there, on a rough, snowy December day, their commanders, instead of staying on the higher ground as they should have done, were induced by a feigned Carthaginian flight to order their 40,000 legionaries to wade across the swollen waters of the River Trebia (Trebbia) and attack him. But the morale of the Roman soldiers was low because they had had no breakfast, and in the morning mist an ambush from the reed beds took them by surprise in flank and rear, so that they were overwhelmed and only a quarter of their numbers escaped the subsequent massacre.

And so already, within only two months, Hannibal had overrun the whole of northern Italy, with the isolated exception of two newly founded Latin colonies at Placentia (Piacenza) and Cremona, which stood firm. It was true that he had lost most of his elephants, and the support he received from the local Gauls was not all he had hoped for; yet as a result of his victories, he was able to increase his force to a total strength of 50,000. And now, from his new north Italian base, he believed the time had come to incite Rome's Italian allies to revolt. Meanwhile at Rome itself, the more prosperous plebeians, who controlled their own council and the national Assembly, were infuriated by the bungling which had lost them the north Italian lands they had fought so hard to win; and their appointment of the reformist 'new man' Flaminius to a second consulship in 217 was a criticism of the Senate's conduct of the war.

Flaminius tried to block the Carthaginian army's southward advance, but early in the year they evaded him by breaking through an unguarded Apennine pass; and then they pressed on through marshy country, in such rough conditions that Hannibal, riding on the sole surviving elephant, lost the sight of an eye through exposure. However, as he ravaged Etruria and seemed to be making for Rome, he drew Flaminius after him and on a foggy April morning trapped his army in a defile between the hills and Lake Trasimene. Surrounded on all three sides, most of the soldiers of these two Roman legions were killed, and Flaminius himself was among the fallen. This victory presented Hannibal with an open, undefended road to Rome itself. However, he did not take the opportunity. This was partly because the total destruction of Roman power might not have been in his own country's interests, for it would only have introduced rival powers from the eastern Mediterranean to fill the vacuum. But in any case, he lacked good siege equipment; and in its absence, the walls of Rome could not be breached by any attacker, especially if he had no supply base near by. And no such base existed, because, to Hannibal's acute disappointment, not one single town of central Italy defected to his side. Rome's system of colonies and allies stood this searching test with admirable firmness.

So Hannibal swerved aside from the city, and instead decided to seek allies in the southern part of the peninsula, which, for the most part, was non-Italian and unromanized. As he marched through Campania and Apulia, relying on their grain-lands for food and on their ports for contact with Carthage, his army was shadowed by a veteran Roman general, Fabius Maximus, now dictator (for the second time). Fabius' reappointment had been arranged, with the concurrence of the Senate, by the unusual procedure of election in the Assembly, since one of the consuls who should have nominated him was dead and the other was cut off from the city. Fabius was a Roman of the old and canny type, and the strategy he now put into effect avoided risking his hastily recruited new armies in any further pitched battles – a policy which earned him the nickname 'of Cunctator (Delayer) – while instead he cut off the enemy's supplies by devastating the surrounding countryside. But this policy of destruction was understandably hated by many Romans and Italians, and lost him the popular support which had brought him to power.

In the following year, therefore, the generalship was removed from him and bestowed on two inexperienced consuls, who were entrusted with the largest force Rome had ever put into the field; they were placed in its joint command, as consuls had never been before, since it had hitherto been the custom for each to command his own separate army. In a supreme effort to end the war at a single blow, they accepted battle on a smooth open plain near Cannae, a small fortress and important supply base near Italy's heel. The Romans believed that their numerical superiority would tell. But the prevailing hot sirocco wind blew blinding clouds of sand into their faces, and they found themselves caught in a pincer movement by the Carthaginians' light troops on either flank and by their cavalry in the rear. Wedged tight in these hopeless conditions, the Roman army, after savage resistance, was almost wholly destroyed. This battle, the bloodiest defeat they ever suffered, provided an unprecedented example of a smaller force successfully enveloping a larger one, a tactic which required perfect co-ordination, and was imitated by the German general von Schlieffen at the outset of the First World War in 1914.

One of the consuls was killed in action, but the other, although a nominee of the Assembly and consequently blamed for everything by later conservative historians, received a courteous reception from his fellow-senators at Rome, and was thanked for not despairing of the Republic. For in the city, despite this catastrophe, morale remained indomitable. Indeed, even before the end of the very same year, under a government now unquestioningly left in the hands of the Senate, Rome's terrible losses were already more than made good by further recruitment, so that Hannibal's victory had failed to repair his numerical disadvantage. Moreover, in order to avert further disastrous pitched battles, Fabius' strategy was seen to be good after all, and underwent revival: the Roman armies were divided into a number of small forces distributed at vital points, like a pack of dogs circling round a lion. Yet Cannae had led, at last, to some of the defections Rome had feared – not, indeed, among its subject allies in the centre of the peninsula, but in the geographically and culturally remoter areas of south Italy and Sicily, where the vitally important cities of Capua, Syracuse and Tarentum all successively went over to the invader (216–213 BC). Nevertheless by a series of mighty sieges, conducted by double cordons of troops supplied with the most scientific equipment, all three of these places were won back again, Capua and Syracuse in 211, and Tarentum in 209.

In 213 or 212, despite all these troubles, Rome emphasized its status as a major power by issuing for the first time, on a large scale, its historic silver coin the *denarius*, which with smaller coins marking its subdivisions, provided a much improved means of meeting the state's financial needs. Nor was it of any avail, in 211, for Hannibal to advance to the outskirts of Rome itself. Accompanied by an escort of cavalry, he rode slowly on his black horse round the walls, watched by the inhabitants. At that very moment, as it happened, the site of his camp, three miles away, came up for auction in the city – and was duly sold at a normal price. Nothing could have shown him more clearly that the Romans, in spite of all the disasters they had suffered at his hands, were still determined to survive and to win.

Because of the remarkable dramas of Hannibal's Italian invasion, the Second Punic War is often looked at as a war fought primarily on Italian soil, with a secondary sphere of operations in Spain. But the Spanish campaigns fought during the same years were a deciding factor in the outcome of the war. For although the Romans had failed to keep Hannibal from crossing the Pyrenees and marching on Italy, they nevertheless succeeded in preventing his younger brother Hasdrubal Barca, whom he had left behind to rule Carthage's Spanish empire, from sending him any reinforcements. This they did by making the fateful decision to fight an active war in Spain itself, despite all the crises which they were undergoing in their homeland.

Rome's Spanish armies were commanded, for the first seven years of the war, by two men named Scipio, the father and uncle of the great Scipio Africanus. In spite of initial offensives by Hasdrubal Barca, the Scipios won a number of successes that enabled them to gain control of the Mediterranean seaboard of the country, moving gradually southwards along its coast until in 211 they captured Saguntum, the original bone of contention: which they then made preparations to use as a base for further advances. Because of these setbacks, Hasdrubal Barca failed on several occasions in attempts to break out across the Pyrenees. Moreover successive drafts of recruits, who would have been very useful to Hannibal's Italian campaigns, had to be diverted from north Africa to his brother's Spanish army instead. Yet the diversion of these troops, which gave such an invaluable breathing space to the hard-pressed Romans in Italy, caused the downfall of the Scipios in Spain, for in 211 both the brothers were successively defeated, and died in battle.

The Carthaginians were now able to take back the regions they had lost south of the Ebro. Yet they did not cross the river; for, after their setback in Italy in the same year, they did not feel strong enough to tackle the defences, somewhat feeble though they were, which the Roman survivors of the Scipios', defeats had erected along its banks. Moreover, as soon became clear, Rome had by no means finished with Spain. For in 210 the Assembly, at last re-emerging from the timidity imposed by its failures against Hannibal, induced the Senate to acquiesce in the appointment of a new and surprising general to command the Spanish armies. This was Publius Cornelius Scipio (later Africanus), son and nephew of the commanders who had perished in Spain the year before. Publius Scipio was only twenty-five. He had therefore held none of the senior offices regarded as necessary prerequisites for such an appointment. Yet he was not untried in war, and his exploits had inspired the conviction that he was the right man for the job.

Once in Spain, he reverted to the attacking strategy of his father and uncle. He chose as his target the enemy headquarters and arsenal at Carthago Nova. While assaulting the town from the land side, he profited by a squall, which had blown up and lowered the level of the lagoon, to send his troops through the shallow waters and scale the fortifications that were undefended on this side – and by this means the whole of Carthago Nova fell into his hands (209). In the following year, he marched into the interior of the country, and engaged Hasdrubal Barca's smaller army at Baecula (Bailen) on the upper Baetis (Guadalquivir). Compelled to fight quickly because he feared the arrival of enemy reinforcements, Scipio divided up his main force and, using his light troops as a screen, fell on the enemy's flanks. This striking demonstration of a novel flexibility in Roman tactics, which showed how carefully Scipio had studied Hannibal's Italian victories, won him the battle.

Yet Hasdrubal Barca escaped, and at last got out of Spain altogether, taking an unexpected land route round the western extremity of the Pyrenees and proceeding onwards to Italy, with the intention of joining his brother Hannibal there. His escape transformed the battle of Baecula from a tactical victory into a strategic defeat. And Scipio did not try to pursue him. Probably his orders from Rome did not allow him to; but even if they did, he was right not to make the attempt, since if he had, he would have exposed himself in difficult country too far from his base, and would have risked losing Spain altogether: and, besides, he would never have caught him in any case. As it was, the departure of Hasdrubal Barca's army ensured final Roman success in the Spanish campaign. This was sealed by a huge battle against his successors in 206, fought at Ilipa (Alcala del Rio, near Seville). Here Scipio introduced a sophisticated variation into his out-flanking tactics by reversing the usual battle order and moving his light auxiliaries from the flanks to the centre of his line. This meant that the men now located on the flanks were his best troops, the legionaries: it was they who now found themselves entrusted with the encirclement of the enemy army, and they carried out their task triumphantly. This time, the victory was conclusive. Many native princes abandoned their alliances with Carthage. And by the end of the year it had lost its Spanish possessions for ever.

And so these most valuable portions of the Iberian peninsula had fallen into the hands of Rome, which annexed them and converted them into two new provinces: the eastern coastal strip of Nearer Spain, and beyond it Further Spain (Baetica) comprising the southern coast and the valley of the Baetis (Guadalquivir). Eight years later, the Roman government appointed two new praetors to administer these territories. A 5 per cent tribute was imposed on grain, resembling the taxes earlier instituted in Sicily. But otherwise, the pattern was different; for it seemed practicable in this more warlike country to impose the duty of military service, so that the country's manpower resources could provide auxiliary units to supplement the legions. Moreover, the Romans developed and expanded Carthaginian mining in the country, which was rightly said to overflow with metals; at Carthago Nova alone, the capital of the Nearer province, the silver mines subsequently employed as many as 40,000 workers at one time. And so a fixed sum in silver was levied on the population in addition to the tribute.

In 206 Scipio established a new town named Italica (Santiponce near Seville), where his veterans were given grants of land: although Italica was not a colony, the foundation of such an Italian-style community overseas established a novel and far-reaching precedent. The purpose of the place was to serve as a fortress against the tribesmen who dwelt in the hinter-land. For in this fierce country the Romans still had an immense military task ahead, which took them 200 years to complete. So it is doubtful if even the enormous revenue they soon found themselves able to collect sufficed to pay for the costs of occupation. Yet at least the Carthaginians had been expelled from this enormously important and strategic territory.

·   ·   ·   ·   ·   ·

Nevertheless, the events that had led to their expulsion seemed, at first, to carry compensating advantages: for the removal of Hasdrubal Barca's army from Spain was Hannibal's gain in Italy. And it came at a very appropriate time. For in spite of their successes in south Italy, the Romans were almost at the end of their resources. In 209, twelve Latin colonies out of the existing thirty had declared their inability to supply any more troops, or the money to pay for them. They had been bled white, and could fight no more. And now, two years later, the arrival of Hasdrubal, fulfilling hopes that the enemy had been cherishing for eleven years, caused alarm throughout Italy. After crossing southern France and the Alps unopposed, he descended into the Po valley, where new Gaulish recruits raised his numbers to 30,000. Then the two Carthaginian brothers moved towards one another intending to join forces.

Meanwhile the Romans, after mobilizing massively yet again in spite of their exhaustion, had an army in the north of Italy and an army in the south. And now they benefited from a great stroke of luck: for captured dispatch-riders of Hasdrubal revealed to them that his meeting-place with Hannibal was to be on Umbrian territory. On receiving this news the southern Roman commander, leaving a force to watch Hannibal, undertook a rapid six-day march up the Adriatic coast to the Umbrian river Metaurus, and on the following morning Hasdrubal heard a double bugle call from the camp of the Romans which told him that their two armies had united. This meant that he was outnumbered by at least 10,000 men. In a desperate attempt to slip through and join forces with his brother, he moved up the Metaurus valley after nightfall. But he lost his way in the dark, and was overtaken among the gorges and slippery crags, and died fighting with almost all his men.

For the first time during the entire long period of the war, the Romans had won a pitched battle in their homeland: and the end of Hannibal's occupation of Italy was now only a matter of time. He learnt what had happened when his brother's head was hurled into his camp. Then he withdrew into the mountains of Italy's toe and stayed there, without emerging, for another four years.

When two of these years had passed (205), Scipio, fresh from his Spanish victories, was elected consul and asked the Senate for permission to invade Africa and attack Carthage directly. The senators were very reluctant, since they still felt apprehensive of Hannibal's continued presence in Italy, and were anxious not to impose further burdens on the allied towns. But when Scipio appealed over their heads to the Assembly, promising vengeance on the Carthaginians for all the sufferings they had inflicted, the Senate gave way, somewhat grudgingly. That is to say they agreed that, whereas Sicily was to be his province, he could also sail to Africa if the interests of the state required it, with two legions in addition to whatever volunteers he could collect. He recruited 7,000 of them, thus bringing his total army up to 30,000; and with this force he landed in north Africa some twenty miles from Carthage (204). There he was joined by a neighbouring prince Masinissa, ruler of part of Numidia (eastern Algeria), who had changed sides with his excellent cavalry.

In the next year Hannibal returned from Italy, his fifteen-year-long invasion at an end. Carthage had begun negotiations for peace with the Romans and the discussions had reached an advanced stage, but Hannibal persuaded his government to break them off. Thereupon Scipio moved inland to sever the enemy capital from its agricultural supplies, and in 202, near Zama seventy-five miles from the city, the final battle of the war was fought. It was not a real climax, because the eventual outcome of the campaign could be in no doubt. But it achieved great fame owing to the calibre of the rival commanders, and because, before the engagement, the two men had a famous meeting, about which nothing is known, except that it was unproductive.

When the battle began, neither side succeeded in outflanking the other, for both were by now thoroughly familiar with tactics of this kind. But the issue was decided by the horsemen of Rome's new Numidian allies, who broke off their pursuit of the enemy's cavalry wings, and fell on their rear, achieving total victory. There were few Carthaginian survivors, but Hannibal was one of them. He recommended to his government that peace should be made immediately, and this was done. The terms were less favourable than they would have been in the previous year if negotiations had not been suspended. The indemnity to be paid by the Carthaginians was doubled, their fleet was limited to ten ships instead of twenty, and Masinissa, who became king of all Numidia, was rewarded with part of their western borderlands. And finally, they were forbidden, henceforward, to engage in any war without the prior consent of Rome.

They had already lost Spain; and now they had ceased to be a major power, and would never become one again. So the Romans had victoriously completed the most decisive single phase of their rise to domination. For the Second Punic War had made it certain that they would remain in control of the entire western Mediterranean region for many hundreds of years to come. For the west, therefore, with the possible exception of the struggles of the twentieth century AD, the Second Punic War proved to have been the most momentous war of all time.

But victory had only been won by feats of unprecedented endurance. In spite of initial disastrous defeats, the Italian dominion built up with such patience by Rome had, on the whole, resisted the temptation to defect, fully justifying the Roman system. Even in the gravest peril Roman and Italian morale and discipline had stood firm, leaving memories of this supreme test which later writers were never tired of recalling. For the solid virtues of many Romans and Italians, working together as loyal, obedient partners within a tradition built up over many generations, had prevailed and won the day.

They won partly, as the historian Polybius says, because no comparable co-operation was to be found among the enemy's mercenaries who were exploited by their bosses much worse than the Romans exploited the Italians, and in consequence lacked the same incentives to loyalty. And another reason why the Romans and Italian soldiers won was because there were more of them. Moreover, their numbers were greatly increased because the property qualification formerly required before a man could become a legionary had been reduced, so that much poorer men could now be called up at public cost. These 'proletarians', as they were called (from *proles*, offspring, hitherto the only offering they had made to the state), were recruited between the ages of eighteen and forty-six, and served in the legions for an average of seven years, so that the old city-militia was turning into something like a professional army.

The men who had officered this new army gave close, hard attention to technical innovations in soldiering, of which Scipio Africanus was the principal author, first in Spain and then in north Africa. His achievements show the careful attention he paid to the tactics which Hannibal had displayed in Italy: and how he even improved on them. He also drilled his army in tactical methods, based on Rome's experience of small-unit hill-fighting during the Samnite Wars. The knack was to allow the three lines of the maniple (of which there were thirty in a legion) to act more or less on their own. Yet there were occasions when the independent action of these three lines, or even of the maniple itself, risked excessive dispersion, and so Scipio also experimented in Spain with a unit combining three maniples, the cohort, which provided greater cohesion, but at the same time still allowed greater flexibility than the larger legion itself. There were also improvements in the construction of the throwing javelin. But the legionaries were also armed with the heavy, excellently made, Spanish cutting swords, which became their most important weapon.

The career of Scipio, on whose initiative all this was done, revealed that the times when all Roman leaders were almost anonymous, brief-tenured representatives of a team, had begun to come to an end. Scipio was a new phenomenon. It was symbolical that he was the first of Rome's generals to be known by the name of the country he had defeated – Africanus. He was also the first to enjoy so long and close a relationship with his army, during the unprecedented ten years when he held high command at the Assembly's wish – at first without the formal qualifications hitherto required for such appointments. His final triumph raised him to the most powerful position any Roman general had ever possessed, pointing manifestly, as later historians noted, to the eventual emergence of other commanders who would use such powers to become autocrats. But Scipio himself did not do so; probably he never thought of doing so, for the time had not come for such thoughts.

Yet already there was something special and distinctive about him. He was a man and a general of rare imagination and initiative – which he employed in the skilful management of men. Sympathetic to the growing influx of Greek culture, he was not afraid to show an un-Roman love of splendour and display, which was deplored by senatorial opinion, but pleased ordinary people; on the coins of captured Carthago Nova his own portrait seems to appear, which was something that had never happened to a Roman before, though individual portrait busts in bronze and marble began to come into their own in this same third century BC. And Scipio possessed that mystical assurance of a direct, personal line to the gods which is always so formidable, and infuriating, a feature in a statesman or soldier. Such convictions made Scipio impatient of petty Roman restraints. Yet at the same time, he also had a keener sense of humour than most Romans. And in a war scarred by many atrocities, he was unusually kind to his defeated enemies. He was an unfamiliar sort of Roman, replacing traditional prudence by a novel individualism, a spirit of adventure.

His enemy Hannibal was a greater general even than his father Hamilcar, and greater even than Scipio, indeed one of the outstanding commanders of all time. That he placed beyond doubt, first, by his initial successes in Italy and the brilliant methods he used to win them, and then by the almost incredibly daring feat of maintaining himself in that hostile, populous country, so far from his home base, for no less than fifteen years. During this period there was ample detailed evidence of his almost unique excellence as a planner and fighter of battles. Employing the Greek device of joint enveloping movements by infantry and cavalry, and combining this with Spanish tactics of ambush and lightning attack, he set the stamp of his own personal genius on both these inheritances. And, above all, he was a leader of men so inspired that, throughout all those foreign years, he never experienced a mutiny. This was astonishing, since, as we have seen, his multi-racial, polyglot armies had little reason to feel allegiance to Carthage: they followed him for himself alone.

It is only as a strategist in the larger sense that the impertinence of hindsight makes it possible to criticize Hannibal. Lack of siege equipment was what caused his ultimate failure; and, even if he could not take this to Italy in the first place, it is hard to see why he could not somehow have secured it afterwards. Moreover, since he needed reinforcements from abroad so acutely, and the land route from Spain remained blocked to him for so many years, it is surprising that he did not challenge Roman naval supremacy by building a fleet; for, after all, the Carthaginian tradition was essentially maritime. But perhaps he was merely realistic in assuming that rivalry with the Romans at sea was now out of the question. And maybe, also, he could not persuade his government to construct a fleet for him, or underwrite him if he constructed it himself.

For, in the large sphere where military and political activities merge, this was one of the things that went wrong for him: he did not receive enough backing from the authorities at Carthage. Worst of all, they could not, or did not, send him sufficient reinforcements. It is possible that he miscalculated by supposing that they ever would. And he had made another miscalculation as well. For although his insight into the psychology of the Romans was often keen enough, he was proved mistaken in his belief that, when he had won battles, their allies and subjects would defect to him *en masse*. This may have been a deliberate gamble; and so may have been the assumption that such defections, when they occurred, would in the end persuade his government to give him fuller support. But if so, neither gamble came off.

Twenty-nine years old when he came to Italy, Hannibal was a wiry, athletic man, trained to run and box and endure hardship, possessed of an iron self-restraint. He was fanatical and superstitious like most of his countrymen. Yet all the same not only his talent, but the integrity of his personal character, caught the fancy of subsequent ages, despite virulent Roman propaganda to the contrary. His final confrontation with Scipio in battle, preceded, it was said, by that mysterious meeting, could not fail to stir people's imaginations for ever more. Yet for most of the war it was not only Scipio he had been fighting against but the corporate strength and endurance of all Rome and its allies. He is one of the world's most noble failures, an altogether exceptional man who took on, in deadly warfare, a nation empowered with rock-like resolution; and that nation proved too much for him. It emerged hardened from the supreme test, and ironically, his most lasting achievement was to confirm and magnify its confidence and power.

# IV

# THE IMPERIAL
# REPUBLIC

# 8

# 'Our Sea'

THE HAPPENINGS OF THE third century BC had brought Rome into forcible contact not only with the Carthaginians but also with the Greeks in southern Italy and Sicily; and the same period had inaugurated its relationships with the Greeks of Greece itself, with repercussions upon the whole future history of the Mediterranean, which within a remarkably short time became a Roman lake.

When Alexander the Great (d. 323 BC), king of the Macedonians who were the Greeks' northern neighbours, conquered gigantic territories far to the east, the ancient cities of the Greek homeland, already brought under Macedonian suzerainty by his father, had still retained their formal independent status, but for the most part faded into relative insignificance. Instead, the important Greek political units of the age now beginning, known as the Hellenistic age to distinguish it from the Hellenic world of the past, were three great monarchies carved out of Alexander's dominions after his death. These were the empires of the Antigonids in Macedonia, the Seleucids whose dominions extended from the Aegean to the Hindu Kush, and the Ptolemies who ruled Egypt and the lands and seas around it. Upon the peripheries of these vast kingdoms, however, there were other much smaller units. It was with these that Rome first came into collision – and first of all, with the states which were its nearest neighbours.

One of these was Epirus (north-western Greece), whose king Pyrrhus had unsuccessfully invaded Sicily and south Italy in 280–275 BC. The next trans-Adriatic state which the Romans encountered was the monarchy of the half-Hellenized Illyrians, who controlled the coast of what is now Dalmatia (Yugoslavia) and expanded southwards into Albania in about 260 BC. The Illyrians must have been alarmed by Rome's establishment in 246 of a Latin fortress-colony just across the strait at Brundusium (Brindisi), located on two arms of the sea penetrating deeply into the land, and possessing the finest harbour on the east coast of Italy. This was during the First Punic War, and the principal intention of the Romans was to close the

Adriatic to Carthaginian shipping. But the new foundation was likely to restrict the Illyrians as well; and sixteen years later, when Rome demanded satisfaction for their assaults on its envoys and the assassinations of Italian merchants, their queen-regent Teuta, a determined and practical ruler, rejected the request.

So the Romans sent troops and ships to bring her to order. The attack, their first direct dealing with a state across the Adriatic, put a stop to Teuta's plans for further expansion, and established a Roman protectorate over Greek towns and tribes on the east side of the strait, which had been grateful for this intervention. Then in 220–219 a Greek adventurer in the area, Demetrius of Pharos, tried to exploit, for his own advantage, the Romans' preoccupation with the coming Second Punic War. But he was expelled by their forces and had to flee from his country. Significantly for the future – for others too were often to make the same mistake – Demetrius had believed himself to be a free agent, whereas the Romans saw him as their client, on the analogy of the patron–client relationship which played such a large part in Roman society.

Demetrius fled to the king of Macedonia, Philip v, who received him (219). So now Rome, at the outset of Hannibal's invasion of Italy, was directly involved with one of the three major Greek powers, the nearest to Italy.

And Macedonia still possessed many of the resources which had led it to Alexander the Great's astonishing victories only a little more than a century earlier. For its territories and dependencies abounded in minerals, timber, grain and wine. Its peoples, too, were fierce and warlike, and could put a large army into the field – even if not as large as the potential strength of the Romans. Besides, Philip V, though impetuous in his political judgements, and capable of wanton atrocities, was a successful commander of troops who had raised his country to its greatest power since the time of Alexander: so that he was once again exercising control, directly or indirectly, over most of the southern regions of the Balkan peninsula.

Naturally enough, he regarded the expansion of the Romans, just across the narrows, with the gravest distrust, and these suspicions were confirmed by the experiences of Demetrius which had obliged him to take refuge at the Macedonian court. And then Philip decided that the Romans' crushing defeat by Carthage at Cannae had given him the opportunity to check them; so he concluded a treaty of mutual assistance with Hannibal (215). In fact neither of the two new allies gave any useful help to the other, Hannibal because he was without a fleet and Philip because, although he had one, it could not stand up against that of Rome. Moreover, Roman warships now proceeded to appear in the Adriatic, and landed men in Greece to foment desultory local hostilities against Macedonian allies and outposts. In 205, therefore, when the victory of the Romans in the Second Punic War was already a foregone conclusion, Philip decided he had better make peace with them for the time being after all. This disillusioned his Greek supporters, without, however, as was soon clear, closing his account with Rome. For one thing, the Romans picked up for themselves some of the allies who had become estranged from Philip, notably the Aetolian confederacy in central Greece. This was one of the leagues of city-states which had grown up in recent years as attempted counterpoises to the power of one or another of the large Greek kingdoms, in the present case its neighbour and natural enemy Macedonia; and by now the Aetolians were the dominant power in central Greece. This was the first formal alliance the Romans had ever entered into on Greek soil. It did not last for long, it is true, but long enough to give them a permanent footing in the country.

The worst problem of the three Greek empires, the Antigonids, Seleucids and Ptolemies, was the debilitating strife that so frequently bedevilled their mutual relations. Philip, still deeply distrustful of the Romans, clearly perceived the perils of these inter-Greek tensions, and therefore concluded a secret treaty with his Seleucid fellow ruler. Despite its lack of tight organization, the enormous Seleucid monarchy, which had introduced numerous Greek settlers into its Syrian capital Antioch and other cities, was potentially the most formidable of the three great states. Moreover, its current ruler, Antiochus III, had earned himself the title of 'the Great, because of the vast conquests by which he had pushed his frontier north-wards and eastwards in a desire to imitate Alexander, of whose speed and dash in warfare he had inherited a good measure.

In 203–202 Philip combined with Antiochus to make a joint attack upon the third major monarchy, Egypt of the Ptolemies, at that time ruled by a boy-king whose overseas dominions the other two kings now began to divide up between themselves. This Ptolemaic kingdom, governed from Alexander's foundation Alexandria, the greatest commercial port and cultural centre in the world, was run by an unparalleled, highly profitable system of centralized state control: and it presented a particularly tempting target to attackers, owing to its abundance of grain, gold, copper, iron and building stones and marbles, and its monopoly of the growth and export of papyrus.

But this sinister alliance between Macedonia and the Seleucids, designed to eliminate the power of Egypt, greatly disturbed the Greek cities, which were convinced that the next to suffer would be themselves. Particular alarm was felt by the two principal second-class powers of the time, which were Rhodes and Pergamum (Bergama). The island of Rhodes, just off Asia Minor's south-west coast, was an extremely prosperous mercantile republic with a large and efficient trading fleet. The Rhodians habitually steered their own course in foreign affairs, and were mainly concerned to preserve the freedom of the seas from aggressors and pirates, while remaining on good terms with everyone else. In this situation, since their island lay so close to the Asian continent from which the great powers could easily subject them to pressure, they liked the estrangement which normally existed between the Seleucids and Antigonids, and felt correspondingly threatened by Antiochus' alliance with Philip, whom they detested, in any case, because of his brutal enslavement of defeated populations. In consequence, they now turned to Rome, and sought to make it share their anxieties. Further persuasion was added by Pergamum, the civilized capital of another very prosperous second-category state, controlling much of western Asia Minor and deriving substantial wealth from its exploitation of natural resources. The royal house of Pergamum, the Attalids, had broken away from the Seleucid empire in the previous century and were justifiably afraid that it would one day try to take them back again. So their current monarch, Attalus I Soter, took the same line as the Rhodians, and joined them in urging Rome to force the Macedonians and Seleucids apart, while at the same time both Pergamum and Rhodes started military action against Philip. Their motives were understandable, yet the outcome of their appeals to Rome was to be the collapse of the entire international Greek system of which they formed so prominent a part.

It seems possible that until it heard the envoys from these states, the Roman Senate was not aware that Philip and Antiochus had entered into an understanding. At all events, the Pergamenes and Rhodians did not find it too hard to convince them that the agreement existed and was undesirable. For if two of the major Greek powers could make friends with one another in order to attack the third, then it seemed that having eliminated it, they might well feel inclined to combine again to attack Rome as well – to which one of these conspiring powers, Macedonia, had already shown hostility on an earlier occasion.

This nervous attitude was significant for the future, because it remained the characteristic motive of many of Rome's military moves from now onwards. These actions would often look like naked imperialism, and in a sense that is how they could be described. But they were caused by frightened and often mistaken Roman suspicions, directed afresh at one new foreign neighbour after another following each successive expansion of Rome's sphere of action and influence. Or rather, the suspicions were mainly felt by the upper classes, the Senate and nobility, and it was they who were in favour of fighting the war against Philip. The members of the Assembly, however, exhausted by the recently concluded eighteen-year-old-long Second Punic War, at first voted solidly against fighting a new foe. But the Senate's warlike policy prevailed, and an ultimatum was delivered to Macedonia.

It must have been a difficult document to frame, especially for the Romans who habitually tried to describe their wars as just: because Philip had done them no direct injury at all. What they demanded, therefore, was that he should indemnify Pergamum and Rhodes; and they insisted also that he should abstain in future from any hostilities against Greek states. This was a startling piece of interference, implying that Macedonia, one of the three great Greek empires, was, like Carthage, no longer entitled to have any foreign policy of its own: in other words that it was a client of the Romans, taken unilaterally under their supervision. There had been hints of this doctrine before, in their dealings with the Illyrians, but never before had it been applied to a major Greek power.

Philip rejected the demand as an impertinence; and so Rome's first important war on Greek soil was under way (200). It was a historic clash between the only military powers in Europe. The first two years' campaigns in Macedonia and Thessaly brought little substantial progress. But then it became clear that the Roman commander Flamininus, consul at the age of only twenty-nine, intended to eject the Macedonians from their three principal fortresses in Greece, and then drive them out of that country altogether, forcing them to retire to their own homeland.

But Philip decided not to await this attack, since he was aware that a war of attrition would show up his numerical inferiority. Instead, therefore, he himself proceeded to move to the offensive, and at the ridge of Cynoscephalae (Dog's Head, now Karadag, in eastern Thessaly) he forced a battle upon Flamininus. Philip's right wing charged successfully downhill, but was then engaged in the rear by the Romans and routed, and the Macedonian cause was lost. In this first direct conflict between two different military traditions, the new flexibility taught by Scipio Africanus had made the legions more than a match for the tightly packed and relatively immobile Greek phalanx. In its defeat, the future of the east Mediterranean world could be read without too much difficulty; although, in this particular battle, the Romans had had the better of the ground, so that the major issue of military principle might still, by Greek optimists, be regarded as open.

Nevertheless, the war was over. After his defeat, Philip was not obliterated by the Romans, because they felt they might need him as a bastion against the Seleucids. But he had to give up his fleet, and his fortresses, and accept total exclusion from Greece. Flamininus filled the vacuum by declaring, at the Isthmian Games in the great mercantile city of Corinth, that the Greek cities were henceforward to be free. This famous Act of Liberation, which could be compared with many similar declarations in the past by Greek monarchs, harmonized with the brilliant young general's respect for Greek culture, since, like Scipio Africanus whom he claimed to rival, he was that new type of Roman who felt an inclination to phil-Hellenism. But sentiment, in so far as it entered into the matter at all, coincided with interest, since the pronouncement was also based on that peculiarly Roman interpretation, of which we have already had other recent hints, of what 'freedom', as applied to such communities, really meant. The Greeks might like to interpret it as complete independence of action. But to the Romans, while it prompted their military evacuation of Greece and ensured its local communities the privileges of self-government, the term was only intended, once again, to mean freedom in the sense of the relationship which a 'free' client possesses with his patron. This was to be the cause of many misunderstandings. But it was clearly understood in 167 BC by King Prusias II of Bithynia in northern Asia Minor. For, as he entered the senate house at Rome, he fell on his face and cried 'Greetings, saviour gods!'

Meanwhile, however, the Declaration of Freedom roused the Greeks to such excitement that the birds, it was said, were stunned by the shout of jubilation that arose. This joy was not, however, universal, since Rome's former allies, the Aetolian League, felt none of it at all. Alone of the Greeks, they had given substantial assistance to Rome, and yet because of the general liberation they had only been allowed to annex an insignificant amount of territory as a reward. In their disappointment, they turned to Antiochus and invited him to bring a Seleucid army to Greece so as to drive out what they described as the new despotism of the Romans (193).

At this time Antiochus' relations with them were poor, since they had told him firmly to keep out of Europe. This was a repetition of the overbearing tactics they had employed in dealing with Philip, though it may have been softened, on this new occasion, by the hint or suggestion that, if he complied, they themselves, in compensation, would not set foot in Asia. Nevertheless, Antiochus ignored their demand, crossing over into European soil and seizing the Propontis (Gallipoli) peninsula in Thrace, which he claimed for himself as territory once owned by his ancestors and belonging to the Seleucids by right as the leading power of the east Mediterranean.

What is more, Rome's ancient enemy Hannibal was now at the Seleucid court. After the Second Punic War, he had led Carthage into an impressive revival; but the Carthaginians had become tired of his strong leadership, and Antiochus allowed him to reside in Seleucid territory. This caused deep suspicion among the Romans; and it was carefully fostered and intensified by the king of Pergamum, now Eumenes II, who deliberately poisoned their relationship with Antiochus just as his father, Attalus, had upset their relations with Philip. This time, in dealing with Antiochus, the Roman Senate did not want war. Yet, as negotiations dragged on, in an atmosphere of increasing tension, it was he who finally lost patience: and he decided to accept the Aetolian invitation. Whereupon in March 192, not content with the corner of Europe he had occupied already, he extended his invasion to Greece itself – although by doing so he made it inevitable that the Senate, for all its reluctance, would send armies to resist him. As it turned out, the Aetolian appeal was imprudent, and his response to it the height of unwisdom, since both provoked the Romans to further expansion. But he probably felt that they must be stopped now or never.

Despite his vast potential reserves of manpower, Antiochus' conduct of the war found him no match for them. Defeated heavily at the historic pass of Thermopylae (191), he was forced to evacuate Greece. Then, in the following year, the Romans defeated him again, this time at sea. This was their last notable naval victory over a foreign enemy in the course of their history; and its immediate result was that it enabled them to land troops in Asia, which they had never done before. And so came Antiochus' final confrontation with the Romans, a land battle at Magnesia (Manisa) in western Asia Minor (190 BC). Scipio Africanus' brother was the nominal Roman commander, but Africanus was there too as his adviser: he had remained politically powerful, and believed strongly that the Greeks should be protected against Antiochus. On the day of the battle, however, Africanus was ill, and the most heroic part was played by Eumenes of Pergamum. For on the left flank of the enormous army of Antiochus it was he who broke the heavy armoured Persian horsemen; and then the Seleucid elephants, stampeded by javelins, charged backwards through their own central phalanx, and the Romans had won an overwhelming victory.

Rhodes and especially Pergamum were its chief beneficiaries while the Aetolian confederacy, which had invited and helped the defeated monarch, was forced to accept a treaty involving the loss of its independence. As for Antiochus, he had to pay the largest indemnity ever demanded by the Romans; and they expelled him from Asia Minor altogether. This, then, was one of the most decisive wars of ancient times, because the Seleucid monarchy, though remaining a continental power in the Middle East, ceased for ever to be a Mediterranean state – leaving the vacuum to be filled by Rome.

Within only a very short time, therefore, the two most powerful Greek kingdoms had been separately engaged and invaded by the Romans, suffering extremely heavy reverses. Nevertheless, the setback experienced by Philip v of Macedonia nine years earlier had not proved fatal or final after all. For in the war that had just been concluded he had fought against Antiochus' Aetolian associates as an ally of Rome, which consequently allowed him to maintain and even partially improve his position.

But then in 179 BC Philip died and was succeeded by his 35-year-old son Perseus. He renewed his father's treaty with the Romans, whom he had no desire to offend. But, at the same time, he took numerous steps to strengthen Macedonia's influence among all its neighbours. Moreover, at a time when Greece was plunged into an economic emergency, he showed sympathy to its many bankrupts, declaring an amnesty for debtors. This could be magnified by the ill-intentioned into an act designed to promote social revolution and undermine the Roman arrangements in Greece. Foremost among those who spread this hostile view abroad was Eumenes II of Pergamum, who, not content with his earlier criticisms of Antiochus, still carried on his father's feud against the Macedonians as well. Indeed in 172 he visited Rome in person, in order to denounce Perseus before the Senate. His denunciation was successful, and in the following year, the Romans drifted once again into war against Macedonia. The feeble pretext was that Perseus had attacked some border chiefs who possessed ties of friendship with Rome. But the real reason was the anxious fear, among its authorities, that he might make a move to disrupt their entire settlement and policy in Greek lands.

As in the previous Macedonian war, the first campaigns were irresolute and inconclusive: Perseus, though vigorous enough in the field, was too indecisive to take his chances, and the Romans, as often, were slow to get going. But by the fourth year of hostilities, the king had finally been obliged to withdraw from his frontier lines, so that the consul Paullus was able to establish himself on the Macedonian plain itself, where he forced the enemy to give battle at Pydna. At first, the assault of Perseus' weighty phalanx of 20,000 men drove the Roman legionaries back. But, as the phalanx charged, gaps opened in its line and into these gaps small Roman units insinuated themselves, while others simultaneously enveloped the Macedonian flanks, where their slashing swords inflicted catastrophic losses on the opposing spearmen. The inferiority of the phalanx to the legions had now been demonstrated even more conclusively than before; and the Macedonian army had ceased to exist.

Perseus surrendered and went on show in Paullus' triumph, and his officials were deported wholesale from the country. Moreover, his monarchy itself was abolished, and the country was divided into four separate republics. This decision, overriding Macedonian nationhood in the roughest and most sweeping fashion, was momentous, for it was the first time that one of the three great successor states of Alexander had succumbed to total destruction at Rome's hands. The recent shift in the relative strength of Romans and Greeks had been displayed with grim directness. Moreover, the new Macedonian republics found themselves bound by an ominous new principle that the 'freedom' which they still possessed did not necessarily mean immunity from taxes. Nevertheless, the financial conditions imposed on them were not excessively severe: and at least the Romans had still refrained from straightforward annexations. For they were not yet willing to apply to the east the provincial system they had inaugurated in western lands. They lacked the administrative machinery needed to impose such a step, and dreaded the responsibility it would involve, still preferring for the time being to act as patrons to client states which remained technically free.

Nevertheless, this was an ominous landmark. Within the space of a single generation the Greek world, hitherto dependent on the balance of power between three large empires, had been irremediably transformed and ruined by the utter defeat of two of those states, one of which had been obliterated: and their place was filled by the Romans, who had entered the lands surrounding the Aegean and were there to stay. Furthermore, another significant move was to follow. For immediately after Pydna, a Roman envoy ordered Antiochus III's successor Antiochus IV Epiphanes, who had captured Alexandria, the capital of Ptolemaic Egypt, to evacuate the city, thus displaying that Rome's conception of its intimate interests now extended to this third major successor state of Alexander as well.

Moreover, owing to the irritable suspiciousness of Rome's leaders there were further tough results of the Macedonian war. For Eumenes II of Pergamum, though he had at first been in favour of Rome's hostilities against Perseus, was later suspected by its leaders of having secretly engaged in negotiations with him, a charge that was probably without foundation, but the suspicion was there all the same. And Rhodes, too, worried about the effect of the war on its maritime trade, had certainly had the effrontery, as the Romans saw it, to offer its services to both parties as mediator, in the hope of restoring peace. After the fighting was over, both Pergamum and

Rhodes felt the Senate's displeasure. As for Pergamum, the Romans started to undermine Eumenes' position in favour of his brother; though they did not persist in this. But Rhodes suffered much more disastrously, since Rome proceeded to convert another island, Delos, into a rival free port, whose rapid rise to commercial supremacy almost completely ruined the trade of the Rhodians. Nor were they any longer in a position to police the seas against pirates – to the eventual great discomfort of Rome itself, which had brought about this result.

Such was the treatment handed out to two loyal, long-standing allies which had momentarily ventured to differ from the Romans about policy. And at the same time others, who had actively supported Macedonia, were penalized by even harsher measures by Rome, which perpetrated enslavements in Epirus and massacres in the Aetolian League, while its Achaean counterpart in the Peloponnese, which had likewise incurred Roman displeasure, had to hand over a thousand detainees who were taken to Italy, including the historian Polybius. All in all, during the first half of the second century BC and particularly as a result of these depredations, Greece lost a quarter of all its inhabitants.

In the years that followed, the attention of the Romans was largely focused on a country at the other end of the Mediterranean, namely Spain. This was, however, nothing new. In the very year in which additional praetors were created to govern the two newly annexed provinces (197), revolts had broken out in each of them, to the south and east of the country, the rebels in both cases receiving assistance from the warlike, well-armed Celtiberians who lived on hilltops in the north-eastern hinterland. Two years later the consul Cato, of whom more will be said later, was sent out to assume the supreme command in Spain; and after extensive operations he succeeded in opening up new lines of communications between the two provincial territories. Yet the Celtiberians still remained defiant; and they were joined by the Lusitanians of Portugal and western Spain. Open hostilities continued at frequent intervals until the father of the famous Gracchi pacified the territory of Celtiberians in 179, by fighting combined, as was unusual at this time, with friendly approaches designed to win the inhabitants' confidence. For the next quarter of a century his settlement held.

But in this 'Wild West' of the empire which invited unscrupulous exploitation, Rome's government was heavy-handed, and in 154–153 both major groups of tribes broke out into rebellion once more; and it was exacerbated by a whole series of murderous breaches of faith by Roman governors over the following years. Moreover, before long a particularly grave situation arose, because the Lusitanians found a guerrilla leader of genius. This man, a shepherd named Viriathus, for the first time mobilized all their tribes into an effective coalition. Next, by the use of small armed bands skilled in making sudden raids and then vanishing, he began to gain repeated victories against the Romans, penetrating their provinces time after time over a period of five years. Yet he failed to achieve the peace terms he wanted, and finally, as a result of two further acts of perfidy by a Roman general, he came to a violent end (140).

Meanwhile, however, the Celtiberians had once again joined the insurgents. Their main base was the hill-fortress of Numantia, the key to the upper Douro region, at the junction of two rivers running between deeply cut banks through heavily forested valleys. From Numantia they withstood Roman attackers for nearly a whole decade. Finally, after a historic eight-month siege, they were starved out by a force of 60,000 Roman soldiers under the command of Scipio Aemilianus, Africanus' adoptive grandson (133). Eighty-five years of fighting in Spain were over at last, and the frontier was pushed up to the high tablelands of central Spain and the line of the middle Douro. The Romans had always been interested in the country as a recruiting ground for excellent auxiliary soldiers, and now this much larger territory was available for the purpose. But the Spanish campaigns which at long last achieved that end had been mainly notable for two disastrous features. One was the unusual military incapacity displayed by Rome, which gave its leaders cause for anxious thought. The other was the horrifying manner in which their commanders, one after another, had gone back on their sworn agreements with the Spaniards, a procedure that even the most xenophobic senators found it impossible to condone.

One reason for Viriathus' early successes had been his successful exploitation of simultaneous Roman crises in the Balkans and north Africa in the 140s BC.

After the last war against the Macedonians, the division of their kingdom into four autonomous but obedient republics had successfully ensured that they would be too weak to do Rome any further harm. But it had also made it certain that they would be too weak to protect themselves; and so it turned out. For in 150 BC a certain Andriscus announced, fraudulently, that he was the son of the late King Perseus, and then, meeting only feeble resistance from the republican militias, he successfully reunited Macedonia and revived the kingship in his own person. The Romans had to intervene to expel him and run him down (148).

And at this point they determined upon a major revision of policy. For since their previous device of partitioning Macedonia into dependent republics had broken down, the whole concept of encouraging Greek communities to become their 'free' but dependent clients – the policy they had been following since the beginning of the century – now seemed ripe for abandonment: and it was decided that the principle of direct annexation, which had provided four provinces in the west, must be imported to these ancient eastern regions as well. It had already caused widespread horror when one of the great Greek monarchies, Macedonia, was destroyed in 167: and now there was a further shock, when the republics into which that country had been divided were directly annexed by Rome. Within this new province a major road was constructed, the Via Egnatia, following an ancient route all the way from the Adriatic to the northern Aegean. This was the first important Roman road in the east. It linked the Macedonian cities to one another and to Italy, and formed part of the defence system of this new Roman possession against barbarian incursions from the north.

On Macedonia's southern flank, in Greece itself, the Romans belatedly sent back to the Achaean League in 150 BC, the 300 survivors of the thousand hostages they had deported seventeen years earlier. Not long afterwards, however, they infuriated the members of the League once again, by allowing the city-state of Sparta, which the Achaeans had earlier compelled to join their confederation, to terminate its membership. This led to violent anti-Spartan and anti-Roman feeling at the League capital, Corinth, a large industrial harbour and key fortress; and when Roman envoys came to the city they were beaten up. However, Achaean hopes that the Romans were too heavily committed elsewhere to be able to retaliate proved misplaced, since the Roman consul Mummius came down from Macedonia with four legions and captured Corinth (146 BC).

By order from his government, the whole place was razed to the ground and all its surviving inhabitants were sold into slavery, while its abundant artistic treasures were shipped off to Rome. This drastic treatment of the city was partly intended as an insurance against social revolution, since the Romans preferred Greek towns to be governed by oligarchies like their own, a preference to which Corinth, dominated by a turbulent proletariat, had failed to conform. But the Romans' brutality was also a demonstration that they would not allow quarrelling Greeks to mishandle their envoys and flout their will. Yet, however much Greece had fallen from its high estate, it was a terrible sign of the new times that one of the most ancient and distinguished centres of Greek and Mediterranean civilization should be blotted out of existence in this way.

The Achaean League, too, was abolished, and Greece and its cities, after the installation of suitable local régimes, were amalgamated with the new province of Macedonia, and made to pay tribute. The long centuries of Greek independence had been brought to an abrupt and violent end.

And in the very same year the independence of the Carthaginian state, too, was likewise terminated by the Romans, and its ancient capital suffered the same fate as Corinth.

Rome's defeat of the Carthaginians fifty-five years earlier, while eliminating their international power, had not prevented them, initially under the guidance of Hannibal, from making a remarkable recovery; they had won back a considerable part of their trade, and had employed improved agricultural methods to increase the profits from their African territories. But the fatal impediment to this revival proved to be Masinissa, the violent, ambitious ruler of neighbouring Numidia, who held his throne as a client of Rome. For throughout half a century, following the Second Punic War, Masinissa, in building up his empire, encroached unscrupulously on Carthage's coastal colonies and wheat-lands, while at the same time ensuring that Rome failed to arbitrate with any effectiveness to stop him. Finally in 150 BC the Carthaginians, driven to desperation, took up arms against him, although their treaty with the Romans had forbidden them to engage in independent warfare. And when Masinissa appealed to Rome, the aged Cato insisted repeatedly to his fellow senators that Carthage must be destroyed. Even if its government's resistance to Masinissa's provocation had technically amounted to an infringement of the treaty, Cato's attitude displayed an irrational vindictiveness and jealous fear, based on senile reminiscences of his own soldiering against Hannibal. But so harrowing were the memories of that dreaded name that the Senate, in spite of strong opposition, gave in to him and war was declared.

The Carthaginians, in this hopeless situation, asked for peace. But as Rome repeatedly raised its price, they instead chose to offer a desperate resistance, which continued for four years. It was terminated in 146 by Scipio Aemilianus,* who, after receiving a special appointment from the Assembly in advance of the statutory age, brought the siege of Carthage itself to a successful, bloody conclusion. Its survivors were sold into slavery; the whole city was demolished, and salt scattered on the site so that it should remain barren and accursed for evermore. This was a measure of the traumatic effect Hannibal had exercised on the minds of the Romans.

All that remained now was to decide what to do with the African territory that had fallen into their hands. Masinissa had died, and they did not want to give these lands to his sons. And so instead, as in Macedonia and Greece, they decided on a policy of annexation. Thus while a number of its cities were allowed to retain nominal independence as Roman clients, the Carthaginian homeland as a whole was converted into the province of Africa, corresponding with the northern part of Tunisia today. The new province possessed immense economic and agricultural wealth. True, it was for psychological rather than economic reasons that this third Carthaginian war had been launched. Yet the African territory won as a result was so overwhelmingly rich in grain that it gradually succeeded Sicily as the principal granary of Rome.

This ruthless obliteration of Carthage, perpetrated in the very same year

* For his later successes in Spain, see p. 123.

as the destruction of Corinth, sent a shudder throughout the civilized Mediterranean world. Roman imperialism could now be seen by all, in its nakedly unconcealed and cynical form. It was a policy which went by the name of the 'New Wisdom'. And, for all its moral defects, its growing employment had achieved astonishing practical results, for within the space of a few years the Romans had become dominant in almost the whole of the Mediterranean: it was indeed *Mare Nostrum*, Our Sea.

# 9

# The New Society

THE FOREIGN POLICY OF these decisive first decades after 200 BC, when
ferocity and authoritarianism were on the increase all the time, was still
directed, except on very few occasions, by the Roman Senate and nobility,
that is to say by those men, patricians and plebeians alike, who numbered
consuls among their ancestors.

In the latter part of the previous century, during the Second Punic War,
the Assembly had on certain rare occasions asserted itself against the
Senate, most conspicuously by insisting upon the appointment of Scipio
Africanus, in which the senators prudently decided to concur. But on
the whole, the first two Carthaginian conflicts had greatly strengthened
the oligarchy's control of affairs. Shortly before these wars had started, the
embryonic Roman social revolution had petered out, when the tribunes of
the people became agents of the nobility instead. And then later on, too,
after Hannibal had been defeated, there was a widespread feeling that it was
this nobility, operating through the Senate, which deserved the credit for
eliminating the gravest danger Rome had ever undergone, and gaining for
it, in the process, extensive and prosperous new territories overseas. Once
won, these provinces came completely under the control of the Senate,
which according to a practice that now became normal appointed as their
governors men who had just served as consul or praetor at Rome, a procedure known as *prorogatio*. But this senatorial grip on the new provinces
was only part of a general phenomenon, for as the third century passed into
the second, despite occasional interventions by the Assembly, the Senate's
control of all Roman policy remained as firm and thoroughgoing as ever
before.

This is confirmed by the statistics of elections to the offices of state: 'new
men', without consular ancestry, remained extremely rare, and government
was virtually run by a close, club-like circle of about 2,000 men, belonging
to less than twenty clans. Philip V of Macedonia expressed his envious
amazement at the friendly solidarity among these nobles and senators.

True, the career and character of Scipio Africanus had introduced strains into the amicable atmosphere, suggesting that it might not last for ever. But so far no substantial deterioration was to be seen.

Indeed, the family of the Scipios themselves was still a living illustration of the system's narrow base. For in less than a hundred years the members of this single family alone gained no less than twenty-three consulships for themselves. And their surviving epitaphs place overwhelming emphasis, not only on public office and military success, but on genealogical descent as well. These great aristocratic houses kept in their cupboards the wax masks of their ancestors who had held high office. The masks were arranged as a family tree, and received religious worship; in family funerals, they were worn by actors engaged to walk in the procession. At such funerals, there were speeches in praise of the dead man and his ancestors, and they have provided us, directly or through intermediaries, with much historical information, highly tendentious although it often is.

Tradition, therefore, remained all-important in Roman education, as Cicero was never tired of emphasizing. And tradition implied reverence not only for people of bygone times but for seniority in the living; so the principle of seniority duly prevailed. For although men could and did hold office fairly young – a praetor at about forty and a consul two or three years later – ex-consuls spoke first in any debate in the Senate, and their experience, which after the wars of the third and second centuries was likely to·be considerable, earned deeper respect than ever before.


So, guided by these men, the Senate reinforced its influence, and in the absence of any effective counterblast retained a position of virtually irresponsible supremacy, becoming even more exclusive and conservative in the process. And this, as we have seen, displayed itself in an ever tougher foreign policy, based on suspicious, ungenerous and often unfounded anxieties. Meanwhile, even if the Assembly might occasionally make itself felt, the vast majority of the people, as usual, were content to leave politics to the politicians.

Yet the nobles remained very vigilant against possible unrest, as a curious religious crisis now revealed. During the emergencies of the Punic Wars the Senate had several times provided an outlet for popular hysteria by the importation of exciting eastern cults more likely than the dry Roman ritual to distract the public from its hardships; once introduced, the new cults could be toned down and domesticated. But then in 186 BC stringent measures were taken to control the emotional, mystic worship of Bacchus (Dionysus). His rites, the Bacchanalia, made known by Roman soldiers returning from the east, had spread extensively throughout Italy, and were especially common in the south of the peninsula. Conducted by conventicles or secret societies, these rituals were believed to be the focus-point not only of sexual immorality but of crime and public disorder. However, the worship had become so deeply rooted that the government saw no possibility of stamping its practice out. Instead, therefore, they ordered that not more than five persons should be allowed to celebrate the Bacchic cult together, and only then after obtaining the Senate's permission.

The nobility, well aware of the importance of religion to its over-all control, at all times meticulously directed and exploited this vital area of social behaviour; and one way in which they chose to do so was by declaring undesirable religious practices, like the Bacchanalia, to be politically conspiratorial and subversive. Such an attitude, however, was ominous for the future, since it produced arbitrary reinterpretations of the law. And what also seemed alarming was the unprecedented scope of the police action by which they enforced these restrictions upon the Bacchic ceremonies throughout allied as well as Roman territory.

In the literary field, too, the nobles and Senate became sensitive about suspected attempts to undermine their supremacy. One of those who suffered was the versatile poet Naevius (*c.* 270–201 BC), a Roman citizen from near Capua. Naevius wrote patriotic works, of which only fragments survive today; they included original tragic dramas about Roman history and legend, and a pioneer epic dealing with the First Punic War, in which he himself had served. But in about 204 BC he committed some fault for which he was imprisoned and went into exile. Perhaps one reason was that the oligarchy still remembered the offence he had caused over thirty years earlier, when he criticized one of the greatest plebeian noble families, the Caecilii Metelli.

Naevius' native ebullience also led him to write comic plays. But here he was outshone by Plautus (*c.* 254–184 BC). With Plautus, who came from backward Sarsina (Mercato Saraceno) in Umbria, we have already reached the precocious zenith of Latin verse comedy: and twenty of his complete plays (with one incomplete) have survived. His models, like those of his few Latin forerunners, were the sophisticated products of the Greek New Comedy of fourth-century BC Athens, familiar to many educated Romans now that contacts with Greek south Italy and Sicily had multiplied. Yet Plautus rewrote these plays and made them almost unrecognizable in the process. For not only was he able, by an astonishing *tour de force*, to weld the still gracelessly cumbrous Latin tongue into the metres of the totally different Greek language, but he wholly abandoned the subtlety of the original Greek comedies in order to give free rein to his own explosive genius for wild, quick-firing, slapstick buffoonery. His success, in the centuries to come, was enormous. And even during his lifetime, although his audiences comprised people at a wide variety of cultural levels, they were prepared to abandon the rival attractions of boxers, dancers, and chariot-races in order to come and laugh at what they heard and saw on Plautus' temporarily erected stages.

Moreover, his plays are filled, for all their farcicality, with oblique but telling social criticism. It takes the form of an exuberant inversion of traditional moral standards: a carnivalesque upturning of reverence for parents, and matrimonial respectability, and conventional depreciation of women and clients – and especially slaves, to whom he gave much larger roles than they had enjoyed in the Greek New Comedy. Yet Plautus, unlike Naevius, escaped upper-class retaliation. For he was careful to claim that his characters and their backgrounds were not Roman but foreign and Greek; so that, superficially at least, it was not Roman institutions at all which were coming under fire.

About fifteen years younger than Plautus was another poet, Ennius (239–169 BC), who like him avoided getting into any trouble with the rulers of Rome – though he not only wrote moralizing 'satire', but ventured to rationalize the traditional mythology and even Jupiter himself, the national god of the Roman state. Born at Rudiae (near Lecce in south-east Italy), a place where Greek and Latin and Italian cultures converged and endowed him, as he said, with three hearts, Ennius served as a soldier in Sardinia at the end of the Second Punic War, and then on the staff of the Aetolian campaign of 189, subsequently gaining the reward of Roman citizenship. A poor man, who enjoyed social life, he was said to have died of gout; but 'unless I have gout', he had remarked, 'I never write poetry'. More indus-trious, however, than this saying implied, and warm-hearted and enthusias-tic as well, he was the first professional literary man Rome ever possessed, and the first to naturalize Greek literary culture.

This was achieved, above all, by his rough, vigorous, colourful *Annals*, an epic poem following the tradition established by Naevius, in which, momentously adapting the Greek heroic metre – the hexameters of the Homeric poems – he chronicled the entire course of Roman history up to his own day. Only a few hundred lines now survive; but they reveal how he gave distinctive expression to the proud, virile energy and sagacious good sense of the imperial Republic of Rome at its best. His compatriots of later generations saw him as the father of Latin poetry and he exercised a profound effect on subsequent historians and literary critics as well.

Ennius had been brought back to Rome from Sardinia in 204 BC by Cato the elder (234–149 BC), who was born at about the same time as the elder Scipio (Africanus), and although a 'new man' without consuls among his ancestors, was bracketed with him as one of the outstanding politicians of his time. But they were also embittered rivals, for the comparative harmony which had hitherto prevailed among senators was coming to an end. There had always been, along with the harmony, struggles for office and prestige, in which each great man's claims were vigorously furthered by his clients, but when such diverse personalities as Cato and Scipio were involved this competitiveness was sharply intensified.

For Cato, taking his stand on antique tradition and rallying the support of many conservative landowners of the day, profoundly objected to the excessive personal reverence accorded to Scipio, whom he regarded as a careerist. Cato also deplored his interest in Greek affairs and debilitating Greek culture (exemplified by his adoption of the Greek practice of close shaving). For, ever since the Greco-Roman contacts of the Second Punic War and increasingly after it had ended, he saw this Hellenism as an evil influence pervading every corner of Roman life: it seemed to Cato outrageous when Scipio's brother brought back from the war against Antiochus the first bronze couches, bedcovers, ornate tables, fine cooking, and cabaret girls ever to be seen in Rome. And Cato had his way, for not long afterwards, in 184, he drove both the Scipios out of public life into retirement; and Africanus died soon afterwards.

Cato's election to the censorship of 184 seemed a remarkable achievement for a 'new man', and earned him the name of Cato the Censor ever afterwards; it also brought the term 'censorious' into our language. The office enabled him to intensify his attacks on Hellenism – and he disguised his own versatile knowledge by inflicting a deliberate pose of boorish ill-manners on his increasingly cultivated fellow senators. As censor he introduced numerous measures of moral and economic reconstruction and purification. Among them was the imposition of new taxes on the extravagance he so greatly deplored. They were designed to ensnare his personal enemies but also, in more general terms, were based on a belief, revived at intervals for hundreds of years to come, that sumptuary legislation of this kind could prove effective.

Cato was also opposed to current tendencies towards the emancipation of women, complaining that wives tyrannized their husbands. Since the previous century a much freer form of marriage had become habitual; and the influx of wealth meant that women began to dress and adorn themselves more luxuriously. Moreover, in certain important families, casualties during the wars had wiped out the male line, so that estates came under female control. This brought heavy frowns to the faces of traditionalists, and in 169 a tribune, strongly supported by Cato, carried a bill insisting on the ancient limitation of women's right to inherit. But the law was easily evaded by nominal transfers of property to collusive trustees; and the 'guardians' through whom women (except Vestal Virgins) were still legally obliged to conduct public business frequently co-operated with their wards, so that unattached women were, in fact, able to control their own affairs.

They were also permitted to attend public entertainments, and, in the more prosperous households at least, they were taught not only the traditional household skills but more academic subjects too. Thus Cornelia, the daughter of Scipio Africanus, not only managed her own estates but presided over a sort of intellectual salon. And women of her rank now played a vital part in political life as well, because their marriages formed the links in the chains uniting the various groups of political allies; and the important meetings between one politician and another took place in their houses.

Cato's disapproval of Cornelia's father Scipio Africanus was only equalled by his distaste for enlightened women like herself. Indeed, his whole way of life was based on the single aim of protecting the traditional social values from further contamination. He himself, although he came from farming stock at Tusculum in Latium, had been brought up in the country of the Sabines, to whose traditional harsh discipline and austerity he ascribed what seemed to him the best features in the character of himself and all Romans, including, above all, their courageous endurance and loyal service to the state. Yet this litigious and vindictive red-headed farmer with the piercing grey eyes was also the epitome of puritanical reaction. But his obsessions were in vain, for although he may have done something, for a time, to re-establish moral responsibility and postpone the lowering of standards, his political programme could not, in the long run, succeed.

Apart from a work on agriculture, very little of what he wrote has survived. Yet his status as a writer is enormous and secure. The gravest loss is his seven-book *Origins*, a history of Rome. Written in Latin, not Greek like all its predecessors, it was the first major achievement in this field, and virtually inaugurated Latin prose as a literary medium. Yet, despite Cato's distaste for the growing intrusion of Greek education – read a bit of Greek literature, he taught his son, but beware that perverse and corrupting race! – he was prepared to supplement his native Italian trenchancy by certain Greek stylistic features and methods of arrangement: which was scarcely surprising after his patronage of the phil-Hellene Ennius.

Nevertheless, Cato always insisted that the Romans were basically different from the Greeks: in contrast to Greek states, he pointed out, Rome owed its national successes not to a few individuals but to the combined genius of a host of different people living and working together with one another. So great was his distaste for the Scipio-type personality cult that in his *Origins*, he actually suppressed the names of great Roman commanders altogether, preferring instead, when describing the Second Punic War, to mention the name of a Carthaginian elephant, Surus. And he correctly identified a very real fault of Roman historiography when he blamed writers for glorifying their own families.

History was closely linked with the government of the Republic: and so was public speaking, at which Cato likewise excelled, exploiting his quick and biting wit to survive no less than fifty political prosecutions. This art was the mainspring of Roman public life and education, and, as in his historical authorship, Cato was not entirely immune from Greek influence, in this case the rhetorical 'art of persuasion' and the technicalities which it imparted. These influences combined with the urgent practical exigencies of speaking in the Assembly, Senate and lawcourts to create that most formidable of instruments, Latin oratory, of which Cato was a pioneer exponent.

As orator, statesman, and defender of austere but narrow morality, Cato remained greatly to the fore throughout these years. His foreign policies were predictably narrow, and under the guise of sagacious common sense he sponsored many of the aggressively chauvinistic measures of the epoch, notably the move to obliterate Carthage. At an earlier date, it is true, an equally vindictive proposal to declare war on Rhodes had not met with his approval.* Yet this, we may be sure, was not because of any sympathy with the island's Greek inhabitants, but because (in contrast to his late enemy Scipio Africanus) he was opposed to further eastern interventions, with all the insidious influences they brought in their wake.

In the campaign against Macedonia which had led to the disgrace of the lukewarm Rhodians, one of the youngest Roman officers was Africanus' grandson by adoption, Scipio Aemilianus (185/4–129 BC). He indulged even more than Africanus in the new Roman taste for Renaissance-style individualism which Cato so greatly deplored. And time after time, in the years to come, it was to Scipio Aemilianus that the Romans turned in a crisis. It was he, in Cato's old age, who won the Third Punic War (146), and then it was he again who finally defeated the Spaniards (133); and for nearly twenty years of Rome's history, although never unchallenged, he remained its key personality and outstanding statesman. He was a man of numerous contradictions, reputedly idle when young yet formidably active in later years. As a speaker he was excellent, as he had to be; and, although not a brilliant general like Africanus, he was an organizer with plenty of drive. Moreover, despite an ironical wit which was inclined to cause offence, he lavished on his friends and on the general public, when he wanted to impress them, a great deal of personal charm. But what was most important about him was his deserved reputation for decent behaviour: he was regarded as a person of integrity, in an age which needed this and knew it.

Yet the career of Scipio Aemilianus, though advancing ambitiously from one honour to another, remained curiously negative all the same. For the troubles of his age, the troubles of a city-state which had become within a short space of time the capital of a vast empire, he had no creative solutions to offer. It seems a missed opportunity that this most brilliant man of his

* Cato had also deprecated the repeated cheating of the Spaniards by Roman commanders, p. 122.

# The family of the Scipios

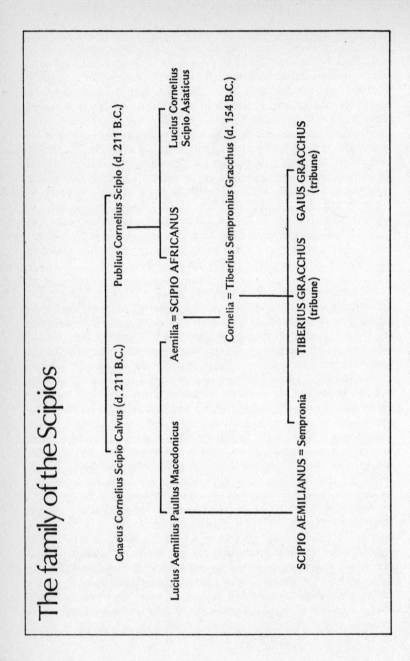

age did not supply some of the reforms which he alone might have succeeded in introducing. Yet this negativeness also had its good side; for it
meant that he never attempted to break out of the Republican system in
order to dominate it himself – as, once again, he probably could have if he
had tried, and as other men did after him. True, his rabble-rousing exploita-
tions of popular appeal, in defiance of the Senate, were a sinister example to
those who came after – and a strain upon the constitution. Yet, like Africanus before him, he was still content to work inside the framework.

An intellectual sympathetic to Hellenism, Scipio Aemilianus had been
educated by a variety of Greek tutors, and was deeply interested in Greek
literature and philosophy: and indeed although there may not quite have
been the 'Scipionic circle' of which Cicero later spoke, men who were in
touch with him played a large role in the partially Hellenized Roman culture of the time. They included not only Greek men of letters, whose
philosophy sometimes implied an idealistic justification for the emerging
Roman commonwealth, but a distinguished Latin dramatic poet, the short-
lived Terence (*c.* 190–159 BC), one of Plautus' successors on the comic
stage. As his last name 'Afer' indicates, Terence came from northern
Africa. He became the slave of a Roman senator, who set him free; and he
gained the friendship of Scipio Aemilianus, who was even rumoured,
probably wrongly, to be part-author of his plays. All six of these survive.
They display a constructional skill which left a strong imprint on the future
theatre of Europe. Their writer is seen to be not only gentler and more
contemplative than Plautus, but also closer to his Greek models and therefore farther away from popular taste. Terence depicts his realistic, amoral,
young heroes with a fashionable philosophical humaneness beneath which
runs an undercurrent of social criticism, more unobtrusive than the running
commentary of Plautus but persistent all the same.

This same note recurs in Lucilius of Suessa Aurunca (Sessa) in Campania (*c.* 180–102), another of Scipio Aemilianus' protégés, who served in
his cavalry in Spain. Lucilius turned his exceptional gifts into the channel
of satire, of which, in its modern sense, he was virtually the founder.
Ennius had written moralizing verses of a mildly satirical kind, but it was
Lucilius, as the 1,300 somewhat rough, crude lines surviving from his
thirty books reveal, who brought his varied and salty mockery to bear upon
contemporary life and letters. A rich and well-connected man, he was no
friend of those who fell from the social standards he upheld. Yet his acute,
incisive mind and irreverent, exuberant humour cut sharply through the
shams and futilities he detected in the contemporary scene. He sensed the
wind of change, and even if he did not like it altogether it found him better
prepared than most, and he lived on until the time when it had gained a
fuller strength.

·    ·    ·    ·    ·    ·

During these years, an ever-increasing stream of coin and bullion flowed into the Roman treasury from countries overseas. In the year after the brother of Scipio Africanus brought back his immense booty from Asia Minor, the Galatians in the centre of that peninsula once again yielded enormous loot (179). Then, in 168, the three-day triumphal procession of the victor of Pydna, Paullus, included 250 waggons of spoils and 300 crowns made of gold. It was a metal which, for the first time, was becoming familiar in Rome, in this form of massive indemnities paid by its defeated foes. And a very large proportion of these new riches found its way into the hands of the senatorial nobility.

The gulf between rich and poor was becoming enormous: and in order to do a little to counteract this trend, the Senate, after Pydna, decided to make an impressive public gesture. Until now, all Roman citizens had been liable to pay the state a direct property tax or *tributum,* which had been levied frequently in emergencies and with particular severity during the Punic Wars. But the Roman public, although prepared to pay indirect taxes (which were not very large), did not consider direct taxation a regular or reasonable part of their obligations as citizens: they would have agreed with Cicero that 'it is a statesman's duty not to impose a property tax upon the people' – that is to say, not to impose it upon Roman citizens, for the corollary was that all necessary direct taxation should be extracted from Rome's subjects in the provinces. When, therefore, the Galatian loot was brought back, the Senate repaid to individual Romans a substantial part or even the whole of the tribute that had been levied on them or their families in the Second Punic War. And then, in 167, the plunder seized after Pydna enabled this form of taxation to be abolished altogether, and it was not reimposed for more than a century to come. This was a popular measure which must have done at least something to lessen discontents arising from the increasing disparities of wealth.

Rome already exceeded all the other cities of the western world in size, and, as this influx of foreign wealth continued, its buildings began to assume a monumental appearance. Greek influence was manifest in a new taste for free-standing porticoes, and for the basilicas or public halls which replaced the old rows of shops beside the Forum and served as markets, meeting places, and courts of justice. The earliest extant example of an Italian basilica happens to be not in Rome itself, but at the Campanian town of Pompeii (?120 BC). It is a large rectangular structure with internal colonnades, which seems originally to have possessed a flat wooden roof. The earliest Roman construction of the same type, which has not survived, was the Basilica Porcia (184 BC) built by Cato the Censor despite his suspicions of Greece. And other basilicas at Rome followed not long afterwards in partial imitation.

At a later date, in the first century BC, these large halls were reconstructed with rounded arches, instead of the rows of flat-architraved columns which had characterized the original basilicas. Although there had been timid earlier attempts at the theme in Greece and Etruria, the arch was a pre-eminently Roman structural form. It could also be created in isolation from arcades; and could even be detached from any buildings at all. The result of the latter process was another typical Roman creation, the free-standing monumental or commemorative arch. Its first recorded examples at Rome, no longer existing today, date from 196 BC, when two such monuments were erected to celebrate victories in Spain. Later in the century there were others. They were the forerunners of the magnificent imperial triumphal arches which can still be seen in many cities.

These developments in the construction of arches and arcades, and of the curving apses and niches and vaults which are likewise among the supreme architectural achievements of the Romans, were made possible by the dis-covery of concrete: which was the most revolutionary of all their revolu-tionary techniques. Until lately, its earliest uses seemed attributable to the final quarter of the second century BC. But recent excavation appears to have ascribed this innovation to a date as early as the first decade of that century. For extensive employment of concrete has been detected in a large market-hall and granary beside the Tiber and the Aventine. This is identi-fied, with probability, as the Porticus Aemilia, built in 193 BC and restored in 174; though concrete was still not used very widely until a generation or two later.

Adhesives of sand, mixed with lime and water, had been known to Greeks in the previous century. But it was only now that the serious exploitation of such materials began, after the Romans had detected the admirable properties of a material available in the soil, a natural, pulverized, volcanic blend of cinders and clay. It is known as *pozzolana* because of its abundance at Puteoli (Pozzuoli near Naples), but quantities are also found close to Rome itself. When good, unadulterated lime was mixed with this product in a kiln, the molten mass became an exceptionally consistent and coherent concrete. This was poured over a rubble 'aggregate' made from chips of stone or brick or pumice, and skilfully graded by weight. The result was a compact, monolithic, almost indestructible mass, extraordin-arily resistant to strains and stresses, impervious to water, and exerting no lateral thrust. It could be concealed from the viewer by the surface applica-tion of facings of marble or stone, and this was usually done. But the fac-ings were purely superficial, and not structurally essential. Gradually, and by a long series of cautious experiments, successive generations of Roman architects would awake to the breathtaking potentialities of this concrete medium, and employ it to build their soaring curvilinear marvels of the future.

But meanwhile, until this confidence had been achieved, arches had to be built more cautiously without using the material. Thus in 144 BC a praetor built Rome's first aqueduct to include arched high-level sectors of appreciable length, the Aqua Marcia, which supplied the city with water from a source thirty-six miles distant: its channel was lined with concrete, but it remained for future aqueducts to embody the material in their arches. For this was only the first stage of a long process of such construction, at the end of which Rome's abundance of running water would be unequalled in its lavishness; nor has any other city ever put it to more spectacular public use, while the provinces, too, would be furnished with aqueducts on a magnificent scale. The Aqua Marcia exemplified the special concern of the Romans of this time for public works of solid, material utility. There was also extensive building of Italian roads; and in Rome itself the streets, although nothing was done to increase their narrow width, were paved with blocks of durable lava from the Alban Mount. The old wooden bridge (Pons Sublicius) across the Tiber, too, was supplemented in 179 BC by the Aemilian bridge resting on piers made of stone, to which an arched superstructure was added in 142.

The growing population of the capital, however, was accommodated in lofty, rickety, jerry-built wooden blocks, lacking adequate light and heat and cooking arrangements and water supply, and subject to frequent destructive fires and floods. For the houses of the rich, on the other hand, wall facings of dressed stone were coming into use. No examples from such an early date survive at Rome itself, but their plan can be recovered from elegant, luxurious houses of this and previous periods at Pompeii. The houses presented plain façades to the street, or let off sections of this frontage space as shops. The rooms are grouped round a central *atrium*, a blend of courtyard and front hall which does not seem to owe its origin to the Greeks but is probably endemic to Italy; it was approached through an entrance passage and covered by a roof containing, normally, a central aperture. The *atrium* housed the family altar and statues. Beyond it were the living and domestic quarters, which might include different dining-rooms for summer and winter; they were often grouped round a colonnaded court (peristyle) containing a small garden – though sometimes the main garden was beyond. Dwellings of this type, which in some regions of Italy continued to be constructed and reconstructed over many generations, were notable for their wall-paintings, of which the earliest surviving examples go back to about 100 BC, though they must have had forerunners. Glazed windows were known, but little used, except in the public bathing establishments which developed later on. Although the provision of water was conceived primarily as a public rather than a private service, the supply directed to the baths and fountains of the towns could also be siphoned off into leaden pipes leading to the better class of private houses.

• • • • • •

The wars that transformed Rome by their plunder also brought sweeping social changes throughout Italy. In some areas of the country, the devastations and confiscations during the fifteen years of Hannibal's invasion eliminated many smallholders altogether. And their ruin was also assisted by other factors, which continued to operate throughout the Mediterranean wars of the second century BC. For in this endless succession of foreign campaigns numerous Italian soldier-farmers were killed; and among those who returned, some brought in malaria, which made many areas uninhabitable, and others could not face the prospect of going back to farming and gravitated to the war-industries of the towns. But above all, whether they returned or not, it was the endless conscription, involving prolonged absence on meagre pay, which set the seal on the collapse of their small properties. For every qualified citizen between the ages of seventeen and forty-six was liable to serve for sixteen years, or even twenty years in emergencies. Between 200 and 168 BC some 47,000 soldiers were in the field each year – including Italians and south Italian Greeks, the total came to 110,000 or 130,000. Nor were the numbers much fewer thereafter. And all these men were lost to their farms at least long enough for their land to fall into decay: and very often this was how it remained permanently.

Much of the soil thus vacated passed in due course into the hands of the Roman state, which came to own by this means one-fifth of the whole Italian peninsula. Once in possession of such a piece of public territory (*ager publicus*), the government could let it out again to private individuals. Those who occupied public land in this way were supposed to pay rent to the state. But its collection was lax, and large numbers of the tenants held on to the properties they had acquired without paying any dues at all. A certain number of these fortunate lessees were smallholders, but many others were large-scale landowners who either took over single big tracts (later known as *latifundia*) or amalgamated a whole network of medium-sized farms. These were men who, during the foreign wars, had accumulated sufficient money to keep up these great estates or groups of properties, and could afford to wait patiently until their endeavours yielded profits. Meanwhile, the ancient legal limitations on the amount of public land any one citizen was permitted to lease were regularly evaded or ignored. So holdings of hundreds of acres became an increasingly prominent feature of the Italian scene; and their wealthy proprietors continued to expand further at the expense of the harassed smallholders round about, by methods ranging from purchases and mortgages to physical violence.

This new phenomenon of the large landowner brought changes in preferred types of agricultural production in certain areas of Italy. For the rising populations of the towns offered them an increased market for their crops, and they responded to the challenge by transforming the traditional modest subsistence farming into large-scale mixed intensive cultivation for purposes of commercial gain. This cultivation was undertaken with the aid of new scientific methods, such as crop-rotation and manuring, and new deep-cutting ploughs, and a new systematic selection of seeds. The city of Rome, where people had begun to eat baked bread instead of porridge, still relied on obtaining its wheat from Campania, which also outstripped Etruria as the industrial centre of Italy. But in certain other parts of the peninsula, the growing of grain, which had remained the staple crop for so long, at last began to lose its supremacy.

Secondary reasons for this development included competitive importation from the granary provinces, and erosion of soil. But above all, the switch from grain was due to a new preference for other farm products that earned more money. For from the middle of the second century BC onwards, grapes had become a more important crop than grain, and olives too were in lucrative demand; the ruin of Carthage made Italy the chief wine and oil producer for the west. Vegetables were also important. But the largest agricultural development of the age, especially in southern Italy, was huge-scale farming and breeding of cattle, to produce meat, cheese, wool and leather. These were enterprises which only the biggest estates were able to undertake, since they alone could provide both the upper and lower grazing required for seasonal migration.

We learn about the agriculture of these years from Cato the Elder's treatise *On Farming (De Agricultura)*, the earliest Latin prose work to have come down to us intact. To own a mixed ranch, insists this hard-bitten farmer-politician, and to work it scientifically, is much the best way to make money. And in this survey, ill-arranged though it is, he gives us a vivid picture of the novel enterprises of the day which combined agriculture with commerce, banking, and various kinds of industry.

The way to run these estates, Cato maintained, was by making good use of slaves. Enormous numbers of these were now available. Slavery had been a recognized institution since the remotest past. Its large-scale exploitation had been introduced to Europe at an early date by the Phoenicians, and then became familiar to the Greeks. Subsequently, as a result of the victorious campaigns of the third and second centuries BC, slaves flooded into Rome: 75,000 as prisoners in the First Punic War, including 25,000 from Agrigentum; 30,000 from Tarentum alone, among the numerous captives of the Hannibalic War; huge numbers of Asiatics after the victory over Antiochus III; 150,000 from Epirus in 167 BC. They were sold in the great slave-markets of Capua and Delos. These enclosures were capable of handling 20,000 slaves a day, and they were kept well stocked not only by the fighting against foreign states but also by kidnappings by pirates, who ever since the unwise reduction of their enemy Rhodes by the

Roman authorities, had infested the eastern Mediterranean, supported more or less secretly by eminent Romans for profit.

Slaves lacked all human rights; and the dramatist Plautus, although expressing himself obliquely, indicated sympathy for their defenceless position in society. Yet household slavery could be relatively humane – and it provided one of the principal channels by which Greek culture came to Rome, supplying the city with its secretaries, teachers and doctors. In the countryside, on the other hand, slaves fared a great deal worse. Cato estimated they ought, on the whole, to receive much the same treatment as farm animals, though more careful attention should be devoted to the care and welfare of an ox, which was not so good at looking after itself as human beings. Often these rustic slaves were kept in chains, and when they became too old to earn their keep by working, Cato was prepared to let them perish. Yet he goes on to say that the most efficient principle of management is to treat *both* animals *and* slaves well enough to enable them to work as hard and as long as they can – which meant giving them more food than, for instance, a 'free' Egyptian peasant was getting. And Cato was gracious enough to permit his male and female slaves to have sex with one another provided they paid him a fee. Furthermore he lent them money with which they themselves could buy slaves of their own whom they could train, at his expense, and then sell – very often to himself. And the slave children of his household were suckled by his wife.

Other employers of slaves on the large plantations were as callous as Cato, but less sensible, and subjected them to appalling ill-treatment. As a result, in spite of the danger of death that this involved, many slaves deserted from their masters and went underground. This was one of the reasons why, at certain periods of the second century BC, the whole structure of the classical Greco-Roman society seemed as if it might crack up and disintegrate. All over the Mediterranean area social strains were acute; and in Italy in particular, slave disturbances recurred at regular intervals from 198 BC onwards.

But the first major crisis occurred in the ranches of Sicily. At the slave-barracks of that island, dangerous groups of fellow-nationals had been imprudently concentrated, and in 135 their inmates broke out into large-scale rebellion. One of its leaders, a talented, mystical Syrian named Eunus, collected an army of 70,000 of his fellow slaves, issued coins describing himself as King Antiochus, and seized a very large part of the island, which he held for no less than three years. Finally the revolt was put down with great slaughter. But meanwhile it had triggered off other disturbances in various territories of the East, from which most of the slaves in Sicily had originated. These outbreaks included a formidable rising at Pergamum. Its last monarch had bequeathed his kingdom to Rome (133) precisely in order to avoid that sort of revolutionary development; but in vain. For a certain Aristonicus led a nationalistic, popular, Pergamene revolt which attracted and enlisted many slaves, as well as free men, before the Romans were able to suppress him.

Nevertheless, despite all these troubles, it was the slaves who made Italy's agricultural plantations work, and prosper, so that the rich became a great deal richer. However, in certain regions of Italy, the effect of this on the 'free' rural poor was disastrous. For not only were they harassed by debt, and dispossessed of their smallholdings, but they could not get work on the large estates which had amalgamated and supplanted these little properties. Earlier on many poor people had migrated to the cities in order to take up industrial jobs, and now immigrants of a more desperate kind were continually doing the same, but still, after they had moved in, remained jobless and impoverished and ready to make trouble. When they had merely been destitute in the remote countryside, the Roman government, rarely noted for its humanitarianism, might remain unmoved. But their presence as potential rioters in the capital carried worrying political implications which meant that something had to be done.

And there was another even more alarming aspect, this time of a military nature. For recruits to the legions had to have certain property qualifications, which this whole considerable section of Roman manpower, seeing that it had become destitute, no longer possessed: so that now, at a time when Rome needed recruits in many different regions, there was a serious dearth of them. Reforms, then, were seen by many to be seriously demanded; and an attempt to provide them could not be long delayed.

# V

# THE FALL OF THE REPUBLIC

# 10

# Reform and War in Italy

TIBERIUS AND GAIUS GRACCHUS, young tribunes of the people, now made spectacular attempts to cure the many ills from which Rome and Italy were suffering. They came from the highest nobility – it would have been impossible for anyone but an influential noble to get far with such an enterprise.

During the middle years of the second century BC the tribunate had begun to revive some of its earlier powers; for certain tribunes were now seen asserting themselves against the Senate. Tiberius Gracchus' brief career came at a time when this revival was under way. He was an idealist. Yet he was also not immune from the characteristic personal hostilities of faction life, since he entertained a private grudge against his cousin and brother-in-law Scipio Aemilianus. However, when Tiberius assumed his tribuneship in 133 BC, Scipio was still absent in Spain: so the new tribune was able to bring forward a measure although Scipio regarded it as unduly radical. This provided for the creation of individual allotments to be carved out of the extensive Italian public land (*ager publicus*) which had come into the possession of the Roman government since the Second Punic War. Of this territory he proposed to leave only 300 acres apiece in the hands of the existing tenants, which was said to be the maximum they were allowed to hold by the terms of a long-ignored law; and the blow was softened by the allowance of an additional 150 acres for every child in the families of these occupants. The rest of the public land was to be distributed in small parcels to poor citizens from Rome. But although the relief of urban poverty may have formed part of Tiberius' intention, his main purpose, against the alarmist background of contemporary slave risings, was to increase the number of free men possessing enough property to qualify them for military service: since he was shocked by the growing shortage of such recruits, as well as by the ineffectiveness of the Roman army, notably in Spain where he himself had been serving four years earlier.

The measure could not be described as overwhelmingly radical: and

Tiberius had the support of many leading men, including his father-in-law the leader of the Senate, and one of the consuls, and the consul's brother who was the richest man in Rome. However, there was also strong opposition to the sort of plans Tiberius had in mind not only from Scipio Aemilianus, but from other senators who were active in the city: and their objections provoked him to pass on to more high-handed behaviour. For at the suggestion of his advisers he decided to short-circuit obstruction to his bill by presenting it direct to the Assembly, without prior reference to the Senate. This was not illegal, and not wholly without precedent: it had been done by Flaminius, a century earlier. Yet that had been an exceptional event, and the procedure remained contrary to custom, which played so great a part in Roman politics.

Moreover, when the measure was vetoed by a fellow-tribune, Octavius, Tiberius induced the Assembly to depose him from his office. Such a motion was wholly without precedent. However, Tiberius, whose counsellors included Greek philosophers familiar with their own country's doctrines of popular rights, could argue that Octavius' veto, flouting the will of the people, was equally unprecedented: as indeed it was, even if he was technically within his rights. At all events the agrarian bill was now passed, and in order to bring it into effect a permanent commission was set up, including Tiberius and his younger brother Gaius, and their father-in-law, who was the leader of the Senate.

The Senate then tried to frustrate Tiberius by withholding any substantial financial backing from the commission. But meanwhile it became known to him, through the channels of his family's hereditary clientships in Asia, that the last king of Pergamum had died and left his kingdom to the Roman people. Thereupon he proposed, or threatened to propose, that the Assembly should be requested to make part of the enormous revenue from this property available to the colonists the commission was hoping to settle. This meant bypassing the Senate once again; and the suggestion struck a grave blow at senatorial control of foreign and financial affairs, which although not based on any explicit legal sanction was hallowed by tradition.

Then, in order to safeguard his legislation against the strong probability of subsequent annulment, Tiberius offered himself for immediate re-election to the tribunate. Now, according to the strict letter of the law, a re-election of this kind, without an interval, was not specifically excluded – it was forbidden for senior magistracies (offices of state), but the tribunate, being an office not of the state but of the *plebs*, was not a magistracy in the technical sense. Nevertheless, the proposed re-election, like Tiberius' way of presenting his bill, was a complete departure from custom. Moreover, as the time for the vote approached, it became clear that he had made too many enemies to win: under the influence of conservative opinion, people were beginning to suspect that his high-handed actions were directed towards seizing personal autocratic control of the state. When, therefore, the Assembly began its electoral meeting on the Capitol, a violent quarrel broke out concerning the legality of the proceedings. Physical brawling soon followed, and a crowd of senators and their clients, with an ex-consul at their head, marched on the Assembly and clubbed Tiberius and 300 of his supporters to death.

It was the first time for nearly 400 years that blood had been shed in Roman civil strife. Tiberius had not, perhaps, actually broken the constitution, but, under provocation, he had subjected it to a variety of strains which senators felt they could not endure. Although, therefore, his intentions and reforms were not revolutionary, he had suffered a violent death – and this was a deeply ominous model for the future. In his brief period of activity, Tiberius Gracchus had initiated, for good or evil, something that he surely did not want: the disintegration of the Roman oligarchic system.

Scipio Aemilianus was glad of his death, and the Senate moved into ruthless action against his partisans. Moreover, Scipio and other senators tried to terminate the activities of the land commissioners. But in this they did not succeed. Friction, it is true, continued, but the efforts of the commission, as inscriptional evidence shows, were actually supported by certain conservatives, who hoped for popularity among the poorer Romans and wanted to demonstrate that their opposition had not been directed against the law itself but only against Tiberius' high-handed methods. And so the commissioners were able to carry on with their work; and their achievements even did something to retard the ruin of the small farmers in certain parts of Italy.

Then one of the commissioners, Gaius Gracchus, was elected tribune for 123. He built many myths on the career of his elder brother Tiberius: but his own aims were more far-reaching. Ingenious, subtle, energetic and passionate, Gaius was a most accomplished orator, and used his oratory and diplomacy to win support from any and every direction. His brother had preferred not to abandon 'the art of the possible' unless he had to. Gaius had no such qualms. And he was able to improve on Tiberius' record by securing his own immediate re-election to a second tribuneship unopposed. The controversy over his brother's efforts to achieve the same end had apparently led to the eventual admission that this was permissible after all. Indeed, there may have been legislation to that effect during the intervening decade. This, however, is uncertain. And there is also some uncertainty about the distribution of Gaius' measures between his two tribunates. But in all probability a good many of them were put forward during the first of the two years, and almost at its outset.

Gaius began, apparently, by reaffirming his brother's agrarian enactment, supplementing it by a measure providing for the foundation of Roman colonies at centres including Tarentum and Capua and Carthage. The Carthaginian proposal, which perhaps came later than the others, was a complete novelty, since overseas colonization was a Greek idea, unfamiliar to the Romans, and many of them found it unwelcome. These colonies, to judge from their locations, were in some cases commercial rather than agricultural, being designed, apparently, for colonists from the urban poor of Rome. Yet Gaius did not cherish the false illusion that all the poor people of the capital could be sent away to become farmer-colonists; and for the benefit of those who remained in the city, he brought forward a law assuring the provision of wheat at a reasonable price, which would be ensured by an official subsidy. This, too, had been customary in the Greek city states. But although moderately framed, and a far cry from the mass bribery of later legislators, the proposal was seen by conservative Romans as alarming state socialism.

Gaius also arranged for the passage of highly controversial bills concerning the lawcourts. In 149, as a result of many political scandals, a new court, the *quaestio de repetundis*, had been established to investigate alleged abuses of power by Roman provincial governors, including illegal confiscations and the acceptance of bribes. In the intervening period, however, many such officials had been far too readily acquitted by the court, since its jurymen, like the defendants, were all senators. In consequence, Gaius Gracchus promoted a measure providing that the juries should henceforward comprise not only senators but knights (*equites*), that is to say, men possessing the property qualification next below the senators. And then this idea was shelved in favour of a law providing that all the jurymen should be knights without any senators at all.

The rise of the knights had been a major phenomenon of recent years. In ancient times, they had been horsemen of the Roman cavalry. But when, in the third century BC, this branch of the citizen army was largely replaced by auxiliaries, the knights retained their social position but changed their function, becoming officers in the legions, for example, and functionaries on the staffs of provincial governors. They did not, however, at this stage form a single homogeneous sector of society, being roughly divided into two categories. The first consisted of prosperous landowners, men who resembled senators except that they were slightly less wealthy. The second group, however, engaged in financial operations – from which the senators were officially debarred, in the vain hope of ensuring that their political functions should remain uncorrupted. These financial knights had a good deal to do. For since republican Rome virtually lacked a civil service, the collection of public revenues – for instance indirect taxes (customs dues, etc.) and the income from public land – was habitually contracted out by the state to the highest bidder, who was then at liberty to reimburse himself as profitably as he could. Such bidders were normally knights; they were known as publicans. They also set out to gain contracts for the construction of public buildings and works and the provision of army supplies, and by using the proceeds from such enterprises to buy tax-contracts, the knights who engaged in such activities could make impressive fortunes.

Conflicts with the Senate sometimes arose, especially when the *publicani* tried to make too much money from these activities, thus impoverishing the provincials and leaving too little loot for the senators. But until the time of Gaius Gracchus, such attempts on the part of the knightly financiers were curbed without too much difficulty. An entirely new situation, however, was created by Gaius' new court consisting wholly of knights, especially as many of its members belonged to the category whose principal interests were financial. Indeed, his action could be said to mark the beginning of what was later called the Equestrian Order as a separate and significant class of knights in the state, whose interests would inevitably clash with those of the senators.

Gaius then struck a further blow for the knights in connexion with the recently annexed province of Asia, the former kingdom of Pergamum. Tiberius Gracchus had wanted to divert its great revenues for the benefit of his land-law. And his brother, too, needed money very pressingly, for his expensive schemes for wheat subsidies and colonies. When the territory had first been annexed, tax immunities had been granted to many of its cities: but Gaius now cancelled them. Since, however, that still did not bring in enough money, he put the collection of Asian taxes up for auction in the capital, thus granting a monopoly of this highly profitable activity to the tax-farming knights or *publicani*. Gaius no doubt believed that this arrangement would benefit the treasury because of the enthusiasm with which these men would extort the required taxes – since they themselves stood to profit from the operation. Indeed, the immense amounts they now proceeded to gain through his measure greatly encouraged the evolution of the *publicani* into powerful companies, thus doing a great deal to ensure the subsequent growth of the knights into a class separate from and hostile to the Senate: so that the governing cadre of the state would henceforward cease to be homogeneous, and would split into two warring parts instead.

Finally, Gaius Gracchus tackled a perilously heated question, the status of Rome's Latin and Italian associates or subject allies. For many of them were labouring under bitterly felt grievances, which had gradually been accumulating for a good many years. In the previous century, the allies had played a massive part in the winning of the Second Punic War, and after it was over the time had been ripe for their admission to Roman citizen rights, or at least to some more equal form of partnership. But the Senate had no desire to bestow the Roman franchise on men whose votes, since they lived so far away, it could not control. So nothing was done to improve their position. On the contrary, from the 180s and 170s onwards, there had been various signs of increased encroachment by Rome. In particular, arbitrary measures had been taken by Roman officials, from whose heavy-handed treatment the allies now felt an urgent desire to seek protection.

Scipio Aemilianus, who had commanded Latin and Italian soldiers in addition to Romans, showed himself to be in favour of the allies' claims. And that was one of the reasons why he had been against Tiberius Gracchus' land-law. His opposition was not just due to plain conservatism, but to the fact that the measure would require many Italian allies to hand over public land they were occupying in excess of the legal limit: they were already upset by their heavy-handed treatment by Roman officials, and this would upset them still further. And that was one of the reasons why, after Tiberius' death, Scipio tried, unsuccessfully, to bring the land-commission to an end.

But this, while endearing Scipio to the Italians, made him extremely unpopular with the urban poor of Rome who had hoped to take over public land. And when he died in 129 there were even rumours that with the connivance of his estranged wife, the sister of the Gracchi, some of these angry Romans had murdered him; though such suspicions were probably unfounded.

An effort was made to appease the Italian allies by proposing that they should have a share of the smallholdings now to be created out of the public land, but the government refused to allow the commissioners to take this step. In consequence, one of their number, the distinguished commander and scholar Fulvius Flaccus, brought forward an alternative proposal (125 BC). What he suggested was that any Italians who wanted Roman citizenship should be given it – which would make them eligible for inclusion in the land distribution: while those who still remained non-Romans should at least become entitled to appeal against oppression by Roman officials. But these ideas, too, came to nothing. However, the Italian question had been well and truly introduced into Roman politics – and the situation was very tense.

So Gaius decided that he could not evade the issue; and in the second year of his tribuneship (122) he put forward a modified version of the proposal of Flaccus, who was now his fellow tribune. According to the new scheme Roman citizenship should be conferred upon all Latins, whereas other Italian communities should be granted the Latin right: which provided that the local civic officials should become Roman citizens, so that the status was a halfway house to the full franchise. But this statesmanlike measure was cunningly outbid by a conservative nominee, Marcus Livius Drusus, the elder, who passed a law providing for the total exemption of holders of the Latin right from capital or corporal punishment by Romans, together with a far more ambitious colonial policy than anything Gaius was proposing. No effort was made to carry this programme out. But Gaius had been undermined, and when he went to supervise his new foundation at Carthage, malevolent rumours about the ill-omened site, which had been dedicated to eternal destruction after the final defeat of the Carthaginians, weakened his position still further.

In consequence, when he tried to secure re-election to a third tribunate in 121, he was rejected. And soon afterwards the end came. For his political enemies now set out to cancel the Carthaginian colonization altogether; and when his supporters vociferously opposed this, a servant of one of the consuls, Opimius, was killed in a scuffle. Thereupon Opimius persuaded the Senate to pass a declaration of public emergency pronouncing that the government was imperilled, and charging the consuls and other high officials 'to see to it that the state took no harm'. On the strength of this injunction he personally led a crowd of senators and knights in a physical attack on Gaius and Flaccus, who were both killed; and then some 3,000 of their supporters were executed after perfunctory trials. The decree that led to these actions, later known as the *senatus consultum ultimum*, was to become a feature of the many disturbed decades that now followed, being variously regarded as a necessary instrument of state or a weapon of illegitimate repression.

Those who held the former view, the conservatives, called themselves the *optimates* (best men), whereas the opposition to emergency decrees was directed by men who were known as *populares*, on the grounds that, following the example of the Gracchi, they were prepared to bypass the Senate in favour of working through the Assembly of the Roman People (*populus Romanus*). Yet the old system of shifting, personal alliances based on kinship, clientship, favour and custom continued to exist – even if somewhat shaken by the Gracchan insistence on points of principle; and the *populares* only came forward intermittently in support of particular measures. That is to say, the two groupings never achieved the clear-cut status of opposed political parties in the modern sense. But the rival tendencies persisted and intensified, and this polarization was another of the results of the activity of the Gracchi.

Because of such developments and the further weakening of the structure owing to the new split between Senate and knights, the demolition of the old constitutional system, which had been started involuntarily by Tiberius, accelerated under Gaius. After their deaths, it appeared at first that they had failed: for the time being, repression held the field, and their plans seemed to have gone completely awry. But the land-commissioners were still not prevented from going on with their work, and, moreover, there were soon going to be other *populares* ready to widen the breaches the Gracchi had opened. And so the two brothers left their ineffaceable and permanent mark on the history of Rome, with the result that within a hundred years after their brief careers the Republic had fallen apart and was no more.

Nevertheless during the final years of the Gracchan crisis the attention of the Romans was not exclusively focused on the capital but was also directed towards Gaul across the Alps, into which they were now decisively drawn.

In the previous century their ally in that country, the Greek city-state of Massilia (Marseille), had brought pressure on them to go to war against Hannibal. Now in 125 BC Massilia, not for the first time, appealed to Rome for help against another set of enemies, the Ligurian tribes of the French Riviera. The Senate responded, and duly suppressed the recalcitrant tribesmen. But in so doing they also came into contact with Celtic tribes of the hinterland, and fought against two of them, the Allobroges and the more powerful Arverni, after whom the Auvergne is named; and each of these in succession they heavily defeated near the Rhône in 121. Cnaeus Domitius Ahenobarbus, who won the first of these battles, stayed on and completed the annexation of the whole of southern Gaul, between the Cévennes and the Alps, with the exception of Massilia and its territory which remained free. A major road, called the Via Domitia after Ahenobarbus, was constructed right across the territory, thus linking Italy by land with Spain, and within the next generation the whole region was converted into a province, known as Gallia Narbonensis after its capital at Narbo (Narbonne).

But meanwhile a more serious operation had to be undertaken on the opposite coast of the Mediterranean, in north Africa. There, in the client kingdom of Numidia – flanking the Roman province of Africa – the successor of King Masinissa had died, and Rome divided the country between two young princes (118). One of them was Jugurtha, who had served under Scipio Aemilianus. He was a noted athlete and horseman and a born soldier, whose mask of breezy bonhomie concealed deep resources of calculated cunning and treachery. The Roman partition had given him only the western and more primitive part of the country. And he not only rejected this settlement, but ordered his troops to massacre the Italian residents in Numidia.

Rome declared war on him; but its first two expeditionary forces achieved nothing at all. It was widely believed that Jugurtha, who became known as the lion of the desert, had bribed the Roman generals. This was not, however, necessarily true, because they may have been merely inefficient. But in any case, a much more competent general now had to be dispatched (107). He was Quintus Metellus, an excellent disciplinarian, who transformed the demoralized Roman army into a powerful machine. But even he, after two years of successful campaigning, failed to induce his

enemy to surrender, and Roman public opinion, not appreciating the difficulties of this desert warfare, secured the appointment of one of his deputies
over his head. This was Gaius Marius, a 'new man' of middle-class origins
from the citizen community of Arpinum east of Rome, who had amassed
wealth as a knight and *publicanus*, and had built up useful political support.
Now, by fomenting the popular discontent against his own chief, he
obtained for himself the consulship for 107 and the supreme command.
These appointments were made by the people which, through the Assemblies, over-rode the Senate's contrary wishes, thus foreshadowing the over-
throw of the oligarchic government during the decades that were to follow.

In order to recruit troops for the war, Marius ignored the property
qualifications for military service (which had already been lowered in the
Second Punic War) and called up propertyless volunteers on an extensive
scale. This inaugurated a period in which volunteer and conscript soldiers
alike, on discharge, began to look to their generals to use their own power to
gain them rewards, since they had no land or money of their own, and could
not rely on getting any from the Senate, which viewed them with suspicion
as potential instruments of sedition. On arrival in Numidia, Marius won
impressive successes that showed him to be an exceptional military commander. Yet, even so, he could not bring about the final defeat of his
enemy. In the end, however, Jugurtha was captured through the treachery
of an African ally, arranged by Marius' lieutenant Sulla; and the Romans
put him to death (104).

Public impatience at the slow course of the Jugurthine war was heightened
by alarming developments beyond the northern frontiers. For despite the
establishment of Roman power in Southern France (Gallia Narbonensis),
the northern defences of Italy had become gravely threatened by two
groups of German tribes, the Cimbri and Teutones. Forced to migrate
from their homes in Jutland by overpopulation and the encroachments of
the sea, these masses of tribesmen spent long years roving along the Elbe
and Danube, and then, over a period of eight years, inflicted defeats on
several Roman armies north and west of the Alps. The culminating setback
was a battle with the Cimbri at Arausio (Orange), at which two incapable
and quarrelsome consuls suffered Rome's most serious military disaster for
over a hundred years (105). Next, the Germans moved on to Spain, still not
venturing to invade Italy which was thus granted a respite of three years.
During this period, Marius made ready to receive them. Then, fully prepared, he crushed the Teutones in a bloody engagement at Aquae Sextiae
(Aix en Provence), where 3,000 of his men concealed on high ground won
the day by unexpectedly launching an attack on their rear (102); then, in
the next year, by a torrid, dusty battle against the Cimbri on the Camp
Raudii near Ferrara in north Italy, in which he inflicted shattering casualties.
And that was the end of the German threat.

Yet the war had instilled in the Romans a terror of the northern barbarians which they never again wholly lost. Moreover, it had brought about
other consequences also. For it had given Marius, elected consul year after
year, the opportunity, not only to achieve unprecedented power for himself,
but to raise the Roman army's equipment and organization to a new level of
efficiency. The *pilum* or thrusting spear which all legionaries carried was
now fitted with a wooden rivet which broke on impact so that the enemy
could not throw the spear back. There were also important developments
in military tactics; in particular the supersession of the maniple, implying
dispersion, by the larger cohort, providing concentration, was now complete. Each cohort contained six centurions of different grades who provided the necessary continuity; men of formidable courage, experience and
initiative, generally promoted from the ranks, who combined the functions
and prestige of a modern company commander and a senior sergeant.
Each cohort had military Standards of its own and each legion possessed its
own silver Eagle, the emblem of Rome. Every one of these units was animated by a new feeling of *esprit de corps*: a feeling, however, which as we
have seen, was increasingly directed by these landless volunteers to the
commander himself rather than to the state, so that his soldiers became
known as 'Marius' Mules'.

Their dependence upon him was immediately put to the test. For, after
their military service was ended, land had to be found to reward them, in
the face of senatorial opposition. To find this land became the task of a
popular speaker named Saturninus: for Marius invoked his help, thus
revealing the potentialities of an alliance between a thwarted military
leader and a demagogue. Elected tribune of the people in 103 and 100 BC,
with some support from the nobility, Saturninus arranged for Marius'
veterans to be assigned large allotments in north Africa and then in
southern Gaul, while others were settled in colonies in Sicily and Greece
and Macedonia. This overseas colonization was modelled on the policy of
Gaius Gracchus, whose system of monthly grain distributions Saturninus
also revived.

He innovated by forcing the senators to agree to his programme, under
pain of exile. But the most significant feature of his activity was the violence
he organized at meetings and in the streets; this marked the beginning of a
new epoch in which such disorders were to become habitual. In this spirit,
Saturninus smoothed the way to his own re-election by hiring toughs to
murder one of his competitors; and then he had a candidate for the consulship assassinated as well. But by now Marius, consul for the sixth time, had
had enough, and withdrew his co-operation. In support of the Senate's
declaration of an emergency, Marius personally raised an improvised force
and led it into action against Saturninus and his friends, who were arrested
and shortly afterwards died by lynching in prison.

This intervention by Marius' soldiery was ominous, for it showed generals of the future they could enlist armies of their own troops and veterans, who were virtually their personal dependants; and they might choose to do this to secure absolute power for themselves. But Marius, although full of ambitions of a more orthodox nature, had no such desire to become an autocrat. He was already, it is true, a portentous and exceptional figure, because no man lacking a consular ancestry had reached such heights ever before. And he adopted a tough, rough manner befitting his self-made career. But he never became the first of the dictator-generals, for their time had not yet arrived. He was rather the last of that series of great commanders, men like the two Scipios, who were still prepared to work within the system. Yet there now followed a period, the opening decade of the first century BC, in which, having offended both sides in turn, Marius was discarded, and played scarcely any part in Roman politics, his heroic foreign wars almost forgotten.

It was a time in which the claims of the Italian allies, which had waxed so strong in the time of Gaius Gracchus, were strongly revived: while the Senate did virtually nothing to deal with the problem. These allies had made a full contribution to the fighting against the Numidians and Germans, and had expected to benefit largely from the colonial schemes of Saturninus. But the plans had been allowed to lapse, and the numerous

Italians who flocked to Rome to riot in favour of their revival had been repressed. That was in 95 BC; four years later matters came to a head, when Marcus Livius Drusus the younger, son of the man of the same name who had opposed Gaius Gracchus, was elected to a tribunate like his father. A person of ostentatious rectitude, the son now proposed a decisive measure granting the full Roman franchise to the Italian allies: and they, in enthusiastic response, declared that he was their patron, and swore an oath declaring that they would be his loyal clients for ever. He also claimed, grandiloquently, to be the patron of the whole Senate as well. But neither the senators nor the knights supported his bill, since another proposal he had made, to the effect that the courts should be shared between both of these groups, was satisfactory to neither. And he was also opposed by the urban voters, who did not want to share their privileges with Italians. Nor did the violent gangs, which, like other politicians of this period, he felt constrained to employ, help to inspire confidence in his moderation or diplomacy. His programme was rejected; and an assassin fatally stabbed him.

The failure and death of Drusus created feelings of such desperate disappointment among the already disaffected Italians that they now plunged the peninsula into an unparalleled and terrible war (90–87 BC). It was known to posterity as the Social War (from *socii*, allies), and sometimes, too, as the Marsian War after one of the central Italian tribes which formed the core of the rebel confederacy.

These peoples, for the most part, wanted full Roman citizenship. But the revolt was also joined by the Samnites and their associates farther south who, still remembering their defeats by the Romans two centuries earlier, increasingly formed much wider aims, directed at nothing less than the restoration of their complete independence. Backed by fighting men of excellent quality and experience, the rebels formed a government at Corfinium (Corfinio), a natural centre of mid-Italian communications. And there they struck silver coins inscribed with the word 'Italia' which was the name they gave to the city: and the name was written in the Oscan letters of the old central Italian language.

The Romans were caught by surprise in the first year of the war, and their enemies were thus able to maintain the initiative in both the central and southern war zones, failing, it is true, to inflict any crippling blow, but pursuing an effective strategy of exhaustion. As for the Romans, for a time they employed Marius as a general, but only as one among others, so that despite successes, he soon withdrew in a huff, because he had not been granted a special overriding commission. Thereafter they relied on other commanders. And these fought dourly back, helped by the Roman and Latin fortress-colonies, which did not join the rebels and by their timely assistance provided the legions with the breathing space they needed. Yet the Romans were increasingly racked by fears that the spread of the rising would threaten their communications with Cisalpine Gaul, which provided a vital recruiting ground – it may have been made a separate province at this very time, so that it might be given a governor who could direct mobilization. If their contacts with Cisalpine Gaul were interrupted, they would be hard put to it to find enough troops to place in the field.

The Roman authorities therefore decided, in mid-war, that it had become necessary to make the political concessions which they had so catastrophically failed to offer in time of peace. In consequence one of the consuls of the year, Lucius Julius Caesar, brought forward a bill conferring the Roman citizenship upon all Italians who had remained loyal, as well as on those who had revolted but were now prepared to lay down their arms. This concession halted the impetus of the rebellion, and in the following year the Romans followed it up by measures extending the franchise to every free man south of the Po, while those communities in Transpadane Gaul (the Cisalpine region lying north of that river) which had not gained privileged status already, were raised to the halfway Latin status which conferred citizenship on their elected officials. Fighting continued for the next two years on several fronts, but from now on the revolt stood no real chance of success: and in the end the war petered out.

It had been a traumatic convulsion, threatening not only the very existence of Rome's Mediterranean empire but the survival of the city itself as the centre of Italy. In the long run, the results of the rebellion were mixed, for whereas Lucius Caesar's law marked a large step towards the unification of Roman Italy as a nation, it also meant that, when the bulk of Roman citizens could no longer make visits to the capital, the old city-state government had become obsolete. In the short term, the Social War caused ruinous damage around the countryside. It also produced a whole further generation of ex-soldiers who would menace the stability of the state unless they were amply rewarded. And it taught soldiers of the future how to fight against their own comrades, on behalf of dubious ideals.

Moreover, the concessions extracted by the Italians during the stress of hostilities proved on closer inspection to be inadequate and illusory. For they had provided that the new citizens should be restricted to only eight, or at most ten, of the thirty-five electoral tribes, thus ensuring that their voting power could always be defeated by the other Roman citizens. This was presumably a last-ditch obstruction by the reactionaries, and in the military crisis of 90 BC the Italians do not seem to have fully appreciated the disabilities it imposed on them. But as the war began to draw to an end, this unfairness became a vital grievance.

In 88 BC, the problem was tackled by the tribune Sulpicius Rufus. He was a friend of the younger Drusus whose efforts had failed three years earlier; and he was a member of the same circle of wealthy, brilliant young nobles. He was also an orator of incomparable dignity, a master of tragic effects. Relying, then, on these advantages, and on devoted groups of armed men parading the streets, Sulpicius put forward a proposal that the newly enfranchised Italian allies should be distributed among all the thirty-five tribes – and he even extended this provision to include freedmen (ex-slaves), who had rarely received any such consideration before, but who might, once included, considerably shift the balance of voting strength. Not surprisingly, Sulpicius' measure encountered the fiercest opposition. So he turned away from his more conservative friends to Marius, who had been skulking disregarded in the wings. And he proposed, in exchange for political help, to secure for Marius the supreme command in an important eastern war.

This was to be fought against King Mithridates VI of Pontus in northern Asia Minor – the first of several wars against that monarch, extending over a period of twenty-five years. A noted hunter, lover and warrior, Mithridates affected Hellenism but was of Persian descent, and the governing nobility of his rich country were Iranian or Iranized, providing fine soldiers from their feudal estates, and especially horsemen. Mithridates had inherited from his father a policy of territorial expansion, and early in his reign he himself extended his kingdom so vigorously that he brought the kingdom of the Cimmerian Bosphorus (Crimea), enormously rich from south Russian grain, under his control, and the Black Sea almost became a Pontic lake. He thus became an active, aggressive rival of the Romans, whose frontiers marched with his own in Asia Minor.

But Mithridates' attempts to annex the neighbouring kingdom of Bithynia, a client of Rome, proved unsuccessful; and Bithynian counter-raids inspired by the Romans caused him such anger that in 88 BC he invaded the province of Asia. And there he caused 80,000 of its Italian and Italian – Greek commercial representatives to be massacred by the local city authorities. Their willingness to comply was a shocking demonstration of Roman unpopularity. Moreover, such Italian businessmen as survived the holocaust were bankrupted by Mithridates' seizure of the province; and the débâcle was profoundly felt in Rome itself, where the reserves of the treasury, which had been greatly dependent on Asian revenues, fell almost to nothing.

After thus gaining control of large regions of Asia Minor, Mithridates crossed the Aegean and occupied Athens and other parts of Greece: so that Roman military retaliation became an even more urgent necessity. The supreme command was entrusted to the 50-year-old patrician Lucius Cornelius Sulla, a man who after a debauched but financially profitable youth had distinguished himself in the Jugurthan and Social Wars, and now assumed the consulship for 88. But the tribune Sulpicius Rufus, by forcible methods, secured Sulla's supersession in the conduct of the Mithridatic campaign by his own new ally, the half-forgotten Marius. However, Sulla, refusing to accept this dismissal, fled to the troops he had been destined to command in Asia Minor (his old soldiers in the Social War), and instead led them successfully in an attack upon Rome itself. It was a fateful moment in history. This was the first march on the capital, and the first civil war, and the first clear example of troops acting out of loyalty to their commander to defy the government. Moreover, Sulla created another precedent by declaring Sulpicius (whose legislation was rescinded) to be an outlaw, and Marius another. A price was set on their heads, and Sulpicius was hunted down and put to death. But Marius escaped, amid great perils, and hid in north Africa.

Meanwhile, Sulla left for Greece, where he twice defeated a general of Mithridates', and then captured the city of Athens, wrecking its port, the Piraeus. Next, remaining aloof from other Roman troops in the area – whose commanders were opposed to him politically – he crossed over into Asia Minor. But once there, instead of pursuing the fight against Mithridates, he negotiated an agreement with him at Dardanus near Troy (85). Although the monarch was obliged to evacuate his conquered territories and pay an indemnity, the terms were mild for a Roman peace, since he was recognized as ruler of Pontus and a friend and ally of the Romans – the major punishment, instead, falling on the wealthy cities of Asia which had collaborated in the murder of Roman citizens, and were now made to pay enormous reparations.

The fact was that Sulla could not afford to expend his troops on prolonging the war: for Rome itself had fallen into the hands of his political enemies. Its government was led, for the next four years, by the patrician Cinna. Like Sulla, whom he now proceeded to outlaw, he had fought creditably in the Social War; and as soon as Sulla had left for the east, he again followed in his footsteps by marching on Rome. Marius, too, came back from his refuge in north Africa to join him, and took the lead in political reprisals, comprising by far the bloodiest civilian massacres that Rome had ever experienced. And shortly afterwards, with his mind partly unhinged, he died (86). His brutal ineptitude had given a classic demonstration that military attainments were not always matched by political skill.

Thereafter Cinna's rule became a good deal better than a largely hostile conservative tradition subsequently admitted. He had to grapple with a grave debt problem, caused by the convulsions of the past few years. This crisis, reviving a theme dominant in earlier Roman history, had come to a head three years earlier when creditors pressing for repayment murdered a praetor who tried to apply old laws against usury; and the situation was aggravated by Mithridates' occupation of Asia, which caused many of the Italian businessmen it had ruined to recall loans and resort to panic-stricken hoarding of whatever money they could collect, thus withdrawing cash from circulation. But in 86 BC a radical bill, remitting three-quarters of all outstanding debts, came into force. The new law was, inevitably, unpopular among that important section of the knights whose financial activities included the launching of loans. But they were appeased by the 'good money' policy of Cinna's government directed against another of their grievances: this was a current depreciation of the silver *denarius*, which had meant that the loans they had made in good coin were repaid in bad, with the result that they incurred enormous losses.

This programme of Cinna's began to win a good deal of support. But it was cut short because in early 84 a mutiny broke out, and he was killed; and the authority of his successors abruptly dwindled.

# Reaction and Breakdown

AT THIS JUNCTURE SULLA, outlawed in Rome, openly rebelled and invaded Italy. Its disintegrating administration was joined by the Samnites – still smarting from memories of the Social War – and with their aid its forces made a final stand outside the Colline Gate of Rome (82). But the outcome was catastrophic to the defenders, and the Samnites fell to a man during the engagement and the butchery of prisoners that followed. Nor were they by any means the only people to be slaughtered, since Sulla organized a mass-murder of his enemies which left even Marius' precedent far behind. For with the help of a bodyguard of 10,000 men known as 'Cornelii', he proscribed and executed a total scarcely short of that same number, including 40 senators and 1,600 knights. Their lands, too, were avidly confiscated by Sulla, to be given to 100,000 of his retired legionaries, settled in numerous large Roman colonies forcibly imposed on the Italian countryside. His nonchalant, devil-may-care manner had always appealed to his soldiers, and now their loyalty in following him against the government was rewarded.

And meanwhile he set about realizing his own highly personal vision of how the nation ought to be reconstructed. For himself he chose the obsolete position of dictator. This office had been incorporated in the earliest republican constitution in order to deal with emergencies; it was not envisaged that its holders would remain in power for more than six months. However, the dictatorship had been abolished at the end of the third century BC, owing to the fear that it might encourage autocracy. Now Sulla unearthed and revived it, for the novel purpose of 'making laws and setting up the state' – and with the equally novel absence of any maximum duration so that he was completely immune from any checks from any quarter. Yet he chose to pass his laws in proper form through the Assembly. And they were numerous. They were also almost uniformly conservative. For Sulla's solution for the troubles of the community, thought out carefully on the advice of his supporting faction, was to restore the flagging authority of the Senate. There was a certain irony in this, because he himself had earlier taken the most decisive step possible to break senatorial power by the naked militarism of his march on Rome. But he was determined that no one else should ever do the same again.

To this end, he decided that one of the principal needs was to break the power of the tribunes of the people who in recent years had so often challenged senatorial control. Henceforward they were not allowed to move any law whatever without the prior approval of the Senate. Moreover, their veto was abolished in criminal cases and limited in other contexts as well, and they were debarred, after their tenure as tribune, from subsequently holding any of the major offices of state, so that the tribunate would cease to attract able and ambitious politicians.

But the most impressive and lasting of Sulla's pro-senatorial achievements was the reconstitution of the law-courts (*quaestiones*), of which the number was increased to at least seven, each dealing with a separate range of crimes. Gaius Gracchus had given the original extortion court to the knights, but Sulla excluded them from it altogether, making the *quaestiones* into a senatorial monopoly. However, this blow was mitigated by the introduction of numerous knights, notably his own Roman and Italian partisans, into the Senate, which he doubled in size to 600.

The rules governing its membership were also overhauled. Men who had held the junior office of quaestor were to become senators automatically, though the quaestorship could not be held until the age of thirty and the praetorship not until forty-two, so that the rise of dangerous young careerists would be slowed down. And Sulla, remembering the illegalities of himself and others, took steps to bring provincial governors under firm senatorial control. In particular, they were forbidden to make war outside the province allotted to them, or indeed to depart for any reason beyond its borders, without previous authorization from the Senate or Assembly. One of the principal weapons against those who strayed was a law of treason, *maiestas* – a crime that had been first defined in 100 BC and was now handled by one of Sulla's new law courts.

It seemed paradoxical that these measures to shore up the ancient oligarchy should be taken by a man who had revived the office of dictator, and who, moreover, surrounded himself superstitiously with the mystic personality cult of an autocrat. And, besides, he lavishly sponsored the vast building activities which traditionally went with this sort of monarchic role, including the construction of the Record Office (Tabularium) of Rome, and the rebuilding of the Roman Senate-house and of the great precinct of Fortuna at Praeneste (Palestrina), the site of one of his civil war victories. These were projects reminiscent of eastern princes. Nevertheless, Sulla still stopped short of complete absolutism. Instead, he decided to abdicate from his dictatorship, becoming consul in 80 BC and returning in the following year to private life in Campania, where he died a year later.

But the memory of this mulberry-faced man, so self-indulgent and yet so energetic, easily moved to laughter and tears, who claimed he never forgot a friend or a foe, remained alive. This was not so much because of his elaborate constitutional scheme. For although he was not blindly intolerant of recent developments, his measures in this field were a putting back of the clock that failed to deal with Rome's essential economic and social problems. Moreover, his assumption that the restrictions imposed on governors and commanders would prove sufficient turned out to be wrong: since in the years to come it was they, and not the state, who could mobilize powerful armies, and make use of them for their own ends. After all, that was just what Sulla had done himself; and that, in the long run, was why he was remembered, because of the callous horrors of his rise to power. Nor were these recollections of his ruthlessness entirely without good effects. For at least they deterred the Romans from repeating large-scale civil war for thirty years.

The failure of Sulla's reconstruction was demonstrated without the slightest delay. For when one of his former officers, Marcus Lepidus, a man of patrician but liberal family with extensive noble backing, became consul in 78 BC, he employed his term of office to bring forward an opportunistic programme for the restoration of the tribunate, which Sulla had so deliberately weakened. Lepidus staked his chances on a possible mass rising of Italians dispossessed by the proscriptions, in which he himself had amassed a fortune. In 77, supported by another disaffected officer in Cisalpine Gaul, he led a considerable force of Etruscan and other malcontents in a dash for the capital, where an emergency decree was passed. His way was barred by a senatorial army and he was defeated at the Milvian Bridge, and shortly afterwards he died.

Far more able was another anti-Sullan, Sertorius, a Sabine who set up an independent government in Spain, where he won over the whole of the eastern seaboard. He also enjoyed widespread support from local tribesmen, among whom his enlightened methods gained him unrivalled popularity, handing on to the future the idea that it might pay after all to treat the provincials decently and attempt their Romanization. He maintained contact with Lepidus, whose followers to the number of 20,000 fled to his colours after the collapse of the rising in Italy.

At the end of 77 BC the Senate felt obliged to strengthen its confrontation with Sertorius by sending out substantial reinforcements under a general only twenty-nine years of age. This was Pompey (Cnaeus Pompeius), who already enjoyed a considerable reputation. His father had been one of Rome's principal officers in the Social War, and Pompey, after serving with him, had built up a strong personal following in central and eastern Italy.

When Sulla arrived from the east, Pompey, who was married to his step-daughter, had joined forces with him. He had then gone on to win victories on Sulla's behalf in Sicily and north Africa, and for these successes, although according to all the rules he was far too young, the dictator had felt reluctantly obliged to grant him a triumph. This, then, was the young man who was now sent to Spain against Sertorius. At first, he achieved no result. But finally, Sertorius was murdered at a banquet by his own un-distinguished lieutenant, whom Pompey then defeated without difficulty and put to death. In this somewhat unmerited fashion he had increased his military renown.

Meanwhile in Italy an event had occurred that inspired great terror among the Romans. It was the last of the series of slave wars extending back to the previous century. But this was a slave war of a special character, because it took place on the Italian peninsula itself. The principal rebels were pro-fessional gladiators, and the outbreak began at Capua, home of one of the largest gladiatorial schools and barracks. It was led by a Thracian named Spartacus, a man of courage and some humanity, who had served as a Roman auxiliary soldier. Slaves of all kinds flocked to join him, and within the space of two years they defeated no less than four Roman armies. Spartacus' hope, in conducting these operations, was that his men might seize the chance to break out and make their way across the Alps, after which they could seek their own homelands in freedom. However, they made no serious attempt to carry out these aims, preferring instead to plunder the rich Italian countryside.

Business interests were gravely damaged by their looting; but the mili-tary respite it provided was turned to good account by the Roman authori-ties. They entrusted the command against Spartacus to the ex-praetor Crassus; he was a former subordinate of Sulla, amiable and flattering, easy of access, a talented wire-puller, who had vastly increased his hereditary wealth in the course of the proscriptions. After meticulously training a force of 40,000 men, Crassus attempted in vain to catch Spartacus in the toe of the peninsula, but finally cornered and killed him in Apulia, crucify-ing 6,000 of his slave followers along the Appian Way (71 BC).

But meanwhile Pompey had been summoned back from Spain to help conduct the operations, and arrived just in time to take part in the man-hunt, which he and his friends magnified into a major military success, eclipsing the victory of Crassus.

At this point the two ambitious men, each with his own army, might well have come to blows. But Crassus, though a daring financial speculator, was a cautious politician, and Pompey, in spite of many irregularities during his earlier career, showed few signs of openly unconstitutional behaviour. In spite, therefore, of a good deal of mutual suspicion, they did not clash, but came to an understanding instead, according to which they would demand election to the consulships of the year 70. Legally speaking, both were unqualified, because neither had disbanded his army as consular candidates were required to do, and besides Pompey, who had not even taken his seat as a senator, was debarred on grounds of his youth. Nevertheless, the Senate had to give way, thus revealing, for the attention of future politicians, how a resolute combination of ambitious men could frustrate the Republic. And so the Assembly duly elected them as consuls.

Setting their disagreements aside, they devoted their year of office to the overturning of Sulla's constitution – a programme which gained them considerable popularity, except, of course, in the Senate. Moreover, its members also had to endure the condemnation of one of their colleagues, Verres, whose prosecution for gross dishonesty during his governorship of Sicily was triumphantly undertaken by the rising orator Cicero. In the same anti-Sullan spirit Crassus and Pompey encouraged the censors of the year to expel sixty-four senators. They also supported a bill reducing the senatorial membership of the jury panels to one-third, and a law proposed by Pompey relieved the tribunate of all the restrictions placed upon it by the late dictator. Almost his whole activity in favour of the traditional order was therefore obliterated, and the old flexibility and anarchy of Roman politics had been fully restored.

During the years that immediately followed, Crassus remained content to stay at home, increasing his financial resources and political influence. But Pompey was waiting for a chance to effect some spectacular increase in his military reputation: and the opportunity was not long in coming. It was provided by the scandalous prevalence of Mediterranean piracy. Ever since Rome had in the previous century shortsightedly weakened Rhodes and its naval police force, pirates had been conducting their operations unimpeded, with the connivance of Roman slave-purchasing interests. Efforts by the government to destroy their harbours on the coast of Asia Minor had not proved effective (102), and during the wars of the eighties, their raids had become more and more audacious. Cyrenaica (eastern Libya) had been annexed and made into a new province, in order to provide bases against the pirates, but in vain: and now they were directly menacing the grain-supply of Rome itself. In 67, therefore, over the heads of the Senate, a tribune put through a bill which entrusted Pompey with the task of suppressing them, and conferred on him, for this purpose, an overriding Mediterranean command, with 120,000 infantry and 500 ships at his disposal. He carried out this enterprise in an operation of lightning rapidity, lasting only three months, during which time he and his officers totally cleared the seas of pirates.

Thereupon another tribune presented a further bill to the Assembly, granting Pompey a general commission to settle the affairs of the near east, and in particular to terminate the hostilities which were still dragging on against Mithridates VI of Pontus. The bill was made law, despite the undiminished reluctance of the Senate, whose dominant position, it was now clear, had virtually ceased to exist. After the peace of 85, Mithridates had rapidly recovered, repelling the officer left behind by Sulla and building up stores of money and supplies, so that when Rome decided to annex adjacent Bithynia in 74, he had marched into that country to forestall them, leaving it garrisoned by a Pontic army. But then the Romans had sent out a general of great ability, a former supporter of Sulla named Lucullus, who expelled the king from Bithynia and even from his own homeland of Pontus (74-70), forcing him to flee to his eastern neighbour and ally Armenia, a country almost new to world history which had recently become a considerable empire.

Lucullus occupied the Armenian capital; but in 68 his troops refused to carry on. This was partly because he had arranged a reorganization of Asian finances, in which Roman business interests had not been allowed to profit as much as they wanted; and at home this had earned him many enemies, who played their part in instigating the mutiny in his army. But on the spot, too, the weather conditions his soldiers had to contend with were intolerable, and, above all, Lucullus, in spite of all his great military talents, was an aristocratic disciplinarian who lacked the ability to get on with the rank and file. In all these unfavourable conditions, his army virtually fell apart. One of the Roman leaders who had accelerated its disintegration, from afar, was Pompey, an old political enemy, and now it was he who took over the command.

On arrival in the field, he proved outstandingly successful – though his strategic gifts were scarcely put to the test. For Mithridates was deserted by his Armenian allies, so that it became possible to defeat him immediately. He contrived to escape to the Cimmerian Bosphorus (Crimea): but there, faced by a rebellion led by his son, he committed suicide. His fight against the Romans had lasted, with intervals, throughout a quarter of a century. It had been important because it involved Rome in the most intractable wars of the age. Moreover, these recurrent crises exerted various other impacts on the Roman scene as well. For example, they forced the government to create long-term, semi-independent commands, with all the attendant perils they posed for the central authority. And Rome's continuing involvement with Mithridates, and its outcome, enormously expanded its commitment in eastern lands.

For Pompey, after sensationally exploring and opening up the hitherto unknown region of the Caucasus (65), now put into effect a sweeping settlement of the affairs of western Asia, involving an immense amount of detailed planning. Pontus was annexed and united with Bithynia, to form a single province. In Syria, the last feeble Seleucid monarch was removed, and his country also, with its great city of Antioch, was taken over and made a province: so that out of the three great successor states of Alexander, Macedonia, the Seleucids, and Egypt, only the last named now remained in a condition of formal independence, although it, too, was already largely subservient to Rome. In the small Judaean kingdom, where there had been dynastic disputes, Pompey captured the ancient capital Jerusalem, causing great and lasting Jewish distress by walking into the Temple; but a member of the reigning Hasmonaean (Maccabee) dynasty was still allowed to rule, as one of Rome's rapidly increasing number of dependent, client monarchs.

This extension of Rome's ancient *clientela* principle to foreign states was nothing new. But Pompey enlarged its application greatly. The client kings were tied to the service of Rome in order to defend its frontiers, and serve as listening posts to the outside world. In return, they were supported by the Romans against internal subversive movements, and allowed a free hand inside their own countries. Thus Rome was spared the trouble and expense of administering these territories; and the formula worked well. Only in Armenia, perhaps, was Pompey mistaken in retaining the local prince instead of annexing the country, for he left it as a future bone of contention between the Romans and powers that lay farther to the east.*

On the site of his victory over Mithridates, he created the new town of Nicopolis, settling a mixed population of veterans, wounded soldiers and local inhabitants. But that was only one of the forty cities he founded or restored throughout the east, in pursuance of the actively urbanizing tradition of the Greek monarchies. Under upper-class leaderships approved by Rome, the cities, new and old alike, were to provide convenient nuclei, not of Romanization because their culture normally remained Greek, but of Roman political influence and *clientela*.

Pompey's reconstruction of the near east far exceeded anything of the kind that any Roman had ever performed before, showing him to be an administrator of the very first order. Indeed, although he still had fifteen years to live, this was easily the greatest achievement of his career, massively standing the test of time and forming the basis of all future reorganizations. And the spectacular honours he received from the eastern communities likewise foreshadowed the imperial personages to come. Moreover, his arrangements were immensely lucrative, both to himself and to Rome. As for his own gains, the spoils of war and gifts from grateful or anxious monarchs and cities† made him a richer man even than Crassus – who had hitherto been the wealthiest man of the day – and gave him a larger host of dependants. And his settlement also vastly enlarged the resources of the Roman treasury, raising the annual revenue of the state by no less than 40

---

* First Parthia (p. 182) and then Persia (p. 283).
† He removed many of their tax immunities.

per cent. The Triumph at his homecoming was celebrated with unprecedented splendour.

While Pompey was away in the east, there had been an uneasy air of suspense at Rome, where people remembered the autocracy Sulla had established when he returned from the same lands; and now they feared that history would repeat itself. Intrigues multiplied, largely prompted by Crassus, who did not act directly against Pompey but financed various needy characters who might work to increase his own personal influence.

One such figure who acquired a good deal of notoriety was Catiline, an impoverished patrician who had supported Sulla but now offered hopes to Sullans and anti-Sullans alike who had become destitute and angry and eager to repair their damaged fortunes. Being an undischarged prisoner on an embezzlement charge, Catiline was debarred from standing for the consulship of 65 BC, and there were rumours that he and others plotted to murder the men who secured election in his place. He was also disqualified from standing for 64, but was admitted to the competition for 63. At this stage Crassus was apparently still willing to back him; but a wide range of conservative senators, and some of their less conservative colleagues as well, were alarmed by the possibility that he might get in. For he seemed to them a flashy and ungovernable person ready for any kind of unscrupulous action that might reverse the setbacks his career had suffered.

In consequence, this large and varied group of worried men banded together to put up a candidate to stand for the consulship against him. The man they selected was Cicero, from Marius' home-town Arpinum. Cicero came from a family which had never provided a consul before, and such 'new men' found it notoriously difficult to gain the office: indeed, none seems to have done so for the previous thirty years. On the other hand, he was an orator of unique brilliance in a society in which oratory was the major part of politics. He had scored a first-class success in 70 in convicting the corrupt governor of Sicily, Verres; and, after that, he had backed the assignment of the eastern command of Pompey, who, despite occasional interruptions and reservations, continued to be his favourite statesman from now onwards.

Now these activities, like his undistinguished origins, might have seemed by no means useful recommendations to the favour of old-fashioned Republicans, or even middle-of-the-road members of the Senate. Nevertheless, men of both these categories rallied to his support against Catiline, whom they regarded as a grave threat to social stability. So Cicero duly won the consulship for 63. His colleague was an insignificant character who had privately favoured Catiline but failed to back him.

At the elections held in 63 for the consulships of the following year, Catiline made a further attempt to gain office, this time with a programme sensational enough to confirm the worst fears, proposing not only sweeping land distribution but a general cancellation of debts. This programme was designed to appeal to bankrupt nobles, veterans and urban poor – indeed, to displaced and discontented persons of every sort. But such proposals scared off not only all conservatives and moderates, but Crassus as well; and Cicero, who equated debt-cancellation with what he considered the worst of all evils, the destruction of private property, helped to secure Catiline's defeat once again. And so now that defeated and disappointed man, estimating that his chances of reaching the top of the tree by legal, constitutional means had vanished for ever, began to move outside the law instead, and plan the subversion of public order. For his intention now was that a force of his discreditable supporters in Etruria, which was full of discontented men ready for violence, should march on Rome in October of this year 63 BC.

However, six days before the date fixed for the coup, rumours of its imminence leaked out, and the Senate passed its emergency decree. Nevertheless, in the absence of concrete proofs of his seditious intentions, Catiline himself, protected by influential friends, was still left at large in the city, and went on plotting revolution. But when Cicero in the first of his four magnificent Catilinarian Orations proceeded to unmask and denounce his aims, Catiline felt it advisable to withdraw from the capital, and took personal command of his followers in Etruria. For Rome had become increasingly uncomfortable for him, since Cicero had won back a number of his supporters by claiming that he intended to burn the city down; and then the orator won back some more by luckily obtaining written evidence of Catiline's revolutionary intentions from Gallic envoys visiting Rome. Thereupon Cicero proceeded to seize five of the leading conspirators in the city, including men of very high rank, and obtained the Senate's approval of their execution, which was immediately carried out – on his orders.

The legality of this action was widely disputed. Cicero himself maintained loudly for the rest of his life that it had been necessary, in order to check an imminent rebellion, and that it was warranted by the Senate's concurrence, as well as by their former emergency decree. On the other hand the Senate was not an executive body but only advisory, so that the deed still remained the responsibility of the consul. And it could be argued against him that it violated a Roman citizen's right to be tried; and, besides, citizens who were not actually caught red-handed under arms, and were not therefore an immediate source of danger, did not look like the enemies of the state against whom alone such summary treatment would have been justified. It seemed, therefore, that Cicero had acted illegally, and this belief among his compatriots affected much of his future career. But in any case, the Catilinarian plot was not the tremendous crisis from which he claimed, for evermore, to have saved the state, but a relatively minor upheaval. It was only important because of the incomparably eloquent speeches and writings Cicero devoted to it, magnifying and defending his own role.

In the final senatorial debate, preceding the execution of the plotters, two statesmen of the future expressed their views, Cato in favour of Cicero's proposal that they should be killed, and Julius Caesar against it. Cato, the great-grandson of the censor of the same name who had been a leading politician of the previous century, was a man of thirty-two, formidable, inhumanly unforgiving, a heavy drinker, and uncompromising in his opposition to all who appeared not to measure up to the traditional system. Gaius Julius Caesar, five years older, was a patrician linked by marriage ties with Marius and Cinna. After a rather late start in Roman public life, and a period in which his shaky finances were bolstered up by Crassus, he had staged a trial demonstrating against senatorial abuses of the emergency decree (63); and in the same year he had obtained, at the cost of heavy outlay, the chief priesthood of the Roman state, an office which, without interfering with its occupant's political career, was a source of extensive prestige and patronage. At the end of the same year, Caesar was about to become praetor; it was at this juncture that he cast constitutional doubts on the propriety of putting the Catilinarians to death. His opinion did not prevail, but he gained valuable allies among those who were afraid of what such high-handed acts might lead to.

For the time being, however, Cicero's policy seemed vindicated, because Catiline moved into open rebellion at the head of his troops. But now that his friends in Rome had been overwhelmed, he no longer had any hope of marching on the city, and instead tried to flee northwards out of the Italian peninsula. But two armies sent by the government, one at either end of the Apennines, caught him in a trap, and he and his followers were destroyed near Pistoria (Pistoia) in January 62 BC. And so Cicero was now, for a brief moment, the hero of the hour.

Cicero became famous in later generations and epochs as the most articulate representative of a remarkable upper-class society which pursued a highly cultured and luxurious way of life derived from the immense accretions of wealth by the imperial Republic and its leaders. The orator himself possessed a mansion on the Palatine Hill and at least eight houses in the country, some just places of rest as he journeyed from place to place, but others elegantly furnished and adorned by wall-paintings and floor mosaics, and housing notable collections of Greek art. Yet he had not been born to this grandeur and lacked the wealth needed to purchase and maintain all these properties; that is to say, he did not himself possess the means to pursue a successful political career. But he was extremely fortunate to have the close friendship and support of an enormously rich knight and banker,

Atticus, who helped him in very many different ways and evidently believed in his political and intellectual aims.

Cicero owed his rise almost exclusively to one single quality. He was one of the most persuasive orators who have ever lived, in an age in which the very core of politics was oratory. The combination of his inborn talents with an elaborate education and training equipped him to speak and write that incomparably eloquent, rotund Latin which persuaded and overwhelmed his listeners in Senate, Assembly and lawcourts alike, and laid the foundations of the subsequent prose of all Europe. His speeches, of which fifty-eight out of over a hundred survive, reflect all the stresses and strains of the crumbling Republic, in which for three decades he lived and worked at the centre of events. They also reveal himself; and so, even more remarkably, do his 800 unique letters, written to Atticus and other friends.

The personage who emerges is humorous and warm-hearted, extravagant, as unable as the next man to see how to make a city-state govern an empire, over-respectful to the nobility to which he did not belong, and intensely eager to tell everyone of his success in stifling Catiline's second-rate coup – an excusable form of self-praise because being a 'new man' he enjoyed no built-in backing of his own. Moreover, Cicero, despite his occasional political successes, did not have the right temperament to be a first-class Roman politician. For one thing, he always took too rosy a view of his own position and influence. And, worse still, he possessed a fatal lawyer-like ability to see both sides of every question, and lacked the ruthless decisiveness that Roman public life required. Yet on two or three occasions in his lifetime, by an excruciating effort, he screwed up his courage to desist from vacillation and stand up and be counted against tyranny, and the last of these stands cost him his life.

For Cicero, despite all his own faults and the faults of his age, had accepted the Greek idea now current among Roman jurists and other thinkers of a Natural Law (*ius naturale*) which was a corollary of the admission of non-citizens to Rome's legal system (*ius gentium*) and ought to be observed by all mankind. That is to say, he was convinced that right is right and wrong is wrong objectively, and that no pronouncements or laws can make them otherwise. And what was most wrong of all, he believed, was for one person to tyrannize others. For, following up the precepts of the Stoic philosophy founded two and a half centuries earlier, he accepted its injunction that men and women should treat one another generously and honestly. They must do so because all human beings have their own personal value and importance. This is because, according to Stoic doctrine, all individuals share a spark of divinity which makes them akin to each other, irrespective of race or status or sex, in the universal brotherhood of humankind.

That was one of the principal elements in the *humanitas* upon which

Cicero insisted, in a series of wonderfully well written treatises on moral themes. Shunning dogma (in accordance with the views of the contemporary Athens Academy), these essays adapted Greek philosophy to Roman life and both exemplified and demanded an enlightenment of mind and character, a recognition not only of one's own unique personality but of the personalities of others. This was the most civilized ideal, for practical purposes of living, that the world had ever seen; it has deeply influenced western thought from his time to our own. And Cicero stressed this ideal with all the more fervent conviction because he believed that the man best equipped to teach the good life was the public speaker. For, as he explains in a number of analyses of that art, every orator must not only be a man of wide and liberal culture, but, if he is to do his job properly, he must also behave decently and well.

Fired by such ideas, and by the momentary acclaim that greeted his victory over the Catilinarians, Cicero adopted a political programme that seemed to him to give practical expression to these doctrines. It envisaged a concept that had been discussed more than once in the previous years, a Concord of the Orders, in which the senators would be permanently allied with the knights of all Italy, municipal men like himself who had become increasingly influential in the state, and had backed him strongly against the anti-social projects of Catiline. However, Cicero himself inadvertently did more than anyone else to ruin the chances of any such Concord becoming a practical possibility. For when Pompey returned from his unparalleled eastern successes, Cicero promptly offended his vanity by reiterating his own achievements as saviour of the country, at a moment when the other man was prepared to think of no other triumphs but his own.

Pompey was arrogant, shifty and aloof. Yet none of the gloomy predictions of his desire to become an autocrat proved correct. Instead, as soon as he landed in Italy, he duly disbanded his troops. By so doing, he indicated clearly that, despite his unquestioned desire for the greatest admiration and position that republican Rome could bestow upon him, he entertained no ambition to become a dictatorial tyrant. Moreover, as Cicero noted, Pompey was now showing a certain readiness to abandon the anti-conservative faction which had given him his appointments since 70, and to side with orthodox senators instead. However, at this stage, he had two requests to make from them. The first was an application for land that could be given to his impatient veterans. This must have been foreseen, and was reasonable. His second request was that all the actions he had performed in the east should be ratified as decisions of the Roman state. This was equally predictable. It could be criticized, certainly, on the grounds that he had largely acted without the customary consultations with Rome. All the same, by straining the tradition a little, his wish might have been granted, in view of the gigantic gains he had brought to Rome.

Nevertheless, a series of obscure metropolitan intrigues now got under way, during which it emerged that very many leading conservatives preferred to take a short-term view and oppose his demand. For they regarded his recent failures to consult the capital, when he was in the east, as just another in a prolonged series of high-handed and illegal acts: while one of their number, the former general Lucullus, added his own vindictive feelings of personal affront, because Pompey had superseded and humiliated him in Asia Minor. Cato, who became tribune in 62, was another of Pompey's opponents. It was true that when Cato wanted to increase the existing free distributions of grain to keep the metropolis quiet while Catiline was still at large, he was willing enough to make use of Pompey's huge new eastern revenue for this purpose. Yet, at the same time, he also used his tribunate to block Pompey's two proposals, deploying his extraordinary powers of obstruction to the full. So, in the face of this pressure, the Senate continually delayed its decision about Pompey's requests; and few things contributed so greatly to the fall of the Republic, which was shortly to follow, as this refusal to give him what he wanted.

The senators also made two further ominous decisions. One of these was in relation to Crassus. After acting ambiguously towards Pompey while he was away in the east, Crassus had come to resent him greatly after his triumphant return: and now he was fully prepared to join with the Senate in blocking his two claims. Yet, in spite of this heaven-sent opportunity to enlist Crassus' support, the senators rebuffed him instead. This happened in regard to a financial matter in which he declared an interest. At the end of 61 BC, a company of tax-gatherers, who were now the most important pressure-group among the knights, were claiming a rebate on the purchase price of Asian revenues they had contracted to collect, since these were proving disastrously less profitable than they had expected; and they persuaded Crassus, as the most influential patron of business interests, to back their request. But Cato, not unreasonably this time, saw their appeal as an outrageous attempt to bend their perfectly clear agreement with the state – merely because it had proved not to bring them as much profit as they had hoped. And so he persuaded the Senate to kill the proposal.

Pompey and Crassus, then, had both been snubbed. And now Caesar was snubbed as well. He had been serving as governor of Further Spain (Baetica), from which he returned to Italy in 60 to become a candidate for the consulate. But because of minor military victories won during his governorship, he had also been awarded a Triumph, and he wanted to celebrate it. His right to do so, however, would have been forfeited by law if in the meanwhile he had entered the city. So he asked leave to stand for the consular elections by proxy instead of in person. Cato, however, ensured that this application should be rejected. And that was not all. It was the practice at this period for the Senate to allocate to the consuls of any given year, even before their election took place and their names were known, the provinces they would be sent to govern at the conclusion of their term of office. And so now the provinces which would go to the consuls for 59 BC were allotted: and it was decided that they should not be ordinary provinces at all, but 'the forests and cattle-drifts of Italy'. This was an abnormally trivial assignment, expressly designed for one possible or probable contingency: that one of the consuls about to be elected would turn out to be Caesar. In other words, it was a deliberate affront directed against him personally.

So the Senate had opposed and offended Pompey, Crassus and Caesar – all three of them: and had thereby displayed that its members no longer possessed the acute judgement that had won Rome the Mediterranean world. What happened next, therefore, seems by hindsight inevitable. For the three men who had all received this treatment buried their differences with one another and joined forces against those who had insulted them. Their agreement took the form of a coalition, informal but potent, at first secret and before long publicly known, which historians describe as the First Triumvirate. Caesar asked Cicero to join this compact, but to his credit he refused. For it was a far cry from the Concord between the Orders which he had been advocating. Far from becoming a partner in the Triumvirate, the Senate was going to be its target and victim; it was so severely weakened that it became, for the first time, a mere political group instead of the effective government of the empire. For almost all power was concentrated in the hands of Pompey, Crassus and Caesar.

Later historical writers saw the event as the end of the Roman Republic; or at least as the beginning of its end. Some of their modern successors have questioned this, pointing out that the triumvirs' control was not absolute, and that the traditional political activities, including more or less freely contested annual elections, still continued for another decade. Yet they only continued under the heaviest of shadows; and the oligarchy never recovered its power again.

# VI

# CAESAR AND AUGUSTUS

# 12

# Caesar

WHEN CAESAR WAS ELECTED to the consulship for 59 BC, the Republic was still able to exhibit faint signs of life by electing an extreme conservative, Bibulus, as his fellow-consul. Nevertheless, Caesar at once pointed the way to Rome's autocratic future by pushing through a series of measures in favour of his fellow triumvirs Pompey and Crassus and himself, in total disregard of the opposition.

One of his first actions as consul was to satisfy Pompey's veterans by a land-bill. When his arch-enemy, Cato, blocked the measure in the Senate, Caesar secured its acceptance in the Assembly by forcible methods, including the beating up of his fellow-consul, which were held against him for the rest of his life. He was supported, however, by his fellow triumvirs, so that his alliance with them came to be revealed, and Pompey married his daughter Julia. Caesar then went on to ensure the ratification of his new son-in-law's eastern arrangements, and they shared an enormously lucrative reward for shoring up a distressed king of Egypt. He also formed the habit of inviting Pompey to speak first in the Senate, rather than Crassus. Nevertheless, Caesar also satisfied Crassus by securing a generous financial concession for his friends the tax-collecting knights, who had been unsuccessfully demanding a rebate on their Asian contracts. And he arranged that in future the proceedings of the Senate (as well as of the Assembly) should be published openly, so that its members' freedom to conduct secret intrigues against him was severely restricted.

It was now the turn of the other triumvirs to help Caesar in his own political career. The governorship of Further Spain from which he was recently back had revealed to him that he possessed exceptional military talents, and these he was now eager to exploit, in order to fulfil his growing ambition to become pre-eminent in the state. Instead, therefore, of the ridiculously unimportant province the Senate had assigned to the consuls for this year, he got himself allotted a much more significant province consisting of Cisalpine Gaul (north Italy) combined with Illyricum (Dalmatia). His

# The family of Caesar

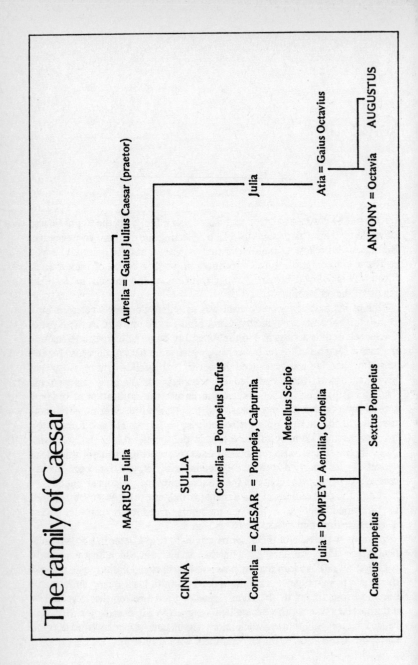

initial purpose was apparently to lead Roman armies north-eastwards, as far as the Rivers Save or Drave, in what is now Yugoslavia.

At this juncture, however, the death occurred of the governor of Transalpine or Narbonese Gaul (southern France). This was a remarkable stroke of luck for Caesar, who saw that region as a far more promising starting-off point for military conquests and arranged for it to be added to the province already assigned to him. He knew it would be best to assume office as provincial governor as soon as his consulship was over, and to retain the job without a break for an indefinite period, since if he became a private citizen even for a moment he would be liable to prosecution for the numerous acts of violence and impropriety he had committed as consul. Before leaving Rome, however, he formed an alliance with a young politician named Clodius, a talented, eccentric radical freelance who he hoped would look after his interests in the capital, with the help of numerous inherited clients, urban gangsters, and trade corporations or guilds (*collegia*), whose exploitation Clodius made into a fine art.

In many parts of their huge unconquered tribal territories lying north of the Transalpine province, the Gauls practised advanced agriculture, animal-breeding and working of metals. But in spite of fine cavalry, their capacity in battle was limited, since once the initial charge of their horsemen and sword-bearing infantry had been held up, their attacks soon degenerated into anarchic disorder. And political cohesion between the tribes, and inside each of them, was weak.

Between the River Seine and the Roman province lived 200 tribes of Celtic race. The most important of them, each surrounded by a ring of lesser dependent peoples, were the Arverni (Auvergne) based on their fortress Gergovia, the Aedui who had succeeded them as the principal allies of the Romans and had their capital at Bibracte (Mont Beuvray above Autun), and the Sequani who were centred upon Vesontio (Besançon). While the shifting relationships between these leading tribes made it clear that Gallic unity was out of the question, their side-by-side existence at least created a certain precarious balance, and, for considerable periods, a sort of peace.

This, however, was now imperilled by the Helvetii, a Celtic people of Germany who had been driven out of their homes into Switzerland and had then decided to migrate westwards, intending to traverse the whole of Gaul until they reached the Atlantic coast, where they hoped to settle. Certain Roman leaders, however, decided that this mass migration must be stopped, since it would threaten the security of the Transalpine province. That was Caesar's ostensible reason for securing the inclusion of that province in his own command. And once his consulship had come to an end, he and the army he had got together hastened northwards.

We know a great deal about the operations that followed from his own *Gallic War*. It was the best account of warfare that had ever been written by a Roman, and retained this supremacy for at least another four centuries to come. This work and his subsequent *Civil War* were entitled 'Commentaries', a term which intentionally falls short of 'Histories', denoting rather a commander's dispatches or memoranda, amplified by informative material and speeches (intended, as always in antiquity, to convey background rather than the actual words employed). Caesar's formidable intellect and lucid, concise Latin transform these ostensibly modest works into masterpieces. His unique inside knowledge carries extraordinary authority, though at the same time the prescribed literary form, as well as his own inclination, encouraged an egotistic approach, allowing little credit to the immense, efficient staff-work behind each of his operations, or to the subordinates who conducted it and commanded his legions. Moreover, Caesar's desire to refute his political enemies at Rome leads to a good deal of distortion, not so much of the actual historical facts, which Caesar, being an excellent propagandist, prefers not to falsify, but of motives, impressions and implications.

At the outset, his numerous critics maintained that the movements of the Helvetii were no concern of Rome, and that his attack on them was a piece of unprovoked aggression without precedent in the whole of Roman history.

But his desire for military prestige left him unmoved by such arguments, and at Armecy beside the River Arroux he wiped out tens and perhaps hundreds of thousands of the Helvetii, while the survivors turned back into Switzerland.

Next, in the same year, he dealt with a rather more plausible menace. The Sequani, at odds with the Aedui, had imprudently invited Ariovistus, chief of one of the tribes of west Germany, to come to their aid, and in 61 BC he had fought the Aedui and heavily defeated them. Two years later, Ariovistus secured recognition as king and ally of the Roman people: and at the time, Caesar favoured this. But soon afterwards the chief's territorial ambitions began to cause widespread alarm among the Gauls, who appealed to Rome; whereupon Caesar, scenting the prospect of another and more dramatic military campaign, reversed his favourable attitude to Ariovistus, and declared that the Gallic appeal must be accepted. At first he was somewhat worried by political disloyalty among some of his own junior officers; but before long he stamped this out. Then, on the plain of Alsace, he engaged the Germans and put them to flight. Ariovistus escaped, but died soon afterwards, and Caesar's friends declared him the triumphant successor of his relative Marius as destroyer of menacing western barbarians.

North of the Seine were the numerous and warlike Belgae, Germans by origin intermarried with Celts. At first they had been content to see the Helvetii and Ariovistus defeated. But when Caesar established his winter quarters on Gallic territory, they grew deeply suspicious of his intentions, and began to mobilize their war potential of 300,000 men. Thereupon Caesar raised two new legions in Cisalpine Gaul, bringing his total up to eight, and prepared to tackle the combined Belgic force. It soon became clear, however, that this had fallen apart, owing to the failure or virtual non-existence of supply services; and in the end only the most powerful of these tribes, the Nervii, was still able to keep an army in the field. They possessed unusually good infantry, but in 57 BC Caesar annihilated them on the River Sambre, after a desperately hazardous battle. As a result of only two seasons of military operations, Gaul already looked incapable of offering any further resistance.

In Rome, Pompey proposed a thanksgiving of unprecedented duration to celebrate these victories of his fellow-triumvir Caesar. Moreover, even the Republican Cicero felt able to second the proposal. But he did so out of gratitude not to Caesar but to Pompey. For Cicero had been in trouble. The executions during his consulship had not been forgotten, especially by Clodius, who also nursed a strong personal grudge against him. As tribune Clodius, dominating the streets and guilds of Rome with his gangs, succeeded in driving Cicero into exile (58). But in the next year he went too far. For one thing, he introduced an unlimited distribution of grain to the population of Rome, entirely without payment, a measure which outbid Cato's earlier measure of the same kind, and seemed to many people excessively radical. And then he showed signs of turning against Pompey, who suspected that Crassus was behind him and, looking round angrily for new allies, recalled Cicero from his banishment.

He came back jubilantly, and hoped that the triumvirate was breaking apart. But disappointment awaited him. For in 56 the three leaders met together at Luca (Lucca) – a place just inside Cisalpine Gaul (which formed part of Caesar's command) that was chosen for the meeting because Caesar did not want to leave his province and face prosecution. At their conference the triumvirs came to a complete agreement once again, and decided how to fulfil their future ambitions. Pompey and Crassus were to become consuls together for the second time in 55. Then Crassus, who was envious of his colleagues' military triumphs, would take up a command against Parthia, an Iranian feudal empire beyond the Euphrates, which had broken away from the Seleucids in the third century BC and was the only substantial foreign power confronting Rome anywhere in the world. Pompey was awarded the rich provinces of Spain for five years and, by a concession anticipating the future arrangements of Roman emperors, was allowed to govern them *in absentia* through subordinates, while he himself remained at Rome and virtually controlled its administration. Caesar's provincial command was likewise prolonged for a further five years, so that he could exploit and extend his new conquests in Transalpine Gaul.

However, it at once became apparent that this country was not yet fully conquered after all. For the Veneti of western Brittany, a people with a powerful fleet, were in rebellion. In the previous years, they had duly surrendered to one of Caesar's officers, a son of Crassus. But then they learnt with anger that Caesar was planning an invasion of Britain, which would seriously upset their control of cross-Channel trade. As a protest, they placed Caesar's requisitioning officers under arrest. But he sent a fleet against them and they were crushed in a battle in Quiberon Bay (56). Expeditions dispatched to Normandy and Aquitania (south-western Gaul) were equally successful, and then early in the next year Caesar threw back a German migration from the east, as he had already done three years before, but with even greater slaughter.

He had prepared for his attack on these Germans by a treacherous breach of faith which caused Cato at Rome to remonstrate; though his motives were political rather than humanitarian, and in any case his objections were not widely shared. Moreover, Caesar at this juncture greatly impressed metropolitan opinion because he built a bridge over the Rhine and led a force across it for a brief stay on the other side, where no Roman commander or troops had ever set foot before. The bridge was a display of his army's superb engineering: but it was also a demonstration that there were no bounds to the frontiers of Rome and his own ambitions.

This last purpose was once again in his mind when, as the Veneti had foreseen, he launched his first expedition to Britain. A subsidiary motive was his desire to lay hands on the considerable, if somewhat exaggerated, wealth of the country, particularly in metals. And he also wanted to harry certain local Belgic rulers on the island – men descended from migrants from northern Gaul who had formed important tribal groupings in Britain, and had supported their continental kinsmen against Caesar. But his main purpose was to eclipse Pompey as a leader of armies to hitherto unknown lands.

Pompey, not to be outdone, later objected that the English Channel was merely an insignificant mudflat. But Caesar had reason to disagree. For when, after embarking from Portus Itius (Boulogne or Wissant), he had landed near Walmer or Deal on the south-east coast of England and had put two legions ashore, many of his eighty ships were heavily damaged on the beach by high tides that he had not foreseen. The ambush that this encouraged the British to attempt was duly beaten off. However, the entire Roman force sailed back to Gaul only eighteen days after its arrival.

The British tribal leaders had agreed to provide hostages. But very few of them were handed over or dispatched, and nothing else had been achieved either. So in the following year, Caesar, after cowing the recalcitrant Belgic Treviri on the Moselle, led a second and larger expedition to Britain. This time he took five legions and 2,000 cavalry on 800 ships – by far the largest fleet the Channel had ever seen, and larger than any it was to see again until 1944. Embarking at the same point as before, he landed a little farther north, near Sandwich, and at once marched into the hinterland. But history repeated itself, for a storm in the night destroyed forty of his ships and disabled most of the rest. So he had to return to the coast to organize repairs, reinforcements and protective measures. Meanwhile the British tribes, dropping their habitual feuds for the moment, had appointed King Cassivellaunus of the Catuvellauni (Hertfordshire) as commander-in-chief of their united forces. But Caesar, beating off guerrillas as he went, forced his way across the Thames – the British tribes at his rear failing to provide a diversion – and stormed the king's capital at Wheathampstead, near St Albans. Then, after a stay of three months on the island, he and his army were transported back to Gaul.

Meanwhile, Cassivellaunus had formally surrendered, given hostages, and promised tribute, and when Caesar told Rome that such remote and exotic peoples had submitted it made impressive propaganda. But he also hoped that he had established a network of client and semi-client states beyond the imperial frontiers, as Pompey had done in the east. Time showed, however, that this had not been achieved; and, as for direct control, Rome did not succeed in annexing any portion whatever of Britain for nearly a hundred years to come.

When Caesar returned to the mainland, he planned to split up his army at a number of separate winter quarters in different regions of Gaul. For it had now become even clearer than before that the conquest of the country was far from complete.

The first trouble that occurred was among the Carnutes, a tribe in the wooded interior round Cenabum (Orléans). Their territory was of particular importance because it contained the principal meeting-place of the Druids, religious leaders who dominated civil and legal and educational affairs throughout Gaul. Among the Belgae, too, in the northern part of the country, outbreaks of rebellion indicated the dismaying possibility that detachments of Caesar's army might be isolated and cut to pieces: one tribe revolted, another massacred a garrison of one and a half legions, and a further garrison under Cicero's brother was only narrowly saved from a hostile horde at Samarobriva (Amiens). And it was in that town that Caesar decided to spend the next winter, instead of moving into Cisalpine Gaul, as had been his custom at the end of each previous campaigning season. Then in 53, at Samarobriva and elsewhere in the north, he summoned three conferences of Gallic chieftains, in an endeavour to stamp out disaffection.

Nevertheless, in the following year the Gauls rose in general revolt. They conferred the supreme command on the only talented leader they produced in these wars, Vercingetorix of the tribe of the Arverni in central Gaul. That winter, Caesar had returned to the Cisalpine part of his command. But now, on hearing the news of the rebellion, he hastened back across the Alps with unexpected speed; and Vercingetorix decided that the only way to stop him was by a scorched earth policy of destroying every Gallic settlement that might provide the Romans with supplies. Caesar directed his attack against the chief fortress of the Arverni, Gergovia. But there he received his first serious setback of the war, and was compelled to break off the siege, while the other principal tribe of the region, the Aedui, was encouraged by his discomfiture to join the insurrection. Caesar had sent his deputy Labienus to the north, but now he summoned him back. Together they besieged Vercingetorix who,. by an unwise decision following a defeat, had retired behind the walls of the fortress of Alesia (Alise Sainte Reine). Huge reinforcements came to relieve him, and for four days Caesar's army had to resist an attack from both directions. But then the Gallic relief forces were routed, and, although there were still resisters to mop up – a process accompanied by dire atrocities – the Great Revolt was at an end.

The Gauls had, on the whole, failed to unite with any effectiveness. And the losses they had suffered were appalling: at least a third of all their men of military age were killed, and another third sold into slavery. And now their large territory, reduced to subject status, was assessed for Roman tribute, at first as a series of client states, dependent on the old Transalpine province in the south, and subsequently as three separate new provinces. By the annexation of this land which forms a bridge between the Inner and the Outer Seas, the whole concept and character of the Roman Empire had been transformed. It was no longer a purely Mediterranean dominion any more, since a vast conglomeration of territories in continental and northern Europe had now been opened up to Romanization.

Caesar had shown himself to be one of the supreme military commanders of all time. But was he a highly original general, or one who perfected a machine he had inherited from earlier commanders? The truth lies somewhere between the two views. He learnt from others all that could be learnt about the workings of the Roman army, but he also left his own stamp on every part of the machine. His powers of endurance were phenomenal. A first-class horseman, he also thought nothing of covering 100 miles a day in a light carriage on terrible roads – while all the time dictating official letters or literary works to relays of secretaries. But his outstanding personal qualities as a commander were speed, timing, and adaptability to suddenly changing circumstances. For his generalship was breathtakingly quick in mind as well as in movement: far too quick for his enemies.

Sometimes this brilliant rapidity produced alarming mistakes and perils. But he became used to extricating himself from such hazards, and achieving total victory by the narrowest of margins. His *Commentaries* pay tribute to the luck for which he was famous. But a commander has to harness the lucky odds in his favour, and that is what Caesar almost invariably achieved. He attracted unbounded admiration from his legions, whom he often addressed with great eloquence, for he was second only to Cicero as an orator. And he linked them to himself still more firmly by doubling their pay.

In Rome, however, during the last four years of his Gallic campaigning, the political situation imposed by the triumvirate had gradually fallen to pieces. As always, Caesar was keeping the closest possible eye on the city through his numerous and effective agents, and by a massive correspondence passing between Rome and Gaul more rapidly, sometimes, than letters do today. But the news that reached him from the capital became increasingly disquieting, since, although Pompey remained nearby, incessant disorders, largely fomented by Clodius, virtually reduced its public life to chaos. Moreover Julia, Caesar's daughter and Pompey's wife, died in 54 BC, so that the links between the two leaders were seriously weakened. And then the triumvirate ceased to exist because their third partner,

Crassus, in his attempt to overcome the Parthians, met with disaster. For at the Mesopotamian town of Carrhae (Haran in south-eastern Turkey), his army was totally defeated by a highly trained force of 10,000 Parthian horse-archers: and when he went to negotiate with their commanders, they put him to death (53). This meant that Pompey and Caesar, with their rival aims and ambitions, now stood alone in direct confrontation.

Early in the following year, Clodius was murdered, and in the resulting emergency Pompey assumed his third consulship, holding the office for some months without a colleague. Some detected in him a taste for permanent one-man rule; but there is no real evidence that this is what Pompey had in mind. In order to retain his friendship Caesar suggested new marriage ties between their families. But Pompey now took a significant decision by rejecting Caesar's proposed bargain and marrying Cornelia, daughter of the highly aristocratic Metellus Scipio, whom he elevated to become his fellow-consul. At least until Caesar was got rid of, conservatives such as Metellus were willing enough to form an association with Pompey, though they hoped to put him in his place later on. And he in his turn, as this new marriage alliance revealed, was no longer averse to them either. That is to say, he was moving away from Caesar, of whom he was increasingly frightened and jealous; though he still could not bring himself to alienate him completely.

As for Caesar's aims, it remained essential to his career, and perhaps even to his survival, that his present governorship should not be followed by a period without office, during which he could be subjected to prosecutions. According to the existing law, the earliest year for which he could aim at a second consulship was 48: so he had somehow to retain his command right up until then. In consequence, he expressed the desire to become a candidate for that consulship, when the time came, *in absentia*. Pompey obligingly agreed to this – while at the same time arranging for his own absentee governorship of Spain to be extended for another five years. But very soon afterwards, he allowed himself to be pushed by his advisers into less friendly measures towards Caesar; and these culminated in a decision that the appointment of a new provincial commander to replace him should be allowed to come up for discussion in the Senate in March 50 BC.

But Caesar had the backing of a young tribune, Curio, who persistently vetoed demands that any such successor should be appointed. And then Curio produced an alternative suggestion: that Caesar should, indeed, resign from his post, but that Pompey should simultaneously resign from his absentee Spanish governorship. This idea seemed attractive to numerous senators, but a small group of diehards ensured its rejection. Near the end of the year, however, the proposal came up for a second time, and Curio induced the Senate to agree to it, by a very large majority – whereupon the diehard faction vetoed it once again. The deadlock was complete; and on the following day one of the consuls, an ultra-conservative, called on Pompey to take up the command of all the forces of the Republic. Pompey accepted the commission 'unless a better way can be found'. and took over two legions which had been about to depart for Syria.

Negotiations continued; but when a message from Caesar arrived in Rome, the young tribune Antony (Marcus Antonius), who had succeeded Curio as his representative, could scarcely induce the senators to allow it to be read: instead they proceeded to pass their emergency decree with Caesar as its target, and Antony and a colleague hastily left Rome for the north. Then on the night of 10 January 49 BC Caesar crossed the small River Rubicon, which formed the border between Cisalpine Gaul and eastern Italy. When he moved across this bridge, taking a single legion with him, he was breaking Rome's law of treason which forbade a governor to lead his troops outside his province – a law which Sulla had formulated precisely with the aim of curbing such acts against the government.

And so, as Caesar himself declared, the die was cast, and the crossing of this little stream was one of the formal turning-points in Roman history. For it meant that the nation was plunged into an empire-wide civil war for which neither side was ready. Yet, in a sense, the real turning-point had come a decade earlier, when the Republic was already, to a large extent, superseded by the autocratic triumvirate. During the intervening years, its inevitable disintegration had accelerated; and now it had entered a catastrophic terminal phase.

But the fifties BC had not all been war and politics. For example, this was also the time when two of the world's outstanding poets completed much or most of their work. The 2,300 surviving lines of Catullus (c. 84–54 BC) were found inscribed on a manuscript discovered at Verona; and this had been his native city, for he, like other writers of Latin poetry at this time, was a product of Cisalpine Gaul. For their formal inspiration, these men went back to the poets of Alexandria whose learned, individualistic, sentimental tendencies had dominated Greek literature during the previous two centuries. But the new, Latin, Alexandrian movement differed considerably from its Greek predecessor in purpose. For the function of the latter had been to revive a tired culture by the injection of novel, topical elements, whereas Roman poetry, despite certain achievements in the past, was still raw and unrefined when these influences overtook it, preparing the way for the technical perfection of Catullus.

Yet although this formal mastery is fully displayed in his jewel-like miniature epics, it was not by these longer poems that he influenced the world of the future, but by his shorter pieces. Some of these give expression to a heartbroken and heart-breaking intensity – inspired by his love for the hopelessly unfaithful 'Lesbia', who was really called Clodia and may have been a fashionable, immoral sister of the politician Clodius. Casting himself free of the impersonal objectivity of the Greeks, the poet feels an irresistible excitement, which he compels his readers to share with him: and the virtuosity and precision of his language heighten the forcefulness of its impact. For Catullus is the product of agonizing tension between a powerful mind and tormented emotions. He responds to the demands of love with an unprecedented seriousness, veering between ecstasy and desperation; and both are communicated with a total intimacy designed for an elite circle of close, like-minded friends. Thus, although his verses fully reflect the lively, dangerous, immoral, precarious social scene of his day, the service of the community is no part of his aim, and the service of its leaders even less: Caesar and Pompey he mentions briefly and contemptuously as irrelevancies, introducing them only because of his fastidious distaste for the upstarts who gained power as their supporters.

His older contemporary Lucretius (*c.* 94–55 BC) does not mention these great men by name at all. It was an extraordinary age which could produce two such totally different poets. Lucretius was an adherent of the philosophy of the Athenian Epicurus (341–270 BC), who had sought to prove that the universe was completely material, consisting of nothing but atoms and the space in which they move. The Epicureans were an austere, unpretentious and unambitious sect who had gained a certain amount of support in Italy, and now had adherents in Rome. But Lucretius, with startling incongruity, transformed the philosopher's undistinguished Greek prose into a burningly impassioned Latin poem on the nature of the universe, *About Reality* or *How Things Are* (*De Rerum Natura*), the only philosophical poem of antiquity that has come down to us intact.

It offers a flashing profusion of visual images, for this poet was a vivid panoramic painter of words. The scientific doctrine he presents is of no more than historical interest today, as a link between Greek and modern atomists. Yet its presentation displays Lucretius as the most original, adventurous, imaginative and dedicated thinker of his day, and perhaps the most formidable intellectual ever to write in the Latin tongue. His interpretation of the universe in a wholly materialistic fashion prompted him to declare, like Epicurus but with a great deal more vigour, that fear of the gods, and above all fear of death, is completely unwarranted and pointless. Yet even if the world is merely a chance pile-up of atoms streaming in a meaningless void, they do not move, Lucretius feels, in a totally predetermined fashion, but on the contrary show independence of movement, and sometimes unpredictably swerve. This means, he concludes, that individual persons are not slaves to fate but remain free agents; and his picture of the triumphs of the human brain and will, which have created civilization, is one of the supreme expositions of what men and women are capable of achieving. Our purpose in life, Lucretius and his master declare, should be happiness. This assertion has damned the Epicureans in the eyes of posterity on the grounds that they are advocating sensuous pleasures; but mistakenly, since, like other philosophies of the day, they equated happiness with something altogether different, namely freedom from disturbance (*ataraxia*), only procurable by the acquisition of the right kind of knowledge.

Caesar and Pompey, the poet must clearly have thought, did not possess this kind of knowledge at all, and it was therefore predictable that he should not refer to them. But he expresses, in forthright terms, the poorest possible view of all the politicians whose rat-race was dragging the Roman Republic down to its final extinction:

> Men lost,
> Confused, in hectic search for the right road,
> The strife of wits, the wars for precedence,
> The everlasting struggle, night and day,
> To win towards heights of wealth and power.

After crossing the Rubicon, Caesar moved forward rapidly into the centre of Italy. He divided his small force into two columns, one of which he himself led to Ariminum (Rimini), where he was joined by the friendly tribunes from Rome, Curio and Antony: and then both his columns pressed on, and one town after another opened its gates to them.

His enemies included most of the senior senators and indeed, theoretically, most of the territories of the empire and this made them too confident. They were also too jealous of Pompey, and would not allow him the powers a commander needed; and they had totally underestimated the capacity of Caesar and his soldiers to complete a rapid invasion of Italy. These troops were highly experienced, after all the battles of the Gallic war; whereas Pompey's veterans, on the other hand, had become less efficient during twelve years of peace, and his best legions, which were in Spain, could give him no help. So, in the face of Caesar's advance, Pompey retreated southwards through the Italian peninsula, while his uneasy allies the consuls fled from Rome, departing in such haste that they even failed to take the reserve treasury with them.

At Corfinium, however, east of Rome, the wealthy nobleman Ahenobarbus, disregarding Pompey's order to retreat and join up with him, endeavoured to make a stand against Caesar, whom he detested. But he was soon compelled to surrender, whereupon Caesar allowed him and the fifty senators and knights who were with him to go free. It was a novel and striking display of clemency to Roman citizens, very different from his earlier treatment of Gauls and Germans. Then in March, only sixty-five days after the campaign had begun, his enemies evacuated Italy altogether: the consuls set out across the Adriatic, followed by Pompey himself who

THE CIVIL WARS

skilfully evaded attempts to blockade him in Brundusium harbour. He was probably right not to persist in forlorn efforts to fight Caesar in Italy, and justified also in making for the eastern provinces; for his favourite strategy was always to fight from carefully prepared positions of superior strength, and in the east he had huge resources to draw upon. Cicero, however, thought his decision was wrong. But all the same, after an inconclusive personal interview with Caesar and prolonged waverings, he decided that Pompey's side was the lesser of the two evils, and obeyed his injunction to join him at Thessalonica (Salonica) in Macedonia.

Caesar could not pursue his opponents yet, for the command of the sea was in their hands and threatened the grain supply of Italy. So Curio, acting on his behalf, seized the wheat-producing island of Sicily, though he was then defeated and killed in north Africa. Meanwhile, Caesar himself, after convening Senate and Assembly meetings at Rome, set off by land to attack Spain, the chief remaining Pompeian stronghold in western Europe; and once there, he cornered and overwhelmed the enemy forces near Ilerda (Lerida).

Meanwhile, in southern Gaul, the Greek city-state of Massilia, which had entrusted its defences to Ahenobarbus after his release, was forced to surrender to Caesar, who allowed the place to remain autonomous but, in fact, brought its long career of independent statehood to an end. He was

still there when he learnt that a mutiny was threatening among four of his
legions at Placentia (Piacenza) in Cisalpine Gaul – a painful incident omitted from his *Civil War*. One of the troubles was that the soldiers deplored
his policy of clemency, since it deprived them of their loot. After quelling
the mutiny by an oration, he paid his second visit of the year to the capital,
where he assumed, for a brief period, his first tenure of the post of dictator,
which Sulla had revived thirty-two years earlier. This enabled him, during
an eleven days' stay in the capital, to fulfil his long-standing ambition of
arranging to become consul in the following year. And his brief dictatorship also gave him a chance to make a start with some of his gravest
administrative problems.

Then, finally, he moved against his opponents in the Balkans, eluding a
flotilla intended to stop him; and after a nerve-racking delay of three
months, Antony managed to reach him from Italy with reinforcements.
Caesar next endeavoured to blockade Pompey's key base Dyrrhachium
(Durrës in Albania), but the attempt was a disastrous failure, and he re-
coiled inland into the Thessalian plain. There, in the largest battle ever
fought between Romans, his superior generalship won the day near
Pharsalus (48). Pompey himself escaped, first by land and then by sea, and
after abortive attempts to land at Aegean ports, decided to proceed to
Egypt; he chose it because the government of the boy king Ptolemy XIII
had backed him against Caesar in the civil war. But as Pompey landed on
the Egyptian coast, he was struck down and assassinated, for the Egyptian
politicians intended to be on the winning side.

And they also wanted to give Caesar no excuse for staying in Egypt; for
he was known to be on his way, in hot pursuit of Pompey, and very soon
afterwards he arrived. His intention was to extort an enormous sum from
this wealthy and still ostensibly independent country. But the official
reason for the visit was to arbitrate between the monarch and his half-sister
Cleopatra VII who had been driven into exile. When, however, Cleopatra,
a highly intelligent 21-year-old charmer, secretly came to see him in
Alexandria, Caesar, over thirty years her senior, took her into the palace and
lived with her as her lover. Thereupon he found himself perilously besieged
by the royal army, which favoured the king. It was not until March of the
following year that the arrival of a relieving force enabled him to bring his
Egyptian enemies to battle, south of the delta of the Nile, and destroy
them. Ptolemy XIII was killed, and Caesar confirmed Cleopatra as queen
of Egypt and a client of Rome and of himself. Then, after a five-day campaign against the son of Rome's old enemy Mithridates VI in Pontus, culminating in total victory at Zela (Zile), Caesar at last returned to Italy and
the capital.

He had been away for a long time, much too long. Antony, his deputy at
Rome, had not been able to stop some of his fellow nobles from getting out

of hand; and Caesar also had a second threat of mutiny to deal with. He
averted it only just in time, for Pompey's death had not meant the death of
his cause, and his sons Cnaeus and Sextus, supported by many prominent
Romans in north Africa and Spain, were now ready for battle. At the height
of winter Caesar crossed over to north Africa, and after a campaign involving many hardships fought a totally successful battle on the isthmus at
Thapsus (Ras Dimas). The enemy commander Metellus Scipio, Pompey's
father-in-law, committed suicide, followed shortly afterwards by Cato,
who committed suicide at Utica, thereby providing the Republicans with a
martyr and a saint.

After a magnificent Triumph in Rome, Caesar left the city again before
the year was over, and made at once for southern Spain. There, in the
following spring, he won a hard and horrifying soldier's battle at an unidentified place named Munda. Labienus, who after serving as his deputy
throughout the Gallic campaigns had joined the other side in the civil
wars, fell in the holocaust, and Pompey's son Cnaeus Pompeius was caught
and killed soon afterwards. His brother Sextus got away, and lived on to
plague Caesar's successors; but as far as Caesar was concerned, the gigantic
and immeasurably costly convulsion of the civil war was over.

Henceforward he employed the title *Imperator* as a special, personal
appellation, not with the meaning of its later derivative 'emperor', but to
show that he was the military commander who totally surpassed all others.

During the brief intervals between these campaigns, and then, when they
were over, in the single year of life that still remained to him, Caesar began
to show that he was a genius, not only as a commander, but as an administrator as well.

The first need, as always in these times, was to reward his ex-soldiers,
whose loyalty, in spite of near-mutinies, had gained him his victory. So
Caesar, who now possessed enormous wealth, settled these retired legionaries in thousands. In the first place he established many colonies in Italy.
But there, if he was to adhere to his much-heralded policy of clemency, he
could only procure a limited amount of land. So he also initiated at least
forty such foundations in the provinces. Among them were the new colonies
of Corinth and Carthage, both rising again out of their destruction just a
hundred years earlier; and both destined to become impressive cities
once more, Corinth as the capital of Roman Greece and Carthage as its
counterpart in Africa and the largest city of all the western provinces.

The new colonies of Caesar included veterans who could always be
called out again for military service, so that these towns became important
bastions of imperial defence – and of potential support for Caesar's régime.
But the settlements were not intended for veterans alone. For the most
original feature of his foundations was the inclusion of civilians as well –

including 80,000 of the capital's penniless unemployed. As well as helping to break down old barriers between Romans and provincials, this meant that Caesar, like no one else before him, had seriously begun to tackle the obstinate problem of the impoverished workless population of the city.

Having founded his colonies, Caesar laid down for them a standard system of local government on Roman lines. The colonies in the east, of which besides Corinth there were relatively few, remained isolated outposts of Romanism in areas which remained predominantly Greek. But more than three-quarters of the new foundations were in the west, and throughout these regions they acted, during the centuries to come, as potent instruments of Romanization. Caesar also gave citizenship liberally on an individual basis, for example to men who practised medicine at Rome.

But the greatest of his achievements, though lacking in melodramatic glamour, was probably his long and patient handling of the problem of debt. This had been an intractable difficulty, time and time again, for more than four centuries. But it had never been so painful and hazardous as it was now. For owing to the disturbances of the past fifty years, many Romans had fallen more grievously into debt than ever, and in spite of sporadic attempts at mitigation over the years, the harsh laws that were still in force cast many of these debtors into total destitution. Caesar, who had been heavily in debt himself, knew very well how things stood; he had seen how the Catilinarian conspiracy was largely supported by desperate debtors, and then he himself had been obliged to grapple with such problems on behalf of the provincials when he was governor in Further Spain.

Yet would-be reformers in this field, as his knowledge of Roman history could warn him, had always found themselves caught in a dilemma. Something had to be done for the victims of the system, whether their misfortunes were their own fault or not. On the other hand, as Cicero was always saying, anything approaching a general cancellation of debts would destroy private property – and thereby usher in chaos.

At the beginning of the civil war the debt crisis had entered a new and even graver phase, because of a shortage of currency: for much coin had been hoarded against better times, and most of what remained was gone to pay the armies. This meant that, whereas men were being urgently requested by their creditors to repay what they had borrowed – and were eager enough to do so, since interest rates had risen from 4 per cent to nearly 12 – they could not find the money, and had to raise it by selling everything they possessed, at the wretched prices which were all they could get in the prevailing emergency. So Caesar, in 49 BC, started upon a long, patient series of attempts to deal with this harrowing situation. First, the hoarding of coin was forbidden – a regulation, admittedly, which could scarcely be enforced, though it did put a certain amount more cash into circulation. Secondly, creditors were compelled by a new measure to accept any land or other property offered them in repayment of their loans, and to accept it at pre-war prices assessed by special commissioners.

Of course, they complained bitterly: whereas the debtors, on the other hand, felt that Caesar could have done a great deal more to help them. However, the fact that both sides were dissatisfied suggests that his proposals were not unreasonable. Yet they caused severe tension at Rome, and he himself was by now at Alexandria, unable to deal with it. Taking advantage, therefore, of his prolonged absence, a trouble-making praetor advocated a moratorium on all repayments of debt and payments of interest; and then another politician, a tribune, made the classic revolutionary proposal that all debts should be cancelled altogether. However the praetor came to a violent end, and the tribune's proposals were halted at the instance of Antony, Caesar's deputy in Italy, by police measures costing 800 lives.

On his return, Caesar, far from pleased, was forced to conclude that his earlier measures, like those of so many previous reformers, had not gone far enough to satisfy the debtors' violent grievances. He therefore decided to cancel all interest due since the beginning of the civil war – in so far as it had not yet been paid, whereas the equivalents of payments that had already been made were to be deducted from future capital repayments. These measures, we are told, wiped out one-quarter of all debts at a single blow.

Once again, a serious loss had been inflicted on creditors. Yet they were obliged to admit that they would never have seen the rest of the money anyway – and that Caesar was not the destroyer of private property his enemies had made him out to be. Indeed, it was a significant feature of the civil war that the most able financiers, unlike senior senators, had mostly chosen to take his side. After his new regulations came into force, financial confidence started to come back, and once more, money began to be freely lent and borrowed. In this field, Caesar had achieved more than any previous Roman statesman; he had broken the back of the Republic's most unmanageable problem.

That was hard, laborious, unspectacular work, but Caesar also had all the appetite of great potentates for splendid spectacles to distract the people from their hardships. Moreover, huge portions of the wealth he accumulated in his victorious wars were spent not only on celebrating Triumphs but on erecting magnificent buildings. A great new hall for public business, the Basilica Julia, was under construction in the Roman Forum; and, close by, another forum named after Caesar himself began to take shape. Its colonnaded precinct flanked a shrine of Venus the Mother (Genetrix), since it was from this goddess, through the mythical Aeneas, that the Julian family claimed to be descended.

There was a statue of Venus in the temple, and beside it he placed a gilt bronze statue of Queen Cleopatra VII. She could see it for herself, because in 46 BC she arrived in the city, with her surviving 13-year-old half-brother (with whom she officially shared the throne) and her infant son Caesarion whose paternity she ascribed, perhaps rightly, to Caesar. The ostensible purpose of her visit was to confirm her father's treaty of alliance and friendship with Egypt's patron Rome. And thereafter, while she stayed on at the capital for the rest of Caesar's life, it is possible to identify certain of his actions which show the influence of herself and her country. For one thing, his plan to establish magnificent public libraries at Rome was based on the world-famous library of the Ptolemies attached to the Museum at Alexandria. Secondly, his ambitious, though incomplete, projects to dig a canal through the Pomptine (Pontine) marshes, south of Rome, and another through the isthmus of Corinth in Greece, must have owed a great deal to Egypt, which was the home of these skills. Furthermore, Caesar's revision of the gravely dislocated Roman calendar, a reform which with minor adjustments has survived until the present day, was directed by an Alexandrian astronomer.

Besides, Cleopatra, to whose Ptolemaic mind the Roman nobleman's ideal of free speech and action seemed absurd and undesirable, may have helped to prompt a trend towards autocratic impatience which people were noticing in the supreme *imperator*. It was true that in his administrative activities he could not and did not act alone, but needed the assistance of the Senate. But it was a Senate modelled according to his own wishes and intentions. Raising its membership from 600 to 900, he enrolled the men who had helped him to gain power – bankers, industrialists, army officers and landowners: and this influx permanently transformed the Senate's character. He also planned to include in its ranks an unprecedentedly large quantity of former officials. This was because he had increased the number of state posts in order to meet the greater needs of the expanded Roman world; and their holders were automatically members of the Senate. Now they, like the other new Senators, were men who were loyal to himself: since although the annual elections to consulships and other offices still continued, those appointed to them were almost invariably the people he wanted. Caesar could do as he liked.

The point was emphasized by the depiction of his own head on the national currency, the first portrait of any living man or woman ever to appear on a Roman coin. And this rising personality-cult was stressed still further by the large number of his portrait-busts which were made and distributed round Italy and the provinces. This marked an important stage in the development of one of Rome's outstanding art-forms. It was an art which had first developed among the Greeks of recent centuries who were interested in personality and literary biography. Like biographers, the Greek sculptors had increasingly desired to stress the unique, private pattern of the personage they were depicting: and when he was a ruler, it was their function to show him to the world as a great man but also as a distinctive individual.

And then the Romans, in their turn, employing very often Greeks or orientals to do the job, but relying also on native Etruscan and other Italian sculptural traditions, showed themselves extremely receptive to these same aims, which coincided with their own interest in national and family history and moral character. From the third century BC onwards, the sculptural portrayals of individuals had received increasing attention in the city; and after 100, Roman portraiture began to become a major art. Portraits also started to appear on the national coinage of the period, which was issued by a committee of three young mint officials of leading families elected each year. Imitating bronze or marble busts or statues, now lost, the designers of these coins first selected early or legendary Roman heroes for portrayal in imaginative fashion; and then, with greater boldness and a close approach to realism, the recently dead, including Sulla. But it marked a decisive stage forward when heads of the living Caesar first appeared on his coins, in January or February 44 BC.

They imitated sculptural portraits – some of which still survive today. It was Caesar himself who gave these sculptors their first really important opportunity. His fine, sensitive features brought out the best in them – and skilful artists could even capture the piercing gaze of his dark eyes. Their task was vitally important because his great position in the state demanded their interpretation of his personality in all its aspects. In this way, then, was launched the great series of portraits of Rome's rulers, which are among its principal artistic gifts to Europe.

The few examples of his surviving busts which can be dated to his lifetime cunningly blend realism with grandeur. For Caesar was as grand as any king. Yet he had no intention of reviving the ancient Roman kingship in his own person, since it was traditionally equated with tyranny. Instead, the constitutional status he chose for himself was the dictatorship, like Sulla before him. From 49 onwards, Caesar was reappointed to this post a number of times, and in 46, by an innovation, for as long as ten years. But then, in February 44 BC, he was appointed dictator for the rest of his life – PERPETVO, as his coins unequivocally assert. This was an exceedingly grave step to have taken. For the conversion of what had originally been intended as an emergency, short-term office into a permanent autocracy meant that the other nobles, however many consulships and other offices they might be permitted to hold, would never again be able to get their hands on the real controls and profits of public life.

But their resentment, evidently, did not weigh with Caesar, who was forming plans that he considered to be of immeasurably greater significance. Above all, he wanted to leave the intrigues of the capital and get back among his admiring, incomparable army. For he was consumed by a desire for further military glory: and it had to come soon, since he was fifty-six and suffered from precarious health, being liable, apparently, to epileptic attacks. But there was still time for him to rival Alexander the Great – and in the same part of the world that Alexander himself had invaded, since Crassus' defeat and death at the hands of the Parthians nine years earlier urgently needed to be avenged. However, a considerable Roman force was first detached to eastern Europe in order to cow the powerful kingdom of Dacia, whose rulers had recently extended their sway from the national homeland in Transylvania (Rumania) as far as the Black Sea. The role of these legions was preparatory. For, once Caesar had suppressed the Parthians and perhaps extended his conquests, like Alexander, into the remotest regions of the orient, it was believed that he intended to wheel back through southern Russia and continental Europe, completing the annexation of Dacia and further vast territories on the way.

But the east was Caesar's first objective, and its provinces witnessed the marshalling of a great Roman army to await his arrival. He was to leave the city on 18 March 44 BC. When this became known, the news brought the growing hostility of the nobles to a head. For whereas it was distasteful enough to be governed by a perpetual dictator on the spot, the prospect of government by his aides or secretaries in his absence was nothing less than intolerable. For it was they who were going to represent him, and enforce his orders, during his prolonged forthcoming absence abroad; and the two chief secretaries, Oppius and Balbus, were not even senators.

There had been suggestions of conspiracies against his life before. But now planning began in earnest. Its chief instigator was Cassius, a proud man who had come over to Caesar in the civil war but did not feel he had been sufficiently rewarded. And Cassius won over another personage who had likewise changed sides, his less dynamic and more philosophically minded brother-in-law Marcus Brutus, who although a special protégé of Caesar was obsessed by the glory of his own legendary forebears as liberators of the Republic. Another leading conspirator was Brutus' distant relation Decimus Brutus Albinus, who had been one of Caesar's principal commanders in the Gallic war and was designated by the dictator for a consulship in the future. With these and others to lead them, the various small separate groups of malcontents coalesced into a single body of sixty determined plotters.

Caesar was perfectly well aware that many noblemen detested him. But a mixture of fatalism and contemptuous pride caused him to ignore the evident threat. Since he had restored the Roman world to prosperity and peace, and since, if he ceased to be at the helm, these benefits would disappear, he professed himself unable to believe that anyone could seriously want him out of the way. Indeed, so little was he concerned with the evident danger to his life that he even disbanded his personal bodyguard of Spaniards, and refused to agree to suggestions that he ought to re-engage them.

Then, three days before he was due to depart for the east, the Senate gathered for a meeting in Pompey's Theatre: and there the conspirators surrounded him and stabbed him to death. Not long before, all senators had sworn an oath of allegiance to the Father of their Country, as Caesar had now come to be called: they were clients bound to protect their patron, just as a son is obliged to protect his own father. But at the moment of supreme reckoning they rushed out of the building, and Caesar lay where he had fallen.

For all his immeasurable abilities as a general and administrator, he had failed, and would probably have continued to fail, to rescue Rome from its major dilemma. It was this. The Republic, obviously, had become impotent, and, that being so, there was no practical alternative to one-man rule. Yet one-man rule was just what the nobles, although themselves incapable of ruling any more, categorically refused to accept; and so they put him to death. It seemed an insoluble problem. Yet there now came another sort of man altogether, who performed the seemingly impossible task of finding a solution after all: he was the 19-year-old Octavian, grandnephew of Julius Caesar who had adopted him in his will as his son.

# 13

# Augustus

AFTER CAESAR'S MURDER, HIS right-hand man Antony, consul in 44 BC, used a variety of methods, including the falsification of the dead man's papers, to gain control of events; and he took steps at the same time to arouse the people against the assassins, Brutus and Cassius, who before long retreated to the east. Yet for all the growing power and popularity of Antony, who in spite of a taste for riotous living was a politician and general of considerable gifts, Cicero, true to his distaste for autocrats large and small, attacked him fiercely in a series of brilliant speeches, the *Philippics*; and with Cicero's encouragement the young Octavian, exploiting his testamentary adoption by his murdered great-uncle Caesar, gradually emerged as a rival to Antony, and gained the support of the Senate.

In April 43 a senatorial coalition including Octavian defeated Antony at Mutina (Modena) in Cisalpine Gaul, and compelled him to withdraw into the Transalpine (Narbonese) province. There, however, he was joined by a number of commanders, including Lepidus (son of the consul of 78 BC), a henchman of Caesar who had succeeded him in the chief priesthood of the state. In November, Octavian, smarting from an unwise snub by the Senate, became reconciled with Antony and Lepidus at a conference in Bononia (Bologna), and the three men were granted a five-year autocratic appointment with the task of reconstituting the government – the 'Second Triumvirate' which, unlike the first, was a formal creation of the state. The institutions of the Republic, from the consulships downwards, still continued to exist. But the power lay with the triumvirs, and this was ratified by law.

After a holocaust of their political enemies, in which 300 senators and 2,000 knights were proscribed and hounded to death, Antony and Octavian crossed the Adriatic and won two battles at Philippi in Macedonia against Brutus and Cassius, both of whom committed suicide (42 BC). Antony was the main victor, though Octavian's prestige was enhanced by the recognition of Julius Caesar as a divinity of the Roman state, since this made his adoptive child the son of a god. Antony assumed control of the eastern provinces and Octavian took over most of the west; but in these regions he encountered serious opposition, first from Pompey's second son Sextus, who was conducting piratical attacks from Sicily, and then from a brother of Antony in Italy itself. Antony and Octavian, however, came to a fresh agreement, confirming the division of the empire between them (40 BC).

But their relations with one another showed increasing signs of strain. This was partly because offence and suspicion were caused in the west by Antony's liaison with the queen of Egypt, Cleopatra VII. In recent years, Rome had become familiar with feminine power. During the last decades of the Republic, women lived in complete freedom. They owned wealth in their own names and looked after it themselves. And this liberty was reflected in their social and domestic arrangements; for instance they now

reclined at dinner like the men. Clodius' sister Clodia had been a famous
beauty who lived hard and fast. And Roman women exerted greatly increased political influence, too. After Caesar's death, Brutus' mother held
a conference to decide what her son and his friends should do, and Brutus
also received exhortations from his masterful wife. But the most strong-
willed of all was Antony's wife Fulvia, who, without consulting her husband, had joined his brother in rebelling against Octavian. However, she
died, and in 40 Antony married Octavian's sister, Octavia: and in these circumstances his simultaneous association with Cleopatra, a descendant of
formidable queens who had more ambitious ideas than any Roman matron,
was unacceptable not only to Octavian, whose family was insulted, but to
conservative Roman opinion in general. Caesar's affair with her had passed
muster, because it was he who remained in control. But people suspected
that the more easy-going Antony, by whom she had two boys and a
girl, was under her thumb – and Octavian spread the word that this was
so.

In 37 a second partial reconciliation between the two men provided for a
five-year renewal of the triumvirate. But the understanding proved short-
lived, since henceforward Antony, abandoning Octavia, lived openly with
Cleopatra, who built up under his overlordship an extensive imperial
system of her own including many client states. Soon afterwards, however,
the balance of Roman power began to change in Antony's disfavour. For an
expedition he launched against the Parthians, in the hope of annexing
Armenia, proved unsuccessful, though he rectified the defeat later.
Octavian's fleet, on the other hand, under his former schoolmate Agrippa
who although unpopular with the nobles was a commander of genius,
totally defeated Sextus Pompeius' fleet off Cape Naulochus (Venetico)
in Sicily (36). At this point, too, the third triumvir Lepidus, seeking
to contest Octavian's western supremacy by force, failed to command
the support of his own legions, and was disarmed and forced into
retirement.*

Octavian's deliberate rivalry with Antony for the eventual mastership of
the Roman world was becoming increasingly apparent, and in 33 the two
leaders exchanged savage propaganda attacks. As this barrage continued,
with unprecedented virulence, into the following year, Antony formally
divorced Octavia, whose brother, in retaliation, published what purported
to be Antony's will containing damaging evidence, probably forged, of the
ascendancy exercised over him by the foreign queen Cleopatra. Each leader
induced the populations under his control to swear allegiance to his cause
and his person, like the oaths sworn by clients to their patrons (32). The
oath sworn by the Italians on this occasion to Octavian (*coniuratio Italiae*)
became a famous precedent for the future. But it scarcely availed to conceal

* He was allowed, however, to retain his chief priesthood until his death in 12 BC.

grave dissatisfaction aroused by his exactions throughout the Italian peninsula.

Having raised as much money as he could, Octavian declared war – not indeed against his compatriot Antony, but against Cleopatra. With her as his companion – and she provided a substantial proportion of his ships and supplies – Antony had brought up his navy and army to guard strongholds along the coast of western Greece. But at the beginning of 31 BC, while it was still mid-winter, Agrippa succeeded in sailing from Italy across the Ionian Sea and capturing decisive strongpoints along the Greek coast, and, after Octavian had also arrived, Antony was finally cornered in the Gulf of Ambracia (Arta). At the battle of Actium, just outside the gulf, he tried to extricate his ships in the hope of continuing the fight elsewhere. But although Cleopatra, and then Antony himself, succeeded in breaking out, only a quarter of their fleet was able to follow them.

Both fled to Egypt, and when it fell to Octavian in the following year, they committed suicide at Alexandria. Their conqueror declared the country a Roman possession, thus eliminating the last survivor of the three Greek monarchies that had succeeded to the heritage of Alexander; and he made it a unique sort of province, under his own direct control. His seizure of Cleopatra's treasure made him wealthier than the Roman state itself. Above all, it enabled him to pay off his veterans, for whom in due course he founded no less than seventy-five colonies, mostly in the west.

The battle of Actium had not been a very spectacular engagement in itself, since the strategic issue had already been settled elsewhere. Nevertheless it was hailed by subsequent writers as one of the most decisive battles ever fought, because it established Octavian's position as master of the entire Greco-Roman world. It also meant that this empire would be dominated, for a very long time to come, by the west, and not the east. By the 'east' we should understand, in this context, not the sinister orient which Octavian's propagandists equated with Antony's dominions, but Rome's eastern provinces and client states, in which the ruling classes were Greek. For Actium firmly kept this Greek half of the empire in the second place. If Antony had won, there might well have been some sort of partnership between Romans and Greeks, under his overall rule. Instead, the future political leadership of the empire lay with Italy and Rome, as Virgil a few years later unequivocally pronounced, while paying tactful tribute, at the same time, to Greek cultural supremacy. It was not until another 300 years had passed that the Greeks started to get some of their own back, after the capital had been shifted to Constantinople and Greek begun to replace Latin as the official language of the Byzantine empire.

From now on, by a long and gradual series of tentative, patient measures, Octavian established the Roman principate, a system of government which, while not dispensing with Republican forms, ultimately depended on himself as the first man of the state (*princeps*), and enabled him to maintain, in all essentials, absolute control over its affairs.

He gradually reduced his sixty legions to the relatively small figure of twenty-eight, that is to say, to about 150,000 men which was all he felt he could pay for, or recruit. In 28 BC he and Agrippa conducted a census of the population for enlistment and taxation purposes, the first of three censuses held during his reign. The soldiers of Augustus' legions in the west were mostly Italians and therefore Roman citizens, but in the east they included many provincials, granted the franchise unofficially on enlistment. These legionaries were supplemented by about the same number of auxiliaries, drawn exclusively from the provinces; and there were already the beginnings of a policy by which they were rewarded by Roman citizenship on their discharge. This was all part of a quietly liberal policy of enfranchisement sponsored by Augustus. In an empire containing between seventy and a hundred million inhabitants, he raised the total number of Roman citizens, including women and children, from about five million to more than six, including an increase of citizens in the provinces from about one million to nearly two.

Remembering that Caesar had been murdered because of his recourse to naked power, he understood that the nobles would only tolerate his autocracy if he concealed it behind acceptable Republican traditions. For the first eight years after his victory at Actium, the constitutional basis of his power remained a continuous succession of consulships. But in the middle of this period, in 27 BC, he pronounced 'the transfer of the state to the free disposal of the Senate and people', thereby earning the misleading, though outwardly plausible, reputation of the restorer of the *res publica*, or ancestral system. At the same time he was granted, for ten years, an area of government comprising not only Egypt, which was his personal domain, but also Gaul (with the Rhine commands) and Spain and Syria, the three territories containing the greater part of the Roman army; and he ruled this huge collection of 'imperial' provinces through governors who were his own subordinates (*legati*).\* The principal remaining provinces remained 'public', administered by nominees of the Senate (proconsuls) in the old customary fashion, though with improved efficiency and honesty – since governors of all types, proconsuls and *legati* alike, and the procurators who governed minor provinces,† were now salaried officials, under close supervision from Rome.

Octavian, however, believed – and this belief was nearly always justified – that the supreme prestige (*auctoritas*) to which his public offices and

---

\* Pompey, likewise *in absentia*, had governed Spain in similar fashion.

† The governor of Judaea, however (annexed in AD 6) was still called *praefectus*; and so was the man in charge of the major but peculiar new province of Egypt.

achievements, and his sonship of the god Julius, entitled him, were sufficient safeguards against any defiance by governors or commanders. Besides, he was always able, directly or indirectly, to control their appointments, just as he was able, when he considered it desirable, to bring unobtrusive influence to bear on elections to the consulships and other state
posts. For these offices continued to exist in ostensibly Republican fashion;
and he contrived that their occupants should comprise an appropriate
blend of nobles and Italian 'new men', including, among both categories,
men who had supported him in the civil war.

Such were the members of Augustus' new Senate, which he reduced in
numbers from Caesar's 900 to the earlier figure of 600. He was elected its
president, and overshadowed it by his grandeur. Yet he did not diminish
the Senate's functions but actually enlarged them, so that it possessed, for
example, its own high court of justice, alongside another new 'imperial'
court presided over by himself. The Senate's strength was no longer political but administrative; the achievement of the new order was to take politics
out of administration for the first time in Roman history. This was only
one of the many acts of transformation that Augustus performed, veiling
them always under the guise of traditionalism.

Four days after the new political arrangements were announced in 27
BC, the ruler's name 'Caesar' was supplemented by the novel designation
'Augustus'. It was a word that carried venerable religious overtones, being
linked with the verb 'increase' (*augere*) which was also the root of *auctoritas* and probably of *augurium*, the practice of divination which lay deep
in Roman tradition. The adoption of this term 'Augustus' to define his new
status as the leader of the nation indicated his superiority over the rest of
humankind and yet avoided dictatorial or divine appellations that would
cause conservatives offence. It is true that, like other leaders before him,
Augustus did not refuse divine status in the provinces, although, officially
at least, his worship there was conducted in conjunction with the goddess Rome: it was an imperial cult which served as an instrument for encouraging loyalty, and was subsequently adopted by the local communities
of Italy itself. Yet at the same time, the ruler also showed his patriotic
reverence for the ancient Roman religion not only, as we have seen, by
adopting a name reminiscent of augury but by reviving many ancient
ceremonials and repairing numerous temples that had fallen into decay
during the prolonged civil wars. He also became chief priest; though meticulously postponing his assumption of this office until the death of its
incumbent Lepidus (12 BC).

Military operations continued in numerous areas, and the eastern frontier
was pushed a large distance forward by the annexation of a huge area of
central Asia Minor under the name of Galatia (25 BC). At the other end of

the empire, however, Mauretania reverted from provincial status to that of a client-kingdom, for such dependent monarchies were still relied upon to play a large part in frontier defence.

Augustus himself visited Gaul and directed part of a campaign in Spain until his health gave out. In 23 BC, he fell ill again, and was thought to be on the point of death. Believing, amid rumours of plots, that the constitutional position was still unsatisfactory, he terminated his series of consulships – which were unpopular with the nobles because they took jobs away from themselves. But he retained his own provinces. Moreover, in order that he should not be without ultimate sanctions in the senatorial provinces as well, he was granted a power (*imperium maius*) which raised him above their proconsuls. But this somewhat novel power, separated altogether from office and its day-to-day preoccupations, was intended for only sparing employment, particularly in crises or on personal visits, though it could also be tactfully exercised on other occasions as well.

Another exploitation of this fruitful idea of authority without office was his permanent assumption of the powers of a tribune of the people (*tribunicia potestas*, 23 BC). Earlier he had accepted certain privileges of the tribunes. The fuller tribunician power he now assumed enveloped him in a popular aura, because of the traditional role of the tribunes as defenders of the oppressed: and he endowed it with special significance by using it to date the years of his principate. For it was the sort of reputation which Augustus needed, because, in spite of legal reforms improving the lot of the poorer classes, he tended to back the established order as the keystone of his political system yet wanted to counteract the impression that this was all he cared about.

Agrippa, too, was granted superiority over the proconsuls, presumably to make sure that these provinces would remain under safe control in case one of the ruler's recurrent illnesses proved fatal. The next to die, however, was not Augustus, but his young nephew Marcellus (23 BC), who had been married to his daughter Julia and seemed destined for further special favours. After his death, Julia became the wife of Agrippa, who continued to travel and fight as the deputy of the *princeps*, and even shared his tribunician power (18 BC). And meanwhile, Augustus too undertook a fresh round of extensive journeys. Important reorganizations were set on foot wherever he went. Moreover, immense popular satisfaction was caused in 20 BC by an agreement with the Parthians who not only returned the legionary standards taken from Crassus thirty-three years earlier, but recognized (though only briefly) Rome's protectorate over Armenia.

Then, in 19 BC, there was some adjustment of Augustus' constitutional powers to allow him to exercise them more freely in Italy, though still in not too open or direct a fashion. And the following two years witnessed social legislation vigorously seeking to encourage morality and marriage and bring the family as an institution under public protection. These endeavours were immortalized by Virgil and Horace; but they did not enjoy the resounding success of his measures in other fields.

We think of Augustus as the inaugurator of an imperial line, the first emperor. Yet the conglomeration of powers which added up to his position as *princeps* was something which could not, constitutionally speaking, be handed on to any other single person after his death. Nevertheless, there was obviously speculation that this was what must happen, as there had already been while Marcellus was still alive. Since his death, Agrippa must have seemed, even more than before, a likely candidate for this succession, and his powers continued to be renewed together with his master's. But the nobles would never have accepted this 'new man'; and Augustus appeared to be indicating a novel, alternative view regarding likely eventual successors when he adopted, as his own children, Gaius and Lucius, the sons of Agrippa and Julia. Yet they were only three and one year old respectively, and Augustus, as time went on, hedged his bets in two ways; first by favouring the careers not of one of them but of both, and secondly by giving important military employment to his grown stepsons, Tiberius and Nero Drusus, the sons of his wife Livia by a previous marriage to a member of the Claudian clan. Marching across the Alps, they occupied large parts of what are now Switzerland, Austria and Bavaria, annexing these territories as the provinces of Noricum and Raetia (16–15 BC). By such operations and others the empire was extended northwards and eastwards from the Alps to its historic, long-lasting frontier along the Danube.

It was probably during this period that an executive committee (*consilium*) of the Senate was established in order to help Augustus to draft senatorial business. His vast burden of work was also gradually lightened by the expansion of his own staff to include, at the higher level, a number of knights. Although this personal staff was still relatively small, its development announced the beginnings of a civil service, which had never existed during the Republic but was destined to become a vital feature of the imperial system. Gradually, too, and by patient trial and error, Augustus reformed the administrative structures of Rome and Italy and the entire empire. Once again, knights played a prominent part, serving not only as the chairmen and members of important commissions at home but as his financial agents (procurators) in every province, and as governors of small provinces and even of one extremely important and special one, Egypt.

In 12 BC Agrippa died, and Augustus, while still furthering the careers of the dead man's children, compelled his widow Julia to marry Tiberius, against the wishes of both of them. During the next three years Tiberius

# The family of Augustus

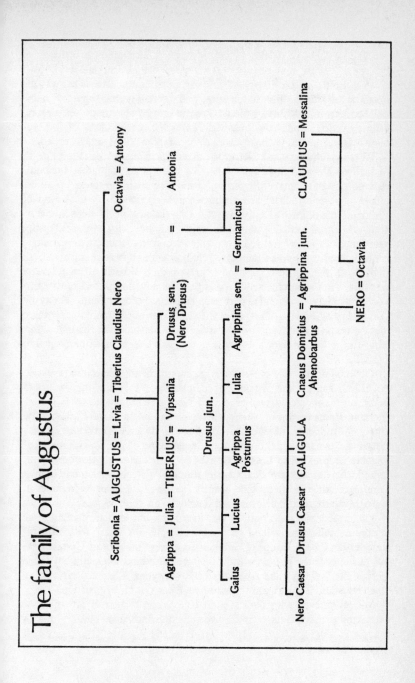

returned to military life, moving northwards the limits of the province of
Illyricum (Yugoslavia) and creating a new middle Danubian province of
Pannonia (Austria and Hungary).* At the same time his brother Nero Drusus
crossed the Rhine and invaded Germany as far as the Elbe. This was the
first step towards the annexation of the country; for it was Augustus' ambition to replace the Rhine by the Elbe as the empire's frontier, thus creating
a much shorter boundary line, within which huge numbers of the previously free, warlike, Germans were to be safely included and absorbed.

Tiberius, who replaced Nero Drusus in Germany on the latter's death
(9 BC), was elevated three years later to a share in his stepfather's tribunician power. But shortly afterwards, at his own wish, he threw up all his
laborious responsibilities and withdrew into retirement on the island of
Rhodes. This dramatic step was ascribed to jealousy of his stepson Gaius,
who was introduced to public life amid great publicity in the following
year; and so was his brother Lucius three years later. But only a very short
time afterwards, by an extraordinary chance, both of these young men were
dead (AD 4, 2). Augustus might have preferred, as hitherto, to keep several
potential heirs simultaneously in play; but he now had to realize that this
could no longer be done. He may have harboured certain doubts about the
personality of Tiberius. But, if so, they had to be forgotten, for now there
was no other possible successor but he. So Augustus adopted him as his
son, with powers which, in everything except prestige, made him equal to
himself.

Tiberius' next task was to fill a large gap in the middle of the proposed
new Elbe–Danube line by taking over Bohemia, at that time the nucleus of
of an unprecedentedly well-organized German empire. In AD 6, a two-
pronged Roman invasion of Bohemian territory was already under way.
But then, suddenly, news came that the recently annexed regions of Illyricum and Pannonia had broken into desperate rebellion, which took three
years to suppress. And the reconquest of the area had only just been completed when disaster struck across the Rhine as well: for a talented German
chief, Arminius, led his people against the unwary Roman commander in
the area, Varus, and killed him and destroyed his three legions. The result
was that the annexation both of west Germany and of Bohemia had to be
postponed indefinitely – and, as it turned out, for evermore: with incalcul-
able results for the future of Europe, since these millions of Germans remained outside the Roman world. Whether the annexation might have been
practicable before, when Augustus had twenty-eight legions, remains an
open question. But with only twenty-five, it was out of the question.

Moreover, even with twenty-eight legions, he had never attempted to
supplement the frontier army by the maintenance of a central strategic

*Later in the reign, the frontier was extended to the river mouth, providing yet another
province, Moesia.

reserve which might have made it possible to deal with this sort of emergency. That was partly because a reserve army of such a kind, if stationed for example in north Italy, might be turned by some ambitious general against himself. Such a contingency was never far from Augustus' mind, or from any later emperor's mind either. He sought to provide against attacks on his own person by creating a permanent bodyguard. Earlier Roman commanders had maintained personal guards, and Augustus developed these precedents by the creation of a standing Praetorian Guard of nine cohorts, which he stationed partly in Rome and partly in other towns of Italy. He also established a city police at Rome consisting of three cohorts (*cohortes urbanae*), under a newly appointed prefect of the city, and a fire-brigade (*vigiles*) was set up as well.

THE PROVINCES AT THE DEATH OF AUGUSTUS (A D 14)

Yet meanwhile he was still finding difficulty in recruiting sufficient men for his legionary force, reduced in size though it was. Nor did he find it easy to pay their salaries or, on retirement, their rewards. These consisted initially of the traditional land-allotments, largely in his Roman colonies, and later, when land began to be exhausted, they had to be paid out in money instead. In AD 6, therefore, he founded a new military treasury, the *aerarium militare*, which was to defray legionaries' retirement pensions from the proceeds of indirect taxes. This was only one of a number of administrative innovations which the ageing and tiring ruler introduced during the last decade of his life, with the help and perhaps the guiding initiative of Tiberius.

In AD 13 Augustus deposited his will at the House of the Vestals at Rome. It included a summary of the military and financial resources of the empire, and an ingenious political testament, his Acts (*Res Gestae*), known also as the Monumentum Ancyranum because its best-preserved copy is on the walls of the temple of Rome and Augustus at Ancyra (Ankara), capital of his new province of Galatia. Then, in the following year, he died, and Tiberius became emperor.

After many earlier successes, Augustus' policy of military expansion had ground to a halt in his last years, and he himself left Tiberius the advice not to continue it. By his reorganization, on the other hand, of the entire machinery of civilian government, he had proved himself one of the most gifted administrators the world has ever seen, and the most influential single figure in the entire history of Rome. The gigantic work of reform that he carried out in every branch of Italian and provincial life not only transformed the decaying Republic into a new régime with many centuries of existence ahead of it, but also created a durable, efficient Roman peace. It was this Pax Romana or Pax Augusta which ensured the survival and eventual transmission of the classical heritage, Greek and Roman alike, and made possible the diffusion of Christianity, of which the founder, Jesus, was born during this reign.

The dilemma Caesar's career had posed – its demonstration that whereas the empire needed one-man rule the nobles would tolerate no such thing – had been miraculously solved by Augustus. He had two things on his side: the Roman people's utter weariness of civil war, and his own subtle mastery of publicity in a wide variety of forms. Although, therefore, in every respect that mattered, he was scarcely less of an autocrat than Caesar had been, he contrived to cloak his absolutism in guises which looked old-fashioned enough to pass muster. True, the humble majority of the population of the empire, who were only concerned with keeping life together, had no time to care about such clever nuances: yet even they were able to appreciate the diminished risks of sudden death. But the people who positively approved of his Republican façade were the nobles, or at least a substantial proportion of their number – despite occasional plots, when they reflected on their loss of political power – and above all others the knights and the members of the enormous middle class, whom this new régime notably benefited and enriched.

Many of the satisfied beneficiaries were not Roman but Italian, for Augustus felt and encouraged a new patriotic feeling for Italy, echoed by Virgil's insistence on the country's identity, which he helped to make as vivid as Rome's. This ideal was very different from the Greco-Roman concepts of Antony and Cleopatra. Augustus' narrower view was based on his own small-town Italian origins; and these were partly responsible, also, for his puritanical social policy, and his antiquarian attachment to the ancient religion.

He summed up this whole pro-Italian, pro-Roman trend of his policy by the title which he chose to have conferred upon himself in 2 BC. It was *pater patriae*, father of his country; Caesar had experimented with the designation, and Augustus adopted it as the climax of all his endeavours and the final expression of his régime. His proclaimed fatherhood of all Romans and Italians went back to the most ancient roots of the community, in which the *paterfamilias* had been the revered key figure. Moreover, by equally antique custom the patrons of clients were often described as their fathers: and in this sense, Augustus, by accepting the title of father of his country, was following up the oath which all Italians had sworn to him in 32 BC. and asserting that all Roman citizens, without exception, were his clients and that he was their patron; thus extending this traditional institution, in his own interests and person, to the whole people of Italy, and to the colonies of Roman citizens in the provinces as well. And by implication he was extending his patronage even more widely, by suggesting that the whole empire, non-Roman and Roman alike, consisted of his clients, and so did the dependent kingdoms beyond. His sympathies, that is to say, were not so narrowly Italian that he took no thought for his other subjects and allies. Indeed, as befitted the author of a number of literary works (now all lost), his chauvinism was modified by a well-informed admiration of Greek culture which Virgil and the other literary personages of the time entirely shared. The conventional view of his character, in ancient times, differentiated between his cruelty in his youthful years and his mildness when he was older. But there was not so much need or occasion for cruelty in his later career as there had been earlier on; and when, even towards the end of his days, harsh measures were needed (for example in the suppression of alleged conspiracies), he often remained ready to apply them. But nothing short of this degree of political toughness could ever have produced such vast results.

His domestic life too, though simple and homespun, was conducted on ruthless lines. It is true that, although unfaithful to his wife Livia, he remained devoted to her. Yet when his daughter Julia and granddaughter of the same name moved in immoral smart circles suspected of subversion, he exiled them one after another, without compunction, and his third grandson, too, suffered banishment and perhaps death as well. And as for his male relatives who acted as his principal helpers, he was loyal to them, but drove them as fiercely hard as he drove himself. He needed them because the burden was so heavy, and he especially needed the exceptional talents of Agrippa and Tiberius in the military sphere because, unlike most famous Romans before him, he himself was not a particularly effective general or admiral, and could be regarded as a coward. Be that as it may, his physical condition was subject to a large number of recurrent weaknesses and disabilities. They were intensified by a well-developed strain of hypochondria; but his ill-health was very real, as well, and when he was young it was only his indomitable will that enabled him to survive – a strange preliminary to such a prolonged and uniquely active career.

Augustus was short of stature, but his fine countenance with its calm and mild expression proved a godsend to the best sculptors of the time, Greeks and Hellenized easterners who devoted to his features a remarkable series of sympathetic, moving interpretations. These portrayals displaying a discreet blend of idealism and realism were reduplicated throughout the empire in thousands of busts and statues and portraits on coins. Less successful, perhaps, though some think otherwise, are the majestic but somewhat stiff reliefs of the Altar of Peace (Ara Pacis), depicting scenes from the patriotic Roman mythology and a religious procession in which the leading figures of the state are seen taking a dignified part.

Augustus was also the greatest of all the adorners of Rome. Something of the monumental, classic grandeur of his buildings can still be seen today in the Theatre of Marcellus and the remains of the massive Augustan Forum. Flanked by huge colonnades and side apses, the new precinct culminated in the Temple of Mars the Avenger – the avenger of his adoptive Father, the god Caesar, who had himself started this precedent of constructing new forums. Outside Rome, too, there were innumerable arches, trophies and other memorials of the Augustan age. And from his wife Livia's mansion on the outskirts of Rome, at Prima Porta, comes a reminder that not all the art of the period was formal and grandiose. For one of the rooms is adorned with wall paintings that create the illusion of an enchanted garden; beyond a trellis are orchards and flowerbeds, in which birds and insects perch among the foliage.

This elegance, and the whole way of living for which it stood, was the product of a new solidity in the finances of the empire. The relationship of the central state treasury, the public *aerarium*, to the treasuries of the provinces, is still imperfectly understood. Augustus, it is true, proudly recorded his own gifts to the state. But the state's profits from running the rich, peaceful, senatorial provinces must somehow have been pumped in the reverse direction, so as to pay for the imperial frontier provinces which required heavy expenditure.

The principal direct taxes paid by the population of the empire, other by than Rome and Italy which enjoyed exemption, were two in number, a levy on all occupiers of land (*tributum soli*), from which came by far the greater part of the revenue, and a poll tax (*tributum capitis*) collected in Egypt, Syria and certain other areas. These taxes were based on the results of censuses, which Augustus organized throughout the provinces. The statistics thus gathered made it possible to fix the sums the state required, so that Augustus, pursuing further a tendency initiated by Caesar, was able to eliminate private tax-farmers from the direct taxation system altogether. Indirect taxes, however – the only dues to which Roman citizens were liable – were still, for the time being, farmed out to contractors as in the past. The most important of these indirect levies were customs dues. But their rates, at 2 or 2½ per cent, were low enough not to hamper commerce.

Its free operation was ensured by a system of fleets which, for the first time, were organized to police the Mediterranean, so that maritime interchanges gained in speed and security alike. But the most important means of communication and organization was provided by the comprehensive network of roads extending throughout Italy and the provinces. These roads were systematically and resourcefully distributed, designed, constructed and drained, with careful adaptation to local materials and conditions. They were made to span rivers by the creation of powerful, soaring bridges; and they penetrated mountains by tunnels that aroused admiration for centuries.

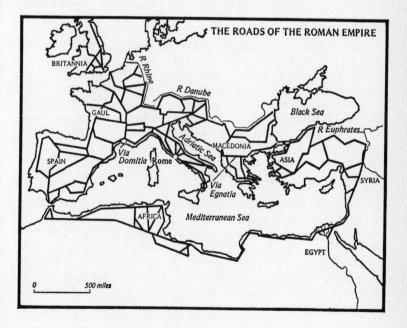

THE ROADS OF THE ROMAN EMPIRE

Already in the later Republic, despite all the disturbances of that period, the great increases in individual wealth had stimulated inter-regional trade, and now, in the favourable circumstances created by Augustus, it became solidly established as a significant economic factor. Italy still took the lead. A fine building at Pompeii, constructed for the guild or corporation of the fullers, shows how efficiently the men engaged in such businesses organized themselves. New industries for woollen goods sprang up in other Italian cities as well, while metal-working at Rome and Capua flourished, and glass-blowing became a prosperous activity in Campania and north Italy alike. The general picture was of relatively small-scale enterprises. But the pottery of Arretium (Arezzo) was an exception, since these products, their red-glazing a trade secret, were widely exported outside the peninsula.

And Italy in return bought a large range of provincial wares, including slaves, grain, metals, marble, linen, papyrus, furs and ivory. For the provinces, too, displayed a greatly increased commercial activity, which is illustrated, for example, by the impressive porticoed Augustan market-place at Lepcis Magna in north Africa. This trade was stimulated by intensified mining operations, increasingly under imperial control. And it was also encouraged by an impressive reform of the currency, retaining the former gold and silver but introducing a new token coinage in two attractive metals, yellow brass and red copper. This coinage was primarily intended, as always, for the needs of the army and the state. But trade benefited too, and coins of Augustus in all metals are found abundantly throughout the western provinces. Many bronze coinages of individual cities were also sanctioned, for example in Spain at the outset of the imperial epoch, and for a much longer period in the eastern provinces, where they circulated alongside the imperial gold and silver for 300 years.

The currency in the precious metals is also found in considerable quantities outside the empire. For there was a picturesquely varied influx of goods from beyond its borders. For example, silk came from China, to be woven and dyed in Syria and combined with a linen warp on the island of Cos; and large numbers of *denarii* found at Coimbatore in southern India had been brought there to pay for pepper. But all these luxury imports from abroad were much less important than exchanges within the empire itself.

Nevertheless, neither now nor at any later period of antiquity did trading ever become the economic basis of the Roman world, for it could never achieve really large dimensions as long as the manufacturers showed so little interest in productive expansion or the technological advances required to achieve it. Instead, they were mostly content with the simple satisfaction of their own material needs; and the continued employment of numerous slaves made labour-saving unnecessary. Moreover, there was no real mass-market to provide an incentive for large-scale endeavours, and capitalism was still embryonic, so that no clear distinction was made between capital and labour costs.

Besides, there were severe practical problems. Fuel was scarce; and transportation, while risky and erratic by sea, was extremely slow and expensive on land. For all these reasons the entire commerce and industry of all the empire together probably never amounted to more than 10 per cent of its total revenue. All the rest came from agriculture: principally wheat, with barley second. Here again, however, the prohibitively heavy cost of land transport hampered development. Methods of cultivation, too, did not advance very much further, and there was no planned reinvestment of agricultural profits. Once again, there was more interest in mere acquisition than in better production.

For example long-term loans to encourage improvements in output were non-existent, and state intervention of any kind to help agriculture remained limited. Nevertheless, the need to provide such support had to figure to a certain extent in the calculations of emperors. This was because, to prevent unrest, they considered it one of their most essential duties (as certain late Republican politicians had already considered it before them) to provide the people of Rome with sufficient grain, at cheap prices. Most of this was imported, especially from north Africa (Tunisia) which had replaced Sicily as the granary of the capital; and an increasing amount began to come from Egypt as well. However, the great increase in the production of cereals in those and other countries did little to improve the depressed situation of their cultivators. The slaves remained slaves; and the huge 'free' agricultural population of the empire likewise did not benefit markedly from the Augustan peace. For the burden of the land-tax, from which the state derived most of its funds, fell mainly upon their shoulders. And even if it might be something of a relief that the government no longer employed intermediaries to collect it, this tax was not progressive in its operation – that is to say, it fell with equal percentual weight on large and small incomes, thus hitting the poor much more heavily than the rich. And additional unfairness was caused by the failure of this form of taxation to take account of different qualities of soil and of fluctuations in annual yields.

So the great bulk of the 'free' population of the Roman world, comprising the inhabitants of the villages and rural areas, remained extremely poor, living at bare subsistence level. They were also, politically, almost non-persons. For the political structure of the empire was still founded on its city-states, no longer wholly independent, like those of earlier Greece, but still enjoying, subject to ultimate dependence on Rome, varying degrees of local autonomy. Each city was allowed to control rural territories of its own, not so large as the increasingly enormous lands which belonged to the emperors, but nevertheless very often of substantial size; and they paid for their own amenities by exploiting such possessions. Yet the inhabitants of these rural zones lacked the privileges enjoyed by the citizens of the towns that ruled over them.

For those citizens, the Pax Augusta was a splendid thing. It meant the triumph of the bourgeoisie – the businessmen and traders and all the people who had a share in the city-state system everywhere and participated in its profits. This whole section of the population had, in effect, taken over the power previously wielded by the old political upper class. And, in Italy especially, Augustus also paid particular attention to the very large, indeed numerically preponderant class of freedmen – ex-slaves and their children. By allowing them, in many cases, to intermarry with full citizens, and by calling upon them to provide priests for the growing local imperial cult, he found them a place in the social and civic system. And they gained for themselves a considerable share in the universal middle-class wellbeing – with the hope of even higher things, for not long after Augustus' time they were becoming state secretaries, and Petronius' *Satyricon* tells how they could make enormous fortunes. Such tycoons, it is true, were exceptional; but many other freedmen, too, fared better than they had ever fared before.

And so, not indeed from the humble farm labourers, but from a considerably wider section of the population than had ever flourished in the previous history of Rome – or for that matter of any other country either – Augustus deserved the compliment that was paid to him in the last days of his life. For as the ship on which he was travelling sailed beside the busy Campanian port of Puteoli (Pozzuoli) it passed a merchant vessel that had just arrived from Alexandria. Thereupon its crew and passengers, wearing white robes and garlands, burned incense and offered a salute to the Father of their Country, crying out that it was to him that they owed their lives, freedom and prosperity.

Alongside Agrippa, the most important of Augustus' advisers – especially in the earlier part of the reign – had been the Etruscan Maecenas (d. 8 BC). Through him, the ruler was able to win the goodwill of some of the greatest and most influential writers the world has ever known, and this approbation they freely expressed, even though all of them displayed a strong vein of independence as well.

Virgil was born in 70 BC near Mantua in north Italy, of a family which seems to have been partly of Etruscan origin. Later, he moved to the region of Neapolis (Naples), where his father, expropriated by the Second Triumvirate (41 BC), came to join him. Virgil first astonished literary circles in Rome by the novelty of his *Eclogues (Bucolics)* (45–37 BC). These ten short poems transmuted into a melodious, evocative Latin the pastoral themes introduced to the Greek literature of Alexandria more than two centuries earlier. This is a timeless, unreal Greek countryside, blended with Italian elements, and designed for sophisticated townsmen; an idyllic rusticity which conflicts in the poet's heart with the need to come to terms with imperial Rome. The fourth poem in the collection, written in a euphoric moment of reconciliation between Antony and Octavian (40 BC), reflects the widespread belief that a saviour was about to appear and rescue the world from its prolonged miseries. He remains unnamed, but elsewhere in the *Eclogues* the task of salvation is attributed specifically to Octavian, the future Augustus.

The four longer *Georgics* that followed (36–29 BC), dedicated to Maecenas, celebrated in verse of a new flexible subtlety the beauties and labours and rewards of the rustic life, and the glorious antiquarian, legendary past of the rich Italian countryside. The *Georgics* are the supreme literary expression of that emotional love for Roman Italy which was a feature of the times and became the centre-point of Augustus' policy and peace: the peace for which he is praised from the heart in these profoundly evocative poems.

Next Virgil turned to heroic epic, in the tradition that went back to Homer. But the sensitive subtleties of his *Aeneid* are very far removed from Homer's ballad-like extroversion. And so is the hitherto unimaginable rhythmical elaboration and sonorous majesty of this poetry, extracting from the Latin language its ultimate, complex potentialities of emotion and sound and artifice. The Trojan Aeneas, escaping from the Greek sack of Troy, is destined for many wanderings and adventures. In north Africa, he encounters the mythical Queen Dido of Carthage, and the sadness of their doomed romance owes less to the Homeric epic than to the more recent Greek poetry of Alexandria, magically transformed. Finally Aeneas reaches Italy. As he lands on its shores, he is taken down by the Sibyl into the underworld, a scene in which the poet discloses his deepest reflections upon the nature of the universe. Then, after a visit to the place that was later to become Rome, Aeneas is compelled to join battle with the peoples of Italy. The wars end in peace, he marries a Latin bride, and Rome's foundation will follow – for this is what the poem is really about.

Its theme is largely war – the *Aeneid* is an *Odyssey* followed by an *Iliad*, this warlike section being indebted to the national, epic tradition of Naevius and Ennius, who had first adapted the Homeric genre to Latin poetry. War leads to peace, and it is the Augustan peace of which Virgil is thinking. For his age, following upon the prolonged nightmare epoch of civil strife, was one of those times in the history of the world when order looked even more important than liberty, and Augustus' feat in bringing peace seemed to Virgil the greatest of all possible national gifts – and most of his contemporaries agreed with him. Yet Aeneas in the poem is only allowed to win his war, and become a true exemplar of the virtues, after he has bitterly suffered: and among his most poignant ordeals is his parting from Dido, enforced by Jupiter and destiny.

Dido is, in one sense, a symbol of Rome's most perilous enemy of the past, her kingdom of Carthage; and those who listened to the poet reciting the *Aeneid* must have thought of that other hostile queen of living memory, Cleopatra. And yet, although Dido's efforts to detain Aeneas are against the divine will, she is portrayed with heart-wringing sympathy – it is almost as if Virgil's sorrow at her tragedy has for the moment got the better of his knowledge that Aeneas acts rightly, indeed inevitably, in leaving her. And the same thing appears to happen again when the poet begins to describe Turnus, the tough leader of Aeneas' Italian foes. For Turnus too is plainly fighting against what is fated to happen, and yet he too is allotted almost more than his share of nobility.

Despite, therefore, the radiant future that will lie ahead for Rome after Aeneas has prevailed, Virgil was telling us that wars turn to dust and ashes and weariness. In the end, he reckoned military conquest lower than the conquest by human beings of their own souls and hearts. He was a man deeply divided within himself. The benefits Augustus had brought to a war-torn world inspired him with deep gratitude. Yet he also knew better than anyone else that such triumphs, like all the Roman triumphs that had ever been, are built on pain.

In 19 BC he was in Greece, where Augustus, who happened also to be there, persuaded him to sail back home in his company. But Virgil fell ill, and after returning across the Adriatic to Brundusium, he died. The *Aeneid* was not quite completed, and, before leaving Italy, he had made his literary executor promise to burn it in the event of his death. Perhaps he felt that the two conflicting ideals which tear the poem apart were too much for its unity. But when he was dead, Augustus gave orders that his wish should be disregarded, and had the *Aeneid* published just as it was.

The second of the outstanding Augustan poets, Horace, was born in 65 BC at Venusia (Venosa) in Apulia, in south-east Italy. His father, who probably came of the hillman stock of Italy's central highlands, had been a slave and subsequently an auctioneer's assistant; he could afford to send his son to a famous school at Rome, from which he moved on to the empire's most favoured centre of higher education, the Academy of Athens. At the battle of Philippi (42 BC) Horace served as an officer on the side of Brutus and Cassius, but after their defeat he returned to Italy. There his family farm, like Virgil's, had been confiscated by the victorious triumvirs; but he obtained a job at Rome and got to know Maecenas.

His *Satires* (35, 30 BC) reject careerism and advocate wisdom through serenity, in the manner of a Greek philosopher. But they vary in theme, and so does another of his poetic collections of this time, the *Epodes* (*c.* 30 BC), which sometimes assail social abuses with a bitterness that is more than just a literary convention. Then, after Maecenas had given him a farm in the Sabine hills, Horace published his famous *Odes* (23, 13 BC), treating of love, wine, nature, friends, moderation and state affairs. While representing himself, in these short poems, as the heir to the Greek lyricists, he displayed a sensitive, economical mastery of words that is wholly Latin and his own. And meanwhile he was also composing his *Epistles* (*c.* 20–15 BC), which were more profound and mature versions of the *Satires*, and incorporated some of the most influential literary criticism the classical world ever produced. The man who emerges from these later works is kindly, tolerant, humane and mild, but by no means lacking in strength, which reveals itself in a spirit of astringent, detached realism: and Horace is a gentle but persistent mocker not only of others, but of himself.

Augustus, against whom he had formerly fought at Philippi, became his friend, through Maecenas. Indeed he later became virtually the court poet, for in 17 BC, two years after Virgil's death, he was asked to compose the *Carmen Saeculare*, a hymn designed for the antique Secular Games, which Augustus had revived to purge the state of the evils and crimes of the past and provide a solemn, religious sanction for his régime and its moral reforms.

Nevertheless, when the ruler offered him the post of his private secretary, he declined; and the praises of the new order throughout his poems are interwoven with tactful but firm assertions of his own personal independence. Horace was as ambivalent, in his own way, as Virgil. Like him, he welcomed Augustus' attempts to revive the old Roman virtues and traditions; and above all, he felt immense gratitude for his termination of the civil wars. Indeed, after the prolonged convulsions of the recent past, this achievement seemed so great to Horace that he had no eye for whatever hardness the new régime might possess. All the same, he always remained his own master, and kept the core of his quiet but distinct personality intact.

Another member of Maecenas' circle was Propertius of Asisium (Assisi) in Umbria, who was junior to Virgil and Horace by about fifteen and ten years respectively. Like them, he had been impoverished by the civil wars, and had Augustus to thank for the revival of his fortunes. Unlike them, however, he devoted his poetical genius and mythological learning, during the greater part of his career, to a theme that had nothing to do with the new régime – the passion of love. On this subject, despite the usual claims to be Romanizing the Greeks, he wrote elegies of a new, obsessive subjectivity, spanning the shifting and obscure border of what is classic and what is romantic. Only in his last writings did he turn to poems of public significance, giving expression to the blend of myth and patriotic antiquarianism which had so greatly attracted Virgil.

This, again, was the inspiration of Livy of Patavium (Padua) (c. 59 BC– AD 17) throughout his entire life. His *History of Rome* from the earliest times is an unparalleled achievement which took forty years to complete. It consisted of 142 'books' (nearly 107 of them are lost) which would have filled some twenty or thirty modern volumes. Writing in fluent, lush prose, and making loftily imaginative, uncritical use of a wide variety of sources, he offers highly coloured evocations of the foundation and early epic age of Rome, and provides many rousing narratives including a superb account of Hannibal's invasion. Rome, as the chosen object and instrument of providential destiny, receives its supreme glorification from Livy; and so does the Roman character, for it is to Livy more than any other writer that we owe our idea of what this was, or rather, of what he and his compatriots wanted and believed it to have been in the past. Rome's traditional heroes and their actions, as he so vividly depicted them, were handed down to later Europe as revelations of what the human spirit can achieve. And the most favoured of these heroes was Augustus, restorer of peace and of the Republican moral standards still greatly respected in the cities of Livy's own Italian northland. It was in this traditional spirit that the ruler himself placed statues of all the victorious Roman generals of ancient times in his resplendent new forum; and to the historian, whom he thus translated into sculpture, he was a friend.

Yet at the same time Livy, like Virgil and Horace, still retains a considerable degree of detachment from the Augustan order. He always felt deep sympathy with humble individuals caught up in the great warlike crises. And when he dealt with the later years of the Republic, we learn from surviving abridgements that he expressed doubts whether Caesar's career was beneficial, and favoured his enemy Pompey by glossing over his youthful brutalities so that Augustus, the adoptive son of the divine Caesar, half-jokingly called him a 'Pompeian'. Besides, there are other strange omissions from these summaries as well. For example, despite his general approval of Augustus' endeavours to revive the old morality, we find no appreciation of the specific reforms which the ruler had already begun to set in motion very shortly after Actium.

On the contrary, Livy, in the introduction to his whole work, shows notable caution about the feasibility of any real return to the glorious past. 'Our defects are unendurable to us', he declares, 'and so are their cures.' At first sight this looks surprisingly unfriendly towards Augustus' aspirations. However, such lack of interest in current changes, combined with nostalgia for the good old times, was not as anti-Augustan as might be thought: since it harmonized with Augustus' own claim that he was not, formally speaking, an innovating autocrat at all, but the restorer of ancient

Republican ways and customs. Livy was therefore free to pursue his romantic idealization of the Rome that had vanished for ever.

The poet Ovid of Sulmo (Sulmona in the Abruzzi) (43 BC–AD 17) was the only one of these writers whose aloofness veered over into catastrophe. Although only some twenty years younger than Livy, he belonged to a very different generation, no longer brought up amid civil war, and although able enough to turn out a patriotic poem, no longer much concerned with Augustan nationalism or morality. Ovid's elegiac couplets look at men and especially women with not unfriendly or altogether untender gaze, although the humour to which his observations move him sometimes seems cold-blooded, or even clinical. Yet this astringency does not strike a chill because of his incomparable genius for vivid description and narrative, which has been one of the greatest influences Rome has exerted upon the culture of the Western world. This gift as teller of stories finds its fullest expression in the *Metamorphoses*, a vast Arabian Nights of every sort of myth and folk-tale and anecdote, written in a lighter version of Virgil's epic metre.

In spite of occasional references to Augustus' glories in these poems, the sort of poetry Ovid was writing did not much appeal to the *princeps*; and so in AD 8 the blow fell, and the poet was exiled to far distant Tomi (Constanța in Rumania). He himself describes the charges that had led to this disastrous result as 'a poem and a mistake'. The poem to which he refers was perhaps *The Art of Love*, far too immoral for the tastes of Augustus, who disapproved of the smart metropolitan society in which such things were cynically talked and laughed about; Ovid's self-indulgent individualism clashed sharply with Augustus' conception of his age. The 'mistake' may have had something to do with the banishment for adultery of Augustus' granddaughter Julia, her lover being executed at the same time for alleged plotting. Perhaps Ovid was accused of having known more than he should: and of having remained silent about it.

He was never recalled from Tomi; and nine years later he died, having occupied his time in writing further, much sadder elegies, in which he obliquely contrasts the spiritual authority of poetry with the supreme temporal power which had punished him. He is part of the reverse side of the Augustan society: the member of the ruling class who rejected the values the ruler told it to adopt: the poet who was not serious or public spirited enough to live in this bracing climate and survive.

# VII

# THE IMPERIAL PEACE

# 14

# The Inheritors of Empire

TIBERIUS, WHOSE UNFAIR DEPICTION is the most brilliant achievement of the historian Tacitus, was a proud member of the ancient Claudian clan who had a splendid record of military and administrative achievement. But he was also grim, caustic and suspicious, and lacked Augustus' talent for public relations. In particular, despite his strongly emphasized desire that the Senate should play its part in imperial decision-making, he found it difficult to get on with senators, both individually and *en masse*.

During the first years of his reign, he employed as his principal generals his nephew Germanicus – whom Augustus had required him to adopt as his son – and his own son Drusus the younger. Both were immediately engaged in the suppression of legionary mutinies which had broken out after his reign began in Germany and Pannonia (northern Yugoslavia) respectively. Subsequently, Germanicus fought three massive but unproductive campaigns against the Germans beyond the Rhine frontier, momentarily repeating the earlier Roman advance as far as the Elbe (AD 14–16). Then he was transferred to a major appointment in the east. This terminated in his death (19), which caused widespread sorrow. Four years later Drusus the younger also died, so that Tiberius had already lost his two principal heirs; there were suspicions that both of them had been murdered, but probably they died natural deaths.

Meanwhile a strong personal position was built up by Sejanus, prefect of the praetorian guard. In 23, this astute Etruscan concentrated the guardsmen, previously dispersed around a number of Italian towns, within a single new barracks at Rome itself. The government displayed continual fear of real or imagined conspiracies, which existing treason laws were employed to suppress, amid complaints about the vagueness of these enactments and their perilous potentialities as weapons of tyranny. Sejanus took the lead in initiating such accusations, and became more powerful still after Tiberius, in 26, retired from Rome to the Campanian island of Capreae (Capri), never to set foot in the city again for the rest of his life.

THE ROMAN LEGIONS IN AD 23

R Rhine
R Danube
PANNONIA
R Euphrates
ILLYRICUM
MOESIA
SPAIN (3)
SYRIA (4)
AFRICA (2)
EGYPT (2)

•••••• Imperial Frontier
•••• Provincial Frontiers
◯ Number of Roman Legions

0        500 miles

Sejanus also encouraged the emperor to detect seditious intentions in
Germanicus' evidently indiscreet widow Agrippina – the daughter of
Agrippa – so that she and her two elder sons (the heirs apparent) were
arrested in AD 29–30 and put to death or forced to commit suicide during
the following years, leaving a young third son Gaius Caesar, known as
Caligula (Little Boots) because of the miniature military uniform he had
worn as a child, as the probable successor to the throne.

Meanwhile Sejanus with some difficulty induced the emperor to promise
him a marriage connexion; and although as praetorian prefect he had
previously been a knight and not a senator, he gained the consulship in 31
as the colleague of Tiberius himself. But his downfall promptly followed.
It appears probable that he was plotting against Caligula, whose succession would mean an end of his ascendancy. At any rate that was the
information that came to Tiberius' ears, and so he secretly transferred the
praetorian command to his own confidant Macro, who arranged for
Sejanus to be arrested in Rome during a meeting of the Senate. This was
done, and its members immediately ordered his execution, which was
carried out and followed by many other deaths among his political friends.

The empire as a whole was still governed well, though on somewhat
static lines, with Augustus consciously employed as model; and it scarcely
felt these metropolitan tremors. Yet the career of Sejanus had been in-

structive. It had displayed the need all emperors were bound to feel for a
helper they could trust; and it had underlined the extreme peril they ran
in trusting such a deputy too much, and delegating too much power to
him. The crisis had also underlined the equivocal position of the army and
particularly of the praetorian guard, which was intended to protect the
ruler but might instead be employed by its prefect to offer a lethal threat
to himself or his relations. As it happened, however, the guard did nothing
to help or avenge Sejanus, and under Macro's direction remained loyal.

Among Tiberius' entourage at Capreae was Caligula; and when in AD
37, at the age of seventy-nine, the emperor died, it was he who became the
next emperor. The transition was arranged by the officers of the praetorian
guard, who thus launched their career as emperor-makers. Their commander, Macro, however, did not long survive, nor did the late ruler's
grandson, who had been left a share of his personal estate, thus incurring
Caligula's animosity.

Caligula was the first emperor to show aversion to the long hours of
laborious duty needed to keep matters under control, preferring instead to
delegate work to the Greek or Hellenized ex-slaves who were his secretaries,
so that he himself could concentrate on a round of amusements instead.
The turning point of his reign came in AD 39 when he formed a powerful
dislike for the Senate, an attitude which became strongly accentuated when
one of their number, the commander in Upper Germany, was detected in a
plot. Caligula himself marched north to organize its suppression, which
was accompanied by executions and banishments in high places.

Irremediably frightened by this narrow escape, Caligula abandoned
proposed expeditions against the still unconquered Germans and British,
and returned to Rome (AD 40). There he gave expression to far-reaching
ideas for the conversion of the tactful Augustan principate into a thoroughgoing autocratic system, on the lines of the absolute monarchies of Greece.
Although honours were showered on him with extravagant lack of restraint,
conspiracies and rumours of conspiracies continued to abound, and
security precautions around his person were sharply intensified. Before long,
however, the praetorian high command decided that he was a bad risk, and
early in the following year a group of its officers murdered him, together
with his wife and infant daughter.

After his death, his 51-year-old uncle Claudius was hailed emperor by the
guardsmen. Handicapped by infirmity – he was probably spastic – he had
obtained no preferment until a belated consulship four years previously,
devoting many earlier years to scholarly pursuits instead. But now, because he was the brother of the much-loved Germanicus and the only surviving adult male of the Julian and Claudian clans, the senior praetorian
officers who killed Caligula had ensured that he should ascend to the throne

in the dead man's place. The Senate, however, which had discussed a possible restoration of the Republic after Caligula's murder, included many members unwilling to accept Claudius, and in the year following his accession they supported a rebellion planned by the governor of Upper Illyricum (Dalmatia). This terrified Claudius just as a similar seditious move had upset Caligula, and the suppression of the plot was followed by another fierce tightening of precautions, and by further measures against senators of dubious loyalty – measures which in turn led to a fresh crop of real or suspected conspiracies, followed by a renewed wave of treason trials.

At the same time, however, the government of Claudius was impressively active in provincial and foreign affairs. Just a century after the reconnaissances of Julius Caesar on the island of Britain, the southern and central regions of England were now occupied, in what was perhaps the

best planned of all Roman conquests, and their annexation as the province
of Britannia immediately followed. Claudius himself came to the country in
AD 43, for the decisive capture of Camulodunum (Colchester), which became the capital of the new province. Mauretania and Thrace were also
taken away from client rule and added to the empire; and colonies were
established in the northern frontier zones and elsewhere. Moreover, there
was a conscious and perceptible liberalization of policies concerning en-
franchisements, and admissions to the Senate, and appointments to offices
of state, for which Gauls in particular were now encouraged to apply. The
emperor also displayed considerable ability for long-term projects. For
example, the grain supply of the city was organized on a permanent
basis, and the port of Ostia underwent reconstruction to facilitate this
traffic.

Claudius himself devoted unremitting absorption to the judicial duties
which were one of the most important functions of an emperor. His predecessor's employment of Greek freedmen as advisers and imperial secretaries was continued and extended, and this was a period when certain of
them, especially Narcissus and Pallas, rose to great power. However,
Claudius still kept such men, for the time being, under his firm personal control and employed a senator, Lucius Vitellius, as his principal counsellor.
For a number of years, too, his young wife Messalina, who had borne him a
daughter, Octavia, and a son, Britannicus, remained more interested in
indulging herself than in exerting power. In 48, however, she was charged,
perhaps rightly, with conniving in an attempt by one of her lovers to seize
the throne or supplant Claudius by Britannicus, and both she and her lover
were put to death.

The initiative in stamping out this conspiracy had been taken by
Narcissus. But his moment of power ended abruptly in the next year, when
Claudius married again, selecting his niece Agrippina the younger, who
had not been Narcissus' preferred candidate. For the rest of his reign the
ageing emperor, overworked, worried about plots, and weakened by infirmity and drink, increasingly lost his command of what was going on. The
government was in the hands of Agrippina and of Pallas – who had supported Agrippina's marriage to Claudius – and of another of her protégés,
the new praetorian prefect Burrus, who came from southern (Narbonese)
Gaul. Obliterating her opponents, Agrippina arranged in AD 50 that her
own 13-year-old boy, by a former marriage to a nobleman, should be
adopted by Claudius as his son, taking the name of Nero: so that it was
evident that he, rather than Britannicus who was four years younger, would
eventually succeed to the throne.

And then Claudius suddenly died (54). It is believed, probably with good
reason, that Agrippina had fed him poisoned mushrooms. At all events,

Nero, with the help of his tutor, the leading writer Seneca, and of the praetorian commander Burrus, succeeded peacefully to the imperial throne. In
view of his youth, it was Agrippina herself who became the effective ruler
of the empire. Her pre-eminence, however, was extremely brief, since already in the following year it was rapidly becoming eroded, and Nero had
started to assume his imperial duties. Yet when certain liberal ideas he
initially proposed, relating to tax reforms and the prohibition of gladiatorial
combats, proved impracticable, he lost interest, and chariot racing, music,
drama and sex seemed more rewarding activities; so that the empire was
largely governed by the harmonious, efficient partnership of Seneca and
Burrus, backed by their senatorial supporters. At the same time, important
military operations against the Parthians took place under the empire's
leading general Corbulo (58–60), and then in Britain the ferocious revolt of
Boudicca (Boadicea) in 60 was put down.

Meanwhile, Nero, fearing that his mother, discontented with her retirement, might encourage a conspiracy, had enticed her to the Campanian
coast, where he caused her to be assassinated (59). Seneca and Burrus may
or may not have been involved in her death, but from now on they found it
increasingly difficult to keep the emperor in order. In 62 Burrus died, and
Seneca, believing it impossible to carry on without his help, went into
voluntary retirement.

The emperor's chief counsellor was now Tigellinus, a seedy figure whom
he had made joint prefect of the praetorian guard; in this capacity he presided over a revival of the treason law, under which a number of prominent
nobles, as in earlier reigns, were executed on suspicion of conspiracy. Nero,
long since estranged from his young wife Octavia, divorced her and put her
to death, marrying a famous beauty Poppaea* – who bore him a short-lived
daughter (63). In the next year Rome was ravaged by a savagely destructive
fire, for which the government penalized the small Christian movement as
scapegoats. Suspicions that Nero himself had been responsible for the fire
were probably unwarranted. But they gained strength when work was at
once started on his new palace the Golden House, designed to extend, with
its parklands, over a wide area of the city, and situated partly on the sites of
houses that had been gutted by the fire.

Furthermore, in 65 the emperor's reputation deteriorated further, when
he carried out a long cherished ambition by appearing in his first public
performance on the stage. Senators were profoundly shocked, and soon
afterwards the first of a series of plots, or alleged plots, against his life was
detected and betrayed. One of its casualties was Seneca; and another was
Tigellinus' colleague as praetorian prefect, in whose place was appointed a
personage as sinister as Tigellinus himself, a certain Nymphidius Sabinus,
who claimed to be Caligula's illegitimate son. In the following year a new

* She had formerly been married to his young friend Otho, the future emperor.

security drive wiped out a group of senators of philosophical republican inclinations, and leading military commanders, too, were compelled to kill themselves. They included Corbulo, who had become a national hero after victories and negotiations which brought peace to the Armenian frontier for half a century to come. But Nero was afraid of such outstanding commanders, and when a major revolt broke out in the turbulent minor province of Judaea, he deliberately assigned its suppression to a man credited with only moderate talents and ambitions, Vespasian.

Meanwhile, the emperor himself was conducting an extended artistic and dramatic tour of Greece. It culminated in his ostensible liberation of the country; this philhellene gesture, echoing an earlier liberation more than two and a half centuries earlier, did not, of course, restore political liberty to the Greeks, but brought them a welcome exemption from Roman taxes. However, during Nero's prolonged absence from the capital, his position became seriously undermined, since provincial governors and army commanders, feeling that their lives were in danger, felt tempted to rebel; and soon after he had finally returned to Rome, Vindex, the governor of Gallia Lugdunensis (central Gaul), broke into open revolt (68). His insurrection, however, was defeated by his colleague from Upper Germany in a battle at Vesontio (Besançon), and he did not survive. But then Galba, governor of Nearer Spain, whose bad relations with Nero's local agents had prompted him to make secret contacts with Vindex, was hailed emperor by the soldiers of the single legion he commanded, and this was confirmed by the Senate at Rome. Nero found himself abandoned even by the praetorian guard, and in June he committed suicide.

Galba, who was about seventy-one years of age, came of a family of resplendent nobility and wealth. Although he now assumed the titles 'Caesar' and 'Augustus' which had been borne by emperors of the Julian and Claudian clans, he was not in any way related to them; and the fact that he was the first ruler to come from outside that imperial house is his principal significance.

When he learnt that Nero was dead, he marched slowly on Rome, where in his absence an incipient *coup* by the praetorian prefect, Nymphidius Sabinus, was easily suppressed. But when the new emperor arrived outside the city in October, he caused a bad impression by killing a number of marines who had come to meet him, and his meanness over money, combined with an unwelcome choice of advisers, rapidly undermined his security. The bad news travelled; and on New Year's Day, AD 69, the army in Upper Germany overthrew his statues and called on the Senate and Roman people to choose a successor. But on the following day, the Lower German forces saluted an emperor on their own account, their governor Vitellius, son of Claudius' chief adviser and the grandson of a knight in the service of Augustus; and the garrison in Upper Germany then accepted their choice.

On hearing what had happened on New Year's Day, Galba decided that, lacking a son of his own, he must adopt an heir from outside his family to offer hope of continuity. This was an important precedent for future emperors, but of no avail to himself because the selection he made, a young man of the same highly aristocratic background as himself, proved immediately disastrous, for it earned the fatal displeasure of Otho. Aged thirty-seven at this time, he had been a close friend of Nero until that emperor had taken his wife Poppaea away from him, and had sent him out to be governor of Lusitania (Portugal): and in that capacity, Otho had been the principal supporter of Galba's revolt, so that, although himself an Etruscan whose Roman nobility was of comparatively recent origin, he now expected the succession to the imperial throne for himself and felt deeply disappointed that another man had been preferred to him. On 15 January, therefore, in singularly brutal circumstances, he had Galba put to death, thus earning notoriety as the first emperor to arrange his predecessor's murder. And Galba's heir and advisers were slaughtered on the same day.

Once these horrors were over, however, Otho's government displayed signs of moderation. Egypt, north Africa and the legions of the Danube and Euphrates declared in his favour. Nevertheless, he must already have known, when he seized power, that Vitellius had likewise been hailed as emperor in Germany. And now Vitellius' legionaries, under his generals Valens and Caecina, moved rapidly southwards in the direction of Rome. In early March, they were already across the Alps; and they had reached the banks of the Po before Otho's advance guard was ready to hold them up. Otho himself left Rome later in the same month, and although reinforcements from the Danubian legions were expected to join him at any moment, he decided that the enemy must be engaged without waiting for them to arrive, the action to be fought by his generals, while he himself should remain at the rear in reserve. However, in the ensuing engagement near Cremona, known as the First Battle of Bedriacum, his commanders were resoundingly defeated. The praetorian guard wanted to fight on in his cause; but he refused to let them, and committed suicide. It was 16 April, and he had reigned for three months.

The Senate immediately recognized Vitellius as emperor, and he followed his generals down towards Rome. Though a man of only average ability, he was more than just the preposterous glutton of tradition, since he had certain ideas of his own. For example, it was only with reluctance that he adopted the traditional titles 'Caesar' and 'Augustus', which had been used by Galba and Otho but seemed to him too reminiscent of the defunct Julio-Claudians. Instead, he preferred to emphasize the consulship to be held permanently, as the basis of his position; and he relied on being able to found a dynasty since, unlike so many of his predecessors, he had a young son of his own. He also endeavoured to strengthen his position by disbanding Otho's praetorian guard in favour of a larger body composed of his own legionaries. However, on arrival in the capital, he learnt that the eastern legions had transferred their allegiance to Vespasian, the governor of rebellious Judaea; and the Danube armies did the same, thus for the first time assuming their historic emperor-making role of the future. So another phase of this prolonged and complex civil war inevitably lay ahead.

The plan Vespasian adopted was that he himself should remain in Alexandria, where he could cut off the supply of grain to Rome; while his principal supporter Mucianus, governor of Syria, was to set out on the long march to the west. But meanwhile a Danubian legionary commander named Primus, who had joined Vespasian's cause, made a sudden dash for Italy, apparently without awaiting orders from his new chief. Vitellius planned to hold the line of the River Po against him, but his former generals, Valens and Caecina, were both unavailable to command his troops, since Valens was ill and Caecina had deserted. In late October, therefore, the almost leaderless Vitellian army, superior in numbers but tired after a forced march of thirty miles, was overwhelmed by Primus in the Second Battle of Bedriacum (Cremona); and as the victors advanced on the capital, Vitellius' remaining forces melted away. Yet he still had active supporters inside Rome itself, and Vespasian's brother Sabinus, who happened to be prefect of the city, had to barricade himself against them on the Capitoline Hill. But he did so in vain, since as Primus' troops forced their way within the walls, his position was stormed by the Vitellians, and he was captured and killed and thrown into the Tiber. And Vitellius himself, too, who had gone into hiding, was discovered by the invading army and lynched.

The Senate promptly declared Vespasian his successor, and a week or two afterwards his main force arrived in the city under the command of Mucianus, who put an end to the ambitions of Primus by superseding him. Reducing the praetorian guard to its earlier and smaller dimensions, Mucianus directed the government in the name of Vespasian, until the new emperor himself reached the city some ten months later.

Soon afterwards, his relative Cerialis put down a serious Gallo-German nationalist revolt against Roman rule which had broken out on either side of the Rhine, under Civilis, a Batavian, and Classicus of the tribe of the Treviri. Farther to the south, Vespasian annexed the Upper Rhine-Upper Danube re-entrant, in order to make the empire's defence line better and shorter. And meanwhile, the emperor's elder son Titus had almost completed the suppression of the First Jewish Revolt, by capturing the rebels' capital Jerusalem (70). In the following year Vespasian and Titus celebrated a magnificent joint triumph.

With the help of Mucianus (until his death some five years later), Vespasian now addressed himself to the reconstruction of the empire and its defences, gravely damaged by the civil wars. He was of rather less distinguished origins than his predecessors, being the son of a Sabine tax-collector of knightly rank. Moreover, he himself had correspondingly plain tastes, and was proud of them. He was a man who, although in basic matters autocratic enough, was easy to get on with and accessible. Yet he worked without stopping; and he decided things by prosaic, common-sense methods which made him one of the most effective of all the emperors. It was no mere coincidence that his three immediate forerunners had only survived for a few months each, after which they all perished violently, whereas his own reign lasted for ten years, at the end of which he died a natural death. For although none of the three others had been lacking in ability, he was a far better ruler than any of them.

Of necessity, his financial policy, after the vast expenditures of the civil wars, had to be stringent: tax-rates were drastically increased, and new sources of revenue invented. Yet Vespasian succeeded in raising funds to strengthen the eastern frontier which was now, after the wars of the previous decade, more heavily garrisoned than before; and he also showed himself a pioneer in the educational field, by endowing new professorships. His provincial policy, too, was liberal since he furthered the Romanization of Spain as Claudius had Romanized Gaul; Vespasian wanted to avail himself of administrative capacity wherever it could be found. And, with this once more in mind, again following in the footsteps of Claudius, he revived the ancient censorship (73-4), utilizing the office not only to purge the Senate of men who had sided against him but also to augment it by many new members, provincials as well as Italians.

His fellow censor was his son Titus, whom, although no one had ever made such use of a member of his family before, he also employed as his praetorian prefect. For Vespasian rightly disregarded rumours that the young man cherished designs against him. Like all emperors as they grew older, he deteriorated in energy and health, but he was able with Titus' help to carry on effectively. Moreover, being the first emperor to have a son of his own blood whose maturity and distinction already fitted him to succeed to the throne, he openly declared his intention of founding a new dynasty with Titus as his heir.

Yet there now followed a period in which his political opponents, mainly old-fashioned aristocratic Republicans who justified their ideas from Greek philosophy, expressed a good deal of hostility to the new dynastic pro-gramme; and Titus rigorously put down a conspiracy in which Vitellius' former general Caecina was involved. This was early in AD 79, which proved to be the last year of Vespasian's life. For during the summer, near his Sabine birthplace, he succumbed to a stomach chill and died.

Titus' tenure of the throne (79–81) was so short that it is impossible to say whether his charm, for which he was famous, would have carried him through a longer period of rule or not. He sent away, for the second time, his mistress, the Jewish princess Berenice, whose liaison with him cannot have been popular in senatorial circles. In the provinces, attention was principally concentrated on Britain, where Agricola, governor from 77, consolidated the Forth–Clyde line, and advanced tentatively as far as the River Tay. At the capital, Titus made himself popular by lavish expenditure. Yet at the very outset of his reign, Italy had been struck by disaster when an eruption of Vesuvius, dormant since before the beginning of history, had buried Pompeii, Herculaneum, Stabiae (Castellamare di Stabia), Oplontis (Torre Annunziata) and other centres, thus providing excavators from the eighteenth century onwards with the richest of all collections of evidence about the ancient world.

Titus died prematurely, at the age of only forty-two. Yet rumours that he was poisoned by his younger brother and successor Domitian were probably unjustified; though it is true that Domitian harboured a strong grudge against him, since he himself, despite stirring adventures at the end of the civil wars, had been given far fewer opportunities of distinguishing himself in subsequent years.

When Domitian now became emperor in his turn, he showed little sympathy with the old Republican forms in which most earlier rulers had clothed their autocracy, but instead followed a meticulously thought-out policy of systematic absolutism. As time went on, and particularly after his adoption of the unprecedented title 'perpetual censor' (84–5), this tendency caused consternation among the senators. As a counterblast, the emperor realized he must achieve popularity with the army; for which he was eager in any case, since he was ambitious to become a conqueror of foreign lands.

Conquest in Britain, however, did not appeal to him, and Agricola's plans to annex part of the Scottish highlands were dropped. But success was achieved in south-western Germany, where the frontier-line, pushed forward by his father, was advanced once again (83). Domitian's principal objective, however, was the kingdom of Dacia (Rumania), whose king Decebalus had almost restored it to the power it had possessed more than a century earlier. Domitian's generals sent to bring him to order suffered a couple of severe defeats. Then, finally, the military situation was restored. Yet Decebalus survived – because of what happened next.

For in 89, within the borders of the empire, the seditious pattern of the previous dynasty now began to repeat itself: and the Roman commander in

Upper Germany rose in rebellion. Domitian swooped down and mercilessly crushed the revolt. But his suspicions of the senators, already considerable, were greatly increased by this traumatic event. Under treason procedures revived for the purpose, a substantial number of leading Romans were executed. They included, as on earlier occasions, men of Republican, philosophical inclinations; but as Domitian, always a nervously irritable man, became increasingly afraid of retaliation, terror began to spread among the rest of the senatorial class. The legionaries, it is true, continued to support him strongly. But among those alienated and frightened were the commanders of his praetorian guard. And they, without the knowledge of their own soldiers, joined his wife Domitia, daughter of the eminent general Corbulo, in a conspiracy which struck the emperor down in AD 96.

The 66-year-old lawyer and former consul, Nerva, who was declared his successor on the very same day, must have been privy to the plot. But it caused such great anger in the army, and especially among the rank and file of the praetorian guard, that after a short interlude he was humiliatingly compelled, in the following year, to hand over Domitian's assassins and allow them to be executed. Immediately afterwards, to save his throne and his life, he adopted a son and heir from outside his own family. He was acting like Galba before him, but his choice was a great deal more successful. It fell on Trajan, aged forty-four, the governor of Upper Germany; his adoption inaugurated a period of over sixty years in which successions to the throne were determined by adoption rather than by birth.*

Trajan's father was descended from Roman settlers in Further Spain (Baetica) and his mother was a Spaniard; he was the first of the emperors to come from a province, and his origin was symptomatic of the rise of the provincial element within the ruling class. For the way to the highest office was now becoming open to all educated men, regardless of race and nationality; at present, westerners such as Gauls and Spaniards were still advancing much more rapidly than north Africans and easterners – though their turn would come later.

Attractive and affable, Trajan possessed the rare qualification of popularity among Senate and army alike. His governmental policies were progressive. In Italy, one of his achievements was the foundation of the *alimenta*, a system of financial provision for poor children. He also lightened the burden of taxation in the provinces; and a series of letters preserved by Pliny the younger, his governor of Bithynia in Asia Minor, display his humane care for the welfare of the provincials – combined with a suspicious preoccupation with internal security, and a paternalistic tendency to inter-

---

* In subsequent cases, however, it was usually reinforced by matrimonial ties – and would never have happened at all if the rulers had had sons of their own.

fere in the affairs of the ostensible self-governing cities, when their finances, as frequently happened, were unsound.

An ever-increasing programme of impressive public works was also carried out on Trajan's orders. The spiral reliefs on his Column at Rome indicate the source of the vast expenditure on such projects: they were paid for by the wealth of conquered Dacia. Domitian had been obliged to leave the country unsubdued. The forces with which Trajan invaded it were even more formidable. He enlarged the Roman army to thirty legions, each of which, moreover, was increased in size; and the auxiliaries who fought alongside them were supplemented by new kinds of native troops (*numeri*), which comprised national units from un-Romanized tribes, equipped with their own arms and including cuirassed horsemen. With this great army, the emperor overran Dacia in two large-scale wars (101–6). Its capital Sarmizegethusa (Grădiştea Muncelului) was captured and destroyed, and Decebalus was driven to suicide. His kingdom became a Roman province, and gigantic sums of gold and silver were seized and brought to Rome, the last really large profits its treasury ever derived from a war. But the end of the Dacian campaign meant that there was a new, long frontier to protect; and from now on the numerical superiority of frontier troops shifted permanently from the Rhine to the Danube and Dacian garrisons.

But there were also the eastern borders of the empire to be considered; and Trajan had decided that the peace concluded half a century earlier with Parthia must be brought to an end, because it had not provided a satisfactory imperial boundary. But when Armenia, the traditional bone of contention between the two states, fell to him with ease (114), he decided to go onwards and annex the whole of Mesopotamia as well, with infinite prospects of conquests ahead, which might make him the first authentic successor of Alexander the Great. Parallel Roman forces simultaneously descended the Tigris and Euphrates, the Parthian winter capital Ctesiphon was taken, and the end of the following year saw Trajan at the Persian Gulf. Never before had a Roman commander marched so far, and it would never happen again.

However, it was a transient success. For far behind the advancing Roman army, in one eastern province after another, the Jews of the Dispersion (p. 263) broke into revolts, encouraged by their numerous co-religionists in Parthian territory temporarily occupied by the Romans. And meanwhile the Parthians themselves rallied their forces, and attacked Trajan's extended lines of communication. He suppressed the rebellions where he could, and even, uniquely, proclaimed the conversion of the kingdom of Parthia into a Roman client state. But this was little more than an empty gesture; and almost immediately he turned back towards home. Either he decided that it had all been in vain – in which case it must have been the hardest decision of his life – or he hopefully believed that he could leave the scene because the arrangements he had recently made would endure; though he can scarcely have been labouring under such a massive delusion. But there is a third possibility also, for perhaps, whatever the military forecasts, his weakened health had made him unable to carry on. For he was ill, suffering from blood-pressure, followed, it would appear, by a paralytic stroke in AD 116 – though it may be that his illness was in part the psychological outcome of failure. At all events, in the following year, in the south-eastern corner of Asia Minor, he died.

Trajan's talent for civil government, the popular aggressiveness of his military policies, and his agreeable accessible personality, had earned him the title of the Best Ruler (*Optimus Princeps*). Yet whereas his Dacian campaigns had brought in a great deal of money, the vastly ambitious Parthian campaigns that followed cost enormous sums with little or no compensating political or military advantages. True, these displays of might may have helped his successors to keep the peace. Yet, by and large, Trajan remains a classic example of a good man carried away by the exciting Roman tradition that conquest was glorious.

His successor Hadrian, a distant relative from the same part of Spain, had accompanied him to Rome at the outset of his reign, and then served him in many important posts, enjoying his special favour. On Trajan's death-bed, it was given out that the emperor had adopted him as his heir, but this, though possible, remains uncertain.

At all events, Hadrian now assumed the imperial powers. Without delay, he decided – as his predecessor may well have decided already – that the newly occupied eastern territories were untenable, and so, unwilling for adventures when he needed to consolidate his own power, he abandoned all that was left of Trajan's temporary conquests and withdrew the Roman frontiers to the Euphrates again, to the dissatisfaction of militarist senators. Then he set out for Rome and subsequently for the lower Danube frontier, where there was trouble. While he was away from the capital, however, four of the most eminent senators, all former consuls, found themselves accused – with how much justification is uncertain – of plotting against his life and were put to death, probably by the independent initiative of his praetorian prefect (118). This treatment of the four ex-consuls permanently damaged his relations with the Senate. Moreover, although he was assiduous in his attentions to that body, it became clear that he did not estimate class and rank very highly.

The remarkable feature of Hadrian's 21-year-long principate was the fact that he spent more than half of it outside Italy, travelling widely throughout the provinces of the empire. His motives for all these journeys were varied. One was pure curiosity; he was the most fanatical of all the many Roman sightseers. But in addition, as the designs selected for his coinage confirm, he had formed a novel conception of what the imperial territories meant. He saw them no longer as a collection of conquered provinces, but as a commonwealth in which each individual province and nation possessed its own proud identity. Yet probably the foremost aim of his travels was to keep the army, in which he maintained a constant and expert interest, in a state of skilled readiness; and he made efforts to improve the living conditions of the soldiers, deprecating the harshness of previous rulers. One of the first fruits of this active military policy, following upon a minor reverse on the British frontier, was the best preserved of all the fortifications of the empire, Hadrian's Wall from the Tyne to the Solway, manned by 15,000 auxiliaries watching over the bare brown hills that rolled away to the still unconquered north.

Fighting in the empire was infrequent. But there was one serious war towards the end of his life, a Jewish rising – not of the Dispersion this time, as in the previous reign, but in the homeland of Palestine itself. For Hadrian's establishment of a Roman colony and temple at Jerusalem, now renamed Aelia Capitolina, after the emperor's family name Aelius, caused great anger among the Jews, and under a talented leader, Bar Kosiba, they launched the ferocious and bloodily suppressed Second Jewish Revolt (132–5). For Hadrian, a keen Hellenist – and himself a talented writer and musician – felt no sympathy with a race which could not, like every other people in the empire, be content with the dominant Greco-Roman civilization and its ideas.

Following up the governmental policies of Trajan, Hadrian aimed, like him, at enlightened centralization: and he pursued it with particular skill. His was a remarkably many-sided personality, full of bold ideas yet at the same time devoted to administrative efficiency, and deeply concerned with justice and the law. Yet he continued to be dogged by the unhappy relations with the senators which had marred his early years. Then, in 136, a dangerous plot, perhaps genuine, resulted in further executions, whereupon Hadrian, who had no son and was sick, decided that he must proceed rapidly with the adoption of an heir. His first choice, who took the name of Aelius after him, died almost at once and was replaced by the 51-year-old Antoninus who soon afterwards, on Hadrian's death, succeeded peacefully to the throne (138).

Antoninus, like his two predecessors, was of western provincial origin, his father being a man of consular descent from Nemausus (Nîmes) in southern Gaul. His reign was aptly summed up by the conferment of the title Pius, indicating devotion to his duty, the gods, his country, and his adoptive father. He also achieved a careful balance in his relations with the Senate, showing deference to its prestige while quietly continuing to centralize the administrative machinery, and taking steps to cut down unnecessary public expenditure. In Britain, he advanced the frontier and constructed a new Antonine Wall from the Forth to the Clyde (141), though subsequently there were outbreaks of raiding within the province. The southern frontiers, too, suffered from occasional unrest and rebellion. Nevertheless, the greater part of the empire enjoyed peace during the twenty-three years of his reign.

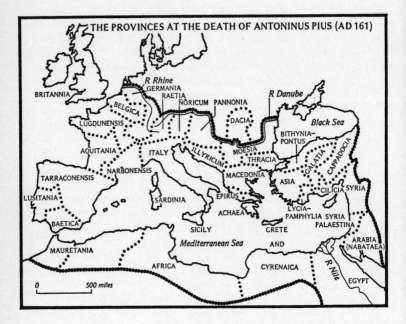

THE PROVINCES AT THE DEATH OF ANTONINUS PIUS (AD 161)

# 15

# Imperial Society

THE SCULPTURAL PORTRAITURE OF private persons, men, women and children, flourished throughout the imperial period.* But above all, it is the emperors of the age and their relations who are depicted in a series of extraordinarily skilful portrait busts, designed to acquaint the peoples of the empire with the personalities their rulers wished to present to them. Augustus had been shown in many guises, but under Claudius a new problem arose, for his knobbly countenance seemed to defy accurate representation. Some sculptors compromised, others idealized. When his stepson Nero succeeded to the throne, they had to think once again how to depict the rapidly increasing grossness of the imperial features; and they achieved remarkable success. Far from minimizing or evading the idiosyncracy of Nero's appearance, they cleverly cherished his peculiarities, and even endowed them with a certain impressiveness, by infusing just that touch of elevation which made the emperor seem, if still a fat lout, at least a lout of slightly superhuman dimensions.

The men who designed the heads on the coins, too, performed triumphs which earned the admiration of the Renaissance, their contrasted interpretations of Nero and the bleak Galba proving particularly noteworthy. Under Vespasian, portrait sculptors and coin engravers had to rise to a new challenge – an emperor who belonged to an unpretentious social class, and wanted to show it. Some artists, it is true, tried to iron out his rugged, whimsical features into something more orthodox. But others depicted them exactly as they were, or even added a touch of amusing caricature. Trajan is shown as an impressive soldier or a responsible and thoughtful administrator. But the most interesting of the male portraits of the epoch comes from the principate of Hadrian. He was partly homosexual (as Trajan also had been), and the posthumous heads of the boy Antinous,

* And Egypt maintained a superb tradition of portrait painting on the panels inserted in mummy cases.

who was loved by him and died young, show a dreamy gaze suggesting the tragedy of that early doom.

Sad, meditative little children of the imperial house are likewise portrayed with keen psychological sympathy, and the women of successive dynasties, too, were made known to the public through the same sculptural medium. The ladies of Vespasian's house evidently did not share their emperor's desire to reflect his middle-class origins, for they are elegant, and frequently change their elaborate hairstyles. The portraits of this age aim at a new smooth, fluent surface texture, enhanced by the subtle use of flesh and hair tints, of which only traces survive today. The sculptors are fond of deep incisions, appropriate to the strong sun and shadow in which their busts and statues originally stood.

The same vigorous interplay of light and shade appears on a relief upon the inner face of the Arch of Titus at Rome, depicting soldiers carrying the spoils taken from the Jerusalem Temple in AD 70; the artist creates the illusion that the procession is viewed through an open frame, silhouetted against the sky. But the outstanding example of this relief sculpture is the continuous series of spiral designs on the Column of Trajan. Towering over the massive new forum designed by his great architect Apollodorus of Damascus, the reliefs, more than a hundred in number, offer a bird's eye view of numerous events in the emperor's Dacian wars. This panorama includes no less than 2,500 human figures, and a wide variety of incidents is selected for illustration – battles and sieges, the capture of prisoners-of-war, visits by envoys, marches and journeys, buildings and fortifications, and above all, events relating to the emperor himself, the addresses he delivered and the sacrifices he made to the gods, and the deeds he performed that illuminated his solicitude and clemency.

Among other great arts of the early empire was the painting of walls: and as a recently discovered example has reminded us, of ceilings as well. The bulk of the pictures that have come down to us are of an earlier date than the great reliefs which have just been mentioned. For they appeared in town-houses at Pompeii and Herculaneum, and in country villas which adjoined those cities at Stabiae (Castellamare di Stabia) and Oplontis (Torre Annunziata) and elsewhere. The eruption of Vesuvius which overwhelmed the region in AD 79 preserved a great many of these paintings; most of those that survive belong to the period immediately preceding the eruption, since much redecoration, displaying a new brilliance and richness in colour, had taken place as a result of earthquake damage in 62. Figure paintings, often derived from lost Greek originals, were greatly in favour; very often they were devoted to the mythological and theatrical themes dear to Nero. Moreover, as in his own Golden House at Rome, an earlier taste for architectural vistas was now revived, displaying a new baroque, scenic illusionism which experimented with effects of spatial recession drawing their inspiration from stage designs.

There are also paintings of romantic landscapes and fantastic Nile scenes, and studies of still life, and portraits. On some walls the overall pictorial design includes painted panels as centre points, but it would have seemed wrong to the architects and artists who planned these houses to spoil their organic structure and décor by affixing detachable panel pictures, like modern canvases, to the walls. Similarly, the floors were meant to be seen without carpets or mats, and instead were covered with vivid mosaics, in large patterns or small, sometimes, like the paintings, reproducing Greek masterpieces of the past. This was one of the most enjoyable and picturesque of Roman arts: when transferred to walls, vaults, niches, apses and ceilings, a process which had already tentatively begun, it led the way to the mosaic decoration which was to line the interiors of Byzantine churches.

These paintings and mosaics adorned large terraced villas opening out upon the sea, and town houses which still retained their traditional grouping round the atrium, though by this time the architectural designs showed increasing variety and elaboration. Sometimes, however, these houses of the rich, for example at Herculaneum, had begun to be divided up by partitions, in order to serve a somewhat less prosperous social class. There were also other forms of housing for the middle class and poor, and on this subject recent researches at Pompeii have yielded a good deal of information, revealing domestic arrangements of considerable variety and a general standard of living never achieved again until the nineteenth century. Quite a lot can also be learnt about the humble accommodation of slaves, both in the town houses and the rural dwellings round about (villae rusticae), which often combined private suites, for the use of their rich and mainly absentee proprietors, with elaborate farms worked by their agents and tenants.

In another respect, too, Pompeii is a uniquely informative source of evidence for the lives of its ordinary citizens. For at the moment when the eruption buried the town (as, no doubt, at all other times as well), the walls of its buildings were covered by many thousands of graffiti which have survived and display extraordinary variety. Very often, there are references to the annual civic elections – which in these smaller towns, unlike Rome, were still hotly contested – and one such election was imminent at the time when the eruption took place. The graffiti also have much to say about current theatrical and gladiatorial events. Moreover, like their counterparts today, they recorded many curious aspects of the loves or erotic fantasies of a great number of individuals.

The lives of the inhabitants of Pompeii are also illustrated by the surviving remains of about 20 inns and 120 bars. At the ancient colony of Ostia, on the other hand, which was the port of Rome, only two inns and fourteen bars have come to light, since the people of this place apparently preferred to drink in the social clubs of their trade corporations (*collegia*). The community was rapidly expanding, to keep pace with a massive development of port facilities. For Claudius, who was eager to direct the skills of his architects and engineers away from showpieces to practical projects, gave the town a new harbour, connected by canals with the Tiber; and temples, baths, warehouses and granaries were constructed. Then, subsequently, Trajan added a landlocked hexagonal inner basin, and Ostia came to handle the largest volume of goods of any ancient Mediterranean city apart from Alexandria.

In these prosperous years, the population grew rapidly, to a total of approximately 100,000. This expansion dictated a revolution in housing for the not particularly wealthy, in the course of which the Pompeii-type dwelling of earlier days was largely replaced by tall apartment blocks which accommodated far greater numbers of people. Made of brick which was no longer concealed, as in the past, by stone or stucco facings, these large buildings were strongly constructed, and relied for their architectural effect on the spacing and scale of their windows, which had panes of selenite or mica or glass and were framed by small external balconies. The interiors of the apartments, adorned with good mosaics and wall-paintings, often contained seven rooms or more, and sometimes as many as twelve. These blocks did not normally possess a private water-supply of their own, but, as at Pompeii, public cisterns fed from the aqueduct were liberally distributed round public places of the town.

In few other cities of the Roman world has substantial housing been excavated, but the Ostian type was no doubt more characteristic than the Pompeian; it was the empire's most important contribution to urban living. And at Rome itself, too, increasing signs of the same sort of apartment blocks have lately come to light, in addition to many other types of residential accommodation. It is true that, up to the second century AD, we still have complaints of rickety, ill-constructed, high-rise tenements in the capital. Some of the worst abuses, however, had been eliminated by Nero, who made efforts to impose a more spacious plan and scale.

He was given this opportunity by the Great Fire of Rome (AD 64) which he was unfairly accused of having started himself to make room for his Golden House (*Domus Aurea*). For this and its parklands took over nearly 400 acres of what had formerly been the most thickly inhabited zone of the city – the largest piece of land that any European monarch has ever carved out of his capital to make a residence for himself. The Golden House, like palaces erected by Greek monarchs of earlier days, was not a single unified structure but consisted of a number of separate pavilions, set

among elegantly designed formal landscapes. The central porticoed building contained an octagonal hall which can still be seen today (though it is
now beneath the ground). It was lit from a round hole in the centre of the
cupola and made unprecedentedly enterprising use of the brick-faced
concrete which had been Rome's greatest architectural discovery.

Nero's successors abandoned the Golden House; but Domitian ordered
the construction of a new imperial residence on the Palatine. In addition
to the private quarters of the emperor, it included state apartments, consisting of two groups of imposing halls, separated from one another by a
colonnade. Domitian also built a magnificent villa looking down on to the
Alban lake, complete with theatre and amphitheatre. It has not survived;
but much can still be seen of a later and considerably more elaborate
country palace erected by Hadrian, near Tibur (Tivoli). Extending for a
mile across the slopes beneath the city, this complex virtually forms a
whole town in itself. The architect exploits the gently undulating site by
ringing every change on the theme of curve and countercurve; and his
impressive mastery of concrete achieves all manner of ingenious, romantic
effects, with nostalgic reminiscences of the Greece the emperor loved. This
Villa of Hadrian, wrote Mortimer Wheeler, 'stripped and shattered though
it be, remains the most fantastic material creation of the Roman genius: of
a particular Roman genius, which had travelled far and experienced much,
and had learnt to temper affairs with sentiment, sentiment with reason'.

And another building which owes its design to Hadrian was Rome's
Pantheon. His reconstruction of Agrippa's original temple is the best
preserved today of all the edifices that the ancient Romans ever built; it is
among the most admirable of all their achievements. The huge colonnaded
portico leads into a rotunda 142 feet high and wide. Its concrete interior
wall contains vaulted niches and recesses which show that by now the
Romans had pretty full trust in their mastery of this material, so that they
could boldly lighten it by inserting such cavities, and the dome that they
superimposed on these walls, surpassing Nero's Golden House, proved
durable enough even to survive the removal of its gilded bronze tiles in the
seventh century AD.

From its circular central opening, a stream of light, smoothly and regularly diffused, descends into the rotunda. The great space is tranquil and
sublime. But unlike an earth-bound Greek temple, it dwarfs men and
women by its hugeness. This cavernous grandeur warns humans that they
are in the presence of all the gods – for that is what 'Pantheon' means, and
its niches were probably intended for statues of the old planetary divinities. And in this astrologically minded age, the central opening of the dome
represented the sun; while the star-like rosettes on its curved internal
surface reflected the majestic rhythm of the heavenly bodies.

. . . . . .

Such was one of the greatest among the innumerable shrines devoted to the religious needs of the Roman population. But ample provision was also made for their pleasures. There were enormous bathing establishments, of which something will be said in describing a later epoch, when the construction of such buildings reached its climax. But there was also another sort of entertainment altogether, provided by the Flavian Amphitheatre. Begun by Vespasian and completed by Titus, it was designed for gladiatorial combats and the slaughter of wild animals, and could also be flooded to stage imitation sea fights. Known much later as the Colosseum, after the colossal statue of Nero that had stood near by, this amphitheatre, the earliest in the city to be built completely of stone, remains, for all its horrific purpose, one of the most marvellous buildings in the world.

These elliptical amphitheatres were like two semi-circular theatres placed back to back. The curving exteriors of Greek theatres had normally displayed two storeys of arcades, and Rome had a theatre with three. But in its final form the Colosseum was extended up to four of these storeys, of which the topmost was walled and windowed, but the three lowest consisted of open arches in continuous arcades. Classical columns are to be seen, engaged in these great rows of arches, but they are only there to provide ornamentation and scale. The essential constructional units are the massive concrete-covered piers which support the arches. The Colosseum displayed with unique majesty the genius of Roman architects for dramatic effects and exerted a vast influence upon the buildings of later Europe.

It provided seats for about 45,000 spectators, and standing room for 5,000 more. The emperor's platform was at the centre of one of the long sides, facing the sections reserved for state officials and the holders of the games. There were also places for foreign envoys, imperial ladies, Vestal Virgins, and priests. The entertainments provided in these arenas remained extraordinarily popular, and rulers found it advisable to arrange and finance such displays on a munificent scale, and to listen patiently to the popular demonstrations and protests and demands which the audiences of pampered Rome, by tradition, seized the opportunity to stage on these occasions. As for the gladiators, their legal and moral status was utterly degraded, but many graffiti bear witness to the admiration and excitement which they none the less provoked in the hearts of the public, especially women.

The pattern of the Colosseum was duplicated throughout the Roman world in other amphitheatres of widely varying dimensions. And indeed, it was these first and second centuries AD, when the Pax Romana gained such remarkable strength, that provided by far the greater part of the immense material remains not only of amphitheatres but of very many other kinds of buildings as well which are still to be seen in Rome and its provinces. For the cities of these regions, abounding in prosperous public-spirited benefactors competing with one another in their lavish contributions to municipal amenities, were entering upon the climactic period of their development, destined, in some areas, never to be equalled again in later times. The consequent orgy of urban construction produced many spectacular achievements, among which Thamugadi (Timgad) and other cities in north Africa may perhaps be singled out, because they have never been built over in later ages and therefore survived on a monumental scale.

Such cities often originated from military camps, but rapidly displayed great advances in industry and commerce. For in these fields of activity, the provinces had truly come into their own, and had begun to eclipse Rome itself. For example, the glass and bronze wares of Italian Capua were superseded by products made in Gaul; and the most important pottery industry was similarly displaced, first to Condatomagus (La Graufesenque) in the south of Gaul (*c.* AD 20) and then to Ledosus (Lezoux in the Auvergne). Next, in the second century AD, the main output of pottery was from the Rhineland, which became before long the principal industrial area of Europe. For the first time in history, this region had caught up with the industrial production of the eastern Mediterranean; while the Danube area, too, along the whole of its length, was developing an east–west commercial axis of great importance for the future. Nor was this kind of

expansion a European phenomenon only, since in Asia as well, and in
Syria where the towns stretched almost uninterruptedly throughout a
single vast urbanized zone, the export trades in textiles and other materials
continued to flourish and multiply.

Yet the fundamental facts of Roman trading remained the same as
before, and were subject to the same limitations: it was still, on the whole,
a hand-to-mouth affair, with no solid capitalistic infrastructure or foundation. And, above all, the basis of the imperial economy was still not commerce but agriculture. In this sphere, at first sight, there were certain
encouraging signs. For example many fruit trees were brought to the vicini-
ties of the Rhine, Danube and Atlantic and planted there; and olives were
introduced into the steppe lands of southern Tunisia and south-east Spain,
which became the principal centres of the empire's production of oil.
Spain also produced and sent abroad a great deal of wine: the Monte
Testaccio on the outskirts of Rome is a mound consisting of fragments of
forty million jars which had once been full of cheap wine imported from
Spanish vineyards.

The rich farmer-landowners possessed and lived in huge residential and
agricultural complexes. Among many hundreds may be named Chiragan
(on the Garonne, in Gaul), covering forty acres and housing four or five
hundred dependants, Anthée (near Philippeville in Belgium), which
included a large villa and twenty other buildings within a thirty-acre walled
enclosure, and Chedworth in Britain, which was another luxurious administrative centre for a substantial group of farms. The owners of such
palaces were very wealthy men: although, on the whole, this was an age not
so much of a few millionaires as of a great many affluent bourgeois.

Nevertheless, in spite of all this development, the basic facts of the
agricultural economy were still much as they had been in earlier years.
For one thing, the placid rhythm of the Antonine world still depended,
though perhaps to a slightly lesser extent, upon slaves; and they were still
wholly excluded from the area of political and social privilege. But excluded
also – and this, too, was no novelty – were the 'free' agricultural workers
who formed an even larger proportion of the population. It was not the
depressed rural poor of the countryside, but the prosperous people of the
cities, who felt loyalty to the imperial régime in response for services
rendered.

In the eighteenth century, the historian Edward Gibbon believed that
the Antonine age witnessed greater happiness and prosperity than the
world had seen before. And he may even have been right, because prosperity had never been very widespread any more than it is now. True,
it was not very widespread in the time Gibbon was writing about either,
for it did not extend to the poor cultivators of the land who comprised

most of the Roman world's inhabitants. Nevertheless, the limited circle of those enjoying favourable conditions had been considerably enlarged. And to that extent, there was some justification in the praises which the second century Asian orator Aelius Aristides, anticipating Gibbon, lavished on the imperial system of the day, eulogizing the lush amenities and secure, universal communications which were owed to the Antonine peace.

Even if the poor did not secure many of these material blessings, at least Roman law, as it entered, under the initiative of Hadrian, upon the first and most creative and philosophical period of its Golden Age, was now doing a good deal to protect them from the worst illegalities of exploitation. For example the treatment of slaves, despite their exclusion from privilege, was controlled by an increasing number of legal safeguards – devised out of a combination of humaneness with a self-interest which saw advantages in their well-being. And the position of the free poor, unprosperous though they remained, likewise benefited from current legal reforms.

These tendencies were apparent in the activity of Hadrian's north African jurist Salvius Julianus. Famous for his concise formulations, Salvius collected and revised the successive edicts which praetors had for centuries been accustomed to pronounce at the outset of their year of office. This meant that, from now on, the edicts could be recognized as permanently valid; and his publication of them diffused a far clearer understanding than had hitherto existed of the legal safeguards to which the subject populations of the empire were entitled.

The same trend was manifest in the work of one of Salvius' pupils and employees, Gaius. For his renowned *Institutes,* the only classical legal work to have come down to us in substantially its original form, include suggestions that their author was especially interested in provincial legislation, and had discussed it previously in writings that have not survived. The study of the law, that is to say, was now displaying a new and much more attentive interest in people who were not Roman citizens: the legal barriers between priviliged citizens and all the rest, for centuries a fundamental feature of Roman life, were becoming eroded.

And yet, despite all these measures, *equality* had come no nearer than it had been before. For all that had happened was that these old civic differences between Roman citizens and the rest were being replaced by another distinction altogether. This perpetuated the division of the community into two main groups, to which the law gave entirely separate treatment. The superior class (*honestiores*) included senators, knights, land-owners, soldiers, civil servants and town councillors. Everyone else belonged to the lower category (*humiliores*), who possessed inferior legal rights and incurred heavier penalties in the courts, including many punishments which only non-citizens had suffered before. Roman law, despite all its concern for equity, had always favoured the upper échelon of society, from which its own practitioners originated; and now, from the time of Trajan or Hadrian onwards, such preferential treatment became crystallized in legal forms. This greater explicitness was ominous, for beneath the tranquil surface of second-century life it confirmed the depressed status of the underprivileged, and thus deepened the basic rift which in the following centuries would bring the empire down.

So inequalities were perpetuated; and this seems paradoxical, seeing that the Roman lawyers were at the same time producing measures displaying a new considerate solicitude. But the inequalities derived from a social system which unchangeably presupposed them, whereas the solicitude stemmed to a considerable extent from that Stoic philosophy to which Cicero had owed much of his moral inspiration in an earlier epoch.

In the imperial age the most eloquent exponent of this system was Nero's minister Seneca (c. 4 BC-AD 65), son of a rhetorician from Corduba (Cordova) in Further Spain (Baetica). In contrast to earlier Roman tragic drama, of which almost all is lost, we have nine tragedies attributed to Seneca. These plays, to which Shakespeare and other European dramatists owe a very great debt, breathe the enlightened tolerance and humanity of Stoicism, including its sympathy for slaves. And more explicitly still, this same spirit pervades Seneca's literary letters and ethical treatises, which the Renaissance came to value for the moral guidance they provided.

He also set the tone for a new phase of Roman literature by his use of scintillating verbal tricks and vivid pointed epigrams, to which the lapidary Latin language so readily lends itself. This same sparkling oratorical 'Silver Latin' style, combined with a similar Stoic viewpoint, was adopted by Seneca's nephew Lucan in his poem, the *Civil War* or *Pharsalia*. Its subject was the struggle between Pompey and Caesar;* but it displayed a philosophical viewpoint, gradually veering towards anti-monarchism, which increasingly broke up his friendship with the reigning emperor, Nero. Despite its many purple patches and digressions, this mordant, powerful poem won great fame in the Middle Ages, and earned its author a place as one of Dante's four Lords of Highest Song.

Nero's fatal displeasure eventually fell both on Seneca and on Lucan: and it descended also on his 'arbiter' of court fashions, Petronius, who wrote a lively, scandalous picaresque novel known to us as the *Satyricon*, that is to say *saturikōn libri*, tales of lascivious behaviour; for here Senecan moralizing takes a rest. The preceding centuries had produced many sorts of Greek fiction including fake biographies, fantastic travel stories, romantic novelettes, satirical efforts in mixed prose and verse, and pornographic

* For the battle of Pharsalus, see p. 191.

sketches. Petronius gathers all these threads together, in a highly entertaining Latin narrative of three disreputable but elaborately educated young homosexuals on the move round the Greek towns of south Italy; and their journey is also intended as a mocking comment on the contemporary Roman social scene.

This work, of which a large portion but by no means all survives, includes poems and prose discussions which give the author his opportunity to offer criticism of currently fashionable writings. And, in addition, Petronius includes oblique, humorous echoes of earlier literary works. Thus the anti-hero's renunciation of women for boys is intended as a burlesque of middle-brow, heterosexual, Greek love romances, and descriptions of the wrath of the phallic god Priapus are a parody of the wraths of the Homeric gods. The *Satyricon* also contains set pieces or short stories, of which the longest and most famous is the 'Dinner of Trimalchio', a self-made, vulgar industrialist of slave origin living in Campania, who emerges as the most entertaining comic figure of all ancient literature. His banquet and reminiscences, as well as the coarse, colloquial remarks of his friends and guests and hangers-on, reflect needle-sharp observation and keen sensual gusto: and incidentally, they provide unique historical material. Although fiction did not qualify as a separate branch of literature in ancient classifications of the subject, it was the most vigorous and creative literary form of the time: and many centuries later, too, in the mixed beginnings of the modern European novel, admiring recollections of Petronius were still to play a great and varied part.

In the generation that followed him, the most original talent was that of Martial (*c.* AD 40–104), the outstanding epigrammatist of the ancient world. Although Spanish, Martial caught the authentic Italian note of riotous, mordant satire, and has imprinted his definition of this term on subsequent European letters. His witty, humane, obscene little poems cast a vivid light upon the social picture of his day.

Juvenal, born in about AD 50 at Aquinum (Aquino) in southern Latium, strikes a grander and also harsher note; and his sixteen long poems reveal him to be one of the supreme masters of the Latin tongue and the foremost of all Roman satirists, who did more even than Martial to found the *genre* as a tradition of the western world. Juvenal had started life as a rather unsuccessful rhetorician; and neither forgetting nor forgiving the relative poverty from which he partially emerged – only partially, for he never obtained adequate recognition – he flays the evils of the contemporary Roman scene with ironical, savagely pessimistic invective. This is ostensibly directed against personages belonging to the past; yet its ferocity is really aimed at the present as well. For although Juvenal wrote during the time of Trajan, in a Rome much more relaxed than it had been under the hated Domitian, the empire still seemed to him a sick, maladjusted organism, overflowing with deplorable men and vicious women.

An equally damaging view of Roman society, once again despite the current Trajanic improvements, was implicit in the work of Tacitus (*c.* AD 55–?*c.* 116), the greatest of Roman historians. Perhaps the son of a tax-collector in one of the provinces of Gaul, he became a well-known advocate; though, as he explained in his *Dialogue on Orators*, in times of imperial peace forensic pleading could no longer flourish as it had under the Republic, and in consequence he moved over to a political and administrative career. But the hazards he and other Romans had undergone under Domitian continued, even after that emperor's death, to prey on the mind of Tacitus, who criticized him posthumously in a biographical essay in praise of his own father-in-law Agricola, governor of Britain who, according to the historian, had received insufficient imperial appreciation for all he had done. Germany, too, was the subject of a special moralizing study of great ethnological interest, the *Germania*, providing a reminder that Tacitus never commits the error of regarding the Roman empire as the only existing world.

Then he turned to his supreme achievement, the narration of Rome's history from the death of Augustus to the death of Domitian (AD 14–96). This survey is divided into the *Histories* and the *Annals*. Of the former work, dealing with the last twenty-eight of those years, only the first part, describing the convulsed Year of the Four Emperors, is still extant. But the greater portion of the subsequently published *Annals*, dealing with the earlier period from Tiberius to Nero, has survived. Tacitus draws upon studies by earlier historians, now lost, but transforms them by the massive power of his own personality; and these haunting, penetrating, moralistic analyses of the men holding such monstrous power in their hands comprise our earliest and only extensive account of the imperial phenomenon. Tacitus was unique for the meticulous care with which he collected and sought to verify and evaluate his facts, far exceeding in this respect the fascinating biographers who were his contemporaries, Suetonius and Plutarch, writing in Latin and Greek respectively. His claim to impartiality, however, cannot be accepted, since his hatred of Domitian, for example, overflows into unfair bias against an emperor he saw as Domitian's forerunner, Tiberius. Incisive, abrupt, tortured and unfailingly stimulating, Tacitus' literary style is also frequently poetical in its vocabulary and construction, echoing tragic drama (which he had at one time attempted to write) in its awareness of the implacability or malevolence of destiny, and in its stress upon the more sinister aspects of the imperial régime.

Nevertheless, these gloomy implications sometimes clash strangely with the more favourable facts which Tacitus was far too good a historian to suppress. Thus he was able, for example, to weigh up objectively the credit side of Roman rule as it appeared to the peoples of the empire. And the relative advantages of absolute monarchy and the old republican system are presented with equal objectivity: so that, in later Europe, not only revolutionaries felt able to claim his support for their cause, but autocrats as well. For if Tacitus felt in his romantically republican heart that one-man rule was wrong, his powerful intellect also told him that Rome could not avoid it.

In consequence, his heroes are often men like Agricola, who quietly got on with their jobs under even the most deplorable of emperors: and this, indeed, was what Tacitus had done himself, and so, before his accession to the throne, had Trajan himself, in whose reign the historian was writing. Yet, in spite of this conclusion reached on rational grounds, Tacitus' spirit was moved by observing how men and women, even in times of tyranny and terror, still find themselves able to rise to remarkable heights of heroism; people like the ex-slavewoman Epicharis who, even under torture, refused to betray her fellow-conspirators against Nero.

Under the Antonines, a very different sort of commentary on the life of the empire was provided by the Greek author Lucian of Samosata (Samsat in south-east Turkey), who wrote a series of adroit and sometimes amusing essays ridiculing such targets as religious charlatans, over-pretentious philosophers and travellers who told exaggerated tales.

His capacity for story-telling was shared in full measure by a contemporary Latin writer of unique gifts, Apuleius. Born in about 123 at Madaurus (Mdaourouch in Algeria), he became one of the leading lecturers in popular philosophy (sophists) who were peculiarly characteristic of this century, gaining such renown, in a number of cases, that they addressed even emperors with confidence and arrogance. Apuleius was the arch-manipulator of an unfamiliar sort of Latin prose: artfully combining the florid with the archaic, for which there was a current vogue, it creates a sort of language that is on the way to the Middle Ages. Moreover, he was also a lawyer and his *Apologia* – one of the few Latin speeches, other than Cicero's, which have come down to us – is a startlingly extravagant defence against charges that he was a magician: which, in Saint Augustine's view, was precisely the right name for him.

The same fantastic, luscious style, incorporating a wealth of Roman and Greek literary echoes, reappears in Apuleius' *Metamorphoses* or *Golden Ass*, the only Latin novel which has survived in its entirety. Adapting, perhaps, a simpler Greek work, but creating something entirely original in the process, the writer tells of a certain Lucius, who is accidentally turned into a donkey and undergoes many other fantastic experiences. The numerous stories this long narrative incorporates include the world-wide Cinderella folk-tale of the fairy bridegroom, which Apuleius combines with the Greek myth of Cupid and Psyche, and his account of their weird, romantic adventures attracted endless admiration and allegorical interpretation in the literatures of later antiquity, and of medieval and renaissance Europe as well.

When Apuleius describes, with all the wealth of his exuberant imagination, how his hero is initiated into the mysteries of the Egyptian goddess, whose merciful hand raises up and saves the fallen souls (*psychai*) of human beings, he seems to be recording a profoundly felt experience of his own. And this is based on an ecstatic empathy with the Mystery faiths and Saviour cults which marked, in a sense, the transition between decaying state paganism and rising Christianity. It was true that the gods and goddesses of the old national religion of Rome still provided a great stimulus to patriotism, and for this purpose were exported to the provinces, where they were deliberately identified with the local, native divinities of each region. Yet they were too sterile to fill the spiritual vacuum during these first centuries of our era when men and women became increasingly preoccupied with the urgent needs of their own souls for something more satisfying, and the enormously widespread acceptance of astrological doctrines, maintaining that everything was irremediably fixed by the stars, was another factor which caused many to turn their panic-stricken attention to other and more comforting sorts of faith instead.

What they turned to, above all, was a passionate belief in certain saviours who would endow their chosen devotees with a life of blessedness after they were dead. For there was a new, rather hopeless humility abroad, a sinking of the heart, an instinct of isolation and defeat: since no reliance could be placed in this world – and this was an age when scientific studies were in total retreat – ever-increasing numbers of peoples throughout the Roman empire pinned their hopes on the next world instead, longing for an individual victory over evil and death in a happy hereafter. It was to these yearnings that the pagan saviour cults responded, with their thrilling, dramatic, sometimes orgiastic ceremonials, their solemn rituals of progressive initiation (*mysterion*), and their holy books claiming unique revelation and knowledge. The strength of these religions was that they were all things to all people; and they were among the most vigorously lively features of contemporary Roman society and thought.

These Mystery Saviour faiths went back to the elaborate secret rituals of Demeter in early Greece, and to the disturbing, frenzied worship of Dionysus, the liberator of mankind, which was celebrated in the *Bacchants* of Euripides. Among the kingdoms of Alexander the Great's heirs this Dionysiac cult, as a setting for Mysteries, became particularly widespread, and its subsequent arrival in Italy, where the god was known as Bacchus, had alarmed the Senate into a repressive reaction (186 BC). But then this religion became accepted among the Romans, and attained enormous popularity. The ecstatic element tended to be toned down into mere hedonism, the afterlife being often depicted as just a jolly party, with facilities for alcoholic and sexual gratification.

More profound excitement, however, was inspired by the mystery cult of Cybele, the ancient divine earth-mother of Asia Minor. Admitted to Roman cult in 204 BC, and later celebrated in an extraordinary poem of Catullus, the worship of Cybele, accompanied by stirring ritual dramas, raised hopes of immortality to a fever-heat of excitement, as the resurrection of her youthful consort Attis, god of all that annually grows and dies, was enacted amid scenes of resplendent pageantry.

Innumerable people throughout the Roman empire believed passionately in Cybele. But even more, like Apuleius, believed in the Egyptian Isis. Accompanying her in the liturgical drama was the god of the underworld, Osiris, who stood like Attis for the birth and death of the year: and the annual Finding of Osiris was the occasion for unrestrained jubilation and excitement. For as the worship of Isis turned into a cosmopolitan Mystery religion, her major festivals provided ceremonies equalling or even exceeding those of Cybele in their theatrical, emotional appeals to ear and eye. Her penitents roamed the streets of the cities intoning hymns, or competed with one another in acts of piety and self-mortification, or contemplated the magnificent images of the goddess and meditated upon her countenance. All barriers of caste and race were thrown down, and distinctions of sex as well, for among these worshippers were great numbers of women. To them the worship of Isis, like many of the successful beliefs of the world, made a direct and specific and powerful appeal: this Goddess of Ten Thousand Names was their own glory, and gave them equal power to men.

From the first century BC, when senators' suspicions of Egyptian ideas failed to keep the cult of Isis out of Rome, right on until the final decline of paganism many hundreds of years later, her faith remained the most widespread of all the religions of the Roman empire, the only Saviour cult which had a real chance of becoming universal.

# 16

# The Jews, Jesus and Paul

THE RELIGION, HOWEVER, WHICH in the end turned out to defeat all the others originated not in Egypt or Asia Minor, the homelands of the cults of Isis and Cybele, but in that other historic centre of religious movements, Palestine.

Nearly a thousand years before the birth of Jesus, this little country had controlled a great empire, under King David and his son Solomon. After them, however, it had split into two kingdoms, a northern (Israel) and a southern state (Judah), which later fell to successive imperial powers, Assyria (721 BC) and Babylonia (597–586 BC) respectively. Subsequently the Persians had taken over the whole territory, and then it came under the Ptolemaic and Seleucid monarchies in turn. Finally, in the second century BC the Jewish nationalist movement of the Hasmonaeans (Maccabees) had broken away from the Seleucids, and succeeded in re-establishing national independence.

In total contrast to the Greeks and Romans, the Jews adhered to a strict monotheism, venerating their ancient holy books with an all-engrossing, literal-minded reverence which declared that every past and present and future happening was a fulfilment of divine prophecy. They believed that their Laws had been handed to Moses on Mount Sinai by God himself, who 'gave him the two tablets of the Tokens, tablets of stone written with the finger of God'. These tablets, forming a Covenant which was the lasting cornerstone of the Jewish conception of history, were held to have been inscribed with the first five books of the scriptures, the Torah (Pentateuch in Greek), which is often translated 'Law' but originally meant instruction by divine revelation. Next in importance to the Torah, in what Christians later named the Old Testament, came the prophets. These glorious figures were credited with deeds and utterances inspired by the Torah and forecast and prefigured by what had been said in it. The Psalms, too, traditionally though erroneously attributed to King David, were invested with similar authority.

And then, in the second century BC, under the Hasmonaean dynasty, arose the most determined, serious and progressive element in the Jewish leadership of the day, the Pharisees or 'Separated'. They opposed the Hasmonaean monarchs, because the latter, in their view, were wrong to combine kingship with the antique high priesthood in their own persons. Yet the Pharisees were not political activists, but favoured submission to the divine will even if this meant endurance of worldly oppression. Although they held that individuals would eventually rise bodily from the dead, they discounted the possibility, which some other Jews were now envisaging, of a violent, simultaneous, universal resurrection, that would bring all life on earth to an apocalyptic end. Nor were the Pharisaic thinkers fundamentalist or fanatical, but on the contrary, while duly stressing the applicability of the Law to all human problems, and insisting as much as anybody on the distinctively religious character of Jewish life, they were also eager to adapt their faith to modern needs, for example by accepting oral interpretations as an integral part of the written canon.

Though the Pharisees' movement remained lay and unofficial, it served as a focus for national Jewish hopes and aspirations. And, in poverty-stricken Palestine, the leading members of the movement, though they themselves mostly were of middle-class origin, often championed the cause of ordinary people and the oppressed; though other Pharisees displayed a tendency to puritanical formalism which earned them charges of complacency. Their strength lay in the synagogues, which existed in every Jewish town. At these focal points of spiritual life, the popular religious universities of the day, the Torah was carefully studied and expounded, and fervent prayers were offered for the revival of the nation.

The Pharisees' agents and assistants were the doctors of the Law or 'scribes' (Sopherim). Qualified jurists with pupils, it was they who decided what details of conduct were required to give practical effect to the Torah. Unpaid laymen and not men of wealth, they gradually became the country's most influential section, in place of the old landed aristocracy. But that aristocracy, too, was still strong. It mainly consisted of a group known as the Sadducees: they followed an unspiritual policy, directed towards the survival of the established order and the avoidance of rebellion; and it was they who controlled the ancient revered Temple at Jerusalem, which after desecration by the Seleucid occupying power had been rededicated by the Hasmonaeans. Moreover, it was from the Sadducee ranks that the high priest was periodically appointed, and the hereditary priests under him who organized the Temple's manifold activities.

In the first century BC the Hasmonaeans were maintained on the throne by Pompey as his clients; but later they succumbed to Antony, who replaced them by a monarch from Idumaea in the south of the country, bearing the name of Herod (37 BC). As a protégé of Antony and thereafter, for a quarter of a century, a dependant of Augustus in his turn, Herod expanded Judaea and made it one of the most prosperous of Rome's client kingdoms. To distinguish him from later Herods, he became known as 'the elder', or the Great. He was a deeply suspicious man, and struck down a number of individuals, including his closest relatives, for fear of possible sedition. Yet under his rule the rest of his subjects were able to flourish – including the greatest of all Pharisee thinkers, Hillel and Shammai.

Herod died in 4 BC, and Jesus had probably been born slightly earlier; the date AD I to which his birth came to be attributed was based on a miscalculation by a sixth-century monk.

Almost all our information about Jesus is contained in the four Gospels (to which the other, non-canonical Gospels do not add very much). Their writers are known as the evangelists, from the Greek word *euangelion*, good news; and they were identified from the earliest times as his apostles Matthew and John, and Saint Paul's companions, Mark and Luke. Yet, despite recent efforts to argue to the contrary, they can scarcely have been the real authors of these writings. Who the authors were, cannot now be determined. Nor do we know where the Gospels were written, or when; probably they reached their final form between thirty-five and sixty years after Jesus' death. But the main difficulty these works present, from the historian's point of view, arises from their intention to edify, to spread belief in the divinity of Jesus: that is to say, they were not designed *primarily* as historical evidence. In attempting, therefore, to extract historical information from what they record, a distinction must be made between those passages which bear the stamp of the early Christian Church and those which seem to go back to Jesus himself. And, contrary to pessimistic estimates, the main lines of his career and thinking and teaching can to some considerable extent be reconstructed.

When Jesus was still a boy, the core of Palestine was directly annexed by the Romans as the province of Judaea (AD 6), governed, as minor provinces sometimes were (along with one major province, Egypt) not by a senator but by a knight, who, in this territory, was known as its prefect. Under his general supervision Rome allowed the Jews a measure of internal self-government, under a council (Sanhedrin) directed by the high priest. Adjoining this Judaean province, to its north and east respectively, were the territories of Galilee and Peraea. These continued to form the princedom of one of Herod the Great's sons, Herod Antipas (4 BC–AD 39), who ruled, as his father had ruled before him, by the grace of Rome.

On the desert fringes of Judaea and Peraea, in about AD 28–29, a mysterious Jewish preacher, John the Baptist, attracted widespread attention by proclaiming to his coreligionists (not to Gentiles) the imminence of the Kingdom, or rather 'kingship', of God. This was not a new idea; despite the scepticism of the Pharisees, many Jews had long believed that their earthly miseries would one day end when the divine rule would be achieved upon earth, and the Lord would usher in universal perfection. They had also emphasized the need for repentance, and so did John, stressing that it must be a total change of heart. When this came to pass, he declared, the sins of Jewish men and women would be forgiven. And he set a seal on the process by performing baptisms in the River Jordan – a new development of the periodical ritual ablutions familiar in ancient Palestine, converted by the Baptist into a once-and-for-all event which radically and permanently transfigured the spiritual nature of its recipients.

One of those who received John's baptism was Jesus – an unquestionably historical happening, since the early Church would have dearly liked to omit it (seeing that Jesus was supposedly sinless) but could not because of its authenticity. He had probably been born not at Bethlehem in Judaea –

a fiction inserted to fulfil an old Testament prophecy – but at Nazareth (or possibly some other small place) in the northern land of Galilee. This was a country of fairly recent conversion to Judaism which produced numerous devout sages, though it was looked down on by Jerusalem as bucolic in its way of life and incorrect in matters of religion.

Soon after John had baptized Jesus, Herod Antipas placed him under arrest as a potential revolutionary: for sedition was rife, especially in these border areas. Thereupon Jesus returned to Galilee and began his mission. It contained, at least initially, the same ingredients as the Baptist's, but with one remarkable amendment. For Jesus, while continuing to proclaim the Kingdom of God, no longer preached, like the Baptist and other Jews before him, that this was imminent, but that *it had already begun to arrive* – by his own agency, on the direct order of God. This conviction was the key to Jesus' entire career. It dominated all his thoughts and actions, and every item of his ethical and social teaching. For example, his many parables – brilliant narratives of imaginary happenings in daily life, endowed with an underlying spiritual significance – derived from and depended upon this single-minded idea.

The same is true of his alleged miracles. These – healings or exorcisms on the one hand, and conquests of nature (such as walking upon water) on the other – were 'signs' in the traditional Jewish sense that they not only prefigured salvation but at the same time actually helped to bring about what they prefigured. And in certain passages of the Gospels it is implied not so much that these miracles 'actually happened' as that their primary significance was symbolic: they were descriptive gestures or enacted parables, once again relating to the inauguration of the Kingdom of God. His healings, in particular (some of which must surely have been authentic), were directly and explicitly linked by Jesus to the forgiveness of sins – conferred by himself, and the product of repentance – which was the accompaniment of this dawning Kingdom.

The Jews, however, regarded the forgiveness of sins as belonging to the One God alone. What they had thought when the Baptist proclaimed this doctrine in connexion with his own baptisms is scarcely known. But when Jesus proclaimed it, once again, as his own personal prerogative, they were shocked because he seemed to be usurping the divine authority and thus infringing upon their cherished monotheism.

Yet Jesus continued to admit that the completion, the full realization, of the Kingdom of God upon earth had not yet taken place; like many other Jewish thinkers he believed that it would take place almost immediately. His entire programme of teachings and preachings was based on these two assumptions: the familiar belief that the Kingdom would be brought into full and final effect on the earth almost at once, and the more startling conviction that he himself, by God's will, was beginning to bring it into effect already, there and then. This second assertion placed everything in a new light. Repentance now meant not only a complete change of heart but a change of heart which specifically accepted Jesus' message about himself.

Later on, the evangelists, and especially Luke, laid special stress on Jesus' compassion. And no doubt he was a deeply compassionate man. But the actions and gestures revealing this quality were, once more, motivated by his total concentration on the Kingdom of God as a haven into which every Jew had the possibility of entering. As for Gentiles, the Kingdom of God was not a concept which would have had any meaning for them, and it does not appear from the Gospels that Jesus, any more than the Baptist, directed his preaching towards them at all, apart from a few isolated individuals who happened to come his way. But owing to his belief that all Jews, indiscriminately, could be admitted to this Kingdom, he paid particular attention to the Jewish poor, because they were 'poor in spirit': that is to say, lacking material strengths of their own, they depended on God's help and were therefore especially accessible to his invitation to enrol in the Kingdom. Sinners, too, received a welcome from him because they too, once they repented, would obtain admission – all the more readily since they lacked the complacency of the consciously virtuous. And forgive your enemy, he amazingly said, and turn the other cheek, because what can possibly be the point of petty worldly enmities in the face of this great, overriding opportunity for all Jews to enrol in the Kingdom together? 'Suffer little children to come unto me', not for any compassionate or sentimental reason, but because their simple, unspoilt directness provided just the approach needed for the ready acceptance of Jesus' message. And he welcomed women around him, too, because it was absurd to suppose that the Kingdom was only open to one of the two sexes. In this respect he differed from the Jewish teachers of the time, the scribes, who were not surrounded by women in this way. Nor did the scribes go outside the synagogues in each town, as he did, in order to preach to a much wider Jewish public.

As a teacher, Jesus was brilliant but unorthodox. He was also, like John the Baptist before him, seen by many of his listeners as heir to the ancient, extinct succession of prophets. And some hailed him as the Messiah or anointed one (Greek *Christos*). This was, according to Jewish tradition, the personage who would eventually come to rescue oppressed Israel, and who, according to more recent theories, would receive the aid of superhuman hosts in performing this task; to harmonize with this warlike view of his function as the liberator of Israel, he was credited with descent (variously described) from the royal house of David. And Jesus was also ascribed a mysterious and variously applied designation, 'The Man' or Son of Man. At certain times in the past, in keeping with a Jewish tendency towards corporate and communal concepts, this term had been used to denote all

Israel, or the remnant of Israel that would be saved, though it may latterly have acquired a more specific reference to a future single individual who would perform this salvation. Some also regarded Jesus as Son of God. All Israelites were in a sense Sons of God, though the term had tended to be applied to great secular and spiritual leaders. But Jesus, whose mother was Mary the wife of Joseph, was believed to have no father but God himself.

But how, in the light of these contemporary ways of thinking, did Jesus see himself? This has been greatly disputed. But it seems probable that he felt that none of these designations – except perhaps the suitably ambiguous 'Son of Man' – sufficed to describe his mission, which he believed to be unique. In holding this belief, he followed other Galilean sages before him, who had likewise claimed an exceptional, personal, intimacy with God. And so did the devotees of Qumran, a semi-monastic settlement near the Dead Sea, whose scrolls, discovered in nearby caves during the past thirty years, have thrown much light on the contemporary, varied Jewish scene: they reveal, for example, the veneration of a Teacher of Righteousness, who had once lived on the earth and would, it was believed, come to live on it again. We have no evidence that Jesus saw himself in just this light, but, like the Teacher of Righteousness whom the dedicated inmates of Qumran revered, he believed that he enjoyed an altogether peculiar relationship with God.

This, like his claim to forgive sins, brought him into collision with the most active Jewish religious group, the Pharisees, and with their associates the scribes. In the face of this opposition, his mission in Galilee, in which he was assisted by his twelve principal disciples (apostles), ended in failure – as he himself openly admitted. And as his support dwindled, the local prince, Herod Antipas, saw a chance to get rid of this preacher, who was not only inconvenient, but also potentially subversive because his insistence on the dawning actuality of direct rule by God himself implied a disloyal attitude to earthly monarchies. Antipas, by this time, had executed the Baptist. And at this juncture, now that Jesus' mission was manifestly unsuccessful, it was probably Antipas once again who compelled him to leave Galilee.

At all events that is what Jesus did; and in about AD 30, or perhaps 33, he proceeded by gradual stages to Jerusalem. He was making his way deliberately to the centre of the Jewish establishment. Yet he knew these leaders would not accept him; and he must, therefore, have foreseen his death – a prospect he seems (though this is not universally agreed) to have clothed in the thoughts of the Suffering Servant eloquently depicted by the prophet Isaiah, while likewise recalling the stories of the martyrs who at different times had died for Israel. Jesus, like other Jews, believed many of his experiences to fulfil the predictions and prefigurations of the Torah and prophets and psalms, and purposefully directed every action to this end: thus his entry into Jerusalem was carefully arranged, in keeping with a prophetic text, to show that his kingship was not of this world. And next, once again in deliberate fulfilment of a scriptural passage, he directly challenged the most politically powerful Jewish group, the Sadducees, by entering their domain, the precinct of the Temple, and driving out of it the traders who did their business there.

In consequence, with the connivance of one of his twelve apostles, Judas Iscariot – who was probably, like others, disappointed by Jesus' refusal of an earthly role – the Sadducees placed him under arrest. He was charged with threatening to destroy the Temple (an unlikely accusation), and was also accused of claiming to be the Messiah and Son of God and King of the Jews – to which he gave no clear answer, since neither an affirmative nor a negative reply would have offered an adequate explanation to such an unsympathetic audience. He was then handed over to the provincial prefect Pilate (Pontius Pilatus). Pilate was reluctant to judge the case, since he had experienced great trouble with Jewish disputes on earlier occasions. But finally he agreed to give judgement, and convicted Jesus of sedition against the Roman imperial throne, on the grounds that he refused to deny that he was King of the Jews. And so Pilate gave orders for his crucifixion.

Three days after Jesus' death on the cross, his followers believed that they saw him resurrected upon the earth, and that he then ascended to heaven. And thus had begun the process by which the failure of his lifetime was converted into triumph after his death – one of the few revolutions in the world's history that has lasted.

But Jesus' posthumous triumph took a long time to become manifest. That it took place at all was due to the extraordinary accident, or act of providence, which made a man of towering gifts into one of the disciples of the crucified Jesus. He was Paul: a Jew of quite different origins from his new master, for whereas Jesus came from Galilee, an appendage of the homeland, Paul belonged to the Dispersion (Diaspora), comprising the communities of Jews in countries other than Palestine. The first Dispersion had taken place in the early sixth century BC after Jerusalem and its Temple had been destroyed by the Babylonians, who took many thousands of Jews away into foreign captivity. Some were later repatriated by the Persians who succeeded to the Babylonian empire, but the Dispersion continued to increase in numbers, particularly when the Ptolemies introduced many Jews into their new city of Alexandria, and then again when the Seleucids, who took their place as rulers of Palestine, settled many families in Asia Minor, and subsequently drove many more out of Judaea by persecution. By the time of Paul, the Jews of the Dispersion were to be numbered in millions, comprising a sizeable minority in many or most of the principal cities of the eastern Roman provinces.

Paul himself came from the self-governing Greek city of Tarsus in Cilicia (south-eastern Asia Minor). He claimed descent from the Jewish tribe of Benjamin, and belonged to a family of strict Pharisees. It seems probable that he spent his youth at his native town, learning his father's craft of weaving goat's hair into tents, carpets and shoes. Tarsus was a centre of advanced Hellenic culture, so that Paul was familiar with Greek, and wrote in that language. The Jews in Greek cities like Tarsus were accorded a quasi-autonomous community status by the Roman authorities. But Paul's family enjoyed a more unusual distinction as well. For they were among that section of the local population, never numerous in such towns, which had been granted Roman citizenship. Perhaps it was Paul's father who had acquired this franchise, either as a reward for services to Rome, or because he had been a slave and was subsequently freed. At all events, although he gave his son the Jewish name of Saul, this was replaced, on occasion, by a Latin equivalent, Paulus – probably chosen because of its resemblance to his original name. Thus the young man possessed the remarkable triple qualification of belonging to the Jewish, Greek and Roman civilizations all at the same time; no one else in ancient history spans, as he does, all those three different worlds.

But above all, he was a Jew, and a very active one: indeed he may well have been a member of an ultra-pious group active in the Dispersion. At all events, soon after the crucifixion, he began to object strongly to Jesus' disciples, and the Messianic claims they were putting forward on his behalf. In accordance with the coercive powers which the Romans delegated to their councils at Jerusalem and elsewhere, the Jewish authorities were pursuing fierce sanctions against these dissidents. And in enforcing these sanctions, Paul tells us that he himself played an active part; perhaps he received his instructions from the local council at Tarsus or Antioch, and set out from one of these cities on his punitive missions.

In any case it was on one such disciplinary journey, perhaps in about AD 36, that he made for Damascus, an important 'free' city of Syria which contained a Jewish community of considerable size. It was the devotees of Jesus among their number whom Paul had been commissioned by his Jewish chiefs to bring to order. But instead – he later declared – while he was on his way to Damascus, a mighty light flashed upon him and blinded him and felled him to the ground; and at the same time he heard a voice. Psychologists describe such experiences under the name of photism, a sensation of light or colour accompanying some other species of sensation, and especially a sound. The sound Paul believed that he heard was the voice of Jesus ordering him to enter Damascus, where he would learn of a new task to perform. When he recovered, therefore, from his blindness, he went on into the city, where Jewish converts to Jesus' doctrines told him to go and preach to the Jews the Good News (Gospel) that Jesus himself had been preaching to them a short while ago. And he gladly accepted this message, since his experience outside the gates of Damascus had utterly changed his attitude to the followers of Jesus, so that, instead of being their remorseless persecutor, he now believed, no less fanatically, that they were right after all.

For what followed we have a remarkable source, the letters of Paul himself, written in Greek. The earliest of these documents perhaps dates back to about AD 50, only twenty years at most after the crucifixion of Jesus, so that they antedate the first of the Gospels by at least sixteen and probably twenty years, and constitute by far the earliest Christian literature. Paul's vigorous, violent personality emerges from these epistles with stunning force; he was a strange addition indeed to the humble and uneducated adherents of the infant church. Despite his powerful intellect, he often wrote paradoxically and ambiguously – his letters were dashed off to meet the current needs of the moment, so that even the one with the greatest claims to a measure of comprehensiveness, the Epistle to the Romans, was not by any means intended as a systematic corpus of his views.

Furthermore, the letters were not primarily written with historical aims in mind. And yet they convey a great deal of invaluable information. Facts can also be derived from the Acts of the Apostles. But this work, from the historian's point of view, is considerably less reliable. It was written much later, under a strong shadow cast by the events of the intervening period, and the first half of its contents largely consists of miracles of which the historian can take no cognisance. Nevertheless, the rest of the book contains a good deal of by no means unreliable historical material.

The letters and the Acts, therefore, taken together, make it possible to give a fairly accurate idea of Paul's career and teaching. It becomes clear that, during the period immediately subsequent to his conversion, the embryonic Jewish movement which had accepted the Messiahship of Jesus was still based upon Jerusalem, the centre of the Jewish faith and the place where Jesus had died. At first it was Peter, Jesus' close personal associate, who headed this Jewish Christian community, and the fairly extensive missionary movement which it began to direct towards its fellow Jews in Judaea and neighbouring lands. But in due course James the Just, the brother of Jesus, took Peter's place. After Paul had been converted, there was, for a time, no split between himself and this group, and he worked as its missionary to its fellow-Jews, first in Arabia (southern Jordan) and later for ten years in Syria and Cilicia.

Then in about 45, with his friend Barnabas, he set out on the first of those far more widespread journeys of his, which so notably exploited the improved communications of the Pax Romana for the benefit of Christianity. This first great journey, lasting several years, took him not only to Syria but to Cyprus and Asia Minor as well. The intention of Paul and

Barnabas was to speak in synagogues to their fellow-Jews. Yet matters did not turn out that way. For one thing the Jews were against him, since they objected to what they regarded as his deification of Jesus, and the rejection of monotheism which this seemed to imply: and they carried their hatred of his teaching even to the lengths of physical violence. Furthermore, a strong disagreement arose between Paul and his own Jewish Christian mother church – a disagreement which before long caused the division of the Christian community into two virtually separate parts, one Jewish and the other of Gentiles, to whom Paul, rejected by the Jews, increasingly addressed his teaching. In particular, the Gentiles who accepted the new faith proved unwilling to undergo circumcision and the dietary restrictions required of Jews: and whereas Paul saw no possibility of enforcing such practices upon them, the Jewish Christians deplored this permissive attitude.

Nevertheless, he set out with a series of different companions on two further huge journeys, during which he addressed himself once again, ever increasingly, to the Gentiles who did not make such injurious objections. These travels covered a period of about eight years, including one and a half years spent at Corinth in Greece, and three at Ephesus (Selçuk) on the west coast of Asia Minor.

On returning to Jerusalem in about AD 58, Paul was subjected to accusaions of blasphemy by the angry Jews, and the Roman authorities arrested him to save his life. While still detaining him at their provincial capital Caesarea Maritima (Sdot Yam), two successive Roman governors deferred a decision on these charges, anxious to evade the obscure but inflammable question at issue. When, however, Paul, as a Roman citizen, requested that this case should be transferred to the court of the emperor Nero at Rome, his appeal was granted; and after an eventful journey, including shipwreck at Melita (Malta), he spent two years in the city, first under informal house arrest and then in prison. Finally, following a trial or trials, instigated this time not by the Jews but apparently by his other enemies the Jewish Christians, he was condemned to death and executed, either in 64 when the Christian community at Rome were persecuted as scapegoats for the city's Great Fire, or possibly a year or two later.

There was something wrong with Paul, what he called his 'thorn in the flesh' – either a physical ailment or more probably a sexual problem, since although, like Jesus, he adopted the un-Jewish practice of enlisting women to help him in his ministry, he wrote somewhat sourly about sex. But the characteristic of Paul which most greatly struck the imagination of those who came after him was his fabulous perseverance and endurance. Wherever he went, he urgently argued, remonstrated, appealed in support of the new sort of Judaism that he believed to have been made necessary and inevitable by Jesus' crucifixion. Oscillating strangely between modesty and self-confidence, he was unimpressive in presence and manner; but he hectoringly repeated over and over again his demands for utter obedience.

It was obedience to a novel cause. For the reason why Paul became converted was that he found he could no longer accept the normal Jewish view that the Torah was the answer to all the problems of life. Criticizing this whole code far more sharply than Jesus – who had merely stated that he came not to destroy the Law but to complete it – Paul denounced its provisions as overburdened with legalism and unrealistic in its demands for perfection. Like other Jews, Paul held that the Fall of Adam had plunged the whole world into evil ways. But unlike them, as he looked round at its ills, and above all at the miseries of the Jewish people in their homeland, he felt that the Torah had, for many centuries, failed to end these tribulations, and was still failing to end them now; so it could not possibly be the answer he was looking for.

That being so, mere oral explications to its doctrines, such as the Pharisees were prepared to offer, did not seem enough. Instead, he felt a total change was needed, something that would turn the whole of this abominable history into complete and abrupt reverse. And in his desperate perplexity, although he had never known Jesus himself, Paul seized on the astonishing, moving tales of his crucifixion and resurrection and ascension, and decided that these reported events possessed exactly the saving power of reversal that he was looking for. That was not, obviously, the same as Jesus had preached, since, when Jesus was preaching, these events had not yet happened. Moreover, in strange contrast to the later Gospels, Paul is almost totally uninterested in any and every supposed occurrence in Jesus' life before the Last Supper. It was his death only, and what followed after his death, that Paul declared to be redemptive (by God's Grace, beside which all human initiatives were nothing). He was very clearly aware that Jews and Greeks alike would find it singularly hard to understand that these happenings *have anything to do with us*. Yet that is what he believed, and what he devoted his life and eloquence to explaining to the outside world. In comparison with the central, overwhelming significance of the redemptive power of Jesus' death and what followed it, the whole Jewish code, in fact all knowledge in any ordinary sense of the word, seemed to him useless and pointless.

Yet many Jews and Jewish Christians alike considered that this rejection of the Law was nothing better than an open invitation to licence, and they therefore refused to join him in throwing the Torah overboard. In consequence, both communities turned against him; and his career seemed to have ended in total failure. His churches for Gentile converts did not prosper, or even in many cases continue to exist. Instead, such Christian communities as survived in the Dispersion preferred to follow the Jewish Christian Church, based on the very code he had spurned. His reputation at the time of his death was at its lowest ebb.

But then the course of events was remarkably changed by the First Jewish Revolt (AD 66–73). The province of Judaea had never been a credit to Rome. Elsewhere in the empire, Roman government, if sometimes unimaginative, had generally been relatively successful, or at least peaceable. In Judaea, on the other hand, successive provincial governors, men lacking senatorial rank and only supported by a small garrison of non-Jewish auxiliaries, had been obliged to grapple with an almost continuous and ever-worsening series of internal crises, embittered by mutual incomprehension of each other's religious attitudes. As a result, an underground terrorist movement developed, or rather several distinct movements; and finally the imprudent actions of one of the governors triggered off open revolt. With all the resources of the Roman empire against them, the rebels had no chance of success. Besides, they chose the worst possible moment for themselves, when Rome had just made a durable peace with its eastern enemy Parthia. For a time, it is true, the Jewish insurgents were given a lucky reprieve by the prolonged Roman civil wars after Nero's death. But the end was bound to come, and the obliteration of Jerusalem and its Temple by Vespasian's son Titus in 70 marked the end of the nation's life in Israel for more than two thousand years.

When the Jews, because of this rebellion, fell into total disgrace with the

Roman occupying power, the Christians in their midst urgently needed to convince the Romans that they themselves lacked any taint of Judaism. But in this respect the split in their ranks proved damaging. For the Jewish Christians, despite all their efforts to prevent this, became discredited in Roman eyes along with the Jews; and so they dwindled gradually into a scattering of insignificant sects, which failed to survive into the modern world. The Gentile Christians, on the other hand, escaped this Roman stigma and lived on, to become the dominant force and theme of the Christianity of the future. Within the first two decades following the revolt, it was they who produced all four Gospels: books which preach a sharp dissociation from the Jews, and present the Jewish Christians, too, as exemplified by Jesus' apostles, in a very unfavourable light.

And so, because of this strange reversal of circumstances, Paul's Gentile mission had prevailed after all. True, much of his own teaching still seemed too daring and provocative, and the *Acts of the Apostles*, which deals with his career, says remarkably little, indeed virtually nothing, about the content of his message. Yet because his ministry had been directed to the Gentiles he had to be rehabilitated. The *Acts*, therefore, chose to praise him, not for his embarrassing views, but on the safer grounds that he was an indefatigable missionary; and 'the greatest example of endurance' was what he remained.

Moreover, later on, at a time when to talk of Jesus Christ and simultaneously practise Judaism had been declared wholly impossible, feelings moved still further in Paul's favour. Indeed, there was an attempt by Marcion, in the second century AD, to raise him to a startling, overriding eminence. But this proved unacceptable, and it was the cautious, sober interpretation of his career that prevailed: he could be praised as an intrepid missionary, but his awkward radical thoughts must be damped down. Yet often, in later years, the reverberations of the true Paul have been heard through this deliberate softening and muffling, and they have sometimes been explosively loud. For by extending Christianity to the Gentiles, it was he who had made it into a world religion. And since then he has been the greatest single source of all its successive spiritual revivals. Whenever the faith has been in danger of flagging, the memory of the man who first spread it far and wide has been revived time after time to give it new life.

# VIII

# TOWARDS A NEW WORLD

# 17

# Collapse and Recovery

WHEN ANTONINUS PIUS DIED in 161, he bequeathed the empire to Marcus Aurelius, his adopted son and the husband of his daughter. But Marcus Aurelius promptly appointed a co-emperor, Verus, who had likewise been an adoptive son of Antoninus but had not hitherto enjoyed the same degree of preferment. This régime of an imperial pair, which lasted until Verus' death in 169, was an important innovation that would be seen again during the centuries to come. However, the two emperors were unequal in stature. For Marcus Aurelius, whose inmost thoughts have come down to us in his *Meditations*, was both phenomenally hard-working and a man of the highest ideals. Verus, on the other hand, though attractive, was a light-weight. Nevertheless, when a crisis arose in the east because of Parthian encroachments on Armenia, it was he who was sent to deal with the situation, and in 163–6 his generals reoccupied Armenia and annexed Mesopotamia.

But at about the time when these campaigns were coming to an end, an event occurred in another part of the imperial frontier lands which heralded the permanent transformation of the world scene. For German and other tribesmen, 'barbarians' as the Romans called them, began to pour across the upper and middle and lower reaches of the Danube in a wide series of formidable, collusive thrusts. In the preceding years, during a long period of relative stability, many of the Germans had outgrown their relatively simple agricultural techniques and become determined, if they could, to abandon their marshy forest clearings for the richer territories that lay within the Roman borders. The fighting which now resulted was more serious than anything of the kind that had been seen before, and it continued to engage the personal attention of Marcus Aurelius for the remaining fourteen years of his life. Breaking through into the provinces of central and eastern Europe, the land-hungry Germans even crossed the Alps into Italy itself, where they destroyed cities and laid siege to the Adriatic port of Aquileia. Almost simultaneously, another German tribe

THE 'BARBARIAN' INVASIONS OF THE 2ND AND 3RD CENTURIES AD

penetrated most of the Balkan peninsula, plundering Eleusis very close to Athens itself.

The Roman armies, though incapacitated by an epidemic brought back from the east – perhaps typhus, the plague or smallpox – gradually and painfully regained control of the military situation. It faced Marcus Aurelius with a financial emergency of almost desperate dimensions. Yet, while pressing ahead with border defence, he also formed two further ideas for dealing with this unprecedented German pressure. One was to admit large numbers of tribesmen into the empire as settlers and potential auxiliary soldiers. This had been done before, for example by Augustus and Nero; and Marcus Aurelius now adopted the policy on a much more systematic scale. In various parts of Italy and the northern frontier provinces, these German settlers were assigned to Roman proprietors or the lease-holders of imperial domains, and legally tied to their new plots of land. The emperors who organized such arrangements have often been accused of barbarizing the provinces. But these settlements can also be regarded as a counterblast to racial prejudices, though not a sufficiently decisive one; and at least they supplied the Roman world with cultivators and soldiers whose services it needed.

Marcus Aurelius' second solution involved the annexation of Marcomannia (Bohemia) and a further province of Sarmatia to its east, providing the empire with frontier defences which were shorter in length and depended on mountains instead of the Danube. But like Augustus before him, who had first formed this intention of annexing Bohemia, Marcus Aurelius never succeeded in carrying out his plan. It was put off, first because of a serious rebellion by his principal eastern general (175), and then because he himself died. After his death, the proposed annexations were abandoned. It is unlikely that they would have been a success, for the easier frontier would scarcely have compensated for the difficulty and expense of recruiting enough troops to garrison such huge and warlike territories. Probably the empire had already expanded to the farthest limits which were practically possible.

Because Marcus Aurelius had a son of his own, Commodus, he elevated him to be his heir, thus abandoning the principle of adoption from outside the family which had been pursued by his four immediate predecessors. Since, however, Commodus' excessive addiction to emotional religions and gladiatorial sports made him one of the most eccentric of Rome's emperors, his father has been blamed for this reversion to the hereditary doctrine. Yet, unlike the four rulers before him, Marcus Aurelius could not have found a generally acceptable candidate outside his own house, so that any adoption would have provoked rival candidatures and civil wars. And they at least were avoided, since, when he died, the transition to Commodus' rule was managed peacefully.

Thereafter, however, the first batch of authentic or rumoured conspiracies against the new emperor came almost at once. They made him extremely hostile towards the Senate. But since, while eagerly developing his own personality-cult, he showed no desire to govern the empire himself, the effective power remained in the hands of successive praetorian prefects. Finally one of them, Laetus, the first north African to hold this post, became convinced that Commodus' growing megalomania and anti-senatorial feeling had become too hazardous, and decided that he must die, and commissioned a professional athlete to murder him.

The city prefect Pertinax was elevated to the throne, but when his martinet discipline and financial meanness quickly angered the guardsmen, Laetus withdrew his support and allowed him to be killed after a three-month reign. The situation recalled what had happened after the termination of Rome's first imperial dynasty, when Galba had likewise acquired a reputation for stringency and failed to establish himself. And from now on the analogy developed further, during the long period of civil war that ensued. The chaotic events of these months served to emphasize, once again, the insuperable flaw in the arrangements governing Rome's imperial successions, a flaw which was to become increasingly disastrous in the years to come.

The successor to Pertinax, a rich senator Didius Julianus, set an unedifying precedent by purchasing the throne at an auction held by the praetorians; soon afterwards, however, he terminated the emperor-making career of their prefect, Laetus, by putting him to death. But from the provinces news came, almost immediately, that two governors had been declared emperor by their legions. They were Severus, a 48-year-old north African, proclaimed at Carnuntum (Petronell) on the Danube in Upper Pannonia, and Niger, whose troops saluted him in Syria. Obeying a command from Severus, the Senate put Didius Julianus to death, after a reign of nine weeks. Then Severus marched south and entered Rome. But, before dealing with his eastern rival Niger, he felt it necessary to conciliate the most influential of the western provincial governors, his fellow-African Albinus in Britain. So he gave Albinus the title of Caesar, which was the equivalent to pronouncing him heir to the throne; although Severus had two sons of his own, Caracalla and Geta, aged five and four respectively. Then he set out for the east and overwhelmed Niger at Issus, at the point where Asia Minor and Syria meet (194). Encouraged by that success, he felt strong enough to declare his own elder son Caracalla his heir after all, thus breaking openly with Albinus, whom he defeated and killed in 197 in a fierce battle at Lugdunum (Lyon).

Although the civil wars were so reminiscent of the strife of 68–9, they had lasted much longer, and proved far more damaging to the empire. The numerous casualties included twenty-nine members of the Senate; and Severus still remained suspicious of the senators who survived, and excluded them from his administrative posts, which he filled with knights of purely military training.

Since the Parthians had given aid to his enemy Niger, and had made inroads into Roman territory, it was against them that Severus next turned (197–9). He captured their winter capital Ctesiphon, and reasserted Rome's claim to Mesopotamia, but did not attempt to repeat Trajan's short-lived advance to the Persian Gulf. Nevertheless, Parthia was dealt an unprecedentedly severe blow, which proved to have weakened it permanently – as Rome would later have reason to regret.

On his accession, Severus had replaced the praetorian guard by his own Danubian soldiers, and doubled its size. And at the same time he had substantially increased the city police (*cohortes urbanae*) as well. Now, moreover, on returning from the east, he stationed a new legion just outside the capital, at Albanum (Albano). This set a novel precedent, for hitherto no legions at all had been stationed in Italy by any previous emperor; and Severus' move has sometimes been interpreted as an African's deliberate indication that Italian supremacy over the provinces was coming to an end. And this was, indeed, gradually happening. However Severus' primary motive, in stationing this unit in Italy, was probably not political but military. It was based on his recognition that the imperial army needed a central reserve capable of being sent wherever it was needed – a reserve that Augustus had omitted to provide for.

He had fixed the number of Roman legions at twenty-eight, later reduced by losses to twenty-five. Trajan had maintained thirty legions, and Severus now raised this total to thirty-three, including a larger proportion of provincials than hitherto. Severus also increased the native soldiery (*numeri*) which had been employed since the previous century, relying especially on mounted archers from Osrhoene (Mesopotamia) and Palmyra (Syria), who were available for dispatch around the empire wherever the need arose. Severus elevated the army to these unprecedented dimensions because he knew that a big and permanent change had taken place: ever since the frontier crisis of Marcus Aurelius, imperial defence had become a far graver problem than ever before.

Besides, another purpose of the enlarged army, in Italy as elsewhere, was to eradicate internal sedition. And with this purpose once again in mind, he took a number of steps to make the officers of the legions a privileged class, and tie them firmly to his own person. In due course, many former soldiers of his new guard were promoted to officer status, which in consequence assumed a more democratic appearance. And the other ranks of the army, too, were considerably better paid and rewarded than hitherto. This was a development which, as we shall see, caused lasting hardship to the taxpayers, and in the end, throughout many areas of the Roman world, virtually wiped out the middle class of society. Yet it was both logical and inevitable if the empire was to face up to its new military problems.

Three years later, Severus took his new army into action, setting out with his wife and two sons for Britain, where tribal attacks had caused the Antonine Wall to be abandoned, and Hadrian's Wall to be breached. The large-scale invasions of Caledonia (Scotland) that he now proceeded to undertake yielded, as usual in this area, no permanent results, but Hadrian's Wall was rebuilt and restored as an effective frontier. Soon afterwards, however, at Eburacum (York), the emperor died (211). He was reported to have given a last piece of advice to his sons: 'Be on good terms with one another, be generous to the soldiers, and don't care about anyone else!' Whether that is authentic or not, he had launched the empire on a new path by giving overall priority to the requirements of a greatly expanded army.

Severus was an extremely purposeful man, determined to exercise rigorous control of all that went on. It is therefore surprising to find that he became as thoroughly dependent on his praetorian prefect as any ruler before him; no doubt the personal burden of empire was so enormous that even the most strongminded ruler found he needed a confidant. And so the

# The family of Septimius Severus

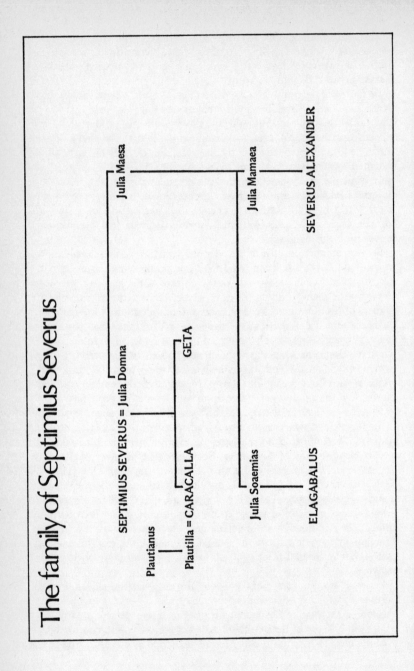

prefect Plautianus, a fellow-townsman of Severus, gained an extraordinary and almost autocratic authority (197). But as he did so the emperor's Syrian wife Julia Domna, an able woman surrounded by a personal court of learned scholars and writers, became his enemy. And Caracalla, too, unhappily married to Plautianus' daughter, came to hate his father-in-law, and in the end brought about his downfall and death (208).

Severus left the empire jointly to his two sons. It was a mistaken arrangement, since they hated one another; and Caracalla, a temperamental and violent young man, almost at once had Geta murdered. Then, in 213, he set out for Germany, where he defeated some of its tribes and bought off others with a subsidy, winning considerable popularity among his troops. Next he set off for the east, identifying himself with Alexander the Great, whose conquests he was eager to rival. Although an attack on Armenia failed, he pushed forward the frontier of Mesopotamia and invaded Media, to its north. But near Carrhae (Haran) he succumbed to an assassin (217). This was his Mauretanian praetorian prefect Macrinus, who was alarmed that Caracalla might be intending to put him to death.

Macrinus' principal claim to fame is that he was the first Roman emperor who had not been a member of the Senate, but was only a knight. His reign was brief and undistinguished. For his conclusion of the Parthian war on not very favourable terms, followed by retrenchments in military pay, made the army look back longingly to the reign of his predecessor; and Severus' Syrian sister-in-law, Julia Maesa, was able to organize a rebellion in which Macrinus was defeated and lost his life. The new emperor was her 14-year-old grandson, known as Elagabalus after El-Gabal, the sun-god of their home town Emesa (Homs), of whom he was the hereditary priest.

When he and his grandmother and mother reached Rome, the young monarch, a promiscuous sexual invert, devoted himself entirely to the worship of his oriental divinity; and his neglect to adapt its cult to the religious institutions of Rome deeply alienated the senatorial class. Alarmed for her own and her family's future, Maesa switched her allegiance to another of her grandchildren, Severus Alexander, the 14-year-old son of her daughter Julia Mamaea; and the two women, by an opportune bribe, induced the praetorians to murder Elagabalus and his mother. Maesa died shortly afterwards, but this unprecedented phase of personal feminine rule went on, since throughout the reign of her son that was now to follow it was Mamaea who ruled the empire. The later tradition that Alexander's reign witnessed a revival of senatorial influence was largely fictitious.

In its later years, Mamaea's government became preoccupied by simultaneous threats on both major frontiers. In 231 she and her son left Rome for the east to repel an invasion of Mesopotamia by the Persians

(Sassanians), who had overthrown the Parthian kingdom and replaced it by their own much superior power.* After heavy losses on both sides, the Romans temporarily recovered their Mesopotamian province. But then Alexander and Mamaea had to return to the west, to deal with a perilous German menace on the Rhine. They attempted to buy off the aggressors, but this proved unpopular with their own officers and cost them their lives (235).

The officer who emerged from the mutiny as emperor, the giant Danubian peasant Maximinus I, might have dealt effectively with Rome's external foes, but the severity with which he treated his own subjects led to his death in 238. In that single year, the empire saw the coinage of no less than seven Caesars. The survivor among them, Gordianus III, was a youth of thirteen whose praetorian prefect governed the empire effectively until the deaths of both of them on an eastern expedition. Then came a renewal of the series of soldier emperors. Their first batch, however, seemed unable to measure up to the formidable accumulation of threats within and outside the imperial borders alike. Philip the Arabian (244-9) sought to distract attention by celebrating the thousandth anniversary of Rome. But Decius (249-51), who came from the same region as Maximinus, overthrew him, and then himself fell to German (Gothic) invaders. His successor Gallus (251-3) had to deal not only with similar onslaughts but with an unfamiliar and prolonged pestilence, perhaps bubonic plague. Finally, as economic disasters proliferated, Valerian (253-60) was captured by the Persians. His son, co-ruler and successor Gallienus (253-68) found himself confronted with internal and external problems of every kind.

The main internal difficulty, throughout the whole of this period, was the proliferation of military usurpers. Between AD 218 and 268 about fifty usurpers assumed the imperial title, either at the capital or in some other part of the empire; and out of the twenty-seven 'regular' emperors of the third century (in so far as they can be distinguished from usurpers), seventeen were killed at the hands of their own people – all but one of them by the troops – and two of the others were forced to commit suicide. Therein lay one of Rome's most grievous and costly problems. The old custom by which its rulers were appointed by the Senate had become a threadbare farce. For in reality, with a few unimportant exceptions, they were placed on the throne by one or other of the armies, after which the Senate was ostensibly asked for its approval – but, in reality, merely received the information. Since local recruitment was now prevalent, the armies on many occasions were stronger in parochial *esprit de corps* than in patriotism. But above all their motive for changing emperors was greed: they felt eager for the lavish gifts which their protégés were always com-

* See below, p. 283.

pelled to distribute. In consequence, the soldiers acclaimed new imperators with ludicrous or tragic frequency; and the previous incumbent was nearly always killed.

This totally unstable situation at the top created paralysis in the empire's defences, not to speak of its finances. For there were constant, costly civil wars. Time after time, a frontier operation against a foreign foe had to be called off because the monarch of the time was obliged to turn back to face a rival Roman army. Sometimes the commanders who found themselves successively elevated to the throne would have lost their lives to their own troops if they had not consented. But much more often, they were willing: the lure of the purple was too great – however briefly it was likely to be worn.

After asserting his claims, a new emperor almost always tried to have a successor available, to give the illusion of dynastic stability. There were two traditional ways in which he could attempt this. One way was to bring forward and promote his own son or another close relation, so that when he himself died there might be a smooth takeover inside the family. The armies, in theory, liked a dynastic succession of this kind, because it ensured the continuity of their pay: although their attachment to any proposed dynasty wore off rapidly if the ruler proved parsimonious, or ineffective in the field. The senators, on the other hand, generally preferred a second method of securing the succession, according to which the ruler, after consulting with themselves, adopted a suitable heir from outside his own house. This procedure had worked well in the second century AD. But during the anarchic years that ensued, there was scarcely an opportunity to give it a try. The fact was that any and every doctrine about how to arrange for a peaceful succession, whether by heredity or adoption, remained theoretical and irrelevant, since all such efforts almost invariably failed.

The Danubian armies were by far the largest in the empire, and during the recurrent civil wars of this epoch it was their candidate, more often than not, who gained the throne. Maximinus I, though stationed elsewhere at the time of his succession, was a Danubian ex-ranker put forward by a unit from his homeland. Decius, too, was born in the same country, of an Italian family. Neither maintained his power for long; the more successful emperors from the Danube region were still to come. But already it was producing most of the best officers in the army, and the best soldiers as well. And when not engaged in promoting the imperial claims of one of their countrymen, they were more patriotic than troops from elsewhere. For their hearts were filled with the frontiersman's proud and emotional confidence that their protection of their own homes was protecting Italy and Rome as well.

In reversal of the situation of early imperial times, the Rhine armies had now become smaller than those of the Danube. That meant that they felt neglected by Rome in favour of the Danubian legions; and this official attitude, they felt, unfairly impeded them from carrying out their defensive tasks, which were terribly severe in the face of German invasions. That was why, in a time of grave crisis, they put forward Postumus (259–68) as an emperor of their own. He set up independent consuls and Senate at Augusta Trevirorum (now Trier) on the Moselle; not only Gaul but Britain and Spain rallied to his cause, and for fourteen years, under himself and his successors, western Europe was a large separatist state, confronting Rome in a cold war which broke at intervals into open hostilities.

The eastern garrisons, too, second only to those of the Danube in size and strength, were equally ready to put forward rulers of their own choice. Elagabalus (218–22), the grand-nephew of a Syrian empress, was a nominee of that country's soldiery. And thereafter a number of emperors and would-be emperors continued to be proclaimed by these eastern armies, including Philip (244–9), the son of an Arabian chief.

But the most vigorous, durable and menacing of the oriental dissidents came from the oasis city of Palmyra (Tadmor), on the borders between Syria and Mesopotamia. Annexed by Rome in the early first century AD, Palmyra possessed a good water-supply and was located at an important desert crossroads; and from the time of Severus onwards, its excellent mounted archers played a strong part in frontier defence. Moreover, when Parthia succumbed to the more dangerous Persians, Palmyra became even more important, indeed indispensable, as a bastion of the empire. Indeed in the reign of Gallienus, its chieftain Odenathus was made the semi-independent commander of Rome's entire defensive system in the east. But when he fell to assassins (266–7) his gifted and learned widow Zenobia declared her total independence, and expanded the dominions she already held in Syria and Mesopotamia by annexing Egypt and the greater part of Asia Minor as well. Then she declared herself Augusta, empress of Rome, and her son was hailed as Augustus (*c.* 270).

The dismemberment of the empire, from which both Zenobia and Postumus had torn enormous territories, could scarcely go farther. Moreover, it came at a time when Rome's external enemies had never been stronger and more menacing.

For the threats from beyond both the eastern and northern frontiers, already productive of anxiety, had begun to increase with appalling sharpness some forty and fifty years earlier, and were still getting graver and graver.

The massive changes in the east have already been briefly mentioned. Way back in the previous century, the situation had first begun to look easier, since Rome's enemies, the Parthians, were gradually declining in strength. This was partly because of their recurring warfare against the Romans; and the invasion of Severus, in particular, weakened their hold over their feudal dependencies. One of these was Persis (Fars) in the deep south of Iranian chauvinism; and in 223–6 its prince Ardashir (Artaxerxes) of the Sassanian dynasty, ruler of a large area extending from the Persian Gulf to Isfahan, invaded Parthia and overthrew the last of its monarchs. His own Sassanian dynasty which replaced it ruled from Ctesiphon in Babylonia, but the religious capital was now at a holy city near Persepolis on Persian territory, the residence of the glorious monarchs of his race eight centuries earlier.

The Sassanians combined pride in this ancient tradition with a willingness to take over Parthian institutions. But the new state was far more formidable and centralized than Parthia. It was also intensely nationalistic, claiming the right to all the Roman empire's eastern territories in the name of its own ancestral inheritance. This aggressiveness, backed by an efficiently centralized administration, enormously worsened the strategic situation of Rome, confronting it with a military threat which equalled the gravest German menaces from the north. For the Persian army, reinforcing the traditional mail-clad Parthian horsemen by recruitment from newly created nobles, was the most up-to-date attacking force of the age. And the Romans failed to reduce this new foe to manageable proportions or bring it to a workable agreement. Their eastern military operations, hitherto something of an imperialistic luxury, now became a direly urgent and hugely expensive necessity.

After initial fierce but indecisive fighting in the frontier regions, Shapur (Sapor) I (c. 234–70) adopted, at his coronation, the provocative title of 'King of Kings of Iran and non-Iran'. He was the most dangerous single enemy the Roman emperors had ever had to confront. Every year, he raided deep into their provinces; and during the first two decades of his reign he launched three major invasions. Mesopotamia and Armenia were overrun and Antioch, the capital of Syria, was temporarily lost to Rome as well. Then, in the last of these campaigns in 260, the Roman emperor Valerian himself fell into Shapur's hands near the Mesopotamian town of Edessa (now Urfa in south-east Turkey). This event, the most inglorious in all Roman history, continued to be emphasized over and over again in Persian propaganda; and Valerian remained a captive for the rest of his life. For his son Gallienus did not succeed in rescuing him, or did not try. The only consolation for Rome was that when its eastern commander Odenathus, the prince of Palmyra, made overtures to Shapur I, the Persian decided to reject them. This decision, and Shapur's savage treatment of the Roman provinces he overran, were imprudences which, by a narrow margin, eventually saved these territories for Rome.

·  ·  ·  ·  ·  ·

During these same disastrous years the Romans' position on the Rhine and Danube boundaries, too, deteriorated gravely. For years, it is true, there had been fighting on either side of the two rivers. But new German peoples appeared, who were far more dangerous than any that had ever been seen there before. They were the Goths. Leaving their Scandinavian homes before the beginning of our era, they had come to the lower Vistula, and then during the second century AD, various pressures forced them onwards in a south-westerly direction, until finally they established themselves near the mouth of the Danube. During their migrations they had acquired some culture and political cohesion, and although remaining weak in army tactics and siegecraft, they absorbed a number of Roman military techniques.

In the 230s – at the very time when the eastern frontier, too, was the scene of perilous new threats – these Goths began to surge across the lower Danube, and the Romans tried to appease them with a subsidy. In the following decade, however, this ceased to be paid any longer; perhaps no money could be found to pay. But the cessation infuriated the Goths who, encouraged by rebellions within the empire, crossed the river again and penetrated far into the Balkans (248). The commander of the Danubian armies, Decius, defeated this invasion with such success that his troops declared him emperor in the following year. But his attempt to reinforce the Danube defences proved inadequate, for in their monarch Kniva the Goths had a leader capable of grandiose strategies, threatening Rome almost as perilously as Shapur at the opposite extremity of the empire; and Kniva's supreme triumph came in the marshes at Abrittus (near Razgrad, west of Varna), where he defeated and slew the emperor Decius himself.

These two menacing foes at either end of the empire, the Germans and Persians, took collusive advantage of each other's attacks on the forces of Rome, which were consequently faced with prolonged, gigantically costly warfare on two fronts that made all previous border operations look trivial in comparison. While Persians overran the orient, and rebellions and epidemics (perhaps bubonic plague) paralyzed Roman defence, the Goths, joined by other peoples, ravaged the Balkans and even drove deep into the central plateau of Asia Minor (253). Moreover, they took to the sea as well, obtaining ships from the Greek coastal cities and swooping on major Black Sea ports, with disastrous effects on the empire's grain supplies. And meanwhile other German tribes, too, joined the onslaught along the entire length of the European river frontiers. Among them was the powerful confederacy of the Franks, who broke right through the Rhine defences, overran Gaul and Spain, and extended their raids as far as north Africa.

Since one man could not face both ways at once, the imperial armies, in such regions as remained to them, were now divided between two commands, anticipating the later division between the eastern and western empires. Valerian took the east and Gallienus the west, and after Valerian's capture by the Persians Gallienus fought on. In the last year of his life (268), utilizing the Heruli – recent arrivals in the Black Sea area – as their sailors, the Goths mustered unparalleled numbers of warriors and ships at the mouth of the River Dniester; and Greece and Asia Minor were ravaged yet again. The invaders, laden with plunder, began to return northwards by the Balkan land-route; and the Roman empire had reached the lowest depths of disarray.

But in fact an extraordinary recovery was about to begin. It was preceded by Gallienus' reorganization of the army. For he had completed the separation of the officer corps from the senatorial career – thus making the military system more professional. And, above all, he had set up a new, mobile, strategic force, based on cavalry, which had now for the first time become an element of primary importance in the previously infantry-dominated imperial army. The headquarters of the new formation was at Mediolanum (Milan), which was now virtually the advance capital of the empire. This troop concentration in Italy was an important extension of the ideas of Severus, who had located a legion on Italian soil. It was also a step which was to have far-reaching effects in later times, both militarily since it at last created a powerful reserve, and politically, because it encouraged a growing tendency to stop seeing Rome as the world centre. Yet such a force, for all its strategic benefits, was at the same time a grave security risk, as was confirmed when its very first commander tried to make himself emperor, and then its second, the future emperor Aurelian, led a successful plot which put Gallienus to death.

Yet Gallienus' new army, at the very end of his life, had won a major military triumph against his foreign foes. For as the Goths returned northwards through the Balkans, he succeeded in cutting them off, winning the bloodiest battle of the century at Naïssus (Niš in Yugoslavia), in which 50,000 enemy soldiers met their deaths (268). And soon afterwards his Danubian successor Claudius II (268-70), when a group of west German tribes, the Alamanni, struck into Italy itself, crushed them beside Lake Benacus (Garda), and then defeated the Goths in further battles, which rightly earned him the title of Gothicus. Then he was struck down by the continuing epidemic and died; but the expulsion of the Goths was completed by an emperor who was an even more brilliant commander, Aurelian, known as 'hand on hilt' (manu ad ferrum). Meanwhile other Germans, too, were continuing to pour through the Brenner Pass: but Aurelian engaged these as well, and overwhelmed them in two battles in northern Italy, at Fanum Fortunae (Fano) and near the fortress of Ticinum (Pavia).

Then Aurelian turned on Queen Zenobia of Palmyra. Asia Minor and Egypt were recaptured and brought back under Roman rule; and he twice defeated her principal general in Syria (271). Palmyra itself fell to him, and then revolted, and then fell again, and the queen walked in golden chains at Aurelian's triumph. And with her walked Tetricus, the last monarch of Postumus' splinter state in the west. For following upon the suppression of Zenobia, Aurelian had immediately moved right across the empire to Gaul and defeated the rebel army on the Catalaunian Plains (near Châlons-sur-Marne), after Tetricus himself had deserted his own soldiers and joined him (224).

Yet Aurelian was still conscious that many perils existed; and he built a new defensive wall round Rome, enclosing all the regions that had been added to the city since the last wall had been built 600 years earlier. More-over, he decided that the defences beyond the lower Danube, heavily in-filtrated by barbarians, were no longer tenable, and in consequence Dacia (Rumania), a province since the time of Trajan, was abandoned, and the frontier brought back to the river, which provided a shorter and stronger boundary. And then another Danubian warrior Probus (276–82) repelled a massive three-pronged German attack on Gaul, and drove other Germans (Vandals) out of the Balkans. Next, his former praetorian prefect Carus (282–3), who succeeded him as emperor, struck north against further hordes of Germans, and then moved east against the Persians, and even temporarily occupied their capital Ctesiphon.

The entire military picture, inside and outside the empire alike, had been transformed out of all recognition within the space of only fifteen years. It was the most extraordinary warlike achievement, or cumulation of varied, simultaneous achievements, in the whole of Roman history. Rome had seemed in a state of such advanced disintegration that recovery could scarcely be imagined. Yet by the exceptional talents of successive Danubian generals, commanding troops as good as any that Rome ever produced, the seemingly impossible had come to pass, and the empire was restored.

Yet the restoration had taken place against a background of fierce economic dislocation; this made it even more remarkable, but it also meant that an enormous human price was paid. At the beginning of the century, Severus and Caracalla had decided that the civilian population must sacrifice every comfort and amenity to ensure the loyalty of the army. And this policy had not been changed.

Moreover, the prevailing hardships were intensified by a collapse of the imperial currency. The ancients expected currency in the precious metals to contain the quantities of fine metal which corresponded to the values attached officially to each denomination; the public refused to tolerate gold and silver coins of token weight. But the Roman government, pressed for funds, could not refrain from lightening the weights of these pieces, and, above all, they adulterated the silver. This had been done for a long time, but in the third century AD the process became so blatant that people would no longer accept the base money with which the market was flooded. In consequence, inflation reached, even by modern standards, preposterous heights: between the years 258 and 275, despite an attempt by Aurelian to stabilize the coinage, prices in many or most parts of the empire rose by nearly 1,000 per cent. The result, for a population also tormented by unprecedented wars and epidemics, was misery.

But what was most serious for the imperial government was that this inflation, which they themselves had inadvertently caused, meant that the wages of soldiers, as of other state employees, were practically wiped out. So successive emperors, in order to protect their very existence, had to employ special methods to augment these perilously diminished pay packets. Among these methods was the distribution of donatives – special money gifts (originally war-spoils), either handed out by emperors at the beginnings of their reigns or on other joyful occasions, or left (and known to be left) in their wills. It had long been customary to supplement army pay by such bonuses; and after the transient predecessors of Severus had been killed because they failed to hand over the donatives they had promised, the third century AD witnessed sharp increases in the size and frequency of these awards. Moreover, they consisted, at least on imperial accessions, not of the contemporary coins of debased silver, but pieces of pure gold. To quell a mutiny after the death of Gallienus, we learn that the soldiers were given twenty of these gold coins each; larger pieces, the imposing gold medallions of the time, were presented to senior officers.

But the huge sums required to pay these donatives had to be obtained by increases in taxation. The land-tax and poll-tax, the direct contributions which provincials normally had to pay, were not the best ways of obtaining such revenue. For these taxes fell unfairly, because non-progressively, upon an agricultural economy like Rome's, and in bad times there was a strict limit to what could be raised by such means. So instead, the emperors, starting apparently with Caracalla, demanded an extraordinary income-tax known as crown money (*aurum coronarium*), originating from a republican custom of levying gold crowns for Triumphs, although now the crowns were commuted into cash. Yet the raising of all this money, from whatever source, was of little avail, because the rapid rise in prices meant that the sums needed for the army were far beyond what any monetary taxes could provide. Accordingly, the Roman government, from the Severan period onwards, also proceeded to raise revenue by other means. First of all they confiscated personal property whenever they had a chance. And secondly, they raised supplementary taxes not in cash but in kind, that is to say by levying supplies of foodstuffs and other goods (*annona militaris*). This had been done before, in national emergencies, but now the practice was organized on a far more systematic scale. And, once collected, the proceeds of these levies in kind were recycled to the troops in the form of free distributions of rations, clothing, and the materials needed to make arms and equipment. As the quality of money deteriorated, these distributions rapidly became the principal means of remunerating the troops.

During the previous century, rations and uniform and arms had been issued to soldiers against deductions from pay, but as the system of payments in kind gained in momentum, it became customary to exempt them from such deductions. As for the civilian populations, who were compelled to hand over these supplies, at first they were paid for what they provided, and as late as the 230s such cash transactions are still recorded. But by that time the money the authorities offered in compensation fell far below the inflated prices the suppliers could have secured for themselves on the free market. Moreover, it was now becoming increasingly rare for the government to offer contributors any payment at all; and by the middle of the third century forced deliveries for the army, without recompense, had become prevalent and normal.

Moreover, for some time before that – apparently from the days of Severus – each province had also been required to hand over food direct to the troops stationed within its borders. Landowners extracted the required products from their tenants, and the leading officials of the cities were ordered to see that their citizens contributed what was demanded. Worst of all, perhaps, was the unforeseeable irregularity of such claims, which fell like thunderbolts upon the population. We have inscriptions recording grievous local discontents, and desperate appeals for relief.

It may seem strange, at first sight, that so vast an empire could not maintain an army of between a quarter and half a million strong without resorting to these assessments reminiscent of a prehistoric non-monetary economy. But now that money had become so much less useful, the army could only be supplied at all by these more primitive methods. In the technologically backward Roman world, food, clothing, weapons and armour were expensive to produce and transport. Yet the soldiers had to have them in huge quantities, and they could only have them if the subjects of the empire contributed the materials. Besides, not only the army but the imperial civil service, too, had to be paid for, and the inhabitants of Rome as well, who, even if the city had lost some of its political power, were allowed to retain a subsidized status, as privileged parasites.

It was against this grim economic background that the great Danubian soldier emperors succeeded so amazingly in restoring Rome's military equilibrium on both sides of the frontiers. But the strain on the civilian population, outside the capital at least, was appalling, and seemed almost impossible to endure.

# 18

# The Climax of the Pagan Empire

YET IT WOULD BE a complete mistake to regard this tumultuous epoch merely as a time of military and economic vicissitudes. On the contrary, it was also an age of extraordinary intellectual and spiritual achievement – in several respects the culmination of the pagan world.

The keynote had been set at the outset of the period by the emperor Marcus Aurelius. He was one of those rulers, rare in human history, whose practical achievements have been eclipsed and outlived by what he wrote. His dramatically intimate disclosures of his deepest thoughts, entitled by editors 'his writings to himself' and later known as the *Meditations*, are the most famous book ever written by a monarch. Their language is Greek, and they are framed in literary form, but they were meant to be private notes, and their author did not intend this highly personal masterpiece of self-scrutiny and self-admonition to be published.

Marcus Aurelius' doctrine was an austere one, and provided no comfort – except that of putting its tenets into practice. For men and women must just strive onwards, he declares, and continue their laborious efforts as best they can, with patient, long-suffering endurance. They must turn inwards and be strong, and draw on their own inner lives and resources, and thus renew themselves and find the courage to get on with their daily existences: and his was almost unendurably burdensome. Life is desperately short and transient, says Marcus Aurelius, a temporary visit to an alien land. And all we have the power to do, as long as it lasts, is to act as responsibly and unselfishly and kindly as we can to those who are our fellow travellers on this transitory enterprise. Much of this is the old Stoicism, but none of its previous devotees, even Seneca or a more recent exponent, the eloquent, lame, ex-slave Epictetus (*c.* 55–135) from Asia Minor, had ever communicated the urgency and hardness of self-reliant moral and social effort in phrases that strike home so poignantly. True, Marcus Aurelius is a fatalist: much, he believes, is predestined and cannot be altered. Yet all the same, much else *can* be altered and improved, by the efforts of our own will – which we must summon up the discipline to use as it should be used. For, as the Stoics had always said, we have a share of the divine spark so that it is only natural and right for us to see each other as kinsmen – as brothers and sisters who should treat each other decently, members of a single cosmopolis of which the Roman empire, for all its imperfections, seemed to its ruler the most complete earthly expression.

Marcus Aurelius sought to reinforce these ideals with a rigorously ascetic attitude typical of the age that was now beginning. Nowhere can one find more relentless attacks on the 'twitchings of appetite' which were all that the pleasures of eye, ear, food and sex appeared to him to amount to. Moreover, as one hard year succeeded to another, his spirit was tortured by ever more serious doubts about his own personal adequacy. All he could do was struggle on, fighting off moods of depression and battling against a sensitive distaste for disagreeable people and sights which made him more human than any other antique Stoic. Left far behind are the bright classical incentives to material achievement, the sunny sense of unlimited power. But in terms of humanly decent principles, translated scrupulously into a consistent way of living, Marcus Aurelius' creed was the culmination of ancient paganism and of Rome.

He had also done much to carry onwards the Golden Age of Roman Law, ushered in earlier in the century by Hadrian. Marcus Aurelius' legal adviser, Quintus Cervidius Scaevola, was a popular consultant jurist who left extensive written works behind him. This practice of writing everything down was fairly new among jurists, based on Greek rather than Roman custom. A high proportion of the lawyers of the day were easterners, and although Cervidius himself probably was not, many of the cases he describes come from provinces of the eastern empire.

Cervidius was also the teacher of the emperor Severus. In his reign this legal Golden Age developed a second phase which, although perhaps less abundantly creative, produced the most far-reaching of all Rome's contributions to posterity: since it comprised the working out, and writing down, of existing principles over the entire field. The writings in which this information was incorporated offer extraordinary insights into the secrets of how the imperial machine worked. Moreover, Severus, following occasional earlier precedents, chose the greatest jurists of the day – perhaps the greatest of all time – as his praetorian prefects. These officials exercised a general control over the imperial finances; and they were also entrusted with vital judicial functions, including both direct and appeal jurisdiction.

One of them, Papinian, who was perhaps from Syria or north Africa and became praetorian prefect from AD 203 until 212, is the most famous name in all Roman jurisprudence. He never wrote a comprehensive treatise, but compiled extensive collections and summaries of legal decisions. Independent, not averse to changing his mind, master of terse and exact

Latin, he produced solutions which are original and closely reasoned, and which give the fullest weight to considerations of equity and humaneness. And then Ulpian, who came from Tyre in Phoenicia, was joint prefect from 222 to 223. His massive works, designed to cover the whole range of the law, are business-like and unaffected and superlatively clear; he displays an easy, reliable mastery of all this gigantic, complicated material. And another praetorian prefect of the time was Paulus. His writings, the most voluminous of all, include the *Opinions* (*Sententiae*). The work that has come down to us under this name may be an anthology taken from a number of his books; and it also contains later interpolations. But as far as we can judge, while falling short of Ulpian's lucid precision, Paulus seems to have excelled him in breadth, independence, and powers of penetrating argument.

When, three centuries later, Justinian's jurists summed up the achievements of Roman Law, more than half the contents of this *Digest* came, directly or indirectly, from these three writers, Papinian, Ulpian and Paulus.

The distinction between the legal treatment of one social class and another, the *honestiores* and *humiliores*, still continued and may even have been intensified. Yet in many other respects, paradoxically enough, these jurists were enlightened. Thus while striving to maintain the fundamental institutions of Roman law – the family, private property, and sanctity of contracts – they also modified these concepts in a philanthropic and democratic direction, corresponding with a new sensitiveness for suffering, of which this age saw so much. Thus Ulpian proclaimed that all human beings are born free – so that slavery is unnatural. And there was an acceleration of already existing tendencies to protect the poor, weak and defenceless.

However, this trend was not exclusively, or even primarily, humanitarian, but directed towards the elimination of all possible causes of discontent or disloyalty which might prevent the maximum exploitation of all classes to serve the state and pay its enormous taxes. Indeed, this fiscal aim was expressly claimed by Caracalla when he published the most famous legal measure of antiquity, known as the *Constitutio Antoniniana* (212–13). With the exception (despite Ulpian) of slaves, it bestowed upon virtually the entire population of the empire the status of Roman citizens, which had hitherto been restricted to Italians and an elite minority of provincials. But the principal purpose of this measure was to increase the numbers of those who had to pay the indirect dues on inheritance and slave-emancipation – these being taxes which fell upon citizens of Rome. And the elevation of almost every free person to citizen rank was not, in fact, a very sensational development. For the differentiation between citizens and non-citizens had become increasingly blurred for a century past, as the lawyers had recognized by their substitution of the altogether different distinction between the two main social classes. So the enactment of Caracalla, although dramatic in its finality, was not so much an epoch-making event in itself as a step in a gradual and already well advanced process of standardization.

Standardization, once again, and a more concrete approach to genuine equality was apparent in a great spread of secondary education during this same third century AD.

And the same approach is illustrated by the amenities provided for the people of Rome, notably the stupendous baths which were inaugurated by Severus but bear the name of his son Caracalla who completed them. There were finally eleven such public baths in the pampered capital, and smaller replicas and variants in almost every town of the empire. They displayed much ingenious multiplicity of function, being designed not only for luxurious bathing at various temperatures, but also for all the diverse social activities of an elaborate community centre, in which many people, belonging to a wide spectrum of social and economic classes, spent a substantial part of each day.

All the features that had appeared in thermal establishments of the earlier empire were to be seen on a massive scale in the Baths of Caracalla, enriched by every sort of novel elaboration. Surrounded by an enclosure containing gardens and open-air gymnasiums and art-collections, the main building was provided with vast unseen services of heating, water supply, and drainage, designed to deal with the needs of 1,600 bathers. The bathing accommodation included a circular domed hot room; and the central feature of the whole complex was a great cross-vaulted central hall or concourse containing a swimming-pool. This hall, measuring 185 by 79 feet, is so large that men and women almost vanish inside its immensity: for all its services to human comfort, this is the architecture not of humanism but of a new age in which the individual is one of a mass. A new age, too, is heralded by the architectural style, since the load of the intersecting vaults, with their increased span and assurance, is carried not on a row of independent columns but on only four enormous piers dividing the hall into three bays – vaults and piers alike being constructed of the concrete which made these enormous, lightly soaring buildings possible.

Nor was third-century architecture the only art to display a strong move away from the traditional classicism; for marked changes were apparent in portrait sculpture as well. This had long been one of Rome's outstanding achievements, and in these difficult times its practitioners rose to heights of originality and psychological skill they had never attained before.

Contrary to what is often believed, these developments started as early as the reign of Marcus Aurelius. His best-known busts, it is true, are as emptily classicizing as any of the less inspired products of the immediately preceding age of Antoninus. But a few of Marcus Aurelius' surviving heads are startlingly different, and give us an almost violent impression of what the author of the harrowing *Meditations* was really like. And, by the same token, the reliefs on the Column of Aurelius at Rome show a different world from the Column of Trajan: a world in which wars are no longer military parades and triumphs, but, as Virgil had known long ago, scenes of horror and tragedy.

Under Commodus and Caracalla the portrait-sculptors of the emperors take a rest from the seriousness of Marcus Aurelius' philosophy, instead providing richly baroque interpretations of these outrageous autocrats. But then, in the years of turbulence and desolation that followed, the artists returned to their search for the inner man and woman, with astonishing results. The clue to these triumphs is their departure from faithfulness to nature. Now that the classical world is on its way out, strict adherence to physical accuracy is subordinated to more intangible, non-naturalistic processes of introspection. As in earlier times, it was the portraiture of the emperors themselves that directed the most original trends and attracted the finest talent, since the propaganda of these rulers demanded that their features, after suitable interpretation, should be made known to the world. But in the mid-third century the emperors were of a new type, tough soldiers, rugged and careworn. And it is evident that each successive ruler was very willing for his subjects to see him laden and afflicted with these cares and anxieties, which were endured on their behalf and enhanced by his artists almost to the point of dramatic caricature.

So these men provide a startling series of portraits, particularly during the ruinous years AD 235–68. Their faces are made to reflect, quite deliberately, the almost unbearable strain to which their vigilant resistance to stave off disaster was subjecting them. The Danubian giant Maximinus I, for example, hated by the senators but a victorious commander of armies, is presented by his sculptor with imposing vividness; his close-cropped hair and beard, sketched with light, rapid pointillist chisel-strokes, reflect the illusionistic techniques of painting.* The personality of Philip the Arabian, too, is revealed in a highly charged impressionistic study of his mobile, suspicious features and flickering brows. There is also a violently asymmetrical, nervously glaring Decius – the subject also of distinguished coin portraits – and the forehead of his successor Gallus is grotesquely furrowed.

A slight stiffening of features, hardening of anatomy, and simplifying of volume have begun to remodel and distort these faces into inorganic forms which correspond not to the human shape but to deeper movements within the soul and the universe. Some portraits emit an aura of intense feeling, almost as though they are representing the tormented visage of a medieval mystic. And tremendous play was made with the eyes, their irises and

---

* Portrait-painting (mummy portraits) continued to develop fruitfully in Egypt at this time.

upward-rolling pupils deeply incised with the sculptor's drill: they were seen as the mirrors of the soul, reflecting its inmost light – the doors by which the viewer could pass straight into the mind of the man or woman who is portrayed. For this was an age in which the torments of practical life were counterbalanced by an intense concentration on spirituality.

We are reminded of the greatest of these pagan spiritual revivals when we see the portrait busts of Gallienus, for they display a temporary regression from the military austerity of his predecessors, displaying him in the guise of a Hellenic philosopher. For he was the friend and patron of Plotinus, the greatest philosopher the Roman empire ever produced.

Born in AD 205, perhaps at Lycopolis in Upper Egypt, Plotinus studied philosophy for eleven years at Alexandria, and after joining an imperial expedition against the Persians settled in Rome as a teacher, remaining there, in touch with the cultivated court of Gallienus, until he eventually retired to Campania, where soon afterwards he died (c. 269–70). His instruction took the form of seminars and discussions, which he recorded in a series of essays written in Greek. They were primarily intended for the guidance of his students, one of whom, Porphyry of Tyre, collected and published them in six books known as the *Enneads*, from *ennea*, nine, because this was the number of treatises in each book.

Plotinus saw living reality as a complex, orderly structure which continuously and perpetually descends in an unbroken succession of stages from its transcendent First Principle. This Principle, the single immaterial source of all existence and all values, pours itself out in an eternal downward rush of generation which brings into being all the different, ordered levels of the world as we know it, in a majestic, spontaneous surge of living forms. Yet this downward radiation has a reverse counterpart as well. For in the endless dance of the universe there is always an upward impetus also, an upsurging towards identification and unification with the First Principle, the One.

The One, as Plotinus conceived it, is beyond thought or definition or language – the negation of number and movement and space and time. And yet in another sense, it is the very opposite of negation, for it is superabundant reality and goodness, absolute and pure. Plotinus' One has been said to be nearer than any other Graeco-Roman philosopher's concept to the God of the Christians. Yet there is no great resemblance, all the same. For it is not, like the Christian God, a power that intervenes in earthly things, since, although their creator, it remains wholly external to them, and outside all the orders of being, 'light above light'. And its creative activity leaves it unchanged, just as the Sun, too, engenders its own encircling illumination while staying undiminished itself.

Yet, remote though the One is, this incessant generation of which it is the agent ensures that every level of the cosmos is intimately linked with every other. Above all the structure of the One is repeated in the structure of human beings, and they all contain within themselves the potentiality of union with the One: their life, like the life of all the universe, is an upward yearning urge, an impulse to climb back to the summit and mingle themselves with the One. The whole philosophy of Plotinus seeks to animate our dulled sense of the supernatural and bring us back to our true nature and source.

The intermediaries in this contact between the One and the human body are Mind and, below it, Soul. Universal Mind is the timeless thought force and Soul the direction which emanates from it, but once again they are not only the divine working organisms of the Universe as a whole but also present within each and every individual person. For, lowly and degraded though our mortal bodies are – since Plotinus shared the increasingly widespread distaste for the corporeal which we have seen in Marcus Aurelius – the souls and minds of every man and woman provide steps by which they can rise to the heights.

Indeed by so doing they can, though only on the rarest occasions, catch a supreme glimpse of the One itself and even reunite with it. They can achieve this by looking within themselves. Many earlier philosophers had spoken in praise of such contemplation. But it was Plotinus above all who saw it as the dynamic device for thinking away the limitations of body and space and time into nothingness, until we merge with the supreme reality itself. And he was confident that he himself, a troubled and urgent man, had more than once, by harsh discipline, experienced this mystic union, in which his personality became truly awakened to what it was.

He is the western world's pioneer of those who have believed they can achieve such ineffable joyous reunion by intellectual discipline alone, without the need for religion or drugs. Many maintain today that such experiences do not, as he believed, genuinely apprehend something that lies outside, but are entirely inward happenings. Yet at all events Plotinus possessed the power to communicate to others this 'blessed fullness' and to endow it with a luminous, enchanting splendour that made all the political and economic disturbances of the day fade away into irrelevance.

Such, then, was one answer to the widespread, painful crisis of human identity throughout the vast and increasingly regimented and tormented Roman world. In this successful search for intimacy in a bottomless universe Plotinus presents paganism, during this final century of its prolonged supremacy, at its noblest. But he offers no likelihood that it could maintain itself, as Christianity was about to do, as a faith for all classes: since his words were manifestly directed to an intellectual and spiritual elite.

·   ·   ·   ·   ·   ·

Yet there was also another pagan belief, during this same epoch, which much more nearly competed with Christ for the control of the western world. This was the cult of the Sun, which was revered by millions of the inhabitants of the Roman empire; and its religion for a time even became the state worship. From the remotest periods of antiquity onwards, people had concluded, from their observation of nature, that they must greet the Sun's orb as a beneficent divinity – and their conviction was confirmed afresh each day as the god rose again. In due course, he had played a part in many writings of the Greeks. He was identified with Apollo; Plato hailed him as the author of all light and life; and from the time of Alexander the Great and his successors the faith in his potency had spread throughout the Mediterranean world. Moreover, there was an ever-increasing tendency to explain the other traditional deities in terms of the Sun, in all but monotheistic fashion.

To Rome, the divinity of the Sun came very early on; and then centuries afterwards, in the superb dome of Hadrian's Pantheon, the central opening, surrounded by star-like rosettes, represented the solar orb. Moreover, the cult of this deity offered flattering analogies to the imperial régime and its resplendent, sun-like leaders. Under Severus, whose wife Julia Domna came from Syria where reverence for the Sun was especially strong, its worship almost took command of the whole state religion. There was a brief interlude when their grandnephew Elagabalus (AD 218–22), to the alarm of conventional Romans, tried to bestow supremacy upon his own local Syrian version of Sun worship, which was accompanied by bizarre, outlandish trappings. But his failure did not delay the continued rise of solar beliefs in more acceptable forms, and the light-filled imagery of Plotinus reveals how deeply such ideas pervaded current thought. Before long, the emperor Aurelian established a massive temple of the Unconquerable Sun as the central and focal point of the entire religious system of the State (274). The birthday of the god was to be on 25 December, and this, transformed into Christmas Day, was one of the heritages which Christianity owed to his cult.

For a time, at a critical juncture, the symbiosis of the two faiths was very close. For Constantine the Great, in the years preceding his Christianization of the empire, and even later while this process was actually under way, concentrated all the resources of a vast bronze coinage upon the single design of the Sun-God, accompanied by the inscription *To the Sun, the Unconquerable Companion* (SOLI INVICTO COMITI) (*c.* 309). At this juncture, the Sun-cult could well have become the religion of the Mediterranean area for an indefinite period ahead. But it did not do so, in the end, because such a divinity was too impersonal, too lacking in urgent human appeal.

. . . . .

Devotees of the Sun themselves felt that this excessive remoteness failed to satisfy their needs, and a branch of the cult came into vogue in order to respond to such yearnings. It was the worship of an ancient Iranian deity, Mithras, who was god of the Morning Light, and from the first century AD onwards was identified with the Sun himself. But unlike the solar cult the ritual of Mithras always retained its private character. State approbation, it is true, was not lacking, but in marked contrast to the Sun's innumerable appearances on the official coinage, Mithras never appeared on the coins at all. Mithraism was not a court religion, and had no public ceremonies or professional priestly class. It was personal – supplying the intimate element which the Sun-faith lacked.

And its popularity increased at great speed, especially at the great cosmopolitan ports and trading centres of the west, where the worshippers at such shrines included numerous merchants. But it was above all the army, and particularly its officers, who accepted and diffused these beliefs. For the Mithras of legend was a hero figure, unconquerable like the Sun himself, a superman for critical times – and he was also an ethical, austere model of conduct, excellently suited to an age of rising asceticism, whose good faith, purity and continence his worshippers must seek to emulate. Moreover, all the excitement inherent in initiations of an elect, which were such a prominent aspect of contemporary religion, was offered by the melodramatic form and staging of his rites.

The worship of Mithras, then, possessed ideas, moral urgency, and intimate emotional force. And its baptisms and sacrifices and communal meals offered resemblances to the rituals and sacraments of the Christians. Yet it was Christianity, instead, that won the day. For the 'biography' that was Mithras' holy book was unconvincing. Above all, it failed to persuade its readers that he had ever really appeared on this earth to provide help for human beings. Sculptors, it is true, displayed him as compassionate, yet his religion still was lacking in the tenderness and sympathy which alone could solace the poor for their misfortunes. Besides, Mithraism had no place for women; and it is they, as the cults of Isis and Cybele and Jesus made clear, who provided the largest numerical support for successful faiths.

Mithras, attending the Iranian Sun-god in eternal opposition to his evil enemy, linked solar theology with the other outstanding pagan movement of the time, that of the Dualists, who believed in the conflict between good and evil powers, contending with each other for the control of the Universe. This belief goes back to very ancient times: to millions of people it has appeared the only possible explanation of what they see in the world with their own eyes. For evil manifestly exists. But how can this be so, if a benevolent and all-powerful God or gods created and controls the world? It seems a glaring contradiction; and many have therefore felt convinced that there must be *two* opposing forces, a good and an evil power, locked in a struggle that has so far, very manifestly, by no means come to an end.

The Athenian dramatists had been racked by the problem, and so were their philosophical compatriots. Then Persian ideas seeped into Greek and Roman lands, explaining the origin of evil in terms of the dualistic struggle. An enormous, fantastic variety of dualistic beliefs gradually arose, but through them all ran the conviction that the world, created by the evil power, has to be condemned and thrown off, and that men and women must seek to escape the imprisoning vileness of the body by purging what is non-spiritual within themselves. For since human souls are fragments of the vast luminous divine light beyond the sky, every person contains a spiritual element too. But the spirit is incarcerated in the body, awaiting its freedom. And to teach how such liberation was to be achieved was the business of the Dualists, known as Gnostics from *gnosis*, knowledge. This was the secret enlightenment they were able to impart to their initiates, who thus gained special privileges in this world, but above all won that salvation in the world to come which was the aim of all the leading religions of the day.

The culminating period of this Dualist movement started in about AD 240, when a young Persian named Mani began to preach, addressing great crowds at his national capital Ctesiphon, and the large Greek city of Seleucia which lay on the opposite bank of the Tigris. A contemporary of Plotinus, Mani taught for thirty years, displaying lofty spiritual and artistic gifts and wide learning. His fundamental principle was this clash between good and evil, Light and Darkness. In the remote past of the Universe, he declared, the Dark had encroached on the Light, and we are still suffering from that invasion, since Primal Man failed to repel it, and his failure and fall were what created our own flawed world. Yet as life still pursues its dirty path, pronounced Mani, there is hope, for the dirt and darkness is slowly being blotted out by Light; and once this process is completed a saviour will return (whom he identified with Jesus Christ, though this was not a Christian religion) and all will be Light once again. But meanwhile the human body, as other philosophers had reiterated, remains an encumbrance. The cosmic conflict could only be won by ascetic self-denial on the part of every human being, in the hope of sloughing off this loathsome world.

Mani was an organizer of genius, and his aim was to found a religious community of his Manichaeans which would embrace the entire earth. In the end, he proved too radical for the Persians, who killed him (*c.* 274–7). Yet by then their empire was filled with his doctrine; and before another century was gone it had permeated huge regions of the Roman world as well.

But the Roman government hated these Manichaeans, for political reasons, because it regarded their Persian origin as deeply suspect and potentially seditious; and so they suffered repression. And later, too, when the Christians made their bid to become the national religion of Rome, Manichaeanism found itself unable to stand up to them either. For it was too passive and pacifist to offer really vigorous rivalry, and too ascetic and anti-social to form a powerful, cohesive church. Besides, the theological solution of the Manichaeans, for all its attractive features, ultimately failed to carry the day. Their story was epitomized in the career of Saint Augustine. As a young man, he became one of them, because he was unable to accept the idea that God, who must be good, could ever have created evil. But after nine years he abandoned this Manichaean allegiance, because he concluded that their division of the deity into two halves was hateful and shocking – and, in consequence, impossible to believe after all.

# The Supreme State and Church

WHILE THESE LAST MANIFESTATIONS of paganism were reaching their climax, the Roman empire had become a very different place.

The first of the two great agents of change was a Dalmatian of humble origin, Diocletian. After rising to become commander of the imperial bodyguard, he successfully asserted his claim to the throne (284), and two years later appointed an old Danubian comrade, Maximian, as joint Augustus. Then, after some years of urgent frontier fighting, he converted this dual régime into a system based on four rulers, the tetrarchy. This he did by nominating two further Danubians as secondary emperors or Caesars, Galerius from Serdica (Sofia) who was to preside over parts of the east under his own ultimate control, and Constantius I from Naissus (Niš) to rule over western areas under Maximian. The tetrarchs had four separate capitals, all endowed with magnificent buildings. For himself, Diocletian selected Nicomedia (Izmit) on the Sea of Marmara, a choice reflecting the increasing strategic importance of the Bosphorus strait; while Galerius resided at Thessalonica (Salonica) in Macedonia. In the west, although the Senate remained at Rome, Maximian's court was at Mediolanum (Milan), and Constantius had his headquarters at Treviri – the former Augusta Trevirorum, now Trier, located at a crossing of the Moselle commanding the natural lines of communication between northern Gaul and the Rhineland. The great basilica and baths and city gate (Porta Nigra) of his capital are still to be seen.

There had been partitions of the empire before, but this arrangement was more elaborate and thoroughgoing, and was intended to be permanent. It was designed to fulfil military needs, and to ensure, in due course, an orderly series of collegiate imperial successions. Nevertheless, although the tetrarchy multiplied authority, it did not officially split it; the empire was still an undivided unit. Legislation was in the name of all four men; the law of one Augustus was the law of the other, and both Caesars were obliged to obey them both.

Constantius and Diocletian put down rebellions in Britain (*c.* 287–96) and Egypt (293–4 and 297–8) respectively and from 302 campaigned successfully across the Rhine and the Danube. And Diocletian and Galerius also fought the Persians; they were defeated at first, but then Galerius eventually won a victory of a completeness granted to few others in Roman history, which he celebrated by the erection of an arch at Thessalonica. In 305 Diocletian, whose health had become precarious, took the unprecedented step of abdicating from the throne, and induced the reluctant Maximian to do the same. They retired into private life at Salonae (Split in Yugoslavia) and in Lucania (south-west Italy) respectively, and Constantius I and Galerius became Augusti in their places.

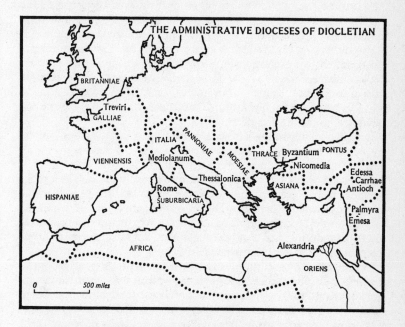

Diocletian had left a remarkable heritage, for he was the greatest imperial organizer since Augustus. One of his reforms was to raise the number of provinces from fifty to a hundred; since their areas were now relatively small, it was hoped that provincial governors would have little opportunity to revolt – especially as their posts were now completely separated from military commands. A further innovation was the grouping of the provinces into thirteen major units or dioceses. These dioceses, which in some cases pointed the way to national identities of the future, were administered by governors-general, and they in turn depended on the four praetorian prefects (one attached to each ruler), who had now become great personages of the civil administration.

Another of Diocletian's tasks, undertaken with the help of his fellow-tetrarchs, was to overhaul the entire structure of the Roman army. Pursuing his predecessors' interest in mobile formations, he created a new mounted guard which consisted mainly of Germans. This guard, known as the *scholae palatinae* after a portico in the place where they awaited the imperial orders, was incorporated into one of the two major branches into which the entire army was now divided. This was the mobile field force; divided into four formations, one for each ruler, these *comitatenses*, 'soldiers of the retinue', included a certain proportion of infantry, but cavalry was their particular strength. The second major division of Diocletian's army was the frontier force, stationed along the much strengthened border-fortifications; in consequence these troops were later known as *limitanei* or *riparienses*, men of the frontier or of the river banks. This frontier army was recruited by systematic annual conscription among Roman citizens. But extensive use was also made of the warlike tastes and various specialist skills of barbarian tribesmen. These recruits included numerous Germans, as well as men from the highlands of Asia Minor. Diocletian also expanded the hitherto somewhat insignificant fleet.

The total military strength of the empire was now half a million or more, a good deal larger even than the expanded army of Severus a century earlier. These massive dimensions made it all the more necessary that the taxes needed to pay the soldiers should be duly gathered in. Throughout the previous half century, these exactions had caused the peoples of the empire immeasurable hardship. Diocletian did not, could not, lessen the burden. On the contrary, he increased it to the very utmost that manpower and food production and transport could bear. But at least he tried to ensure that the levies were distributed fairly.

In particular, he issued an edict fixing maximum prices for all goods and transport costs, and maximum wages for all workers throughout the empire (301). It seemed to Diocletian that the only chance of establishing sufficient stability to enable the taxes to be brought in – and the dishonesty of army contractors reduced – was by this insistence on stationary price levels. His edict on this subject, the most valuable of all ancient economic documents, was something quite new to the Roman empire, though similar measures had occasionally been attempted in Greece. However, the tetrarchs neither owned nor controlled the means of production and consumption, and consequently proved unable to enforce their orders. The result was that goods disappeared from the market; and so inflation resumed its inexorable course. In order to combat it, Diocletian and his colleagues had already made a determined attempt to issue a reformed, stable coinage (*c.* 294), and it was in terms of this currency that the edict was framed. But he lacked the silver and gold needed to issue sufficient coins in these metals, so that the artificial relation he established between these and the token base metal issues proved untenable, and the price of commodities in terms of the latter continued to shoot up at an appalling rate.

But the emperors also made another attempt to lighten the miseries of the harassed taxpayers. What had afflicted them particularly gravely was the irregularity and suddenness of the demands which had descended on them. To eliminate this unpredictable element, Diocletian and his colleagues placed the whole tax-collecting process on a novel, systematic, and regular basis. Henceforward, the sums and supplies required were no longer announced at varying, arbitrary intervals, but instead a new and revised announcement was published every year. So although people might not be any better off, at least they knew where they stood. Individual Greek communities, in the past, had experimented with annual budgets; but this was the first time the idea had been applied on this massive empire-wide scale. The preparations of the budget were placed in the hands of the four praetorian prefects, who thus, in addition to their duties as supervisors of the governors-general of the dioceses, retained the position of the principal finance ministers of the empire which their predecessors had occupied during the previous century.

The taxation system for which they now became responsible was still based overwhelmingly on agriculture, as in the past. But an effort was made to mitigate the unfairness of the old system in which variations between harvests and qualities of soil had been ignored. For a new method of assessment was now worked out, according to which agricultural land was divided into units of measurement deliberately calculated to take varying crops and qualities and regions into account; and it was on this basis that the periodic censuses of empire were henceforward to be conducted.

However, this new arrangement was not as effective as it might have been, because of the many imponderables and complexities involved; and it also had a sinister side-effect. For it caused a marked advance in a process of which there had already been signs earlier, the compulsion of the populace to stay at work, on a hereditary basis, in the places where they were registered. Under Diocletian and his successors this principle was broadened to ensure that the tenants of large estates did not escape such compulsions; and they were also extended outside the agricultural field, to include members of guilds or corporations, and government employees of every kind.

In order, then, to maintain the imperial defences, a totalitarian state had been devised, theoretically almost as thoroughgoing as the police system advocated by Plato; though there was no practical likelihood that every coercion and prohibition thought out by the emperors and their jurists could ever be brought into effect.

All these measures of coercion were directed towards a more efficient mobilization of resources against internal rivals and foreign foes. Imperial publicity does not refer to the former peril directly, since there was a tacit propaganda assumption that the Roman army could not be anything but loyal. But there was continual, increasing emphasis on the tetrarchs' role as triumphant defenders against their numerous external enemies. From now on, imperial coin propaganda concentrates remorselessly on this first and most imperative demand that the Roman people had to make of its rulers – victorious leadership and prowess. For these personages, who alone stood between themselves and catastrophes even worse than those they were already undergoing, understandably seemed larger than other human beings. And this aggrandizement was reflected in imperial ceremonial which developed into a formidable pattern far removed from the early principate and closer in spirit to the contemporary, Persian, rival and foe.

Thus the mighty palace-fortress at Salonae (Split), to which Diocletian withdrew after his abdication, centred upon a grandiose Hall of Audience. Beneath the arch which surmounted its façade the retired, revered emperor made his public appearances as if framed by the vault of heaven; and as he paused, bejewelled and haloed, before entering and taking his throne in the shrine-like Hall, and momentarily stopped again as he left, the assembled multitude accorded him homage as if he was the image of divinity itself.

Such, it was now felt, must be the treatment accorded to the men who represented the ancient, renowned and now revived Roman state: and through them it was the state itself which was glorified. For the most Roman and patriotic of all cults was the worship of Rome herself, and Diocletian, son of the loyal Balkan provinces, gave even more massive and widespread publicity to this concept than any other ruler before him. For when he reorganized the imperial coinage, he and his fellow-rulers expressed this idea without cessation, on the token pieces, made of bronze with a light coating of silver, which circulated throughout the empire. The slogan they chose for duplication on all these millions of coins celebrated the Genius of the Roman People (GENIVS POPVLI ROMANI) – an antique idea personifying that particular principle, virile yet coming from a source beyond human eyes, which enabled the life of Rome and Romans to continue from generation to generation.

This principle seemed, above all, to be embodied in the emperors themselves. To describe them officially as gods, in these spiritually minded times, did not always seem suitable and decorous – and, besides, the multitude of past deified princes had downgraded this sort of symbolism. But there was also a long precedent for describing the rulers instead as companions of a god: and it was in pursuance of this formula that Diocletian and Maximian pronounced Jupiter and Hercules to be their special personal companions, and the patrons of their respective houses. The divinities they thus selected were above all else patriotic in their appeal: and in this monotheistic epoch which allowed most of the Olympians to fade into an amorphous amalgam, national propaganda concentrated its efforts upon deities, such as Jupiter and Hercules, who fulfilled the time-honoured roles of protectors of the Roman leaders and their people.

This revival of paganism, on an even more emphatically national basis than before, was accompanied by violent persecutions of the faith which had become its principal competitor – Christianity. Moreover, as already for the greater part of the third century, these official attacks corresponded with the wishes of a considerable section of the public. For, as the pagan cults were increasingly identified with patriotism, popular hatred of the supposedly unpatriotic Christians attained new and formidable dimensions.

Since the composition of the Gospels 200 years earlier, the Christian community, though still only a small minority of the total population, had grown steadily. By AD 200 it had gained a sense of permanent identity by establishing the components of the New Testament, a canonical scripture which had eliminated a host of deviant writings and was refreshingly more manageable than the multitudinous, confusing holy books of other religions. Efforts had also been made to harmonize Christian doctrines with those of the ancient pagan philosophers, first by Justin of Neapolis in Samaria (d. 165-7), who represented the faith as summing up all that was best in antiquity, and subsequently at the Christian school of Clement of Alexandria (c. 150-215). And then, in his compatriot and pupil Origen (d. 254-5), the church for the first time found a theologian who had thoroughly mastered Plato and other Greek thought, and had received personal instruction from the head of a philosophical school – a teacher, incidentally, whom he shared with the pagan Plotinus. But at the same time, among more uncompromising Christians, there was also vigorous hostility to this whole classicizing, philosophical approach, for example from the fierce north African Tertullian (c. 160-228).

But while these and many other controversies flourished within the ranks of Christianity, its membership and structure were quietly expanding all the time. Origen saw the church as parallel to the empire, and it was indeed almost a state within a state. It was still, basically, an urban institution: for while its extension to rural areas in Africa and the east produced fanatical nonconformists such as Tertullian, the main strength of the Christian community lay in the lower and middle classes of the cities. And it was in the ancient city-states of Asia Minor, in particular, that the church most rapidly established vigorous nuclei, from which it could expand to other eastern territories. But Christian missionary activities had also, at a very early date, extended to the west as well, and in the third century the process accelerated. At Rome itself, for example, the numbers of Christians probably rose from about ten thousand in AD 200 to three or four times that total a century later.

As time went on, the local communities of the Church had come under the autocratic control of bishops. This growing importance of the episcopacy took power away from the local elders and, in the west, from the mass of lay members as well. But it also made for much more efficient organization. The first of the important bishops in north Africa, Cyprian (d. 258), whose see was Carthage, felt emboldened by this impressive system to boast of the united, dynamic solidarity of Christians of every status and grade. And despite all the doctrinal disputes within their ranks, his praise was justified; for the church possessed a solidarity, a tightness of organization, that was unrivalled in any contemporary religion. This showed itself in welfare measures that knew no social distinctions, and displayed a scope and range which left Jewish and Greco-Roman precedents – charities and mutual assistance clubs – far behind. These beneficent arrangements, their financial basis solidly established in a bank, earned the reluctant admiration even of pagans; and, later on, the emperor Julian the Apostate, who hated Christianity, attributed its success to the effectiveness of its philanthropic activities.

Yet the Christians, from an early date, had encountered opposition. The Greek population of the east had never liked them, any more than it liked the Jews, because of their deliberate self-separation from the rest of the community: in which the followers of Jesus declared themselves to be mere strangers and sojourners. As a result of this attitude, the Greeks remained largely ignorant of their customs, and in consequence launched extraordinary accusations against them, including charges of obscenity and even of cannibalism.

Moreover, in the west, too, as Christianity gradually became better known, the same sort of hostility towards its followers began to develop among the inhabitants of the cities. And in these regions, this same unfriendly attitude spread to imperial administration as well. Indeed, when the Roman government became able to distinguish the Christians from the Jews, it liked the Jews rather better: for at least their religion was an ancestral heritage, whereas no such excuse was available for the Christians. Already in AD 64, under Nero, they were blamed for the Great Fire of Rome. But that was a feeble charge, and in reality what was being held against them, as Tacitus points out, was that they seemed to 'hate the human race'.

Nevertheless, apart from such exceptional occasions, the emperors were normally concerned to cool the temperature rather than heat it; and so, for another century or more, they remained on the whole more inclined to protect the Christians from the hostile public than to take the initiative in convicting them of any crime. Trajan wrote instructions on the subject to Pliny the younger, governor of Bithynia. 'They are not to be hunted out, he ordered; 'any who are accused and convicted should be punished, with the proviso that if a man says he is not a Christian and makes it obvious by his actual conduct – namely by worshipping our gods – then, however suspect he may have been with regard to the past, he should gain pardon from his repentance.'

Under Marcus Aurelius, however, the inhabitants both of Gaul and Asia Minor took violent exception to the Christian communities in their midst, blaming the military, economic and natural disasters of the time on their unpatriotic detachment from the common cause. Not long afterwards, Severus subjected them to the first co-ordinated, empire-wide sanctions, forbidding them to conduct missionary activities, and imposing stringent penalties on converts. Tertullian, in response, uttered open defiance against the government, declaring that no official position in the state ought to be held by any true Christian. Then there was a lull. But before long anti-Christian animosities began to intensify once again. For in 235 Maximinus I, desiring to find scapegoats for crises and earthquakes, exiled rival Christian popes (bishops of Rome) to Sardinia, and employed a new rigorousness in enforcing regulations against the sect, and particularly against its clergy. Then, as the imperial authorities became more and more desperately harassed by all their problems, the competent organization of the Christians, relatively few though they were, seemed more and more a cause of provocation, and Decius, hailed in a recently discovered inscription as 'Restorer of the Cults', declared himself unable to countenance their refusal to join in communal corporate pagan observances. He therefore demanded of every Christian a single performance of the traditional religious rites: once that had been made, the local Sacrificial Commission handed out a Certificate of Sacrifice (*libellus*), of which specimens have been found in Egypt.

The members of the Church, being mainly city people, found it hard to escape notice, and were dangerously vulnerable. Many, it is true, succeeded in evading the tests. But a considerable number of others, when subjected to this pressure, lapsed from their faith, at least for the time being. Others, however, who were called upon to sacrifice refused to do so, and were put to death. Martyrdom had glorious Jewish precedents; and, besides, Christians who underwent the ordeal felt they were imitating the sufferings of Christ himself, and of Peter and Paul. Shrines of martyrs were established and revered, on the analogy of pagan heroes, and provided great encouragement to the faithful: in the words of Tertullian 'the blood of Christians is seed'. And then the emperor Valerian, engulfed in an even graver military and financial situation than Decius had been, revived his anti-Christian plan and extended it to include large-scale confiscations of church property.

But his son Gallienus called a halt to this persecution, launching a policy of tolerance which lasted for forty years, during which the Church established itself on an increasingly firm basis. This caused alarm to pagans such as Plotinus' pupil Porphyry, whose work *Against the Christians* attacked them with unprecedented ferocity. And Porphyry's friends were among the instigators of the Great Persecution that now followed in AD 303. It was launched by Diocletian and, above all, by his Caesar Galerius, whose views on conformity were those of a military martinet. The motive of the persecutors was passionate enthusiasm for the old Roman religion and tradition and discipline, in the interests of imperial, patriotic unity. In consequence, as never before, the aim of these arch-regimenters was the total extirpation of Christianity. It was a struggle to the death between the one faith and the other, the old order and the new.

The first of Diocletian's edicts forbade all assemblies of Christians for purposes of worship, and ordered the destruction of their churches and sacred books. Then two further edicts, in the eastern provinces, commanded that the clergy, unless they sacrificed to the gods of the state, should be placed under arrest. Next, a fourth proclamation extended this requirement to every member of the Christian Church (304). And when, shortly afterwards, Diocletian abdicated his eastern throne in favour of Galerius, the suppression of recalcitrants was intensified still further. Bureaucracy and army joined forces to maintain these anti-Christian measures over a period of ten years, not so much in western Europe where few casualties occurred, but throughout the eastern provinces and in Africa. And although there were apostasies once again, resistance was on the whole resolute and defiant, and there were perhaps 3,000 martyrs altogether.

As soon as Diocletian had abdicated in 305, the regular, planned succession to the tetrarchy broke down in hopeless confusion, revealing that the system had no power to survive at all when supported no longer by his exceptional personality. Amid a welter of joint, competing occupants of the various palaces, Constantine I, son of the Danubian Constantius I, emerged to defeat Maxentius (the son of Maximian) in 312 at Rome's Milvian Bridge, thereby becoming sole emperor of the west; and in the following year Licinius gained unchallenged control of the east. Then in 323-4 Constantine won three great battles against Licinius and became the only ruler of the Roman world until his death in 337.

Constantine the Great was a man of impetuous and wide-ranging energy who felt utterly convinced of his duty to govern and change the world. Against a continuing background of exaction and inflation, he carried on the

# The family of Constantine

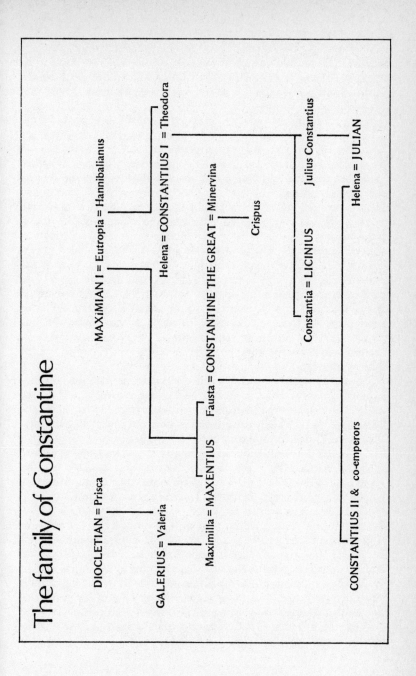

DIOCLETIAN = Prisca

GALERIUS = Valeria

Maximilla = MAXENTIUS

MAXiMIAN I = Eutropia = Hannibalianus

Fausta = CONSTANTINE THE GREAT = Minervina

Helena = CONSTANTIUS I = Theodora

Crispus

Constantia = LICINIUS

Julius Constantius

Helena = JULIAN

CONSTANTIUS II & co-emperors

reforming activity of Diocletian over a very wide field, enlarging taxation and bureaucracy, tying more and more people to their jobs on a hereditary basis, and generally advancing the formidable process of regimentation in every way. Indeed, whereas Diocletian's plans had been conceived to meet a series of emergencies, Constantine's were intended for a stable monarchy that would last for all time.

In particular, he continued to reorganize the army, which received ever-increasing commemoration on his coins and medallions. Like Diocletian before him, he greatly enlarged the proportion of Germans among the troops, since, after fighting successfully in their country himself, he appreciated their peculiar qualifications for tackling their own hostile compatriots on the other side of the frontier. High favour, therefore, went to German generals, and other ranks as well. For example, the praetorian guard, which had fought against Constantine on Maxentius' side, found itself abolished altogether, after an existence of nearly 350 years, and was replaced by the largely German mounted guard (*scholae palatinae*) created by Diocletian. Furthermore, many other Germans and Sarmatians, admitted inside the empire as settlers, were drafted into elite cavalry and infantry corps of the new field army, of which the effectiveness as a central striking force and strategic reserve was substantially increased; and it was placed under the command of a pair of new officers, the Master of Horse and the Master of Foot. The frontier garrisons, too, were rearranged and enlarged, and recruitment was enforced by severe penalties which caused widespread terror.

With the same military needs in mind, Constantine confirmed his predecessors' conclusion that Rome was no longer a suitable capital for the empire. An emperor who lived there was poorly placed to maintain control, at one and the same time, over the two vital imperial boundaries, the Rhine–Danube line in the north and the Euphrates in the east. Earlier rulers, feeling the same, had already from time to time established their residences at places more accessible to the frontier zones. Mediolanum (Milan) was a favourite choice, and Constantine himself had dwelt in a number of other centres, including Treviri (Trier), Arelate (Arles) and Ticinum (Pavia), as well as Sirmium (Sremska Mitrovica) and Serdica (Sofia) in his own native Balkans. But now he decided that the ideal site for simultaneous supervision of the Danube and Euphrates defences was the city of Byzantium on the strategic Bosphorus strait; and there he founded Constantinople, on the site where Istanbul is today (324–30).

Like Rome which formed its model, the new city was given a forum and a Senate of its own, and its people received free distributions from the grain-fleet which had served the ancient capital. It was true that Rome lost none of its privileges, and at first Constantinople and its senators ranked only second. Nevertheless, Constantine intended to make it the new metropolis of the empire; and by this revolutionary decision the scene was set for the Middle Ages.

Constantine also carried through a second and even more far-reaching and fateful revolution. This was the conversion of the empire from paganism to Christianity. The persecutions initiated by Diocletian and Galerius had not achieved their aim; and as they ran their course it became clear that the pagan community regarded the whole campaign as exaggerated, disliking the Christians rather less than they disliked the tyrannical government. And so Galerius, during his terminal illness, had issued, in conjunction with Constantine and Licinius, the Edict of Serdica (Sofia) granting freedom of worship to all members of the Christian faith (311). For the first time, that is to say, they were granted a measure of legal recognition.*

Meanwhile, in the west, Constantine's victory at the Milvian Bridge (312) was won, as he later asserted, under the auspices of the Cross, and in the following year he and Licinius, in the Edict of Mediolanum (Milan), echoed Galerius' pronouncement of tolerance towards the Christians. Constantine always felt a strong, impulsive need for a divine companion and sponsor. For a time the Sun-god, whose worship was ancestral in his family, had been his choice. But although this deity continued to be depicted on the coins until 318–19, Constantine had already disclosed, at the time of the Edict of Mediolanum, his own personal adherence to Christianity; and the One Supreme Power, to whom the literature and inscriptions of the time made numerous vague allusions, was identified, more and more explicitly, with Jesus.

And so Constantine, speaking of 'the most lawful and most holy' religion of Christ, initiated over a period of years a series of measures openly favouring its adherents. Christian priests, other than those of dissident sects, were exempted from municipal obligations, and imperial funds were sent to subsidize churches in the provinces. At Rome, the bishop, or Pope, was lodged in the Lateran palace, and the Church borrowed imposing features from the court ceremonial and was granted its own jurisdiction. Church and state were to be run in double harness. However, as the emperor became increasingly conscious of his own sacred mission, the successive Councils of Arelate (Arles) (314) and Nicaea (Iznik) (325) showed that it was he who was the master. At Nicaea, he attended the council meetings himself, and in the intervals between the sessions he went down among the bishops and joked with them in bad Greek.

And yet, at the time when Constantine raised the Christian community to these lofty heights, its position throughout the empire had been relatively insignificant: the church had lacked political and social and economic power

* Delayed in the east for two years because Galerius' successor Maximinus II Daia (defeated by Licinius) refused to concur.

alike. Its elevation, therefore, to become the ruling section of the empire was one of the most surprising phenomena in Roman history. The emperor's motives have been endlessly analysed and discussed. But it appears that he and his advisers experienced a growing conviction that, however uninfluential the Christians might be at present, the course of events was working, or could be made to work, in their favour: since they alone possessed the universal aims and efficient, coherent organization which, in the long run, could unite the various conflicting peoples and classes of the empire in a single all-embracing 'Catholic' (i.e. universal) harmony. It was in that belief that he launched his ecumenical missionary drive – and, as time went on, became increasingly intolerant of other faiths.

So Constantine's Christianization of the empire, though it still bears the appearance of a rash and unexpected step, was based on far-reaching states-manlike calculations. Nevertheless it would be mistaken to regard Constan-tine's personal conversion as coldly calculating and nothing else. On the contrary, he was a profoundly religious and emotional man. But why did he choose the Christian religion and not, for example, the Sun worship to which he had been earlier devoted? The reason was that he felt a powerful need for a personal saviour; and in this the cult of the Sun was deficient. Mithraism, it is true, attempted to fill the gap. But its key-figure lacked one indispensable feature. For Mithras, like other pagan saviours, was never thought to have actually appeared on earth and formed part of the history of men and women. But Jesus was believed to have done just this and to have intervened to save them, in the most dramatic and moving way pos-sible. That made him by far the most satisfying saviour of all; and it explains why Christianity won the struggle over the minds and hearts of Constantine and his subjects. The paintings in the catacombs, and reliefs and other works of art of the period, demonstrate the point clearly: for it is in his role as saviour and as worker of the miracles which brought salvation to indivi-duals and symbolized it for the whole world, that they chose to portray him.

But it may still, perhaps, be wondered why the faith which succeeded the pagans as the dominant faith of the Western world was Christianity and not Judaism. For Judaism, too, had such a great deal to offer; and it had revived very effectively from the consequences of the Second Revolt (AD 132–5), and become strong once again in the third century AD. And besides, the two faiths, parent and offspring, had so much in common. They both, unlike the pagan cults, offered a philosophy as well as a cult; and more than 90 per cent of Christian ethics had already appeared in the Jewish scriptures. Moreover, the social and philanthrophic services of the two religions were once again comparable, though the centralized arrange-ments of Christian bishoprics were more efficient than the local efforts of individual Jewish communities and presbyteries. The Christians also excelled in their presentation of a truly universal charity and compassion and consolation, embracing even the sinners and the destitute. True, all these features are also found in certain areas of Jewish theology and social thinking. But they are presented more vividly in the books of the New Testament. Yet above all, once again, it was for another reason that they prevailed over Constantine, and then the Roman world: because of the Christians' saviour, and his personal intervention upon the earth, a feature which the Jews, like the Sun-worshippers and Mithraists, could not offer.

Constantine himself did not treat the Jews too badly. But the Christian rulers of the next generation regarded them with less tolerance than the pagan emperors before him. They must be allowed to exist, because Jesus had been a Jew; yet their lives should be made miserable, because they had killed him. And nonconformist Christians, belonging to sects which would not follow the official line, ran into trouble as well. For in the words of Constantine's spokesman Eusebius, the first ecclesiastical historian, nothing was so infuriating to God as divisions in the Church – they were like cutting the body of Christ into pieces.

Constantine himself was baptized at the very end of his life, after postponing this step, like many of his co-religionists, until his death-bed when he could sin no more. By that time, the Christian revolution throughout the empire was well advanced. His conversion, which had prompted it, was seen by Petrarch, in the fourteenth century, as the great dividing line between antiquity and the ages that lay ahead: and, indeed, he had brought a whole new world into being. Constantine himself was profoundly aware of the vastness and holiness of this task: he saw himself as the thirteenth apostle of Jesus, and as God's Messianic regent upon earth.

It is in this guise that he is displayed in a colossal marble head which stands in the courtyard of the Palazzo dei Conservatori on Rome's Capitoline Hill. Here is the man at whose court, resplendent and hieratic, men spoke in hushed tones of his 'Divine Face' and 'Sacred Countenance'. The sculptor has conceived this countenance as a holy mask, a cult object foreshadowing the icons of the coming Byzantine empire: an overpowering image animated with the presence of God, and empowered to repel the demons lurking in every pagan idol. The head is nine feet high, and weighs nine tons. It formed part of a huge seated statue, of which the wooden body and glittering robe of gilded bronze have not survived.

This vast figure, reducing ordinary individuals to nothingness beside its hugeness, stood in one of the apses of the Basilica Nova. This was a secular building, the heir to the old market-basilicas – social, judicial and commercial meeting places beside the Forum. Yet it was a basilica with a difference. Mainly constructed by Maxentius, after whom it is often named, it was altered by Constantine who changed the principal orientation from the long to the short axis. The Basilica Nova was based on the bold idea of isolating the central cross-vaulted hall familiar in Roman baths and converting it into an independent structure. After the fashion of the Bath-halls of Caracalla and Diocletian, it consisted of only three bays, separated by huge internal piers. The lofty nave and aisles, lit by huge half-circular windows anticipating the Romanesque cathedrals of the future, were no longer roofed by flat ceilings, like the old market-basilicas, but surmounted, like the halls of the baths, by great curving, intersecting barrel vaults. The Basilica Nova, of which three lofty spans remain today, represented the climax of Rome's greatest architectural achievement: its discovery how to exploit the significance of interior space.

But the future lay with another sort of basilica, not secular but ecclesiastical. For Constantine's religious transformation stimulated the greatest architects of the day to serve the requirements of the new national faith; and these magnificent successors of the humble house-churches of the past were their major creations. Like the Basilica Nova, they were rectangular and longitudinal. But, in contrast to that building, they contained side aisles separated from the loftier nave, not by a few massive piers carrying rounded arches, but by long rows of columns supporting flat architraves. And flat, too, was the ceiling that surmounted this central nave, since the cross-vaults of the Basilica Nova would have distracted the essential concentration of Christian churches on drawing the eye towards the east. For the great colonnades created a single irresistible tide of nave and aisles flowing onwards towards the cross on the canopied altar, and to the apse which rose skywards beyond, enshrining the throne of the bishop, the representative of God. This culminating point of the Christian basilica was glimpsed from afar by those who entered the building from the west, and saw the rays of the rising sun pouring through the windows of the apse upon the celebrant who stood facing his congregation. In the rest of the building there was holy penumbra, in which gilt mosaics and be-jewelled objects lavishly glistened.

Little can be seen of Constantine's basilica-churches today, since they were demolished by later generations in favour of the monuments they themselves were eager to erect upon the same sacred sites. Yet his grandiose basilicas in their day comprised in their totality the greatest architectural accomplishment of any single man in Roman history. At his new foundation of Constantinople, he founded the Church of the Holy Wisdom (Santa Sophia), later replaced by Justinian's even mightier building. At Rome, too, which retained enormous spiritual importance as the burial place of the martyred Peter and Paul, there was the Basilica of St Peter (*c.* 333-7), lit by sixteen great windows and flanked by massive transepts.

And, before St Peter's, Constantine had already built, alongside the Lateran palace, which was the residence of the Popes, the church that was called after himself, the Basilica Constantiniana, which later bore the name of St John Lateran instead, and became the cathedral of the city.

Beside it was erected a centralized octagonal baptistery, which became the prototype of many others and has survived today. And Constantine built much larger centralized churches as well, which, like his basilicas, represented a major architectural revolution – and which, like them again, have suffered the fate of total disappearance. They included the cross-shaped Holy Apostles at Constantinople and the palace church of the Golden Octagon at Antioch, dedicated to Harmony – the divine power that creates unity within the empire, and the Christian community, and the universe. In Palestine, too, there were great Constantinian buildings: the Holy Sepulchre at Jerusalem combined both the longitudinal and centralized formulas, since it was a rectangular basilica built to enclose a circular martyr's shrine.

Constantine was determined to achieve hereditary succession to his throne, but his endeavours to arrange this were less successful than anything else he attempted. In 326, on reports of a plot, he ordered the execution of his wife and his eldest son by an earlier marriage. Then he groomed for the succession the three boys who remained to him, together with the two sons of a half-brother. Within thirteen years after his death, however, all these five had been eliminated, except one, who was Constantius II.

While prodigious monetary inflation and taxation continued within the empire, Constantius fought against Persia, and then turned to the west to put down usurpers. Meanwhile he was converting Constantine's acrobatic establishment of Christianity into a lasting reality. He himself, however, belonged to the Arian sect (regarding Christ, being the Son, as younger than God and inferior), which was overtaken by Catholicism;* and his attempts to grapple with the theological disputes that were splitting the state apart did not bear fruit. Constantius appointed his cousin Constantius Gallus to be his Caesar and presumptive heir, residing at Antioch; but in 354, on suspicions of disloyalty, he recalled Gallus and put him to death. Then he appointed a new Caesar, this time in the west, namely the dead man's half-brother Julian, who won an important series of campaigns against the Germans and restored the Rhine frontier. Thereupon his troops proclaimed him emperor, and conflict with Constantius II was inevitable; but before the clash came, the emperor died (361), and Julian succeeded in his place.

He had reacted strongly against his Christian background, and is known as the Apostate because he abandoned the faith altogether. He noted that his Constantinian relatives, steeped in crime, had failed to practise what they preached; and he spoke, as an outsider, for the financially depressed gentry of the ancient Greek towns of Asia Minor, who felt a distaste for the glaring affluence of the court, and despised its intellectual confusions as uncultured. Instead, Julian, in his youth, had derived from men of learning, including his tutor and a well-known philosopher of the day, a passion for classical literature and for the deities of the pagans; and these admirations emerge strongly from his surviving speeches, essays and letters, in which he manipulates the Greek language of his day with confidence and skill.

When he came to the throne, he openly professed adherence to the beliefs of the pagans, and reinstituted their cults, endowing them with substantial grants-in-aid and an organization intended to compete with the Christians. He also proclaimed general toleration of all religions. However, not only was the Christian Church deprived of its financial

* Athanasius, bishop of Alexandria (five times exiled) headed the fight against Arianism.

privileges, but in the religious disorders that followed, their members were penalized more severely than the pagans; a particularly controversial measure forbade them to teach in the schools. To strike a further blow against their faith, Julian offered encouragement to the Jews, whose lot had become worse under the Christian régime; and he even planned to allow the reconstruction of the Temple at Jerusalem, destroyed nearly three centuries earlier. Another reason for this move may have been a desire to protect the rear of his army from Palestinian revolts during forth-coming eastern campaigns. But owing to the absence of any real enthusiasm on the part either of Julian or the rabbis, who were content with their teaching centres in the synagogues, this plan to elevate the Jews, at the expense of Christianity, came to nothing.

And the same, indeed, was true of the whole of his angry anti-Christian campaign. He believed he possessed a divine mission to heal a sick society. But his character, a curious blend of opportunism and preciosity, was alien from any diplomatic compromise; and he was so deeply imbued with classical traditions that he found it hard to reach out and understand the common man of his day. His Canute-like attempt to roll back the Christian tide was too archaistic to prevail.

In other directions he succeeded better, for he was a hard-working and conscientious administrator. He did what he could to revive the declining fortunes of the city-states in the eastern part of the empire – the communities from which much of his political support was derived. He temporarily put an end to the inflation, probably by placing an extensive gold coinage in circulation. And, above all, he made a courageous attempt to cut down the ever-growing and all-encroaching imperial bureaucracy.

But his major ambition was to deal drastically with the Persians, who had become menacing once again during his predecessor's reign. After elaborate preparations, Julian marched eastwards in one of the most determined invasions of Persian territory for centuries, and won a victory (363). But his column was constantly harassed by the enemy, and in one of these skirmishes he received a wound from which he died in the Zagros foothills. His successor, a Danubian officer, Jovian (363–4), reversed both his principal policies, negotiating an unpopular peace with the Persians, and restoring Christianity – of which he was a pious adherent – as the religion of the empire.

# IX

# THE
# TRANSFORMATION
# OF EUROPE

# 20

# The Fall of the Western Empire

IN AD 364 THE army acclaimed Valentinian I, another Danubian, as emperor; and he was the last impressive ruler the western empire had. Valentinian was tall and vigorous, with fair hair and grey-blue eyes, and even if his opponents sneered at him as a man of barbarous origins, he had received a thorough education. Although jealous, cruel and easily angered and frightened, and often at sea in his judgement of civilian officials, he was a fine soldier and an energetic organizer. He disliked the Roman aristocracy, and felt an unusually strong sense of duty towards the poor. More unusual still, he tolerated differences of religious opinion.

Concluding that in the interests of national defence there should be a second emperor besides himself, Valentinian gave the east to his brother Valens, who took up residence at Constantinople. He himself kept the west, ruling at Mediolanum (Milan) though the Senate still remained at Rome. His treasury was impoverished by the division, since revenue from the richer eastern provinces ceased to flow in. Nevertheless, at his death eleven years later he left the western empire stronger than ever: no one could have believed that it would shortly be entering upon the final phase of its life.

Valentinian achieved this excellent result by dealing vigilantly with a host of successive emergencies. First, the Germans had burst across the Rhine, seizing the fortress of Moguntiacum (Mainz). But the emperor defeated them three times, and then marched up the Neckar valley and won a major victory in the Black Forest. Remaining in the north for seven years, he constructed a complex new system of defences and weakened his enemies by deliberately stirring up dissensions between one tribal group and another. Meanwhile, numerous Germans continued to be admitted as settlers within the western frontiers. In 374–5 Valentinian repelled and avenged another great incursion of Germans across the middle and upper Danube. Not long afterwards, however, while listening to the insolent words of German envoys, he burst a blood-vessel and died, leaving his throne to his 16-year-old son Gratian.

THE EMPIRE IN THE 4TH AND 5TH CENTURIES AD

R Rhine
Black Forest
R Neckar
Treviri
Campi Catalaunii
Moguntiacum
R Danube
Mediolanum
Arverna
R Po
Aquileia
Arelate
Ravenna
Tolosa
Rome
Ostia
Hadrianopolis
Constantinople
Carthage
Thagaste
Hippo Regius
Bethlehem
Alexandria

Frontier between
Western and
Eastern Empires

0        500 miles

Three years later the other, eastern Roman empire suffered a setback of unprecedented gravity. Beyond its borders, two great German states had taken shape, the Ostrogoths ('bright Goths') in the Ukraine, and the Visigoths ('wise Goths') based upon what is now Rumanian territory. But a non-German people living farther away, the Huns, had burst through into the lands of these two peoples in about AD 370. The Ostrogothic state crumbled before the onslaught of their formidable cavalry, and 200,000 Visigoths, too, were driven by the Hunnish invaders across the Danube into the eastern Roman empire, where its authorities permitted them to settle. Incensed, however, by their unjust treatment at the hands of these functionaries, the Visigothic chieftain, Fritigern, broke into revolt and ravaged the Balkans, while other northerners forced their way across the Danube in their wake (376). Valens marched rapidly from Asia to deal with the crisis, and passed to the attack at Hadrianopolis (Edirne, Adrianople) in Thrace. But the Visigothic cavalry drove off the horsemen of the Romans, and the imperial infantry fell almost to a man. Valens himself perished; and his corpse disappeared without trace.

His nephew Gratian, emperor in the west, had failed to reach the scene in time to help him. And now he appointed, to succeed Valens at Constantinople, a new colleague, Theodosius I, the 32-year-old son of a Spanish land-

# The family of Valentinian 1

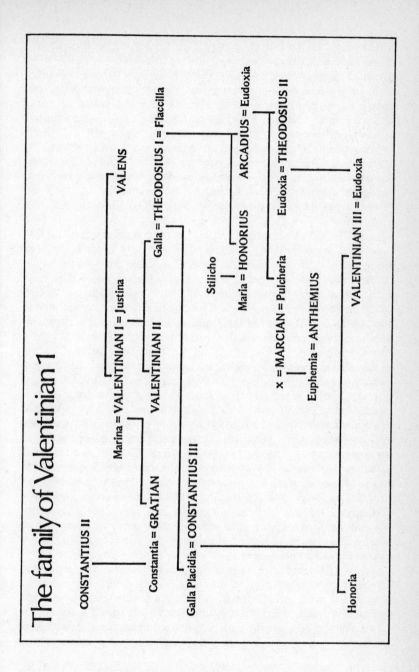

owner and general. For the next decade Theodosius ruled the eastern empire, and added to it by inducing his western counterparts to cede the greater part of the Balkan peninsula. Then, putting down two usurpers in the west, he momentarily reunited the two imperial thrones before his death in 395. Theodosius was blond and elegant and eager to please, but greedy, extravagant and unreliable, veering from brutal judicial sentences to quick pardons, and from frenzied activity to idleness. He became known as 'the Great' because of his insistence on rigorous Christian orthodoxy. This was one of the main features of his reign; the other was the acceptance, despite the disaster at Hadrianopolis, of a mass of Visigothic settlers within the imperial borders (382). There they could live under their own rulers, but must supply soldiers and agricultural workers for the Romans – the first of a series of German nations on which this allied, 'federate' status was conferred.

After Theodosius' death the empire was once again divided, and this time the division became permanent. The east went to his 18-year-old son Arcadius (395–408), and the western throne at Mediolanum to his younger son Honorius, aged eleven (395–423). Both boys, as they grew older, turned out to be unintelligent and incompetent, and the task of ruling the two empires fell to their regents. The effective ruler of the west was Stilicho, half-Roman and half-German, who was married to Honorius' cousin. Although he was a general of unusual brilliance and vigour, Stilicho's career, which might have saved the west for a time, was darkened by two clouds. The first was his hostility to the eastern empire, where he arranged that his counterpart as the guardian of its young emperor, Rufinus, should be assassinated. The second flaw in Stilicho's reputation was his unwillingness to deal firmly enough with the Visigoths' new ruler Alaric, who was not yet quite a king but a chieftain of the old type whose ability won him special prestige. Alaric had shown his aggressive intentions by a series of invasions deep into Italy itself (401–3) – events which induced the timid Honorius to move his capital from Mediolanum to the Adriatic coastal town of Ravenna, which was protected by marshes from the land side and provided an escape route by sea. Yet Stilicho, instead of resolutely proceeding against Alaric, preferred to keep him sound and strong as a counterpoise to the eastern Roman state. And indeed in 405, after destroying an Ostrogothic invasion of Italy, Stilicho developed plans for military action against the eastern government.

But on 31 December of the following year his designs were interrupted by the gravest and most fateful of all the German invasions of the west. For on that day a mixed army of men from a number of different tribal groups – Vandals, Suevi, Alans, Burgundians – crossed the ice on the frozen Rhine, and sweeping aside half-hearted resistance plundered Moguntiacum (Mainz) and Treviri (Trier) and many other border towns.

Next the invaders fanned out into Gaul beyond, continuing to ravage wherever they went and marching on throughout the entire country as far as the Pyrenees. With only a few exceptions, of which Tolosa (Toulouse) was one, the Gallic cities did not put up a fight. It proved a decisive break-through, because the Rhine barrier could never again be repaired.

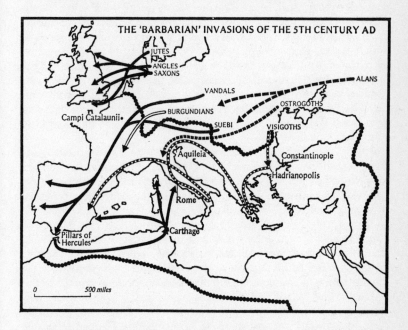

THE 'BARBARIAN' INVASIONS OF THE 5TH CENTURY AD

Stilicho did nothing effective to block the invaders, at first because he was still preoccupied with his plans for invading the east, and then because the shock-waves of the German onslaught threw up several usurpers in the Roman armies that were supposed to repel them: one of these men crossed over to the continent from Britain, which henceforward, denuded of troops, passed gradually into the hands of Saxon immigrants who had been allowed to settle in the country. Stilicho was under heavy pressure from the Visigoths, whose leader Alaric insisted that he should be given 4,000 pounds of gold from the western imperial treasury. Stilicho com-pelled his reluctant Senate to agree, but soon afterwards found himself accused of plotting, in collusion with Alaric, to place his own son on the throne. Although this may not have been true, a mutiny was fomented against him, and his supporters were massacred. He himself went to the emperor at Ravenna; but Honorius had him put to death (408). For half a century to come, no German was to follow in his footsteps as commander-in-chief in the west. But meanwhile, as the immediate sequel of his death, the Roman troops began to slaughter the families of their federate German fellow-soldiers, who, in consequence, went over to the Visigoths.

Their leader Alaric, cut off from the helpful contacts which Stilicho had maintained with him, went on demanding money and land and, when his demands were rejected, he marched in three successive years right up to the outskirts of Rome. On the first occasion he was appeased by large payments, on the second he set up a puppet emperor within the walls; and when he arrived for the third time the gates were treacherously opened to admit him. Thereupon his army moved in and occupied the city, which had not been taken by a foreign foe for nearly 800 years. Its capture by Alaric horrified the entire Roman world, yet although much wealth was plundered, and fires were started in various areas, the number of buildings that were burnt down was not very great. For the Visigoths only stayed in Rome for three days.

After that, taking the emperor's half-sister Placidia with him, Alaric departed and moved on towards the south of Italy, planning an invasion of north Africa. But he turned back and died, and was buried deep in the bed of an Italian river, so that his body should never be found and subjected to impious treatment.

The dominant Roman military leader of the next decade was Constantius (III), a long-necked, broad-headed general from the region of the Danube. In the year after Alaric's sack of Rome, Constantius courageously took the initiative. First, he put down no less than three rival claimants to the throne and established himself at the capital of one of them, Arelate, which now replaced devastated Treviri as the principal city of the western provinces. Next, in 413, Constantius granted one of the invading German tribes, the Burgundians, the status of allies and federates, and allowed them to live on the west bank of the middle reaches of the Rhine.

Meanwhile, however, the Visigoth Ataulf, brother-in-law and successor of Alaric, had moved his people out of Italy and settled them in the fertile lands of south-west Gaul. To prove his good intentions towards the empire, he married Honorius' half-sister Placidia, whom his predecessor had abducted from the city. But Honorius withheld his agreement to the marriage, and Constantius forced Ataulf to withdraw into Spain, where he was killed (415). Then his brother Wallia, after he returned Placidia to the Romans, was permitted to take his Visigoths back to south-western Gaul, where they were granted federate status, with Tolosa (Toulouse) as their capital (418). Honorius also proclaimed the delegation of his authority in Gaul to a regional administration at Arelate in which Romans and Visigoths were intended to collaborate. But the scheme was only rarely effective (p. 339).

Constantius had married Placidia in the previous year – against her will, though she provided him with a son. His position was now very powerful, and early in 421, Honorius proclaimed him joint emperor of the west. However, the eastern empire refused to recognize this unilateral appointment. This greatly angered Constantius III; but he had no opportunity to try conclusions with them, since, after a reign of only seven months, he died. Had he lived, he would have continued to provide vigorous administration. But he could never have been on good terms with Constantinople, so that it is doubtful whether his survival would have reversed the gathering process of western decline.

A quarrel now broke out between Honorius and Placidia, who sought refuge at the eastern capital, accompanied by her 4-year-old son Valentinian (III). But when Honorius died of dropsy in 423, an eastern army helped her to return to Italy and defeat a usurper, and the child became emperor in the west (425–55). During the first years of his titular rule, Placidia exercised autocratic control. But there was also another striking figure to be reckoned with, Aetius, a Danubian from Durostorum (Silistria in Rumania). As a young man he had been a hostage in the hands first of the Visigoths and then of the Huns, experiences which had given him valuable insight into these two leading foreign peoples of his time. Then, after Honorius' death, he had led a large force of Huns to try to block the return of Placidia. Subsequently, he made his peace with her government; but before long she began to find his power excessive. He took an army to north Africa, on which the Romans depended completely for their grain. At this time the country was under the semi-independent control of Boniface, a strange blend of saint and medieval knightly adventurer. Like Aetius, Boniface had at first been opposed to Placidia but had then made his peace with her, whereupon she deliberately set the two men at odds with each other. She offered her own support to Boniface. But in the ensuing hostilities he was wounded and died (432). Aetius now became the unchallenged commander-in-chief; and before long he began to be stronger than Placidia.

His most urgent task was to check the Vandals, a German people who had moved from Gaul into Spain and then across the strait into the vital territories of north Africa (429). Their king Gaiseric was a leader whose single-minded, far-sighted diplomacy and willpower faced the Romans with the most intractable German problem they had ever experienced. A joint army of the western and eastern empires sent against him failed dismally, and since the northern frontiers of Gaul were now breached, and peasant revolts, too, had broken out within that country, the western government felt obliged to offer him peace. A treaty was drawn up according to which the Vandals were granted federate status in Mauretania and Numidia (Morocco and western Algeria).

But this time it was a federate status which was not far removed from complete independence. And four years later, Gaiseric revealed this situation in unmistakable terms, when he invaded the historic nucleus of Roman north Africa, comprising the grain-lands of Tunisia and north-eastern Algeria; and the ancient capital Carthage itself fell into his hands (439). It was the second city of the western Roman world; and its loss was a blow that made the dissolution of the empire lamentably apparent. At this point, the government of Ravenna felt compelled to make a revised treaty with Gaiseric. Under its terms, he retained the regions he had lately seized, while ostensibly giving Mauretania and Numidia back to the western empire. But instead he broke his word and kept everything. Furthermore, he now abandoned even the pretence of federate status and instead began to rule openly over his own sovereign state, which was torn away from Roman suzerainty altogether. This was an unprecedented phenomenon; and Gaiseric was also unique among the Germans in possessing a fleet of his own, which struck terror far beyond north Africa's shores and menaced Italy itself, severing the unity of the Mediterranean for the first time for over 600 years. Gaiseric contributed more to the collapse of the western Roman empire than any other single man. And Aetius, although successful elsewhere in transplanting and resettling the Burgundians, was powerless to stop him.

This was also the time when the Huns, who had hitherto supplied Aetius with many of his soldiers, began to be the enemies of the Romans instead, fighting first against the eastern empire and then against the west. The Latin historian Ammianus Marcellinus saw them as deceitful, violent, greedy savages, abnormally competent as horsemen. By the early fifth century they had built up an empire of enormous dimensions, stretching all the way from the Baltic to the Danube. In 434 this entire territory was inherited by Attila and his elder brother, whom Attila soon put to death. Evil-tempered, arrogant and tireless, this square, flat-nosed little man earned the name of 'the Scourge of God', for during his nineteen-year reign he came to play almost as large a part as Gaiseric in the downfall of the Roman world.

At first, however, during the 440s, he remained on friendly terms with Aetius, concentrating his attacks on the eastern empire, which he compelled to conclude two treaties on increasingly unfavourable terms. Then, however, a new ruler at Constantinople refused to subsidize him any longer, and Attila finally turned against the west in order to make up this financial deficiency by looting. He was given a pretext to intervene when the sister of Valentinian III appealed to him to rescue her from a wedding with another man whom she did not like. The Hun chose to interpret this as a proposal that he himself should become her husband, and when his demand for a dowry consisting of half the western empire was turned down he marched on Gaul. There, on the Catalaunian Plains near Châlons-sur-Marne, he was confronted by a combined army of Aetius' Roman troops and federated Germans. The German units were partly provided by the Visigoths, and their king was one of the many who fell in the mutual slaughter that followed. Yet he fell in the moment of victory – the greatest victory of Aetius' career. It was the only battle Attila ever lost in his life; and it caused him to evacuate Gaul.

But Gaul's gain meant terror for Italy, since he and his Huns crossed the Alps in the following year, sacking Mediolanum and other leading cities. This time Aetius had no imperial army to send against him. Yet as Attila was preparing to cross one of the Po tributaries, Pope Leo I arrived on the scene from Rome; now that the city no longer contained an imperial court, its bishops, the popes, were political potentates. Pope Leo made effective use of his authority, requesting an interview with Attila and persuading him to withdraw from Italian soil. Presumably he convinced the king that owing to famine and pestilence the Huns would not be able to feed off the land. In any case, they turned back, and Italy was free of them.

Two years later, Attila died. His empire fell apart between his quarrelling sons; and before long their army faced a rebellion from their German subjects south of the Danube, and suffered an overwhelming defeat. The surviving Huns retreated far to the east (455), and were never a great power again.

But by that time Aetius was dead, for Valentinian III, falsely persuaded that he was treasonable, had murdered him with his own hand (454). Throughout two decades and more Aetius had laboured to keep the destroyers of the Western world in check. For a time he was almost successful: but with his assassination its terminal crisis had begun.

Only six months later, two of Aetius' barbarian retainers struck down Valentinian in revenge. In spite of his personal insignificance, his death was, in its way, as decisive as the killing of Aetius. For the emperor had no heir, so that his dynasty, which had exceptionally lasted for nearly a century, expired with him.

The year of his death already brought immediate catastrophe. For Gaiseric the Vandal, whose navy dominated the seas, landed in person at Ostia, and captured the city of Rome itself. He remained for two weeks, extracting loot far beyond Alaric's briefer plundering; and on his departure he removed thousands of captives including Valentinian's widow and two daughters.

The western empire had just twenty-one more years to live. During that period, as many as nine more or less legitimate rulers could be counted. Belonging to a variety of different families, most of them could claim only the barest minimum of power; and six came to violent ends.

Within the rapidly dissolving government of Ravenna, the predominant personage was now the supreme commander Ricimer. For the first time since Stilicho, a German had become the commander-in-chief again. Yet his origin was still felt to disqualify him from wearing the imperial purple itself: so instead, for the next fifteen years, Ricimer was the power behind the throne. He set up emperor after emperor, and then repeatedly unmade them as well, thus greatly intensifying the general instability. His most able protégé was Majorian (457–61), who fought well against the Germans in Gaul and Spain, but then suffered a serious naval reverse at Gaiseric's hands which caused Ricimer to put him to death. The German's next candidate, who was supported by Constantinople as well, suffered a similar fate, followed shortly afterwards by the death of Ricimer himself.

After three more transient reigns, which witnessed the loss of a loyal remnant of Gaul to the now independent Visigoths, a new military commander gave the Ravenna throne to his own son. The youth bore the historic names of Romulus Augustus, but was generally known by the diminutive version Augustulus. Yet Romulus only remained emperor for the briefest of periods, because of the intervention of a German general, Odoacer, who commanded a force of his Danubian compatriots in Italy. For Odoacer now decided to request, within that peninsula, the federate status and land grants which other Germans had succeeded in acquiring in

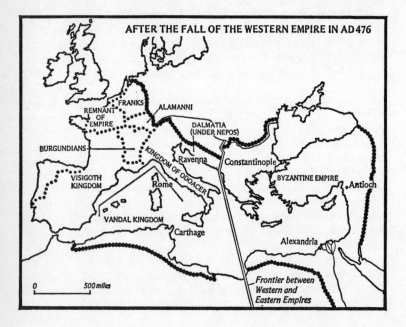

other territories of the west. When his claim was rejected, his soldiers saluted him as their independent ruler: not as Roman emperor however, but as their king.

Seizing Ravenna, Odoacer declared Romulus to be deposed, and dismissed him into pensioned retirement. This time, however, no attempt was made to appoint a new Augustus in the west. Instead, at Odoacer's bidding, the Roman Senate transferred the imperial insignia to Zeno, who occupied the throne at Constantinople (474–91). Zeno demurred, because the penultimate, transient, emperor of the west, Julius Nepos, his nominee, was still alive in Dalmatia. But since the eastern empire, at this time, was troubled by internal dissensions, Zeno took no action against Odoacer, who, while politely placing the heads of Zeno (and his nominee) on his coins, continued to rule Italy (with the co-operation of the nobles) as an independent monarch, like the kings of the Vandals and Visigoths.

In consequence, later historians fastened on this year 476 as the date at which the long declining western empire finally fell. In recent times, there has been a tendency to minimize the significance of this particular event, since, after all, it was only one more landmark in a series of destructive developments, and not a very spectacular landmark at that; and, besides, the system created by Odoacer in Italy was not unlike the arrangements which other German tribes had already made in Gaul and Spain. Nevertheless this forced abdication of the last man to occupy the throne at Ravenna did have a meaning, for it signified that the last remaining country of the west, and its metropolitan territory at that, had become just another German kingdom. The western Roman empire had fallen; or it had become something else. At any rate it was no more.

# 21

# The Fatal Disunities

THE WESTERN EMPIRE WAS no more because it had succumbed to its external enemies. Yet these would not have been too formidable to overcome if it had still possessed sufficient internal strength. But when the murderous blows were struck, the government could no longer muster the force to ward them off. This was because Italy and the whole western world were hopelessly disunited within. The disunities assumed various shapes and forms. Each one of them, in itself, was damaging. In combination they made resistance to the external onslaughts impossible.

One prime cause of disunity was the failure of the rulers to control their generals. This, of course, was nothing new. It had been a defect inherent in the imperial system from the very beginning, since the Romans, for all their political skill, had never devised a workable system for ensuring a peaceful transition from one ruler to the next. This defect was a standing temptation to many of their own commanders, beckoning them to make a violent bid for the immense stake of autocratic power. Under the dynasty of Valentinian I, at least ten and possibly thirteen men from outside his house made lunges at the throne. They were all unsuccessful in the end, but all had enjoyed a considerable measure of acceptance for a time; and the struggles to put them down severely weakened the already strained resources of imperial manpower and revenue. In the words of an acute contemporary historian, Ammianus: 'What fury of foreign peoples, what barbarian cruelty, can be compared with the harm done by civil wars?'

And yet, despite these troubles, Valentinian I and his kinsmen had presided over a period of comparative internal calm. At first sight, it is surprising that this should have been so, since not one of these emperors, after himself, was of sufficient calibre to carry such an enormous burden with personal distinction, and the later incumbents were almost unrelievedly dim. Yet the family remained on the throne for the record period of ninety-one years. And the measure of stability which this unbroken continuation had provided could readily be appreciated after the dynasty had gone: for chaos at once prevailed. However this assumed the form, no longer of usurpations, but of a régime in which even the most ostensibly legitimate emperors were mere figureheads depending on powerful German generals. The throne passed with ludicrous rapidity from one puppet to another, and the old Roman failure to secure peaceful successions had become a major factor in the dissolution of the western empire which followed so soon afterwards in 476.

While the armies of the empire were seeking to assert themselves against one another, they were failing to perform the tasks of imperial defence that were required of them. For they collapsed before foreign invaders who were, theoretically, much their inferiors in numbers and equipment: the sort of enemies that Rome had often encountered before, and defeated. Alaric and Gaiseric may have commanded no more than a mere 40,000 and 20,000 warriors respectively; whereas, according to the Record of Official Posts (*Notitia Dignitatum*), the two Roman empires between them disposed of no less than 500,000 soldiers. And half of these belonged to the west, being stationed, for the most part, on or near the Rhine and Danube borders.

However, such statistics are deceptive. For one thing, as much as two-thirds of the western empire's total army consisted, not of the high-grade field force, but of the less mobile and less respected frontier troops – and it was from their ranks, moreover, that the heavy casualties in the field force had to be replenished as best they could. The result was that in terms of active, effective strength, the western Romans could scarcely mobilize bigger numbers than their foes. Stilicho, in 405, led a force of not many more than 20,000, and even 15,000 was considered a substantial total for a Roman field army of the time.

This numerical weakness was largely due to the increasing failure of the imperial authorities to enforce conscription. During the earlier part of the fourth century AD this had been the principal source of recruitment, and Valentinian I, for example, conscripted strenuously every year. But the exempted categories were cripplingly numerous; not only slaves, as always, but senators, bureaucrats, clergymen, and many others were entitled to opt out. Efforts to recruit the remainder of the population, therefore, had to be intensive. Even the men who worked on the emperor's vast estates found themselves called up. Yet other landlords, though required to provide recruits in proportion to the size of their estates, firmly resisted such demands, or only sent the men they were content to lose. And they had some excuse for resentment at being fastened on because little attempt was made to conscript the inhabitants of the cities, who, especially if they came from Rome, were deemed useless as soldiers; so that the burden fell on the rural population, with the inevitable result that agricultural production suffered, and would have suffered more still had there not been widespread evasion of the draft.

Becoming convinced, for such reasons, that ordinary measures of conscription would no longer avail, the government introduced new and stringent rules – including the insistence that if a man's father had been a soldier he himself must become one too. This doctrine of hereditary obligation had already been put into practice earlier, with application to a wide variety of professions; and now it was directed towards the military career, in so far as the authorities had the power to assert their will, with ever-increasing sternness. For, as Saint Ambrose remarked, military service was no longer considered a patriotic duty, but a servitude – to be shunned. By the 440s it had become impossible to attempt any call-ups whatever except in the gravest emergencies. And a decade later we hear of no more western citizens being drafted at all.

And yet this failure occurred despite the most strenuous efforts to make army life attractive. There had been endeavours on these lines in a number of earlier reigns. Such reforms had been sharply censured by conservatives, and Valentinian I and Theodosius I, too, were charged with treating the soldiers much too indulgently; for example when they allowed them to earn extra pay as workers on the farms. However, these inducements were varied by heavy threats, including instructions that those who sought to escape military service by amputating their thumbs should be burnt alive. Yet neither the stick nor the carrot tempted men to seek the life of a soldier in such a perilous and dislocated world.

The result was, as a law of 409 reveals, that the hereditary defenders of the frontier posts just melted away. The cities were left unguarded even when invaders were almost in sight; and the encouragement of local defence groups proved effective only rarely. True, a fine general like Stilicho or Aetius could still win his battles. But on many other occasions the imperial troops were doomed to defeat before they had even caught a glimpse of a German or Hun soldier. Besides, in the frontier garrisons in particular, they were exploited by their officers, who grabbed much of their pay: and this left them unenthusiastic for battle. But this was only one small aspect of a wider phenomenon: the empire no longer inspired its soldiers to fight vigorously for its survival.

Failing, therefore, to mobilize enough satisfactory recruits, the government decided that if it could not get men it would get money. And so, from the fourth century onwards, it accepted cash sums in lieu of manpower, from those who wanted to avoid serving, and from their landlords as well. It took these sums in order to pay for German soldiers, to supplement and replace the elusive provincials. This, in itself, was not new. There had long been Germans in the Roman army; and their enrolment had been considerably increased by Diocletian and Constantine. At that time, they were

mostly recruited under personal contract, on an individual basis, to serve
under Roman officers; and for the most part they fought well, seeing the
empire not as an enemy but as an employer.

But then in 382 Theodosius I extended the process decisively, and transformed it. For the German 'allies' or federates whom he now enlisted were
not merely individual soldiers any longer, but whole tribes, each recruited
under its own chieftains who paid their men in cash and goods received
annually for the purpose from the emperor. Once introduced, this new
federate participation in the army grew apace. It was widely criticized as an
undermining influence, and yet, since other forms of recruitment had
failed, it was probably the best remedy available. And yet it proved a
failure, and its failure helped to bring the western empire down.

One reason why it failed was the total lack of sympathy between the army
and civilians. Rather than fight, the soldiers preferred to terrorize the rest
of the population, who consequently loathed them.

Besides, the people resented the military for other reasons as well.
Above all else, the burden of taxation they had to undergo in order to
keep this army in existence was appallingly heavy, so heavy that its im-
positions alienated the poor from the state for ever. The laws of Theodosius
I, for example, show a passionate desire to increase the extortion of revenue
by every possible means. 'No man', he pronounced in 383, 'shall possess
any property that is exempt from taxes.' Harsh regimentation, for this same
purpose of paying the army, had been a fact of Roman life for nearly 200
years. But now each successive emperor continued to turn the screw a little
tighter still.

Besides, the payment of these huge taxes was only one part of the contribution a citizen had to make to the state. There was also widespread
requisitioning of his personal services. For example, he was compelled to
supply coal and wood, and to boil lime, and to help keep public works and
buildings in repair. This mobilization of compulsory labour became more
stringent all the time; and violence and torture were employed to prevent
evasions. Yet, at the same time, as in the military draft, there were far too
many exemptions, which privileged social groups found it excessively easy
to obtain; and there was also a great deal of corruption, as numerous ineffective attempts to prevent it reveal.

It was unquestionable that, in some form or other – cash or kind or
personal services or all three – huge contributions *had* to be raised, since
otherwise the army, and empire, were not going to be able to survive. But
does the historical fact that this purpose was not, in the end, achieved
prove that the required amounts were too great to be raised – that their
collection was a practical impossibility?

No, probably the taxes could have been brought in, if only the system for levying them had been less inefficient. It was inefficient because it was so intolerably oppressive, leaving tax-dodging as the only alternative to destitution. And it was not only oppressive but unfair, since the worst sufferers were, as always, the agricultural poor. The unfairness of the land-tax, from which the state drew nine-tenths of its income, had always meant that they were hit much harder than the rich, and despite Diocletian's attempts to introduce sliding scales of crops and harvests, this situation was still substantially unchanged. Indeed, it had become worse. For by 350 the sums exacted from this principal source of revenue had multiplied three-fold within living memory, and after that the situation deteriorated still further. Moreover, the most important tax in kind, utilized for many years to pay government employees, had to be paid in the form of grain, so that once more it was the agricultural population that suffered. True, subsequently there was a change of method, as a result of which levies in kind were increasingly commuted to gold once again. But that was of no assistance to the labourers in the fields who had no gold, and were once again suffering from a galloping inflation. Moreover they were still crippled by the general adverse conditions that had always restricted the economy of the ancient world – costly transportation and stagnant technology, supplemented now by a shrinkage of cultivable land owing to encroachments by the invasions.

Slavery was not the major problem of the age. It is true that in certain territories, such as the Middle Danube region and Mauretania, slaves were still numerous enough to make a substantial contribution to the labour force. However, this did not so much increase the total number of workers available as depress the 'free' poor still further, since they could not compete with this unpaid labour and dropped out of the market altogether. Besides, such areas with abundant slaves were somewhat exceptional. In most other parts of the empire, at this epoch, there was no longer enough slave labour to make any appreciable difference to the economic picture one way or the other. Such slaves as there were sometimes helped the empire's various enemies, and sometimes went round looting. But their role in the history of the period was relatively unimportant. It was on the impoverished 'free' men and women of the rural countryside that the full horrors of the situation descended. They and the government were oppressed and oppressor, face to face in destructive and suicidal hostility. It was largely because of this rift that the taxes needed to support the army were not, could not be, paid in. And since that could not be done, the western empire failed to find defenders, and collapsed. This was perhaps the gravest and most disastrous of all the disunities that afflicted the Roman world.

It also brought about radical changes in the structure of society. For when the small farmers and agricultural labourers could no longer make both ends meet, they sought protection where they could find it. Thus whole villages formally placed themselves under the patronage of individual army officers, who, in return for the services of the villagers, were prepared to parley on their behalf with the imperial tax collectors. More numerous, however, were the communities which chose not officers but local landowners as their patrons. And many individual civilians did the same on their own personal account: small farmers who abandoned their homes and land in desperation, and fled within the walls of the nearest great estate. This had happened before, during the troubles of the third century, but now the process repeated itself on a vast scale.

Since agricultural labour was so scarce, the landowners were content to receive these people, who defrayed their keep either by paying a cash rent, or by handing over a proportion of the crop they were allowed to grow, or by contributing the labour of their hands. Although their surrender was unconditional, at first, like the clients of the army officers, they could often rely on their new patrons to chase the tax authorities away. But later the landowners did an unholy deal with the western government, and the refugees found themselves on the tax-lists once again. And so the emperors were glad to attempt, though without complete success, to prevent these tenants from moving away without their landlord's consent, so that they were wholly subjected to his control – and so were their children after them. Such men were not exactly slaves, but foreshadowed the serfs of the middle ages.

One of the emperors who published such restrictions was Valentinian I. He, for his part, was not prompted by any desire to grind the faces of the poor, but was acting from motives of plain realism, since if there was one thing worse than being frozen into one's occupation it was being frozen out of any job or food at all – and from that fate at least the landowners saved their refugee tenants. Moreover, in other respects, Valentinian displayed notable concern for the welfare of the poorer classes, to which he himself had belonged. In particular, he appointed functionaries described as Defenders of the People (368–70). Somewhat resembling the Ombudsmen of modern countries, these officials were designed to protect the underprivileged 'against the iniquities of the powerful'. The praetorian prefects were ordered to nominate such a Defender in every town of the western empire, and the emperor himself required to know the name of every man who received such an appointment. Unfortunately, however, his successors watered the project down, transferring the selection first to city councillors – the very men responsible for collecting the taxes – and then to committees on which the landowners were heavily represented.

The scheme had failed. But there were still writers prepared to speak up for the oppressed. John Chrysostom, bishop (patriarch) of Constantinople (c. 354–407), was painfully aware of the gulf between rich and poor.

And above all Salvian, presbyter at Massilia (Marseille) (*c.* 400 – after 470), saw God chastising the world for its sins – which he equated with material oppression. The age he lived in, like the later 1800s, was one in which poverty was regarded as blameworthy and disgraceful. Salvian fiercely rejected that stigma; and indeed he was so determinedly radical that no social class gained his favour except the totally destitute, whose abominable treatment by the government and the rich alike he deplored with intense forcefulness and unrelieved gloom.

The consequence of the conditions he so eloquently describes was that thousands of people despaired of making an honest living at all, and went underground to form travelling gangs of robbers and bandits. Gaul, in particular, experienced a succession of large-scale disturbances of such a kind. Indeed, such bands operated almost on the scale of a nationwide rising, in which tenants and slaves alike revolted in unison against the land-lords and authorities. We learn that these Bagaudae – an old name by which they called themselves – held their own People's Courts, 'where capital sentences are posted up on an oak-branch or marked on a man's bones'. And can you wonder that there were such terrorist gangs? asked Salvian, blaming these widespread disorders unreservedly upon the ruthlessness of the governing class.

Far back in the distant past, whole aeons away it seemed, was that not totally imaginary golden age when the various classes of the Roman state, even if never truly united because of the yawning economic differences, had at least been able to live together without seeking each other's annihila-tion. Now, instead, the empire had come to a time like the nineteenth century, when Disraeli made a character in his novel, *Sibyl*, remark: 'I am told that the privileged and the people formed two nations.' But in the nineteenth century the social structure managed to avoid disintegration: whereas in the fifth century it had crumbled, opening a breach through which the external enemy could batter his way in.

Yet the western empire might still have held together, brushing aside the claims of the poor, if only the rich and the government had more frequently seen eye to eye with one another. They colluded, it is true, in ensuring that the tenants on the large estates should be allowed no freedom or rights. But in general there was very little sympathy between the imperial authorities and the upper class. In the declining Roman world this class, the topmost layer of the population, consisted of men entitled to describe themselves as senators. And even if the Senate, as such, did not count for a great deal more than it had in the earlier empire, its individual members were now more powerful than they had ever been before. Those who attended the Senate-house at Rome did not see much of the emperor, whose residence was at Milan and later in Ravenna. But this gave them (as it gave the Popes in the same city) a certain independence of action. Constantine the Great knew the value of these senatorial dignitaries, mainly pagan though they still were; and so, while excluding them from his army, he courted their acquiescence in his policies by offering them lucrative civilian posts, and preserving and even enhancing the pompous dignity of their consulships and other sinecures.

Class-consciousness and snobbery were enormous. Yet the senatorial order was not altogether closed to newcomers. Moreover, the term 'senator' had come to be extended beyond those who actually sat in the Senate at Rome to several thousand additional aristocrats living outside the capital and, in many cases, outside Italy. Such men, the owners of enormous properties, may have been five times wealthier, on an average, than their forerunners of earlier imperial epochs. Their estates, to which so many displaced persons fled for shelter, were like small kingdoms in themselves, self-contained economic and social units packed with farm-workers, slaves, artisans, guards, bailiffs and hangers-on. In Gaul there was a particularly massive concentration of about 100 powerful landowners who, with Honorius' concurrence, virtually assumed control of the country, and later, with the support of the Visigoths, briefly proclaimed one of their own number as emperor (455).

The noblemen and noblewomen of the later empire were magnificent personages. But they were not particularly addicted to vicious high living – a good deal less so than their forerunners three and four centuries earlier. So the idea that the western world collapsed because of orgies, a theory beloved of modern moralists and makers of spectacular films, must be abandoned. There were many more orgies earlier, when the empire had been doing well, than later when it was faring badly. More serious is the accusation that the senators of the fourth and fifth centuries stood aloof from public life. For many of them held no office of state, preferring instead to remain at home and enjoy their properties at leisure. In Rome and the provinces alike, they failed to pull their weight in state affairs. True, towards the very end of the western empire there was a change, because by then the landowners had become more powerful than the emperor himself, and some of them successfully invaded his councils. But even then many others still remained apart, living idly on their own estates and oblivious of any wider claims upon their time.

Salvian, among others, felt this profoundly, and declared that the higher a man's status might be, the greater were his obligations, and the greater his guilt when, as so often, he fell short of them. For by this sin of omission such a man was betraying the empire, and contributing to its fall. And indeed, in spite of lip-service to the romantic concept of Eternal Rome, many noblemen were not prepared to lift a finger to save the reality. On the contrary, they often actively undermined its welfare, by rebuffing imperial officials, harbouring deserters and brigands, and taking the law into their own hands, to such an extent that they even maintained their own private prisons. Valentinian I objected to this practice, with some determination; but his successors – the emperors who made an arrangement with the landowners about the tenants – virtually had to give in. And yet, even so, these upper-class personages still frequently remained hostile to the government, scoffing at the Augusti as uncultured, and detesting their ministers.

In the vain hope, then, of keeping their armies in the field, the imperial authorities ruined the poor and alienated the rich. They also alienated and then very largely destroyed the solid segment of the population that came in between – the middle class. This had once been the backbone of the Greek city-states, and later on it had fulfilled the same role in the Roman empire as well; since that too was a network of city-state communities. But the external invasions and internal rebellions of the third century AD had dealt this middle class terrible physical blows, while the accompanying monetary inflation caused their endowments to vanish altogether. And then, from the next batch of emperors, those who came later on in the same century, and grimly pursued the enormous tasks of reconstruction, the old-fashioned ideals of this bourgeois section of the community received little sympathy. Their public work programmes cut to nothing or severely restricted, the cities of the empire began to assume a very dilapidated appearance; and then in the fourth and fifth centuries, despite contrary efforts by Julian and others, their position continued to worsen, and the old urban civilization, especially in the west, plunged into a sharp decline.

The nucleus of the middle class had been provided by the *curiales*, who comprised the members of the city councils (*curiae*) and their sons and descendants. Once they had been munificent benefactors of their cities; but those days were gone for ever. For nowadays by far their most important function was to carry out the orders they received from the central government, and above all to collect its revenues. It was the duty of the councillors, and of their offspring when their turn came, to extract from their fellow-citizens the taxes in cash and kind demanded by the state, and to compel them to join the army.

That is to say, they had virtually become imperial agents. This meant that they had to act toughly, and social critics such as Salvian of Massilia deeply blamed them for doing so. Yet the councillors' own personal situation, too, had become acutely difficult, since they had to make up any shortfall themselves. This meant that from the third century onwards wealthy men became increasingly reluctant to serve on the city councils. It also meant that, since few new families were willing to be enlisted in such a burdensome cause, these memberships more and more often assumed a hereditary character: a situation encouraged by the imperial government, which insisted, as in so many other sections of the community, that the sons of councillors should follow in the footsteps of their fathers.

But such insistence, although reiterated with almost neurotic regularity, did not prevent these *curiales* from deserting wholesale from their posts: and indeed the entire middle class of the western empire, of which they formed such an essential part, was almost wiped out of existence. In a society which had always so largely depended on this class, its destruction left a vacuum which nothing could fill, and signified that from now onwards the population of these territories for the most part consisted of very rich and very poor. No doubt, the traditional urban civilization had always exhibited a disequilibrium, since the towns were parasites upon an agrarian economy. Nevertheless, that was the system on which the ancient world had been founded, and its virtual erasure contributed substantially to the destruction and transformation of that world.

So throughout the last two centuries of the Roman west there was an ever-deepening loss of personal freedom and prosperity for all, except the very prosperous and powerful. The western empire had become a military camp in a perpetual state of siege, where each man was assigned a place he and his descendants must never desert. The authorities sought to impose maximum regimentation, to pay for the army and prop up the imperial structure. And yet all that they thereby achieved was to hasten the ruin of what they wanted to preserve, by destroying all the individual loyalty and initiative which alone could have achieved its preservation.

Moreover, this suicidal process was accelerated by the vast size and deteriorating quality of the civil service employed to regiment the remainder of the population. It was a self-perpetuating body, because like the town councils and so many other institutions, it became hereditary. Since the beginning of the fourth century there had been a new imperial aristocracy of service, enabling the rulers to make use of a body of helpers loyal to themselves. Before long, however, the civil servants of this new brand, who knew how greatly they were needed in order to collect the required revenue, gained confidence, and betrayed an unobtrusive, but none the less persistent, defiance of their rulers.

Valentinian I and some of his successors tried to halt this trend, declaring that the civil servants owed obedience as much as any soldiers. Yet the emperors failed to prevent this rampant bureaucracy from gradually encroaching on their own imperial power and finally reducing it to almost total paralysis. It is true that some of the provincial governors and governors-general, as well as some of the praetorian prefects who supervised their activities, were conscientious enough. But others, more numerous than in earlier days, were callously inhumane and monsters of corruption – partly because the western empire was too poor to give them decent pay. The laws

of the time made feverish attempts to reduce this unmanageable official-
dom to order; but the very repetitiousness of such measures shows how
ineffective they must have been.

These regulations are known to us because they were collected in AD
438 in the code of the eastern ruler Theodosius II, accepted also by his
western colleague Valentinian III. This Theodosian Code contains enactments of both empires dating back a century and more. And they are
remarkably revealing. For although some are humane and enlightened,
many others display an almost hysterical repressive violence which
augured badly for the survival of the weaker of the two states, the empire of
the west. And, once again, these laws are monotonously repetitive – proof
that they were circumvented, disobeyed and ignored. The government was
overwhelmed by the situation, and powerless to improve it. And the lawyers
of the period who composed such strident documents were evidently a
great deal less impressive than their counterparts of earlier times. Moreover, the administration of justice, like the other operations of bureaucracy,
was undermined by bribery. An anonymous fourth-century writer *On
Matters of Warfare* (*De Rebus Bellicis*) concludes his essay with an appeal to
the emperors of his day: 'Put a stop to dishonest litigation!'

The rulers whose orders produced all these unproductive edicts often
lived extremely cloistered lives, disastrously lacking in contact with all their
subjects in the outside world. At the two courts of Ravenna and Constantinople, ceremonial and adulation were elaborate, and the eunuch-chamber-
lains who controlled admission to the imperial presence were regarded with
implacable hostility, not only by the ruling class but by all others, too, who
encountered their arrogance. In vain the official coinage poured out streams
of rousing patriotic slogans, which sank to extraordinary depths of unreal-
ism and unpersuasiveness. There is unceasing stress on Glory, and
emperors ferociously declare themselves 'triumphant over the barbarian
nations', when the very reverse was the case. Between the heads of the two
Roman states and their subjects, there was a lamentable failure of
communication.

Even so, however, the downfall of the western empire would have been
delayed if only it had co-operated better with its more successful eastern
counterpart. But co-operation was often poor, or non-existent. There was
an ancient, endemic mutual dislike between the Latin-based and Greek-
based halves of the Roman world, and the rulers of the two sections often
seemed reluctant to come to each other's assistance, and much readier to
offer a stab in the back instead.

This situation was at its worst just after the death of Theodosius I had
left the two régimes divided once again, and this time divided sharply and
finally. For the commander-in-chief of his son Honorius in the west,

Stilicho, felt obsessive hostility towards the eastern empire, where he even had his counterpart Rufinus assassinated. Nor, as we have seen, did he act strongly enough against the Visigoth Alaric, since he always regarded the government at Constantinople as the foremost of his enemies. When, long after his death, the west proved willing to accept an eastern nominee for its throne (AD 467), it was already too late. Decades of mutual ill-will had sapped the strength of the western empire beyond repair, and soon afterwards it ceased to exist.

Another reason why it fell was because of a disastrous failure to assimilate the Germans in its midst, or achieve a workable arrangement with their leaders. These German immigrants had constantly increased in numbers: a decisive moment came in 382, when Theodosius I allowed entire tribes to reside on imperial territory in Thrace as autonomous federate units, committed to serving in the Roman army under their own chiefs. And then again early in the fifth century, when the Visigoths and Burgundians settled in Gaul, there were once more formal partitions of land, in which the local Roman proprietors handed over a third of their arable ground to the settlers; and later this proportion was doubled.

In these developments, one can detect the origins of the independent European nations of the future. Yet when these Germans had first begun to establish themselves on imperial territory, they felt no ambition to become independent of Rome or spurn its institutions, only desiring to obtain a share of its benefits, and, above all, cultivable soil. Even the Visigoth Alaric, who went down to history as the captor of Rome, had at first aimed at a new form of co-existence, and a single German–Roman people. And his son Ataulf (410–15) formulated the same ideal with great explicitness, stating that he had formerly wanted to establish a Gothic empire in place of the Roman state, whereas now, instead, he 'aspired to the glory of restoring the fame of Rome in all its integrity, and of increasing it by means of the Gothic strength'.

But the Roman response to this unprecedented offer of partnership was inadequate. True, there were a few writers, inspired by pagan or Christian universalism, who paid lip-service to multi-racial unity. But lip-service was all that it was, because even they could not restrain themselves from expressing, like so many other authors of the time, a deep repugnance for the personal characters and habits of the barbarians. Even Salvian, who bravely supported co-existence on the grounds that these noble savages were better than corrupt Roman society, commented on the nauseous smell of the Germans' bodies and clothing, and described the Goths as perfidious, the Alamanni as drunkards, the Saxons, Franks and Heruli as wantonly brutal, and the Alans as rapacious lechers. Similarly Sidonius Apollinaris, the highly literate bishop of Arverna (Clermont Ferrand), while lavishly flattering successive Visigothic monarchs and observing that he and they had a common interest in saving the empire, nevertheless objected fastidiously to the noisy, skin-clad Goths, and tattooed Herulians, and Burgundians who stank of the rancid butter they smeared on their tow-haired skulls.

Valens' governors and military commanders subjected the immigrant Visigoths to unconcealed, rapacious exploitation. But what was almost worse was that the Romans generally imposed on these new, unwelcome and disconcerting neighbours a kind of spiritual and social apartheid. The German immigrants seemed to them an unabsorbable lump of branded, sub-human outcasts; and so they set them apart, beyond a wall of contempt and distaste. For instance, a law of 370 set a total veto on intermarriage; and even the wearing of barbarian clothes by Romans was stringently forbidden. This deliberate detachment, moreover, was greatly accentuated by religious divergences, since the Arian form of Christianity, which was adopted by the Germans, appeared to the churches of Rome and Constantinople* to deny the divinity of Jesus and was condemned as heretical.

Only Aetius, if he had lived, might have reversed the general trend, for he knew the Germans well, and handled them with tact. But he came too late, and he was struck down: whereupon hostility to the Germans became the rule. Some of them, in response to this treatment, behaved with apologetic humility. But many more reacted by refusing to become Romanized after all. Thus the scheme of enlisting units of Germans in the army proved a failure and foundered: disliked and despised, they retaliated by hating the people whose glories they had once hoped to share. True, the individual German soldiers in *Roman* units generally remained loyal. But the federate troops, despite good service on occasion, came to be in a condition of almost perpetual turbulence and revolt. In 409 and 422 they acted with treasonable disloyalty. And thereafter they got increasingly out of hand, and presented a perilous hazard.

Instead of a new unity between Romans and Germans, a deadly disharmony prevailed. In modern times, a few generations ago – when racial explanations were fashionable – it was maintained that Rome fell because its ethnic purity suffered pollution. The opposite is rather the case. Despite intermixtures with many peoples over the course of the centuries, the tough character of many Romans had not changed – as their continuing achievements testify. Indeed, the trouble was rather that, psychologically, they had not changed enough: if only they had been able to adapt themselves to getting on with the Germans, the western empire might have been preserved.

What happened instead was painfully displayed by the rise of Gaiseric the Vandal. For he, far from talking of co-existence and partnership within

* For the distinction between western Catholic and eastern orthodox, see pp. 347, 354.

the empire, raised his north African state to an uncompromising, virulently hostile independence, fiercely including both the great Roman landowners and the non-Arian clergy in his attacks. And at the same time King Euric of the Visigoths (466–484/5) was making his people in Gaul and Spain into another wholly independent nation, and once again subjecting the members of the official Church to vigorous oppression. His legal Code (475) rejected any kind of amalgamation between the German and Roman peoples in his kingdom, declaring them utterly separate and distinct from one another. So now segregation was the policy on both sides. The opportunity for a constructive union had been lost, and it was dramatically appropriate that the last emperor of the west was forced to abdicate in the year immediately following the publication of Euric's code.

There were also various other causes of the downfall of the western empire, secondary and peripheral, though not altogether unimportant. One of these was the proliferation of drop-outs who refused to participate in communal and public life. For there were many people who found the social and economic situation intolerable and in consequence went underground and became the enemies of society. And a large number of them became hermits and monks and nuns, who abandoned the company of their fellow human beings and, in the manner of modern Jesus people or followers of gurus, divorced themselves from society, shaking the dust of the imperial system off their feet as completely as if they had never been part of it all.

The monastic movement had its beginnings in Egypt, but it was introduced to the western empire by Athanasius, bishop of Alexandria, who arrived in Rome in about 341, accompanied by two Egyptian monks. Then the popularization of the ascetic ideal in the west was carried farther by St Martin of Tours (c. 330–97), a Danubian who founded monasteries in Gaul. And St Jerome, from Stridon in Dalmatia (c. 348–420), in addition to his immense services to Christian scholarship, wrote an account of the sort of lives led by hermits and monks, based on his own experience as creator of a monastic society at Aquileia in north-east Italy (370–3) and later at Bethlehem in Palestine. Then, early in the following century, John Cassian, founder of a monastery at Massilia (c. 415), wrote works which induced many a nobleman to make the transition from senator to monk. By this time, however, the monastic life often was no longer the end of a career, but led to a bishopric; for monasticism had become respectable, and was on its way to the prestige conferred upon it by St Benedict (c. 480–547). But in its earlier days it had attracted those who wanted to escape from the community; and at all times, for all its steadfast attempts to maintain Christianity's spiritual commitment in face of an insidious society, it deprived the state of greatly needed manpower and revenue.

On a long-term view, what proved particularly disadvantageous was the celibacy the monastic career entailed, since this, by lowering the birth-rate, still further diminished the numbers of potential soldiers. Moreover, this urge to the celibate life, already noticeable during the previous two centuries, extended far outside the circle of monks and nuns; and preachers of the calibre of Augustine and Jerome defended it eloquently as an ideal to be aimed at by ordinary people. But it was an ideal which imposed yet another division upon a society that was profoundly divided already. The government knew this and made warning noises against the men and women who had embraced this profession of withdrawal. However, it took no forcible steps to bring them back.

Against those, on the other hand, who did not adhere to the same religion as themselves – and even to the same branch of the same religion – the authorities practised violent coercion. This was possible because Church and state were bound in a close alliance, established by Constantine the Great. The state was, at first, the controlling partner: as one of Valentinian I's bishops admitted, 'the state is not in the Church, but the Church is in the state'. Nevertheless, the imperial court having moved elsewhere, the bishops of Rome, the Popes, were left free to become great men on their own account. And another bishop, not of Rome but of Mediolanum (Milan), raised the power of the hierarchy to a new peak. This was Ambrose, who occupied the see from 374 until his death in 397. Ambrose presided over a grandiose programme of ecclesiastical building and rediscovery of martyrs; and he had two famous clashes with Theodosius I – from both it was the bishop who emerged victorious. After his death, the ecclesiastical initiative returned from Mediolanum to Rome, whose Popes Innocent I (401-17) and Leo I (440-61) treated with Alaric and Attila respectively; the latter with triumphant success. And in his time, too, mighty Roman churches were under construction.

It was Pope Leo's view that collaboration between state and Catholic Church was a bargain beneficial to both, uniquely capable of binding the disunited Western world together. But not everyone agreed; and in fact the alliance turned out to have the opposite effect. This was because of the excessive, violent zeal with which the civil leaders, acting upon the requests of their spiritual partners, pressed conformity upon the pagans. For by such means they transformed differences of opinion into irremediable hostilities. Valentinian I was very unusual, since he stood against this policy, preferring universal toleration. But shortly after his death there was a great symbolic moment in the war against paganism when his son Gratian expelled the pagan statue of Victory from the Senate-house (382). After his death, there was once again keen debate on the subject; but the Christian view prevailed. And then Theodosius I passed a whole series of laws endeavouring to obliterate paganism altogether. In north Africa, however, religious riots broke out among the pagans because their temples had been closed: but this only spurred the bishops of the region to demand further and even more hostile legislation, in order to 'extirpate the last remnants of idolatry'.

One of the ecclesiastics who took the lead in exerting this pressure on the secular power was Augustine, the outstanding churchman and intellectual and writer of his age. Augustine was born at Thagaste (Soukh Ahras in Algeria) in 354 of a Christian mother, who converted his father. The young man received a careful education in north Africa and became professor of rhetoric at Mediolanum. After passing through a variety of religious convictions, recaptured in his passionately introspective and self-critical *Confessions*, he was ordained a priest at Hippo Regius (Annaba), where he became bishop four years later, in 395. And now he came out in favour of coercing pagans – and back-sliders from Christianity to paganism as well: for Christ, he declared, like a general, must use military methods to recall deserters to his army.

The pagans were being worn down. But an attempt by one of their western sympathizers to seize the throne in 392–4 gave the authorities a serious shock, and then Alaric's capture of Rome in 410 invested paganism with a new lease of life, since the disaster was widely attributed to the empire's Christian régime. That was the argument which Augustine's *City of God* sought to refute: the immediate stimulus of the work was an urgent need to stem this new pagan revival. Thereafter, acts of imperial repression against the supposed peril continued well on into the 440s. These coercive measures did in the end almost succeed in extirpating paganism. Yet at first, during the crucial years of the earlier fifth century, this persecution had intensified the very disunities it was designed to eliminate; and it had thus played its part in the destruction of the western Roman empire.

Equally divisive and destructive were the conflicts within Christianity itself. It had been Constantine's conviction that unity among all Christians was urgently necessary, not only because God and Jesus were indivisible, but because church unity was the best way of uniting the whole empire. Yet disputes within the Church continued to abound, relating to clerical celibacy, the Fall of Man and the nature of the Holy Spirit: and the east, as always, stressed the singleness of the supreme deity, while the west emphasized the divinity of Jesus which the Arians seemed to be decrying. It seemed, therefore, to the historian Ammianus Marcellinus, that 'no wild beasts are such enemies to mankind as are most of the Christians in the deadly hatred they feel for one another.' Valentinian I, it is true, remained as tolerant to 'heretics' within the Christian ranks as to pagans outside them. But his successors displayed a very different attitude, especially Theodosius I, who issued repeated laws and edicts against nonconformist

Christians. And Augustine, brooding on his own earlier spiritual devia-
tions, concluded that Christian heretics as well as pagans must be brought
into the fold by force. He quoted the scriptural text: 'give opportunity to a
wise man and he will become wiser'. But 'opportunity' was only a euphem-
ism for violent suppression: and it was in the same spirit that Pope Leo I
later declared that 'truth, which is simple and one, does not admit of
variety'. Manichaeans and Jews, too, continued to fare much worse under
the Christian emperors than under their pagan predecessors. But persecution, as always, deepened rather than closed the rifts, and made the united
loyalty, which the empire so desperately needed, even more of a will-of-
the-wisp than ever.

Moreover, the psychological attitudes of pagans and Christians alike were
equally unhelpful to the government in its unsuccessful struggle to ensure
national survival. For the pagans, on the whole, relied too complacently
on the glories of the past; and the Christian theologians preached doctrines
that deprecated the importance of serving the State.

To take the pagans first, their ancient educational habits were very far
from dead. Indeed, their purveyance of the classical tradition still held the
field virtually unopposed. For the Christians had no rival educational
theory or practice to offer: even Constantine himself fervently assumed the
patronage of the old system, without showing any desire to broaden its
scope. And so in the great universities of Rome and Mediolanum and
Carthage, and the famous municipal schools of Gaul, the professors adhered
to the classical pattern of the Seven Liberal Arts: or rather, since four of
them were no longer much taught,* they concentrated on the remaining
three, Grammar, Rhetoric and Dialectic. Indeed, throughout the entire
fourth century, there was a significant resurgence of these traditional
subjects; though, as the middle class decayed, the pursuit of such studies
became increasingly limited to the aristocracy, whose cultural and literary
attitudes, as revealed in their refined and cliquish poems and letters, remained
fixed in an almost uniform sterility.

These works display a romantic, nostalgic feeling for eternal Rome – the
'Invicta Roma Aeterna' of coins and medallions. Though no longer the
governmental centre of the world which had taken its name, the ancient
city was now symbolic of that world in a novel and significant manner. This
was denoted by the term 'Romania', which came to signify the whole heritage of Roman culture in the Latin west, in distinction from Gothia,
Francia, Alamannia. Emperors and officers and humbler people alike who
had originated in far distant provinces and had scarcely, if ever, set foot in
the city, were now thinking of themselves as 'Romans' with passionate
emphasis. Less than a decade after the city had fallen to Alaric, the Gallo-

* Arithmetic, Geometry, Astronomy, Music.

Roman poet Rutilius Namatianus still felt able to discern a Rome of higher
reality, which could never falter or fall:

> No man will ever be safe if he forgets you;
> May I praise you still when the sun is dark.
> To count up the glories of Rome is like counting
> The stars in the sky.

Rutilius was a pagan, but contemporary Christians too, felt the impact of
the classical past very strongly. It is true that they also engaged in incessant
debate about the extent to which they should draw upon this pagan heritage. Augustine, for example, in spite of his immense admiration of the
*Aeneid*, contrasted *your* Virgil with *our* Scriptures. Yet he also, like others,
recalled that even the ancient Israelites had been permitted to 'spoil the
Egyptians' and take their women as concubines: and that, therefore, according to the same reasoning, he and his fellow-Christians were entitled to
abstract what they could from the pagan writers.

But the trouble about this deeply ingrained veneration of the past was
that it tempted people to see every contemporary event in terms of *previous*
Roman happenings. In order to ram these comparisons home, the writers
call continually upon a wide range of precedents, taken from the entire
range of their country's glorious history. Thus, when the pagan, classicizing Claudian of Alexandria, the leading poet of the age, wants to write
flatteringly about his own contemporaries, he can never stop comparing
them to the Scipios and Catos and Brutuses. 'If we have any discernment at
all,' advised a learned writer Macrobius, 'we must always revere antiquity.'
And indeed, the very last western emperor of all was named both Romulus
and Augustus.

Yet this propensity for looking backwards, with such singleminded
passion, led directly to catastrophes. When, for instance, the pagan historian
Ammianus writes of the recent defeat of the Romans by the Visigoths at
Hadrianopolis (376), he at once compares the disaster to German invasions
half a millennium earlier: his point is that such tribulations had occurred
before and had been overcome – so that there is no reason why they should
not be overcome once again. And later on, Rutilius Namatianus made
exactly the same point. Yet the analogy was fallacious, since the German
invasions five centuries previously had never offered even the slightest
threat to the empire's actual survival, whereas now the degree of magnitude
had altogether changed: the blow suffered by Valens at Hadrianopolis in
378 indicated a plight far more desperate than had ever existed before. But
the complacent nostalgia of Roman education made it impossible to face
up to such novel situations with any adequate or constructive response.
'Your power is felt wherever the sun's light shines', declared Rutilius about
Rome. But he was wrong, since the Roman west was approaching final

collapse; countermeasures of the most determined kind were urgently required, and attitudes such as his distracted attention from this necessity.

The great Christian theologians, on the other hand, men of superior brains and character who in earlier times would have joined the public service instead of the Church, were often guilty of a different but equally serious disservice to the state: namely, the active discouragement of Christians from working on its behalf, either in a peaceful or a warlike capacity. This attitude, easily justifiable from the New Testament, had been natural enough in the old days when the civil authorities were engaged in persecuting Christianity. But it is remarkable that, even after the empire had become Christian, the leaders of the Church should still persist in their old conviction that Christianity was incompatible with state service. And yet that is what happened: a series of Popes continued to pronounce that to work for the government was perilous to a man's soul, and St Martin of Tours, founder of monasteries in Gaul, asked to be released from the Roman army because he was Christ's soldier and could not fight for his country. When such views took hold of the population, the power of the empire to resist its foes was weakened.

It was sapped further by Augustine. He was not, it is true, a pacifist; indeed he conceded that a literal interpretation of Christ's saying 'turn the other cheek' would ruin the state. But the massive twenty-two books of his *City of God* undermined patriotism by more insidious means. For in this supreme literary masterpiece of the later Roman empire, from which medieval thinkers derived a large proportion of all they knew about the ancient world, he called up all the resources of pagan philosophy and Christian doctrine alike to make a sharp distinction between the earthly city and its counterpart in heaven. Plato and Paul had told of such ideal cities before, but Augustine, writing soon after Alaric's sack of Rome, described the concept with a vividness that was altogether new. And he infused it with a distinct unhopefulness about the future of any and every terrestrial state. He had felt this before, and now it seemed to him more than ever that Christianity was the crop coming just before the icy frosts of winter – frosts which would freeze the nations of the world to death.

True, his 'earthly city', which contains not only the sinners of this world but unrighteous men and women anywhere in the universe, is a wider concept than the Roman empire. All the same, Augustine's pessimism carries gloomy implications for the future of Rome's civilization – or rather, for the *human endeavour* which was needed to maintain it. For his doctrine of Grace, adapted from Saint Paul, maintained that by our own unaided will, without God-given aid, human beings are incapable of achieving anything at all. It was a decisive break with the optimistic, humanistic attitudes of the classical world. And it was deeply resented by men such as

Pelagius, a British or Irish theologian who, in the spirit of Cicero, laid strong counter-emphasis on individual effort. Violent controversies ensued: and the Pelagians were suppressed.

Augustine had cut Rome firmly down to size. Its interests could no longer be held paramount: 'Please pardon us if *our* country, up above, has to cause trouble to *yours* . . . You would acquire still greater merit if you served a higher fatherland.' And, indeed, as he grew older, Augustine came more than ever to reject any identification between Christianity and empire. In terms of world politics, he did not prevail, because the identification had come to stay. But his influence was widespread, and his refusal to believe in a Christian empire was part and parcel of the west's failure to defend itself against its enemies and stave off its own collapse.

# 22

# The Aftermath

WHEN ROME'S RULE CRUMBLED in the west, it left the Visigoths ruling the south-west of Gaul as well as Spain, and the Burgundians in control of south-eastern Gaul, while another group of German communities, the Franks, had established themselves in the north of the country. The Visigoths and Burgundians, however, whose Arian 'heresy' was alien to the local Catholic populations and their bishops, were overcome in 507 by the Franks, whose pagan chief and founder of the Merovingian dynasty, Clovis of Turnacum (Tournai) (c. 482–511), had embraced the Catholic brand of Christianity with 3,000 of his warriors. He was sent the emblems of a Roman consul by the eastern Roman emperor; yet his kingdom was not a dependency of Constantinople, but the independent nucleus of a future nation-state. Clovis and his successors extended this Frankish dominion both to the east and to the south, where Mediterranean Gaul gave them strength and culture.

Later Merovingian monarchs, however, gradually became puppets of their successive Mayors of the Palace, of whom one, Pepin the Short, finally deposed his overlord and founded the Carolingian dynasty (751), named after his father Charles Martel. Then a ruler of that house, Charlemagne (772–814), broke with his family's previous policy of peaceful missionary penetration by undertaking repeated military campaigns and forcible conversions throughout the northern regions of Europe. Permanent inspectors were dispatched to the 300 counties of his realm; and a legislative assembly was summoned twice a year. Finally, Charlemagne declared himself Roman emperor and had himself crowned at Rome by Pope Leo III (800).

In Spain Euric (466–85) and Alaric II (485–507) had fully established the power of the Visigoths; and after the collapse of the Gallic portion of their empire to Clovis this Visigothic kingdom assumed a more national, Spanish character. Nevertheless, there remained a division between the Catholic south of Spain – with its Roman law and Roman, Byzantinized cities such as Hispalis (Seville) – and the new settlers, who were governed from their capital at Toletum (Toledo) and retained their own Arian religion and legal codes. However, the Visigothic régime prospered, especially under Leovigild (586–86) who annexed additional regions of the peninsula and became the first monarch in a former Roman province to strike an independent national coinage of his own. Then his successor Reccared (586–601) turned from his Arian faith to the Church of Rome, thus founding Iberian Catholicism.

But Islamic power, spreading in a gigantic explosion across north Africa after the death of the Prophet Mohammed (632), soon impinged forcibly on Spain. For in 711 the country was invaded by the Mohammedan prince Tarik, whose successors asserted Moslem control throughout the southern part of the peninsula, relegating the Christian Spanish monarchy to its northern regions for centuries to come.

Meanwhile in Italy, after Odoacer had asserted virtual independence of Constantinople, his Ostrogothic successor Theoderic (493–526) brought unaccustomed peace and prosperity to the land. He solicitously retained the Roman civil administration, and Latin literature greatly flourished, producing such writers as Boethius and then Cassiodorus who served as bridges between the culture of the past and the medieval civilization which was dawning. Moreover, although the Ostrogothic régime was not Catholic but Arian, the Roman Church continued to gain in power; and its Pope Gelasius I wrote to the eastern emperor: 'the world is ruled by two things, the sacred authority of the priesthood and the kingly power'.

In north Africa, however, the relations of the independent Arian kingdom of the Vandals both with Catholicism and with Constantinople were subject to violent vicissitudes. But this state did not maintain itself for long, for by the middle of the sixth century, the eastern empire's general Belisarius blotted it out of existence; and then Belisarius and his successor Narses destroyed its Ostrogothic counterpart in Italy as well.

For the eastern empire, named Byzantine after the original name of Constantinople, remained, unlike the western, very much in existence. When the two realms had been finally separated between the offspring of Theodosius I, Arcadius and Honorius, the advisers of the former in the east had with difficulty warded off an Ostrogothic threat. During the long reign of Arcadius' son Theodosius II (408–50) which followed, power at Constantinople was chiefly exercised by his mother Pulcheria. Noting the sack of Rome by Alaric, the eastern government erected new walls round its capital, and the Huns were bought off with increasingly large sums. But Pulcheria's Thracian husband Marcian, when he subsequently became emperor (450–7), refused to pay Attila's subsidy, thus launching him against the west instead. After Marcian's death, a German general gave the

Byzantine throne to another Thracian, Leo I (457–74), who saved his empire from the German soldiery by calling in troops from Asia Minor; and their commander, his son-in-law Zeno, became his successor (474–91).

It was in Zeno's reign that the western empire became extinct. But the eastern empire did not; and it nominally assumed control of the west, though in practice Zeno refrained from interfering. But one of the chief events of his time was a quarrel between the ecclesiastical authorities in Rome and Constantinople, reflecting a dispute which was to rack Christendom for centuries to come and would eventually result in the permanent division between Catholic and Orthodox. On Zeno's death his widow gave the throne to a rich nobleman, Anastasius I (491–518), who shored up a difficult financial situation.

Then Justin I (518–27), in whose time the Slavs appeared as a major threat in the Balkans, became the founder of a new dynasty and elevated his nephew Justinian I to the regency and the throne (527–65). The guiding spirit of one of the most creative epochs in human history, Justinian also built some of the world's greatest buildings; at Constantinople his church of the Holy Wisdom (Santa Sophia), which replaced Constantine's basilica of the same name, still stands, a fitting symbol of the profoundly religious Byzantine ethos. The last emperor to speak Latin better than Greek,

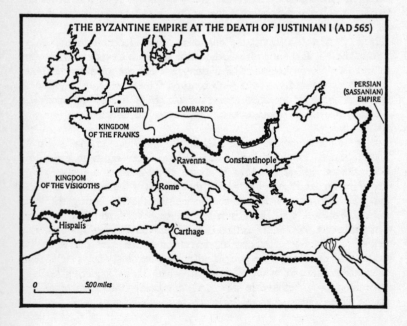

THE BYZANTINE EMPIRE AT THE DEATH OF JUSTINIAN I (AD 565)

Justinian instigated the compilation of a Latin Corpus of Civil Law in which a committee of sixteen men summed up and adapted the whole legal experience of Rome, condensing three million lines of earlier law books into 150,000. The reign had its fair share of troubles, including riots in the capital and one of the severest outbreaks of bubonic plague in recorded history. Yet all the time Justinian's indefatigable administration, controlling and consulting the Church, continued to adjust the imperial system to the tasks of the future, with impersonal and ruthless benevolence. Moreover, he held his own against Persia, soon to fall to the Arabs but now reaching the height of its power. And, as we have seen, Justinian also recovered Italy and north Africa, thanks to the genius of his generals Belisarius and Narses.

These western reconquests proved impossible to maintain. Yet the eastern Roman or Byzantine empire continued to exist for an extraordinary duration of time. For with only a brief interval from 1204 to 1261, when its central region came under the domination of crusaders, it went on existing until its capital fell to the Ottoman Turkish sultan Mohammed II in 1453. Many times throughout its millennial career, it served as the bulwark of western civilization against the east; and throughout almost the entire period Constantinople was by far the largest and most splendid and most learned city in Europe. Although its culture was Greek, and its superb art was a highly original blend of Roman, Greek and oriental elements, the Byzantine emperors saw themselves as the heirs of ancient Rome, and called themselves 'Kings of the Romans'.

But why did this eastern, Byzantine, monarchy outlast its western counterpart by nearly a thousand years? Why did these two halves of the originally united empire experience such totally separate and distinct destinies? For one thing, the western realm was far more vulnerable to external attack owing to its geographical location. It had to guard the long frontiers of the upper and middle Danube and the Rhine, whereas the Byzantine empire only had the lower Danube to cover – thus remaining relatively free to deal with menaces arising from the Asian east. Besides, if the western emperor failed to hold his river barriers, he had no second line of defence to fall back upon, and Italy and Gaul and Spain lay wide open to the invaders: whereas to force the Bosphorus, guarded by the impregnable defences of Constantinople, was beyond the capacity of any hostile power.

Furthermore, the eastern empire possessed a sounder social and economic structure than the west, embodying fewer glaring disunities. It did not, for example, suffer in the same way from enormously wealthy noblemen, who grudged both men and money to the government and the army. Moreover, as did not happen in the west, the middle class, the traditional nucleus of ancient society, survived its vicissitudes throughout many of the dominions of Constantinople in tolerable economic conditions: and by employing this class to man a professional civil service that was more effective than its western counterpart the Byzantine authorities managed to gather in a much higher proportion of the national income than the court of Ravenna was ever able to collect. Besides, in contrast to the position today, the east was both more populous and better cultivated than the west; and its provinces had survived the ravages of the third-century invasions with far greater resilience.

In addition, the internal political stability of the eastern empire was far greater. During a whole century and a half from AD 365, its internal peace was only broken by five usurpers (three of them in the same reign), a remarkable contrast to the proliferation of such rebels in the west. True, Constantinople had its troubles, notably savage ecclesiastical divisions. But it could weather them, owing to its inherently superior situation in other respects. That was why it was the west that fell, or had to assume new political forms, whereas the east was able to survive for another thousand years.

# Epilogue

AS FAR AS OUR sources, multiple but elusive, allow us to find out what happened in the ancient Roman empire, we have seen a rise from nothing to long ages of diverse and splendid efflorescence, and then a massive fall or radical change. It is a story that has extended from the establishment of diminutive Tiber villages to the creation and maintenance of an enormous multi-racial society, followed by its fragmentation into units foreshadowing the nations of the modern world.

With modifications, much of Rome continued to live on within these successor states – language, government, law, Church, literature, art and habits of thinking and living. And of these persistent Roman elements western civilization has remained very conscious ever since, recalling and cherishing them in one revival and renaissance after another. Yet in politics, as in art, the repetitions have never been exact, since the backgrounds can never be repeated: and that again is why, although the Roman experience unmistakably still carries lessons and warnings for today, their exact form and significance is sometimes problematical.

One thing that is clear is that we do not always want to relive the experience of the Romans: although sometimes what they did is entirely to be admired and envied, in other respects they were detestable. For most of what they achieved was based upon the use of force; the culture which has given us their unequalled masterpieces was created and maintained, in the last resort, by violent means which modern societies could not, or should not, tolerate today. So that we are still left with the unanswered question how the acute ethnic problems that still bedevil the equally large, or larger, political units of our own day can be solved without the use of such unacceptable methods. Here we should look at the second stage of the Roman process, for its forcible stages were habitually followed by phases of political settlement at which this people and its rulers displayed a sagacity to which no study of our own times, or for that matter any other times either, reveals an effective parallel. That is to say, after conquering or absorbing a territory, the Romans generally then proceeded to administer it, if not with a great deal of social justice as the term is understood today, at least in a remarkably pacific fashion which conferred a degree of prosperity that such countries had never known before.

Another aspect of society in which the Roman experience raises thought-provoking questions – even if, once again, it does not always supply the answers – concerns the relationships between the individual and the community. In the heroic days of the Roman Republic, community spirit was enormous, and its whole tradition prevented the rise of any individuals to extraordinary importance; it was not entirely eccentric of Cato the elder, when he was writing military history, to prefer to omit the names of Roman generals altogether. In the last days of the Republic things were changing, as the rise of an admirable portrait sculpture clearly hinted. Under the imperial régime that followed, the opposite extreme to the Republic was reached, as personality-cult ran riot, focused on the larger-than-life figures of the rulers themselves.

The modern historian demurs here, protesting that although this glaring spotlight was evidently directed upon the emperors, they did not, as individuals, exert all the influence ancient writers supposed upon the historical process, which went its own way regardless of them under the influence of ineluctable social and economic factors. And there is certainly some measure of truth in that, since Suetonius' highly personal *Twelve Caesars* alone would give us a ludicrously inadequate picture of what was going on. But, equally, we must not exaggerate our reaction in the other direction, as we are inclined to do under the pressure of modern sociological thinking, not to speak of our distaste for the dictators we have seen in our own time. Indeed, it is these modern dictators themselves who warn us that it would be a mistake to react too forcibly against Suetonius and the others. For, granted that Stalin, for example, in a sense reflected the current trends and tendencies around him, it would clearly be wrong to argue that those tendencies would have impelled world history along precisely the same course if he had never existed. Roman history offers the same warning, in no uncertain terms. Without, for example, the very peculiar personalities and individual gifts of Augustus and Constantine, it would not have gone the same way at all.

The story of Rome, that is to say, shows that individuals do count. And that does not only apply at the most exalted level either. The historian Tacitus, bemoaning the imperial autocracy, admits freely that it left room for superb courage and achievement among ordinary citizens. And Roman poetry, in spite of all the powerful ties that bound its writers to their state and society, emerges as something far more private and personal than the community-minded poetry of classical Greece.

Even though Roman history needs no updating to make it valuable and exciting, all the same, in our own late 1970s, it is perhaps this aspect of it which most forcibly strikes the mind in the end. We in western Europe, and America as well, are living in times when official assessments of the desirable and practicable extent of individual freedom are sometimes being reduced and eroded with unprecedented speed and thoroughness. How do the Romans stand on this? Now it is true that, although their unique legal capacity contributed greatly to the democracies of the future, they scarcely even began to achieve what is regarded as democracy today, in any of the current interpretations of the term; and indeed, the lower and by far the greater part of the social pyramid comprised a vast, inarticulate majority, living scarcely above the level of bare survival, as they had lived in all other societies as well, ever since the beginning of time. If we are disposed to make moral judgements, and the historian should not always refuse to, we may regret that this was a barrier the Romans did not break. Nor, of course, did any other nation until the modern age, and only partially then.

But, having duly taken note of that, let us consider what they *did* accomplish. What their whole immense story shows us is not only what a tightly knit community can achieve by mutual co-operation, but also the possibilities of self-expression for individuals within that community. For even if the large, suppressed majority still failed to benefit, Rome did achieve an unprecedentedly massive measure of personal self-realization and achievement at least among all the other and formative elements in its society: politicians, writers, artists, thinkers, architects, engineers, lawyers, and men of affairs. And it is that tradition which wins our respectful admiration and causes us to be proud that we are among its inheritors.

# NOTES

PART I  ETRUSCAN ROME

*Chapter 1 Rome and Etruria*

ITALY: the name is probably a Hellenized form of the Italian *Viteliu* (calf land), a name originally restricted to the southern half of the peninsula's toe. SALT ROUTE: extended inland by Via Salaria (from *sal*, salt) from Rome to Reate (Rieti) in the Sabine country. HILLS OF ROME: originally raised by action of Ciminian and Alban volcanoes. MIDDLE AND LATE BRONZE AGE: used to be named after Terramara (*terra marna*, rich black soil) settlements south of the Po. LATIUM: the name 'Latini' was first applied to a tribal group on the Tiber north of Rome. CATTLE MARKET OF ROME: Forum Boarium. INDO-EUROPEAN speech in Italy; probably originated from common source in Danube area. IRON AGE: includes 'Villanovans' named after a small town near Bologna. INHUMERS of Latium formed part of widespread Italian Fossa Culture, which reached its climax in the 7th century BC. PALATINE (*Roma quadrata*, square Rome): two archaic cisterns and rock-cut postholes, cf. remains on Alban Hills. ROME'S ORIGINS: it was believed that, after the sack of Troy in the Trojan War (*c.* 1100 BC), one of the Trojan leaders, Aeneas, had made his way to Italy where he founded Lavinium and his son Ascanius (Iulus) founded Alba Longa, of which Rome was a much later offshoot. Probably the Etruscans devised the Aeneas link between the Trojan saga and their own Asian origins. FOUNDATION OF ROME: 814 BC (Timaeus), 753 (Varro), 751 (Cato the elder), 748–7 (Fabius Pictor), 729 (Cincius Alimentus). ETRUSCANS' ORIGINS: Herodotus placed their coming more than three centuries too early, perhaps telescoping early Iron Age and Etruscan immigrants. The suddenness of the finest orient-alizing tombs from *c.* 700 suggests a new historical situation. (At least some in-fluences crossed the Apennines from the north, notably to Vetulonia.) ETRUSCAN LINK WITH CARTHAGE: two gold plates from Pyrgi (Santa Severa) inscribed in Etruscan (*c.* 500) are matched by one in Phoenician (Carthaginian?). GREEK AND SOUTH ITALIAN LINKS: Not only Ionians at Graviscae, but pottery from Cumae (mid-6th century) at Tarquinii, Caere. METALS: from *c.* 400 much iron smelted at Populonia opposite Ilva (Elba); Volaterrae (Volterra) was the capital of a metal-rich zone. VOLTUMNA shrine: possibly at Montefiascone.

SEPTIMONTIUM: Palatium, Velia, Fagutal, Germalus, Caelius, Oppius, Cispius, the last two being spurs of the Esquiline; eight including the low-lying Subura, between Esquiline and Viminal. POMOERIUM: boundary; also understood to mean the strips inside and outside the wall. The Capitoline Hill was not inside the *pomoerium*. ETRUSCAN TRADE WITH ROME: 7th-century *graffiti* from Forum Boarium (Cattle market) reflect this. By 650 Rome had close relations with Etruscanized Falerii (Civita Castellana), another frontier town 28 miles north, centre of a diversified group of Faliscan towns.

*Chapter 2 The Etruscan Monarchy*

GREEKS IN CAMPANIA: first on island of Pithecusa (Latin Aenaria, now Ischia; Euboeans, *c.* 775) then Cumae (*c.* 750), Neapolis and Dicaearchia (Latin Puteoli, now Pozzuoli). ETRUSCAN-CAMPANIAN LEAGUE of twelve cities led by Capua: perhaps legendary. ETRUSCANS IN LATIUM: not conquered until after Campania, because it was so swampy? Tarquinii inscription (*elogium*) boasts of conquest of nine Latian cities; Tusculum means 'Etruscan city', and Praeneste (Palestrina) tombs show a dominant Etruscan class fifty years before the Tarquins at Rome. CUNICULI: rainwater had to be enticed into them with great speed because the surface loam was very precious and had to be saved. PATERFAMILIAS: any male citizen who had no living ancestor in the male line. ANTHROPOMORPHISM: Varro said that making statues in Greek fashion undermined people's fear of the gods. LEGENDARY KING-LIST: Romulus, Numa Pompilius, Tullus Hostilius, Ancus Marcius, Tarquinius Priscus, Servius Tullius, Tarquinius Superbus. 'REX': also inscribed on cup now found near the Regia, which *may* be *c.* 530-510 BC. Words related to *rex* are found in other Indo-European languages as well. THREE EARLIEST TRIBES: Tities, Ramnes, Luceres. SENATE: the meaning of *patres conscripti* is disputed. According to tradition, there had been, in earlier days still, a Senate of only 100 members. POLITORIUM: 117 tombs now found; including Etruscan remains. LATIN LANGUAGE: craftsman's inscription on gold *fibula* from Praeneste (Palestrina), late 7th century; *cippus* from Roman Forum (Black Stone), late 6th century. TARQUINS: the diviner (*haruspex*) Tarquitius Priscus is mentioned on an inscription (*elogium*) of Tarquinii. Five other Etruscan cities, including Clusium (Chiusi), were believed to have fought against Tarquinius Priscus, as allies of the Latins. 'Tarpeian' cliff on Capitoline Hill='Tarquinian'. Iron model of axes and *fasces* of *c.* 600 BC found at Vetulonia. Etruscan pottery of *c.* 530-520 BC at Rome (S. Omobono) comes from Vulci. CALENDAR of Numa: probably of time of Tarquins. The names Aprilis (April) and Idus (day of month) are Etruscan. SERVIAN TRIBES: the urban tribes (and Four Regions) are: Suburana (Sucusana), Esquilina, Collina, Palatina. The Capitoline Hill was not included in the Four Regions. COMITIA CENTURIATA: its establishment is sometimes attributed to after 450 or *c.* 366 BC. SERVIAN INFANTRY CLASSES: first three infantry of line, last two light-armed. Then came five classes of unarmed. EARLY HOPLITE SHIELD: Fabriano (near Gubbio). SENATE of 300: based on 3 tribes and 30 *curiae*. ALBA LONGA from 10th century BC controlled line of future Via Appia. Its existence may not antedate Rome's, but its importance does. Its destruction (doubted by some) was attributed to King Tullus Hostilius. Its leading families in Rome; Julii, Tullii. OSTIA AND PONS SUBLICIUS (from *sublicae*, piles):

legendary attributions to King Ancus Marcius. DIANA: like Artemis was identified with the moon. MASSILIA: founded from Ionian Phocaea (Foca). GREEK INFLUENCE in Latium: shown by some of the early bronze statuettes now discovered at Gabii (Castiglione: see below). GREEK ALTAR OF HERCULES (*Ara Maxima*) presided over commerce: imports in 6th century were paid for by Rome in salt, timber and slaves. CAPITOLINE TEMPLE: Statue of Jupiter (Tinia in Etruscan): made by Vulca of Veii. Platform of *cappellaccio* without mortar. The temple had flanking colonnades unlike the 'normal' Etruscan temple described by Vitruvius. Jupiter, Juno and Minerva (identified with the Greek Zeus, Hera and Athena) had already been grouped on the Capitolium Vetus on the Quirinal (whose god Quirinus was identified with Romulus). EXPANSION OF TARQUINIUS SUPERBUS: Gabii guarded the eastern flank of Latium against the Sabines: treaty celebrated on coin of Augustus. Antium (Anzio), Ardea and probably Lavinium seem to have accepted Roman military leadership (temporarily). Garrisons (of allies?) at Pometia (Pomezia), Circeii (S. Felice Circeo), Signia (Segni). DOWNFALL OF SUPERBUS: ascribed to love-affair (with woman), Athenian Hippias (510 BC) (with boy). ARICIA: became leader of the league of Ferentina. DESTRUCTION OF ETRUSCAN TOWN: late 6th century S. Giovenale, near Viterbo. PORSENNA: perhaps an Etruscan title (purthna). CLUSIUM: was at the southern end of the Val di Chiana. (A modern theory identified Porsenna's city instead with Marsigliana d'Albegna or Orbetello, on the coast.) ETRUSCAN RAIDER-SETTLERS IN ROME: Mastarna (from *magister*, general ?) and Caeles Vibenna. CUMAE BATTLE: the Syracusan victor was Hiero I. MARZABOTTO: on flood plain of River Renus (Reno); grid-iron street plan. ADRIA: gave its name to Adriatic Sea. SPINA: built on piles amid a network of canals. ETRUSCAN WRITING IN EUROPE: Scandinavian runes in the Middle Ages were still based on Etruscan letters.


## PART II THE UNITY OF ITALY AND ROME

### Chapter 3 The Unification of Italy

LATINS: by 500 the original 50 or more communities were reduced to 10 or 12. LAVINIUM: at least 13 altars of *c.* 500 BC and large statues, archaic Latin inscription to Castor and Pollux. Lavinium first developed parallel to the Alban communities, then rose as they declined. TUSCULUM: its leader Octavius Mamilius was believed to have been Tarquinius Superbus' son-in-law. CASSIAN TREATY: 493 BC (Latins); made by Spurius Cassius Vecellinus. ARDEA: home of legendary Italian (Rutulian) leader Turnus in Virgil's *Aeneid*. Perhaps Ardea, like Lavinium, had for a time been in Roman hands at an earlier date. OSCAN: alphabet derived through Etruscan alphabet from Chalcidic (Euboean) Greek. VOLSCI: originated in upper Liris (Garigliano) valley west of Fucine lake and moved across Lepini mountains towards Rome. They were the tribe of the legendary heroine Camilla in Virgil's *Aeneid*. ANTIUM: captured 338, the beaks of its ships were the first war prizes to embellish Rome, placed on the speaker's platform (*rostra* = beaks) in the Forum by Gaius Maenius. ALGIDUS: just beyond Grottaferrata. LATIN COLONIES: the earliest were Cora (Cori, dated to 501),

Signia (Segni, 495), Velitrae (Velletri, *c.* 494), Norba 492. There were about fourteen of these *priscae Latinae coloniae* by 338. The term *colonus*, from *colere* to cultivate, reveals an agricultural motive. SABINES: had probably begun to descend the Tiber valley in 8th century. Their towns included Reate (Rieti), Cures (near Via Salaria), Amiternum (S. Vittorino). FETIALES: presided over international relations; no war was acceptable to the gods unless in defence of Rome or its allies. ETRUSCANS in 5th-century Rome: there are Etruscan names of consuls in Fasti 509-490 and 461-448; in 492 grain had been imported from Etruria. Archaeological evidence shows waning of Etruscan contacts *c.* 475-450 BC. FIDENAE: the tradition of a very early (regal) Latin colony here is uncertain. VEII: Rome had arranged for a flag to be flown on the Janiculum hill in case of attack. Veii had a tunnel piercing a ridge leading to the Tiber valley 17 miles north of Rome, also another short cut to the river halfway to Ostia. FABII: continuous consulships *c.* 485-479/7 BC, then ten-year gap. They shared their leading position with the family of the Licinii. CREMERA BATTLE: legendary details suspiciously similar to those of the battle of Thermopylae between the Greeks and Persians (480 BC). CENSORS' period of office ended in *lustrum* (cleansing). Censors were appointed at intervals of five years from 209 BC onwards. They took over the selection of senators from the consuls. CAMILLUS: reputedly dictator five times, military tribune with consular power five times, four Triumphs. JUNO REGINA: this transfer of a deity is *evocatio*. EXPANSION AFTER VEII: Capena and Falerii annexed; four new rustic Roman tribes. CELTS: La Tène style (from Swiss type-site) succeeds Hallstatt *c.* 500 BC. The La Tène Celts invented horse-drawn carts. GAULS: sack of Rome mentioned by Theopompus (*c.* 350) and Aristotle. Further raids in 360s, 350s and 340s, which caused the Italian peoples to turn to Rome. Subsequently the Gauls of North Italy became skilful agriculturalists. CAERE: ports: Pyrgi (Santa Severa), Alsium (Palo), Punicum (Santa Marinella). Raided by Dionysius I of Syracuse *c.* 384. HOSTILITY TO VEII: Greek imports to Caere had increased from *c.* 630, and those to Veii had decreased, perhaps because of Roman territorial gains from the latter. HOSPITIUM with Caere: *c.* 386(300?). Rome joined Caere in sending 500 colonists to Sardinia and Corsica (*c.* 386 or 378/7). WALL OF SERVIUS (4th century): of Grotta Oscura tufa. CIRCUS MAXIMUS: believed to have dated from regal times. LATIN COLONIES after Gallic invasion: Nepet (Nepi) and Sutrium (Sutri) *c.* 383-382, formerly dependencies of Falerii. TUSCULUM: its consuls at Rome: Mamilii, Fulvii, Fonteii, Juventii, Porcii. PRAENESTE: the Via Praenestina led to Rome; it was an Etruscanized Latian town like Satricum (Conca), Lanuvium (Lanuvio), Velitrae (Velletri). FORTUNA: the 'bringer' (from *ferre*), later identified with the Greek Tyche (Chance). CAPUA: its bronze work was praised by Cato the censor in 2nd century BC. TIBUR: on River Anio (Aniene); dominated Via Valeria. SAMNITES: belonged to Sabellian group of peoples; they were believed to have originated from Sabine Amiternum (S. Vittorino). CIVITAS SINE SUFFRAGIO: private rights included the right to exchange citizenship on moving from the one city to the other (*ius migrandi* or *mutandae civitatis*), limited in 3rd century BC (to prevent too much immigration to Rome) and abolished in 2nd century (cf. *ius exsilii*). Latin colonies privileged in 338: Ardea, Circeii, Nepet, Norba, Setia, Signia, Sutrium – half of the *priscae Latinae coloniae*. SABINES: after revolt of 290, some were enslaved, and the rest given *civitas sine suffragio*. CALES: Roman citizen settlers were not a loss to Rome's military manpower because they had mostly been beneath the property qualification – and besides they could now serve in the Cales quota. Cales was one of a small number of Latin colonies allowed in the 3rd century to coin silver. The others were Suessa Aurunca (Sessa), Paestum (formerly Posidonia), Signia and Alba Fucens (Albe). LATIN COLONIES: Cosa: polygonal walls, with corbelled gateway, such as also survive at Signia. OSTIA: Town wall of Fidenae tufa. TARRACINA: Volscian Anxur. SAMNITE TRIBES: Caraceni, Pentri, Caudini, Hirpini. NEAPOLIS: issued coins on behalf of Rome in the later 4th century, inscribed 'of the Romans' in Greek. VIA APPIA: by 244 BC extended to Brundusium. By the end of the 3rd century, seven major roads led to and from Rome. THIRD SAMNITE WAR: the Lucanians had appealed to Rome. The Samnites won a victory near Luceria (Lucera) (294), and the Romans near Aquilonia (Lacedogna) (293). MANIPLE: *manipulus*, handful, from a bundle of straw tied to a pole to act as a flag. Each maniple contained two centuries of 80 men, each divided into ten mess units sharing a tent and a mule. GLADIATORS: first called 'Samnites'; later they also included Thracians and Gauls. TREATIES AFTER SAMNITE WARS: also with seven Etruscan cities, to make them part of defence system against the Gauls (280). Sometimes, too, in the later 3rd century, the Romans made truces of varying duration with Etruscan cities, instead of permanent treaties. Alliances were extended to Umbria, Picenum, the Marsi and N. Apulia. 50,000 SQUARE MILES controlled by Rome: included 10,000 square miles of Roman and 5,000 of Latin territory. The system included partial, though not necessarily always conscious, borrowings from Sparta, the Panhellenic league, Thessaly, Aetolia, Achaea and the Athenian empire. COINAGE: *aes grave*, true coins of defined face value, developed from *aes signatum* of central Italy (of later 4th century, consisting of flat bars of varying size with a design on one side). This in turn had evolved from shapeless unstamped *aes rude*, valued purely by weight, which had partially replaced cattle as a medium of exchange in the 5th century BC.

*Chapter 4 The Class Struggle*

CONSULS: perhaps at first for a time there was only one, possibly known as the *praetor maximus*. DICTATORS: may have developed from *praetor maximus*: nominated by a consul on the Senate's proposal with subsequent ratifying law. Only a few of the recorded early dictatorships seem to be genuine. LEGISLATION: remarkable in that it could be initiated by all three branches (magistrates, Senate and Assemblies). PATRONS: evidence of patron or client could not be enforced against the other. PLEBEIANS: allegedly plebeian consuls *c.* 502–500 BC may not have been plebeians at all but patricians. PATRICIANS: out of 53 5th-century *gentes* only 29 still appear in 4th century: by 300 BC they formed less than one-twentieth of the population. AGITATIONS FOR LAND: go back to *c.* 486 BC. Livy records seven between 441 and 410. Until the Apennines were conquered, there was a lack of summer pastures. CERES: temple probably on site of S. Maria Cosmedin. The cult was looked after by two plebeian aediles, assistants of the tribunes of the people (two patrician curule aedileships were created in 367 BC). TYRANTS: allegedly tried to seize power at Rome in 478, 431, 376 BC.

GREEK TRADE: Athenian commerce with Rome fell off sharply 450–400. APOLLO: temple of *c.* 431 in Flaminian Fields, on site of previous shrine (Apollinar). EPIDEMICS: anthrax? FOOD: five shortages of grain reported 508–411 BC. In about 4th century coarse emmer wheat was partly superseded by more highly evolved bread wheat; and vine and olive growing had been learnt from the Greeks – though the need for heavy initial outlays slowed down development. DEBT: cf. problems of 4th-century Greece. SECESSIONS: allegedly 494, 449, 448, 342, 287 BC. Menenius Agrippa reputedly appeased the plebeians in 494. OATH of plebeians: *lex sacrata*, hence probably erroneous tradition of secession to Mons Sacer (just beyond River Anio). TRIBUNI PLEBIS: originally 2, or 4, or 5: 10 by 449 BC. CONCILIUM PLEBIS: generally known as *comitia plebis tributa* after *c.* 287. The *comitia populi tributa* was founded in imitation of this (it elected quaestors, curule aediles, etc.). PLEBISCITA: in *c.* 449 BC (?) all such future measures that received the prior sanction of the patrician senators (*patrum auctoritas*) were recognized as universally binding. Unconditional validity from 339 (?) and/or 287. DECEMVIRI: names of first team (except one) seem authentic, but not second team (including some plebeians). TWELVE TABLES: traditionally ten published by the first team of decemvirs, plus two 'unjust' ones by the second. A formal procedure of appeal (*provocatio*) carrying no guarantee of admission may have existed by the time of the Tables. LAWS OF 449: Leges Valeriae Horatiae. MEASURE OF 447: the two quaestors (junior financial officials), previously appointed by the consuls, were to be elected by the *Concilium Plebis*. Two were added in 421 when plebeians admitted. It is often uncertain whether measures reported in the tradition were conceded by the patricians as having force of law or merely asserted by the plebeians as a right. RESTORATION OF CONSULSHIP: Leges Liciniae Sextiae. One of the tribunes, Lucius Sextius Lateranus, may have become the first plebeian consul in 366. These two tribunes supposedly limited land ownership to 300 acres (500 *iugera*), but this tradition may be a false reflection of later political disputes. CENSORS: Lex Publilia of 339 BC laid it down that one must be a plebeian. It was not until 131 that two plebeian censors were appointed. NOBLES: also included those descended from a *tribunus militum consulari potestate*. DEBT MEASURES: allegedly 351, 352, 342, 326 (?). The Lex Genucia (342) had tried to veto usury, at least temporarily. CONCORD: Camillus' temple was at the foot of the Capitol, near the Forum. LEX POETELIA: 326 or possibly 313 BC. It also permitted mortgage on land. AQUA APPIA: followed by Anio Vetus (272) from Sabine hills, tunnelled with short bridges and an inverted siphon. NEW NOBILITY: its hegemony was upheld by the Fabii Maximi who controlled the Senate in the early 3rd century BC.

## PART III  ROME AGAINST CARTHAGE

*Chapter 5 First Wars Against Foreign Powers*

TARENTUM: at its zenith under the philosopher–scientist Archytas, early 4th century. Its attempt to mediate in the Second Samnite War (*c.* 314 BC) had been rebuffed by Rome. VENUSIA: on upper Aufidus (R. Ofanto), probably 6,000 settlers. Latin colony at Hadria or Hatria (Atri) at the same time, and Roman colony at Sena Gallica (Senigallia) a few years later. THURII: former Sybaris. GREEK HELPERS OF TARENTUM in later 4th century: Archidamus II of Sparta, Alexander I of Epirus, Cleonymus of Sparta. PYRRHUS: capital at Ambracia (Arta); completed Hellenization of Epirus. His army included 3,000 Thessalian cavalry, 2,000 archers. HERACLEA: detached from Tarentum by Rome by favourable treaty (*c.* 278). AUSCULUM: Pyrrhus was threatening the Latin colonies of Venusia and Luceria. BENEVENTUM: called Malventum until made a Latin colony in 268, at same time as Ariminum (Rimini): they were the two farthest colonies from Rome yet to be founded. Beneventum split Samnium in half. EGYPT: Roman treaty with Ptolemy II in 273; Rome had made an agreement with Rhodes in *c.* 306. SILVER COINAGE: didrachms inscribed ROMANO., issued at south Italian mint after 280. Coins of *c.* 269 issued at Rome had type of wolf and twins. CARTHAGE: 4th-century population 400,000–500,000, compared to 100,000–150,000 at Rome, 200,000 at Tarentum. CARTHAGINIAN SICILY: Panormus founded early 7th century; principal port Motya near Lilybaeum (Marsala). CARTHAGINIAN SARDINIA: recent discoveries (e.g. Monte Sirai) show importance *c.* 600. Chief port Nora was much older. CORSICA: Greeks defeated off Alalia (Aleria) *c.* 535 BC. Corsica went to the Etruscans and later to the Carthaginians. CAERE: Carthaginian presence at its ports Pyrgi and Punicum. TUNISIA: fertile valley of River Medjerda (Bagradas), beside which was second city Utica (Henchir bou Chateur), traditionally older. WEST AFRICA: e.g. explorations of Hanno before 480 BC. AGRICULTURAL STUDIES: 32-book work of Mago, translated by order of Roman Senate in later 2nd century BC. CARTHAGINIANS AT ROME: perhaps the Altar of Hercules (*Ara Maxima*) beside the Tiber was founded with a view not only to Greek but to Carthaginian associations (Hercules being identified with the Semitic deity Melkart). TREATIES WITH ROME: according to one theory the first treaty was with the Etruscans not the Romans. MESSANA: dominated since 288 BC by Mamertini ('men of Mars'), Campanian mercenaries of Syracusan Agathocles. ROMAN FLEETS: by 311 a flotilla; 267 four *quaestores Italici* (at Ostia, etc.) responsible for it. FIRST PUNIC WAR: in 262 Rome took Segesta and Agrigentum (Agrigento); their capture was a turning point. QUINQUEREMES: better than obsolete triremes in which, although there were less rowers, every one of them had to be a skilled oarsman. Two Carthaginian warships have now been found under the sea off Lilybaeum (Marsala), including one that apparently dates from the First Punic War. REGULUS: according to legend, rather than urge the Roman Senate to make peace, he went back voluntarily to be tortured and killed by Carthaginians. LAST PHASE: Carthaginian successes by young Hamilcar Barca (248–242), badly supplied from home. PROW: on bronze *as*, from *c.* 240–235 BC. PEACE TREATY: veto on Carthaginian presence in Italian waters was for benefit of Greek cities in South Italy. SICILIAN PROVINCE: quaestors set up at Syracuse and Lilybaeum (Marsala). INDIRECT TAXES: levied by the cities especially on imports and exports. They also derived income from monopolies. WAR OF THE MERCENARIES (Truceless War): started at Sicca Veneria (El Kef). Liby-phoenicians and Numidians joined; promises had been broken by Hanno the Great and landlords.

*Chapter 6 The Changing Roman World*

GLADIATORS: in 358 BC, 307 Roman prisoners had been slaughtered as human sacrifices at Tarquinii (Tarquinia). Capua (S. Maria Capua Vetere) and Puteoli (Pozzuoli, the former Dicaearchia) in Campania had the largest amphitheatres known until the Colosseum. GREEK WORKS OF ART: first seen in triumph of Lucius Papirius Cursor, captor of Tarentum in 272. Manius Valerius Messalla showed paintings of his Sicilian victories in 264. LIVIUS ANDRONICUS: when freed, he took on his former owner's name, as was the custom. Ulysses (Odysseus) had long been regarded as an Italic hero. Livius may have become Rome's first schoolmaster. *Ludi Scaenici* were now added to *Ludi Romani* (240) (religious *Ludi Tarentini*, later known as *Ludi Saeculares*, were believed to have been introduced in 348 or 249?); they purified the city at intervals of time (often the passage of a century), by propitiatory ceremonies to the underworld deities. LAW: the founder of Roman juristic literature was Sextus Aelius Paetus Catus (consul 198 BC). IUS GENTIUM: probably provincial governors played a part in its formulation as well. PLEBEIAN COUNCIL *(concilium plebis, comitia plebis tributa)*: based on 35 tribes by 241 BC. GAULS: *ager Gallicus* annexed in *c.* 283, after Roman defeat at Arretium (Arezzo) in 284. Invasion by Boii, Lingones, Insubres, Taurini, Gaesati in 225.

*Chapter 7 The Invasion by Hannibal*

HAMILCAR BARCA had seized hilltop Ercte or Heirkte behind Panormus (Palermo) (M. Pellegrino or M. Castellaccio) as base for raids in First Punic War, and had joined with his political enemy Hanno the Great in terminating the War of the Mercenaries (Truceless War). Drowned in River Helice in Spain. CARTHAGO NOVA: originally Mastia. SAGUNTUM: 16 miles north of Valentia (Valencia). Aemilii and Scipios led Roman war party. MASSILIA: perhaps Roman ally since 386; also an ally of Saguntum. EBRO TREATY: Romans were prepared to agree because of Gallic threat at home. ROMAN MANPOWER 218 BC: perhaps out of a total population of Italy of 3 million, with 2 million slaves (?) (plus population of 1,400,000 in Cisalpine Gaul), there were 270,000–300,000 adult Roman and 640,000 allied males. ALPS: crossed by Hannibal somewhere between Little S. Bernard and M. Genèvre passes (probably a pass of M. Cenis or M. Genèvre group). All his 37 elephants seem to have survived the crossing, although they then did not last long. PLACENTIA: just east of the point where River Trebbia, flowing down from Apennines, joins the Po. 217 BC: 11 legions were put into the field, including 4 to block road to Rome. Hannibal penetrated through Collina Pass, and then on between Pistoria (Pistoia) and Faesulae (Fiesole). FABIUS MAXIMUS: first dictatorship in 221. In 217 he was duped into letting Hannibal move from Campania to Apulia. CANNAE: near south bank of Aufidus (River Ofanto). Hannibal had forced battle by seizing valuable depot of stores and chose open plain to show the Romans they had nothing to fear from reserves. He allowed his convex crescent (or *échelon*) to become concave under the pressure of the Roman centre. The consuls were Lucius Aemilius Paullus and Gaius Terentius Varro. 215 BC: 25 legions raised. CAPUA: the rebellious city, together with its dependencies Atella (Aversa) and Calatia (S. Giacomo alle Gallazze), issued coins of its own, inscribed in the Italic Oscan language. The rebellion gave Hannibal sorely needed men, weapons, supplies, and base; its suppression enabled Rome to reinforce Spain. SYRACUSE: betrayed by Spanish officer to Marcus Claudius Marcellus, the 'Sword of Rome', despite the engineering skill of Archimedes. TARENTUM: taken by Hannibal by treachery (citadel remaining in Roman hands), plundered by Romans on recapture. THE TWO CORNELIUS SCIPIOS (father and uncle of Africanus): Publius failed to stop Hannibal's departure for Spain, then was defeated at Ticinus and Trebia, and returned to Spain 217; and Cnaeus, sent to Spain 218, where he won a naval victory off the Ebro in 217. The brothers defeated Hasdrubal Barca near Ibera (Ebro) in 215, but in 211 Publius was killed on the upper Baetis (Guadalquivir) and Cnaeus at Ilorci (Lorqui) behind Carthago Nova. PUBLIUS SCIPIO JUNIOR (Publius' son, later Africanus): the first private citizen to be invested with proconsular *imperium*. ILIPA (206): Hasdrubal (son of Gisgo) and Mago (brother of Hannibal) were the defeated Carthaginian commanders. TAX ON SPAIN: mints for silver coinage opened at Osca (Huesca), etc. SPANISH AUXILIA: cavalry and slingers from Baleares (Balearic islands). ITALICA: Baetis navigable by sea-going vessels for 140 miles up to there, then by smaller boats up to Corduba (Cordova) plain. REBELLIOUS LATIN COLONIES: included Ardea, Cales, Alba Fucens: they were punished by a double draft in 204. The farms of Italy were so exhausted that wheat had to be imported from Egypt (208–207). METAURUS: preceded by forced march (240 miles in 6 days) of Gaius Claudius Nero. SCIPIO IN AFRICA: first victory at Great Plains (Campi Magni, near Souk el Kremis, on upper Medjerda [Bagradas]). ZAMA (REGIA): battle probably in plain of Draa-el-Metnan (S.W. of Sicca Veneria). HANNIBAL AND THE HOME FRONT: his victories had at first silenced the Carthaginian oligarchy, but after Rome's recovery of Capua his political opponents became much stronger. Lines of maniple operating independently: Baecula, Ilipa, Campi Magni. PORTRAITURE: Etruscan portraits at Clusium and Caere. From 3rd century, Hellenistic Greek portraits also gradually exerted an influence.

## PART IV  THE IMPERIAL REPUBLIC

### Chapter 8 'Our Sea'

ALEXANDER THE GREAT: son of Philip II (359–336 BC). The principal states of Alexander's Hellenistic successors were named after their monarchs Antigonus I, Seleucus I Nicator, and Ptolemy I Soter (Lagid house). ILLYRIANS: took Scodra (Skhöder) and Lissus (Leš, *c.* 260), Corcyra (Corfu, 229). ROMAN PROTECTORATE: Apollonia (ancient, rich and strategic port in Bay of Valona), and Dyrrhachium (Durazzo, Durrës: formerly Epidamnus, 229). The Romans relieved Apollonia in 214. MACEDONIA: had united almost all Greece by alliance with Achaean League and conquest of Sparta (222). PEACE WITH PHILIP V (205): Peace of Phoenice. AETOLIAN LEAGUE: protectorate over Delphi in 3rd century. They made peace with Philip V in 206 because Rome had not helped them sufficiently. ANTIOCHUS III: acquired Armenia and regained Parthia and Bactria as vassal kingdoms, crossed Persian Gulf, and entered Kabul valley

(212–206). RHODES AND PERGAMUM: defeated Philip V by sea off Chios (201).
FORTRESSES OF PHILIP V: Demetrias (near Volos), Chalci<sup>s</sup>, Corinth. CYNOSCEPH-
ALAE: 8,000 Macedonians killed, 5,000 captured. Philip, weak in cavalry, gave his
infantry no flank guard. FLAMININUS: had been at Tarentum (205–204) where he
won the goodwill of the Greeks. HANNIBAL: leading official (*suffete*) of Carthage
c. 196 BC. At Antiochus' court he was rumoured to be planning a fresh invasion
of Italy. MAGNESIA: the Roman commander was Lucius Cornelius Scipio (who
took the name Asiaticus). Antiochus had 75,000 men to face 30,000 Romans.
The Roman victory was preceded by another at sea at Myonnesus (Çifitkale).
The peace of Apamea in Phrygia (Dinar, 188) was concluded by Cnaeus Manlius
Vulso after he had subdued the Galatians (descendants of Gaulish immigrants)
in the centre of Asia Minor. Subsequent Seleucid decline caused independent
development of Pontus, Armenia, Parthia, Judaea. PERSEUS: Third Macedonian
War. Romans failed to dislodge him from Tempe in 171 and 170 but succeeded
in 169 BC. Two years after Pydna he died at Alba Fucens. EPIRUS: was raided
for slaves by the Romans because it had not helped them effectively. REPUBLICS
of Macedonia: land tax reduced by half, iron and copper worked by contractors,
gold and silver mines reopened after 10 years. Illyria too was subdivided, into
three republics. ANTIOCHUS IV EPIPHANES: ordered to leave Ptolemy VI's Egypt
by Gaius Popillius Laenas (168). RHODES AFTER PYDNA: Eumenes II's brother
was Attalus II Philadelphus (160–138 BC). DELOS: was also to gain greatly from
the destruction of Corinth in 146. ACHAEAN LEAGUE: had gone over to Rome in
198 but relations had often been strained since then. SPAIN: land communications
with Italy were secured by development of Po valley, 200–150 BC. CELTIBERIANS:
a major group of peoples formed by fusion of Iberian population with Celtic
invaders. FATHER OF GRACCHI: Tiberius Sempronius Gracchus: founded native
town Gracchuris near Ebro (179). Carteia (El Rocadillo), for sons of soldiers,
was the first Latin colony outside Italy (171). VIRIATHUS' final base was among
the Carpetani, N.W. of Toletum (Toledo). His soldiers were settled at Valentia
(Valencia, 138). NUMANTIA: surrounded by Scipio Aemilianus (consul for the
second time in 134 after special legislation) with seven camps and a 5-mile-long
double ring wall. A red layer of burnt material shows the town was burnt to
the ground. PACIFIED SPAIN: a major strategic road was built from c. 120 BC from
the Pyrenees to Gibraltar (in Spain the road system did not radiate but followed
the periphery of the peninsula). ANDRISCUS: Fourth Macedonian War; he overran
Thessaly, and was caught in Thrace. MACEDONIAN PROVINCE: included Epirus
and Thessaly: alliances were made with Thracian chiefs. VIA EGNATIA: from
Apollonia to Thessalonica (Salonika); by 130 it was continued in Asia Minor.
CORINTH: the local autocrat, Critolaus, was its commander. CARTHAGE: in 191
offered immediate payment of 40 further instalments of its indemnity; and gave
much free grain for Roman forces in the east. MASINISSA: his empire extended
from Mauretania to Cyrenaica. Rome offered adjudications in the 160s and 150s
which did not hamper him. But he was ignored in the Third Punic War, and
died in 148 BC. CATO AND CARTHAGE: opposed by Publius Scipio Nasica Corculum, who regarded it morally salutary to have an enemy to fear. THIRD
PUNIC WAR: Carthage initially surrendered and handed over hostages and war-
material, but on hearing that the city must be destroyed decided to fight.

AFRICAN PROVINCE: 5,000 square miles with capital at Utica (Henchir bou Chateur) which had joined the Romans. Seven cities were left 'free'. Governors went there by an extension of their year of urban office (*prorogatio*, first in 326 BC, by this time general). If the wind was right, Ostia was only a 48-hour sail.

## Chapter 9 The New Society

'NEW MEN' AS CONSULS: 16 out of 262 from 264 to 134 BC, 8 out of 108 from 200 to 146 BC. The 200 consuls between 233 and 133 BC included 99 from 10 families, 159 from 15 families. AGE LIMITS (minimum) of magistracies: Lex Villia Annalis (180 BC). Possibly the same law required an interval of two years between senior magistracies. NEW CULTS: Aesculapius (Asclepius) from Epidaurus after plague in 292, Venus Erycina from Eryx (Erice) in Sicily 215, Cybele from Asia Minor in 205-204. In 139 Jews were banished by the *praetor peregrinus*. TRAGEDIES ABOUT ROMAN HISTORY AND LEGEND: *fabula praetextata*. COMEDY: owed something to rudimentary Italian song-and-dance and dramatic sketches of the past. Naevius' comedies were mainly *palliatae* (adaptations of Greek New Comedy) but also *togatae* (about Roman themes). Mime (*fabula riciniata*) was staged at Rome before 200 BC. SLAVES: in 217 the Saturnalia was turned into a Hellenized festival in which slaves temporarily changed places with their masters. ENNIUS: Rudiae was subject to Greek and Latin influences from Tarentum and Brundusium (Brindisi) respectively. Ennius was brought home from Sardinia by Cato the elder (204) and was with Marcus Fulvius Nobilior in Aetolia (189). The *Annals* are in quantitative dactylic hexameters. 31 lines of his 4 or 6 books of *Satires* have survived. He was the uncle of Pacuvius of Brundusium (died *c*. 130), who disputed the title of the greatest Roman tragedian with Accius of Pisaurum (Pesaro) (died after 90 BC). SCIPIO AFRICANUS: after the obscure 'Trials of the Scipios' (187, 184?), relating to misuse of public funds, Africanus withdrew, ill, to his farm at Liternum (N. of Cumae) in Campania, where he died soon afterwards. PERSONALITY CULT: from 2nd century state officials were permitted to erect statues of themselves in public places. Delos became an important centre of Greek sculpture which influenced Rome. CATO THE ELDER: his career was made by the clan of the Valerii, enemies of the Scipios. LUXURY: the taste for it spread after the public had seen the loot in the *ovatio* (minor Triumph) of Marcus Claudius Marcellus (211) and the Triumphs of Cnaeus Manlius Vulso (187) and Lucius Aemilius Paullus Macedonicus, victor of Pydna. Mass-imports of Greek works of art (as well as the voting of divine honours to Romans in the east) had started in the later 3rd century BC, and much statuary came in after the sack of Corinth (146). AGAINST WOMEN'S LIBERATION: Lex Voconia (164). In 195 Cato had opposed the repeal of the wartime Lex Oppia (215) restricting female dress and jewellery. In 102 BC there was the first public funeral ceremony (*ovatio*) for a woman. ROMAN HISTORIES IN GREEK: Quintus Fabius Pictor, Lucius Cincius Alimentus (both took part in the Second Punic War). EDUCATION: secondary schools taught by *grammatici* were opened after the Second Punic War. SCIPIO AEMILIANUS' associates included Panaetius of Rhodes (*c*. 185-109), who placed a new emphasis on human individuality and (incidentally) helped to adapt Stoicism to Roman

public life, and Polybius of Megalopolis (*c.* 200 – after 118), Greek historian
of Rome. COMEDY: Caecilius Statius (*d.* 168 BC) a Gaulish (Insubrian) ex-slave,
rated as the greatest comic dramatist in the following century. TAXES: There may
have been irregular levies of direct taxation (*tributum*) in the 180s. Italians also
had to pay indirect taxes (*vectigalia*) including rents on public land, mines, and
saltworks, a 5 per cent tax on freeing slaves, and customs dues (*portoria*) (Puteoli
[Pozzuoli, formerly Dicaearchia], which grew in the Second Punic War and became
a Roman colony in 194, was a leading customs station and port). BASILICAS
(often with galleries, *exedrae* and clerestories; early Roman examples 184,
179, 170) are now believed to have evolved from the porticoes of the Hellenistic
Greeks (directly imitated in Rome 196 (?), 167, 146 BC). There were two types:
(1) with long side facing an open area (e.g. Alba Fucens, Ardea, Cosa), (2)
longitudinal, with entrance at short side (e.g. Pompeii). ARCHES IN ROME:
the earliest were erected by Lucius Stertinius (196 BC), in Circus Maximus and
Forum Boarium (Cattle market); then 190, 120. The oldest surviving arch in
Italy is at Cosa (Ansedonia, *c.* 150), with a triple opening. Imperial triumphal
arches at Rome: of Titus, Septimius Severus, Constantine. CONCRETE IN
TEMPLES: Concord (121), Castor and Pollux (117). AQUA MARCIA: built from
head of Anio valley by praetor Quintus Marcius Rex who also repaired older
aqueducts. ROADS: Via Aemilia (187 BC) continued the Via Flaminia from
Ariminum (Rimini) to Placentia (Piacenza). BRIDGES: after the Pons Aemilius,
the Pons Mulvius (Ponte Milvio) was built to carry the Via Flaminia (109).
STONE FACINGS: marble apparently first used for Temple of Jupiter Stator
(149 BC). POMPEII HOUSES: Italian (Samnite) phase 4th century (e.g. House of
Surgeon) replaced by Hellenistic Greek phase mid-3rd century. Incrustation
style of wall painting (from *crusta*, slab of marble, which this imitates): earliest
surviving examples at Pompeii and Cosa from *c.* 100 BC. SMALLHOLDERS
generally found south Italy (except Greek south coast) unattractive, though small
grid units (*c.* 120) have been detected in Apulia. But small holdings were still
extensive in the mountains and Campania and the Po valley. MALARIA (especially
prevalent in Maremma and Pomptine [Pontine] Marshes) had perhaps been
introduced by Carthaginian soldiers in the Second Punic War. LIMITATION
ON LAND-OWNERSHIP: Leges Liciniae Sextiae (366 BC), though recorded details
are anachronistic. GRAIN: poorer people ate either coarse bread (ground husks
and all) or porridge of meal (often millet) and water. CAMPANIA: e.g. Francolise
near Capua contained *villae rusticae* (residences with farms) at Posta (end
2nd century) and S. Rocco (mid-1st century), recently excavated. ETRURIA:
e.g. farmhouse at Villa Sambuco (near S. Giovenale, end 2nd century), now being
excavated. GRAIN COMPETITION: from Sicily and north Africa, mainly felt in
Roman area and some coastal towns. WINE: probably already exported *c.* 230 BC
(red Latian), later spread widely; the first known vintage dated from the consulship of Gaius Opimius (121 BC). VEGETABLES: turnips, beans. Also fruit (especially figs). CATTLE: Italians rarely ate meat – and it was mainly pork when they
did. SLAVES: there is a 4th-century BC painting of a woman with a slave from
Neapolis (Naples). The First Slave War provoked unrest in Delos, Laurium
in Attica (silver mines), Macedonia, Pergamum. SOLDIER'S PAY: *c.* 170-122 BC:
5 *asses* a day with deductions for food, clothes and arms. COLONIES AFTER 200:

Cisalpine Gauls forced to give up half their territory. Mutina (Modena) and Parma Roman colonies in 183, Bononia (former Felsina, now Bologna) and Aquileia Latin colonies in 189 and 181. But Latin colonies then lapsed because of unwillingness of settlers to accept the limited Latin franchise. But Roman colonies, too, ceased to be founded for many years. Roman citizens were reluctant to sacrifice rentals of *ager publicus* to go to either sort of colony. DEBTORS: if they possessed land, it could be sold up, and they forfeited many citizen rights. But there were also many poor and discontented in the towns.

# PART V THE FALL OF THE REPUBLIC

## Chapter 10 Reform and War in Italy

REASSERTION BY TRIBUNES: successful clashes with consuls and Senate 151, 149, 138. The Lex Aelia and Lex Fufia (*c.* 150?) in retaliation gave officials the right to obstruct plebeian assemblies by the announcement of unfavourable auspices (*obnuntiatio*). LAND PROBLEMS: the amount of *ager publicus* in illegal possession was considerable, but much inflated by rumour. TIBERIUS GRACCHUS, to increase free labour, made slave labour a target for criticism. GRUDGE AGAINST SCIPIO AEMILIANUS: because Scipio had advised the Senate to reject a treaty which Tiberius, as quaestor in Spain in 137, had made to save the army of Gaius Hostilius Mancinus. TIBERIUS' FACTION: included his father-in-law the *princeps senatus*, Appius Claudius Pulcher. Some senators supported Tiberius because they were displeased by the appointment of Scipio Aemilianus to Spain. Tiberius was also supported by a Stoic philosopher, Gaius Blossius, of a prominent anti-Roman family from Cumae. PERGAMUM: Attalus III Philometor was its last king: after his death Eudemus visited Tiberius Gracchus of whose father Pergamenes had been clients. MURDER OF TIBERIUS GRACCHUS: the physical attack was led by Publius Cornelius Scipio Nasica Serapio. LAND COMMISSION: 76,000 allotments made 132-125; number of citizens rose eventually from 319,000 to 395,000. By 111 BC all public land in Italy was allotted except rich Campania. RE-ELECTION TO TRIBUNATE: Gaius Papirius Carbo, tribune 131, had sought to pass bill authorizing this (though it had never been legally impermissible), but Scipio Aemilianus frustrated him; possibly a subsequent law in the early 120s carried out Carbo's intention. A further measure of Carbo, extending the secret ballot to legislative assemblies, was passed and played a part in the later break-up of oligarchic power. COLONIES OF GAIUS GRACCHUS: Neptunia (Tarentum) and Scolacium (Squillace), under the toe of Italy, look like commercial sites. ALLIED GRIEVANCES: shared by Latins who since *c.* 128 had lost right to move from one city to another (*ius migrandi*) in favour of a new 'Latin right' by which only local officials (magistrates) became Roman citizens. LAW COURTS: the *quaestio de repetundis* was established by a Lex Calpurnia of 149 BC. SENATORS DEBARRED FROM FINANCE: Lex Claudia *de nave senatorum* (218 BC): this was one reason why they instead seized money in the provinces. SCIPIO AEMILIANUS' WIFE: Sempronia, sister of Gracchi. FULVIUS FLACCUS' LAND BILL: according to one view Tiberius Gracchus, too, had intended to distribute land to Italians, though many of them had not approved of his measures. MASSILIA: given security by Rome's occupation of Po valley 200–150 BC. ARVERNI: under Bituitus, defeated by Quintus Fabius Maximus, who also became patron of the Allobroges and took their name 'Allobrogicus'. The Aedui, the rivals of the Arverni, had taken the side of Rome. VIA DOMITIA: an ancient route, already improved before 124. MASINISSA'S SUCCESSOR: Micipsa, succeeded by Adherbal and Jugurtha. JUGURTHA BETRAYED: by King Bocchus of Mauretania. ARAUSIO: the consuls were Cnaeus Mallius Maximus and Quintus Servilius Caepio. AQUAE SEXTIAE: Roman colony since 124 BC. For many years after the battle there was a bumper crop on the blood-soaked, corpse-filled soil. CAMPI RAUDII: probably not near Vercellae (Vercelli) as believed. Marius was joint commander with Catulus; 120,000 Germans were killed. ARMIES OF MARIUS: standing and short-term Roman armies were now distinguishable from each other. Marius' soldiers ('mules') carried 100 lbs of weapon rations, cooking-pots, stakes for palisades, etc. CANDIDATE MURDERED: Gaius Memmius, standing for consulship of 99 against Glaucia, who supported Saturninus (and died with him). ITALIAN CLAIMS: Lex Licinia Mucia of 95 BC, setting up enquiry into aliens illegally claiming to be citizens, was construed by the Italians as a snub. REBEL CAPITAL: moved from Corfinium to Bovianum (Boiano) and then Aesernia (Isernia). CISALPINE GAUL: a province in 91 or 89 BC or possibly under Sulla. LEX JULIA: followed up by other laws (Calpurnia, Plautia Papiria, Pompeia). MITHRIDATES VI: had gained the grain-rich Cimmerian Bosphorus (Crimea) and most of the sea coast from Danube to Caucasus but was resisted by King Nicomedes IV Philopator of Bithynia (*c.* 94–75 BC). In 88 Mithridates pronounced that any debtor killing his (Italian) creditor would have half his debt remitted. SULLA defeated Mithridates' general Archelaus at Chaeronea and Orchomenus, and after the peace caused the Marian general Fimbria to commit suicide. MURDERED PRAETOR: Sempronius Asellio (89 BC). DEBT LAW: cancelling three-quarters of all debts, passed by Lucius Valerius Flaccus, who was then murdered in Asia in a mutiny caused by Fimbria. CURRENCY LAW: credit was claimed by Marius' nephew Marcus Marius Gratidianus.

### Chapter 11 Reaction and Breakdown

SULLA: had already began to legislate against the Senate and tribunes in 88 BC. Roman colonies, of which the creation had been resumed since *c.* 128, after a long intermission, were now much larger: one of Sulla's veteran colonies was Pompeii, settled to punish it for siding against him in the civil war, but relations between the old and new populations were tense, as they also were at the Sullan colony of Praeneste (Palestrina), formerly strongly anti-Sullan. Quaestors were now increased to 20, praetors from 6 to 8. Sulla encouraged and regularized the current practice of sending (proroguing) men who had just held office to provincial governorship as pro-magistrates (proconsuls, propraetors). Consuls now ceased to be basically military officials. TRIBUNES: prohibitions of their veto in special circumstances were multiplied. Their judicial powers were also curtailed. LEPIDUS (78–77 BC): his supporter in Cisalpine Gaul was Marcus Junius Brutus. Lepidus was defeated at the Milvian Bridge by Catulus and died shortly afterwards from grief owing to his divorce. SERTORIUS: his followers swore an oath (*devotio*) not to survive him. Metellus Pius was initially sent against him.

Sertorius was murdered by Perperna. POMPEY: son of Pompeius Strabo. After bringing 3 legions from Picenum to help, he had killed Cnaeus Papirius Carbo in Sicily and defeated Cinna's son-in-law Cnaeus Domitius Ahenobarbus in north Africa. Pompey married Sulla's step-daughter Aemilia (d. 80), and then later a close connexion of the Metelli, Mucia, whom he divorced in 62. SLAVE REVOLT: the joint leader with Spartacus until 72 was Crixus, a Thracian. VERRES CASE: Cicero defeated the leading orator of the day, Quintus Hortensius Hortalus. JURY LAW: the Lex Aurelia (70 BC) divided panels equally among senators, knights and *tribuni aerarii*, the next class below the knights in property qualification. PIRATE WARS: Marcus Antonius (102 BC), Pompey under Lex Gabinia (67). Cilician command (later province; S. E. Asia Minor) created to deal with pirates in 102, enlarged 64. Crete was added to the province of Cyrenaica in 67. MITHRIDATIC WARS: second conducted by Murena (81), third by Lucullus (74) and Pompey (Lex Manilia, 66). Lucullus had reduced accumulated interest on debts of Asian cities and forbade creditors to seize more than a fixed proportion of the sums due. ARMENIA: Tigranes I the Great (after 100-*c*. 56 BC). JUDAEA: Pompey reappointed Hyrcanus II (high priest 76-67, high priest and ethnarch [secular prince] 63-40). NEW MEN: the last certain *novus homo* to win the consulship had been in 94 BC. CICERO'S FELLOW-CONSUL: Gaius Antonius Hybrida. BANKRUPT NOBLES: competition for office was intense (and canvassing expensive), because only 2 out of the 20 annual quaestors could later become consuls. GALLIC ENVOYS (63): from the tribe of the Allobroges. EXECUTED CATILINARIANS: included ex-consul Publius Cornelius Lentulus Sura. PISTORIA: won by Petreius (62); Gaius Antonius Hybrida remained in his tent allegedly ill. CAESAR'S MARIAN LINKS: Caesar married Cinna's daughter Cornelia, and his father's sister had been Marius' wife. EMERGENCY DECREE CASE: trial of Gaius Rabirius (63). HOUSES OF IST CENTURY BC: the characteristic form of wall paintings of the time ('Second Style') displayed illusionistic architectural vistas (e.g. Boscoreale bedroom in Metropolitan Museum, New York, and newly discovered villa at Oplontis [Torre Annunziata]). CICERO'S EDUCATION: studied philosophy and rhetoric at Rome, Athens and Rhodes. Schools of rhetoric (higher education) had begun at Rome early in 1st century BC. LAW: Quintus Mucius Scaevola Pontifex (d. 82) published the first systematic treatise on civil law. PHILOSOPHY: Zeno came from Citium in Cyprus. Cicero followed the belief of a later Stoic, Posidonius of Apamea in Syria (Kalat-el-Mudik; *c*. 135-50 BC), that philosophy had been the inventor of the civilized arts and supported the view of the contemporary New Academy at Athens (descended from Plato's Academy) that dogma must be avoided. CONCORD OF THE ORDERS: slogan used by the historian Macer, who agitated for popular rights as tribune in 73. Cicero broadened it into a general concept involving moral responsibility and embracing moderates in the country towns (*consensus Italiae*). LAND INTRIGUES (63 BC): Cicero opposed the major agrarian bill of Rullus, which may or may not have been directed against Pompey. The veterans asked for a renewal of the Lex Valeria of 86 scaling down debts by three-quarters. CATO'S GRAIN DOLE (62): cf. occasional measures in Hellenistic Greece. TAX-GATHERERS (*publicani*) had strengthened their position after the First Mithridatic War by lending money to the Asian cities to pay tax arrears and indemnities.

## PART VI  CAESAR AND AUGUSTUS

### Chapter 12 Caesar

LAND LAW (59 BC): extended to rich Campania by hotly contested *Lex Campana*. Bibulus attempted to obstruct legislation by *obnuntiatio* (proclamation that the auspices were ill-omened), under the Leges Aelia and Fufia (?c. 150). But refuse was emptied over his head in the Forum, and his official bundle of rods (*fasces*) were broken. EGYPTIAN KING HELPED BY CAESAR: Ptolemy XII Auletes (80–51 BC). CAESAR'S COMMAND: Lex Vatinia. GAUL: 'three parts' (according to Caesar): Belgae, Celts, Aquitani. ARIOVISTUS: of a Suebian tribe, perhaps the Triboci. He had defeated the Aedui in 61 at Magetobriga (Moigte de Broie?), and it was they who led the appeal to Caesar against him. CLODIUS: guilds or corporations (*collegia*), often composed of men practising the same trade, were normally permitted to exist subject to senatorial sanction: they had, however, been suppressed in 64 BC for political action, but were revived by Clodius. He financed his grain-dole out of the annexation of Cyprus organized by his political enemy Cato the younger (58). There were 320,000 recipients by c. 46 BC. CICERO EXILED: in 58 by the agency of Clodius (who bore him a grudge for destroying his alibi in a lawsuit concerning Clodius' desecration of the cult of the Good Goddess [Bona Dea] in 61); he was brought back in 57 by Pompey. PARTHIA: centred on Media (N. Iran); Ecbatana (Hamadan) was the capital of the Arsacid royal house, Ctesiphon (in Babylonia) their winter residence. The Parthians ruled from the Euphrates to the Indus and controlled the caravan routes from the far east. SON OF CRASSUS: Publius Licinius Crassus. QUIBERON BAY: the victor was Decimus Junius Brutus Albinus. GERMAN TRIBES suppressed in 56: Usipetes and Tencteri. BELGIC REVOLTS (54): by Treviri; and Ambiorix of Eburones (Ardennes) massacred garrison at Aduatuca. CONFERENCES (53): Samarobriva (Amiens), Lutetia (Paris), Durocortorum (Reims). VERCINGETORIX: pan-Gallic command conferred at Bibracte, capital of Aedui (52). FINAL OPERATION (51): Uxellodunum (Pay d'Issolu in Dordogne). CONQUERED GAUL: Gallia Comata (later divided into three provinces plus two German commands): road-system based on Lugdunum (Lyon), founded in 43. ARMY PAY: became 225 *denarii* per annum. CARRHAE (53): the victor was Surenas, ruler of Seistan (E. Iran and S. W. Afghanistan) as Parthian vassal. In the battle, his horse archers were kept supplied by swift Arabian camels carrying reserves of arrows. The Parthians also employed cataphracts (heavily mailed horsemen with large spears), CLODIUS MURDERED (52): by the gangster Milo, originally pro-Pompeian but now convicted on Pompey's initiative (in spite of Cicero's defence speech) and exiled to Massilia. POMPEY'S COMMAND (49): proposed by the consul Gaius Claudius Marcellus with the support of the two consuls designate. RUBICON: R. Pisciatello (?). ALEXANDRIANS (Greek, 3rd century BC): Callimachus, Apollonius Rhodius, Theocritus, Euphorion. Their Roman followers were called the Neoterics. ATOMISTS (Greek): Leucippus, Democritus (5th century BC). LUCRETIUS ON POLITICS: II 10–13 (translated by R. Humphries). CAESAR'S INVASION: second column moved on to Arretium (Arezzo). RESERVE TREASURY: in Temple of Saturn. ILERDA: the Pompeian commanders were

Afranius and Petreius. ADRIATIC FLOTILLA eluded by Caesar: commanded by Bibulus, who died soon afterwards. POMPEY MURDERED: by Ptolemaic general Achillas and two Roman officers. CLEOPATRA: a remarkable linguist, but did not trouble to learn Latin. ARMY RELIEVING CAESAR: Mithridates of Pergamum, and Jewish contingent. VICTORY IN ASIA MINOR: at Zela (Zile) against Pharnaces II. This was the occasion of Caesar's saying 'I came, I saw, I conquered' (*veni, vidi, vici*). SECOND THREAT OF MUTINY (47): the legionaries followed Caesar from Campania to Rome where he pacified them. CAESAR'S SETTLEMENTS: a veteran with 3 children usually received rather more than 6 acres. Colonies in provinces remained provincial soil and paid land tax. His civilian colonies included Corinth, Carthage, Urso (Osuna in Spain). (Gades [Cadiz] was the first provincial city to receive the franchise without a settlement, as a *municipium*). Some colonies, notably in Narbonese Gaul and Further Spain, were given the intermediate Latin right, i.e. their magistrates became citizens. In Cisalpine Gaul the regions south and north of the Po received Roman citizenship and 'Latin right' respectively. MEDICINE: the first regular school at Rome was founded by Asclepiades of Bithynia, *c.* 40 BC. DEBT: the praetor, Caelius (a correspondent of Cicero), also proposed the abolition of house rents for one year (48), and the tribune, Dolabella, urged their total abolition. Caelius started a rising with Milo and was executed at Thurii (Sybaris). Dolabella survived (until 43). CAESAR'S WEALTH: his gold coinage, issued by Aulus Hirtius, was probably the largest in Roman history. After the Gallic War the price of gold had fallen by one-quarter. CLEOPATRA'S HALF-BROTHER with her at Rome in 46: Ptolemy XIV. She murdered him in 44. CAESAR'S LIBRARIES: organized by the learned writer Marcus Terentius Varro (116–27 BC); by the 4th century AD there were 29 libraries in Rome, 9 of which are known to us. CALENDAR: reorganized by Sosigenes; adjusted by Augustus and Pope Gregory XIII (1582). PORTRAITURE: coins of the early 1st century BC had displayed idealized portraits of early Romans; the first coin-portraits of the recently dead were of Sulla and his fellow-consul of 88 BC, Quintus Pompeius Rufus, on a coin of their grandson named after the latter (54 BC). CAESAR'S BUSTS (of his lifetime): e.g. at Castello d'Agliè (Turin). MAGISTRATES: Caesar increased praetors from 8 to 16, aediles from 4 to 6, quaestors from 20 to 40. EASTERN EXPEDITION (44 BC): 16 legions, 10,000 cavalry and archers. In anticipation of Caesar's absence all major appointments were fixed two years ahead. CAESAR'S SECRETARIES (knights): Gaius Oppius, biographer, and the wealthy Lucius Cornelius Balbus from Gades (Cadiz). BRUTUS: *praetor urbanus* in 44, Cassius *praetor peregrinus* (less important). On a coin of *c.* 54 BC issued when he was a young moneyer, Marcus Brutus had boasted of his descent from the legendary liberators Lucius Brutus (believed to have expelled Tarquinius Superbus) and Ahala (alleged to have put down the tyrant Maelius, 440–439 BC). CAESAR'S MURDER: two senators, only, claimed to have moved to his defence: Gaius Calvisius Sabinus and Lucius Marcius Censorinus.

*Chapter 13 Augustus*

NAME: Gaius Octavius, then Gaius Julius Caesar (Octavianus). LEPIDUS: at first retained Narbonese Gaul and Further Spain (assigned to him by Caesar), lost

them after Philippi, was given Africa in 40. SEXTUS POMPEIUS: set up independent rule based on Sicily (43). ANTONY'S BROTHER: Lucius Antonius, captured
after siege of Perusia (Perugia) (41). ALLIANCE: between Antony, Octavian
and Lepidus (40): Treaty of Brundusium. BRUTUS' mother Servilia (mistress of
Caesar, presided over political salon) held conference at Antium (Anzio) (44);
Brutus' wife was Porcia, daughter of Cato and widow of Bibulus. FULVIA:
formerly married to Clodius and Curio. RECONCILIATION: between Antony and
Octavian (37); Treaty of Tarentum. CLEOPATRA'S EMPIRE: established 37,
amplified at Donations of Alexandra (34). Its titular rulers included her son,
allegedly by Caesar, Ptolemy XV Caesar (Caesarion) and her children by Antony.
ANTONY'S CLIENTS: Asander (Cimmerian Bosphorus, 41–17 BC), Herod the
Great (Judaea), Amyntas (Galatia), Polemo I (Pontus), Archelaus (Cappadocia).
PARTHIAN WARS: Parthian invasion of Syria 41–40 BC, successful expedition by
Ventidius 38, disastrous Roman retreat 36; Armenia occupied by the Romans 34.
SEXTUS POMPEIUS' END: fled to Asia Minor, killed 35. ACTIUM: preceded by
Agrippa's seizure of Methone. VETERANS' REWARDS: paid by Octavian (Augustus)
himself for nearly 30 years, mainly from civil war spoils. COLONIES: of Octavian
(Augustus): mainly in west (those in Spain issued numerous local coinages), but also
a few in east, e.g. in newly annexed province of Galatia (Lycaonia, Pisidia). His colonies unlike Caesar's were almost exclusively military. MANPOWER: by the time of
Augustus' death the free adult male population of Italy, including Cisalpine Gaul
(part of Italy since 42 BC) was perhaps $1\frac{1}{2}$ million (no more than in 218 BC). But the
total number of slaves in Italy, including women and children, may have been as
high as four million. IMPERIAL PROVINCE(S): Upper and Lower Germany were
commands rather than provinces. AUGUSTAN NOBLES: the princeps had married
Livia (38 BC), of a noble clan and formerly married to the member of another,
Tiberius Claudius Nero, by whom she had two sons, Tiberius and Nero
Drusus. AUGUSTAN 'NEW MEN': tended to become army commanders and
suffect consuls, i.e. those replacing, during the course of each year, the more
important 'ordinary' consuls, who were generally noble (though many upper-
class families were dying out). The Lex Valeria Cornelia of AD 5 on election
procedure enhanced the dignity (not power) of the upper class. SENATORS:
excused attendance at age of 60. WORSHIP OF AUGUSTUS: with the goddess
Rome, first at Pergamum (Bergama) in Asia and Nicomedia (Izmit) in Bithynia;
provincial councils (*koina*, concilia) presided. In Rome, an altar was erected
to the *numen* (divine power) of Augustus (AD 13) and his *genius* was worshipped
with *lares publici*, protective deities of Rome. His image was carried with military
standards and received the homage of the troops. SPAIN: Lusitania (Portugal
and W. Spain) became a separate province during the reign of Augustus and
Tarraco (Tarragona) became the capital of Nearer Spain (Hispania Tarraconensis).
TRIBUNICIAN POWER: also practical advantage, e.g. right to convene Senate.
TRAVELS: Agrippa in east, Gaul, Spain (23–21, 20–19), Augustus in Sicily, Greece,
Asia (22–19). In 20 BC Armenia was (temporarily) reduced to client status, amid
great applause. MARRIAGE LAWS: *lex de maritandis ordinibus* and *lex de adulteriis
coercendis* (18 BC) reinforced by Lex Papia Poppaea (AD 9) which introduced still
stronger incentives to marriage. KNIGHTS: Caesar had increased their employment
as chief advisers and officers. DEATH of Agrippa: a fragment of Augustus' funeral

oration has now come to light. Nobles shunned the occasion. BOHEMIA: centre of empire of Maroboduus (Marcomanni who supplanted Boii *c.* 8 BC). ARMINIUS: a chieftain of the Cherusci and a Roman citizen, ambushed Publius Varius at the Teutoburg Forest (Saltus), near Detmold. Tiberius and Germanicus were then sent to consolidate the Rhine frontier. PRAETORIAN GUARD: included inner group of mounted *speculatores* (messengers, intelligence agents), and was supplemented by a separate bodyguard of Germans. PREFECT OF THE CITY: temporary appointments during the reign were followed by creation of permanent post (? *c.* AD 13). FIRE BRIGADE (*vigiles*): eventually of 7,000 freedmen (AD 6). MILITARY PENSIONS: because of financial shortages, fixed term enlistments (20 years legionary, 25 auxiliary) often had to be prolonged. MONARCHY: easterners thought of Augustus as monarch (*basileus*), though that title does not appear on coins. EXILED BY AUGUSTUS: his daughter Julia (2 BC) and granddaughter Julia (AD 8), and his grandson, Agrippa Postumus (AD 7), whose death in AD 14 was ordered either by Augustus or Tiberius. ARA PACIS: consecrated 13 and dedicated 9 BC. PRIMA PORTA PAINTINGS: Museo Nazionale delle Terme, Rome: cf. a branch of the Pompeian Second Style. Soon afterwards the Third Style (*c.* 20 BC–AD 20) showed more illusionistic landscapes, and panel paintings amid fantastic architecture. TAXES: Caesar had abolished tax-farming and tithes in Asia Minor and probably Sicily, substituting fixed *tributum soli*. *Tributum* was paid in some provinces by all adults and in others by adult males. FLEETS: principal stations at Misenum and Ravenna. ROADS: by 2nd century AD there were more than 50,000 miles of first-class roads in the empire and over 200,000 miles of lesser roads. BRIDGES: e.g. Alcantara bridge over Tagus, with 18 arches of which 6 remain. TUNNELS: e.g. of Occeius at Cumae (¾ mile), and Neapolis-Puteoli (½ mile). TRADE: normal rate of interest on a good security fell to 4–6 per cent, the lowest level of ancient times. WOOL: Pompeii (building for Guild of Fullers dedicated by its woman patron the priestess Eumachia), Parma, Mediolanum (Milan), Patavium (Padua). GLASS-BLOWING: recently invented in Sidon (Saida) in Phoenicia. EARTHENWARE: of coarser variety at Mutina (Modena) and Aquileia. FOREIGN TRADE: reflected by Latin and Greek words surviving in German, Semitic, Pahlevi, Iranian, Irish, and even a few in Indian and Mongolian. LEPCIS MAGNA: founded by Carthage in 6th century BC to oppose the Greeks. COINAGE: brass (*orichalcum* = zinc alloy) and copper replaced discredited bronze (lead and tin alloy, terminated in 80s BC except for special issues) in official coinages. The local city currencies of bronze were supplemented, for a time, by a few of silver. Client kingdoms had coinages of their own, in silver and bronze (and gold in the Cimmerian Bosphorus [Crimea]). LAND TRANSPORT: it did not pay to cart grain more than 50 miles. Diocletian's Edict of Prices shows that a 1,200-pound wagon load of wheat would double in price in 300 miles. FREEDMEN: marriages with free-born were largely recognized (18 BC); they also became priests (*Augustales*) of the cult in which Augustus was associated with the Lares. MAECENAS: probably from aristocracy of Arretium (Arezzo); he played a major political part up to the battle of Actium, and therefore acted more than once as the absent Augustus' representative at Rome. He was sloppy and soft according to Seneca, a keen ball-player according to Horace. ECLOGUES OF VIRGIL: most were loosely modelled on

Theocritus of Syracuse (*c.* 300–260 BC). GEORGICS: poetical and patriotic, but contained information based on agricultural handbook of Marcus Terentius Varro (*Res Rusticae*, 37 BC). AENEID: romantic element cf. Apollonius Rhodius of Alexandria, *Argonautica* (3rd century BC). Latin bride of Aeneas: Lavinia. HORACE (65–8 BC): *Epodes* and *Odes* (including *Carmen Saeculare*) in lyrical metres (latter claimed Alcaeus [born *c.* 620 BC] as model), *Satires* and *Epistles* (including *Ars Poetica*) in hexameters. His Sabine farm perhaps identifiable near Digentia (Licenza), 22 miles N.E. of Rome. PROPERTIUS (born 59–47 BC) claimed Callimachus of Cyrene (*c.* 305–240) as model. A contemporary elegist was Tibullus (55 or 48–19 BC), whose patron was the soldier, statesman, and orator Marcus Valerius Messalla Corvinus (64 BC–AD 8). LIVY: alternatively his dates could be 64 BC–AD 12. His history ended in 9 BC. OVID'S: tragedy the *Medea* is lost.

## PART VII   THE IMPERIAL PEACE

### Chapter 14 The Inheritors of Empire

THE EAST: Cappadocia (E. Asia Minor) and Commagene (N.W. Syria) annexed (AD 17). DEATH OF GERMANICUS: Cnaeus Calpurnius Piso, imperial governor of Syria, was accused of his murder in the Senate and although innocent of this charge (but guilty of sedition) killed himself. TREASON CHARGES: under the Lex Julia maiestatis, probably passed by Julius Caesar. SEJANUS: son of Lucius Aelius Strabo of Volsinii (Orvieto); for a time they were joint praetorian prefects. Before Sejanus became consul in AD 31 he had been granted the rank of praetor. SONS OF GERMANICUS AND AGRIPPINA THE ELDER: Nero Caesar (d. AD 31), Drusus Caesar (d. 33) and Gaius (Caligula, later emperor). GRANDSON OF TIBERIUS: Tiberius Gemellus, killed by Caligula in 38. REVOLT IN UPPER GERMANY (39): under Cnaeus Cornelius Lentulus Gaetulicus. Also executed was Caligula's brother-in-law and heir-apparent Marcus Lepidus; Caligula's sisters Agrippina junior and Julia Livilla were banished. CALIGULA'S WIFE (fourth and last): Caesonia. CLAUDIUS: son of Nero Drusus (Drusus the elder, brother of Tiberius) and Antonia. REVOLT IN DALMATIA (42): Lucius Furius Camillus Scribonianus. BRITAIN: invasion prompted by death of Cunobelinus (*c.* AD 9–40/43; Shakespeare's Cymbeline) of the Catuvellauni, overlord of S.E. England. By 47 the frontier was the Fosse Way (Lindum [Lincoln] – South Devon). The revolt of Cunobelinus' son Caratacus ended in 51 and veterans were settled at *colonia* Camulodunum (Colchester) in 50 (also at Colonia Agrippinensis, now Köln). But the capital of Britain was later moved from Camulodunum to the much larger Londinium (330 acres). Perhaps 6,000 miles of roads were built in the first four decades of the British province. MAURETANIA: gradually pacified after murder of its client king Ptolemy at Rome in 40. THRACE: made a province after the murder of its last client prince in 46. Lycia (S. Asia Minor) was also annexed as part of province Lycia–Pamphylia (43). GAULS: nobles were brought into the Senate (by *adlectio*) and all Roman citizens in Gaul were permitted to stand for office in the capital, following a speech by Claudius, largely preserved on a bronze tablet at Lugdunum (Lyon). MESSALINA: great-niece of

Augustus. Her lover, executed in 48, was Gaius Silius. NERO'S NAME: originally Lucius (his father was Cnaeus) Domitius Ahenobarbus. NERO'S AMUSEMENTS: early in his reign he associated with *pantomimi* (male ballet-dancers). He was also interested not only in music but in chariot-racing (of which there were four main factions). BOUDICCA: her revolt was suppressed by Gaius Suetonius Paulinus (60). TIGELLINUS' FELLOW-PREFECT: Faenius Rufus, executed in 65 with Seneca, after a plot to place Gaius Calpurnius Piso on the throne. PHILOSOPHICAL REPUBLICANS: Thrasea Paetus, forced to commit suicide in 66. CORBULO'S PEACE: Tiridates I of Armenia was jointly sponsored by Rome and Parthia. After these wars, the Euphrates garrison was permanently increased at the expense of the Rhine and Danube. VINDEX: defeated by the eminent Verginius Rufus, commander in Upper Germany, who refused the throne for himself (as again in the following year, 69). GALBA'S ADVISERS: Vinius, Laco, Icelus. GALBA'S HEIR: Lucius Calpurnius Piso Licinianus. OTHO: of princely family from Ferentium (Ferento) in Etruria. GALLO-GERMAN REVOLT: captured major Rhine base of Vetera (near Birten) in 70; the whole river line to Argentorate (Strasbourg) or beyond was lost. Cerialis recovered Classicus' capital Augusta Trevirorum (Trier), destroyed the Gallic empire, and drove the Batavians back home. UPPER RHINE – UPPER DANUBE RE-ENTRANT: Agri Decumates. FIRST JEWISH REVOLT: Masada resisted until 73. VESPASIAN'S ORIGIN: from Sabine town of Reate (Rieti). SPAIN: S. province of Baetica received Latin rights, and between AD 74 and 84, 350 Spanish towns received municipal charters. TAXES: in provinces were sometimes doubled by Vespasian, and Greek immunities revoked. EDUCATION: Quintilian of Cala-gurris (Calahorra in Spain) was the first salaried professor of rhetoric. Teachers received tax rebates like doctors. OPPOSITION TO VESPASIAN: supported by Stoic and Cynic ideas. Helvidius Priscus executed. PLOT OF CAECINA (79): allied with Eprius Marcellus, leading orator and Vespasian's adviser. VESPASIAN'S DEATH: at Aquae Cutiliae (Bagni di Paterno). BERENICE: daughter of Agrippa I and sister of Agrippa II (N. Palestine and S. Syria), had supported Rome in the First Jewish Revolt. BRITAIN: Fishbourne Villa had probably been built for the old age of Cogidubnus of the Atrebates (*c.* 43–75), a client king within the frontiers. FORTH–CLYDE LINE: forts at Camelon and near Cadder and Mumrills. VESUVIUS ERUPTION (79): Pliny the elder, admiral and historian and scientist, died of suffocation on the beach (described in a letter of his nephew Pliny the younger to the historian Tacitus). AGRICOLA UNDER DOMITIAN: advance beyond Firth of Forth (fortress at Inchtuthil) in 83. 'MONS GRAUPIUS' site of Roman victory (84): probably not far short of the Moray Firth. Signal stations on road east from Ardoch may mark the frontier after withdrawal following Agricola's recall. Vindolanda (Chesterholm) is also a Domitianic fort (recent discoveries of limewood tablets). S.W. GERMANY under Domitian: by the end of his reign the frontier (*limes*) road ran from near Bonna (Bonn) down River Neckar to meet the Danube in Raetia. DACIAN BATTLES: Oppius Sabinus, governor of Moesia, was killed in 85, and Cornelius Fuscus, praetorian prefect, in 86 or 87; then Roman victory at Tapae (Iron Gates) in 88. REVOLT IN UPPER GERMANY (89): by Lucius Antonius Saturninus. Afterwards Domitian converted the Upper and Lower German commands into formal provinces. TRAJAN'S ORIGINS: born at Italica

(Santiponce) in Baetica (S. Spain) in 53. PROVINCIAL ORIGINS: in 90 the first known eastern consul was elected, and in 94 the first pair of consuls both to possess provincial backgrounds. ALIMENTA: at Veleia (Velleia in north Italy) Trajan supported 245 boys and 34 girls born in wedlock and 2 illegitimate children. ADMINISTRATION: *curatores* of one or several cities, perhaps already under Domitian, then at Caere (Cerveteri, 113). Pliny, like a governor of Achaea (Greece) in the same reign, had special powers as *corrector*. There was a new distinction between civilian and military careers in the equestrian ranks of the government service. TRAJAN'S ARMY: 400,000 strong. The first cohort of each legion was doubled in size. There was also a new intelligence organization (*frumentarii*), and a mounted bodyguard of *equites singulares* (500, later 1,000), mainly German and Danubian (from Pannonia). TRAJAN'S DACIAN WARS: new Roman colony adjacent to old site of Sarmizegethusa, near Toteşti, *c.* 110. On the frontier fortifications (Limes Dacicus), *castella* (e.g. Buciumi, near Cluj) have unusually elaborate gates. The Danube bridge designed by Apollodorus over 1,000 yards long, was built of stone piers and segmental timber arches. EASTERN FRONTIER: Arabia Petraea (Nabataea: west Jordan and Sinai) annexed 105-6; Bostra (Busra) replaced Petra as capital. Later in the century Gerasa (Jerash) became an increasingly important town. JEWISH DISPERSION REVOLTS: Cyrene, Cyprus, Egypt; the aim in the first two was the extermination of the Greeks. Henceforward Jews were forbidden in Cyprus. Revolts were also formented by the Parthian King Osroes in the Jewish communities of Babylonia. PARTHIAN ATTACKS IN ROMAN REAR: Mesopotamia, Armenia, Adiabene (Assyria). Was Trajan obliged to abandon his conquests even before the Jewish revolts? PARTHIAN CLIENT KING at Ctesiphon: Parthamaspates. HADRIAN'S ORIGIN: born at Gades (Cadiz) in Baetica (S. Spain) in 76; his paternal grandfather had married Trajan's aunt. PLOT OF THE FOUR CONSULARS (118): including the Mauretanian Lusius Quietus, who had suppressed the Babylonian Jews and governed Judaea. They were executed by the praetorian prefect Attianus. PROVINCES: a great series of coins honoured individual provinces and Hadrian as their visitor (*adventui Augusti*) and restorer (*restitutori*). The temple of Divus Hadrianus (Hadrianeum), erected in the Campus Martius after his death, displayed sculptural representations of the provinces. DEFEAT IN BRITAIN: a legion was lost some time between 117 and 122. HADRIAN'S ARMY: Hadrian introduced, or increased, heavy armoured cavalry (*cataphracts*), borrowed from the Sarmatians (nomads related to the Scythians); and he extended the use of irregular 'national' *numeri*. FORTIFICATIONS: Hadrian built a stone wall on the Numidian as well as the British frontier and constructed a continuous wooden palisade in Raetia and Upper Germany. HADRIAN'S WESTERN WARS: minor risings in Britain and Mauretania. AELIUS CAESAR: his original name was Lucius Ceionius Commodus. ANTONINUS 'PIUS': he insisted on the deification of Hadrian, though the Senate was not enthusiastic. ANTONINUS' WALL in Britain: (AD 142): but the frontier was retracted more than once, and definitively before the end of the century. ANTONINUS' WARS: disturbances in 139-142 among Brigantes (Yorkshire; some Britons were transplanted to the Agri Decumates and organized in *numeri* there) and in Numidia, Mauretania, Syria, Palaestina (Judaea), Egypt, Dacia (partitioned into three provinces).

*Chapter 15 Imperial Society*

ARCH OF TITUS: the spoils from the Jerusalem temple include the Menorah (seven-branched candlestick), silver trumpet, and golden table of the Shewbread. COLUMN OF TRAJAN: in colonnaded court flanked by Greek and Latin libraries behind the Basilica which occupied the north side of Trajan's Forum, completed in AD 113 according to the plan of Apollodorus. POMPEII: a so-called 'fourth' style from *c*. AD 50 comprised a great many varied themes, including more imaginative versions of the architectural vistas of the 'second' style. Wall-decorations also include stucco. MOSAICS: the favourite mosaic pavements in Italy (1st-3rd centuries) were black and white. Figured, overall designs are conspicuous, e.g. in north Africa. Wall-mosaics already appear on Pompeian fountains. SLAVE ACCOMMODATION: so-called House of Menander (Pompeii), and Villa of Agrippa Postumus (outside Pompeii), cf. Pliny the younger's villa at Laurentum. OSTIA: most of the apartment houses (of which more than 200 have been identified) incorporated shops. Ostia replaced Puteoli (Pozzuoli) as Italy's principal west coast port. OTHER HOUSING: Bulla Regia (Hammon Daradji) in north Africa (a Roman colony for veterans under Hadrian) shows an experiment in underground housing to resist summer and winter climatic extremes. NERO'S GOLDEN HOUSE: architects Severus and Celer. Separate pavilions, cf. Prytaneum of Antigonus II Gonatas at Pella (Palatitsa) in Macedonia and Hadrian's Villa at Tibur (and Sultans' Seraglio at Istanbul). DOMITIAN'S PALACE: architect Rabirius. HADRIAN'S VILLA: adorned with masterpieces of Greek sculpture and of the Hadrianic school which it influenced. PANTHEON: made little impression in antiquity but exercised great influence on the Renaissance. TEMPLES: the buildings at Heliopolis (Baalbek) in Syria were exceptionally grand. ROMAN BATHS: Agrippa, Titus, Trajan (later Caracalla, Diocletian): cf. four so far discovered at Pompeii, two at Herculaneum. VESPASIAN'S BUILDINGS: Forum and Temple of Peace; he reconstructed the Capitoline temple, and started work on the Colosseum. COLOSSEUM: fourth storey is of blind arcading broken by windows. EARLIER AMPHITHEATRE: the building of Titus Statilius Taurus at Rome in 29 BC had been partly of wood and partly of stone, but there were earlier stone amphitheatres at Pompeii, etc. Pompey had built Rome's first stone theatre (53 BC) and Augustus built the three-storey Theatre of Marcellus (13 BC). There were three imperial training schools for gladiators at Rome, also at Capua (Santa Maria Capua Vetere) and Ravenna and Praeneste (Palestrina) (unless this was still privately owned). Even Petuaria (Brough-on-Humber) had its amphitheatre. THAMUGADI: founded in AD 100 by Trajan as a Roman colony for veterans and originally designed on camp lines, later greatly expanded; the most complete African remains, next to Lepcis Magna (which was likewise colonized by Trajan). TRADE: Greeks and Syrians supplemented their virtual monopoly of the Mediterranean carrying trade by taking over a large share of the outlying routes. RHINELAND: e.g. Tres Tabernae (Rheinzabern) and Augusta Trevirorum (Trier), with Colonia Agrippinensis (Köln) as glass-blowing centre. SLAVES: by 2nd century, it was ceasing to be profitable to employ slave-gangs in agriculture and mining. Emperors received petitions from slaves as from every other category of the population. AELIUS ARISTIDES of Mysia (AD 117 or 129-181 or later). TO ROME: cf. Pliny the elder, 'the immense majesty of the Roman peace'. SALVIUS JULIANUS: of Pupput (?) near Hadrumetum (Sousse), *c.* AD 100–69; also wrote *Digesta*, in 90 books. GAIUS (lawyer): born under Trajan (?), perhaps from a Greek province. HADRIAN: salaried jurisconsults were members of his *consilium*. LEGAL REFORMS: there were also improvements in the legal status of women. HUMILIORES: liable to flogging, torture, summary execution; lacked right of appeal to emperor which all *honestiores*, not only citizens, possessed. The dichotomy was already to some extent recognized by the time of the leading jurists Labeo (d. AD 10/11) and Ateius Capito (d. 22). SENECA: his father was Seneca the elder (*c.* 55 BC–AD 37–41). The younger Seneca was the author of a scientific work, the *Natural Questions*. His alleged correspondence with St Paul is a 4th-century forgery. PETRONIUS: plausibly identified with Titus Petronius Niger, consul *c.* AD 61. His poems seem, in part at least, to be derisive parodies of Lucan and Seneca, on whose retirement Petronius became prominent. Set pieces: also 'The Widow of Ephesus'. His writing is ignored by Tacitus (who describes him as *arbiter elegantiae*) and fiction is not included in Quintilian's survey of Latin literature. Other Domitianic poets were Statius (*Thebaid, Silvae*), Silius Italicus (*Punica*) and Valerius Flaccus (*Argonautica*). TACITUS: his name appears to have been Publius Cornelius Tacitus. It is disputed whether the *Annals* were published late in Trajan's reign (as is usually believed) or early in Hadrian's. LUCIAN of Samosata (Samsat in S.E. Turkey; born *c.* AD 120): his works, in Greek, developed a special variety of the dialogue, based on Cynic and other antecedents. SOPHISTS of 2nd century AD: the 'Second Sophistic' (the First was in the 5th century BC). ARCHAIC REVIVAL: the New Speech (*elocutio novella*), sponsored by Fronto (*c.* AD 100–66), the tutor of Marcus Aurelius and leading Roman orator of his day. ASTROLOGY: in vogue in eastern Mediterranean since 2nd century BC; spread to Italy late in the following century. SCIENCE: virtually its last figure was Galen of Pergamum (AD 129–99), who summarized the ancient knowledge of medicine. DEMETER: her Mysteries were centred on Eleusis in Greece. DIONYSUS (Bacchus): wall-paintings in Villa of Mysteries outside Pompeii, 1st century BC. CYBELE: poem on myth of Attis by Catullus. Bloodbaths of animals (*taurobolium, criobolium*) originated in Asia Minor and first appeared in the west in 2nd century AD. Before Cybele, the mystery cult of Asclepius (Aesculapius) had been imported to Rome after a plague (293 BC, from Epidaurus). ISIS: the Egyptian gods gained the imperial cachet under Hadrian.

## Chapter 16 The Jews, Jesus and Paul

ISRAEL (kingdom): fell to Assyria 721 BC. JUDAH: fell to Babylonia 597–586 BC. PROPHETS: the 'major' prophetic books are those of Isaiah (multiple authorship), Jeremiah and Ezekiel (and Daniel in the English Bible). TEMPLE: Antiochus IV Epiphanes set up a statue of Olympian Zeus in the Holy of Holies (168 BC). The temple was reconsecrated by Judas Maccabaeus (165–164 BC) and rebuilt in 22–18 BC by Herod the Great (37–34 BC) whom Antony had placed on the Judaean throne to succeed the Hasmonaean Mattathias Antigonus (40–37), a client of Parthia. JESUS'S BIRTH: misattributed to AD 1 by Dionysius Exiguus from Scythia (S. Russia) (AD 500–60). NON-CANONICAL GOSPELS: e.g. of *Thomas, Eve, Mary,*

*James, John, Judas, Matthias, Peter, Philip.* JUDAEA: ruled by prince (ethnarch) Archelaus (4 BC–AD 6), by Roman prefects (knights) from AD 6–41, then (after interlude under King Agrippa I, AD 41–4) by Roman procurators (knights) from AD 44 until First Jewish Revolt; thereafter by senior (senatorial) governors. SON OF MAN: *bar nasha.* QUMRAN: Dead Sea Scrolls of various dates up to dispersal of sect in First Jewish Revolt. APOSTLES: Peter, James and John the sons of Zebedee, Andrew, Philip, Bartholomew, Matthew, Thomas, James the son of Alphaeus, Thaddaeus (or Judas), Simon the Zealot, and Judas Iscariot (meaning, 'of Kerioth'). FULFILMENT OF O.T.: Typology. PONTIUS PILATUS: prefect of Judaea AD 26–36. DISPERSION: Ptolemy I Soter had introduced many Jews and Samaritans (dissident Jews from northern Palestine) into Alexandria, and Antiochus III the Great settled 2,000 Jewish families in Asia Minor. EARLIEST LETTERS (EPISTLES) OF PAUL: probably *I and II Thessalonians* (c. AD 50), though some place *Galatians* in c. 49. ACTS OF THE APOSTLES: perhaps written towards AD 90. PETER: supposedly martyred in Rome under Nero, though his career after the first years following Jesus's death is uncertain. JAMES THE JUST: put to death by the Jewish high priest Annas II in AD 62. PAUL AND PAX ROMANA: cf. rabbinical story that God had created the Roman peace simply so that Jews might study the law undistracted. PROCURATORS OF JUDAEA WHO DETAINED PAUL: Antonius Felix (52– c. 60) and Porcius Festus (c. 60–2). JEWISH CHRISTIANS: their decline was accelerated after the Second Jewish Revolt under Hadrian. The smaller sects into which they split included the Ebionites. GOSPELS: written for Gentile Christians, though Matthew possibly envisaged a Jewish readership as well. MARCION of Sinope (Sinop) in N. Asia Minor came to Rome c. AD 137.

## PART VIII  TOWARDS A NEW WORLD

### Chapter 17 Collapse and Recovery

MARCUS AURELIUS AND VERUS: originally Marcus Annius Verus and Lucius Ceionius Commodus respectively. Antoninus Pius had adopted them at Hadrian's wish in 138 (Verus was the son of Aelius Caesar). EPIDEMIC: exanthematous typhus or bubonic plague? NORTHERN ENEMIES OF AURELIUS: Marcomanni (German) and Sarmatians (or Jazyges, non-German) to their S.E. The Germans burnt Opitergium (Oderzo in N. Italy) in 170. REVOLT IN EAST (175): Avidius Cassius. DEATH OF MARCUS AURELIUS: at Vindonissa (Windisch) or Sirmium (Sremska Mitrovica). HEIR OF MARCUS AURELIUS: he passed over Pompeianus, married to his daughter Lucilla. She conspired against Commodus in c. 182 and was exiled and killed. COMMODUS' PRAETORIAN PREFECTS: Perennis 182–5, Cleander 186–9, Laetus 191. DIDIUS JULIANUS: won throne at auction against Sulpicianus, city prefect. SEVERUS: from Lepcis Magna, which he splendidly rebuilt. Just over half the senators were now provincials, and about one-third of these provincials were north African. CITY TROOPS INCREASED: Severus also trebled the watch (*vigiles*). 'CARACALLA' = a Celtic or German tunic; his original name was Bassianus, later officially called Marcus Aurelius Antoninus. PARTHIAN WAR: But Severus twice failed to take the desert fortress of Hatra.

BRITISH WAR: Severus built a new legionary fortress at Carpow on the River Tay (above Abernethy). CARACALLA'S WIFE: Plautilla. NORTHERN WARS: Alamanni (mentioned for first time) defeated and Chatti (?) bought off in 213. ELAGABALUS: his original name was Varius Avitus Bassianus (after his father Varius Marcellus); later officially called Marcus Aurelius Antoninus, like Caracalla. ELAGABALUS MOTHER: Julia Soaemias. SEVERUS ALEXANDER: his original name was Alexianus. His father was Gessius Marcianus. NORTHERN FRONTIER: garrison weakened by Severus Alexander's eastern wars. MAXIMINUS I: elevated by a Danubian unit at Moguntiacum (Mainz). SEVEN CAESARS IN 238: Maximinus I, Maximus Caesar (his son). Gordianus I and II Africanus (in Carthage), Balbinus and Pupienus (known as Maximus) (in Rome), Gordianus III Pius (238-44, prefect Timesitheus d. 243/4). Gordianus III fought in the east but was murdered at Zaitha near the Euphrates, probably at the instigation of his successor Philip. MILLENNIUM: Secular Games (Ludi Saeculares) AD 248. DECIUS: from southern Pannonia; he assumed the name of Trajanus. EPIDEMIC (starting under Gallus, 251-3): this plague(?) continued to recur often until at least 270. SONS: promoted by Severus, Maximinus, Philip, Decius, Valerian, Carus. PHILIP'S FATHER: Marinus in Trachonitis (S.E. of Damascus). VALERIAN: followed brief reign of Aemilianus (253). ZENOBIA: her son Vaballathus Athenodorus was made Augustus. Her chief minister was the Syrian philosopher Longinus. LAST PARTHIAN KING: Artabanus V. SASSANIANS: after Sasan, grandfather of Ardashir. Their holy city was Istakhr, ancient residence of the Achaemenids. SHAPUR I'S INVASIONS OF ROMAN EMPIRE: 242/4, between 250 and 256, 259-60. GOTHIC INVASIONS: as far as Marcianopolis (Provadiya, W. of Varna, 248); and as far as Ephesus (Selçuk) and Pessinus (Balhisar, 253). FRANKS: plundered Tarraco (Tarragona), capital of Nearer Spain (Hispania Tarraconensis). HERULI: originally from Scandinavia. Some had migrated to Rhine area, most to Black Sea. MOBILE FORCE: the first commander Aureolus, a Dacian, revolted against Gallienus but surrendered to the next emperor Claudius II Gothicus, who killed him. NAISSUS: probably the victory was won by Gallienus rather than after his death by Claudius II Gothicus, to whom it was also attributed by later historians. ALAMANNI: had been defeated by Gallienus in c. 258-60 but settled in the Agri Decumates, which the Romans permanently evacuated. CLAUDIUS II'S BROTHER: Quintillus (270). ZENOBIA'S DEFEATS: Zabdas defeated at Antioch and Emesa (Homs) in 271. AURELIAN'S WALL at Rome: 12 miles long, with 16 gates and 381 rectangular towers; originally 20 feet high. Built by civilian labour. AURELIAN'S SUCCESSOR: Tacitus (275-6), an elderly senator; defeated the Goths in Pontus but was killed by his troops or committed suicide. CARUS: defeated Germans (Quadi) and Sarmatians on Danube and captured Ctesiphon. He was the first emperor to omit to request senatorial approval of his accession. AURUM CORONARIUM: gold crowns had been offered to eastern and Hellenistic conquerors and Roman generals of 2nd century BC. COMPLAINTS: e.g. from Burunum (South-el-Khmis, Tunisia) to Commodus; from Lydian tenants probably to Severus (both these were from imperial estates); Scaptopare (Kyustendil in Bulgaria) in 238; Aragueni (Phrygia) to Philip, and many protests on Egyptian papyri. Probably the later practice of taking refuge on the great country estates had already begun; e.g. Kaua (Mauretania), cf. a great 3rd-century peristyle house near Colonia Agrippinensis (Köln) with grain warehouse. But private munificence towards cities largely ceased in the later 3rd century.

## Chapter 18 The Climax of the Pagan Empire

EPICTETUS (c. 55-135): from Hierapolis (Pamukkale) in Phrygia. MARCUS AURELIUS: recognized occasional heavenly guidance. His view of the cosmopolis was partly derived from the Stoic Posidonius who held that inner tensions preserve it as a composite whole. SEVERUS' PRAETORIAN PREFECTS: under Antoninus Pius, too, they had regularly been prominent jurists. PAPINIAN: joint prefect with Plautianus 203-5. Executed by Caracalla in 212. ULPIAN: had been Papinian's assessor. Killed by mutinous praetorians in 223. PAULUS: pupil of Cervidius Scaevola; Papinian's assessor, and may have been briefly joint prefect with Ulpian. Wrote 320 books. CONSTITUTIO ANTONINIANA: our version (a Greek papyrus) may be a policy statement, not the original *constitutio* itself. A class known as *dediticii* (capitulants) was excluded along with slaves; perhaps it principally comprised people recently and forcibly settled within the empire (known as *laeti*), though there was also a category of freed slaves described as *dediticii*. Ostensible aim of the *Constitutio*: 'so that the Gods, with more worshippers, would favour the pious Roman people more'. Nevertheless the national law of the Greek past continued to assert itself against imperial law, at least until Diocletian systematically enforced the latter. BATHS OF CARACALLA: the reservoir could hold 2,688,000 cubic feet of water. MARCUS AURELIUS' PORTRAITS: some show blank, Antonine classicism, but a few are in a novel, tense, style: e.g. from arch of c. 178 (vanished) celebrating Marcomannic triumph, and gold head from Aventicum (Avenches in Switzerland) at Lausanne. MARCUS AURELIUS' COLUMN: style originally foreshadowed, in part, by reliefs from lost Column of Antoninus. PORTRAITS: Commodus as Hercules in Palazzo dei Conservatori, Rome; Caracalla in Museo Archeologico Nazionale, Naples; Maximinus I in Ny Carlsberg Glypothek, Copenhagen (his coin-portraits carry realism almost to the point of caricature); Philip in the Vatican; Decius in Capitoline Museum, Rome; Trebonianus Gallus in Metropolitan Museum, New York; Gallienus in Museo Nazionale delle Terme, Rome. PLOTINUS: studied in Alexandria under the Platonist Ammonius Saccas who also taught Origen and Longinus. PORPHYRY (c. AD 232-305) from Tyre (Sur): pupil first of Longinus then of Plotinus. SUN CULT: traditionally went back in Rome to King Numa Pompilius. Identified with Apollo as in Greece since about 5th century BC. MITHRAS: as god of light, was patron of truthful dealings and obligations. He supported the god Ahuramazda against Ahriman. MANI: arrested by Persian king Bahram I and died at Gundeshapur (c. 274/7). Kartir, chief Magus and architect of the state religion, prevailed.

## Chapter 19 The Supreme State and Church

DIOCLETIAN: succeeded the sons of Carus, Numerian (probably killed by his praetorian prefect Aper) and Carinus (killed after a battle with Diocletian near River Margus [Morava]). REVOLT IN BRITAIN: Carausius (c. 287-93; he apparently controlled N.E. Gaul), Allectus (c. 293-6; defeated by Constantius I's praetorian prefect Asclepiodotus). Some forts of Britain's Saxon shore may date from this period. OTHER NORTHERN SUCCESSES: Constantius I in Germany (302–4), and five victories of Diocletian on Danube (from 302). REVOLTS IN EGYPT: the second proclaimed the usurper Domitius Domitianus (297–8). PERSIAN WAR (296–8): Diocletian and Galerius were defeated by Narses I near Carrhae (Haran), but Galerius seized Armenia, and then Ctesiphon, and annexed five small provinces. MAXIMIAN'S RETIREMENT: the palace at Piazza Armerina in Sicily may possibly have belonged to him, or to his son Maxentius. DIOCESES (*dioeceseis*): each under a *vicarius*, i.e. officially a deputy of the praetorian prefects (in whose favour the power of the *vicarii* subsequently declined). PRICE EDICT (*edictum de pretiis*): the most complete copy is from Aezani (Emet) in Phrygia (Asia Minor). CURRENCY REFORM OF DIOCLETIAN: underestimated the value of the precious metal coinage in relation to the base metal issues, so that the price of commodities in terms of the latter rose sharply. CEREMONIAL: the name of Diocletian's imperial council was changed from *consilium* to *consistorium*, because its members no longer sat but stood in his presence. SALONAE: the palace covered 9 acres. Its plan was based on a blend of Roman camps, city walls and civil architecture. COMPANIONS OF THE GODS: Commodus had displayed Hercules as his companion (*comes*) on coins and medallions. CLEMENT OF ALEXANDRIA: 'how may a rich man be saved?' ORIGEN: taught by Leonides (his father), Pantaenus, Clement and Ammonius Saccas (also the teacher of Plotinus). His numerous works included a refutation of the pagan Celsus. TERTULLIAN: born in or near Carthage. He joined the extreme, ascetic, Montanist movement. CYPRIAN: executed in 258 during Valerian's persecution. JEWS: began to be outnumbered by Christians in 2nd century AD. Although Severus forbade proselytism by Jews (as by Christians), their good relations with Rome were cemented in Syria Palaestina (the former Judaea) by the recognized national leader (patriarch) Judah I ha-Nasi, 'the prince' (AD 135–219). There was extensive synagogue-building in Galilee (Chorazin, Capernaum, Kefr Bir'im): cf. at Dura Europus on the Euphrates. Exilarchs, the counterpart of the Palestinian patriarchs, presided over flourishing communities of Babylonian Jews in 3rd century (Nehardea, Sura, Pumbeditha, Machuza near Ctesiphon). DECIUS' PERSECUTION: Pope (bishop of Rome) Fabian was executed. DIOCLETIAN'S PERSECUTION: neo-Platonist Hierocles, governor of Bithynia and Egypt, was one of its leaders, and also wrote against the Christians. SUCCESSORS OF DIOCLETIAN: Constantius I (305–6), Galerius (305–11), Severus II (306–7), Maxentius (306–12), Maximian (second reign 306–8, third attempt 310), Maximinus II Daia (308–13; nephew of Galerius), Constantine I (the Great) (312–37), Licinius (312–24; from the new Dacia, south of the Danube): but Constantine and Licinius had first been declared Augusti in 306 and 308; respectively. CONSTANTINE THE GREAT'S MOTHER: (Saint) Helena, a barmaid from Bithynia; she became a pious Christian (at an uncertain date) and died in c. 328. GERMAN WARS OF CONSTANTINE: against Franks, Alamanni, etc. (306–13). CONSTANTINOPLE: did not have a large population until c. 360. By the end of the century it had 4,388 private residences. For church buildings, see below. CHRISTIANIZATION: in the latest edition of the Edict of Serdica, the name of Licinius was omitted. The Edict of Milan consisted of regulations of Constantine and Licinius which were issued when the latter visited Mediolanum (Milan) to marry Constantine's half-sister Constantia, and subsequently repeated by Licinius in a proclamation at Nicomedia (Izmit) (though Licinius, quarrelling with Constantine, later reverted to persecution). African milestones with the Christian Chi-Rho symbol date from 317–19. A vault-mosaic in the Mausoleum of Julii under St Peter's at Rome identifies Christ and the Sun. King Tiridates III of Armenia had joined the Christian faith and imposed it on his country when restored to its throne in 298. SUPREME DEITY (*Summus sanctus deus*): revered by Hierocles and invoked by troops of Licinius before his victory over Maximinus II Daia at Tzirallum (near Edirne) in Thrace in 313. CHURCH FUNDS: an extension of the private wealth of the emperor rather than of state funds. CHRISTIAN COMMUNITIES: the best organized and biggest were at Antioch and Alexandria. DISSIDENT CHRISTIANS: e.g. the Donatists of north Africa, who condemned all who had sacrificed to pagan deities in Diocletian's persecution and were eventually persecuted by Constantine (316–21); he built an important church at Cirta, renamed Constantina (now Constantine). CHRISTIAN CATACOMBS AT ROME: Sts. Callixtus, Sebastian, Domitilla, etc. JEWS: catacombs at Rome (some to be opened before long to the public); Via Appia Pignatelli, Villa Torlonia, Vigna Rondanini. The treatment of the Jews deteriorated under Constantius II (337–61), especially after the rebellion of Patricius in Palestine. HOUSE-CHURCHES: church at Dura-Europus on Euphrates (232) was built to succeed a place of worship in a private house. But purpose-built churches preceded Diocletian's persecution. BASILICAS: Trajan's timber-roofed Basilica Ulpia was widely imitated; cf. fine Basilica of Severus at Lepcis Magna. LATERAN: from family of Plautii Laterani. It may not have become the papal cathedral immediately. ST PETER'S: built over shrine of St Peter of which the surviving structure dates from *c.* AD 160-170. Constantine also transformed the *cella memoriae* of St Paul into the Basilica Ostiensis (St Paul Outside the Walls). His great Roman churches were all located outside the walls so as not to offend the pagans. HOLY APOSTLES, CONSTANTINOPLE: under its conical roof, the remains of Constantine the Great, the 'thirteenth apostle', lay for a time. GOLDEN OCTAGON, Antioch: forerunner of palace-church of Aquisgranum (Aachen), etc. PALESTINE (Syria Palaestina): in addition to the Holy Sepulchre there were further great churches of Constantine at Jerusalem (on the sites of the Nativity and the Ascension, initiated by his mother Helena), as well as at Bethlehem and Hebron. Such combinations of centralized and longitudinal designs reached their climax in Justinian I's Santa Sophia (Aya Sofya) at Constantinople. ALLEGED PLOT OF 326: by Constantine's wife Fausta and eldest son Crispus (by his previous wife Minervina; Caesar since 316) executed. CONSTANTINE'S SUCCESSORS: sons Constantine II (337–40), Constantius II (337–61) and Constans (337–50), and nephews (both killed immediately after his death) Delmatius and Hannibalianus (made King of Kings in Armenia). CONSTANTIUS II'S PERSIAN WARS: Shapur II (309–79) thrice attacked the fortress of Nisibis in Mesopotamia (Nüsaybin, S.E. Turkey) without success but was then diverted by a nomad threat on his eastern frontier. REVOLTS AGAINST CONSTANTIUS II: Magnentius, Vetranio, Nepotianus (all in 350; Magnentius reigned until 353), Silvanus 355, Julian 360. GALLUS (Constantius): put down revolts in Syria Palaestina (Patricius) and Isauria (S. Asia Minor) but was recalled and put to death at Pola in Istria (Pula in N.W. Yugoslavia).

JULIAN'S GERMAN VICTORIES (356–9): over Alamanni, whom he defeated at Argentorate (Strasbourg) in 356, and over Franks. REBELLION OF JULIAN (360): at Lutetia (Paris). JULIAN'S EDUCATION: by eunuch Mardonius and pagan philosopher Maximus (at Ephesus); also at Athens. RESTORATION OF JERUSALEM TEMPLE: ostensibly abandoned because of inflammable gases. JULIAN'S ADMINISTRATION: bureaucracy and bodyguard and secret police (*agentes in rebus*) were greatly reduced, and he attempted to revive the cities and their councils. PERSIAN WAR: Julian was killed while marching to meet a reserve army. JOVIANUS: originated from Singidunum (Belgrade). He surrendered Nisibis and Singara (on Jebel Sinjar), and Galerius' gains in the east.


# PART IX  THE TRANSFORMATION OF EUROPE

## Chapter 20 *The Fall of the Western Empire*

VALENTINIAN I'S ORIGIN: from Cibalae (Vinkovci in Yugoslavia). HIS NORTHERN CAMPAIGNS (365–73): successive headquarters at Lutetia (Paris), Ambianum (Amiens [formerly Samarobriva]: to deal with attacks by Saxons, Picts and Scots on British provinces), Treviri and Sirmium (Sremska Mitrovica) (with interlude to crush revolt of Firmus in Africa, 373–5; there was also a later African revolt under Gildo, 398). GRATIAN and VALENS had to give Italy, Illyricum and north Africa to Gratian's brother Valentinian II, hailed emperor at Aquincum (Budapest) (375–92). THEODOSIUS I'S ORIGINS: from Cauca (Coca) in Spain. REVOLTS AGAINST THEODOSIUS I: Magnus Maximus (383–8), a Spaniard, in Britain, Gaul and Spain (he overthrew Gratian), Eugenius (392–4), a protégé of Arbogast who had Valentinian II murdered but was killed in battle of Frigidus (River Vipacco or Wippach, tributary of Isonzo). STILICHO'S WIFE: Serena. OSTROGOTHIC INVASION (405): Radagaisus, defeated at Faesulae (Fiesole). ALANS: nomadic pastoralists from between River Volga and River Don. USURPERS AFTER INVASION: e.g. Constantine III (407–11), elevated in Britain, established capital at Arelate (Arles). Honorius had probably settled Saxons in Britain as *foederati*, in exchange for military service. Its communities were still economically linked to the continent in *c.* 420–30. STILICHO'S DEATH: after mutiny at Ticinum (Pavia). ALARIC'S PUPPET AT ROME: Priscus Attalus (409). ALARIC'S DEATH: at Consentia (Cosenza), buried in River Busento. CONSTANTIUS III'S ORIGINS: from Naïssus (Niš in Yugoslavia). BURGUNDIANS: kingdom based on Borbetomagus (Worms) (*c.* 406); transplanted to Sabaudia (Savoy) in 443. ATAULF'S DEATH: at Barcino (Barcelona). WESTERN USURPER (423–5): Johannes. ATTILA: his elder brother was Bleda. VALENTINIAN III'S SISTER: Honoria. CATALAUNIAN PLAINS: the Visigothic King Theoderic I, who had developed the powers of the monarchy, was killed. POPE LEO I: met Attila on the River Mincius (Mincio). HUN DEFEAT BY GERMANS: on River Medao (unidentified). GERMANS pressed forward near Lake Constance. MAJORIAN'S DEFEAT by Gaiseric: off Carthago Nova (Cartagena). MAJORIAN'S SUCCESSOR: Anthemius, nominated by eastern emperor Leo I. LAST WESTERN EMPERORS: Olybrius (472), Glycerius (473–4), Julius Nepos (474–5; d. 480 in Dalmatia), Romulus Augustus ('Augustulus', 475–6). LOYAL REMNANT OF

CENTRAL GAUL: Auvergne, with its capital at Arverna (Clermont-Ferrand; formerly Augustonemetum), lost by Julius Nepos to Visigothic King Euric (474). Arelate fell in 476. FATHER OF ROMULUS: Orestes, a Roman who had been Attila's secretary. 'FALL': the term 'Middle Ages' (from 476 or 395, 406, 610, 800, 842?) was first used by Prof. C. Kellner of Halle in 1688. Abbé Ferdinando Galiani (1744): 'The Fall of empires: what can that mean? Empires, being neither up nor down, do not fall.' GERMAN APPROVAL OF 'FALL' : Beatus Rhenanus (15th-16th century); cf. the Dutch jurist and historian Hugo Grotius (16th-17th century). ZENO'S WESTERN NOMINEE: Julius Nepos.

## Chapter 21 The Fatal Disunities

NOTITIA DIGNITATUM: List of senior officers of state and army, with their staffs, in the western and eastern empires (AD 395). Great estates: e.g. Burgus Julius near Carthage (on mosaic in Bardo Museum, Tunis); cf. Burgus of Leontius at confluence of Dordogne and Garonne; and earlier three-storeyed fortress at Pfalzel (4th century). DEFENDERS OF PEOPLE: Letter of Valentinian I to his praetorian prefect Petronius Probus. Selection of Defenders was transferred to city councillors by Theodosius I, then to committees including land-owners by Honorius. SALVIAN: probably born at Treviri (Trier); wrote On the Governance of God (De Gubernatione Dei). BAGAUDAE: Tibatto (435, raised slaves), physician Eudoxius (440s, fled to Huns); also in Spain, where they were crushed by Aetius in 454. Their People's Courts: mentioned in verse-drama Querolus ('The Protester'). GAULISH LANDOWNER AS EMPEROR: Avitus (455) at Arelate; coronation attended by Visigothic king Theoderic II (453–66). DE REBUS BELLICIS: anonymous treatise explaining plans for the reform of the administration and the army; apparently addressed to the emperors Valentinian I and Valens. ALARIC: had wanted a single German–Roman people according to the Gothic historical summarizer Jordanes. ATAULF on German–Roman co-operation: reported by a citizen of Narbo (Narbonne) to the chronicler Orosius. SIDONIUS APOLLINARIS (c. 430–88) of Lugdunum (Lyon); praised the Visigothic monarchs Theoderic II and Euric (having fought against the latter in 471–5). DISLOYALTY OF FEDERATES: in 409 they failed to prevent other Germans from crossing into Spain, and in 422 they deserted to the Vandals there. MONASTICISM: first made famous by St Antony (born in upper Egypt c. 251), who organized his followers into groups during the persecution of Galerius (305–6). MONASTERIES of St Martin of Tours: Ligugé near Pictavi (Poitiers; formerly Limonum) c. 360, and then Marmoutier near Civitas Turonum (Tours; formerly Caesarodunum). Martin, who came from Savaria in Pannonia (Szombathely in Hungary), followed St Antony's ideal of partly eremitical and partly communal life. After 400 Honoratus established a monastery at Lérins near Cannes. JEROME'S numerous works include translation of Bible into Latin (the Vulgate). JOHN CASSIAN: writer of Institutes and Conferences which exercised great influence on St Benedict of Nursia (Norcia) abbot of Monte Cassino (died c. 547). CHURCH IS IN THE STATE: Bishop Optatus of Milev (Mila in Algeria). MEDIOLANUM (Milan) in later 4th century: 5 huge churches: SS. Nazaro, Simpliciano, Giovanni in Conca, Tecla, Lorenzo. Ambrose, bishop of Mediolanum, unearthed two pairs of saints there and one at

Bononia (Bologna). ROMAN CHURCHES in mid-5th century: e.g. S. Maria
Maggiore (Basilica Liberiana) of Sixtus III (432–40). FORCIBLE CONFORMITY:
based on interpretations of texts of Luke's Gospel and Paul's Epistles. VICTORY
DEBATE (384): between Ambrose and the pagan aristocratic Roman orator and
writer Symmachus (c. 340–402). AUGUSTINE'S BACKGROUND: his parents were
Patricius and Monica and he was educated at Thagaste, Madaurus and Carthage.
He was then in Rome for one year as a teacher before going to Mediolanum
(Milan) in 386. PRO-PAGAN USURPER, 392–4: Eugenius. SURVIVAL OF PAGANISM:
gladiatorial combats may have continued until 439–40, duels of men against
wild animals until 498 and contests between wild animals until 681. AUGUSTINE
ON 'OPPORTUNITY': to Vincentius, Donatist bishop of Cartennae (Ténès).
'YOUR' VIRGIL: letter to Nectarius of Calama. 'INVICTA ROMA AETERNA':
e.g. on gold medallion of client Priscus Attalus. RUTILIUS NAMATIANUS: poem
*De Reditu Suo* (On his Return). MACROBIUS: probably pagan, perhaps from north
Africa; his works included extant *Saturnalia* (? c. 430), academic symposium in
seven books. POPES AGAINST GOVERNMENT SERVICE: Siricius (385–99), Innocent I
(401–17). PELAGIUS: died after 419. He wrote commentary on Pauline epistles.
70 tracts supporting his viewpoint are the work of his followers. AUGUSTINE
DISSOCIATES CHURCH FROM STATE: influence of lay Donatist theologian
Tyconius, author of *Rules* and interpreter of St Paul.

## Chapter 22 The Aftermath

CLOVIS: son of Childeric I, ruler of a tribe of Salian Franks. He had remained loyal
to his treaties with the Romans, but won the battle of Vouillé against the Visigoths, whose king Alaric II, son of Euric, was killed. Clovius had defeated a last
west Roman outpost at Suessiona (Soissons on N. France) in 486. He was sent
consular insignia from Constantinople by Anastasius I. CHARLES MARTEL:
threw back a Moslem invasion from Spain (732). CHARLEMAGNE: the Holy
Roman Empire only disappeared in 1806. SEVILLE: formerly Hispalis: its bishop
Isidore (602–35), a prolific writer, was one of the principal links between the
ancient world and the Middle Ages. NORTH AFRICA: the Islamic armies started
their advance westwards from Egypt in 640 and had conquered the whole of
north Africa by 711. OSTROGOTHS: took one-third of Italian land for their own
use. The populations were kept apart. Theoderic the Ostrogoth, like the
Burgundians and Visigoths, placed the head of the Byzantine emperor Anastasius I
on his coins. BOETHIUS (c. 480–524): held high office but was then imprisoned
and executed by Theoderic. He wrote *On the Consolation of Philosophy* in
prison. CASSIODORUS (c. 490–583): senator, consul, encyclopaedist, theologian,
founded religious community at Vivarium (Coscia di Staletti) in his native
Calabria. GELASIUS I TO EASTERN EMPEROR: Anastasius I. BELISARIUS: occupied
Carthage and captured Vandal king Gelimer (533); then in Italy 533–40 and
546–9. NARSES: Pers-Armenian eunuch: completed conquest of Italy 550–4,
then administered it from Ravenna to 567. Justinian's generals also recaptured
parts of southern Spain. ARCADIUS' ADVISERS: Rufinus, Eutropius, Anthemius.
THEODOSIUS II: bought off Huns 422, sum increased 434, 443. EASTERN EMPEROR
LEO I: given the throne by Aspar the Alan. ZENO: from Isauria in Asia Minor;
his original name was Tarasicodissa. At first for a few months co-emperor with

his son Leo II (474). ANASTASIUS I: from Dyrrhachium (Durrës in Albania). His major reform of the coinage marked the beginning of the Byzantine system. JUSTIN I: from a village near Naïssus (Niš in Yugoslavia). BALKANS: Bulgars crossed the Danube and menaced Constantinople in 679. CORPUS OF JUSTINIAN I: *Digest* (50 books with 432 titles from 2,000 works), *Codex* (imperial statutes, 2 editions), *Institutes* (elementary), *Novellae* (new laws). Undertaken by a commission of 16 members, mostly presided over by Tribonian of Side (Eski Antalya, S. Asia Minor) (d. 542/5). PERSIA: large areas of the Byzantine empire were lost to the Persian King Chosroes II Parvez (590–628). LOSS OF JUSTINIAN I'S WESTERN CONQUESTS: N. Italy settled by Lombards (568) for two centuries; Pope Gregory the Great (590–604) (the last intellectual to combine western and Greek culture) negotiated directly with them. Hopes of a united empire were further shattered by movement of Slavs into the Balkans (7th century), separating Italy from the east, and by the loss of north Africa to the Arabs (8th century). CRUSADERS AT CONSTANTINOPLE, 1204–61: the 'Latin Empire'. TURKS: the Seljuk Turks defeated the Byzantines at Manzikert in 1071. The Ottoman Turks began to encroach on the empire under the founder of their dynasty Osman I (1288–1326). FALL OF CONSTANTINOPLE (1453): the end of the 'Middle Ages' (or this has been dated to 1440, 1492, 1515, 1548). USURPERS IN EASTERN EMPIRE: Procopius (365–6, distant relation of Julian the Apostate), Basiliscus (475–6), Marcian (479), Leontius I (484–8) (these three all in Zeno's reign), and Vitalian (513–15).

# ANCIENT SOURCES

## 1 LATIN HISTORICAL WRITERS

AMMIANUS MARCELLINUS, *c.* AD 330–95; born at Antioch in Syria (Antakya in S.E. Turkey). History (*Rerum Gestarum libri*) of years AD 96–378 (Books 14–31 about AD 353–78 survive).

CAESAR, Gaius Julius, 100–44 BC. Dictator, seven books of *Commentaries* on Gallic War (eighth is by Aulus Hirtius), three on *Civil War* (the concluding books on African, Alexandrian and Spanish wars are by other authors).

CASSIODORUS, *c.* AD 490–583; born at Scylacium (Squillace) in S. Italy. Extant examples of his numerous works include the *Chronica*, a brief summary of Roman history to AD 519. See also JORDANES.

EUTROPIUS, fourth century AD. Survey (*Breviarium*) of Roman history from beginning to AD 364.

FLORUS, ANNAEUS (?), second century AD; born in North Africa. *Epitome* of Roman history to wars of Augustus.

HISTORIA AUGUSTA, ostensibly the work of six authors (probably pseudonyms); apparently of the later 4th century AD. Partly fictitious 'biographies' of Roman emperors, Caesars and usurpers from AD 117 to 284 (gap for 244–59).

ISIDORE, bishop of Hispalis (Seville), AD 602–36. Numerous works included history to his own times (*Chronica Majora*) and a history of the Goths.

JEROME, SAINT (Eusebius Hieronymus), *c.* AD 348–420; born at Stridon in Dalmatia. His historical works include a *Chronicle* of ancient events and short biographies of Christian writers (*De Viris Illustribus*).

JORDANES, mid-6th century AD; probably a Goth from the lower Danube. Summaries of Gothic and Roman History, former summarizing the *Gothic Histories* of Cassiodorus (q.v.).

LIVY (Titus Livius), 59 BC–AD 17 or 64 BC–AD 12; born at Patavium (Padua in N. Italy). History of Rome (*Ab Urbe Condita*, to 9 BC) in 142 books, of which 35 are extant, covering the periods 753–243 and 219–167 BC. From the lost books we have fragments and excerpts, and there are two sets of abridgements.

NEPOS, Cornelius, *c.* 99–24 BC; born in North Italy. Out of various works 24 short biographies survive.

OROSIUS, Paulus, early 5th century AD; probably born at Bracara Augusta

(Braga in Portugal). Christian Chronicle (*Historiae adversum Paganos*) in 7 books from the Creation to AD 417.

SALLUST (Gaius Sallustius Crispus), *c.* 86–35 BC; born at Amiternum (San Vittorino in central Italy). Monographs on Catilinarian conspiracy (*Bellum Catilinae*) and Jugurthine War (*Bellum Iugurthinum*) in addition to lost *Histories*.

SUETONIUS (Gaius Suetonius Tranquillus), *c.* AD 69–104 (?); probably from Hippo Regius (Annaba in Algeria). Writings include *Biographies*, *De Vita Caesarum* (The Twelve Caesars), *De Viris Illustribus* (including *De Grammaticis et Rhetoribus*), *De Poetis* (at least 3 survive), *De Oratoribus* (15, summary of one survives), *De Historicis* (one of 6 survives).

TACITUS, Publius Cornelius, *c.* AD 56 – before or after 117; probably of Gallic or North Italian origin. *Histories* of the years AD 69–96 (?): out of 12 or 14 books, 4 and part of the fifth survive (on the Civil Wars, AD 69–70). Then *Annals* covering the years AD 14–68; out of 18 or 16 books, 10 (minus parts of 3) survive (on Tiberius, part of Claudius' reign, and most of Nero's). Previous works included a biography of his father-in-law, *Agricola*, and the *Germania* and *Dialogue on Orators* (*Dialogus de Oratoribus*).

VALERIUS MAXIMUS, wrote in 30s AD. Moral and rhetorical history (*Facta ac dicta memorabilia*) in 9 books.

VELLEIUS PATERCULUS, *c.* 19 BC–after AD 30; of Campanian origin. Compendium of Roman history (*Historiae Romanae*) to AD 30.

## 2  GREEK HISTORICAL WRITERS

APPIAN, 2nd century AD; probably born at Alexandria in Egypt. History of Roman conquests to Trajan, in 24 books of which nos. 6–9 (mostly) and 11–17 are complete.

DIO CASSIUS (Cassius Dio Cocceianus), *c.* AD 155–235; from Nicaea (Iznik in N.W. Turkey). Roman History to AD 229, in 80 books of which nos. 36–54 (68–10 BC) are preserved, 55–60 (91 BC–AD 46) exist in abbreviated form, 17 and 79–80 in part. Xiphilinus (11th century) epitomized from book 36 onwards and Zonaras (12th century) gives the gist of 1–21 and 44–80.

DIODORUS SICULUS, lived under Caesar and Augustus; from Agyrium (Agira) in Sicily. World history (*Bibliotheke*) to Caesar's Gallic War in 40 books, of which 1–8 and 11–20 are fully preserved and the remaining books fragmentary.

DIONYSIUS, worked under Augustus; from Halicarnassus (Bodrum in S.W. Turkey). His writings included *Roman Antiquities* to outbreak of First Punic War, in 20 books of which the first 10 survive.

EUSEBIUS, *c.* AD 260–340; of Caesarea Maritima (near Sdot Yam in Israel). His writings included *Church History*, extended in latest edition to AD 324, and eulogistic life of Constantine the Great.

HERODIAN, early 3rd century AD; from Syria. Roman History from AD 180 to 238, in 8 books.

JOSEPHUS, FLAVIUS, AD 37/8 – after 94; of Jewish, Pharisaic, origin. *Jewish War* (about the First Jewish Revolt), Greek translation in 7 books of lost Aramaic original; *Jewish Antiquities* in 20 books, a history of the Jews from the Creation to just before the First Revolt; his *Life*, an autobiographical defence; and *Against Apion*, a 2-book work attacking anti-Semitic writers from the 3rd century BC.

NICOLAUS, later 1st century BC; from Damascus in Syria. Court historian of Herod the Great (37–4 BC); his works included a *Universal History* to Herod's death of which portions are preserved.

PLUTARCH (Lucius (?) Mestrius Plutarchus), before AD 50 to after 120; of Chaeronea in Greece. Numerous writings include 23 pairs of 'parallel lives' of Greeks and Romans, and lives of the Caesars, of which only *Galba* and *Otho* survive.

POLYBIUS, *c*. 200–118 BC; of Megalopolis in Greece. *Universal History* of the years 220–144 BC in 40 books, of which we have the first 5, a large part of book 6, substantial portions of 7–16, and smaller extracts from most of the others, comprising altogether nearly a third of the whole work.

PROCOPIUS, *c*. AD 500 – after 562; born at Caesarea Maritima (near Sdot Yam in Israel). *History of the Wars of Justinian* in 8 books and censorious *Secret History*.

THEODORETUS, *c*. AD 393–466; bishop of Cyrrhus (Kurus in S.E. Turkey). Writings included *Church History* from Constantine the Great to AD 428, and *Religious History* containing biographies of ascetics.

ZONARAS, Johannes, 12th century AD; monk at Hagia Glyceria in the Princes' Islands (Kizil Adalar). *Universal Epitome of Histories* to AD 1118, now in 18 books, excerpting Dio Cassius, Plutarch, etc.

ZOSIMUS, *c*. AD 500; a pagan, possibly from Ascalon (Ashkelon) or Gaza in S.W. Palestine. *Historia Nova* from Augustus to AD 410.


## 3   OTHER SOURCES

(i) Other historians and biographers, whose works in this field are now lost or mainly lost but detectable through intermediaries. Of particular importance (among very many) are the Latin writers Cato the elder (234–149 BC), Licinius Macer (died 68 BC), Pliny the elder (AD 23–79), Pollio (76 BC – AD 4), Valerius Antias (1st century BC) and Varro (116–27 BC); and, in Greek, Cincius Alimentus (late 2nd century BC), the emperor Claudius (10 BC–AD 54), Fabius Pictor (late 2nd century BC), and Posidonius (*c*. 135–50 BC).

(ii) Other Greek and Latin authors of a primarily non-historical character whose works nevertheless contain historical information, notably Augustine, Cicero, Lucan, Salvian, Seneca the younger, Sidonius Apollinaris, Virgil, etc., etc.

(iii) Inscriptions.

(iv) Papyri, mainly from Egypt.

(v) Graffiti, especially at Pompeii.

(vi) Coins, of the Roman state and its enemies, and local communities and client kingdoms, and of the neighbours and enemies of the Roman empire.

(vii) Commemorative medallions of the Roman state and local communities.

(viii) Works of art and architecture and engineering.

(ix) Remains of agricultural and commercial and industrial activities.

# BIBLIOGRAPHY

AFRICA, T. W., *The Immense Majesty: A History of Rome and the Roman Empire* (New York 1974)
ALFÖLDI, A., *Early Rome and the Latins* (Ann Arbor 1965)
ANDRÉ, J. M., *Le siècle d'Auguste* (Paris 1974)
ARNOTT, P. D., *An Introduction to the Roman World* (London 1976)
BADIAN, E., *Roman Imperialism in the Late Republic*, 2nd ed. (Oxford 1968)
BAILEY, C. (ed.), *The Legacy of Rome* (Oxford 1924)
BALSDON, J. P. V. D., *Life and Leisure in Ancient Rome* (London 1969)
BALSDON, J. P. V. D., *Roman Women* (London 1962)
BALSDON, J. P. V. D. (ed.), *The Romans* (London 1965)
BANTI, L., *Il mondo degli etruschi*, 2nd ed. (Rome 1969) (*Etruscan Cities and their Culture*, London and Berkeley 1973)
BENGTSON, H., *Einführung in die alte Geschichte*, 6th ed. (Munich 1974) (*Introduction to Ancient History*, London and Berkeley 1975)
BIANCHI BANDINELLI, R., *Rome: le centre du pouvoir* (Paris 1969) (*Rome the Centre of Power: Roman Art to A.D. 200*, London 1970)
BIANCHI BANDINELLI, R., *Rome: la fin de l'art antique* (Paris 1970) (*The Late Empire: Roman Art A.D. 200–400*, London 1971)
BLOCH, R., *Les origines de Rome* (Paris 1959) (*The Origins of Rome*, London 1960)
BOAK, A. E. R. and SINNIGAN, W. G., *History of Rome to A.D. 565*, 5th ed. (New York 1965)
BOETHIUS, A. and WARD-PERKINS, J. B., *Etruscan and Roman Architecture* (Harmondsworth 1970)
BRAUER, G. C., *The Age of the Soldier Emperors* (Park Ridge 1975)
BRILLIANT, R., *Roman Art from the Republic to Constantine* (London 1974)
BRISSON, J. P., *Carthage ou Rome* (Paris 1973)
BRUNT, P. A., *Social conflicts in the Roman Republic* (London 1971)
CALABI, I., *L'uso storiografico delle iscrizioni latine* (Milan 1953)
CAMBRIDGE ANCIENT HISTORY, vols VII–XII (Cambridge 1928–39)
CARCOPINO, H., *La vie quotidienne à Rome à l'apogée de l'empire* (Paris 1939) (*Daily Life in Ancient Rome*, Harmondsworth 1956)
CARSON, R. A. G., *Coins of Greece and Rome*, 2nd ed. (London 1970)

CARY, M. and SCULLARD, H. H. *A History of Rome*, 3rd ed. (of Cary's *History*) (London 1975)

CASSON, L., *Travel in the Ancient World* (London 1974)

CHARLESWORTH, M. P., *The Roman Empire* (Oxford 1951)

CHEVALLIER, R., *Les voies romaines* (Paris 1972) (*Roman Roads*, London and Berkeley 1976)

CHRIST, K. (ed.), *Hannibal* (Darmstadt 1974)

CHRIST, K., *Römische Geschichte: Einführung, Quellenkunde, Bibliographie* (Darmstadt 1973)

CLARKE, M. L., *The Roman Mind* (London 1956)

COARELLI, F. (etc.), *Le città etrusche* (Milan 1973) (*Etruscan Cities*, London 1975)

COWELL, F. R., *Everyday Life in Ancient Rome* (London 1961)

CROOK, J. A., *Law and Life of Rome* (London 1967)

CUNLIFFE, B., *Rome and the Barbarians* (London 1975)

DILKE, O. A. W., *The Ancient Romans: How they Lived and Worked* (Newton Abbot 1975)

DOREY, T. A. and DUDLEY, D. R., *Rome against Carthage* (London 1971)

DOWNEY, G., *The Late Roman Empire* (New York 1969)

DUDLEY, D. R., *The Romans* (London 1970) (*Roman Society*, 1975)

EARL, D., *The Moral and Political Tradition of Rome* (London 1967)

ERRINGTON, R. M., *The Dawn of Empire: Rome's Rise to World Power* (London 1972)

FERGUSON, J., *The Religions of the Roman Empire* (London 1970)

FINLEY, M. I., *The Ancient Economy* (London 1973)

FINLEY, M. I. (ed.), *Slavery in Classical Antiquity* (London 1960)

FOWLER, W. W., *Rome*, 3rd ed. (Oxford 1967)

FRIEDLÄNDER, L., *Darstellungen aus der Sittengeschichte Roms*, 10th ed. (Leipzig 1922) (*Roman Life and Manners under the Early Empire*, London 1965 ed.)

GAGÉ, J., *Enquêtes sur les structures sociales et religieuses de la Rome primitive* (Brussels 1977)

GAGÉ, J., *Les classes sociales dans l'empire romain* (Paris 1969)

GARZETTI, A., *L'impero da Tiberio agli Antonini* (Rome 1960) (*From Tiberius to the Antonines*, London 1974)

GENTILI, B. (etc.), *Storia della letteratura latina* (Rome 1976)

GIBBON, E., *History of the Decline and Fall of the Roman Empire* (London 1776–88)

GRANT, M., *The Climax of Rome*, 3rd ed. (London 1974)

GRANT, M., *The Fall of the Roman Empire* (Radnor (Pennsylvania) 1976)

GRANT, M., *The Jews in the Roman World* (London 1973)*

GRANT, M., *Roman History from Coins*, 2nd ed. (Cambridge 1968)

GRANT, M., *Roman Literature*, 3rd ed. (Harmondsworth 1964)

GRANT, M., *The World of Rome*, 3rd ed. (London 1974)

GRIMAL, P., *La civilisation romaine* (Paris 1960) (*The Civilization of Rome*, London 1963)

GRIMAL, P. (etc.), *Der Hellenismus und der Aufstieg Roms* (Frankfurt-am-Main 1965) (*Hellenism and the Rise of Rome*, London 1968)

* See also *Jesus* (1977) and *Saint Paul* (1976) for short bibliographies.

GRUEN, E. S. (ed.), *The Image of Rome* (Englewood Cliffs 1969)

HADAS, M., *A History of Rome* (New York 1956)

HAMMOND, M., *The Antonine Monarchy* (Oxford 1959)

HAYWOOD, R. M., *Ancient Rome* (New York 1967)

HEICHELHEIM, F. M. and YEO, C. A., *History of the Roman People* (Englewood Cliffs 1962)

HEURGON, J., *Rome et la Méditerranée occidentale ·jusqu'aux guerres puniques* (Paris 1969) (*The Rise of Rome*, London 1973)

HEUSS, A., *Römische Geschichte*, 2nd ed. (Braunschweig 1964)

HIGHET, G., *The Classical Tradition*, 2nd ed. (Oxford 1967)

HOMO, L., *Le haut-empire* (Paris 1941)

JOLOWICZ, H. F., *Historical Introduction to the Study of Roman Law*, 2nd ed. (Cambridge 1972)

JONES, A. H. M., *The Decline of the Ancient World* (London 1966)

JONES, A. H. M., *A History of Rome through the Fifth Century* (London 1968)

JONES, A. H. M., *The Roman Economy* (Oxford 1974)

JONES, A. H. M., *The Later Roman Empire* (Oxford 1964)

KAEHLER, H., *Rom und sein Welt*, 2nd ed. (Munich 1968–70) (*Rome and her Empire*, London 1963)

KELLY, J. M., *Roman Litigation* (Oxford 1966)

KIENAST, D., *Augustus* (Darmstadt 1977)

KJELLBERG, E. and SAFLUND, G., *Grekisk och Romersk Konst* (Stockholm 1958) (*Greek and Roman Art*, London 1968)

KRAFT, H. (ed.), *Konstantin der Grosse* (Darmstadt 1974)

KUNKEL, W., *Römische Rechtsgeschichte*, 6th ed. (Köln 1971) (*An Introduction to Roman Legal and Constitutional History*, 2nd ed., Oxford 1973)

LE GALL, J., *La religion romaine de l'époque de Caton l'ancien au règne de l'empereur Commode* (Paris 1975)

LEVI, M. A. and MELONI, P., *Storia romana dagli etruschi a Teodosio*, 4th ed. (Milan 1968)

LEWIS, N. and REINHOLD, M., *Roman Civilization: A Sourcebook* (New York 1955)

LOT, F., *La fin du monde antique et le début du moyen age* (Paris 1927) (*The End of the Ancient World*, 2nd ed., London 1966)

LUTTWAK, E. N., *The Grand Strategy of the Roman Empire* (Baltimore 1977)

MCDONALD, A. H., *Republican Rome* (London 1966)

MACDONALD, W. L., *The Architecture of the Roman Empire* (New Haven 1956)

MACMULLEN, R., *The Roman Government's Response to Crisis A.D. 235–337* (New Haven 1976)

MACMULLEN, R., *Roman Social Relations 50 B.C. – A.D. 289* (New Haven 1974)

MANSUELLI, G., *Etrurien und die Anfänge Roms* (Milan 1963) (*Etruria and Early Rome*, London 1966)

MARKUS, R. A., *Christianity in the Roman World* (London 1974)

MAROTTI, I., *Letteratura latina* (Bologna 1976)

MARROU, H. I., *Histoire de l'éducation dans l'antiquité*, 2nd ed. (1948) (*History of Education in Antiquity*, London, reprint 1977)

MARSH, F. B., *A History of the Roman World from 146 B.C. to 30 B.C.*, 3rd ed. (London 1963)

MARTIN, J-P. *La Rome ancienne : 753 avant J.C. – 395 après J.C.* (Paris 1973)

MASSON, G. A., *A Concise History of Republican Rome* (London 1973)

MATTINGLY, H., *Roman Coins*, 2nd ed. (London 1960)

MATTINGLY, H., *Roman Imperial Civilization* (London 1957)

MAZZARINO, S., *La fine del mondo antico* (Milan 1959) (*The End of the Ancient World*, London 1966)

MILLAR, F., *The Emperor in the Roman World* (London 1977)

MILLAR, F. (etc.), *Das Römische Reich und seine Nachbarn* (Frankfurt-am-Main 1966) (*The Roman Empire and its Neighbours*, London 1967)

MOMMSEN, T., *Römische Geschichte*, 1854–6, 1886, ed. K. Christ (Darmstadt 1976); (*History of Rome* [London 1913], abridged ed. 1960)

NASH, E., *Pictorial Dictionary of Ancient Rome*, 2nd ed. (New York 1968)

NICOLET, C., *Le métier de citoyen dans la Rome républicaine* (Paris 1976)

OGILVIE, R. M., *Early Rome and the Etruscans* (London 1976)

OGILVIE, R. M., *The Romans and their Gods* (London 1969)

OXFORD CLASSICAL DICTIONARY, 2nd ed. (Oxford 1970)

PALANQUE, J-R., *Le bas-empire* (Paris 1971)

PALLOTTINO, M., *Etruscologia*, 7th ed. (Milan 1972) (*The Etruscans*, Harmondsworth 1975, from 6th ed.)

PALLOTTINO, M. (etc., eds.), *Popoli e civiltà dell' Italia antica* (Rome 1974)

PALMER, R. E. A., *The Archaic Community of the Romans* (Cambridge 1970)

PAOLI, V. E., *Vita Romana*, 10th ed. (Florence 1967) (*Rome : its People, Life and Customs*, London 1963)

PARKER, H. M. D., *A History of the Roman World from A.D. 138 to 337*, 2nd ed. (London 1958)

PASSERINI, A., *Linee di storia romana in età imperiale*, 2nd ed. (Milan 1972)

PAYNE, R., *Ancient Rome* (New York 1970)

PEROWNE, S., *The End of the Roman World* (London 1966)

PETIT, P., *Histoire générale de l'empire romain* (Paris 1974)

PICARD, G., *Empire romain (Architecture universelle)* (Fribourg 1965)

PIGANIOL, A., *L'empire chrétien*, 2nd ed. (Paris 1972)

PIGANIOL, A., *Histoire de Rome*, 5th ed. (Paris 1962)

RADICE, B., *Who's Who in the Ancient World*, 2nd ed. (London 1973)

RAFFALT, R., *Grosse Kaiser Roms* (Munich 1977)

REMONDON, R., *La crise de l'empire romain* (Paris 1964)

ROSTOVTZEFF, M., *Social and Economic History of the Roman Empire*, 2nd ed. (P. M. Fraser) (Oxford 1957)

ROULAND, N., *Clientela : Essai sur l'influence des rapports de clientèle sur la vie politique romaine* (Aix-Marseille [dissertation] 1977)

SALMON, E. T., *A History of the Roman World from 30 B.C to A.D. 138*, 6th ed. (London 1968)

SCHMIDT, J., *Vie et mort des esclaves dans la Rome antique* (Paris 1973)

SCULLARD, H. H., *The Etruscan Cities and Rome* (London 1967)

SCULLARD, H. H., *From the Gracchi to Nero*, 4th ed. (London 1976)

SCULLARD, H. H., *A History of the Roman World from 753 to 146 B.C.*, 3rd ed. (London 1961)

SHERWIN-WHITE, A. N., *The Roman Citizenship*, 2nd ed. (Oxford 1973)

SIMON, M., and BENOIT, A., *Le Judaïsme et le Christianisme antique* (Paris 1968)

SMALLWOOD, E. M., *The Jews under Roman Rule from Pompey to Diocletian* (Leiden 1976)

STARR, C. G., *Civilization and the Caesars* (Ithaca [N.Y.] 1954)

STARR, C. G., *The Emergence of Rome*, 2nd ed. (Ithaca [N.Y.] 1965)

STRONG, D., *Roman Art* (Harmondsworth 1976)

SUTHERLAND, C. H. V., *Roman Coins* (London 1974)

SYME, R., *Roman Papers* (Oxford 1977)

SYME, R., *The Roman Revolution* (Oxford 1939)

TEMPORINI, H. (ed.), *Aufstieg und Niedergang der antiken Welt* (Berlin 1972) (many parts)

THOMAS, J. A. C., *Textbook of Roman Law* (Amsterdam 1977)

TOYNBEE, J. M. C., *The Art of the Romans* (London 1965)

TURNER, E. G., *The Papyrologist at Work* (Durham, N. Carolina 1976)

VOGT, J., *Die römische Republik*, 6th ed. (Freiburg 1973)

VOGT, J., *Der Niedergang Roms* (Zurich 1965) (*The Decline of Rome*, London 1967)

WALBANK, F. W., *The Awful Revolution* (Liverpool 1969)

WATSON, A., *Rome of the Twelve Tables* (Princeton 1975)

WATSON, G. R., *The Roman Soldier* (London 1969)

WHEELER, R. E. M., *Roman Art and Architecture* (Rome 1964)

WHITE, L. (ed.), *The Transformation of the Roman World* (Berkeley 1966)

WILKINSON, L. P., *The Roman Experience* (New York 1975)

ZANKER, P. (ed.), *Hellenismus in Mittelitalien* (Göttingen 1976)

# TABLE OF DATES*

BC
625–600    Arrival of Etruscans at Rome.
[586       Jerusalem captured by the Babylonians (Nebuchadnezzar).]
578–534(?) Reign of Servius Tullius.
[c. 563–483 Life of Gautama Buddha]
[c. 551–479 Life of Confucius.]
535        Etruscans and Carthaginians defeat Phocaean Greeks off Alalia.
524        Etruscans defeated off Cumae.
[510       Tyrant Hippias expelled from Athens.]
507(?)     Tarquins expelled; Republic begins.
506(?)     Etruscans defeated by Latins and Cumaeans at Aricia.
496        Romans defeat Latins at Lake Regillus.
494(?)     First Secession of the plebeians. Establishment of tribunes of the people.
493        Cassian Treaty with Latins.
479        Veii defeat Romans at River Cremera.
471        Creation of tribal assembly (concilium plebis).
451–450    The decemvirates and Twelve Tables.
449        Valerian–Horatian Laws.
444        Institution of military tribunes with consular powers.
443        Institution of censorship.
431        Aequi defeated on Mt Algidus.
[431–404   Peloponnesian War between Athens and Sparta.]
425        Fidenae taken from Veii.
396        Fall of Veii.
[c. 388    Plato founds Academy at Athens.]
387        Gauls defeat Romans at River Allia and capture the city.
378        'Servian Wall'.
367–366    Licinian–Sextian Laws; first plebeian consul.
343–341    First Samnite War.
340–338    Latin and Campanian War.
339        Publilian Laws.

* Until the 4th century BC, Italian dates are only approximate.

BC

| | |
|---|---|
| [334–323 | Conquests of Alexander the Great.] |
| 328–302 | Second Samnite War. |
| 321 | Defeat by Samnites at the Caudine Forks. |
| 312 | Censorship of Appius Claudius. Via Appia and Aqua Appia. |
| 298–290 | Third Samnite War. |
| 295 | Samnites defeated at Sentinum. |
| 297 | Hortensian Law. |
| 280–275 | War with Pyrrhus. |
| [c. 274–232(?) | Rule of Asoka in India.] |
| 264–241 | First Punic War. |
| 241 | Victory off Aegates Islands. Annexation of Sicily. |
| 241–238 | War of Mercenaries (Truceless War) against Carthage. |
| 238 | Annexation of Sardinia and Corsica. |
| 237 | Hamilcar Barca goes to Spain. |
| 232 | Flaminian land law. |
| 226 | Ebro treaty with Hasdrubal Barca. |
| 225 | Gauls defeated at Telamon. |
| 218–201 | Second Punic War. |
| 218–216 | Defeats at River Ticinus, River Trebia, Lake Trasimene and Cannae. |
| 215–209 | Revolts of Capua, Tarentum, Syracuse. |
| 207 | Hasdrubal defeated at River Metaurus. |
| 206 | Victory of Scipio Africanus at Ilipa. |
| [206 BC – AD 220 | Han Dynasty in China.] |
| 202 BC | Victory of Scipio Africanus at Zama. |
| 200–196 | Second Macedonian War. |
| 197 | Philip v defeated at Cynoscephalae. |
| 192–189 | War against Antiochus III. |
| 190 | Antiochus III defeated at Magnesia. |
| 171–168 | Third Macedonian War. |
| 168 | Perseus defeated at Pydna. |
| 149–146 | Third Punic War. |
| 146 | Destruction of Carthage and Corinth. |
| 139–132 | First Slave Revolt in Sicily. |
| 133 | Scipio Aemilianus captures Numantia. |
| 133–129 | Pergamum left to Rome and annexed as province of Asia. |
| 133 & 123–122 | Tribunates of Tiberius and Gaius Gracchus. |
| 121 | Defeat of Arverni and Allobroges in Gaul. |
| 112–105 | Jugurthine War. |
| 104–100 | Second Slave Revolt in Sicily. |
| 102–101 | Marius defeats Teutones and Cimbri. |
| 91 | Tribunate and murder of Marcus Livius Drusus the Younger. |
| 91–87 | Social (Marsian) War. |
| 90 | Julian Law conferring rights upon Italians. |

BC
| | |
|---|---|
| 88 | Sulla marches on Rome. |
| 88–4 | First Mithridatic War. |
| 81 | Second Mithridatic War. |
| 81 | Dictatorship of Sulla. |
| 81–72 | Revolt of Sertorius in Spain. |
| 74–63 | Third Mithridatic War. |
| 73–71 | Slave revolt of Spartacus. |
| 70 | Consulships of Pompey and Crassus. |
| 67 | Gabinian Law gives Pompey pirate command. |
| 66–3 | Manilian Law gives Pompey Mithridatic command. Eastern settlement. |
| 63 | Consulship of Cicero. Conspiracy of Catiline. |
| 60 | 'First Triumvirate' of Pompey, Crassus and Caesar. |
| 59 | First consulship of Caesar. |
| 58–51 | Caesar's Gallic War. |
| 53 | Crassus defeated and killed by Parthians at Carrhae. |
| 49–45 | Civil War. Caesar's victories at Pharsalus (followed by death of Pompey), Thapsus, Munda. |
| 44 | Perpetual dictatorship and assassination of Caesar. |
| 43 | Second Triumvirate of Antony, Octavian and Lepidus. Death of Cicero. |
| 42 | Deaths of Brutus and Cassius, defeated at Philippi. |
| 36 | Octavian eliminates Sextus Pompeius and Lepidus. |
| 31 | Octavian and Agrippa defeat Antony and Cleopatra at Actium. |
| 30 | Deaths of Antony and Cleopatra. Egypt annexed. |
| 27 BC – AD 14 | *Augustus (Octavian).* |
| 25 BC | Annexation of Galatia. |
| 19 | Death of Virgil. |
| 16–9 | Annexations to Danube and Elbe. |
| 8 | Death of Horace. |
| [6–4 (?) | Birth of Jesus.] |
| AD 6–9 | Revolts in Pannonia and Illyricum. |
| 9 | Arminius defeats and kills Varus at Teutoburg Forest. |
| 14–37 | *Tiberius.* |
| 19 | Death of Germanicus. |
| [c. 30 or 33 | Crucifixion of Jesus.] |
| 31 | Execution of Sejanus. |
| 37–41 | *Caligula (Gaius).* |
| 41–54 | *Claudius.* |
| 41–6 | Annexation of Mauretania and south-eastern England (Britannia) and Thrace. |
| [c. 45–58 | Missionary journeys of Paul.] |
| 54–68 | *Nero.* |
| 61 | Revolt of Boudicca (Boadicea) in Britain. |
| 63–6 | Settlement of Armenian question with Parthia. |

AD

| | |
|---|---|
| 65 | Pisonian conspiracy and deaths of Seneca and Petronius. |
| 66–70 | First Jewish Revolt (First Roman War). |
| 68–9 | *Galba, Otho, Vitellius*. Civil Wars. |
| 69–79 | *Vespasian*. |
| 79–81 | *Titus*. |
| 79 | Destruction of Pompeii and Herculaneum by eruption of Vesuvius. |
| 80 | Inauguration of Colosseum at Rome. |
| 81–96 | *Domitian*. |
| 96–8 | *Nerva*. |
| 98–117 | *Trajan*. |
| 106 | Annexation of Dacia. |
| 113–17 | Trajan's eastern campaigns. |
| 115–c. 118 | Revolts of Jewish Dispersion in Cyrene, Cyprus and Egypt. |
| 117–138 | *Hadrian*. |
| 122 | Hadrian's Wall in Britain. |
| 132–5 | Second Jewish Revolt (Second Roman War). |
| 138–61 | *Antoninus Pius*. |
| 142 | Antonine Wall in Britain. |
| 161–80 | *Marcus Aurelius and Lucius Verus* (d. 169). |
| 162–6 | Parthian War. |
| 166–72, 177–80 | Marcomannic and Sarmatian Wars. |
| 180–92 | *Commodus*. |
| 193 | *Pertinax, Didius Julianus*. |
| 193–211 | *Septimius Severus*. |
| 194 | Defeat of Pescennius Niger at Issus. |
| 197 | Defeat of Clodius Albinus at Lugdunum. |
| 197–9 | Parthian War. |
| 208–11 | British Wars. |
| 211–17 | *Caracalla and Geta* (d. 211 or 212) |
| 212 | The Constitutio Antoniniana conferring general citizenship. |
| 212 | Death of jurist Papinian. |
| 217–18 | *Macrinus*. |
| 218–22 | *Elagabalus*. |
| 222–35 | *Severus Alexander*. Rule of Julia Mamaea. |
| 223 | Deaths of Julia Maesa and jurist Ulpian. |
| c. 226 | Persians (Sassanians) overthrow Parthians. |
| 235–8 | *Maximinus I Thrax*. |
| 238 | *Gordianus I* and *II Africanus* proclaimed in Africa; *Balbinus* and *Pupienus*. |
| 238–44 | *Gordianus III*; rule of Timesitheus (*d. 243*). |
| 241–72 | Sapor I. Sassanian King of Persia. |
| 244–9 | *Philip the Arabian*. |
| 248 | Millenary Games in Rome. |
| 249–51 | *Trajanus Decius*. Persecution of Christians. |
| 251 | Decius defeated and killed by Goths at Abrittus. |

AD

| | |
|---|---|
| 251–3 | *Trebonianus Gallus*. Epidemic begins. |
| 253 | *Aemilian*. |
| 253–60 | *Valerian and Gallienus*. German and Persian invasions. |
| 257 | Renewed persecution of Christians. |
| 259–73 | Usurpation of Postumus and successors in western provinces. |
| 260 | Valerian captured by Persians. Sole reign of *Gallienus*. |
| 261–7 | Odenathus viceroy of the east. |
| 267 | Zenobia independent ruler in the east. |
| 268 | Goths defeated at Naissus. |
| 268–70 | *Claudius Gothicus*. |
| 269 | Decisive victories over Goths. |
| c. 270 | Death of Plotinus. |
| 270–5 | *Aurelian*. |
| 270 | Dacia abandoned. |
| 271 | Wall of Aurelian started at Rome. |
| 273 | Zenobia defeated. Capture of Palmyra. |
| 274 | Tetricus, emperor in Gaul, defeated at Catalaunian Plains. Temple of Sun-god at Rome. |
| 275–6 | *Tacitus*. |
| 276–82 | *Probus*. |
| 277–9 | Victories on Rhine and Danube. |
| 277 | Death of Mani. |
| 282–3 | *Carus*. |
| 283–4 | *Carinus and Numerian*. |
| 284–305 | *Diocletian and Maximian (286)*. |
| 286–296 | Usurpations of Carausius (d. 293) and Allectus in Britain. |
| 293 | Constantius I (d. 306) and Galerius (d. 311) appointed Caesars. |
| 297–8 | Persian War. |
| 301 | Edict on Prices. |
| 303–11 | Great Persecution of Christians. |
| 311 | Edict of Serdica (Sofia). |
| 312 | Constantine I the Great defeats Maxentius at the Milvian Bridge. |
| 312–37 | *Constantine I the Great and Licinius (d. 324)*. |
| 313 | Edict of Mediolanum (Milan) in favour of Christians. |
| 324–30 | Foundation of Constantinople. |
| 325 | Council of Nicaea. |
| 326 | Execution of Fausta and Crispus. |
| 337 | *Accessions of Constantine II (d. 340), Constantius II (d. 361), and Constans (d. 350)*. |
| 350–3 | Usurpation of Magnentius in the west. |
| 357 | Julian defeats Germans near Argentorate. |
| 360–3 | *Julian the Apostate*. Restoration of paganism. |
| 363–4 | *Jovian*. |
| 364–75 | *Valentinian I. Valens* emperor in the east. |
| 373–97 | Ambrose bishop of Mediolanum (Milan). |

AD

| | |
|---|---|
| 375 | *Gratian* (d. 383) and *Valentinian II* (d. 392) emperors in the west. |
| 378 | Valens defeated and killed by Visigoths at Edirne (Adrianople). |
| 378–95 | *Theodosius I.* |
| 382 | Altar of Victory removed from Senate-house. |
| 383–8 | Usurpation of Magnus Maximus in the west. |
| 389 | Jerome's foundation of a religious house at Bethlehem. |
| 392–4 | Usurpation of Eugenius in the west. |
| 395 | *Arcadius* (d. 408) emperor in the east and *Honorius* (d. 423) in the west. |
| 395–408 | Stilicho commander-in-chief in the west. |
| 395–430 | Augustine bishop of Hippo Regius. |
| 404 | Ravenna becomes the capital of the western empire. |
| 405 | Stilicho defeats the Ostrogoth Radagaisus at Faesulae. |
| 406 | German invaders cross the Rhine. |
| 408–50 | *Theodosius II* emperor in the east. |
| 410 | Capture of Rome by Alaric the Visigoth, and his death. |
| 413 | Burgundians settled by Constantius (III) on west bank of Rhine. |
| 418 | Visigoths granted federate status with Tolosa as capital. |
| 425–55 | *Valentinian III* emperor in the west; rule of Placidia (to *c.* 432) |
| 428–77 | Gaiseric king of the Vandals. |
| 432–54 | Aetius commander-in-chief in the west. |
| 434–53 | Attila joint and then (445) sole king of the Huns. |
| 438 | The Theodosian Code. |
| 439 | Capture of Carthage by Gaiseric, who declares his Vandal kingdom independent. |
| 450–7 | *Marcian* emperor in the east. |
| 451 | Aetius and the Visigoths defeat Attila at the Catalaunian Plains. |
| 452 | Attila's invasion of Italy halted by Pope Leo I. |
| 455 | Sack of Rome by Gaiseric. |
| 456–72 | Ricimer commander-in-chief in west, makes and unmakes emperors. |
| 457–61 | *Majorian* emperor in west, wins victories but is defeated by Vandals. |
| 457–74 | *Leo I* emperor in the east. |
| 474–91 | *Zeno* emperor in the east. |
| 475 | Code of Euric, king of Visigoths, who declares himself independent. |
| 475–6 | *Romulus Augustulus*: last emperor at Ravenna (*Nepos* d. 480). |
| 476–93 | Odoacer (Herulian) king of Italy. |
| 481–511 | Clovis king of the Franks. |
| 491–518 | *Anastasius I* emperor in the east (Byzantine emperor). |
| 507–711 | Visigothic kingdom in Spain. |
| 518–27 | *Justin I* Byzantine emperor. |
| 524 | Death of Boethius. |

AD

| | |
|---|---|
| 527–65 | *Justinian I* Byzantine emperor. |
| 528–39 | Justinian's *Digest*. |
| 533 | Belisarius reconquers north Africa from the Vandals. |
| 535–53 | Belisarius and Narses reconquer Italy from the Ostrogoths. |
| 547 | Death of St Benedict. |
| 568 | Lombards invade north Italy. |
| c. 583 | Death of Cassiodorus. |
| 590–604 | Pope Gregory I the Great. |
| 632 | Death of the Prophet Mohammed. |
| 636 | Death of Isidore of Seville. |
| 637–711 | Arabs take Sassanian Persia, north Africa and most of Spain. |
| 678–717 | Arabs repelled from Constantinople. |
| 732 | Charles Martel defeats Arabs in France. |
| 751 | Lombards capture Ravenna. |
| 800 | Charlemagne crowned emperor by Pope Leo III. |
| 962 | Otto I crowned emperor by Pope John XII. |
| 1204–61 | Crusaders occupy Constantinople (Latin Empire). |
| 1453 | Fall of Constantinople to Ottoman Turks of Mohammed II. |
| 1806 | Abolition of Holy Roman Empire. |

# INDEX

# INDEX

AACHEN, *see* Aquis-granum
Abernethy, 385
Abrittus, 284
Academy (Athens), 172, 218, 379
Accius, 370
Achaea (Roman posses-sion), *see* Greece
Achaean League, 124, 364, 368 f.
Achillas, 376
Acra Leuce, 97
Actium, 202 f., 220, 377 f.
*Acts of the Apostles,* 265, 269, 384
Adherbal, 373
Adiabene, *see* Assyria
Adria, 33, 362
Adrianople, *see* Hadrian-opolis
Adriatic Sea, 7, 13, 78, 94, 105, 114 f., 124, 189, 273, 362, 376; *see also* Ionian Sea
Aduatuca, 375
aediles, 364, 376
Aedui, 179, 181, 184, 373, 375
Aegates Is., 85
Aelius (Lex Aelia and Lex Fufia), 372, 375
Aelius Caesar, 239, 381, 384
Aelius Paetus Catus, Sex-tus, *see* Paetus

Aemilia, 374
Aemilianus (emperor), 385
Aemilii, 61, 367
Aenaria, *see* Pithecusa
Aeneas, 23, 195, 217 f., 360, 379
Aequi, 38 ff.
*aerarium, see* treasury
Aesernia, 373
Aetius, 327 ff., 334, 344, 390
Aetolian League, 115, 118 ff., 122, 130, 236, 368, 370
Aezani, 387
Afghanistan, 368, 375
Afranius, Lucius, 375
Africa (province, Tunisia), 125, 152, 154, 159, 164, 192, 215, 232, 236, 247 ff., 275 f., 284, 290, 305 f., 308, 326 ff., 345 ff., 353, 355, 368, 370 f., 374, 377, 382, 384, 388 f., 391 ff.
Africa, West, 82, 84, 366
Agathocles, 366
*agentes in rebus, see* secret police
Ager Gallicus, 94, 367; *see also* Gaul (N. Italy)
*ager publicus, see* state land
Agri Decumates, 380 f., 385
Agricola, Cnaeus Julius, 235, 252 f., 380, 394

agriculture, farming, 7, 9 f., 23, 41, 52, 62, 77, 81 f., 86, 94, 125, 132, 139–42, 145 f., 148, 215, 243, 248, 303, 334, 336 f., 363–6, 368, 371, 395; *see also* drainage, grain, oil, wine
Agrigentum, 140, 366
Agrippa I, 380, 384
Agrippa II, 380
Agrippa, Marcus Vipsan-ius, 201 ff., 205 f., 212, 216, 226, 245, 377, 382
Agrippa, Menenius, 365
Agrippa Postumus (grandson of Augustus), 211, 378, 382
Agrippina the elder, 226, 379
Agrippina the younger, 229 f., 379
Agrippinensis, Colonia, 382, 385
Agyrium, 394
Ahala, Gaius Servilius, 376
Ahenobarbus, Cnaeus Domitius (consul 122 BC), 152
Ahenobarbus, Cnaeus Domitius (consul 54 BC), 189 f.
Ahenobarbus, Cnaeus Domitius (consul AD 32), 380

Ahenobarbus, Cnaeus Domitius (son-in-law of Cinna), 374
Ahriman, 386
Ahuramazda, 386
Alalia, 366
Alamanni, 285, 343, 348, 385, 387, 389
Alans, 324, 343, 389, 391
Alaric I, 324 ff., 329, 333, 343, 346 ff., 350, 353, 389 f.
Alaric II, 352, 391
Alba Fucens, 364, 368 f., 371
Alba Longa, 27 f., 32, 360 f.
Alban Mount, 10, 27 f., 38 f., 138, 360, 362
Albanum, 276
Albinus, Clodius, 276
Alcaeus, 379
Alcantara, 378
Alesia, 184
Alexander I of Epirus, 366
Alexander III of Macedonia (the Great), 78, 80, 113, 115, 118, 121, 167, 197, 202, 237, 254, 279, 296, 368
Alexander, Severus, 279 f.
Alexandria, 118, 121, 187, 191, 194 f., 202, 217, 233, 244, 263, 294, 305, 316, 345, 349, 375, 377, 379, 384, 386 ff., 393 f.
Algidus, 39, 362
alimenta, 236, 381
Alimentus, Lucius Cincius, 370, 395
Allectus, 386
Allia, R., 44
allies, Italian (socii), 55 f., 149 ff., 156 ff.; see also Social War
Allobroges, 152, 373 f.
alphabet, 14, 23, 362
Alps, 7, 99, 105, 152 f., 164, 184, 206, 232, 273, 367
Alsium, 363
Ambianum, 389

Ambiorix, 375
Ambracia, 202, 366
Ambrose, St, 334, 346, 390 f.
Amiternum, 363, 394
Ammianus Marcellinus, 328, 332, 347, 349, 393
Ammonius Saccas, 386 f.
amphitheatres, see architecture, gladiators
Amyntas, 377
Anastasius I, 354, 391 f.
Ancus Marcius, 361 f.
Ancyra, 210
Andriscus, 123, 369
Anio, R., 363, 365, 371
Annas II, 384
annona militaris, see taxation
Anthée, 248
Anthemius (emperor), 389
Anthemius (praetorian prefect), 391
Antias, Valerius, 395
Antigonids, 113, 115 f.
Antigonus I Monophthalmus, 368
Antigonus II Gonatas, 382
Antigonus, Mattathias, 383
Antinous, 241
Antioch (Syria), 115, 167, 264, 283, 315, 383, 388, 393
Antiochus, see Eunus
Antiochus III the Great, 115 f., 118–21, 140, 368 f., 384
Antiochus IV Epiphanes, 121, 369, 383
Antium, 39, 51, 362, 377
Antonia, 379
Antoninus, Marcus Aurelius, see Aurelius, Caracalla, Elagabalus
Antoninus Pius, 239 f,. 273, 381, 384, 386
Antonius, Lucius (brother of Marcus), 200, 377
Antonius, Marcus (Mark Antony), 187, 189, 191,

194, 199–202, 211, 217, 257, 374, 377, 383
Antonius Hybrida, Gaius, 374
Antony, St, 390
Apamea (Phrygia), 369
Apamea (Syria), 374
Apennine Mts, 7, 38 f., 47, 52 f., 95, 100, 170, 360, 364, 367
Aper, 386
Apion, 395
Apollodorus, 242, 318 f.
Apollonia, 368 f.
Apollonius Rhodius, 375, 379
apostles (list), 384
appeal (provocatio), 71, 365, 383
Appian, 394
Appian Way, see Claudius Caecus, Appius, and roads
Apuleius, 253 f.
Apulia, 79, 101, 164, 218, 364, 367, 371
Aquae Cutiliae, 380
Aquae Sextiae, 153, 373
aqueducts, 70, 138, 244, 365, 371
Aquileia, 273, 345, 372, 378
Aquilonia, 364
Aquincum, 389
Aquinum, 251
Aquisgranum, 388
Aquitania, 182, 375
Ara Maxima, 29, 362, 366
Ara Pacis (Altar of Peace), 212, 378
Arabia, Arabs, 265, 280, 282, 293, 355, 375, 381, 392
Aragueni, 385
Arausio, 153, 373
Arbogast, 389
Arcadius, 324, 353
Archelaus (ethnarch of Judaea), 384
Archelaus (general of Mithridates VI), 373

Archelaus (king of Cappadocia), 377
Archidamus II, 366
Archimedes, 368
architecture, 14, 23, 136 ff., 212, 214, 243–7, 291 f., 300, 313–16, 346, 354, 359, 367, 371, 374, 378, 382, 385–8, 390 f., 395
Archytas, 365
Ardashir (Artaxerxes), 283, 385
Ardea, 38, 362 f., 368, 371
Ardoch, 380
Arelate, 310 f., 326, 389 f.
Argentorate, 380, 389
Arians, 316, 344, 347, 352 f.
Aricia, 28 f., 32, 38, 49, 362
Ariminum, 189, 366, 371
Ariovistus, 181, 375
Aristides, Aelius, 249, 382 f.
Aristodemus, 31
Aristonicus, 142
Aristotle, 363
Armecy, 181
Armenia, 166 f., 201, 205, 231, 237, 273, 279, 283, 368 f., 374, 377, 381, 387 f., 391
Arminius, 208, 378
army, 22, 28 f., 37, 42 ff., 50, 53, 56, 70, 78, 97, 104, 107 f., 118, 120 f., 139, 148, 154, 185, 197, 203, 208 f., 237, 239, 276 f., 280, 282–8, 302, 308, 310, 333 ff., 339, 341, 344, 358, 361, 364, 367 f., 371, 373, 375, 377, 381, 390; see also recruitment, veterans
Arno, R., 13
Arpinum, 153, 168
Arretium, 214, 367, 375, 378
Arroux, R., 181
Arsacids, see Parthia
Artabanus V, 385

Arverna (Augustonemetum), 343, 390
Arverni, 152, 179, 184, 373
Asander, 377
Ascanius (Iulus), 360
Asclepiades, 376
Asclepiodotus, 386
Asellio, Sempronius, 373
Asia (province, former kingdom of Pergamum), 146, 148, 166, 173, 177, 373 f., 377 f.
Asia Minor, 13 f., 116, 158 f., 165, 173, 204, 238, 255, 263–6, 276, 282, 284 ff., 289, 302, 305, 307, 316, 322, 354, 369 f., 376 ff., 383 f., 391 f.; see also names of provinces and regions
Asisium, 219
Aspar, 391
Assembly (*comitia*), 22, 25, 58 f., 64, 66, 71 f., 83, 94, 100 f., 103, 105, 117, 125, 127 f., 133, 146 f., 151, 153, 161 f., 165, 171, 177, 190, 361, 367; see also Council, plebeian
Assyria (Adiabene), 13, 25, 256, 381, 383
astrology, 245, 254, 383
Ataulf, 326, 343, 389 f.
Ateius Capito, Gaius, see Capito
Atella, 367 f.
Athanasius, 316, 345
Athens, 16, 31, 46, 65, 129, 158 f., 172, 188, 218, 274, 298, 362, 364 f., 374, 389
Atlantic Ocean, 82, 179, 248
Atrebates, 380
Attalids, 116
Attalus I Soter, 116, 119
Attalus II Philadelphus, 369
Attalus III Philometor, 372

Attalus, Priscus, 391
Attianus, Publius Acilius, 381
Atticus, Titus Pomponius, 171
Attila, 328 f., 346, 353, 389 f.
Attus Clausus, see Clausus
*auctoritas*, 59, 203 f., 365
Aufidus, R., 365
*Augustales*, 378
Augusta Treverorum, see Treviri
Augustine, St, 253, 299, 346–51, 391, 395
Augustonemetum, see Arverna
Augustus, 198–221, 225 ff., 232, 241, 252, 258, 274 f., 349, 358, 362, 376–80, 382, 393 f.
Aurelian, 285 f., 296
Aurelius (Lex Aurelia), see Cotta
Aurelius, Marcus, 273 ff., 277, 289 f., 292 f., 295, 307, 383 f., 386
Aureolus, 385
*aurum coronarium*, see taxation
Ausculum, 79, 366
Aventicum, 386
Aventine Hill, 28 f., 32, 43, 45, 62 f., 65, 67, 137
Avidius Cassius, Gaius, 384
Avitus, 390

BABYLONIA, 256, 263, 283, 375, 381, 383, 387
Bactria, 368
Baecula, 103, 368
Baetica, see Spain
Baetis, R., see Guadalquivir
Bagaudae, 338, 390
Bagradas, R., see Medjerda
Bahram I, 386
Balbinus, 385
Balbus, Lucius Cornelius, 376

Balearic Islands, 368
Baltic Sea, 328
Bar Kosiba (Kochba), 239
Barcids, 96
Barcino, 389
Barnabas, St, 265 f.
Basiliscus, 392
Batavians, 233, 380
Bedriacum, 232 f.
Belgae, 181, 183 f., 375
Belisarius, 353, 355, 391
Benacus, Lake, 285
Benedict, St, 345, 390
Beneventum, 79, 366
Berenice, 235, 380
Bethlehem, 259, 345, 388
Bibracte, 179, 375
Bibulus, Marcus Calpur-
 nius, 177, 375 ff.
Bilbilis, 177
Bithynia, 118, 158, 166,
 236, 307, 376 f., 387
Bituitus, 373
Black Forest, 321
Black Sea, 158, 197, 284 f.,
 385
Black Stone (*Lapis niger*),
 361
Bleda, 389
Blossius, Gaius, 372
Boadicea, see Boudicca
Bocchus I, 373
Boethius, 353, 391
Bohemia, 208, 274 f., 378
Boii (Bohemia), 378
Boii (Cisalpine Gaul),
 367
Bologna, see Bononia, Fel-
 sina
Bolsena, Lake, 15
Boniface, 327
Bonna, 380
Bononia, 199, 360, 372,
 391; see also Felsina
Borbetomagus, 389
Boscoreale, 374
Bosphorus, Cimmerian
 (Crimea), 158, 166, 373,
 377 f.
Bosphorus, Thracian, 310,
 355
Bostra, 381

Boudicca (Boadicea), 230,
 380
Bovianum, 373
Bracara Augusta, 393 f.
Brenner Pass, 285
Brennus, 44 f.
bridges, 28, 32, 41, 52,
 138, 182 f., 213, 361,
 365, 371, 378, 381; see
 also Milvian Bridge
Brigantes, 381
Britannia, Britain, 43,
 182 ff., 227–30, 235,
 239, 252, 276 f., 282,
 301, 325, 351, 379, 381,
 386, 389
Britannicus, 229
Brittany, 182
Bronze Age, see metals
Brough on Humber, see
 Petuaria
Brundusium, 113, 189,
 218, 364, 370, 377
Brutus, Lucius Junius,
 376
Brutus, Marcus Junius
 (*legatus* 77 BC), 373
Brutus, Marcus Junius
 (Quintus Caepio Brutus,
 praetor 44 BC), 197,
 199, 201, 218, 349,
 376 f.
Brutus Albinus, Decimus
 Junius, 197, 375
Buciumi, 381
Bulgars, 392
Bulla Regia, 382
bureaucracy, see civil ser-
 vice
Burgundians, 324, 326 f.,
 343 f., 352, 389
Burgus Julius, of Leon-
 tius, see Julius, Leon-
 tius
burial, 10 f.
Burrus, Sextus Afranius,
 229 f.
Burunum, 385
Busento, R., 389
Byzantine empire, 202,
 353–6, 391 f.; see also
 Constantinople

CADDER, 380
Caecilii Metelli, see
 Metelli
Caecilius Statius, 371
Caecina Alienus, Aulus,
 232 ff., 380
Caeles Vibenna, see Vi-
 benna
Caelian Hill, 10, 16, 28,
 33, 45, 361
Caelius Rufus, Marcus,
 376
Caepio, Quintus Servilius,
 373
Caere, 16 f., 22, 43–6,
 49, 82, 360, 363, 366,
 381
Caesar, Gaius Julius, 170,
 173 f., 177, 179–99, 204,
 210, 212 f., 220, 228,
 250, 354 ff., 379, 393 f.
Caesar, Lucius Julius
 (Lex Julia, 90 BC), 157,
 373
Caesarea Maritima, 267,
 394 f.
Caesarion (Ptolemy XV
 Caesar), 195, 377
Caesarodunum, see Tur-
 onum, Civitas
Caesonia (wife of Cali-
 gula), 227, 379
Calagurris, 380
Calama, 391
Calatia, 367 f.
Caledonia, see Scotland
calendar, 23, 195, 361, 376
Cales, 50 ff., 364, 368
Caligula, 226 ff., 379
Callimachus, 375, 379
Calpurnia, Lex (149 BC),
 see Piso Frugi, Gaius
 Calpurnius
Calpurnius (Lex Calpur-
 nia 90 BC), 373
Camelon, 380
Camilla, 362
Camillus, Marcus Furius,
 43, 46, 68 f., 71, 363,
 365
Camillus Scribonianus,
 Lucius Furius, 379

Campania, 8 f., 18 f., 23, 31 ff., 39, 47–50, 52, 89, 101, 135 f., 140, 162, 214, 216, 225, 230, 294, 361, 367, 370 ff., 375 f., 394
Campi Catalaunii, Flaminii, Magni, *see* Catalaunii, Flaminii, Magni
Campus Martius, 381
Camulodunum, 229, 379
canals, 195; *see also* drainage
Cannae, 101 f., 115, 367
Capena, 363
Capernaum, 387
Capito, Gaius Ateius, 383
Capitol, Capitoline Hill, 10, 16, 23, 29, 31, 43 ff., 147, 233, 313, 361 f., 365, 382
Capitolium Vetus, 362
Cappadocia, 377, 379
Capreae, 225
Capua, 18, 47 f., 50, 52, 86, 89, 102, 129, 140, 148, 164, 214, 247, 361, 363, 367 f., 371, 382
Caracalla, 276, 279, 286 f., 291 ff., 314, 382, 384, 386
Caraceni, 364
Caratacus, 379
Carausius, 386
Carbo, Cnaeus Papirius, 374
Carbo, Gaius Papirius (tribune 131 BC), 372
Carbo, Gaius Papirius (Lex Plautia Papiria), 373
Carinus, 386
Carnuntum, 276
Carnutes, 184
Carpetani, 369
Carpow, 385
Carrhae, 186, 279, 375, 387
Carteia, 369
Cartenna, 391

Carthage, 11, 80–8, 96–106, 108 f., 113 ff., 117, 119, 124 f., 148, 151, 192, 217 f., 306, 328, 348, 360, 366–9, 371, 376, 378, 387, 390 f.
Carus, 286, 385 f.
Cassian Treaty (with Latins), *see* Cassius Vecellinus, Spurius
Cassian, John, *see* John Cassian
Cassino, Mt, 390
Cassiodorus, 353, 391, 393
Cassius, Gaius Avidius, *see* Avidius
Cassius Dio, *see* Dio
Cassius Longinus, Gaius, 197, 199, 218, 376
Cassius Vecellinus, Spurius (Cassian Treaty with Latins), 37 f., 362
Cassivellaunus, 183
catacombs, 312, 388
Catalaunii, Campi, 286, 329, 389
Catilina, Lucius Sergius, 168 ff., 172 f., 193, 394
Cato the Censor, Marcus Porcius, 122, 125, 130–3, 136, 140 f., 170, 358, 360, 369 f., 395
Cato of Utica, Marcus Porcius, 170, 173, 177, 182, 192, 349, 374 f., 377
cattle-market (Forum Boarium), 16, 62, 89, 360 f., 371
Catullus, 187 f., 255, 383
Catulus, Quintus Lutatius, 373
Catuvellauni, 183, 379
Cauca, 389
Caucasus Mts, 166, 373
Caudine Forks, 52
Caudini, 364
Celer, 382
Celsus, 387
Celtiberians, 97, 122 f., 369

Celts, 43 f., 363, 369, 375; *see also* Gaul, Gauls
Cenabum, 184
Cenis, Mt, 367
censors, censorship, 42, 68, 70, 131, 165, 234 f., 363, 365; *see also* census
Censorinus, Lucius Marcius, 376
census, 21, 24, 203, 213; *see also* censors
*centuriata, comitia, see* Assembly
Cerialis Caesius Rufus, Quintus Petillius, 233, 380
Cervidius Scaevola, Quintus, *see* Scaevola
Cévennes, Mts, 152
Chaeronea, 373, 395
Chalcis, 362, 369
Châlons-sur-Marne, *see* Catalaunii, Campi
Charlemagne, 352, 391
Charles Martel, 352, 391
Chatti, 385
Chedworth, 248
Cheragan, 248
Cherusci, 378
Chiana, Val di, 362
chief priest (*pontifex maximus*), 90, 170, 201, 204
Childeric I, 391
China, 214
Chios, 369
Chorazin, 387
Chosroes II Parvez, 392
Christians, Christianity, 210, 230, 254, 258–69, 294–9, 305–8, 311–17, 324, 344–57, 383 f., 387–91, 393 ff.; *see also* Jesus, Jewish Christians
Chrysostom, St John, *see* John Chrysostom
Cibalae, 389
Cicero, Marcus Tullius, 19, 30, 128, 135 f., 168–72, 174, 181, 190, 199, 250, 253, 349, 351, 374 ff., 395

Cilicia, 264 f., 374
Cimbri, 153
Ciminian Mts, 360
Cimmerian Bosphorus (Crimea), *see* Bosphorus
Cincius Alimentus, Lucius, 360
Cinna, Lucius Cornelius, 159 f., 170, 374
Cinna Magnus, Lucius Cornelius (Lex Valeria Cornelia), 377
Circeii, 362 f.
Circus Maximus, 45, 363
Cirta (Constantine), 388
Cisalpine Gaul, *see* Gaul
Cispian Hill, 361
Citium, 374
citizenship, Latin, 39, 46; *see also* Latin right
citizenship, Roman, 39, 46, 51, 91, 149 f., 156 f., 169, 193, 203, 211, 213, 229, 249, 264, 267, 291, 364, 371 f., 376, 378 ff., 383; *see also civitas sine suffragio*
city police (*cohortes urbanae*), 209, 276
city prefect (*praefectus urbi*), 209, 233, 378
civil service (bureaucracy), imperial, 206, 229, 288, 303, 308, 317, 333, 341 f., 353, 356, 389
Civilis, Gaius Julius, 233
*civitas sine suffragio* (half-citizenship), 49, 55, 92, 363 f.
Civitas Turonum, *see* Turonum, Civitas
clan (*gens*), 19, 21, 40 f., 59, 61, 364
Classicus, Julius, 233, 380
Claudian, 349
Claudii, 61, 206, 225, 227, 231 f.; *see also* Drusus, Marcellus, Nero, Pompeianus, Pulcher
Claudius I, 227, 229, 231, 234, 241, 244, 379, 394 f.

Claudius II Gothicus, 285, 385
Claudius, Appius (decemvir), 63
Claudius, Quintus (Lex Claudia), 372
Claudius Caecus (the Blind), Appius, 70 f., 79; *see also* aqueducts, roads
Clausus, Attus (Appius Claudius Sabinus Inregillensis), 40
Cleander, 384
Clement of Alexandria, 305, 387
Cleonymus, 366
Cleopatra VII Philopator Philadelphus, 191, 195, 200 ff., 211, 376 f.
client states, 84, 86, 118, 121, 125, 167, 183, 191, 195, 205, 229, 237, 257 f., 377–81, 383, 395
clients (individual), *clientela*, patronage, 60 f., 66, 72, 84, 118, 146, 151, 156, 179, 211, 337, 364
Clodia, 187, 201
Clodius Albinus, *see* Albinus
Clodius Pulcher, Publius, 179, 181, 185 f., 188, 201, 375, 377
Clovis, 352, 391
Clusium, 32, 44, 361, 368
Clyde, R., 235, 240, 380
Cogidubnus, 380
*cohortes urbanae, see* city police
Coimbatore, *see* India
coinage, coins, 55, 79, 83, 85, 102, 108, 141, 160, 193–6, 214, 239, 286 ff., 293, 297, 302 ff., 310, 317, 342, 348, 364, 366, 368, 373, 376 ff., 381, 387, 392, 395
*collegia, see* corporations
Collina Pass, 367

Collina, Porta, 161
Collina (tribe), 361
Colonia Agrippinensis, 379
colonies, Latin, 39, 50–3, 94, 101, 105, 156, 362 f., 366, 369, 371 f.
colonies, Roman, 50 f., 94, 101, 148 f., 151, 154, 156, 161, 192 f., 202, 209, 211, 229, 239, 366, 371 f., 373, 376 f., 381 f.
Colosseum (Flavian Amphitheatre), 246, 367, 382
*comitia centuriata, curiata, populi tributa, see* Assembly
*comitia plebis tributa, see* Council, plebeian
Commagene, 379
*commercium* (right of), 92
Commodus, 275, 293, 384–7
*concilium plebis, see* Council, plebeian
Concord, 69, 71, 172, 174, 365, 371, 374
concrete, 136, 245, 371
Condatomagus, 247
Consentia, 389
*consilium principis, consistorium, see* Council, imperial
Constance, Lake, 389
Constans, 388
Constantia, 388
Constantina, *see* Cirta
Constantine I the Great, 296, 308, 310–16, 334, 339, 346 ff., 354, 358, 371, 387 f., 394 f.
Constantine II, 388
Constantine III, 389
Constantinople (Byzantium, Istanbul), 202, 310, 314 f., 321 f., 327 f., 331, 337, 342 ff., 352–6, 382, 387 f., 391 f.
Constantius I Chlorus, 300 f., 308, 386 f.

Constantius II, 316, 388
Constantius III, 326 f., 389
Constantius Gallus, see Gallus
*Constitutio Antoniniana*, 291 f., 386
consuls, consulship, 57 f., 68, 101, 127 f., 169, 173, 196, 199, 203 f., 226, 232, 282, 339, 352, 363 f., 370, 372, 377, 381
*conubium* (right of), 92
Cora, 362
Corbulo, Cnaeus Domitius, 230 f., 236, 380
Corcyra, 368
Corduba, 250, 368
Corfinium, 156, 189, 373
Corinth, 13 f., 46, 118, 124, 126, 192 f., 195, 266, 369 f., 376
Cornelia (daughter of Cinna), 374
Cornelia (daughter of Metellus Scipio), 186
Cornelia (mother of the Gracchi), 132
Cornelii (bodyguard), 161
Cornelii (family), 61; see also Nepos, Scipios, Sulla
corporations (guilds, *collegia*), 179, 214, 244, 303, 375, 378
*correctores*, 381
Corsica, 81 f., 87, 96, 363, 366
Coruncanius, Titus, 90
Cos, 214
Cosa, 50, 364, 371
Cotta, Lucius Aurelius (Lex Aurelia), 374
Council, imperial (*consilium principis*), 206, 383, 387
Council, plebeian 64, 71 f., 93 f., 365, 367, 372
Councils, city, see *curiae*
Councils, provincial (*concilia*), 377

Crassus, Lucius Licinius (Lex Licinia Mucia), 337
Crassus, Marcus Licinius, 164 f., 168 ff., 173 f., 177, 182, 186, 197, 205, 375
Crassus, Publius Licinius (son of Marcus), 182, 375
Cremera, R., 41, 363
Cremona, 100, 232 f.
Crete, 374
Crispus, 388
Critolaus, 369
Crixus, 374
crown money, see taxation
Crusades, 392
Ctesiphon, 237, 276, 283, 286, 375, 381, 385, 387
cult, imperial, see deification
Cumae, 8, 18, 23, 31, 33, 47, 62, 360, 362, 370, 372, 378
*cuniculi*, see drainage
Cunobelinus, 379
*curatores*, 381
Cures, 363
*curiae* (city councils), *curiales*, 340 f., 389
*curiae* (wards), 222 f., 361
*curiata, comitia*, see Assembly
Curii, 68
Curio, Gaius Scribonius, 186 f., 189 f., 377
Cursor, Lucius Papirius, 367
customs dues, see taxation
Cynics, 380, 383
Cynoscephalae, 117 f., 369
Cyprian, St, 306, 387
Cyprus, 265, 374 f., 381
Cyrene, Cyrenaica, 165, 369, 374, 379, 381
Cyrrhus, 395

DACIA, 197, 235, 237 f., 242, 380 f., 385, 387
Dalmatia (Upper Illyricum), 113, 177, 228, 300, 345, 379, 393

Damascus, 242, 264 f., 385, 395
Danube, R., Danubians, 153, 206, 208, 232 f., 237 f., 247 f., 273, 275 f., 280 ff., 284 ff., 288, 293, 300 f., 308, 310, 317, 321 f., 326–30, 333, 336, 345, 356, 360, 373, 380 ff., 385, 387, 392 f.
Dardanus, 159
David, 256, 261
Dead Sea, Dead Sea Scrolls, 262, 384
Deal, 183
*De Rebus Bellicis*, see *On Matters of Warfare*
debt, 62, 67–71, 120, 159 f., 169, 193 f., 365, 372 ff., 376
Decebalus, 235, 237
decemvirs, 42, 65, 67 f., 365
Decii, 68
Decius, Trajanus, 280, 284, 293, 307 f., 385 ff.
Decumates, Agri, see Agri Decumates
*dediticii*, 386
Defenders of the People, 371, 390
deification, 199 f., 204, 220, 266, 304, 377, 381
Delmatius, 388
Delos, 122, 140, 369 ff.
Delphi, 43, 45, 368
Demetrias, 369
Demetrius of Pharos, 114 f.
Democritus, 375
Diaspora, see Jews
Dicaearchia, see Puteoli
dictator, dictatorship, 57, 68, 101, 161 f., 191, 196 f., 204, 363 f., 367
Didius Julianus, see Julianus
Dido, 217 f.
Digentia, 379
Dio Cassius, 394 f.
dioceses (administrative), 301, 303, 387

Diocletian, 300–4, 308, 310 f., 314, 334, 336, 378, 382, 386 ff.
Diodorus Siculus, 394
Dionysius I, 363
Dionysius Exiguus, 383
Dionysius of Halicarnassus, 20, 394
Dionysus, *see* Bacchus
Dispersion, Jewish, *see* Jews
Dniester, R., 285
doctors, *see* medicine
Dolabella, Publius Cornelius, 376
Domitia, 236
Domitian, 235 ff., 245, 252, 380 f., 383
Domitianus, Domitius, 387
Domna, Julia, 279, 296
Domus Aurea, *see* Golden House
Don, R., 389
Donatists, 388, 391
donatives, 287
Dordogne, R., 390
Douro, R., 98, 123
drainage, irrigation, 16, 19, 41, 195, 361
Drave, R., 179
Druids, 184
Drusus Caesar (son of Germanicus), 379
Drusus, Marcus Livius, *see* Livius
Drusus the elder (Nero Drusus), 206, 208, 377, 379
Drusus the younger, 225
dualism (Gnosticism), 297 f.
Dura-Europus, 387 f.
Durocortorum, 375
Durostorum, 327
Dyrrhachium, 191, 368, 392

EBIONITES, 384
Ebro, R., 98, 99, 103, 367, 368 f.
Eburacum, 277

Eburones, 375
Ecbatana, 375
Ecnomus, Cape, 84
Edessa, 283
Edirne, *see* Hadrianopolis
education, 66, 90, 132 f., 141, 218, 292, 348, 367, 370, 374, 376, 380
Egypt, 13, 80, 113, 118, 121, 140, 167, 191, 195, 200, 202 f., 206, 215, 232, 241, 255 f., 282, 286, 294, 307, 345, 366, 368, 375, 381, 383, 385, 387, 390 f., 394 f.
Elagabalus, 279, 282, 296, 385
Elba, I., *see* Ilva
Elbe, R., 153, 208, 225
elephants, 78 f., 99 f., 119, 132, 367
Eleusis, 274, 383
*elocutio novella*, 383
emergency decree of Senate (*senatusconsultum ultimum*), 151, 154, 169 f., 374
Emesa, 279, 385
emperor worship, *see* deification
Ennius, 130, 132, 135, 217, 370
Ephesus, 29, 266, 383, 385
Epicharis, 253
Epictetus, 289, 386
Epicurus, Epicureans, 188 f.
Epidaurus, 370, 383
epidemics, 62, 64, 274, 280, 284, 287, 365, 384 f.
Epirus, 78, 113, 122, 140, 366, 369
Eprius Marcellus, Titus Clodius, *see* Marcellus
*equites*, *see* knights
*equites singulares*, 381
Ercte, 367
Eryx, 370
Esquilina (tribe), 361
Esquiline Hill, 10, 16, 26, 45, 361

Etruria, Etruscans, 8 ff., 12–33, 37, 40–4, 47, 49, 53, 57, 65 f., 82, 85, 89, 95, 100, 136, 140, 163, 169, 225, 232, 360–4, 366, 371, 380
Euboea, 361 f.
Eudemus, 372
Eudoxius, 390
Eugenius, 389, 391
Eumachia, 378
Eumenes II, 119 f., 369
eunuchs, 342, 391
Eunus (Antiochus), 141
Euphorion, 375
Euphrates, R., 182, 232, 237 f., 310, 375, 380, 385, 387 f.; *see also* Syria
Euric, 345, 352, 390 f.
Euripides, 254
Eusebius, 313, 394
Eutropius (historian), 393
Eutropius (minister of Arcadius), 391
*evocatio*, 363
exilarchs, 387
ex-slaves, *see* freedmen
ex-soldiers, *see* veterans

FABIAN (POPE), 387
Fabii, 41, 61, 363, 365
Fabius Maximus Allobrogicus, Quintus, 373
Fabius Maximus Verrucosus Cunctator, Quintus, 101 f., 367, 373
Fabius Pictor, Quintus, 360, 370
Fabriano, 361
*fabulae* (types of drama), 370
Faenius Rufus, 380
Faesulae, 367, 389
Fagutal, 361
Falerii, Faliscans, 361, 363
family, kinship, 19 ff., 24, 40, 59 ff., 128, 132, 151, 206, 211, 329, 332, 361, 370; *see also* clan, women
famine, 62, 64

Fanum Fortunae, 285
farming, see agriculture
*Fasti*, 57, 363
Father of the Country, *pater patriae*, 211, 216
Fausta, 388
federates, *foederati*, 324, 326, 328, 330 f., 335, 343 f., 389 f.
Felix, Marcus Antonius, 384
Felsina, 33; see also Bononia
Ferentina, League of, 362
Ferentium, 380
Festus, Porcius, 384
*Fetiales*, 40, 363
Fidenae, 4 f., 363 f.
Fides, Fidius, 40, 60, 87
Fimbria, Gaius Flavius, 373
Fire, Great, 230, 244, 267, 306
fire-brigade, see watch
Firmus, 389
Fishbourne, 380
Flaccus, Gaius Valerius (poet), see Valerius
Flaccus, Lucius Valerius (Lex Valeria), 373 f.
Flaccus, Marcus Fulvius, 150 f., 372 f.
Flaminian Fields, 365
Flamininus, Titus Quinctius, 117 f., 369
Flaminius, Gaius, 94 f., 100, 146
Flavian Amphitheatre, see Colosseum
Flavius, Cnaeus, 71
fleet, navy, marines, 39, 51, 78, 84 f., 99, 108 f., 116, 165, 183, 191, 201, 213, 231, 302, 328, 330, 366, 378
Florus, 393
*foederati*, see federates
Fonteii, 363
Fora, Imperial (Augustus, Caesar, Trajan, Vespasian), 194, 212, 382

Forth, Firth of, 235, 240, 380
Forum Boarium, see cattle-market
Forum Romanum, 10, 16, 20, 44, 64, 136, 194, 361 f., 375
Fossa culture, 360
Fosse Way, 379
Four Regions, Rome of the, see Septimontium
France, see Gaul
Francolise, 371
Franks, 284, 343, 348, 352, 385, 387, 389, 391
freedmen, ex-slaves, 70, 158, 216, 227, 229, 371, 378
Fregellae, 52
Frigidus, R., 389
Fritigern, 322
Fronto, Marcus Cornelius, 383
*frumentarii*, see secret police
Fucine Lake, 362
Fufius (Lex Aelia and Lex Fufia), 372, 375
Fulvia, 201, 377
Fulvii, 363; see also Flaccus, Nobilior, Plautianus
Fuscus, Cornelius, 380

GABII, 31, 40, 362
Gabinius, Aulus (Lex Gabinia), 374
Gades, 96, 376, 381
Gaesati, 367
Gaiseric, 327–30, 333, 344 f., 389
Gaius Caesar (grandson of Augustus), 206, 208
Gaius (Caligula), see Caligula
Gaius (jurist), 249, 383
Galatia, 136, 204, 210, 369, 377, 384
Galba, 231 f., 236, 241, 275, 380, 395
Galen, 383

Galerius, 300 f., 308, 311, 387, 389 f.
Galilee, 259 f., 262 f., 387
Gallia, see Gaul
Gallienus, 280, 282 f., 285, 287, 294, 308, 385 f.
Gallus, Constantius, 316, 388
Gallus, Trebonianus, 280, 293, 385 f.
Games, 11, 90, 118, 219, 243, 367, 385
Garonne, R., 248, 390
Gaul, Cisalpine; Gauls in N. Italy, 7, 33, 43 ff., 47, 53, 64 f., 94 ff., 99 f., 105, 157, 163, 177, 181 f., 184, 187, 191, 199, 363, 367, 371 ff., 376 f.
Gaul, Transalpine (France), 29, 99, 105, 152 ff., 169, 179–85, 189, 192, 197, 199, 203, 205, 229, 231, 233 f., 236, 239, 247 f., 252, 282, 284, 286, 300, 307, 325 ff., 330 f., 338 f., 343 ff., 348, 350, 352, 355, 364, 374, 379 f., 389 f., 393 f.
Gelasius I, 353, 391
Gelimer, 391
Gemellus, Tiberius (grandson of emperor Tiberius), 227, 379
Genèvre, Mt, 367
*gens*, see clan
Genseric, see Gaiseric
Genucius, Lucius (Lex Genucia), 365
Gerasa, 381
Gergovia, 179, 184
Germalus, 361
Germanicus, 225 ff., 378 f.
Germany, Germans, 153, 155, 181 f., 189, 208, 225, 227, 231 ff., 235 f., 252, 273 ff., 279 f., 282–6, 302, 310, 321 f., 324 f., 327–30, 333 ff.,

Germany, Germans –*cont.* 343 ff., 349, 352, 373, 375, 377–81, 384, 387, 389 f.; *see also* Danube, federates, Rhine, and names of German peoples

Geta, 276, 279

Gibraltar, 96, 369

Gildo, 389

Gisgo, 368

gladiators, 89, 164, 243, 246, 364, 367, 382, 391

Glaucia, Gaius Servilius, 373

Glycerius, 389

Gnostics, *see* dualism

Golden House (Domus Aurea), 230, 242–5, 382

Gordianus I, II Africanus, 385

Gordianus III Pius, 280, 385

Gospels (canonical, non-canonical), 259, 261, 383 f., 391

Goths, 280; *see also* Ostrogoths, Visigoths

Gracchuris, 369

Gracchus, Gaius Sempronius, 145, 147–51, 154 ff., 162, 372

Gracchus, Tiberius Sempronius (consul 177 BC), 122, 369

Gracchus, Tiberius Sempronius (tribune 133 BC), 145 ff., 149 ff., 372

graffiti, 243, 361, 395

grain, granaries, 62, 86, 116, 125, 140, 148 f., 165, 214 f., 229, 243, 336, 365, 369, 371, 374 f., 378, 386

Gratian, 321 f., 346, 389

Graupius, Mons, 380

Graviscae, 13, 360

Greece (Roman territory and province of Achaea), 123, 154, 158, 192, 195; 218, 231, 266, 274, 285, 377, 381, 395

Gregory I the Great, 392

Guadalquivir (Baetis), R., 103 f., 368

guilds (*collegia*), *see* corporations

Gundeshapur, 386

HADRIA, 366

Hadrian, 238 f., 241, 245, 249 f., 290, 296, 381–4

Hadrianopolis (Adrianople, Edirne), 322, 324, 349

Hadrumetum, 383

Halicarnassus, 20, 394

Hamilcar Barca, 96 ff., 108, 367

Hannibal, 98–106, 108 f., 114 f., 119, 125, 127, 139, 152, 220, 367 ff.

Hannibalianus, 388

Hanno (explorer), 366

Hanno the Great, 366 f.

Hasdrubal (son of Gisgo), 368

Hasdrubal (son-in-law of Hamilcar), 97 ff.

Hasdrubal Barca (son of Hamilcar), 102–5, 368

Hasmonaeans (Maccabees), 167, 256 f., 383

Hatra, 384

Hebron, 388

Helena, St, 387 f.

Helice, R., 367

Heliopolis, 382

Helvetii, 179 ff.

Helvidius Priscus, *see* Priscus

Heraclea, 366

Herculaneum, 235, 242 f., 382

Herod Antipas, 259, 262

Herod the Great, 257 ff., 377, 383, 395

Herodian, 394

Herodotus, 14, 360

Heruli, 285, 343 f., 385

Hibernia, *see* Ireland

Hierapolis, 386

Hiero I, 362

Hiero II, 83, 86

Hierocles, 387 f.

Hillel the elder, 258

Hippias, 362

Hippo Regius, 347, 394

Hirpini, 364

Hirtius, Aulus, 376

Hispalis (Seville), 353, 391, 393

*Historia Augusta*, 393

Homer, 90, 130, 217, 251

homosexuality, 241, 251, 279, 362

*honestiores*, 249, 291, 383

Honoria, 389

Honorius, 324–7, 339, 342, 353, 389 f.

Horace, 206, 218 f., 378 f.

Horatius Cocles, 32

Hortensius, Quintus (Lex Hortensia), 71

*hospitium publicum*, 45, 363

Hostilius Mancinus, Gaius, *see* Mancinus

Hostilius, Tullus, *see* Tullus

*humanitas*, 171 f.

*humiliores*, 249, 291, 383

Huns, 322, 327 ff., 334, 353, 389 ff.

Hyrcanus II, John, 374

IBERA, 368

Iberians, 97, 369

Iberus, R., *see* Ebro

Icelus (Servius Sulpicius Marcianus), 380

Idumaea, 257

Ifach, Cape, 96

Ilerda, 190, 375

Ilipa, 104, 368

Illyricum, Illyrians, 113 f., 117, 208, 368 f., 389; *see also* Dalmatia (Upper Illyricum), Pannonia (Lower Illyricum)

Ilorci, 368

Ilva, I. (Elba), 360

*Imperator*, 192, 195

Inchtuthil, 380

India, 78, 214

Indus, R., 375

industry, *see* trade, technology

inflation, *see* coinage, prices

inhumation, *see* burial

Innocent I, 346, 391

Insubres, 367, 371

interest, rate of, 193, 378

Ionia, 360

Ionian Sea, 202; *see also* Adriatic Sea

Ireland (Hibernia), 351

Iron Age, *see* metals

Iron Gates, 380

irrigation, *see* drainage

Isauria, 388, 391

Isidore, 391, 393

Islam, *see* Moslems

Israel, Israelites, *see* Jews, Judaea

Issus, 276

Istakhr, 385

Istanbul, *see* Constantinople

Italica, 104, 368, 380

*iudicia publica, see* lawcourts

Iulus, *see* Ascanius

JAMES THE JUST, ST, 265, 384

Janiculum Hill, 41, 363

Jazyges, 384

Jerome, St, 345 f., 390, 393

Jerusalem, 167, 234, 239, 242, 257, 262 f., 265 f., 315, 317, 382, 388 f.

Jesus Christ, 210, 258–69, 297 f., 306, 311 ff., 344, 347, 383 f.; *see also* Christianity

Jewish Christians (Judaeo-Christians), 265–9, 384

Jews, 167, 233, 235, 237, 239, 256–69, 306, 312 f., 317, 348, 370, 376, 380 f., 383 f.; *see also* Judaea

Johannes (usurper), 389

John Cassian, 345, 390

John Chrysostom, St, 337

John Hyrcanus II, *see* Hyrcanus

John the Baptist, St, 259 ff.

Jordan, R., 259

Jordanes, 390, 393

Joseph, 262

Josephus, 394 f.

Jovian, 317

Judaea (Syria Palaestina), 167, 203, 231, 233, 256–69, 315, 317, 345, 369, 374, 377, 381; *see also* Jews

Judah I ha-Nasi (the Prince), 387

Judaism, *see* Jews

Judas Maccabaeus, 383

Jugurtha, 152 f., 158, 373, 394

Julia Augusta, *see* Livia

Julia (daughter of Augustus), 205 f., 378

Julia (daughter of Julius Caesar), 177, 185, 211

Julia (grand-daughter of Augustus), 211, 221, 378

Julia, *see* Domna, Livilla, Maesa, Mamaea, Soaemias

Julia, Lex, *see* Caesar, Lucius Julius

Julia (wife of Marius), 374

Julian the Apostate, 306, 316 f., 340, 388 f., 392

Julianus, Didius, 276, 384

Julianus, Salvius, *see* Salvius

Julii, 195, 227, 231 f., 361, 388; *see also* Caesar, Nepos

Julius, Burgus, 390

juries, *see* lawcourts

jurisprudence, *see* Law, Roman

*ius gentium, naturale*, 92 f., 171, 367

Justin I, 354, 392

Justin of Neapolis, 305

Justinian I the Great, 291, 314, 354 f., 388, 391 f.

Jutland, 153

Juvenal, 251 f.

Juventii, 363

KABUL, *see* Afghanistan

Kartir, 386

Kaua, 385

Kefr Bir'im, 387

Khosrau, *see* Chosroes

kingship, Roman, 11, 15, 19

knights (*equites*, equestrian order), 26, 148 f., 151, 153, 156, 160, 162, 170, 172 f., 177, 206, 210, 226, 231, 234, 276, 279, 374, 376, 381, 384

Kniva, 284

LABEO, Marcus Antistius, 383

Labienus, Titus, 184, 192

Laco, Cornelius, 380

Laenas, Gaius Popillius, 369

Laetus, Quintus Aemilius, 275 f., 384

language, 9, 15, 38, 65, 82, 90, 129, 132, 156, 171, 217, 219 f., 250, 342, 354, 357, 361, 378

Lanuvium, 363

Lapis Niger, *see* Black Stone

Lars Porsenna, *see* Porsenna

Lateran church, palace, 311, 315, 388

Lateranus, Lucius Sextius (Leges Liciniae Sextiae), 68 f., 365, 371

*latifundia*, 139

Latin Empire, 392

Latin right, 150, 157, 372, 376, 380

Latium, Latins, 8–19, 26 f., 29, 31 ff., 37–40, 44, 46–52, 55, 62, 69, 149 f., 217, 251, 360 ff., 371 f., 379; *see also*

Latium, Latins – *cont.*
  colonies, Latin, and
  Latin right
Laurentum, 382
Laurium, 371
Lavinia, 379
Lavinium, 37 f., 360, 362
Law, Jewish, *see* Jews
Law, Roman, 64–7, 90–3,
  249 f., 290 ff., 302, 311,
  341 f., 345 ff., 352 f.,
  355, 357, 359, 364 f.,
  367, 386, 392
lawcourts, juries, 59, 93,
  132 f., 148, 162, 165,
  171, 204, 342, 372–5
Lazio, 9, 13; *see also*
  Latium
Lebanon, *see* Phoenicia
Ledosus, 247
*legati* (subordinate com-
  manders), 182, 203
legends, *see* myths
Lemnos, 14 f.
Lentulus Gaetulicus,
  Cnaeus Cornelius, 379
Lentulus Sura, Publius
  Cornelius, 374
Leo I (emperor), 354, 389,
  391
Leo I (Pope), 329, 346,
  348, 389
Leo II (emperor), 392
Leo III (Pope), 352
Leonides, 387
Leontius I, 392
Leontius, Burgus of, 390
Leovigild, 353
Lepcis Magna, 214, 378,
  382, 384, 388
Lepidus, Marcus Aemil-
  ius (consul 78 BC), 163,
  373
Lepidus, Marcus Aemilius
  (son-in-law of Cali-
  gula), 379
Lepidus, Marcus Aemil-
  ius (triumvir), 199, 201,
  204, 376 f.
Lepini, Mts, 362
Lérins, 390
Lesbia, 187

Leucippus, 375
Lex Campana, 375
libraries, 195, 376, 382
Liby-phoenicians, 366
Licinia Mucia, Lex, *see*
  Crassus, Lucius Lici-
  nius, *and* Scaevola Pon-
  tifex, Quintus Mucius
Liciniae Sextiae, Leges,
  *see* Stolo, Gaius Licinius
  *and* Lateranus, Lucius
  Sextius
Licinii, 363; *see also* Cras-
  sus, Macer, Stolo
Licinius (emperor), 308,
  311
Ligugé, 390
Ligurians, 152
Lilybaeum, 366
Limonum, *see* Pictavi
Lindum, 379
Lingones, 367
Liris, R., 38, 52, 362
Lissus, 368
Liternum, 370
Livia (Julia Augusta), 206,
  211 f., 377
Livilla, Julia, 379
Livius Andronicus, Luc-
  ius, 90, 367
Livius Drusus the elder,
  Marcus (tribune 122
  BC), 149
Livius Drusus the
  younger, Marcus (tri-
  bune 91 BC), 156 f.
Livy, 220 f., 364, 379, 393
Lombards, 392
Londinium (London), 8,
  379
Longinus, Gaius Cassius
  (assassin of Caesar), *see*
  Cassius
Longinus, Cassius (philo-
  sopher), 385 f.
Luca, 182
Lucan, 250, 395
Lucania, Lucanians, 77 f.,
  301, 364
Luceres, 361
Luceria, 364, 366
Lucian, 253, 383

Lucilius, Gaius, 135
Lucilla, 384
Lucius Caesar (grandson
  of Augustus), 206, 208
Lucretius, 188 f., 375
Lucullus, Lucius Licin-
  ius, 166, 173, 374
*ludi*, *see* Games
Lugdunum, 276, 375, 379,
  390
Lusitania, 122, 232, 377
Lutetia (Paris), 8, 375, 389
Lycaonia, 377
Lycia, 379
Lycopolis, 294
Lydia, 14, 385

MACCABEES, *see* Hasmon-
  aeans
Macedonia, 113–18, 120–
  5, 127, 133, 154, 167,
  199, 300, 368 f., 371,
  382
Macer, Gaius Licinius,
  374, 395
Machuza, 387
Macrinus, 279
Macro, Naevius Sutorius,
  226 f.
Macrobius, 349, 391
Madaurus, 253, 391
Maecenas, Gaius, 216–19,
  378
Maelius, Spurius, 376
Maenius, Gaius, 362
Maesa, Julia, 279
Magetobriga, 375
Magna Graecia, 13, 18, 77
Magnentius, 388
Magnesia ad Sipylum,
  119, 369
Magni, Campi, 368
Magnus Maximus, 389
Mago (agricultural writer),
  366
Mago (brother of Hanni-
  bal), 368
*maiestas* (treason), 162,
  187, 225, 230, 379
Majorian, 330, 389
Malaca, 81
malaria, 139, 371

Mallius Maximus, Cnaeus, *see* Maximus

Malventum, *see* Beneventum

Mamaea, Julia, 279 f.

Mamertini, 366

Mamilii, 363

Mamilius, Octavius, 362

Mancinus, Gaius Hostilius, 372

Mani, Manichaeans, 298 f., 348, 386

Manilius, Gaius (Lex Manilia), 374

Manlius Vulso, Cnaeus, *see* Vulso

Mantua, 33, 216

Manzikert, 392

Marcellus, Gaius Claudius, 375

Marcellus, Marcus Claudius (consul five times 215–208), 368, 370

Marcellus, Marcus Claudius (son-in-law of Augustus), 205 f., 212, 382

Marcellus, Titus Clodius Eprius, 380

Marcellus, Varius, 385

Marcian (emperor), 353

Marcian (usurper), 392

Marcianopolis, 385

Marcianus, Gessius, 385

Marcianus, Servius Sulpicius, *see* Icelus

Marcii, 68; *see also* Ancus, Censorinus, Rex

Marcion, 269, 384

Marcomanni, 274, 378, 384, 386; *see also* Bohemia

Marcus Aurelius, *see* Aurelius

Mardonius, 389

Maremma, 371

Margus, R., 386

marines, *see* fleet

Marinus, 385

Marius, Gaius, 153–6, 158 f., 168, 170, 181, 373 f.

Marius Gratidianus, Marcus, 373

Marmara, Sea of, 300

Marmoutier, 390

Maroboduus, 378

marriage, *see* women

Marsala, *see* Lilybaeum

Marsian War, *see* Social War

Marsi, 156, 364

Martial, 251

Martin of Tours, St, 345, 350, 390

Marzabotto, 33, 362

Masada, 380

Masinissa, 106, 125, 152, 369

Massilia (Massalia), 29, 96, 98, 152, 190, 338, 345, 367, 373, 375

Mastarna, 362

Mastia, *see* Carthago Nova

*materfamilias*, *see* family, women

Mattathias Antigonus, *see* Antigonus

Mauretania, 205, 229, 279, 327 f., 336, 369, 373, 379, 381, 385

Maxentius, 308, 310, 314, 387

Maximian, 300 f., 305, 308, 387

Maximinus I Thrax, 280 f., 293, 307, 385 f.

Maximinus II Daia, 311, 387 f.

Maximus Caesar, 385

Maximus, Cnaeus Mallius, 373

Maximus of Ephesus (philosopher), 389

Maximus, *see* Fabius, Magnus, Pupienus, Valerius

medallions, 287, 310, 348, 387, 391, 395

Medao R., 389

Media, 279, 375

medicine, doctors, 141, 193, 376, 380, 383

Mediolanum (Milan), 285,

310, 321, 324, 329, 338, 346, 348, 378, 387, 390 f.

Medjerda (Bagradas), R., 85, 366, 368

Megalopolis, 371

Melita, 267

Memmius, Gaius, 373

Menenius Agrippa, *see* Agrippa

Mercenaries, War of the (Truceless War), 87, 96, 366 f.

Merovingians, 352

Mesopotamia, 13, 237, 273, 276 f., 279 f., 282 f., 381

Messalina, Valeria, 229, 379 f.

Messalla, Manius Valerius, 367

Messalla Corvinus, Marcus Valerius, 379

Messalla Volesus, Lucius Valerius (Lex Valeria Cornelia), 373

Messana, 82 f., 366

metals, 9, 14, 16 f., 26, 41, 55, 80, 97, 104, 116, 136, 214, 336, 360, 369, 371, 376, 378, 382

Metaurus, R., 105, 368

Metelli, Caecilii, 129, 374

Metellus, Quintus Caecilius, 152 f.

Metellus Pius, Quintus Caecilius, 373

Metellus Pius Scipio, Quintus Caecilius, 186, 192

Methone, 377

Micipsa, 373

military tribunes with consular powers, *see tribuni militum consulari potestate*

Milo, Titus Annius, 375 f.

Milvian Bridge, 163, 308, 311, 371, 373

Mincius, R., 389

Minervina, 388

mines, *see* metals

Misenum, 378

Mithridates VI Eupator Dionysus, 158 ff., 166 f., 191, 373 f.
Mithridates of Pergamum, 376
Moesia, 208, 380
Moguntiacum, 321, 324, 385
Mohammed (Prophet), 353; see also Moslems
Mohammed II (Ottoman sultan), 355
Monica, St, 391
monastic movement, monks, nuns, 345 f., 350, 390
Mons Sacer, 365
Montanus, Montanists, 387
Moray Firth, 380
mosaics, 243 f., 382
Moselle, R., 183, 282, 300
Moslems, Islam, 373, 391
Motya, 366
Mucia, 374
Mucia Licinia, Lex, see Scaevola Pontifex, Quintus Mucius
Mucianus, Gaius Licinius, 233 f.
Mummius Achaicus, Lucius, 124
Mumrills, 380
Munda, 192
Murena, Lucius Licinius, 374
Mutilus, Marcus Papius (Lex Papia Poppaea), 377
Mutina, 199, 372, 378
Mycenae, 13
Mylae, 84
Myonnesus, 369
Mysia, 382
myths, legends, 11 f., 22 ff., 37, 43, 66, 130, 212, 217, 360 f., 370

NAEVIUS, 86, 129 f., 217, 370
Naissus, 285, 300, 385, 389, 392

Namatianus, Rutilius, see Rutilius
Nao, Cape, 96
Naples, see Neapolis
Naples, Bay of, see Campania, Cumae
Narbo, 152, 390
Narbonese Gaul, see Gaul
Narcissus, Claudius, 229
Narses (Narsah) I, 387
Narses (general of Justinian I), 353, 355, 391
natural law, see ius gentium, naturale
Naulochus, 201
navy, see fleet
Nazareth, 259
Neanderthal man, 9
Neapolis (in Samaria), 305
Neapolis (Naples), 18, 52, 216, 361, 364, 371, 378
Neckar, R., 321, 380
Nectarius, 391
Nehardea, 387
Nemausus, 239
Nemorensis (Nemi), Lake, 32
Neoterics, 375
Nepet, 363
Nepos, Cornelius, 393
Nepos, Julius, 331, 389 f.
Nepotianus, 388
Nero (emperor), 241 f., 246, 250, 252 f., 267 f., 274, 306, 380, 382, 384, 394
Nero, Gaius Claudius, 368
Nero, Tiberius Claudius, 377
Nero Caesar (son of Germanicus), 379
Nero Drusus, see Drusus the elder
Nerva, 236
Nervii, 181
New Carthage, see Carthago Nova
new men (novi homines), 127, 130, 168, 204, 206, 370, 374, 377
nexus, see debt
Nicaea, 311, 394

Nicolaus of Damascus, 395
Nicomedes IV Philopator, 373
Nicomedia, 300, 377, 388
Nicopolis (Pontus), 167
Niger, Pescennius, 276
Nisibis, 388 f.
Nobilior, Marcus Fulvius, 370
Nora, 366
Norba, 363
Noricum, 206
Normandy, 182
Notitia Dignitatum, 333
novi homines, see new men
Numa Pompilius, 361, 386
Numantia, 123, 369
Numerian, 386
Numidia (Africa Nova), 99, 106, 125, 152 f., 155, 327 f., 366, 381
Nursia, 390
Nymphidius Sabinus, Gaius, 230 f.

OATHS, vows, curses, 19, 63, 123, 125, 198, 201, 211, 365, 373
obnuntiatio, 375
Occeius, 378
Octavia (sister of Augustus), 201
Octavia (wife of Nero), 229 f.
Octavian (Octavius, Gaius), see Augustus
Octavius, Mamilius, see Mamilius
Octavius, Marcus, 146
Odenathus, 282 f.
Odoacer, 330 f., 353
oil, olives, 82, 140, 365
Olybrius, 389
On Matters of Warfare (De Rebus Bellicis), 342, 390
Opimius, Gaius, 151, 371
Opitergium, 384
Oplontis, 235, 242, 374
Oppian Hill, 361
Oppius, Gaius (Lex Oppia), 197, 370, 376

Oppius Sabinus, Gaius, see Sabinus
optimates, 151
oratory, 132 f., 147, 168, 170 ff., 185, 252, 380, 383, 391, 394; see also sophists
Orchomenus, 373
Orestes, 390
Origen, 305, 386 f.
Orosius, 390, 393
Osca, 368
Oscan, 38 f., 47, 156, 362, 368
Osman (Othman) I, 392
Osrhoene, 277
Osroes, 381
Ostia, 28, 51, 229, 244, 329, 361, 363 f., 366, 370, 382
Ostrogoths, 322, 324, 353, 389, 391
Otho, 230, 232 f., 380, 395
Ottoman Turks, see Turks
ovatio, 370
Ovid, 221, 379

Pacuvius, 370
Paestum, 364
Paetus Catus, Sextus Aelius, 367
paintings, 13, 212, 241-4, 293, 367, 371, 374, 378, 382
Palatina (tribe), 361
Palatine Hill (Palatium), 10, 16, 45, 170, 245, 360 f.
Pallas, Antonius, 229
Palmyra, 277, 282 f., 286
Pamphylia, 379
Panaetius, 370
Panhellenic League, 364
Pannonia, 208, 225, 276, 381, 385, 390; see also Danube
Panormus, 81, 85, 366 f.
Pantaenus, 387
Pantheon, 245, 296, 382
pantomimi, 380
Papia Poppaea, Lex, see

Mutilus, Marcus Papius, and Secundus, Quintus Poppaeus
Papinian, 290, 356
papyri, papyrus, 116, 214, 385 f., 395
Paris, see Lutetia
Parma, 372, 378
Parthamaspates, 381
Parthia, 167, 182, 186, 197, 201, 205, 230, 237 f., 268, 273, 276, 279 f., 282 f., 368 f., 375, 377, 380 f., 383 f.
Patavium, 220, 378, 393
pater, see family, Father of the Country
patriarchs, Jewish (of imperial epoch), 387
patricians, 60-4, 67 f., 70 ff., 93 f., 158 f., 170, 364
Patricius (father of Augustine), 391
Patricius (Jewish rebel), 388
patrons, see clientela
Paul, St, 263-9, 307, 314, 350, 383 f., 391
Paulinus, Gaius Suetonius, 380
Paullus, Lucius Aemilius, 367
Paullus Macedonicus, Lucius Aemilius, 120, 136, 370
Paulus (jurist), 291, 386
Pelagius, 351, 391
Pella, 382
Pentri, 364
Pepin the Short, 352
Peraea, 259
Perennis, Tigidius, 384
Pergamum, 116 f., 119-22, 141 f., 146, 369, 371 f., 376 f., 383
Perperna, Marcus, 374
Persepolis, 283
Perseus, 120 f., 123, 369
Persia, Persians, 119, 158, 167, 256, 263, 279 f., 282-6, 294, 298 f., 301,

304, 316 f., 355, 363, 388, 392
Persian Gulf, 237, 276, 368
Persis, 283
Pertinax, 275
Perusia, 377
Pescennius Niger, see Niger
Pessinus, 385
Peter, St, 265, 307, 314 f., 384
Petra, 381
Petreius, Marcus, 374, 376
Petronius Niger, Titus (Petronius Arbiter), 216, 250 f., 383
Petronius Probus, see Probus
Petuaria, 382
Pfalzel, 390
Pharisees, 257 ff., 262, 264, 394
Pharnaces II, 376
Pharos I. (Dalmatia), 114
Pharsalus, 191, 250
Philip II, 368
Philip V, 114-20, 127, 368 f.
Philip the Arabian, 280, 282, 293, 385 f.
Philippi, 199, 219, 377
Phocaea, 362
Phoenice, 368
Phoenicia, 13, 80 ff., 140, 291, 360, 378
Phrygia, 385 ff.
Piazza Armerina, 387
Picenum, 364, 374
Pictavi (Limonum), 390
Pictor, Quintus Fabius, 395
Picts, 389
Pietas, pius, 60, 239, 381
Pilatus, Pontius, 263, 384
Piraeus, 159
pirates, 116, 122, 140, 165, 200, 374
Pisaurum, 374
Pisidia, 377

Piso, Cnaeus Calpurnius, 379

Piso, Gaius Calpurnius, 380

Piso Frugi, Gaius Calpurnius, 372

Piso Licinanus, Lucius Calpurnius (adopted son of Galba), 232, 380

Pistoria, 170, 367

Pithecusa, 361

Placentia, 100, 191, 367, 371

Placidia, Galla, 326 f.

plague, see epidemics

Plato, 296, 303, 305, 350, 374, 386 f.

Plautia Papiria, Lex, see Silvanus, Marcus Plautius and Carbo, Gaius Papirius

Plautianus, Gaius Fulvius, 279, 386

Plautii Laterani, 388

Plautilla (wife of Caracalla), 279

Plautus, 129 f., 135, 141

plebeians, 60–72, 90, 93 f., 129, 146, 364 f.

plebiscita, 64, 365

Pliny the elder, 380, 383, 395

Pliny the younger, 236, 307, 380 ff.

Plotinus, 294 ff., 305, 308, 386

Plutarch, 252, 395

Po (Padus), R., 7 f., 33, 44, 94 f., 100, 157, 232 f., 329, 360, 367, 369, 371, 373, 376

Poetelius Libo Visolus, Gaius (Lex Poetelia), 69 ff., 365

Pola, 388

Polemo I, 377

Politorium, 23, 28, 361

Pollio, Gaius Asinius, 395

Polybius, 53, 59, 85, 98, 107, 122, 371, 395

Pometia, 362

pomoerium (city boundary), 16, 361

Pompeianus, Claudius, 384

Pompeii, 136, 138, 214, 235, 242 ff., 371, 373, 378, 382 f., 395

Pompeius, Cnaeus, junior, 192

Pompeius, Sextus, 192, 200 f., 377

Pompeius Magnus, Cnaeus (Pompey the Great), 163–8, 172 ff., 177, 182 f., 185–92, 198, 203, 220, 250, 257, 374 ff.

Pompeius Strabo (Lex Pompeia), 373 f.

Pons Aemilius, Mulvius, Sublicius, see bridges, Milvian Bridge

pontifex maximus, see chief priest

Pontine (Pomptine) Marshes, 195, 371

Pontius Pilate, see Pilatus

Pontus, 158 f., 166, 369, 377, 385

Popes (bishops of Rome), 307, 311, 315, 338, 346, 350, 387, 391

Poppaea Sabina, 230

Poppaeus Secundus, Quintus (Lex Papia Poppaea), see Secundus

populares, 151

population, 49, 203, 244, 366 f., 372, 377

Populonia, 14, 360

Porcia (wife of Brutus), 201, 377

Porcii, 363; see also Cato

Porphyry, 294, 308, 386

Porsenna, Lars, 32, 362

portraiture, see coins, sculpture

Portus Itius, 183

Posidonius, 374, 386, 395

Postumus, 282, 286

pottery, vases, earthenware, 9, 13, 25 f., 214, 247, 378

praefectus praetorio, urbi, see praetorian prefect, city prefect

Praeneste, 47 ff., 162, 361, 363, 373, 382

praetors, 46 f., 57, 68, 86, 88, 91 f., 104, 127 f., 159, 162, 249, 364, 370, 373, 376

praetorian guard, 209, 225, 227, 233, 236, 378

praetorian prefect, 225 ff., 229 ff., 234, 236, 238, 277, 279 f., 290 f., 301, 341, 380 f., 384, 386, 390

prices, inflation, 286 f., 302 f., 308, 316 f., 336, 376, 378, 387

priests, 20, 64, 71, 279, 297; see also chief priest, Jews

Prima Porta, 212, 378

Primus, Marcus Antonius, 233

Princes' Islands, 395

Priscus Attalus, see Attalus

Priscus, Helvidius, 380

Probus (emperor), 286

Probus, Petronius, 390

Procopius (historian), 395

Procopius (usurper), 392

proletarii (propertyless volunteers), 107, 153 f.

Propertius, 219, 379

Propontis, 119

prorogatio, 127, 370, 373

provocatio, see appeal

Prusias II, 118

Ptolemies (Lagids), 80, 113, 115, 118, 121, 195, 256, 376

Ptolemy I Soter, 368, 384

Ptolemy II Philadelphus, 366

Ptolemy VI Philometor, 369

Ptolemy XII 'Auletes', 375

Ptolemy XIII Philopator Philadelphus, 191

Ptolemy XIV Philopator Philadelphus, 376
Ptolemy XV Caesar, see Caesarion
Ptolemy (of Mauretania), 379
public land, ager publicus, see state land
publicani, 149, 153
Publilius Volero (Lex Publilia), 365
Pulcher, Appius Claudius, 372
Pulcher, Publius Clodius, see Clodius
Pulcheria, 353
Pumbeditha, 387
Punic War, First, 83 ff., 87, 89 ff., 94, 96, 99, 113, 129, 136, 140, 366 f., 394
Punic War, Second (Hannibalic), 98–109, 114 f., 117, 119, 125, 127 f., 130 ff., 136, 140, 145, 149, 153, 367 f., 370 f.
Punic War, Third, 124 f., 133, 369
Punicum, 82, 363, 366
Pupienus (Maximus), 385
Pupput, 383
Puteoli (Dicaearchia), 137, 216, 361, 367, 371, 378, 382
Pydna, 120 f., 136, 369 f.
Pyrenees, Mts, 97, 102 f., 325, 369
Pyrgi, 82, 360, 363, 366
Pyrrhus, 78 ff., 82, 113, 366

QUADI, 385
quaestiones, see lawcourts
quaestors, 162, 365 f., 373, 376
Querolus, 390
Quiberon Bay, 182, 375
Quietus, Lusius, 381
quinqueremes, 366
Quintilian, 380, 383
Quintillus, 385

Quirinal Hill, 10, 16, 26, 31, 45, 362
Qumran, 262, 384

RABIRIUS (ARCHITECT), 382
Rabirius, Gaius, 374
Radagaisus, 389
Raetia, 206, 380 f.
Ramnes, 361
Raudii, Campi, 153, 373
Ravenna, 324 f., 328, 330 f., 338, 342, 356, 378, 382, 391
Reate, 360, 363, 380
Reccared, 353
recruitment, 42, 107, 142, 145, 153 f., 157, 203, 280, 302, 333 ff., 340, 346, 368
Regia, 21, 23, 361
Regillus, Lake, 37
Regions, Four, see Septimontium
Regulus, Marcus Atilius, 85
religion (pagan), 14, 19 ff., 23, 27–32, 37, 40, 43, 58, 60, 62, 66, 128–31, 194 f., 204, 210 ff., 218, 239, 254 ff., 275, 279, 295–9, 303 ff., 308, 311 ff., 316 f., 321, 346–9, 361–7, 370 f., 375, 377 f., 383, 386 ff., 391
Renus (Reno), R., 362
Res Gestae Divi Augusti, 210
Rex, Quintus Marcius, 371
rex sacrorum, 21
Rhine, R., 182, 203, 208, 225, 233, 237, 247 f., 280 f., 284, 300 f., 310, 321, 325 f., 333, 356, 378, 380, 385
Rhodes, 116 f., 120 ff., 133, 140, 165, 208, 366, 369 f., 374
Rhône, R., 99, 152
Ricimer, 330
roads, 16, 23, 39, 41 f., 52,

70, 124, 152, 164, 213, 215, 360 f., 363 f., 369, 371, 373, 378 ff.
Roma quadrata, see Palatine Hill
'Romania', 348
Romulus, 21, 349, 361 f.
Romulus Augustus (Augustulus), 330 f., 349, 389 f.
Rubicon, R., 187, 189, 375
Rudiae, 130, 370
Rufinus, Flavius, 324, 343, 391
Rufus, Faenius, 380
Rufus, Lucius Verginius, 380
Rufus, Publius Sulpicius, 157 ff.
Rufus, Quintus Pompeius (consul 88 BC), 376
Rufus, Quintus Pompeius (tribune 52 BC), 376
Rullus, Publius Servilius, 374
Rumania, see Dacia
Rutilius Namatianus, 349, 391
Rutuli, 362

SABAUDIA, 389
Sabellians, 363
Sabines, 39 f., 47, 49, 70, 132, 219, 234 f., 360, 362–5, 379 f.
Sabinus, Flavius, 233
Sabinus, Gaius Calvisius, 376
Sabinus, Gaius Nymphidius, see Nymphidius
Sabinus, Gaius Oppius, 380
Saccas, Ammonius, see Ammonius
Sadducees, 257, 263
Saguntum, 98 f., 367
Saint Bernard Pass, 367
Salaria, Via, see roads, salt
Sallust, 394
Salonae, 301, 304, 387

salt, 8, 19, 41 f., 125, 360, 362, 371

Salvian, 338 ff., 343, 390, 395

Salvius Julianus, Lucius, 249, 383

Samaria, Samaritans, 305, 384

Samarobriva, 184, 375

Sambre R., 181

Samnites, 47, 52–5, 69 ff., 77 ff., 89, 107, 156, 363–6

Samosata, 253, 383

San Giovenale, 362, 371

Sandwich, 183

Sanhedrin, 259

Sapor (Shapur) I, 283 f., 385

Sapor (Shapur) II, 388

Sardinia, 81 f., 87 f., 96, 130, 307, 363, 366, 370

Sarmatia, Sarmati, 274, 381, 384 f.

Sarmizegethusa, 237, 381

Sarsina, 129

Sasan, 385

Sassanians, *see* Persians

Satricum, 363

Saturninus, Lucius Antonius, 380

Saturninus, Lucius Appuleius, 154 f., 373

Savaria, 390

Save, R., 179

Saxons, 325, 343, 386, 389

Scaevola, Quintus Cervidius, 290, 386

Scaevola Pontifex, Quintus Mucius (Lex Licinia Mucia), 373 f.

Scandinavia, 284, 362, 385; *see also* Jutland

Scaptopare, 385

Scipio, Cnaeus Cornelius (uncle of Africanus the elder), 102 f., 368

Scipio, Publius Cornelius (father of Africanus the elder), 102 ff., 368

Scipio Africanus the elder,

Publius Cornelius, 102–9, 118, 123, 127 f., 130–3, 155, 368, 378

Scipio Africanus the younger (Aemilianus), Publius Cornelius, 123, 125, 133, 135, 145 f., 150, 152, 155, 369, 372

Scipio Asiaticus, Lucius Cornelius (brother of Aemilianus), 131, 136, 369 f.

Scipio Nasica Corculum, Publius Cornelius, 369

Scipio Nasica, Serapio, Publius Cornelius, 372

Scipios, 128, 367, 370; *see also* Cornelii

Scodra, 368

Scolacium, 372

Scotland, (Caledonia), Scots, 277, 389

scribes, Jewish, 257, 261

sculpture, 14, 195 f., 212, 236, 241 f., 292 ff., 368, 370, 376, 382, 386

Scylacium, 393

Scythia, 44, 381, 383

secessions, 63, 67, 365

secret police (*speculatores, frumentarii, agentes in rebus*), 378, 381, 389

Secular Games, *see* Games

Secundus, Quintus Poppaeus (Lex Papia Poppaea), 377

Segesta, 366

Seine, R., 179

Seistan, 375

Seius Strabo, Lucius, 379

Sejanus, Lucius Aelius, 225 f., 379

Seleucia on the Tigris, 298

Seleucids, 113, 115 f., 118 ff., 167, 182, 256, 263, 369

Seleucus I Nicator, 368

Seljuk Turks, *see* Turks

Sempronia, 372

Sempronius Asellio, *see* Asellio

Sena Gallica, 366

Senate, 22, 58–61, 70 ff., 83, 94 f., 98, 100 f., 103, 105, 116–20, 122, 125, 127 ff., 133, 135 f., 145 ff., 151, 153 f., 156, 161 ff., 165 f., 168 f., 171, 173 f., 177, 186, 190, 195, 199, 203 f., 206, 225, 227–36, 238 f., 254, 275 f., 279 f., 282, 310, 321, 331, 338 f., 346, 361, 363, 365 f., 372 ff., 377, 379, 381, 384

*senatusconsultum ultimum*, *see* emergency decree

Seneca the elder, Lucius Annaeus (rhetorician), 383

Seneca the younger, Lucius Annaeus (writer, adviser of Nero), 230, 250, 289, 378, 380, 383, 395

Sentinum, 53

Septimontium, 16, 24, 26, 28, 361

Sequani, 179, 181

Serdica, 300, 310 f., 387

Serena, 389

Sertorius, Quintus, 163 f., 373 f.

Servilia (mother of Marcus Junius [Quintus Caepio] Brutus), 201, 377

Servilius Caepio, Quintus, 373

Servius Tullius, *see* Tullius

Seven Hills, 16, 45

Severus (architect), 382

Severus II, 387

Severus Alexander, *see* Alexander

Severus, Septimius, 276 f., 279, 283, 285–8, 290, 292, 296, 307, 371, 384–8

Seville, *see* Hispalis

Sextius Lateranus, Lucius, *see* Lateranus

Shammai the elder, 258

Shapur I, II, *see* Sapor

Sibyl, 217
Sicca Veneria, 366, 368
Sicily, 50, 65, 79, 81-8, 96, 104 f., 113, 125, 129, 141, 154, 164 f., 190, 200 f., 215, 366 f., 370 f., 374, 377; *see also* Magna Graecia
Side, 392
Sidon, 13, 378
Sidonius Apollinaris, 343, 390, 395
Sierra Leone, *see* Africa, West
Signia, 362 ff.
Silius, Gaius, 380
Silius Italicus, 383
Silvanus, Marcus Plautius (Lex Plautia Papiria), 373
Silvanus (usurper), 388
Singara, 389
Singidunum, 389
Sinope, 384
Sirai, M., 366
Siricius, 391
Sirmium, 310, 384, 389
Sixtus III, 391
slaves, slave wars, 61, 135, 140 ff., 145, 164 f., 214 f., 243, 291, 336 f., 362, 367, 370 ff., 374, 377, 382, 390
Slavs, 354, 392
Soaemias, Julia, 385
Social (Marsian) War, 156-9, 161, 163
*socii, see* allies
Solomon, 256
Solway Firth, 239
sophists, 253, 383
Sosigenes, 376
Spain, 7, 29, 43, 80 ff., 96-9, 102-8, 122 f., 133, 136, 145, 153, 164, 173, 177, 182, 186, 189 f., 192 f., 198, 203, 205, 214, 231, 234, 236, 238, 248, 250, 282, 284, 322, 326 f., 330 f., 345, 352 f., 355, 367 ff., 372, 376 f., 380 f., 385, 390 f., 393

Sparta, 16, 46, 85, 364,366
Spartacus, 164, 374
*speculatores, see* secret police
Spina, 33
Split, *see* Salonae
Stabiae, 235, 242
state land (*ager publicus*), 62, 87, 139, 145, 372
Statilius Taurus, Titus, *see* Taurus
Statius, Caecilius, *see* Caecilius
Statius, Publius Papinius, 383
Stertinius, Lucius, 371
Stilicho, Flavius, 324 f., 330, 333 f., 343, 389
Stoics, 171, 250, 289 f., 370, 372, 374, 380, 386
Stolo, Gaius Licinius (Leges Liciniae Sextiae), 68 f., 365, 371
stone (building), marble, 31, 45, 116, 362 ff., 371, 382; *see also* concrete
Strabo, Lucius Seius, *see* Seius
Strabo, Pompeius, *see* Pompeius
Stridon, 345, 393
stucco, 244, 382
Subura, 361
Suburana, Sucusana (tribe), 361
Suessa Aurunca, 135, 364
Suessiona (Soissons), 391
Suetonius (biographer), 252, 358, 394
Suetonius Paulinus, Gaius, *see* Paulinus
Suevi, 324, 375
Sulla, Lucius Cornelius, 153, 158 f., 161-6, 168, 187, 191, 196, 373 f., 376
Sulmo, 221
Sulpicianus, Titus Flavius, 384
Sulpicius Rufus, Publius, *see* Rufus
Sura, 387
Surenas, 375

Surus, 132
Sutrium, 363
Sybaris, *see* Thurii
Symmachus, Quintus Aurelius, 391
Syracuse, 33, 83, 102, 362 f., 366, 368, 379
Syria, 13, 115, 141, 167, 203, 214, 248, 265, 276 f., 282 f., 286, 290, 296, 377, 379, 381 f., 385, 394 f.

TABULARIUM, 162
Tacitus (emperor), 385
Tacitus (historian), 225, 252 f., 306, 358, 380, 383, 394
Tagus, R., 98, 378
Tapae, 380
Tarasicodissa, *see* Zeno
Tarchna, 22
Tarentum, 77 ff., 90, 102, 140, 148, 365-70, 377
Tarik, 353
Tarpeian Rock, 361
Tarquinii, 13, 16, 22, 45, 360 f., 367
Tarquinius Priscus, 22, 24, 30, 361
Tarquinius Superbus, 22 ff., 30 ff., 37 f., 57, 361 f., 376
Tarquitii, 22, 361
Tarquitius Priscus, 361
Tarracina, 51, 364
Tarraco, 377, 385
Tarsus, 264
Taurini, 367
Taurus, Titus Statilius, 382
taxation, 21, 24, 86 ff., 104, 131, 136, 148 f., 173, 177, 203, 209, 212 f., 215, 234, 252, 277, 287 f., 291, 302 f., 316, 335 ff., 340, 366, 368 f., 371, 374, 376, 376, 378, 380, 385
Tay, R., 235, 285
technology, 214 f., 248, 288, 336

Telamon, 95
Tempe, 369
Tencteri, 375
Terence, 135
Terramara, 360
Tertullian, 305, 307, 387
Testaccio, Monte, 248
tetrarchy (imperial), 300, 302, 304, 308, 387
Tetricus, 286
Teuta, 114
Teutoburg Forest (defeat of Varus), 208, 378
Teutones, 153
Thagaste, 347, 391
Thames (Tamesis), R., 183
Thamugadi, 247, 382
Thapsus, 192
Theocritus, 375, 379
Theoderic (Ostrogoth), 353, 391
Theoderic I (Visigoth), 389
Theoderic II (Visigoth), 390
Theodoretus, 395
Theodosius I the Great, 322, 324, 334 f., 342 f., 346 f., 353, 389 f.
Theodosius II, 342, 353, 391
Theopompus, 363
Thermopylae, 119, 363
Thessalonica, 190, 300, 369, 384
Thessaly, 117, 191, 364, 366, 369
Thrace, 119, 164, 229, 322, 343, 353 f., 364, 369, 374, 379, 388
Thrasea Paetus, Publius Clodius, 380
Thurii, 78, 366, 376
Tibatto, 390
Tiber, R., 8 ff., 13, 15 f., 28 f., 41 f., 44, 47, 51, 137 f., 233, 244, 357, 363, 366
Tiberius, 206, 208, 210, 212, 225 ff., 252, 377 f., 394

Tibullus, 379
Tibur, 29, 47, 49, 245, 363, 382
Ticinum, 285, 310
Ticinus, R., 100, 368
Tigellinus, Gaius Ofonius, 230, 380
Tigranes I the Great, 374
Tigris, R., 237, 298
Timaeus, 360
Timesitheus, 385
Tiridates I, 380
Tiridates III, 388
Tities, 361
Titus, 233 ff., 242, 246, 268, 371, 382
Toletum, 353, 369
Tolosa, 325 f.
Tomi, Tomis, 221
Torah, *see* Jews
Tours, *see* Turonum, Civitas
Trachonitis, 385
trade, 13, 17, 29, 33, 41, 77, 80, 92, 125, 140, 148, 214 f., 247 f., 362, 365, 375, 378, 382, 395
Trajan, 236–9, 241 f., 244, 250–3, 276 f., 286, 293, 307, 380–3, 388, 394
Trajanus Decius, *see* Decius
Transalpine Gaul, *see* Gaul (France)
Transpadane Gaul, *see* Gaul, Cisalpine
Trasimene, Lake, 100
treason, *see* maiestas
treasury (*aerarium*), 158, 167, 212, 237, 375
treasury, military (*aerarium militare*), 209
Trebia, R., 100, 367 f.
Trebonianus Gallus, *see* Gallus
Tres Tabernae, 382
Treviri (city, Augusta Trevirorum), 282, 300, 310, 324, 326, 380, 382, 389
Treviri (tribe), 183, 233, 375

trials, *see* lawcourts
tribes (Roman), 21 f., 24, 64, 158, 361
Triboci, 375
Tribonian, 392
*tribuni aerarii*, 374
*tribuni militum consulari potestate*, 42, 67, 363, 365
*tribuni plebis*, 63, 72, 145 ff., 151, 162, 165, 194, 364 f., 372 ff., 376
tribunician power, 205, 208, 377
*tributum, see* taxation
Trifanum, 48
Trimalchio, 251
Triumphs, 168, 173, 192, 194, 363
Triumvirate, First, 174, 185, 187
Triumvirate, Second, 199, 201, 216
Troy, 159, 217, 360
Truceless War, *see* Mercenaries, War of
Tullii, 361
Tullius, Servius, 24, 26, 28 ff., 45, 59, 361
Tullus Hostilius, 361
Tunisia, *see* Africa (province)
Turks, Ottoman, 355, 392
Turks, Seljuk, 392
Turnacum (Tournai), 352
Turnus, 218, 362
Turonum, Civitas (Caesarodunum, Tours), 345, 350, 390
Tusculum, 37, 40, 46, 49, 68, 132, 361, 363
Twelve Tables, 64–8, 70 f., 91, 365
Tyconius, 391
Tyne, R., 239
Tyre, 13, 80, 291, 294, 386
Tzirallum, 388

UKRAINE, 322
Ulpian, 291, 386
Umbria, 53, 105, 129, 219, 364

Urso, 376
Usipetes, 375
Utica, 192, 366, 370
Uxellodunum, 375

VABALLATHUS ATHENO-
DORUS, 385
Valens (emperor), 321,
344, 349, 389 f.
Valens, Fabius, 232 f.
Valentia, 367, 369
Valentinian I, 321, 332 ff.,
337, 340, 346, 389 f.
Valentinian II, 389
Valentinian III, 327 ff.,
342, 389
Valerian, 280, 283, 285,
307 f., 385, 387
Valeria, Lex, see Flaccus,
Lucius Valerius
Valeria Cornelia, Lex, see
Messalla Volesus, Luc-
ius Valerius, and Cinna
Magnus, Lucius Corn-
elius
Valerii, 370
Valerius Antias, see Antias
Valerius Flaccus, 383
Valerius Maximus, 394
Vandals, 286
Varro, Gaius Terentius,
367
Varro, Marcus Terentius,
11, 360 f., 376, 379
Varus, Publius Quincti-
lius, 208, 378
Vatinius, Publius (Lex
Vatinia), 375
Vecellinus, Spurius Cas-
sius, 362
vectigalia, see taxation
Veii, 14, 16 f., 40-6, 68,
362 f.
Veleia, 381
Velia, 361
Velitrae, 363
Velleius Paterculus, 394
Veneti, 182 f.
Ventidius, Publius, 377
Venusia, 77, 218, 365 f.
Vercellae, 373
Vercingetorix, 184

Vergilius Maro, Publius,
see Virgil
Verginius Rufus, Lucius,
see Rufus
Verona, 187
Verres, Gaius, 165, 168,
374
Verus, Lucius, 273, 384
Vesontio, 179, 231
Vespasian, 231, 233 ff.,
241 f., 246, 268, 380,
382
Vesuvius, Mt, 235, 380
Vetera, Castra, 380
veterans, ex-soldiers, 62,
94, 104, 139, 153, 157,
161, 167, 169, 172, 192,
202, 209, 373, 376 f.,
382; see also colonies,
Roman
Vetranio, 388
Vetulonia, 360 f.
Viae, see roads
Vibenna, Caeles, 362
vigiles, see watch
villae rusticae, see agricul-
ture, architecture
Villanovans, 360
Villius, Lucius (Lex Vil-
lia), 370
Viminal Hill, 16, 26, 45,
361
Vincentius, 391
Vindex, Gaius Julius, 231,
380
Vindolanda, 380
Vindonissa, 384
vines, see wine
Vinius, Titus, 380
Virgil, 12, 23, 27, 33, 50,
202, 206, 210 f., 216-21,
293, 349, 362, 378 f.,
395
Viriathus, 122 f., 369
Visigoths, 322, 324-7,
329 ff., 339, 343 ff., 349,
352 f., 389 ff.
Vistula, R., 284
Vitalian, 392
Vitellius (emperor), 231-4
Vitellius, Lucius, 229, 231
Vitruvius, 362

Vivarium, 391
Voconius (Lex Voconia),
370
Volaterrae, 360
Volga, R., 389
Volsci, 38 ff., 47, 49, 51,
362
Volsiniensis, Lake, see Bol-
sena
Volsinii, 379
Voltumna, Shrine of, 15,
360
Vouille, 391
vows, see oaths
Vulca, 362
Vulci, 361
Vulso, Cnaeus Manlius,
369 f.

WALLIA, 326
walls, 26, 45, 239 f., 277,
286, 361, 363 f., 381,
385
Walmer, 183
watch (vigiles), 209, 378,
384
wharves, 29, 62, 65
Wheathampstead, 183
White Promontory, see
Acra Leuce
wine, 82, 140, 248, 365,
371
women, marriage, 19 f.,
66, 92, 131 f., 141,
200 f., 205, 236, 255,
261, 267, 279, 290, 345 f.,
370, 377, 381, 383

XANTHIPPUS, 85
Xiphilinus, 394

ZABDAS, 385
Zagros Mts, 317
Zaitha, 385
Zama, 106, 368
Zela, 191, 376
Zeno (emperor), 331, 354,
390 f.
Zeno (Stoic), 374
Zenobia, 282, 286, 385
Zonaras, 394 f.
Zosimus, 395